Quality of Life in Mental Disorders

Second Edition

For Neal Adams
with all the best wishes
for this important work
in spreading
person centred care

John Vásquez

Quality of Life in Mental Disorders

Second Edition

Editors

Heinz Katschnig
Medical University of Vienna, Austria

Hugh Freeman
Green College, Oxford, UK

Norman Sartorius
Geneva, Switzerland

John Wiley & Sons, Ltd

Other Wiley Editorial Offices

John Wiley & Sons Inc., 111 River Street, Hoboken, NJ 07030, USA

Jossey-Bass, 989 Market Street, San Francisco, CA 94103-1741, USA

Wiley-VCH Verlag GmbH, Boschstr. 12, D-69469 Weinheim, Germany

John Wiley & Sons Australia Ltd, 42 McDougall Street, Milton, Queensland 4064, Australia

John Wiley & Sons (Asia) Pte Ltd, 2 Clementi Loop #02-01, Jin Xing Distripark, Singapore 129809

John Wiley & Sons Canada Ltd, 22 Worcester Road, Etobicoke, Ontario, Canada M9W 1L1

Wiley also publishes its books in a variety of electronic formats. Some content that appears in print
may not be available in electronic books.

British Library Cataloguing in Publication Data

A catalogue record for this book is available from the British Library

ISBN-10 0-470-85601-7
ISBN-13 978-0-470-85601-7

Typeset in 9/11pt Times by Integra Software Services Pvt Ltd, Pondicherry, India
Printed and bound in Great Britain by Antony Rowe, Ltd, Chippenham, Wiltshire
This book is printed on acid-free paper responsibly manufactured from sustainable forestry
in which at least two trees are planted for each one used for paper production.

Contents

List of Contributors

Michaela Amering   Department of Psychiatry, Medical University of Vienna, Währinger Gürtel 18-20, A-1090 Vienna, Austria

Matthias C. Angermeyer   Department of Psychiatry, University of Leipzig, Johannisallee 20, 04317 Leipzig, Germany

Jose Luis Ayuso-Mateos   Department of Psychiatry, Universidad Autonoma de Madrid, Servicio de Psiquiatría, Hospital Universitario de la Princesa, c/ Diego de Leon 62, 28006 Madrid, Spain

Daniela Q.C.M. Barge-Schaapveld   Rijksstraatweg 681, 2245 CB Wassenaar, The Netherlands

Margaret M. Barry   Department of Health Promotion, National University of Ireland, Galway, University Road, Galway, Ireland

Marion A. Becker   Louis de la Parte Florida Mental Health Institute, Department of Mental Health Law and Policy, University of South Florida, 13301 Bruce B. Downs Blvd, MHC 2735, Tampa, FL 33612, USA

Julio Bobes   Department of Psychiatry, University of Oviedo, Julián Clavería, 6-33006 Oviedo, Spain

Dan Chisholm   Department of Health System Financing (FER), Evidence and Information for Health Policy (EIP), World Health Organisation, 1211 Geneva 27, Switzerland

Jason P. Connor   Department of Psychiatry, School of Medicine, The University of Queensland, Princess Alexandra Hospital, Ipswich Road, Woolloongabba, Queensland 4102, Australia

Philippe A.E.G. Delespaul   Department of Psychiatry & Neuropsychology, Maastricht University, PO Box 616, 6200 MD Maastricht, The Netherlands

Ulrike Demal   Department of Psychiatry, Medical University of Vienna, Währinger Gürtel 18-20, A-1090 Vienna, Austria

Marten W. deVries   Department of Psychiatry & Neuropsychology, Maastricht University, PO Box 616, 6200 MD Maastricht, The Netherlands

Ronald J. Diamond   Department of Psychiatry, University of Wisconsin Medical School, 6001 Research Park Blvd, Madison, WI 53719, USA

Gerald F.X. Feeney   Alcohol and Drug Assessment Unit, Division of Medicine, Princess Alexandra Hospital, Ipswich Road, Woolloongabba, Queensland 4102, Australia

Hugh L. Freeman   21 Montagu Square, London W1H 2LF, UK

María Paz García-Portilla   Department of Psychiatry, University of Oviedo, Julián Clavería, 6-33006 Oviedo, Spain

Barry Gurland   Stroud Center for Study of Quality of Life, Columbia University, Tower 3-30F, 100 Haven Avenue, New York, NY 10032, USA

Eva Jané-Llopis   Prevention Research Centre, Academic Centre for Social Sciences and Department of Clinical Psychology, University of Nijmegen, PO Box 9104, 6500HE Nijmegen, The Netherlands

Heinz Katschnig   Department of Psychiatry, Medical University of Vienna, Währinger Gürtel 18-20, A-1090 Vienna, Austria, Ludwig Boltzmann Institute for Social Psychiatry, Spitalgasse 11, A-1090 Vienna, Austria

Sidney Katz   Stroud Center for Study of Quality of Life, Columbia University, Tower 3-30F, 100 Haven Avenue, New York, NY 10032, USA

Reinhold Kilian   Department of Psychiatry II, University of Ulm, BKH-Günzburg, Ludwig-Heilmeyer Str. 2, 89312 Günzburg, Germany

Monika Krautgartner   Department of Psychiatry, Medical University of Vienna, Währinger Gürtel 18-20, A-1090 Vienna, Austria

Antonio Lasalvia   Department of Medicine and Public Health, Section of Psychiatry and Clinical Psychology, University of Verona, Policlinico "G.B. Rossi", P.le Scuro 10, 37134, Verona, Italy

Julian Leff   Department of Mental Health Sciences, Royal Free and University College Medical School, London and TAPS Research Unit, 69 Fleet Street, London NW3 2QU, UK

Anthony F. Lehman   Department of Psychiatry, University of Maryland School of Medicine, 701 West Pratt Street, Baltimore, Maryland 21201, USA

Gerhard Lenz   Department of Psychiatry, Medical University of Vienna, Währinger Gürtel 18-20, A-1090 Vienna, Austria

Jeffrey A. Lieberman   Department of Psychiatry, College of Physicians and Surgeons, Columbia University, 1051 Riverside Drive, New York, NY 10032, USA

David Mechanic   Institute for Health, Health Care Policy & Aging Research, Rutgers University, 30 College Avenue, PO Box 5070, New Brunswick, NJ 08903-5070, USA

Juan E. Mezzich   Department of Psychiatry, Division of Psychiatric Epidemiology and International Center for Mental Health, Mount Sinai School of Medicine, New York University, Fifth Ave. & 100th Street, Box 1093, New York, NY 10029-6574, USA

Nancy A. Nicolson   Department of Psychiatry & Neuropsychology, Maastricht University, PO Box 616, 6200 MD Maastricht, The Netherlands

Chijs van Nieuwenhuizen   Youth Forensic Psychiatric Hospital 'De Catamaran', PO Box 909, 5600 AX Eindhoven, The Netherlands

Gabriel Pantol   Department of Neurology, North Shore University Hospital, Manhasset, NY, USA

Fritz Poustka   Department of Child and Adolescent Psychiatry, J.W. Goethe University Frankfurt, Deutschordenstrasse 50, D-60590 Frankfurt/M., Germany

Mirella Ruggeri   Department of Medicine and Public Health, Section of Psychiatry and Clinical Psychology, University of Verona, Policlinico "G.B. Rossi", P.le Scuro 10, 37134 Verona, Italy

Luis Salvador-Carulla   University of Cadiz, San Marcos 6, Jerez 11403, Spain

Norman Sartorius   14, Chemin Colladon, CH-1209 Geneva, Switzerland

John B. Saunders   Department of Psychiatry, School of Medicine, The University of Queensland, Royal Brisbane Hospital, Herston, Queensland 4019, Australia

Klaus Schmeck   Department of Child and Adolescent Psychiatry, University of Ulm, Steinhövelstr. 5, D-89075 Ulm, Germany

Margit M. Schmolke   German Academy for Psychoanalysis, Tengstr. 20, 80798 Munich, Germany

Franklin R. Schneier   Anxiety Disorders Clinic, New York State Psychiatric Institute, 1051 Riverside Drive, Unit 69, New York, NY 10032, USA

Beate Schrank   Ludwig Boltzmann Institute for Social Psychiatry, Spitalgasse 11, A-1090 Vienna, Austria

Maria D. Simon   Ludwig Boltzmann Institute for Social Psychiatry, Spitalgasse 11, A-1090 Vienna, Austria

Peter Stastny   Albert Einstein College of Medicine, Bronx Psychiatric Center, 3050 White Plains Road, USA, Bronx, NY 10467, USA

T. Scott Stroup   Department of Psychiatry, University of North Carolina, Chapel-Hill, NC 27599-7160, USA

Durk Wiersma   University Medical Center Groningen, Department of Psychiatry, PO Box 30.001, 9700 RB Groningen, The Netherlands

Anastasia Zissi   Department of Sociology, University of the Aegean, Limnou 1 and Archipelagous, 81100 Mytilene, Lesbos, Greece

Preface to the First Edition

Quality of Life has only recently been recognised as the central purpose of health care. While a widely valued concept, there is still insufficient agreement about the definition of quality of life, about its measurement, particularly in the field of mental health, and about the manner in which the results of assessing quality of life can best be used.

Since the term embraces a whole spectrum of uses and meanings, and is employed both as a fashionable catch-phrase and a scientific concept, it needs careful scrutiny. All too easily it can become a vague label for a state of subjective well-being, with doubtful scientific value. The annual publication of more than 2000 quality of life publications in medical journals – and the number is steadily increasing – documents both the enormous interest in this field and the wide range of uses of the term. A common denominator to these papers seems to be their emphasis on the long-neglected, subjective view of the patient.

This book brings together chapters that examine the definitions and limits of the concept of quality of life. The authors explore it both as it is now and as it could be applied to the field of mental health in the future. Because well-being and subjective satisfaction with various life domains are a core feature of most quality of life definitions, the relationship between psychopathological symptoms and quality of life had to be carefully considered. This is especially salient when it comes to practically measuring quality of life, because many instruments contain psychopathological symptoms. Some of these are, in fact, psychopathological rating scales with the addition of a new label 'Quality of Life', but with little additional heuristic value.

When applying the 'Quality of Life' concept to mental health the strengths and weaknesses of the concept become especially obvious. Its strengths lie in its potential for integrating the views of different players in the mental-health-care field, while its weaknesses reside in its openness – it still designates a *field of interest* rather than a clearly defined *scientific concept*. More than readers might expect, therefore, the contributions to this book deal with conceptual and methodological issues. Indeed, ten of the twenty-four chapters do address such issues – some arguing mainly that quality of life research has generally been too much concerned with psychometrics and too little with conceptual issues.

What about a depressed patient who sees himself as deprived of all social support, while objectively sufficient support actually exists? How are we to judge a schizophrenic patient's assessment of his quality of life as good, while he is living on the streets of New York? Finally, if a manic patient feels on top of the world, his subjectively experienced 'Quality of Life' is excellent, but he will soon suffer from the consequences of his manic misjudgements of reality. These few examples show that while taking the subjective view of the patient into consideration signifies a tremendous progress in somatic medicine this is not enough in psychiatry. Therefore, most authors in this volume stress that the quality of life concept should be multidimensional, with role functioning and environmental living conditions – material and social – as additional dimensions to subjective well-being and satisfaction. It is argued that this multidimensionality is especially salient in the area of community psychiatry, where quality of life assessment is necessarily action-orientated.

Heinz Katschnig, Vienna
Hugh Freeman, Oxford
Norman Sartorius, Geneva

August 1997

Preface to the Second Edition

Since the publication of the First Edition of this book interest in the quality of life concept has been steadily increasing in the scientific community. In 2004 alone, a MEDLINE count produced more than 7000 papers, a more than threefold increase over a similar count in 1995. The raised interest in the specific relationship between quality of life and mental disorders is also documented by the fact that the First Edition of this book has been translated into Spanish, Italian and Japanese.

Despite significant advances of knowledge and numerous publications there is still insufficient agreement about the definition of quality of life, about its measurement, particularly in the field of mental health, and about the manner in which the results of assessing quality of life can best be used. This book brings together the most advanced thinking about these issues, including in particular ideas about moving from the assessment of quality of life to targeted actions aiming at its improvement.

The Second Edition has been thoroughly revised. The chapters contained in the First Edition have been completely updated and five new chapters have been added, dealing with new developments in measurement of quality of life, quality of life and substance abuse, as well as quality of life issues relevant to real world pharmacological trials, mental health services research and the promotion of mental health.

We would like to extend our gratitude to Beate Schrank and Evelyn Obermosterer for their careful work on the manuscripts and to Andrea Baier and Martin Tribe of John Wiley & Sons for handling the production of this book so effectively.

Heinz Katschnig, Vienna
Hugh Freeman, London
Norman Sartorius, Geneva

January 2005

Section I
INTRODUCTION

1

How Useful Is the Concept of Quality of Life in Psychiatry?

Heinz Katschnig

THE RISE OF THE QUALITY OF LIFE CONCEPT IN MEDICINE

Very few diseases or illnesses do not disturb well-being – the very etymology of the words makes this clear: one is not 'at ease' and one is 'ill' and not 'well'. Quite a few diseases also disturb functioning in daily life and in social roles – sickness leave from work and early retirement are examples of society accepting that a sick person is not able to fulfil his/her work roles. Finally, especially in chronic illnesses, external resources, both social and material (the latter being often referred to as 'standard of living'), are taxed.

For a long time, medicine has been accused of becoming 'technocratic' and not paying enough attention to the psychosocial implications of disease. Forty years ago, Elkinton (1966), in referring to Francis Bacon ('The office of medicine is but to tune this curious harp of man's body and reduce it to harmony'), criticised today's medicine as doing the 'tuning with unprecedented skill' but having 'trouble with the harmony'. He went on to ask: 'What is the harmony within a man, and between a man and his world – the *quality of life* – to which the patient, the physician, and society aspires?'

The concept that is now widely used, in medicine in general as well as in psychiatry, to capture these non-disease aspects of an affected person's life is that of 'quality of life' (QoL) or, more specifically, 'health-related quality of life' (HRQL). The first documented use of the term 'quality of life' in a medical journal can be found in the *Annals of Internal Medicine* of 1966, where Elkinton published an editorial with the title 'Medicine and the Quality of Life', which discussed problems of transplantation medicine.

It took some time before the concept became as popular as it is today. A MEDLINE search for the first edition of this book showed only slowly increasing numbers of these articles during the 1970s and 1980s, but a steep rise in the 1990s to over 2000 publications in 1995. Tracking down this development up to 2004 shows not only an undiminished interest in the field but also a veritable explosion of publications on QoL. For 2004, a MEDLINE count produced over 7000 papers. In 1992, a scientific journal *Quality-of-Life Research – An International Journal of Quality of Life Aspects of Treatment, Care and Rehabilitation* was founded, and an International Society of Quality of Life Research is already holding its twelfth annual meeting in 2005. 'Quality of life' is clearly an established feature in medicine.

In some sense, the World Health Organization's definition of health is a precursor of today's QoL concept. Shortly after the Second World War, this organisation put forward its well-known definition of health, which stressed that 'health is a state of complete physical, mental and social well-being and not merely the absence of disease or infirmity' (World Health Organization, 1948). More recently, WHO

Quality of Life in Mental Disorders, Second Edition   Edited by H. Katschnig, H. Freeman and N. Sartorius
© 2006 John Wiley & Sons, Ltd

has jumped on the quality of life 'bandwaggon' and has completed work on a generic assessment instrument for QoL (Orley and Kuyken, 1994; WHOQOL Group, 1998a, 1998b).

Another notion, that of the 'biopsychosocial model of disease', proposed by Engel (1977) to counterbalance the deficiencies of the 'reductionist' biomedical model (and also the limits of the psychosomatic model), has not reached anything like such a wide acceptance in the medical literature. The number of papers published using the term 'biopsychosocial' are minimal compared to the number of QoL papers. It is not possible here to analyse why this is the case (see McLaren, 1998). However, it cannot just be the vagueness of this concept, since it shares this with the concept of QoL.

The concept of QoL is not yet defined in a uniform way, lacks clarity and even creates confusion. It is justified to say that it is a term describing a field of interest rather than a single variable – much as the term 'disease' does – and that there is no simple way of measuring QoL, just as there is no simple way of measuring disease. The term QoL is used in many different connections. For instance, it has been popular with politicians for a long time, as the 1964 election campaign statement by Lyndon B. Johnson illustrates: 'These goals cannot be measured by the size of our bank balances, they can only be measured in the quality of life that our people lead' (Rescher, 1972). It is a concept in social indicator research (Rapley, 2003), where it has many different meanings, ranging from the notion of the welfare of a whole nation at one end of the spectrum to the concept of individual happiness at the other. In medical QoL research, the term refers to a loosely related body of work on psychological well-being, social and emotional functioning, health status, functional performance, life satisfaction, social support, etc., whereby normative, objective and subjective indicators of physical, social and emotional functioning are all used. However, no generally accepted definition exists.

Despite this unclear state of affairs, or perhaps because the term is so loosely used, the QoL concept seems to have an intuitive appeal for many different parties who are involved in managing health and disease. QoL seems to be understood by everyone: by patients and their family members, by professionals (biologically orientated as well as psychosocially and sociologically minded), by the pharmaceutical industry and regulatory bodies, by politicians and by the general public. Who does not strive for a good quality of life? It seems that the concept could have a significant integrative potential in today's health care environments, which are characterised by ever-increasing conflicts and debates on costs and outcome. It also provides a 'potential breath of fresh air' in our understanding of health, illness and health care institutions, as Albrecht and Fitzpatrick (1994) have diagnosed.

In the health care field, the term 'quality of life' has become a rallying cry for all those who strive to integrate patients' experience of their life during illness into clinical care, mainly by relying on patients' subjective assessment of their QoL. In somatic medicine, this is certainly appropriate, since a subjective view of this kind had been neglected by medicine for a long time. In fact, the concept of QoL is mostly used with the qualification 'subjective', to emphasise this point. Corresponding to this notion, most QoL assessment methods are either straightforward self-rating scales or, if applied as an interview, explicitly pick up the patient's point of view. It will be argued below that while this approach is certainly also needed for persons suffering from mental disorders, in this case, the assessment of the subjectively perceived QoL needs to be supplemented by 'objective' measures, including the assessment of functioning and of external resources, both social and material.

One reason for the rise of the QoL concept in medicine was certainly growing consumer dissatisfaction with medical treatment, starting in the 1960s and 1970s. This was also a major driving force behind the development of the advocacy and self-help movement, with its emphasis on the needs of patients in their daily lives. A specific aspect of this dissatisfaction was that in the effort to prolong life at any price and by focusing exclusively on treatment, medicine tended to overlook basic human needs of its patients, such as well-being, autonomy and a sense of belonging. 'Add life to years and not only years to life' has become the slogan of this movement. In the meanwhile, these discussions have ramified into complex ethical and political problems, such as questions of patients' rights (Barofsky, 2003a) and the problem of euthanasia (Farside and Dunlop, 2001).

The medical specialty where the QoL concept gained first prominence was oncology, where with the arrival of 'aggressive' treatments the question arose as to whether one should trade off a longer survival time (with unpleasant treatments) for a better QoL (without treatment). 'I'd rather die with my own hair on' says a character in David Lodge's novel *Paradise News* (1992, p. 26), when asked why she refuses chemotherapy for cancer. In psychiatry, similar issues have been prevalent for a long time. The question whether 'the cure is worse than the disease' arose, for instance, in asylum psychiatry (Wing and Brown, 1970), as well as in the treatment of schizophrenia with conventional neuroleptics (Gardos and Cole, 1976); both observations helped to fuel the 'antipsychiatric' movement of the 1970s.

The roots of the QoL concept reside largely outside medicine, in the psychological happiness research tradition (Diener *et al.*, 1999; for more details see below) and the social indicator movement of the 1960s and 1970s. At that time, social scientists, philosophers and politicians began showing interest in the concepts both of 'quality of life' and 'standard of living'. This was mainly in response to perceived inequalities in the distribution of resources and well-being in society and because of concern with population growth and developmental problems in poor countries (Albrecht and Fitzpatrick, 1994). In addition, the evolution of the welfare state stimulated research on social indicators and well-being, especially on the quality of work, family life and leisure, thereby not having so much the individual, but whole groups of persons, including whole nations, in focus (Drewnowski, 1974; Erickson, 1974; Andrews and Withey, 1976; Campbell, Converse and Rodgers, 1976; Rapley, 2003).

The emphasis of today's medical QoL research on subjectivity and on individual persons' well-being and satisfaction with life (or specific life domains), as well as on the individual's perception of his/her daily functioning, is more related to the happiness than to the social indicator research tradition. In social indicator research, subjective well-being is just one of many different indicators of the QoL of the population under study, and indicators of standard of living are regarded as equally important, assuming that well-being is strongly influenced by the latter (see also Angermeyer and Kilian, Chapter 2 in this volume, and Barge-Schaapveld *et al.*, Chapter 8 in this volume).

MEASURING HEALTH-RELATED QUALITY OF LIFE

It seems that no field in medicine has produced so many instruments to measure the same notion as QoL researchers have (see, for example, the compilation by Salek, 1999). Often, the mix of items included in individual questionnaires is not based on any rationale and includes, in variable proportions, items on physical, emotional and social well-being, social and emotional functioning, satisfaction with different life domains, health status, etc. It is no exaggeration to say that often the only unifying aspect seems to be the letter 'Q', contained in the acronyms of QoL instruments. When asked what QoL is, one cannot resort to the somewhat cynical statement used in relation to intelligence, that 'intelligence is what the intelligence test measures'. Quality of life would be a different concept, depending on which instrument is used. In contrast to this neglected question of validity, there seems to be an over-concern with psychometric and reliability issues (Cox *et al.*, 1992; Hunt, 1997). Also, in accordance with the predominant approach of HRQL research (that the patient's subjective experience of his/her illness and life should be elicited), but also because of the tendency to keep research expenses low, most HRLQ instruments are self-rating scales.

In a first phase of health-related quality of life research in the 1970s and early 1980s, either existing psychological well-being scales were used or new ones were specifically developed for this purpose. Examples are the Affect Balance Scale (ABS) by Bradburn (1969), the Quality of Well-Being Scale (QWBS) by Kaplan, Bush and Berry (1976) and the Psychological General Well-Being (PGWB) index by DuPuy (1984). This particular development has connections to the 'happiness research' tradition within psychology, where well-being is not only discussed in terms of the absence of negative factors (such as depressed mood) but as a positive concept whose determinants are studied (Diener, 1984; Ryff, 1995; Diener *et al.*, 1999; see also Barge-Schaapveld *et al.*, Chapter 8 in this volume, and Katschnig *et al.*, Chapter 11 in this volume). This is a very popular topic, documented by the fact that a recent special issue of *TIME* has covered this field comprehensively (17 January/7 February 2005). The more 'cognitive' notion of satisfaction with life and specific life domains, an integral part of most QoL instruments, is related to the issue of happiness and well-being (see Zissi and Barry, Chapter 3 in this volume).

From the 1980s onwards, in addition to the assessment of well-being and satisfaction, instruments for assessing functioning in daily life were developed. This development is usually subsumed under the term 'health status research' (for a more detailed discussion of the three roots of modern QoL research – the social indicators, happiness and the health status research tradition – see Barge-Schaapveld *et al.*, Chapter 8 in this volume). Well-known examples of 'health status research' instruments are the Sickness

Impact Profile (SIP) (Bergner *et al.*, 1981), the Nottingham Health Profile (NHP) (Hunt and McEwen, 1980) and the SF-36 (Ware and Sherbourne, 1992). Although these instruments do not use the term 'quality of life', studies employing them are today generally regarded as belonging to the field of health-related QoL research.

Among HRQL instruments, two groups are usually distinguished: the 'generic', which can be applied to persons suffering from any disease (such as the WHOQOL, developed by the World Health Organization; WHOQOL Group, 1998a, 1998b), and disease-specific instruments, such as the QLQ-C30 (Aaronson *et al.*, 1993), developed for the European Organization for Research and Treatment of Cancer (EORTC). Among the latter, there are also specific instruments for measuring QoL in mental disorders (see Lehman, Chapter 6 in this volume, and van Nieuwenhuizen, Chapter 7 in this volume).

A criticism made of HRQL instruments is that they do not address widely valued contextual aspects of life that are not generally regarded as health-related, such as income, freedom and social support, which are dealt with by the social indicator research tradition (Rapley, 2003), and focus, instead, on directly disease-related aspects of well-being and subjectively evaluated functional capacity (Guyatt, Feeny and Patrick, 1993). As will be argued below, this narrow, subject-centred concept is not appropriate for the mental health field. Some think that it is not appropriate either for somatic disorders (see Rapley, 2003, and Barofsky, 2003b). For persons suffering from mental disorders, the QoL concept is only useful if it encompasses the aspects mentioned above and other environmental factors, since income, lack of autonomy (e.g. because of lack of money) and low social support are all intrinsically related to psychopathology and life issues. What is required in the field of mental health is a broad and multidimensional concept of QoL and related measurement methods, which include a wide array of aspects of life. Thus, rather than using a single index approach, a profile is more appropriate here (Bullinger, 1993).

QUALITY OF LIFE AND MENTAL DISORDERS

Over the last 50 years, the concept of a person suffering from a mental disorder has fundamentally changed in psychiatry – from someone being totally overwhelmed by the disorder and having to stay in a mental hospital for the rest of his/her life to someone who is able to live outside the hospital, 'in the community', for most of the time. The discovery of psychotropic drugs has played an important, but by no means the only, role in this process (Katschnig, 2001). Community psychiatry has contributed to the emergence of new diagnostic concepts like the 'multiaxial' approach and new ideas of causation and management like the 'vulnerability–stress–coping model'. However, the public stereotype about mental disorders still reflects the old psychiatric view, with prejudices about dangerousness, irrationality, chronicity, incurability, unpredictability of behaviour and lack of competence. The repeated attempts of psychiatry to fight these prejudices by anti-stigma campaigns give evidence of this discrepancy between the new ways of thinking within psychiatry and the old concepts in the public domain.

Recently, two Oscar winning films have depicted persons who suffer from mental disorders and were nevertheless extremely successful in life. In one of them, *A Beautiful Mind*, the Nobel Prize winner John Nash was shown to be afflicted with schizophrenia; in the other, *The Aviator*, the Hollywood tycoon and aircraft constructor Howard Hughes appeared repeatedly and drastically as suffering from severe compulsions and phobias. Both could perhaps have been even more successful without their disorder, and one wonders whether these protagonists were happy. Yet the remarkable message in these widely distributed films is that a person suffering from a mental disorder is not completely overwhelmed by it, but has 'healthy parts' in his/her personality and can make use of these.

One could argue whether or not these two prize-winning films represent correctly what mental disorders are, just as one could claim that John Nash and Howard Hughes are not typical of most persons afflicted with a mental disorder and wonder who would really have liked to live their lives as shown in these films. In a sense, though, these stories set the stage for the present book. It is about how people suffering from mental disorders live their daily lives, how 'good' or 'bad' this life is at some times and at others; it is also concerned with how they view their lives, their well-being, their functioning and their resources; how satisfied they are with these aspect of their lives; and how good their functioning and resources are by external standards. Finally, there is the question of how they integrate the 'symptoms' and the 'disorder' into their lives.

Following de-institutionalisation and the development of community psychiatry, in the early 1980s psychiatry was at the forefront of QoL research by carrying out studies on patients with persistent mental disorders living in the community (Malm, May and Dencher, 1981; Baker and Intagliata, 1982; Bigelow *et al.*, 1982; Lehman, Ward and Linn, 1982; Heinrichs, Hanlon and Carpenter, 1984; see also Angermeyer and Kilian, Chapter 2 in this volume, and Lehman, Chapter 6 in this volume). Later on, the momentum was somewhat lost, before renewed interest appeared in the 1990s.

For a long time, psychiatry has been especially prolific in assessing non-disease aspects of its patients without calling these aspects 'quality of life', but rather 'impairment', 'disability', 'handicap', 'social functioning', 'social adjustment', 'satisfaction', 'social support', etc. To measure these aspects, several instruments have been developed – one well-known example is the Psychiatric Disability Assessment Schedule (DAS), published by the World Health Organization (WHO) in 1988. In fact, a rich literature on defining and measuring such non-medical aspects of psychiatric disorders already existed more than 20 years ago (Weissman *et al.*, 1981; Katschnig, 1983). However, these concepts did not come to the forefront of discussion to the same extent as QoL has now done.

A related issue is the so-called 'multiaxial' diagnostic systems developed for mental disorders. The WHO has published a multiaxial presentation of the ICD-10 Classification of Mental and Behavioural Disorders, which includes one axis on disabilities and another on contextual factors (Janca *et al.*, 1996; World Health Organization, 1997; see also Mezzich and Schmolke, Chapter 9 in this volume). Though a Global Assessment of Functioning (GAF) scale is included in all versions of the *US Diagnostic and Statistical Manual* (latest version DSM-IV TR; American Psychiatric Association, 2000), it seems that neither the ICD-10 nor the DSM-IV axes are widely used in clinical practice.

There is one major problem, however, of applying the currently prevalent QoL concept to persons suffering from mental disorders. The mainstream concept of QoL in medicine, with its emphasis on subjective well-being and the patient's own satisfaction, is less separated from psychiatric concepts of mental disorders than it is from medical concepts of somatic disease. In psychiatry, the main focus of interest is the very subjective experiences of the patients; at least these subjective experiences are intimately related to psychopathological symptoms and mental disorders.

When examining the myriads of health-related QoL instruments available today, it becomes evident that most of them include items that can straightforwardly be considered as psychopathological symptoms, mainly from the field of depression and anxiety. This is not surprising, given the already discussed mainstream philosophy of today's QoL research with its emphasis on well-being and patients' subjective views. This is where the title of this article comes from. Is it useful to apply such a QoL concept and its instruments in psychiatry? One could even go further and ask whether it makes sense to apply it to patients suffering from mental disorders? These and related issues will be explored below.

USING THE QoL CONCEPT IN PSYCHIATRY: SOME SENSITIVE ISSUES

The remainder of this chapter will focus on sensitive issues that arise in applying the quality of life concept and its measurement techniques, primarily developed for somatically ill patients, to those suffering from mental disorders. Topics to be discussed include: (a) 'subjective' versus 'objective' measures, (b) the problem of the inclusion of psychopathological symptoms in QoL instruments, (c) the necessity to go beyond subjective well-being and satisfaction measures, (d) multiarea assessment and the needs of psychiatric patients and (e) aspects of the relationship between time and QoL.

'Subjective' and 'Objective' Measures of QoL

When dealing with mental disorders, the widely accepted position of concentrating on the subjective perspective of the patient (Gill and Feinstein, 1994; Schipper, Clinch and Olweny, 1996) is prone to measurement distortions. Reports about subjective well-being tend simply to reflect altered psychological states, as Katschnig *et al.* (1996) and Atkinson, Zibin and Chuang (1997) have shown for depression (see also Katschnig *et al.*, Chapter 11 in this volume). In addition, subjective reports about functioning in social roles and about material and social living conditions may be distorted for several reasons, which I would like to call 'psychopathological fallacies'.

There are at least three such 'psychopathological fallacies' which may distort both the perception by a psychiatric patient of his/her quality of life and the communication of his/her perception to others: the 'affective fallacy', the 'cognitive fallacy' and the 'reality distortion fallacy'. The most important of these fallacies is the affective one (see also Katschnig *et al.*, Chapter 11 in this volume). It has been shown that people use their momentary affective state as information in making judgements of how happy and satisfied they are with their lives in general (Schwarz and Clore, 1983). A depressed patient will usually see his/her well-being, social functioning, and living conditions as worse than they appear to an independent observer (Kay, Beamisch and Roth, 1964; Beck, 1976) or to patients themselves after recovery (Morgado *et al.*, 1991). The opposite is true for a manic patient who, quite naturally, rates his/her subjective well-being as excellent, but also evaluates the social functioning and the environmental living conditions as unduly favourable.

Mechanic *et al.* (1994) have shown that depressed mood (in addition to perceived stigma) is a powerful determinant of a negative evaluation of subjective QoL in patients suffering from schizophrenia (see also Pukrop *et al*, 2003). Both in research and clinical practice, the affective fallacy can lead to wrong conclusions. For instance, in general medicine, QoL measures might disguise the presence of a comorbid depression, which, as a consequence, might not be discovered and therefore not treated (Jacobson, de Groot and Samson, 1997). In research on the effectiveness of antidepressant drugs, the very improvement of symptoms implies that the patient views the self, the world and the future more positively (Beck, 1976); this will automatically show up in a QoL instrument measuring subjective well-being and satisfaction with life, leading investigators to conclude that a specific drug does not only improve symptoms but also QoL – which in some sense is true, but is basically a tautological statement.

The reality distortion and cognitive fallacies are less problematic, since they are more readily recognised. At times, patients suffer from delusions and hallucinations, whereby perception of oneself and of one's surrounding is distorted by these very symptoms. Taking a deluded or hallucinating patient's judgement on his/her quality of life as granted would constitute the reality distortion fallacy. The cognitive fallacy concerns wrong evaluations by patients who are unable to assess intellectually their life situation, as is the case, for instance, in dementia and mental retardation.

Thus, while the patient's own view seems to be necessary, the question arises whether the subjective view is sufficient to assess QoL in persons suffering from a mental disorder. Becker, Diamond and Sainfort (1993) (see also Becker and Diamond, Chapter 10 in this volume) contend that in the field of psychiatry, QoL assessment has to be carried out not only via the patient but also via professional helpers and key informants – as a rule family members and friends. Accordingly, in addition to a patient version, the authors also provide a 'professional' and a 'carer' version of their Wisconsin QoL Index (W-QLI). There is empirical evidence for this position: Sainfort, Becker and Diamond (1996) have demonstrated that such assessments differ between patients and their relatives. Barry and Crosby (1996) (see also Zissi and Barry, Chapter 3 in this volume) have shown that persons suffering from schizophrenia, when moved from a mental hospital to the community, showed no improvements in life satisfaction ratings, despite 'objectively' improved living conditions and increased leisure activities.

These observations warrant the conclusion that additional evaluations by professionals and by family members and friends are necessary to complement the patient's own subjective assessment. However, assessment by other persons is not *per se* objective, and the term 'objective' may be misleading. 'External assessment' is probably more appropriate than 'objective assessment', since even such an evaluation might reflect the subjective view of the assessors themselves.

The QoL assessment issue brings into the forefront a basic problem of psychiatry – the necessity to reflect the different viewpoints that exist in society, e.g. about whether a psychiatric disorder is present or not and whether something should be done about it or not. Most often, there is disagreement in this matter between the patient, his/her family, professionals and society at large, and such disagreement should at least be documented (see also Sartorius, Chapter 27 in this volume).

The Necessity to Account for the Inclusion of Psychopathological Symptoms in QoL Instruments

The above issue becomes even more salient in the light of the next problem. Most QoL instruments used in medical patients – besides assessing functioning and satisfaction with different life domains, like work, leisure and sexual functioning – also contain 'emotional' items, mostly relating to the field of depression and anxiety. Some authors even speak of an 'emotional–function domain' or of a 'pleasant affect' versus 'unpleasant affect' component (Diener *et al.*, 1999). Here, the psychological tradition of measuring QoL by 'well-being measures' becomes tautological, since, if the item content of both measures is largely overlapping, QoL measures are necessarily correlated with measures of psychopathology.

The use of QoL as an outcome measure in clinical trials and evaluative studies has increased over recent years but, given the lack of a clear-cut definition and the very broad concept of QoL, there is a danger that therapeutic strategies are promoted on the basis of ill-demonstrated benefits for QoL itself. One example is the Quality of Life Scale (QLS) by Heinrichs, Hanlon and Carpenter (1984), which has often been applied in clinical trials of the atypical neuroleptics to show improvement in QoL. An analysis of the item content of the QLS shows that it mainly describes negative symptoms. Another example is the Quality of Life in Depression Scale (QLDS) by Hunt and McKenna (1992), which contains many depressive symptoms (see Katschnig *et al.*, Chapter 11 in this volume). A cautionary stance should therefore be taken by regulatory bodies (who increasingly demand that a new drug is not only improving symptoms but also QoL) to make sure that it is not just a new label (QoL) which is glued on an old bottle (symptoms).

Such an overlap in item content between different instruments purporting to measure different issues, tellingly called 'measurement redundancy' (Monroe and Steiner, 1986), is not uncommon in psychiatry. A remarkable example is the Global Assessment of Functioning (GAF) scale included as Axis V in DSM-IV-TR (American Psychiatric Association, 2000). Meant to be used for assessing 'functioning', the GAF scale nevertheless contains psychopathological symptoms in such a manner that it is not possible to find out whether a specific score is due to a high level of symptomatology or to dysfunction in daily life.

In conclusion, if QoL is studied in the mental health field, it is strongly recommended that the presence of psychopathological items in QoL instruments used for a specific study should be controlled, i.e. to check the correlations found between QoL measures and psychopathological symptoms for possible spuriousness because of simple item overlap. Also, when studying QoL in somatic disorders, at least depressive and anxiety symptoms should be assessed, in order to evaluate their possible impact on the QoL measures. This is especially important in view of the high comorbidity of somatic with mental disorders, especially if the former are chronic (Jacobson, de Groot and Samson, 1997).

The Necessity to Go Beyond Subjective Well-Being and Satisfaction Measures

While relying on subjective well-being and satisfaction measures is thus highly problematic, if QoL is to be assessed in persons suffering from mental disorders, the exclusion of contextual factors from most HRQL measures is an even greater problem.

Calman (1984) has elegantly defined QoL as 'the gap between a person's expectations and achievements'. This gap can be kept small in two ways: living up to one's expectations or lowering these expectations. Lowering one's expectations is an adaptational psychological process. Happiness research has shown that most people are happy and that, by and large, this does not depend a great deal on environmental factors (Diener *et al.*, 1999). Obviously, a large gap between expectations and achievements is not easily bearable, and most people lower their expectations (or do not have too high expectations to start with); otherwise the finding that people living in Detroit and Madras, the rich and the poor, the young and the old are on average equally happy could not be explained (unless it is all genetics).

However, 'achievements' do not depend only on subjective factors, but also on the actual opportunities available in one's environment. Especially, if QoL assessment is to lead to specific actions and not just regarded as another outcome measure of therapeutic interventions, then the inclusion of environmental factors seems necessary. It is contended here that QoL understood in this way has to be differentiated at least according to three components: psychological well-being/satisfaction, functioning in social roles and contextual factors (both social and material).

Assessing functioning in social roles, as is done by health status instruments, takes the environment partly into consideration (see Wiersma, Chapter 4 in this volume; Fossey and Harvey, 2001). What is lacking in today's HRQL research is more of the social indicator research tradition which builds environmental factors and opportunities, social and material, into QoL measures (Romney and Evans, 1996). Becker and Diamond (Chapter 10 in this volume) provide an example of how this can be achieved in the mental health field.

The need to include such contextual factors into the assessment of QoL is especially pressing in the case of persons suffering from mental disorders, where such factors interact with the patient's disorder more than in somatic disorders. Income, social support and living conditions (also called 'standard of living') can be intimately related to psychopathology (see Freeman, Chapter 5 in this volume).

The needs assessment approach in social psychiatry brings in the environment (Brewin et al., 1987; Phelan et al., 1995). Also, community psychiatry as such includes the environment into its spectrum of helping activities. Working with family members, providing a day structure and offering jobs are only a few such examples. Katschnig et al. (Chapter 11 in this volume) have developed an action-orientated framework for assessing QoL in depressed patients, which includes the aforementioned three components of well-being/satisfaction, functioning and contextual factors. They give examples of how helping activities could be classified according to these components: some act on psychological well-being (e.g. antidepressants), some on role functioning (e.g. social skills training) and some on environmental circumstances (e.g. providing money or housing). Also, public health programmes aimed at the promotion of mental health and improvement of the QoL of whole populations do in fact take all these factors into consideration (see Jané-Llopis and Katschnig, Chapter 28 in this volume).

The Needs of Persons Suffering from Mental Disorders and Multiarea Assessment of QoL

One could argue that the way society has dealt with the mentally ill over most of the last hundred years interferes with basic human needs. While keeping patients with persisting mental disorders in mental hospitals might have had the advantage of fulfilling the most basic human needs (physiological needs such as food and security needs such as shelter), higher human needs such as that for autonomy were neglected in this setting (Maslow, 1954). On the other hand, at the end of the twentieth century, in the era of community psychiatry, patients with persisting mental disorders do have the possibility of gaining autonomy, but often at the possible expense of not getting their basic human needs fulfilled.

Psychiatric patients have the specific problem of being stigmatised when they declare themselves as being mentally ill, which seems necessary if they want to obtain the means for survival including their additional needs for treatment (drugs, social security benefits, etc.). However, such stigma jeopardises autonomy, since patients are excluded from society, while qualitative research shows that they want to be 'one of us' (Barham and Hayward, 1991). Many psychiatric patients are thus in a no-win situation as far as the fulfilment of their needs is concerned, and many give up some of their expectations and 'cut their coat to their cloth' (see Mechanic, Chapter 26 in this volume).

In addition to having specific additional needs for treatment, psychiatric patients are disadvantaged since they usually have fewer resources to cope with life problems, fewer social and cognitive skills, and fewer environmental assets, especially money. In many studies on the QoL of schizophrenic patients in the community, lack of money is a prominent complaint, probably because it stands for autonomy.

A salient issue that becomes especially important in psychiatry is the use of single QoL index measures, as opposed to a QoL profile (Bullinger, 1993). Both for planning interventions and assessing outcome in a single patient and in clinical trials, a structured multidimensional use of the QoL concept is necessary, which covers different specific life domains, such as work, family life, money, etc. Some psychiatric QoL instruments separate such domains from each other (e.g. the Q-LES-Q by Endicott et al., 1993, and the W-QLI by Becker, Diamond and Sainfort, 1993), while others do not. For economic evaluation, a single index might be convenient, but this approach simplifies matters to such a degree that it becomes more difficult to understand what the figure obtained actually means (see Chisholm, Salvador-Carulla and Ayuso-Mateos, Chapter 25 in this volume).

Instruments for assessing patients' needs are in fact multidimensional, like the Camberwell Assessment of Need, (CAN) (Phelan et al., 1995) and the Needs for Care Assessment instrument of the Medical

Research Council Unit in London (NCA-MRC) (Brewin *et al.*, 1987), implying that different actions are necessary for different needs in different life areas. A specific Management Orientated Needs Assessment (MONA) instrument following these lines has actually been developed by Amering, Hofer and Rath (1998) in Vienna. This instrument also covers the possibility that the patient regards one life area as less important than another in terms of actions to be taken (see also Angermeyer and Kilian, Chapter 2 this volume).

Quality of Life and Time

HRQL assessments usually refer to a specific point in time or time period. However, there are quite a few time aspects involved when making such assessements.

Firstly, the question arises of whether the meaning of QoL remains the same in an individual person over time. As has been shown by Bernhard *et al.* (2004), the meaning of QoL does not remain constant over time in patients who undergo treatment for severe diseases – especially the weight given to QoL domains changes over distinct clinical phases. Also, Morgado *et al.* (1991) found that, after remission, depressed patients reassess their social adjustment as having been wrongly evaluated too negatively while they were still in their depressive episode.

Secondly, each of the three different components of quality of life – subjective well-being and satisfaction with different life aspects, objective functioning in social roles and environmental living conditions (standard of living, social support) – has different time implications. Subjective well-being, which is largely dependent on the actual affective state, can fluctuate quickly; functioning in social roles may break down rather quickly, though more often it takes some time. Environmental living conditions – both material and social – change only slowly in most cases. Thus, a depressed patient whose subjective well-being declines quickly while depression is worsening may still go on to function in his/her social roles. Even if this person does break down in functioning, the material living conditions and social support might still be unchanged for some time. On the other hand, once social functioning has deteriorated, owing to the long duration of the disease, while environmental assets, both material and social, have diminished, a patient might recover quickly in his/her psychological well-being, but not in social role functioning. Also, it might take some time before environmental living conditions are re-established, if they are at all.

If 'quality of life' is equated with 'subjective well-being', then 'changes in quality of life' might be observed after short psychopharmacological intervention. However, if functioning in social roles is being considered, the chances are less clear-cut that drugs might lead to quick improvement. Finally, if social support and material living conditions are to improve again, it will probably take much longer and need other than psychopharmacological interventions.

A third, more complex, time issue can best be described by Calman's (1984) gap between a person's expectations and achievements. If this gap is small, QoL is high. In this perspective, for each person, the issue arises of what is more important to him/her: a good quality of life today or one tomorrow? In Calman's terms: keeping the gap narrow now or tomorrow? There are numerous ways for persons suffering from mental disorders to achieve a short-term harmony between expectations and achievements: the use of quickly acting psychotropic substances (such as tranquillizers or alcohol) being the most common of these. In the long term, of course, substance abuse might develop and lead to a widening of this gap, following a vicious circle which implies decreased psychological well-being, loss of functioning in social roles, and deteriorating environmental and social living conditions. In the era of the predominant use of the first generation neuroleptics, patients experienced exactly this dilemma: while the prophylactic use of neuroleptics decreased the frequency of relapses, the side effects were often so disturbing that many patients were in the dilemma of having to choose between sustaining the side-effects 'now' (i.e. the immediate 'costs') and then have a good QoL 'tomorrow' (i.e. the future benefits), or not experiencing side-effects 'today' and having an increased risk of relapse 'tomorrow'. It seems that quite a few patients preferred the 'better quality of life now' versus the 'better quality of life tomorrow'. The new atypical antipsychotics might have changed this situation.

A final QoL issue in relation to time concerns the influence of a long duration of a disorder on the subjective assessment of QoL. Many persons suffering from long-term mental disorders report themselves satisfied with life conditions that would be regarded as inadequate by external standards. It has been repeatedly observed that such patients adapt their standards downwards, as we have noted above when discussing Calman's gap. Adding this phenomenon to the psychopathological fallacies described above, I would like to call it the 'standard drift fallacy': if one cannot possibly achieve one's aims, these aims are changed. Such patients remind us of the fox in the fable, concerning the grapes he cannot reach.

Barry, Crosby and Bogg (1993) (see also Zissi and Barry, Chapter 3 in this volume) have demonstrated that patients who have lived for a long time in a psychiatric hospital are more or less satisfied with their lives. Leff (Chapter 20 in this volume) reports that a substantial proportion of patients in two psychiatric hospitals were satisfied to stay there. However, after having moved to community homes, they did not want to go back into the hospital, probably due to the increased autonomy they re-experienced in the community, after having 'forgotten' it while in hospital. Wittchen and Beloch (1996) have shown that persons suffering from social phobia rate their QoL as worse in the past than in the present, probably because they tend to be satisfied with what they have achieved, although this is far below the standards of the general population. A similar finding is reported by Davidson *et al.* (1994) on persons meeting only subthreshold criteria for social phobia; a closer look at the data showed that they were disadvantaged in many respects, but did not find it worthwhile reporting this.

Dubos (1970) made the interesting observation that 'adaptability is an asset for biological survival, but paradoxically, the greatest threat to the quality of human life is that the human species is so immensely adaptable that it can survive even under the most objectionable conditions'. While Dubos is referring to the human species, the same thought can today be applied also to individuals who suffer not only from an illness, but also from a bad quality of life: should one just add years to life or also life to years, even if that means that there will be fewer years? However, going beyond Dubos: can one perhaps survive 'under the most objectionable conditions' because one can still be subjectively satisfied by lowering one's expectations or by experiencing or giving a special meaning to one's life?

FROM ASSESSMENT TO ACTION

Coming back to the title of this article, how useful then is the concept of QoL in psychiatry? To answer this question, we must ask for what the QoL concept and its concomitant measurement instruments are and can be used. Albrecht and Fitzpatrick (1994) have identified four such uses in relation to medicine: (a) as an outcome measure in clinical trials and health services research, (b) for assessing the health needs of populations, (c) for the planning of clinical care of individual patients and (d) for resource allocation.

Today, the most common of these uses seem to be the first two in this list. QoL measures are increasingly employed as an outcome variable in clinical trials, not the least because regulatory authorities are asking for this type of information (Spilker, 1996; see also Angermeyer, Kilian and Katschnig, Chapter 17 in this volume, and Stroup and Lieberman, Chapter 18 in this volume); a similar use as an outcome measure can be found in health services research (Oliver *et al.*, 1996; see also Lasalvia and Ruggeri, Chapter 21 in this volume). Secondly, studies describing QoL in various diagnostic groups, in clinical settings and in epidemiological surveys, are increasing in number and are usually carried out with the purpose of demonstrating how large the 'burden' of a specific mental disorder is (see the chapters on QoL in specific mental disorders in Section IV of this volume).

Of the two other uses of the QoL concept described above, the allocation of resources, i.e. economic analyses, is dealt with extensively in a separate chapter of this book (Chisholm, Salvador-Carulla and Ayuso-Mateos, Chapter 25 in this volume). The fourth use, that of planning the clinical care of individual patients, deserves special attention here.

Today, in clinical trials and health service research QoL measures are often included in order to describe effects of treatments or of special ways of delivering these treatments. However, as a rule, they are not themselves a target of intervention. In this respect some new developments are under way which may have far-reaching consequences for the whole health field, including not only treatment and rehabilitation but also prevention, and finally also the promotion of health.

The use of QoL instruments in everyday clinical practice to improve clinicians' awareness of patients' disabilities and general well-being, while having been judged as uncommon in the early 1990s

(Deyo and Carter, 1992), seems to gain ground now. One reason for this development is the advent of computer assisted monitoring in clinical practice (Espallargus, Valderas and Alonso, 2000; Higginson and Carr, 2001; Velikova 2004). Other developments can also be observed that might contribute to changing the traditional disease-orientated clinical paradigm not only in research but also in daily practice.

For instance, Frisch (2000) uses the term 'quality of life therapy', which he links to specific assessments by his structured Quality of Life Inventory (QOLI), i.e. the QoL assessment is taken as a basis for specific QoL interventions, meaning interventions that focus on enhancing QoL – in much a similar way as psychiatrist elicits psychopathological symptoms, makes a diagnosis and then decides which specific psychiatric treatments are to be used. The difference in Frisch's approach (which he exemplifies for the case of depression) is his focus on QoL instead of symptoms.

Another new development in clinical settings which focuses on interventions in non-disease aspects is so-called 'motivational interviewing' (MI) (Miller and Rollnick, 1991). MI aims to change the life-styles of patients and is used mainly in the substance abuse field, but increasingly also in other health areas (Britt, Hudson and Blampied, 2004).

While in MI the term QoL is not directly used, one could nevertheless say that this technique aims to improve QoL. The same holds true for ongoing activities in the mental health care field. The so-called 'recovery movement' de facto also puts emphasis on QoL interventions, without calling them as such (Anthony, Rogers and Farkas, 2003; see also Stastny and Amering, Chapter 23 in this volume). In Vienna we have developed Management tools and services for improving QoL in persons suffering from mental disorders that included their families. Amering et al. (1998) have produced a specific Management-Orientated Needs Assessment (MONA) instrument. A new psychoeducational tool for use in schizophrenia focuses as much on QoL issues as on disease aspects ('Knowing, Enjoying, Living better'; Amering, et al., 2002), and a family-orientated residential facility functions as a 'school for living with schizophrenia' (Pension Bettina; Katschnig and Amering, 1996). These and similar programmes of community mental health services elsewhere emphasise empowerment, advocacy and self-help (see also Stastny and Amering, Chapter 23 in this volume). This philosophy is in line with the principles of 'promotion of mental health', which can be regarded as a means of improving QoL in whole populations – in healthy persons and those at risk for and those already suffering from a mental disorder (see Jané-Llopis and Katschnig, Chapter 28 in this volume).

Obviously, activities are going on and still developing in the field of mental health care, which regard QoL as equally important as disease aspects. The emphasis of regulatory authorities to require QoL data for new treatments to be admitted to the market is also a sign of increasing awareness of QoL needs of persons suffering from diseases. From this it can be concluded that the concept of QoL is de facto regarded as being useful in the health care field, including mental health care.

However, what about the assessment instruments, especially those used in relation to mental disorders? It has been argued above that methods and instruments developed for assessing QoL in somatic medicine cannot be simply transferred to the mental health field and that some instruments designed specifically for assessing QoL in mental disorders can be methodologically flawed. Also, it has been stated that the use of the QoL concept in psychiatry is only meaningful if its assessment is carried out in a complex and differentiated way, which includes the interaction of the individual with the environment.

In the age of 'evidence-based medicine', studies using unsophisticated assessment instruments may lead to premature conclusions about the improvement of QoL, even if the design of such studies seems to be in order. To avoid such wrong conclusions it is suggested here that

1. Wherever possible, three assessments should be carried out: (a) one by the patient, (b) one by a family member or friend and (c) one by a professional.
2. The inclusion of psychopathological items in QoL instruments should be made explicit and correlations should be controlled for the influence of such items.
3. Three components of QoL should be distinguished: (a) subjective well-being/satisfaction, (b) functioning in activities of daily living and in social roles and (c) living conditions (material, i.e. 'standard of living', and social, such as social support). These components should be all assessed.

4. Different life domains should be assessed separately ('multiarea assessment'), since a person's quality of life might be excellent in one life domain (e.g. family) and inferior in another (e.g. work). Also, helping actions have to address those segments of life that are most in need of assistance.
5. The assessment of change of QoL should consider the different 'speeds' of change inherent in the different components (well-being/satisfaction, functional status, contextual factors), as well as the possible downward drift of standards to which patients with persistent mental illness compare their actual situation.

In psychiatry, the art and science of QoL assessment consists in capturing a patient's quality of life midway between the two extremes of writing a novel on the one hand and summarising QoL into a single index on the other and also between external assessments and the indispensable subjective view of the patient. It has to be stressed that, despite the caveats put forward above, in the mental health field the subjective view of the patient should become a prominent voice in discussing the aims of interventions, both on the individual and the service/political level. Concepts such as 'empowerment' (Stastny and Amering, Chapter 23 in this volume) and 'trialogue' (patients, caregivers and professionals discuss – outside the traditional familial therapeutic and institutional context – the experiences and consequences of psychosis and ways to cope; Amering, Hofer and Rath, 2002) should be given more prominence, especially in the case of persons with persistent mental disorders living in the community. A sense of control and participation is, after all, one of the aspects of quality of life that is most valued, not only by all of us but also by persons suffering from mental disorders (Mechanic, Chapter 26 in this volume, and Leff, Chapter 20 in this volume).

Nine years ago, the introductory article in the first edition of this book ended with the statement that the future would show whether QoL research was a fashionable and transient movement at the turn of the twentieth century or a serious endeavour with profound implications on the daily practice of medicine, on outcome assessment in clinical trials and health services research, on health needs assessment of populations and on resource allocation. Today, the topic of QoL is not only still around but the tremendous increase in publications indicates an ever-growing interest. One might still ask the question, though, of whether this increased interest is still a sign of a passing fad. One sometimes gets the impression that the introduction of new and the application of existing QoL assessment instruments amounts to a *l'art pour l'art* exercise. It is contended here that in an action-orientated field like medicine and psychiatry, QoL assessment should be action orientated. In some sense and in (perhaps too poignant) brevity one could formulate the wish that in the QoL field 'quantity' should turn more into 'quality'.

REFERENCES

Aaronson, N.K., Ahmedzai, S., Bergman, B. *et al* (1993). The European Organization for Research and Treatment for Cancer QLQ-C30: a quality-of-life instrument for use in international clinical trials in oncology, *J. Natl Cancer Inst.*, **85**, 365–376.

Albrecht, G.L. & Fitzpatrick, R. (1994). A sociological perspective on health-related quality of life research, in *Advances in Medical Sociology*, Volume 5, *Quality of Life in Health Care* (Eds G.L. Albrecht and R. Fitzpatrick), pp. 1–21, Jai Press Inc., Greenwich, Connecticut, London.

American Psychiatric Association (2000). *Diagnostic and Statistical Manual of Mental Disorders*, Fourth Edition, *Text Revision (DSM-IV-TR)*, American Psychiatric Association, Washington, DC.

Amering, M., Hofer, H., & Rath, I. (2002). The 'First Vienna Trialogue' – experiences with a new form of communication between users, relatives and mental health professionals, in *Family Interventions in Mental Illness: International Perspectives* (Eds H.P. Lefley & D.L. Johnson), Praeger, Westport, Connecticut, London.

Amering, M., Hofer, E., Windhaber, J., Wancata, J., & Katschnig, H. (1998). MONA – a new instrument for Management Oriented Needs Assessment, in *Book of Abstracts* of the VI World Congress of the World Association for Psychosocial Rehabilitation, Hamburg, p. 28.

Amering, M., Sibitz, I., Gössler, R. & Katschnig, H. (2002) Wissen – Geniessen-Besser leben, in *Ein Seminar für Menschen mit Psychoseerfahrung*, Psychaitrie-Verlag, Bonn.

Andrews, F.M. & Withey, S.B. (1976). *Social Indicators of Well-Being America's Perception of Life Quality*, Plenum Press, New York.

Anthony, W., Rogers, E.S. & Farkas, M. (2003). Research on evidence-based practices: Future directions in an era of recovery, *Community Ment. Health J.*, **39**, 101–114.

Atkinson, M., Zibin, S.H. & Chuang, H. (1997). Characterizing quality of life among patients with chronic mental illness: a critical examination of the self-report methodology, *Am. J. Psychiatry*, **105**, 99–105.

Baker, F. & Intagliata, J. (1982). Quality of life in the evaluation of community support systems, *Evaluation Progm. Plann.*, **5**, 69–79.

Barham, P. & Hayward, R. (1991). *From the Mental Patient to the Person*, Routledge, London.

Barofsky, I. (2003a). Patients' rights, quality of life, and health care system performance. *Quality of Life Res.*, **12**, 473–484.

Barofsky, I. (2003b). Book Review of 'M. Rapley: *Quality of Life Research: A Critical Introduction*', *Quality of Life Res.*, **13**, 1021–1024.

Barry, M.M. & Crosby, C. (1996). Quality of life as an evaluative measure in assessing the impact of community care on people with long-term psychiatric disorders, *Br. J. Psychiatry*, **168**, 210–216.

Barry, M.M., Crosby, C. & Bogg, J. (1993). Methodological issues in evaluating the quality of life of long-stay psychiatric patients, *J. Ment. Health*, **2**, 43–56.

Beck, A.T. (1976). *Cognitive Therapy and the Emotional Disorders*, International University Press, New York.

Becker, M., Diamond, R. & Sainfort, F. (1993). A new patient focused index for measuring quality of life in persons with severe and persistent mental illness, *Quality of Life Res.*, **2**, 239–251.

Bergner, M., Bobbit, R.A., Canter, W.B. & Gilson, B.S. (1981). The Sickness Impact profile: development and final revision of a health status measure, *Med. Care*, **19**, 787–805.

Bernhard, J., Lowy, A., Mathys, N., Hermann, R. & Hürny, Chr. (2004). Health related quality of life: A changing construct?, *Quality of Life Res.*, **13**, 1187–1197.

Bigelow, D.A., Brodsky, G., Stewart, L. & Olson, M.M. (1982). The concept and measurement of quality of life as a dependent variable in evaluation of mental health services, in *Innovative Approaches to Mental Health Evaluation* (Eds G.J. Stahler & W.R. Tash), pp. 345–366, Academic Press Inc., New York.

Bradburn, N.M. (1969). *The Structure of Psychological Well-Being*, Aldine, Chicago, Illinois.

Brewin, C.R., Wing, J.K., Mangen, S.P., Brugha, T.S. & MacCarthy, B. (1987). Principles and practice of measuring needs in the long-term mentally ill: The MRC Needs for Care Assessment, *Psychol. Med.*, **17**, 971–981.

Britt, E., Hudson, S., & Blampied, N.M. (2004). Motivational interviewing in health setting: a review, *Patient Education and Counseling*, **53**, 147–155.

Bullinger, M. (1993). Indices versus profiles – advantages and disadvantages, in *Quality of Life Assessment: Key Issues in the 1990s* (Eds S.R. Walker & R.M. Rosser), pp. 209–220, Kluwer Academic Publishers, Dordrecht, Boston, London.

Calman, K.C. (1984). Quality of life in cancer patients – an hypothesis, *J. Med. Ethics*, **10**, 124–127.

Campbell, A., Converse, P. & Rodgers, W. (1976). *The Quality of American Life*, Russell Sage, New York.

Cox, D., Fitzpatrick, R., Fletcher, A. *et al* (1992). Quality of life assessment. Can we keep it simple?, *J. R. Stat. Soc. A.*, **155**, 353–393.

Davidson, J.R.T., Hughes, D.C., George, L.K. & Blazer, D.G. (1994). The boundary of social phobia: Exploring the threshold, *Arch. Gen. Psychiatry*, **51**, 975–983.

Deyo, R. & Carter, W. (1992). Strategies for improving and expanding the application of health status measures in clinical settings, *Med. Care*, **30**, MS176–MS186.

Diener, E. (1984). Subjective well-being, *Psychol. Bull.*, **95**, 542–575.

Diener, E., Suh, E.M., Lucas, R.E. & Smith, H.L. (1999). Subjective well-being: Three decades of progress, *Psychol. Bull.*, **125**, 276–302.

Drewnowski, J. (1974). *On Measuring and Planning the Quality of Life*, Mouton, The Hague.

Dubos, R.J. (1970). *Reason Awake: Science for Man*, Columbia University Press, New York.

DuPuy, H. (1984). The Psychological General Well-Being Index, in *Assessment of Quality of Life in Clinical Trials of Cardiovascular Therapies* (Ed. N. Wenger), pp. 170–183, Le Jacq, New York.

Elkinton, J. (1966). Medicine and the quality of life, *Ann. Internal Med.*, **64**, 711–714.

Endicott, J., Nee, J., Harrison, W. & Blumenthal, R. (1993). Quality of Life Enjoyment and Satisfaction Questionnaire: A new measure, *Psychopharmocal Bull.*, **29**, 321–326.

Engel, G.L. (1977). The need for a new medical model: A challenge for biomedicine, *Science*, **196**, 129–136.

Erickson, R. (1974). Welfare as a planning goal, *Acta Sociologica*, **17**, 32–43.

Espallargus, M., Valderas, J.M. & Alonso, J.M. (2000). Provision of feedback on perceived health status to health care professionals: A systematic review, *Med. Care*, **38**, 175–186.

Farside, B. & Dunlop, R.J. (2001). Is there such a thing as a life not worth living?, *Br. Med. J.*, **322**, 1481–1483.

Fossey, E.M. & Harvey, C.A. (2001). A conceptual review of functioning: Implications for the development of consumer outcome measures, *Aust. N. Z. J. Psychiatry*, **35**, 91–98.

Frisch, M.B. (2000). Improving mental and physical health care through quality of life therapy and assessment, in *Advances in Quality of Life Theory and Research* (Eds E. Diener & D.R. Rahtz), pp. 207–241, Kluwer Academic Publishers, Dordrecht, Boston, London.

Gardos, G. & Cole, J.O. (1976). Maintenance antipsychotic therapy: Is the cure worse than the disease?, *Am. J. Psychiatry*, **133**, 32–36.

Gill, T.M. & Feinstein, A.R. (1994). A critical appraisal of the quality of life instruments, *J. Am. Med. Ass.*, **272**, 619–626.

Guyatt, G.H., Feeny, D.H. & Patrick, D.L. (1993). Measuring health-related quality of life, *Ann. Internal Med.*, **118**, 622–629.

Heinrichs, D.W., Hanlon, E.T. & Carpenter Jr, W.T. (1984). The quality of life scale: an instrument for rating the schizophrenic deficit syndrome, *Schizophrenia Bull.*, **10**, 388–398.

Higginson, I.J. & Carr, A.J. (2001). Measuring quality of life: Using quality of life measures in the clinical setting, *Br. Med. J.*, **322**, 1297–1300.

Hunt, S.M. (1997). The problem of quality of life, *Quality of Life Res.*, **6**, 205–212.

Hunt, S.M. & McEwen, J. (1980). The development of a subjective health indicator, *Sociol. Health and Illness*, **2**, 231–246.

Hunt, S.M. & McKenna, S.P. (1992). The QLDS: a scale for measurement of quality of life in depression, *Health Policy*, **22**, 307–319.

Jacobson, A.M., de Groot, M. & Samson, J.A. (1997). The effect of psychiatric disorders and symptoms on quality of life in patients with Type I and Type II diabetes mellitus, *Quality of Life Res.*, **6**, 11–20.

Janca, A., Kastrup, M., Katschnig, H., Lopez-Ibor, J.J., Mezzich, J.E. & Sartorius, N. (1996). The ICD-10 multiaxial system for use in adult psychiatry: Structure and application, *J. Nerv. Ment. Dis.*, **184**, 191–192.

Kaplan, R., Bush, J. & Berry, C. (1976). Health status: Types of validity and the index of well-being', *Health. Serv. Res.*, **11**, 478–507.

Katschnig, H. (1983). Methods for measuring social adjustment, in *Methodology in Evaluation of Psychiatric Treatment* (Ed. T. Helagason), pp. 205–218, Cambridge University Press, Cambridge.

Katschnig, H. (2001). Sociology and psychiatry, in *Psychiatry* (Eds. M. Sabshin & F. Holsboer), Volume 4.4, *International Encyclopedia of the Social and Behavioral Sciences* (Eds N.J. Smelser & P.B. Baltes), pp. 12277–12283, Pergamon, Oxford.

Katschnig, H. & Amering, M. (1996). Neutralität und Autonomie – Leitbilder für die Kooperation mit Angehörigen schizophrener Patienten in einem familienorientierten Wohnheim, in *Integrative Therapie der Schizophrenie* (Eds W. Böker and H.D. Brenner), pp. 377–383, Verlag Hans Huber, Bern, Göttingen, Toronto, Seattle.

Katschnig, H., Simhandl, C., Serim, M., Subasi, B., Zoghlami, A. & Jaidhauser, K. (1996). Depression-specific quality of life scales are flawed, in *New Research Abstracts*, APA Annual Meeting, 4–9 May 1996, New York. p. 160

Kay, D.W.K., Beamisch, P. & Roth, M. (1964). Old age mental disorders in Newcastle-upon-Tyne, II. A study of possible social and medical causes, *Br. J. Psychiatry*, **110**, 668–682.

Lehman, A.F., Ward, N.C. & Linn, L.S. (1982). Chronic mental patients: The quality of life issue, *Am. J. Psychiatry*, **139**, 1271–1276.

Lodge, D. (1992). *Paradise News*, Penguin Books, Harmondsworth.

McLaren, N. (1998). A critical review of the biopsychosocial model. *Aust. N. Z. J. Psychiatry*, **32**, 86–92.

Malm, U., May, P.R.A. & Dencher, S.J. (1981). Evaluation of the quality of life of the schizophrenic outpatient: a checklist, *Schizophenia Bull.*, **7**, 477–487.

Maslow, A.H. (1954). *Motivation and Personality*, Harper and Row, New York.

Mechanic, D., McAlpine, D., Rosenfield, S. & Davis, D. (1994). Effects of illness attribution and depression on the quality of life among persons with serious mental illness, *Social. Sci. Med.*, **39**, 155–164.

Miller, W.R. & Rollnick, S.R. (1991). *Motivational Interviewing: Preparing People to Change Behaviour*, Guilford Press, New York.

Monroe, S.M. & Steiner, S.S. (1986). Social support and psychopathology: interrelations with preexisting disorders, stress, and personality, *J. Abnormal Psychol.*, **95**, 29–39.

Morgado, A., Smith, M., Lecrubier, Y. & Widlocher, D. (1991). Depressed subjects unwittingly overreport poor social adjustment which they reappraise when recovered, *J. Nerv. Ment. Dis.*, **179**, 614–619.

Oliver, J., Huxley, P., Bridges, K. & Mohamad, H. (1996). *Quality of Life and Mental Health Services*, Routledge, London.

Orley, J. & Kuyken, W. (Eds) (1994). *Quality of Life Assessment: International Perspectives*, Proceedings of the Joint Meeting organized by the World Health Organization and the Foundation IPSEN, Paris, 2–3 July 1993, Springer, Heidelberg, New York, London, Paris, Tokyo, Hong Kong, Barcelona, Budapest.

Phelan, M., Slade, M., Thornicroft, G., Dunn, G., Holloway, F., Wykes, T., Strathdee, G., Loftus, L., McCrone, P. & Hayward, P. (1995). The Camberwell Assessment of Need: The validity and reliability of an instrument to assess the needs of people with severe mental illness, *Br. J. Psychiatry*, **167**, 589–595.

Pukrop, R., Schlaak, V., Moller-Leimkuhler, A.M., Albus, M., Czernik, A., Klosterkotter, J. & Moller H.J (2003). Reliability and validity of quality of life assessed by the Short-Form 36 and the modular system for quality of life in patients with schizophrenia and patients with depression, *Psychiatry Res.*, **11**, 63–79.

Rapley, M. (2003). *Quality of Life Research: A Critical Introduction*, Sage Publications, London.

Rescher, N. (1972). *Welfare. The Social Issues in Philosophical Perspective*, University of Pittsburgh Press, Pittsburgh, Pennsylvania.

Romney, D.M. & Evans, D.R. (1996). Toward a general model of health-related quality of life, *Quality of Life Res.*, **5**, 235–241.

Ryff, C.D. (1995). Psychological well-being in adult life, *Current Directions in Psycholog. Sci.*, **4**, 99–104.

Sainfort, F., Becker, M. & Diamond, R. (1996). Judgments of quality of life of individuals with severe mental disorders, *Am. J. Psychiatry*, **153**, 497–502.

Salek, S. (Ed.) (1999). *The Compendium of Quality of Life Instruments*, John Wiley and Sons, Chichester, New York.

Schipper, H., Clinch, J.J. & Olweny, C.L.M. (1996). Quality of life studies: Definitions and conceptual issues, in *Quality of Life and Pharmacoeconomics in Clinical Trials* (Ed. B. Spilker), pp. 11–23, Lippincott-Raven Publishers, Philadelphia, New York.

Schwarz, N. & Clore, G.L. (1983). Mood, misattribution, and judgments of well-being: Informative and directive functions of affective states, *J. Personality Soc. Psychol.*, **45**, 513–523.

Spilker, B. (1996). *Quality of Life and Pharmacoeconomics in Clinical Trials*, Lippincott-Raven Press, New York.

Velikova, G. (2004). Use of electronic quality of life applications in cancer research and clinical practice, *Expert Rev. of Pharmcoeconomics and Outcomes Res.*, **4**, 403–411.

Ware, J.E. & Sherbourne, C.D. (1992). The MOS 36-Item Short-Form Health Survey (SF-36), *Med. Care*, **30**, 473–483.

Weissman, M.M., Klerman, G.L., Prusoff, B.A., Sholomskas, D. & Padian, N. (1981). Depressed outpatients: Results 1 year after treatment with drugs and/or interpersonal psychotherapy, *Arch. Gen. Psychiatry*, **38**, 51–55.

WHOQOL Group (1998a). The World Health Organization Quality of Life Assessment (WHOQOL): Development and general psychometric properties, *Social Sci. Med.*, **46**(12), 1569–1585.

WHOQOL Group (1998b). Development of the World Health Organization WHOQoL-BREF quality of life assessment, *Psychol. Med.*, **28**, 551–558.

Wing, J.K. & Brown, G.W. (1970). *Institutionalism and Schizophrenia: A Comparative Study of Three Mental Hospitals 1960–68*, Cambridge University Press, Cambridge.

Wittchen, H.U. & Beloch, E. (1996). The impact of social phobia on quality of life, *Int. Clin. Psychopharmacol.*, **11**,15–23.

World Health Organization (1948). *Constitution of the World Health Organization*, Basic Documents, WHO, Geneva.

World Health Organization (1988). *Psychiatric Disability Assessment Schedule (DAS)*, WHO, Geneva.

World Health Organization (1997). *The Multiaxial Presentation of the ICD-10 for Use in Adult Psychiatry*, Cambridge University Press, Cambridge.

Section II
CONCEPTUAL ISSUES

2

Theoretical Models of Quality of Life for Mental Disorders

Matthias C. Angermeyer and Reinhold Kilian

INTRODUCTION

While subjective satisfaction was sporadically used as an outcome criterion of mental health services since the 1960s (Fairweather, 1969; Test and Stein 1978), it was only in the early 1980s that some authors started to give theoretical consideration to the meaning of quality of life (QoL) in general and in the field of psychiatry in particular (Malm, May and Dencker, 1981; Baker and Intagliata, 1982; Bigelow *et al.*, 1982; Lehman, Ward and Linn, 1982; Lehman, 1983a, 1983b; Tantam, 1988). A common feature of these contributions was the assumption that the scope of QoL goes beyond classical disease-related measures, such as symptoms, impairments and disabilities, to include also patients' subjective experience of their objective living conditions.

> As we see it, the challenge is to describe and assess our patients patterns of existence. A wide range of factors in the social and material environment, together with the subjective, contribute to their overall QoL. We must assess this full range of factors to have a comprehensive view of our patients. Existence is more than symptoms and behaviour, more than happiness; more than adjustment; role performance, and social skills; more than admissions, relapses, days in hospital, and burden on the family. These are parts of existence, but they are not all (Malm, May and Dencker, 1981).

Notwithstanding these common basic assumptions, there are considerable differences about the way that objective conditions are related to subjective perceptions and by which additional factors this relationship might be influenced. At least three distinct models can be identified for the specification of this relationship: (a) satisfaction, (b) combined importance/satisfaction and (c) role functioning.

THE SATISFACTION MODEL

According to the satisfaction model developed by Lehman, Ward and Sinn (1982) and Baker and Intagliata (1982) – with reference to the work of Campbell, Converse and Rodgers (1976) and Andrews and Withey (1976) – QoL consists of three components, 'personal characteristics, objective life conditions in various life domains and the satisfaction with life conditions in these various domains' (Lehman, 1988). Although the theoretical background of the model was not explained, it is apparently based on the supposition that the level of QoL experienced by an individual depends on whether or not his actual living conditions comply with his/her needs, wants and wishes. Unfortunately, this model neglects the question of which needs, wants and wishes people in the target population 'really' have. Therefore, if a patient has a high degree of satisfaction with a particular domain of life, there could be at least three possible interpretations. Firstly, it might be a good fit between what he/she wants and what is obtained within this particular domain; secondly, this life domain might carry such little importance for the patient that his/her satisfaction is not affected by the objective conditions; and thirdly, the patient might have adapted his/her wants and wishes to the perceived opportunities, in which case the apparent satisfaction really represents resignation.

Only if the first of these is correct could the measuring of satisfaction be accepted as a valid indicator of QoL. Therefore, the two other possibilities must first be systematically excluded if unequivocal conclusions are to be drawn from the data.

THE COMBINED IMPORTANCE/SATISFACTION MODEL

One step towards solving the problem of the pure satisfaction model is the combined importance/satisfaction model, which incorporates both the subjective satisfaction of the patients together with an assessment of the importance that a particular life domain carries for him/her. According to Becker, Diamond and Sainfort (1993) 'existing scoring systems (of quality of life) do not allow for cultural diversity or reflect the fact that various aspects of life are not equally important to everyone (because) giving equal weight to different individual domains implicitly assumes that all the domains have equal value' (Becker, Diamond and Sainfort, 1993). Inasmuch as people differ in their individual values and preferences, the objective conditions of particular aspects of life will also affect their subjective QoL in different ways. Thus, for a person with low aspirations for occupational advancement, promotional opportunities will not be an important criterion of job satisfaction, whereas for one with high aspirations, it will be the most important one. Hence, the same degree of job satisfaction will carry a completely different subjective meaning for these two persons. Without an assessment of the importance that a specific life domain or a single part of this domain holds for the patient, it will be impossible to explain why those living under totally different conditions express the same degree of satisfaction.

Even though this combined importance/satisfaction model considerably enlarges the predictive power of the QoL concept, it does not solve all the problems of interpretation mentioned above. While emphasising the significance of individual values and preferences, this model disregards the dynamic character of those attitudes. From social psychological research in the area of cognitive dissonance, it is well known that persons are able and willing to change their values and preferences in the face of environmental pressure. Like the fox in Aesop's fable, who devalues the grapes that he cannot reach, many people try to avoid or reduce cognitive dissonance by devaluating those things or goals that subjectively seem unattainable. Therefore, one cannot exclude the possibility that the low importance of a certain life domain, as mentioned by a patient during a QoL interview, does in fact represent a resigned adaptation to his unsatisfactory living conditions.

THE ROLE-FUNCTIONING MODEL

In contrast to the approaches described above, the role-functioning model of QoL is explicitly based on the theory that 'happiness and satisfaction are related to the social and environmental conditions required to fill basic human needs' (Bigelow *et al.*, 1982). Proceeding on Maslow's assumption (1954) that human needs include such basic requirements as food, shelter and safety, as well as such higher-order needs as affiliation, esteem, autonomy and self-actualisation, these authors develop a person–environment model of QoL: 'The environment consists of opportunities through which the individual may satisfy his or her needs. The opportunities are such material opportunities as housing and food, but, more important, they are social opportunities.' These social opportunities are embedded into such social roles as friends, spouse, employee, parent, etc., which on the one hand can be used by the individual to satisfy his/her psychological needs but which on the other hand are associated with demands or performance requirements. 'For example, in the parent role, one must protect, nurture, defend, and instruct. In the work role, one must concentrate, be able to withstand stress, get along with colleagues without excessive conflict, be punctual etc.' Because of this link between environmental opportunities and demands, the degree to which an individual can satisfy his/her needs depends on that person's cognitive, affective, behavioural and perceptual abilities to meet the demands of different social roles.

> Thus we have an exchange economy in which, (a) it is demanded that each individual performs, using his or her abilities, and (b) it is provided that the individual will also have opportunities to have his or her needs satisfied. To the extent that adequate satisfaction and performance are achieved, the individual is adjusted to his or her environment and enjoys a good quality of life' (Bigelow *et al.*, 1982).

With the incorporation of role theory into the concept of QoL, Bigelow *et al.* (1982) increased the theoretical comprehension of the association between subjective well-being and environmental conditions. Nevertheless, some critical points remain, particularly with the application of the model to assessment of the QoL of mentally ill people. One problem is that the model supposes that human needs are universal and stable properties, even though Maslow had emphasised the dynamic nature and culture-boundedness of these needs. Within his theory of the hierarchical nature of human needs, it was suggested that the emergence of the higher-order psychological needs depends on the satisfaction of the basic ones, especially that for safety (Maslow, 1954). Moreover, as a consequence of the permanent non-satisfaction of a basic need, e.g. for safety, as perceived by an individual, this one may come to dominate the need structure of this individual in a pathological manner. Since many forms of psychiatric disorder are associated with such pathological domination by the need for safety, it seems inadequate to focus any theory of QoL of the mentally ill only on the satisfaction of higher-order needs.

A second problem results from the implicit assumption that only conventional roles provide opportunities for the satisfaction of the needs of mentally ill persons. However, since such people have particular needs due to their illness, e.g. for nurturing, protection, financial benefit, medication, therapy, etc., they are obliged to meet some of the demands of the sick role (Parsons, 1951, 1958; Arluke, 1988; Segall, 1988), such as seeking the help of an expert, compliance with treatment, adaptation to the rules of treatment facilities and, last but not least, proving their inability to secure their own subsistence.

Therefore, regarding the role theory as a concept of QoL, it seems necessary to include questions about the illness-related needs of mentally ill people and the degree to which these particular needs can or cannot be satisfied by conventional role performance within such a concept. Further, it seems to be important to assess the patient's engulfment in the sick role (Lally, 1989) and the degree to which the subjectively perceived demands of this role restrict his/her capability to meet the demands of conventional roles (Scheff, 1966).

TOWARDS A DYNAMIC PROCESS MODEL OF QUALITY OF LIFE IN MENTAL DISORDER

Summarising the above-mentioned criteria, even though all existing theoretical concepts of QoL of the mentally ill will emphasise the central importance of patients' subjective assessments of their objective living conditions, the dynamics and factors influencing these subjective assessment processes have been largely neglected. In our view, the starting point for analysis of these dynamics should be a developmental model of subjective human need satisfaction that takes into consideration both sociocultural factors and those influential factors based on individual personality development.

The model shown in Fig. 2.1 is based on the assumption that subjective QoL represents the result of an ongoing process of adaptation, during which the individual must continuously reconcile the level of aspiration (Lewin *et al.*, 1944), his/her own desires and goals, with environmental conditions and the personal abilities to meet the social demands associated with the fulfilment of these desires and goals. Within this model, satisfaction will not be regarded as the outcome, but rather as the steering mechanism of this process. QoL research founded on the measurement of subjective satisfaction appears to support the fundamentally trivial fact that most people possess a relatively great ability to keep their level of satisfaction relatively stable – at least in the long run – by means of both cognitive and conative activities, even in the light of constantly changing environmental circumstances. This means that if an individual feels dissatisfied because a discrepancy is perceived between individual values and

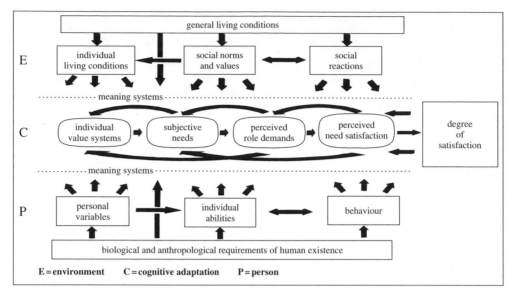

Figure 2.1   The dynamic process model of quality of life

preferences and actual living conditions, this dissatisfaction can be reduced either by changing the environmental conditions or by changing the personal values and preferences. From everyday experience, we know that humans continuously use both strategies, in varying combinations. Because of this non-recursive nature of the need-satisfaction process, using measurements of subjective satisfaction as indicators of QoL will not permit us to differentiate between the QoL of an individual who reduces expectations to such an extent that they will be satisfied with very poor circumstances, objectively speaking, and that of someone who is satisfied with life due to the realisation of all aspired-to goals.

There were intentions, initially associated with the concept of QoL of the mentally ill, to attach more emphasis to the subjective perspectives of these individuals, when assessing their living conditions (Baker and Intagliata, 1982; Lamb, 1982; Diamond, 1985). However, reducing this subjective dimension to simply measuring expressed satisfaction seems to add little extra value. The studies described above indicate that the ability to maintain a particular level of satisfaction remains largely intact, even in the presence of severe psychiatric disorders. The question therefore arises under which conditions and in which form is it meaningful and necessary to consider subjective perspectives when assessing the QoL of the mentally ill. However, clarification of this question first demands outlining the general requirements for assessing the quality of human living conditions. The first prerequisite for such an assessment is the supposition of a universal system of basic human needs (Maslow, 1954; Griffin, 1986). The second is to take a normative setting as the basis for those modes for satisfying the basic needs that can be considered adequate.

The different theoretical models of human needs that have been developed by philosophers, political and social scientists, and anthropologists, despite their theoretical differences, all include the following categories:

1. Physiological needs, which consist of all those resulting from the biological constitution of human beings, i.e. for food, water, air, shelter from natural forces, sexuality, etc.
2. The need for emotional relationships with other people
3. The need for social acceptance
4. The need for accomplishment and meaning

However, even though these four categories can be accepted as the framework for a general conceptualisation of quality of human life, they do not constitute a sufficient basis for its assessment. When assessing an individual's living conditions, it is not enough to assume an abstract need for food or emotional relationships. Instead, explicit standards should be defined with regard to the particular living arrangement by which these needs might be satisfied adequately. Such standards of quality, however, can rarely be established solely on the basis of objective needs, but must largely be guided by commonly accepted norms and value systems. From a more objective point of view, the assessment of QoL will be possible by comparing the objective living conditions of an individual with these general standards of need satisfaction within the society to which the individual belongs.

The purpose of including the subjective view, when assessing QoL, was related mainly to the fact that an individual's system of values and preferences is not determined entirely by the general normative system of his surrounding society. These individual systems are always shaped also by personal characteristics and individual experiences. Disregarding the subjective aspect of QoL would neglect the fundamental principle that in pluralistic societies everyone has the right to attempt the achievement of happiness in their own fashion. However, the central problem of including this viewpoint is that due to the dynamic nature of the need satisfaction process, individual systems of values and preferences can be the result of coercive environmental or personal conditions that are incompatible with the principle of personal freedom. If, for example, an individual who has grown up under deprived material or psychosocial conditions expresses a very low aspirational level, it would be inappropriate to interpret his/her relative satisfaction with these conditions as an expression of the individual value system, and therefore assess the quality of the living arrangements as 'good'. To solve this problem, it seems necessary to define criteria that assess the quality of the adaptational process of individual need satisfaction itself. If we accept the universal nature of the need categories presented above, it seems plausible to assess the quality of the adaptational process of human need satisfaction against the background of how a personal system of values and preferences enables the individual to satisfy the basic needs included in these categories.

In general, there will be two ways in which an individual's ability to satisfy basic human needs might be limited by their personal system of values and preferences: firstly, by the complete suppression of one or more of these basic needs and, secondly, by using strategies for the satisfaction of one need which lead to restrictions on the ability to satisfy others. This first form of a maladaptive need satisfaction process might be rare, emerging only under very unfavourable developmental circumstances. Nevertheless, it could be of great importance in the case of chronic mental illness. The second form, on the other hand, will be found to a greater or lesser degree within the need structure of most people. Referring to the development of restrictive need structures as 'maladaptive' does not imply that delaying the satisfaction of a particular need in favour of another one will generally be undesirable. On the contrary, in the course of their lives, people must continuously use such strategies in order to deal with conflicting needs. Therefore, a 'maladaptive' structure of this kind should rather suggest that an individual has lost the ability to re-establish the balance between different basic needs.

Before discussing the general methodological consequences of these theoretical notions for the assessment of subjective QoL, the developed model will be applied to the particular situation of the chronically mentally ill.

APPLICATION OF THE MODEL TO MENTAL DISORDER

Taking the situation of a chronically mentally ill person as the starting point, his/her objective opportunities of achieving a high level of QoL, measured against general normative standards, will clearly be more or less limited. Adjusting the individual aspirational level to actual opportunities in life is thus a prerequisite for the afflicted individual to be able to lead, in his/her own view, a tolerable life despite the handicaps. The development of this adaptational process will be very important for the subjective assessment of chances in life by the affected person. At best, this adaptational process will enable the patient to take advantage of those opportunities for improving the overall life situation which are objectively available, in spite of the degree of impairment. At the worst, this process will lead to an extreme reduction in aspirational level, which limits the individual's ability to satisfy even the most elementary human needs.

When considering the possible influential factors on this adaptational process, it is important to differentiate between the factors directly resulting from psychiatric disorders and those resulting from environmental conditions, including social reactions to those affected. Factors directly related to the illness, such as the time of first onset or the frequency and severity of psychiatric symptoms, will affect the adaptational process primarily through impairment of the individual's perceptual, physical and social abilities to fulfil the demands of conventional social roles. How a patient adapts their aspirational level to these impairments will depend largely on social reactions to the impairments themselves. Commonly, people with a reduced ability to fulfil social role demands will nevertheless be able to satisfy their essential needs, since every society supplies particular role patterns for such people. Most modern societies have institutionalised sick role patterns for those members who are not able to fulfil conventional role demands because of physical or mental illness (Parsons, 1951). As with conventional roles, sick role patterns link particular rights concerning the satisfaction of needs with particular duties, which must be fulfilled by the afflicted individual. However, in contrast to conventional roles, sick role patterns correspond to the particular needs and abilities of ill people. As an example, conventional role patterns commonly connect the satisfaction of material needs with the fulfilment of occupational role demands. In contrast, sick role patterns release the individual from the demands of the worker's role by substituting the demands of the patient role, including the duty to comply with medical treatment. Depending on how the duties and rights of the sick role are defined, the patient can expect to be supplied with the means for the satisfaction of material needs, without fulfilling occupational duties, e.g. by social benefits. This will occur if he/she is willing to accept the duties associated with that right, such as to prove mental impairment through the expertise of a psychiatrist.

The influence of sick role patterns on the aspirational level of mentally ill patients has been analysed within an ethnographic study by Estroff (1981). This author found that while the rights attached to the sick role, e.g. for financial benefits from the social security system, enable patients to satisfy their material needs, the duties connected with these rights, e.g. to prove their inability to work regularly, also restrict the satisfaction of their need for social acceptance:

> The customary acquainting interrogative in our culture soon focuses on work or on what one does. How could a client converse with a stranger for more than a moment without revealing the disability-connected means of income? The client was caught in but another Catch-22. If he or she revealed being on SSI (Social Security Disability Insurance), others presumed differentness, and more particularly, inadequacy. If he exposed the source of his income but did not appear disabled (or even denied problems), others became resentful, even hostile, at the life of leisure lived at the taxpayer's expense (Estroff, 1981).

This example illustrates that the influence of sick role patterns on the patient's aspirational level depends not only on formal rights and duties but also on informal social attitudes. Because the utilisation of the rights of the sick role, despite its legitimacy, is often coupled with negative social attitudes, afflicted individuals are frequently forced to choose between waiving their rights or accepting stigmatisation or social devaluation. Irrespective of which alternative a patient will choose, the choice will result in a reduction of the aspirational level below the degree directly determined by the severity of his/her illness-related impairment.

Beyond the example of social security benefits, this general dynamic can also be demonstrated in connection with the utilisation of psychiatric care, complementary psychosocial services and medical treatment. Despite the fact that all of these facilities have been created for the purpose of reducing the burden of psychiatric disorder, in particular by enabling patients to live outside hospital, they often produce unintended outcomes that restrain the realisation of objective opportunities for need satisfaction. Based on their qualitative study on the living situation of psychiatric patients in the community, Barham and Hayward (1991) observed that:

> ... in participants' experience of services the significant questions that concerned them about the value and direction of their lives were left unaddressed or obscured. Medication was judged to be beneficial but delivered crudely, as the primary form of intervention, it became a currency that devalued participants' efforts to re-establish their personhood and resist entrapment in an unremitting state of mental patienthood. For the most part services appeared to offer participants a form of protective containment within the identity of a community mental patient. As our participants saw it, such containment did not generally provide a means or stepping-stone to a more meaningful form of inclusion in social life as much as confirmation of their own marginalisation and lack of social worth.

These conclusions, like those of Estroff, suggest that patients must often cope with a conflict between their illness-related needs, such as for psychiatric care, medical treatment or complementary services, and their need for maintaining at least a partial normal social identity. As one possible way of coping with this conflict, many such patients reduce their aspirations to a very low level. While some of those observed by Barham and Hayward and by Estroff preferred to live under very poor material and psychosocial conditions because they refused to accept their dependency on community mental health services, others accepted dependency and the duties of the patient role, but relinquished their efforts towards living a normal life.

These empirical examples generally suggest that the subjective QoL of people with chronic psychiatric disorders depends to a great extent on the degree to which they are able to satisfy their illness-related needs, such as psychiatric care or medication, without interfering with the satisfaction of universal basic human needs, such as social acceptance or emotional relationships. Therefore, to assess the QoL of these people, it would be desirable to combine measures of both their objective living conditions and their subjective degrees of satisfaction with an assessment of their subjective meaning system and need structures. Such comprehensive data should enable us to ascertain what strategies people with chronic mental disabilities have developed for satisfying their different needs, despite their objective deprivation, and for dealing with conflicts between illness-related needs and general human needs. The next step must be to examine how the development of these strategies has been influenced by both environmental and personal factors. Against the background of this information, it should be possible to assess, firstly, whether or not these individual strategies for need satisfaction enable patients to take full advantage of their objective opportunities and, secondly, through which interventions, either on the environmental or the personal level, this ability might be improved.

RECENT RESEARCH

Since the first edition of this book, a huge number of new studies on QoL in mental disorder has been published and it seems that, meanwhile, QoL has become established as an outcome measure of the effectiveness of mental health services (Holloway and Carson, 2002; Pinikahana *et al.*, 2002). However, conceptual confusion still seems to persist about the weak relationships between subjective living conditions and subjective QoL (Atkinson, Zibin and Chuang, 1997; Röder-Wanner and Priebe, 1998; Trauer, Duckmanton and Chiu, 1998; Zissi, Barry and Chochrane, 1998; Rössler *et al.*, 1999; Ruggeri *et al.*, 2001, 2002; Bechdolf *et al.*, 2003). Few attempts have been made to improve the theoretical understanding of the process by which individuals with psychiatric disorders evaluate their living conditions (Katschnig, 1997, 2000; Zissi, Barry and Chochrane, 1998; Kilian and Angermeyer, 1999; Franz *et al.*, 2000; Franz, Meyer and Gallhofer 2002).

Some authors have stressed the importance of personality factors (Zissi, Barry and Chochrane, 1998; Eklund, Bäckström, and Hansson, 2001) as mediator variables between objective living conditions and subjective QoL. Although some empirical evidence for the role of personality factors exists, current studies suggest that the effects of these variables are rather non-specific, in the sense that the effects of them were found, regardless of what kind of personality factors were included in the models. A positive self-concept and perceived autonomy were found by Zissi, Barry and Chochrane (1998) to be mediators related to objective living circumstances as well as overall subjective well-being. However, Eklund, Bäckström and Hansson (2001) proposed a model with direct effects of personality factors and objective QoL indicators only partially mediated by a 'self-factor', which included a sense of coherence, self-esteem and perceived control, and the severity of psychopathology. By contrast with the personality mediator model, the gap model of QoL explicitly refers to the adaptation processes discussed above (Welham, Haire and Mereer 2001). As these authors have suggested, the relationship between objective living conditions and subjective well-being depends on a person's ideal life circumstances and the subjective importance of this concept for that individual.

Even if the gap model seems capable of taking adaptation into account, it leaves the main questions raised above unanswered. Firstly, inclusion of importance in the model disregards the fact that subjective importance may also be susceptible to adaptation (Franz, Meyer and Gallhofer, 1999). Secondly, if both the ideal life circumstances and the importance are affected by adaptation, the weighted gap between ideal and actual life circumstances will be affected by adaptation in the same way. Therefore, it will make no difference whether subjective QoL or the importance-weighted gap will be assessed. The social comparison approach suggested by Franz *et al.* (2000) seems to be more fruitful. Based on the finding that long-term psychiatric hospital in-patients reported a higher subjective QoL than short-term in-patients or out-patients, these authors examined how both the patient groups and people from the general population compare their living situation with that of other people. It was found that short-term mentally ill in-patients compared their living situation mainly with that of healthy people, while long-term patients compared their situation mainly with that of other long-term patients. On this basis, the authors presumed that the experience of restricted and deprived living conditions induces a process of psychological accommodation that should be taken into account in the interpretation of QoL data. In addition to supporting the role of adaptation in the process of subjective QoL, this study provides some clues about the mechanism of the adaptation process, indicating that the level and the duration of restricted living conditions play a crucial role.

To obtain a deeper knowledge of the manner in which people with severe mental illness adapt to their particular living circumstances, problem-focused qualitative interviews were undertaken with 100 persons suffering from chronic schizophrenia living in Leipzig (Riedel *et al.*, 1998; Kilian *et al.*, 2000, 2001a, 2001b, 2003). Using the results of qualitative content analysis, the authors found that in several areas of life, such as work, leisure, social relationships and medical treatment, most of the participants adapted their expectations and aspirations to a level far below that of healthy people. In terms of their occupational situation, most were unemployed or receiving disability pensions. Nevertheless, only a very small minority expressed any hope of getting back into paid employment, while the majority accepted their deprived situation as irreversible and were satisfied with having enough money to survive (Riedel *et al.*, 1998). Social integration of the study participants was found to be more heterogeneous than occupational status. While nearly one-quarter of the participants perceived themselves as fully socially integrated, the rest described their situation as being more or less excluded from the main society. However, among these not fully integrated persons, only a minority expressed a wish to become reintegrated into normal social life. The majority had accommodated to their marginal social position as a member of a mental patient subculture, withdrawn within the family or complete loners. Again, the authors found that accepting deprived living conditions was accompanied by a high level of satisfaction (Kilian *et al.*, 2000, 2001a). In terms of psychiatric services, the majority of participants described out-patient treatment which consisted mainly of receiving drugs, in many cases without really knowing what these drugs were for and without any hope of improvement in their health status. As in the other areas of life, the level of satisfaction with this psychiatric treatment was generally high. Moreover, further quantitative analysis of qualitative data revealed that overall life satisfaction was positively related to an acquiescent acceptance of poor psychiatric treatment (Kilian *et al.*, 2001b, 2003).

CONCLUSIONS

Altogether, empirical evidence for the dynamic adaptation model of QoL was found to be strong in recent research. Nevertheless, by contrast to some authors (Gill and Feinstein, 1994; Oliver, Holloway and Carson, 1995; Hunt, 1997; Leplège and Hunt, 1997), we do not conclude that QoL is useless as an outcome criterion for the effectiveness of medical services. On the contrary, the insight it has contributed into the mechanisms of adaptation make the concept of QoL particularly useful, both in relation to possibilities and limitations. In terms of possibilities, QoL research has shown that adaptation of the level of aspiration takes time (Lewin *et al.*, 1944). Therefore, the time an individual needs to adapt expectations to changed environmental conditions (including his/her own mind and body) should be regarded as the necessary time-window for QoL assessment. Therefore, one should not expect a medical or psychosocial intervention to cause permanent improvement of the subjective QoL. Even if the intervention is highly effective, it may cause only a short-term improvement until the individual has adapted his/her aspiration level to the new situation.

Support for this hypothesis comes from studies of Zissi, Barry and Chochrane (1998), who found that subjective QoL of mentally ill patients was affected by perception of change rather than by the evaluation of current living conditions. Moreover, an analysis of the factors influencing the subjective QoL of people with schizophrenia over a period of 2.5 years showed that this was affected by the idiosyncratic changes of objective QoL indicators, while the cross-sectional differences of these indicators between study participants did not affect subjective QoL (Kilian *et al.*, 2004). From these results, it can be concluded that although the relationship between objective living conditions and subjective QoL is weak, we can expect at least a short-term improvement of subjective QoL after an improvement of objective living conditions.

Regarding the limitations of QoL as an outcome indicator, it has to be remembered that QoL is a comprehensive concept encompassing all dimensions of human life. Therefore, one cannot expect to change general QoL by a clinical intervention focused on a particular dimension of mental illness, such as the reduction of psychopathological symptoms (Kilian and Angermeyer, 1999). On that basis, the emerging tendency to include subjective QoL as an outcome measure for the evaluation of any medical intervention seems to make little sense. Instead, the potential to affect any dimension of QoL must be carefully considered in the planning of any medical or psychosocial intervention study. If there is any reason to believe that one or more particular aspects of QoL may be affected, then the instrument that is most suitable for the assessment of these particular aspects should be included in the study.

REFERENCES

Andrews, F.M. & Withey, S.B. (1976). *Social Indicators of Well-Being. America's Perception of Life Quality*, Plenum Press, New York.

Arluke, A. (1988). The sick-role concept, in *Health Behavior. Emerging Research Perspectives* (Ed. D.S. Gochman), pp. 169–179, Plenum Press, New York, London.

Atkinson, M., Zibin, S. & Chuang, H. (1997). Characterizing quality of life among patients with chronic mental illness: A critical examination of the self-report methodology, *Am. J. Psychiatry*, **154**, 99–105.

Baker, F. & Intagliata, J. (1982). Quality of life in the evaluation of community support systems, *Evaluation Prog. Plann.*, **5**, 69–79.

Barham, P. & Hayward, R. (1991). *From the Mental Patient to the Person*, Tavistock/Routledge, London, New York.

Bechdolf, A., Klosterkötter, J., Hambrecht, M., Knoost, B., Kuntermann, C., Schiller, S. & Pukrop, R. (2003). Determinants of subjective quality of life in post acute patients with schizophrenia, *Eur. Arch. Psychiatry Clin. Neurosci.*, **253**, 328–335.

Becker, M., Diamond, R. & Sainfort, F. (1993). A new patient focused index for measuring quality of life in persons with severe and persistent mental illness, *Quality of Life Res.*, 2, 239 251.

Bigelow, D.A., Brodsky, G., Stewart, L. & Olson, M. M. (1982). The concept of quality of life as a dependent variable in evaluation of mental health services, in *Innovative Approaches to Mental Health Evaluation*. (Eds W. Tash & G. Stahler). pp. 345–366, New York Academic Press, New York.

Campbell, A., Converse, P.E. & Rodgers, W. L. (1976). *The Quality of American Life*, Russell Sage, New York.

Diamond, R. (1985). Drugs and the quality of life: The patients 'point of view', *J. Clin. Psychiatry*, **46**, 29–35.

Eklund, M., Bäckström, M. & Hansson, L. (2001). Personality and self-variables: Important determinants of subjective quality of life in schizophrenia out-patients, *Acta Psychiatrica Scand.*, **108**, 134–143.

Estroff, S.E. (1981). *Making it Crazy. An Ethnography of Psychiatric Clients in an American Community*, University of California Press, Berkeley, California.

Fairweather, G.W. (1969). *Community Life for the Mentally Ill. An Alternative to Institutional Care*, Aldine Publishing Company, Chicago, Illinois.

Franz, M., Meyer, T. & Gallhofer, B. (1999). Are importance ratings useful in the assessment of subjective quality of life in schizophrenic patients?, *Int. J. Meth. Psychiat. Res.*, **8**, 204–211.

Franz, M., Meyer, T., Reber, T. & Gallhofer, B. (2000). The importance of social comparisons for high levels of subjective quality of life in chronic schizophrenic patients, *Quality of Life Res.*, **9**, 481–489.

Gill, T.M. & Feinstein, A.R. (1994). A critical appraisal of quality of life measurements, *J. Am. Med. Ass.*, **272**, 619–626.

Griffin, J. (1986). *Well-Being. Its Meaning, Measurement, and Moral Importance*, Oxford University Press, Oxford.

Holloway, F. & Carson, J. (2002). Quality of life in severe mental illness, *Int. Rev. Psychiatry*, **14**, 175–184.

Hunt, S.M. (1997). The problem of quality of life, *Quality of Life Res.*, **6**, 205–212.

Katschnig, H. (1997). How useful is the concept of quality of life in psychiatry?, *Curr. Opinion Psychiatry*, **10**, 337–345.

Katschnig, H. (2000). Schizophrenia and quality of life, *Acta Psychiatrica Scand.*, **102**, (Suppl. 407), 33–37.

Kilian, R. & Angermeyer, M.C. (1999). Quality of life in psychiatry as an ethical duty: From the clinical to the societal perspective, *Psychopathology*, **32**, 127–134.

Kilian, R., Lindenbach, I., Löbig, U., Uhle, M. & Angermeyer, M.C. (2000). Social integration as a dimension of quality of life of people with chronic schizophrenia living in the community: A qualitative analysis, in *Public Health Research and Practice. Report of the Public Health Research Association Saxony 1998–1999* (Eds G. Heeß-Erler, R. Manz & W. Kirch), S. Roderer, Regensburg.

Kilian, R., Lindenbach, I., Löbig, U., Uhle, M. & Angermeyer, M.C. (2001a). Self-perceived social integration and the use of day centers of persons with severe and persistent schizophrenia living in the community: A qualitative analysis, *Social Psychiatry and Psychiat. Epidemiol.*, **36**, 545–552.

Kilian, R., Lindenbach, I., Löbig, U., Uhle, M., Petscheleit, A. & Angermeyer, M.C. (2001b). Psychiatrists' role, effectiveness of treatment and treatment participation as perceived by persons with chronic schizophrenia in outpatient treatment: An analysis of consumer empowerment in mental health services by means of qualitative and quantitative methods, in *Public Health Research and Practice: Report of the Public Health Research Association Saxony 2000–2001*, (Eds N. Merker, P. Göpfert & W. Kirch), pp. 211–245, S. Roderer Verlag, Regensburg.

Kilian, R., Lindenbach, I., Löbig, U., Uhle, M., Petscheleit, A. & Angermeyer, M.C. (2003). Indicators of empowerment and disempowerment in the subjective evaluation of the psychiatric treatment process by persons with severe and persistent mental illness: A qualitative and quantitative analysis, *Social Sci. Med.*, **57**, 1127–1142.

Kilian, R., Dietrich, S., Toumi, M. & Angermeyer, M.C. (2004). Quality of life in persons with schizophrenia in out-patient treatment with first- or second-generation antipsychotics, *acta Psychiatrica Scand.* **110**, 108–118.

Lally, S.J. (1989). Does being in here mean there is something wrong with me?, *Schizophrenia Bull.*, **15**, 253–265.

Lamb, H.R. (1982). *Treating the Long-Term Mentally Ill*, Jossey-Bass, San Francisco, California.

Lehman, A.F. (1983a). The well-being of chronic mental patients. Assessing their quality of life, *Arch. Gen. Psychiatry*, **40**, 369–373.

Lehman, A.F. (1983b). The effects of psychiatric symptoms on quality of life assessments among the chronically mentally ill, *Evaluation and Prog. Plann.*, **6**, 143–151.

Lehman, A.F. (1988). A quality of life interview for the chronically mentally ill, *Evaluation Prog. Plann.*, **11**, 51–62.

Lehman, A.F., Ward, N.C. & Linn, L.S. (1982). Chronic mental patients: The quality of life issue, *Am. J. Psychiatry*, **139**, 1271–1276.

Leplège, A. & Hunt, S.M. (1997). The problem of quality of life in medicine, *J. Am. Med. Ass.*, **278**, 47–50.

Lewin, K., Dembo, T., Festinger, L. & Sears, P.S. (1944), Level of aspiration, in *Personality and the Behavior Disorders*, (Ed. J.M. Hunt), pp. 333–378, The Ronald Press Company, New York.

Malm, U., May, P.R.A. & Dencker, S.J. (1981). Evaluation of the quality of life of the schizophrenic outpatient. A checklist, *Schizophrenia Bull.*, **7**, 477–486.

Maslow, A.H. (1954). *Motivation and Personality*, Harper & Row, New York.

Oliver, N., Holloway, F. & Carson, J. (1995). Deconstructing quality of life, *J. Ment. Health*, **4**, 1–4.

Parsons, T. (1951). *The Social System*, Free Press, Glenco, Illinois.

Parsons, T. (1958). Definitions of health and illness in the light of American values and social structure, in *Patients, Physicians, Illnesses* (Ed., E.G. Jaco), Free Press, Glencoe, Illinois.

Pinikahana, J., Happel, B., Hope, J. & Keks, N.A. (2002). Quality of life in schizophrenia: A review of the literature from 1995 to 2000, *Int. J. Ment. Health Nurs.*, **11**, 103–111.

Riedel, S.G., Lindenbach, I., Kilian, R. & Angermeyer, M.C. (1998). 'Weg vom Fenster' – Die Selbstbeurteilung der beruflichen Situation chronisch schizophren Erkrankter in den neuen Bundesländern ('Out of the game' – The vocational situation of chronic schizophrenic individuals in the new German länder), *Psychiatrische Praxis*, **25**, 286–290.

Röder-Wanner, U.U. & Priebe, S. (1998). Objective and subjective quality of life of first-admitted women and men with schizophrenia, *Eur. Arch. of Psychiatry and Clin. Neurosci.*, **248**, 250–258.

Rössler, W., Salize, H.J., Cucchiaro, G., Reinhard, I. & Kernig, C. (1999). Does the place of treatment influence the quality of life of schizophrenics?, *Acta Psychiatrica Scand.*, **100**, 142–148.

Ruggeri, M., Warner, R., Bisoffi, G. & Fontecedro, L. (2001). Subjective and objective dimensions of quality of life in psychiatric patients: A factor analytical approach, *Br. J. Psychiatry*, **178**, 268–275.

Ruggeri, M., Gater, R., Bisoffi, G., Barbui, G. & Tansella, M. (2002). Determinants of subjective quality of life in patients attending community-based mental health services. The South-Verona Outcome Project 5, *Acta Psychiatrica Scand.*, **105**, 131–140.

Scheff, T.J. (1966). *Being Mentally Ill. A Sociological Theory*, Aldine, Chicago, Illinois.

Segall, A. (1988). Cultural factos in sick-role expectations, in *Health Behavior. Emerging Research Perspectives* (Ed. D.S. Gochman), pp. 249–260, Plenum Press, New York, London.

Tantam, D. (1988). Review article: Quality of life and the chronically mentally ill, *Int. J. Soc. Psychiatry*, **34**, 243–247.

Test, M.A. & Stein, L.I. (1978). *Training in Community Living: Research Design and Results in Alternatives to Mental Hospital Treatment*, Plenum Press, New York, London.

Trauer, T., Duckmanton, R.A. & Chiu, E. (1998). A study of the quality of life of the severely mentally ill, *Int. J. Social Psychiatry*, **44**, 79–91.

Welham, J., Haire, M. & Mereer, D. (2001). A gap approach to exploring quality of life in mental health, *Quality of Life Res.*, **10**, 421–429.

Zissi, A., Barry, M.M. & Chochrane, R. (1998). A mediational model of quality of life for individuals with severe mental health problems, *Psycholog. Med.*, **28**, 1221–1230.

3

Well-Being and Life Satisfaction as Components of Quality of Life in Mental Disorders

Anastasia Zissi and Margaret M. Barry

INTRODUCTION

Over the past two decades, there has been a growing emphasis on quality of life (QoL) in the mental health literature. The QoL concept is now clearly recognised as providing an evaluative framework against which to assess the outcomes of care provision and offers a useful means of incorporating the client's perspective into the evaluative process. However, despite the increasing importance of QoL, the theoretical conceptualisation of this concept for people with long-term mental health problems remains poorly developed. While substantial progress has been made in developing scales and measures of subjective well-being, the more fundamental question of how people with chronic mental health problems come to assess this concept remains largely unexplored. The growing number of research studies in this area have generated little theory, and few of the empirical findings have been related to an overall theoretical framework (Barry and Zissi, 1997).

The need for a more coherent theoretical conceptualisation of QoL for people with chronic mental health problems is evidenced by the fact that many of its basic concepts remain ill-defined, thereby limiting their usefulness in practical application. There is a need to have a clearer understanding of the defining characteristics of concepts such as subjective well-being and life satisfaction, and to examine the nature of their interrelationship within a formulated theoretical model. How one approaches the assessment of such a broad concept as subjective QoL can very much influence the nature of the results obtained (Cheng, 1988). A coherent theoretical framework is necessary to guide research development in this area, both in terms of methodology and in facilitating the use of QoL measures as effective tools in service planning and evaluation. Fabian (1990) highlighted that the appropriate use of quality of life as a programme evaluation tool entails an understanding of the theoretical and methodological issues underpinning the relevant measures. To date, however, there has been relatively little attention directed to such theoretical development.

This paper addresses the theoretical and methodological issues in evaluating QoL for people with chronic mental health problems. It develops further the mediational model of QoL proposed by Barry (1997) and examines the potential role of mediators of subjective QoL, including an appraisal process that intervenes between external life conditions and subjective evaluations.

Quality of Life in Mental Disorders, Second Edition Edited by H. Katschnig, H. Freeman and N. Sartorius

THEORETICAL MODELS OF SUBJECTIVE WELL-BEING

The theoretical base for QoL research with people with chronic mental health problems derives mostly from the seminal work of Campbell, Converse and Rodgers (1976) and Andrews and Withey (1976) in their large-scale national surveys of quality of life in the United States. This approach to measuring QoL involves assessing both global well-being and life quality in specific life areas, incorporating both subjective and objective indicators. Andrews and Withey's 'domains-by-criteria model' outlines a life domain structure and sets out a number of criteria by which each of the QoL domains are evaluated. In operationalising their model, Andrews and Withey (1976) employed a combination of satisfaction ratings and affect scales in several life domains, to measure subjective QoL.

This approach to measuring QoL has been adapted by researchers in relation to people with chronic mental health problems, most successfully by Lehman (1983a, 1988). He developed a general QoL model, based on the original national survey data and adapted many of the measures originally used by Andrews and Withey (1976) and by Campbell, Converse and Rodgers (1976). According to Lehman's model, QoL is ultimately 'a subjective matter, reflected in a sense of global well-being' (Lehman, 1983a, p. 369). The experience of general well-being is viewed as being a product of three types of variables: personal characteristics, objective QoL in various life domains and subjective QoL in the same domains. Lehman's Quality of Life Interview (Lehman, Ward and Linn, 1982; Lehman, 1988), which is one of the best validated and most widely used scales, is based on this conceptual model and includes a structured interview format, comprising objective and subjective data covering nine life domains in addition to measures of general well-being.

Both Lehman's model and Andrews and Withey's 'domains-by-criteria model' place much importance on subjective well-being in their conceptualisation of QoL and both models rely heavily on ratings of life satisfaction as a means of assessing perceptions of subjective well-being. This raises a number of important questions. Is life satisfaction indeed the critical dimension along which to measure subjective well-being? Are the two concepts equivalent? Do life satisfaction measures give an understanding of how individuals arrive at their judgements of QoL? What are the methodological implications of employing satisfaction measures in the context of service evaluation? Given the increasing usage of QoL measures based on these models, it is timely to consider whether the existing empirical findings validate the models and to examine critically the findings concerning the key determinants of subjective well-being for people with chronic mental health problems.

In examining these issues, this paper draws on existing QoL research and explores the application of a mediational model of QoL in interpreting the QoL perceptions of people with chronic mental health problems resettled in community settings in Greece. The findings of this cross-sectional study, which examines the mediational model's predictions, are presented. As the details of this investigation are reported in Zissi, Barry and Cochrane (1998), the findings reported here will be summarised so as to illustrate the key issues raised.

METHODOLOGICAL ISSUES CONCERNING THE USE OF LIFE SATISFACTION MEASURES

Life satisfaction measures have become an increasingly popular means of understanding and measuring subjective well-being. The approach of operationalising subjective QoL as life satisfaction has also been applied to people with chronic mental health problems. Many of the QoL scales currently used with psychiatric populations employ life satisfaction ratings as measures of subjective QoL (Malm, May and Dencker, 1981; Baker and Intagliata, 1982; Lehman, 1983a; Oliver et al., 1997). Current findings show that these scales can be reliably used with a psychiatric population and that the measurement of subjective QoL for people with chronic mental health problems behaves simi-larly to measurements in the general population (Bigelow et al., 1982; Lehman, 1988). However, most studies using these measures have not been very successful in identifying the predictors of life satisfaction or in delineating the relationship between life satisfaction and the more general concept of subjective well-being. In reviewing the life satisfaction data from studies of people with chronic mental health problems, a number of anomalies or discrepancies can be seen in the research findings.

The majority of studies report that most demographic characteristics show only modest relationships, if any, to measures of life satisfaction (Baker and Intagliata, 1982; Lehman, 1983a), a conclusion that is also drawn from QoL research with general populations (Andrews and Withey, 1976; Campbell, Converse and Rodgers, 1976; Zautra and Goodhart, 1979). Other variables that have been examined in relation to perceived QoL are clinical and psychosocial variables, levels of unmet needs and levels of social support. Cross-sectional investigations of the relationship between clinical characteristics and QoL have reported an association between psychopathology and subjective QoL, specifically depression (Lehman, 1983a; Atkinson, Zibin and Chuang, 1997; Holloway and Carson, 1999) and severe florid symptomatology (Oliver *et al.*, 1997). Similarly, a number of studies have reported an association between role functioning and subjective QoL (Andrews *et al.*, 1990; Barry and Crosby, 1996; Farragher, Carey and Owens, 1996; Ruud, Martinsen and Friis, 1998), with a few exceptions indicating a low (Tempier *et al.*, 1997) to moderate relationship (Trauer, Duckmanton and Chiu, 1998). Despite these associations, the relevant evidence demonstrates that psychopathology, social functioning and QoL are conceptually distinct constructs (Corrigan and Buican, 1995; Barry and Crosby, 1996; Oliver *et al.*, 1997). Research findings suggest that while quality of life may be unrelated to satisfaction with services, unmet clinical and social needs are negatively associated with QoL among people with persistent and severe mental health problems (Bengtsson-Tops and Hansson, 1999; Slade *et al.*, 1999; Wiersma and Van Busschbach, 2001). The amount of social support provided in different treatment settings has also been found to influence the levels of perceived QoL for people with severe mental health problems (Roessler *et al.*, 1999). While this population report lower levels of perceived social support in comparison to the general population (Caron *et al.*, 1998), higher levels have been reported by clients in community settings, a factor, among others, found to be significant for subjective QoL evaluations.

The relationship between the objective and subjective indicators of QoL for people with chronic mental health problems appears to be weak, a finding that also corresponds to general population data (Campbell, Converse and Rodgers, 1976). The nature of the relationship between the two indicators is obviously complex, and it would appear that there is not a one-to-one mapping between objective conditions and their subjective evaluation. Glatzer (1991) reports that individuals may experience feelings of satisfaction and deprivation at the same time. The occurrence of this disjunction between the objective and subjective components of QoL points to the need for further exploration of the mediating mechanisms by which these different constituent elements are appraised. As current theoretical models do not help explain the nature of the interrelationship between objective conditions and their subjective evaluation, it would seem important in the development of QoL research to examine the possible mediators of subjective well-being for people with chronic mental health problems and to delineate those factors that determine how individuals perceive and judge their QoL.

If satisfaction levels are unrelated to objective conditions, the question arises as to how satisfaction measures should be interpreted. Studies of the life satisfaction of people with chronic mental health problems typically report high levels of satisfaction, with the majority of clients reporting being 'mostly satisfied' in most life areas (Baker and Intagliata, 1982; Lehman, Ward and Linn, 1982). Whether these high levels of satisfaction can be accepted at face value as an expression of satisfaction with current QoL or whether they may be attributed to other factors is unclear. To use the terms applied by Campbell, Converse and Rodgers (1976), there may be difficulty in distinguishing between the satisfaction of success and the satisfaction of resignation. This may be especially the case when the objective life conditions fall below generally acceptable standards.

Yet despite the clustering of positive responses, life satisfaction measures do succeed in highlighting those life areas where most dissatisfaction exists, e.g. finance, health (Baker and Intagliata, 1982; Lehman, 1983a) and frequency of contact with family (Barry, Crosby and Bogg, 1993). However, the assumptions inherent in the use of satisfaction scales with a chronic psychiatric population have been questioned. Assessing satisfaction may involve a cognitive judgement concerning discrepancy between one's current situation and one's aspirations (Michalos, 1985). This judgement is likely to be affected by expectation levels, aspirations and comparison with others. Fabian (1991) points out that restricted life experiences can constrain the ability to draw the comparisons required for making subjective evaluations of life quality and that reported satisfaction may be more indicative of prior experience and current expectations.

This point is particularly important in relation to people with chronic mental health problems, many of whom may have suffered severe role constriction in their lives as a result of the illness or spent large portions of their life in psychiatric institutions. Low aspirations and depressed expectation levels may lead individuals to report satisfaction with life conditions considered inadequate by social norms. Quality of life research in the general population has examined the effects of aspirations, expectations and values on an individual's QoL evaluations (Andrews and Withey, 1976; Campbell, Converse and Rodgers, 1976); however, this area has not been explored with psychiatric populations. Understanding the link between these internal standards and satisfaction outcomes will lead to a better understanding of how individuals attach meaning to their experiences, as well as how these internal standards shift in response to external changes.

There are a whole host of factors affecting the reporting of life satisfaction, such as social desirability effects and an acquiescent response set. Currently, relatively little is known about the dynamics of reporting satisfaction among psychiatric populations. The majority of studies have been cross-sectional in nature and are not informative about changes in levels of life satisfaction over time or the accommodation of internal standards to changes in external conditions (Barry and Zissi, 1997).

Life satisfaction measures have been found to be sensitive to the effects of the psychiatric state (Lehman, 1983b), though the sensitivity of satisfaction measures to changes in external or internal life circumstances over time is not well documented. The majority of studies are cross-sectional and are not informative about changes in levels of life satisfaction over time or the accommodation of internal standards to changes in external conditions. While QoL studies of the impact of resettlement from hospital to the community, usually involving a considerable degree of change in residents' lives, have reported changes in the objective QoL indicators, corresponding changes in the subjective indices have not been evident. For example, a prospective study of the impact of resettlement on the QoL of long-term hospital patients from North Wales by Barry and Crosby (1996) reported that dramatic changes in the clients' lives following resettlement were not captured by life satisfaction measures. The findings from this repeated-measures study suggest that improvements in QoL following resettlement were evident in the objective QoL indices, the qualitative data and other outcome measures used in the study, but were not reflected in the satisfaction ratings, which remained relatively stable. Interpreting these findings raises the question as to whether the lack of change in the satisfaction measures is due to the failure of the service programmes to impact on the subjective well-being of clients, or is due to the insensitivity of the measures. The relative stability of life satisfaction measures over time and across situations has been addressed by Cheng (1988), who queries their appropriateness for the purposes of programme evaluation. This author argues that the effects of programme interventions may not be readily captured by life satisfaction scales and that large-scale interventions may be needed in order to bring about any change in satisfaction measures. Longitudinal studies are required to test empirically the sensitivity of these measures and to develop further the theoretical conceptualisation of subjective QoL. These methodological issues highlight the difficulties that may be encountered when using life satisfaction scales for the purpose of programme evaluation.

A MEDIATIONAL MODEL OF QUALITY OF LIFE

Drawing on the relevant information in the literature and based on empirical QoL findings obtained from a large-scale resettlement research project in North Wales (Barry and Crosby, 1996), a mediational model that focuses on the potential link between self-related constructs and subjective evaluations of QoL was proposed by Barry (1997) as a guide to understanding and interpreting QoL data. The disjunction between objective and subjective components of QoL suggest that there is a need for models that link objective indices (external conditions) with more psychological (internal) factors that may be more central in the structure of subjective QoL evaluations. There is a need to identify intervening variables and to assess their potential contribution to the process by which subjective evaluations of QoL are formulated.

In particular, there is a need to determine the extent to which external changes impact on the lives of people with chronic mental health problems in a perceptible manner and how these changes then mediate the subjective appraisal of QoL. To this end, the individual's perception of change, when comparing different treatment and living settings, may need to be incorporated in QoL assessments. Arns and Linney (1993) identified the concept of 'change' as a better predictor than other, more static, measures in the assessment of subjective well-being of people with chronic mental health problems. The importance of self-related constructs has also been identified. Arns and Linney (1993) reported an indirect impact of self-esteem, through self-efficacy, on life satisfaction. Levels of autonomy have also been found to be influential in promoting QoL in Mercier and King's study (1993). Rosenfield (1992) highlighted the importance of control and reported that programme interventions providing economic independence and empowerment affect QoL because of their relationship to the individual's sense of mastery.

These studies point to the importance of psychological constructs and cognitive mechanisms in the way in which individuals perceive and articulate their QoL responses. Their findings, which are based on studies from both community and hospital populations, underline the significant role that cognitive mechanisms and internal referent concepts could play in explaining how respondents arrive at their relevant judgements, and how they attach meaning to their experiences. Specifically, levels of expectation, levels of aspirations and perceived control were found to be significant predictors of community respondents' life domain satisfaction (Gutek *et al.*, 1983). In addition, perceptions of mastery, self-efficacy, self-esteem, self-worth and personal autonomy are identified as critical components in the QoL of individuals with chronic mental health problems (Rosenfield, 1992; Arns and Linney, 1993; Boevink *et al.*, 1994; Mechanic *et al.*, 1994). The contribution of these concepts to perceived subjective well-being more generally has been widely discussed in the social psychology literature (Bandura, 1977; Pearlin and Schooler, 1978).

Barry's theoretical model of QoL incorporates within a unified conceptual framework the main mediating variables that have been shown to play a role in subjective evaluations. The proposed model hypothesises that: (a) an appraisal process, involving variables such as expectations, aspirations and comparison standards, intervenes between objective conditions and subjective QoL evaluations and (b) this appraisal process is influenced by a number of interrelated variables, among which are self-related constructs, which mediate the impact of internal and external life changes on perceived QoL.

The key feature of the model, as outlined in Fig. 3.1, is an emphasis on understanding how subjective evaluations are articulated, by proposing the contribution of an 'appraisal process'. It is hypothesised that this process is mediated by a number of interrelated variables, including self-efficacy, self-esteem

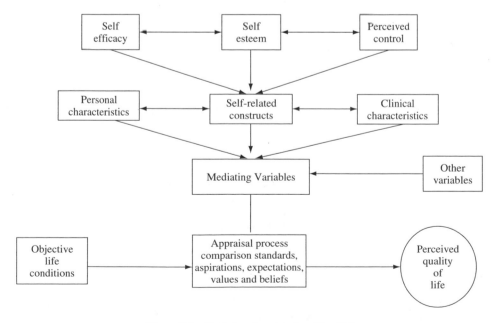

Figure 3.1   Mediational model of quality of life

and perceived control. This mediational model appears to offer a constructive way of integrating a range of variables and provides a potential framework to bridge the gap between external objective conditions and subjective evaluations of QoL.

EMPIRICAL INVESTIGATION

A cross-sectional study examining the impact of resettlement on the well-being of former long-term psychiatric in-patients in Greece was carried out four years after the move from hospital (Zissi, 1997; Zissi and Barry, 1997; Zissi, Barry and Cochrane, 1998). The residents' subjective experience of the resettlement process and their current QoL in the community settings were examined. The mediational model depicted in Fig.3.1 was used to guide the development of the QoL assessments and to examine the impact of both perceived change and internal referents on the subjective QoL evaluations.

Sample and Settings

The sample is comprised of former long-term psychiatric in-patients who had been moved from psychiatric hospitals in Greece to community-based hostels ($n=99$). Of the sample, 54 residents completed the QoL interview. The settings were 12 highly supervised community-based hostels, distributed throughout the Greek mainland (see Zissi, 1997, for further details).

Development of the Quality of Life Schedule (Greek Version)

The original Lehman's Quality of Life Interview (Lehman *et al.*, 1982, 1988) and the Bangor Quality of Life Schedule (Barry, Crosby and Bogg, 1993), together with the mediational model proposed by Barry, constituted the main frameworks for the development of the Greek quality of life schedule. The purpose of the Modified Quality of Life Schedule (Greek version) was to assess the perceived QoL of long-term psychiatric clients in Greece, incorporating the measurement of self-related constructs, as outlined in the model, across the various life domains. The main consideration in developing the modified schedule was to introduce additional items, including: self-related constructs, simplified complex evaluative judgements, 'transition' and 'expectation' scales and the exploration of individuals' subjective experiences and aspirations through applying open-ended questions. The modified version consists of 147 items and retains the same basic structure as Lehman's scale, i.e. objective and subjective indicators across a number of life domains, together with mediator variables. The subjective indices include five-point satisfaction scales, five-point transition scales of perceived change and five-point expectation scales. The methodological development of the QoL mediators in the modified quality of life schedule was the main task. Items exploring internal experiences of self-concept and perceived autonomy were developed and incorporated across life domains in order to assess how subjective well-being in different life domains is mediated by these experiences. These items were adapted from existing global measures of the relevant concepts, such as self-esteem and self-efficacy. Operationalisation of the relevant QoL mediators was guided by the need to base these constructs on the everyday experiences and life concerns of people with chronic mental health problems. This was achieved by incorporating the items across various life domains. The modified schedule was found to have good face and content validity (Zissi, 1997) and the internal consistency reliability of the objective, subjective and mediator variables across the various life domains was found to be satisfactory, comparing well with levels reported by Lehman (1983a) and Barry, Crosby and Bogg (1993). Further details on the development of the measures can be found in Zissi, Barry and Cochrane (1998).

Analysis

The relationship between objective indices, QoL mediators (self-concept and autonomy), perceived 'change' and perceived overall subjective psychological well-being was examined by using a series of regression analyses. Perceived 'change' refers to perceived comparisons between current conditions and the previous experience in hospital. The relationship between age, levels of dependency, depression and perceived overall subjective psychological well-being was also examined. The main form of analysis was multiple regression, with overall subjective well-being as the dependent variable. Age, functional characteristics (levels of dependency and depression), objective indices (family, social contacts, leisure activities, physical health and safety), QoL mediators (perceived autonomy and self-concept) and perceived 'change' were the independent variables. An Overall Subjective Well-Being (OSWB) index was computed by taking the mean of the reported levels of satisfaction across five life domains (living conditions, social relations, leisure activities, family, physical health), together with the reported satisfaction with life in general. The internal consistency reliability of the overall subjective well-being index was satisfactory with Cronbach's alpha = 0.61.

Bivariate Analysis

For the purpose of the main analysis, a bivariate correlational analysis was conducted between age, functional characteristics, objective indices, QoL mediators and perceived 'change' with overall subjective well-being. These correlations were obtained following the reliability analysis of the relevant scales. Perceived 'change' was most highly correlated with overall subjective well-being, though the correlation with QoL mediators (self-concept and perceived autonomy) is slightly lower. The objective indices were not found to correlate significantly with overall subjective well-being, whereas a modest correlation was obtained between levels of dependency, as measured by the Total General Behaviour score of the REHAB (rehabilitation evaluation – Hall and Baker) scale (Hall and Baker, 1984) and overall subjective well-being. No significant correlations were found between psychopathology, as measured by KRS (Krawiecka rating scale) (Krawiecka, Goldberg and Vaughan, 1977), and overall subjective well-being. Finally, a modest correlation was obtained between age and overall subjective well-being. A one-way analysis of variance revealed no relationship between gender and overall subjective well-being, $F = 2.50$, DOF (degrees of freedom) = 1.41 (NS, or not significant).

Main Analyses

To examine the utility of objective indices, QoL mediators (self-concept and perceived autonomy) and perceived 'change' in predicting overall subjective psychological well-being, the different sets of independent variables were initially entered independently in a series of multiple regression analyses. The main results are summarised in Table 3.1. It may be seen that perceived 'change' ($F = 21.58$, DOF = 1.34, $P < 0.0001$) and QoL mediators, self-concept and perceived autonomy ($F = 11.88$, DOF = 2.31, $P < 0.0005$) independently account for a high proportion of the variance in overall subjective psychological well-being. While the objective indices, frequency of family contact, objective social contacts, objective leisure activities, objective physical health and objective safety, account for a very

Table 3.1 Summary of multiple regressions of objective indices, QoL mediators and perceived 'change' on overall subjective well-being

Variables[a]	Multiple R	R^2	β	DOF	F (P)
Objective indices	0.30	0.09		5,27	0.54 (NS)
Family			0.18		
Social contacts			0.11		
Leisure activities			0.17		
Health			−0.03		
Safety			−0.01		
QoL mediators	0.66	0.44		2,31	11.88 < 0.0005
Self-concept			0.29		
Autonomy			0.45		
'Change'	0.62	0.39	0.62	1,34	21.58 < 0.0001

[a] Sets of variables entered separately.

small and statistically non-significant proportion of variance ($F=0.54$, DOF$=5$, 27, NS). A multiple regression on overall subjective well-being of the combined effects of self-concept, perceived autonomy and perceived 'change' account for 48% ($F=8.28$, DOF$=3$, 27, $P<0.0005$) of the variance in overall subjective well-being. With regard to age, levels of dependency and depression, the results indicate that both age ($F=4.17$, DOF$=1.41$, $P<0.05$) and levels of dependency ($F=4.76$, DOF$=1.41$, $P<0.05$) explain small, but statistically significant, amounts of variance in overall subjective well-being. Interestingly, depression fails to account for any statistically significant proportion of variance in overall subjective well-being in the present sample ($F(1,30)=0.54$, NS).

Looking at the role of the objective indicators in the structure of the QoL data, it was found that these indicators explained a substantial and statistically significant amount of variance in self-concept ($F=3.19$, DOF$=5$, 24, $P<0.05$) and in perceived 'change' ($F=4.16$, DOF$=5$, 23, $P<0.01$). Objective indicators failed to account for any statistically significant variance in perceived autonomy. However, objective leisure indices appeared to have a strong association with levels of perceived autonomy ($\beta=0.38$). The results of the analysis are also graphically presented in Fig. 3.2.

Given the strong predictive power of perceived 'change' in the structure of the QoL data, stepwise regression analysis was applied in order to examine the combined effects of the three sets of variables: levels of dependency, objective indices and QoL mediators in predicting perceived 'change'. The

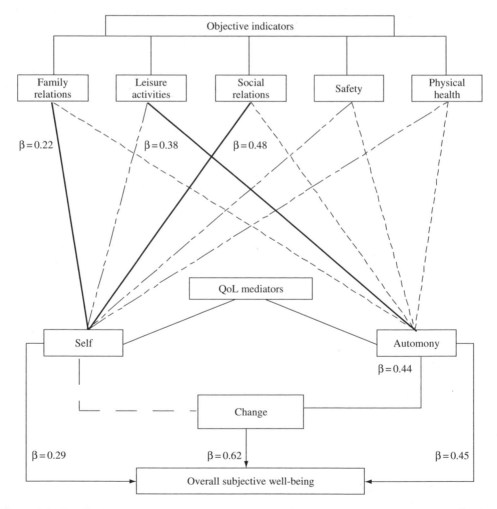

Figure 3.2 Empirically supported mediational model of QoL. Broken lines represent non-significant β values. (Personal variables: age $\beta=0.30$; levels of dependency $\beta=-0.32$; depression $\beta=-0.13$)

results of this analysis indicate that perceived autonomy is the best predictor, explaining 39% of the variance ($F_{change} = 14.94$, $P < 0.001$), followed by frequency of family contact, which adds a statistically significant proportion of variance ($F_{change} = 5.68$, $P < 0.001$) and, finally, levels of dependency adds a smaller, but statistically significant, amount of variance ($F_{change} = 5.45$, $P < 0.001$).

CONCLUSIONS AND FUTURE DIRECTIONS

The findings from the Greek study suggest that both perceived change and the QoL mediators of self-constructs and perceived autonomy were most influential in the construction of subjective QoL evaluations. Within the model, the strongest association was between perceived change and subjective well-being. Perceived improvements in residents' lives, consequent on the move from hospital to community settings, had the most predictive power in the residents' evaluation of their current QoL. The analysis demonstrated the importance of the QoL mediators of self-concept and perceived autonomy in the structure of the QoL data. The objective indicators were found to have no predictive power on subjective well-being directly. However, given the relationships between objective and self-related constructs and perceived change, the influence of the objective indices can be said to be indirect. Depression was found to have no influence on the structure of the QoL data, whereas levels of dependency were found to have an impact on both perceived subjective well-being and perceived changes. The less-dependent residents reported more perceived changes in their lives since resettlement and also enjoyed a greater sense of subjective well-being. Perceived autonomy, frequency of family contacts and level of dependency were found to be the key variables in explaining residents' perceived changes in their lives.

The present analyses are based on data from a cross-sectional study and are therefore limited in the extent to which the predictions of the model may be fully tested. A longitudinal study with a larger sample is needed to test the model more fully and validate its predictions and hypothesised direction of effects. However, the findings from this preliminary analysis are generally supportive of the model and reveal some interesting relationships. They suggest that: (a) self-related constructs and perceived change are directly and strongly linked with subjective well-being evaluations and (b) an appraisal process, as captured by the transition scales, intervenes between external life conditions and subjective evaluations of QoL. This appraisal process is influenced by a range of variables, but mainly by the construct of autonomy. It is clear that self-related constructs serve a mediating role between external life conditions and perceived subjective well-being, and that an appraisal process intervenes between objective conditions and their subjective evaluations. Residents were able to register changes in their lives and to articulate comparisons between their previous conditions and current circumstances. These comparisons between life in hospital and in the community had the most predictive power in the overall index of subjective psychological well-being. Explicitly measuring the variable of perceived change in this study permitted an exploration of how the changes in external living conditions were perceived and appraised by individual residents.

The overall framework of the mediational model, together with the findings from the Greek study reported here, fit well with a psychosocial model of intervention and may prove useful in exploring how service input impacts on clients' self-perceptions, thereby affecting their QoL. Self-esteem, self-efficacy and sense of mastery have long been recognised as critical factors in the long-term success of rehabilitation (Shaffer and Gambino, 1978; Rosenfield, 1987). However, it is surprising how little is known about the way that service programmes affect clients' self-perceptions. Individuals with chronic mental health problems experience damaged self-esteem (Estroff, 1989), low levels of perceived self-efficacy (Hays and Buckle, 1992), stigma and feelings of powerlessness and hopelessness (Rosenfield, 1989). Thus, psychosocial interventions designed to build clients' capacities and personal resources have an important role to play in the rehabilitation process. An example is programmes that begin to repair clients' damaged self-images by helping them to fulfil new roles and identities as community members (Arns and Linney, 1993). Together with supports for economic independence and empowerment (Rosenfield, 1992), these programmes have been shown to have a positive effect on clients' sense of control and hence on the subjective quality of life. The findings reported above support the contention that interventions which raise clients' self-concept and autonomy are likely to also raise overall subjective well-being.

Subject to further testing using more sophisticated statistical techniques, the mediational model appears to have important implications for interpreting QoL data from people with chronic mental health problems, and for the planning, delivery and evaluation of mental health programmes. The model provides a direction along which to build a theoretical and empirical foundation for understanding the dynamics of QoL assessments and perceptions. However, the role of broader social, political and economic factors on perceived QoL also needs to be acknowledged. Kilian and Angermeyer (1999) note that the scope of QoL research must be widened in various ways and that the clinical perspective must be complemented with a societal one. Political factors, such as social policy, the organisation of the mental heath care system, economic and social factors, and the role of public attitudes may also significantly influence the QoL of people with mental health problems. A broader mental health promotion framework (World Health Organization, 2002) incorporating these diverse influences at the individual, community and societal levels brings a useful perspective to understanding the complex interactions between clients' perceptions, internal referents, care environments and the broader social determinants in influencing quality of life and social well-being.

REFERENCES

Andrews, R.F. & Withey, S.B. (1976). *Social Indicators of Well-Being: Americans' Perceptions of Life Quality*, Plenum Press, New York.

Andrews, G., Teeson, M., Stewart, G. & Hoult, J. (1990). Follow-up of community placement of the chronic mentally ill in New South Wales, *Hosp. Community Psychiatry*, **41**(2), 184–188.

Arns, P.G. & Linney, J.A. (1993). Work, self, and life satisfaction for persons with severe and persistent mental disorders, *Psychosocial Rehabil.*, **17**, 63–79.

Atkinson, M., Zibin, S. & Chuang, H. (1997). Characterizing quality of life among patients with chronic mental illness: A critical examination of the self-report methodology, *Am. J. Psychiatry*, **154**, 99–105.

Baker, F. & Intagliata, J. (1982). Quality of life in the evaluation of community support systems, *Evaluation and Progm. Plann.*, **5**, 69–79.

Bandura, A. (1977). Self-efficacy: Toward a unifying theory of behavioural change, *Psycholog. Rev.*, **84**, 191–215.

Barry, M.M. (1997). Well-being and life satisfaction as components of quality of life in mental disorders, in *Quality of Life in Mental Disorders* (Eds H. Katschnig, H. Freeman & N. Sartorius), pp. 31–42, John Wiley & Sons, Chichester.

Barry, M.M. & Crosby, C. (1996). Quality of life as an evaluative measure in assessing the impact of community care on people with long-term psychiatric disorders, *Br. J. Psychiatry*, **168**, 210–216.

Barry, M.M., Crosby, C. & Bogg, J. (1993). Methodological issues in evaluating the quality of life of long-stay psychiatric patients, *J. Men. Health*, **2**, 43–56.

Barry, M.M. & Zissi, A. (1997). Quality of life as an outcome measure in evaluating mental health services: A review of the empirical evidence, *Social Psychiatry Psychiat. Epidemiol.*, **32**, 38–47.

Bengtsson-Tops, A. & Hansson, L. (1999). Clinical and social needs of schizophrenic outpatients living in the community: The relationship between needs and subjective quality of life, *Social Psychiatry and Psychiat. Epidemiol.*, **34**, 513–518.

Bigelow, D.A., Brodsky, G., Stewart, L. & Olson, M. (1982). The concept and measurement of quality of life as a dependent variable in evaluation of mental health services, in *Innovative Approaches to Mental Health Evaluation* (Eds G.J. Stahler & W.R. Tash), pp. 345–366, Academic Press, New York.

Boevink, W., Wolf, J., Nieuwenhuizen, C. & Schene, A. (1994). The quality of life of the long-term mentally ill: A conceptual exploration, Paper presented at the 7th European Symposium on *Quality of Life and Disabilities in Mental Disorders*, Vienna, 7–9 April 1994.

Campbell, A., Converse, P.E. & Rodgers, W.L. (1976). *The Quality of American Life*, Russell Sage Foundation, New York.

Caron, J., Tempier, R., Mercier, C. & Leouffre, P. (1998). Components of social support and quality of life in severely mentally ill, low income individuals and a general population group, *Community Ment. Health J.*, **34**(5), 459–474.

Cheng, Sheung-Tak (1988). Subjective quality of life in the planning and evaluation of programs, *Evaluation and Progm. Plann.*, **11**, 123–134.

Corrigan, P.W. & Buican, B. (1995). The construct validity of subjective quality of life for the severely mentally ill, *J. Nerv. Ment. Dis.*, **183**, 281–285.

Estroff, E.E. (1989). Self, identity, and subjective experiences of schizophrenia: In search of the subject, *Schizophrenia Bull.*, **15**, 189–196.

Fabian, E.S. (1990). Quality of life: A review of theory and practice implications for individuals with long-term mental illness, *Rehabil. Psychol.*, **35**, 161–170.

Fabian, E.S. (1991). Using quality of life indicators in rehabilitation program evaluation, *Rehabil. Counseling Bull.*, **34**, 344–356.

Farragher, B., Carey, T. & Owens, J. (1996). Long-term follow-up of rehabilitated patients with chronic psychiatric illness in Ireland, *Psychiat. Serv.*, **47**(10), 1120–1122.

Glatzer, W. (1991). Quality of life in advanced industrialised countries: the case of West Germany, in *Subjective Well-Being* (Eds F. Strack, M. Argyle & N. Schwarz), pp. 261–279, Pergamon, Oxford.

Gutek, B.A., Allen, H., Tyler, T.R., Lau, R.R. & Majchrzak, A. (1983). The importance of internal referents as determinants of satisfaction, *J. Community Psychol.*, **11**, 11–120.

Hall, J.N. & Baker, R. (1984). *REHAB*, Vine Publishing Company, Aberdeen.

Hays, J.R. & Buckle, K.E. (1992). Self-efficacy among hospitalized mentally ill patients, *Psycholog. Rep.*, **70**, 57–58.

Holloway, F. & Carson, J. (1999). Subjective quality of life, psychopathology, satisfaction with care and insight: An exploratory study. *Int. J. Social Psychiatry*, **45**(4), 259–267.

Kilian, R. & Angermeyer, M. (1999). Quality of life in psychiatry as an ethical duty: From the clinical to the societal perspective, *Psychopathology*, **32**, 127–134.

Krawiecka, M., Goldberg, D. & Vaughan, M. (1977). A standardised psychiatric assessment scale for rating chronic psychotic patients, *Acta Psychiatrica Scand.*, **55**, 299–308.

Lehman, A.F. (1983a). The well-being of chronic mental patients: Assessing their quality of life, *Arch. Gen. Psychiatry*, **40**, 369–373.

Lehman, A.F. (1983b). The effects of psychiatric symptoms on quality of life assessments among the chronically mentally ill, *Evaluation and Prog. Plann.*, **6**, 143–151.

Lehman, A.F. (1988). A Quality of Life Interview for the chronically mentally ill, *Evaluation and Progm. Plann.*, **11**, 51–62.

Lehman, A.F., Ward, N.C. & Linn, L.S. (1982). Chronic mental patients: The quality of life issue, *Am. J. Psychiatry*, **139**, 1271–1276.

Malm, U., May, P.R.A. & Dencker, S.J. (1981). Evaluation of the quality of life of the schizophrenic outpatient: A checklist, *Schizophrenia Bull.*, **7**, 477–488.

Mechanic, D., McAlpine, D., Rosenfield, S. & Davis, D. (1994). Effects of illness attribution and depression on the quality of life among persons with serious mental illness, *Social Sci. Med.*, **39**, 155–164.

Mercier, C. & King, S. (1993). A latent variable causal model of the quality of life and community tenure of psychotic patients, *Acta Psychiatrica Scand.*, **89**, 72–77.

Michalos, A.C. (1985). Multiple discrepancies theory (MDT), *Social Indicators Res.*, **16**, 347–443.

Oliver, J.P.J., Huxley, P.J., Priebe, S. & Kaiser, W. (1997). Measuring the quality of life of severely mentally ill people using the Lancashire Quality of Life Profile, *Social Psychiatry Psychiat. Epidemiol.*, **32**, 76–83.

Pearlin, L.I. & Schooler, C. (1978). The structure of coping, *J. Health and Social Behaviour*, **19**, 2–21.

Roessler, W., Salize, H.J., Cucchiaro, G., Reinhrd, I. & Kernig, C. (1999). Does the place of treatment influence the quality of life of schizophrenics?, *Acta Psychiatric Scand.*, **100**, 142–148.

Rosenfield, S. (1987). Services organization and quality of life among the seriously mentally ill, *New Directions for Ment. Health Serv.*, **36**, 47–59.

Rosenfield, S. (1989). The effects of women's employment: Personal control and sex differences in mental health, *J. Health and Social Behaviour*, **30**, 77–91.

Rosenfield, S. (1992). Factors contributing to the subjective quality of life of the chronic mentally ill, *J. Health and Social Behaviour*, **33**, 299–315.

Ruud, T., Martinsen, E.W. & Friis, S. (1998). Chronic patients in psychiatric institutions: Psychopathology, level of functioning and need for care, *Acta Psychiatrica Scand.*, **97**, 55–61.

Shaffer, H. & Gambino, B. (1978). Psychological rehabilitation, skills-building and self-efficacy, *Am. Psychologist*, **33**, 394–396.

Slade, M., Leese, M., Taylor, R. & Thornicroft, G. (1999). The association between needs and quality of life in an epidemiologically representative sample of people with psychosis, *Acta Psychiatric Scand.*, **100**, 149–157.

Tempier, R., Mercier, C., Leouffre, P. & Caron, J. (1997). Quality of life and social integration of severely mentally ill patients: A longitudinal study. *J. Psychiatry Neurosci.*, **22**(4), 249–255.

Trauer, T., Duckmanton, R.A. & Chiu, E. (1998). A study of the quality of life of the severely mentally ill, *Int. J. Social Psychiatry*, **44**(2), 79–91.

Wiersma, D. & van Busschbach, J. (2001). Are needs and satisfaction of care associated with quality of life? An epidemiological survey among the severely mentally ill in the Netherlands, *Eur. Arch. Psychiatry and Clin. Neurosci.*, **251**, 239–246.

World Health Organization (2002). World Health Report on *Reducing Risks, Promoting Healthy Life*, WHO, Geneva.

Zautra, A. & Goodhart, D. (1979). Quality of life indicators: A review of the literature, *Community Ment. Health Rev.*, **4**, 1–10.

Zissi, A., Barry, M.M. & Cochrane, R. (1998). A mediational model of quality of life for individuals with severe mental health problems. *Psycholog. Med.*, **28**, 1221–1230.

Zissi, A. & Barry, M.M. (1997). From Leros Asylum to community-based facilities: levels of functioning and quality of life among hostel residents in Greece, *Int. J. Social Psychiatry*, **43**, 104–115.

Zissi, A. (1997). From Leros Asylum to community-based hostels: Quality of life, levels of functioning and the care process among psychiatric residents in Greece, Unpublished Doctoral Thesis, University of Birmingham.

4

Role Functioning as a Component of Quality of Life in Mental Disorders

Durk Wiersma

INTRODUCTION

The multidimensional concept of quality of life (QoL) contains aspects of physical, psychological and social well-being, but is not yet well defined. Any broad consensus on the definition and explanation of QoL is lacking. There is nevertheless the recognition that social well-being or social function is an important dimension, although many disagree as to how this dimension should be conceptualised and operationalised. 'Social function' is indeed an ambiguous term, carrying different meanings, which are partly individually, partly collectively focused (see Tyrer and Casey, 1993; Mueser and Tarrier, 1998). This is expressed by such terms as 'cooperation', 'affability' and 'bonding' versus 'community', 'status' and 'social class'. Tyrer and Casey define social function as 'the level at which an individual functions in his or her social context, such function ranging between self-preservation and basic living skills to the relationship with others in society'. They point to various factors that affect social function but should not be confused with it, such as personality, intellect, symptoms or circumstances. Mental disorders are strongly associated with social dysfunctioning, which is particularly the case with schizophrenia and the major affective disorders, but also with personality disorders.

For a long time, social dysfunctioning was considered an epiphenomenon and part of the disease process; criteria for the diagnosis of a mental disorder were, and still are, often derived from the domains of work and social relationships. However, there are at least two related reasons why social functioning deserves a closer look. Firstly, there is growing evidence that the courses of symptomatology and social dysfunctioning may vary relatively independently (Hurry and Sturt, 1981; Casey, Tyrer and Platt, 1985; De Jong et al., 1986; Wohlfarth et al., 1993; Glynn, 1998). A well-known example is the patient with paranoid psychosis or manic-depressive psychosis who may function well in his/her social roles. Another example is the social disablement of a schizophrenic patient, which is characterised more by his/her social disabilities than by his/her persistent psychiatric symptoms. The former may require a different kind of intervention from usual, e.g. psychosocial rehabilitation focusing on cognitive and social abilities that are crucial for a more independent life. Therefore, separate measurement of these disabilities would be justified, so that the right choice of treatment can be made.

Secondly, there is an increasing trend to treat patients in the community instead of in mental hospitals (Freeman and Henderson, 1991; Wiersma et al., 2002), but this changing orientation needs careful evaluation with respect to its consequences. To what extent is survival in the community possible and

Quality of Life in Mental Disorders, Second Edition   Edited by H. Katschnig, H. Freeman and N. Sartorius
© 2006 John Wiley & Sons, Ltd

what is the QoL there? Are community programmes better than hospital treatment, and for whom? Some data show that the risk of rehospitalisation of schizophrenic patients seems to be lower in a community care than in a hospital-based system (Sytema, Burgess and Tansella, 2002), but increasing concerns are raised as to the consequences of the deinstitutionalisation process (see Munk-Jorgensen, 1999). Therefore, a separate measurement is justified for the evaluation of outcome, as well as costs and benefits.

Social dysfunction as a consequence of disease or disorder has been conceptualised in terms of (social) disabilities and (role) handicaps, but the usual diagnostic systems of the *International Classification of Diseases* (ICD) (World Health Organization, 1992a, 1992b) and the *Diagnostic and Statistical Manual of Mental Disorders* (DSM) (American Psychiatric Association, 1987, 1994; Skodol *et al.*, 1988) offer no adequate solution to the problem of classification and assessment of social dysfunctioning. This chapter will discuss two conceptual models of disability and role functioning that characterise a person's integration into the community – an aspect that is of the utmost importance for psychiatry and mental health care.

CONCEPTUAL MODELS OF DISABILITY IN ROLE PERFORMANCE

The World Health Organization (WHO) has been active in developing a conceptual framework to study the consequences of diseases and disorders in terms of functional disabilities and social handicaps that are experienced, as well as the effectiveness of health care to handle these kinds of problems. In 1980, it produced the *International Classification of Impairments, Disabilities and Handicaps* (ICIDH) (World Health Organization, 1980) for trial purposes and in 2001 a major revision of it, the *International Classification of Functioning, Disability and Health* (ICF), which has officially been endorsed by the World Health Assembly for international use. The ICF has been developed to provide a scientific basis for studying health and health-related states, outcomes and determinants, to establish a common language and to provide a systematic coding scheme for health information systems. It can serve various purposes – as a tool for statistics, research, clinical work, social policy and/or education. While the ICD classifies health conditions (disease, disorder, injury) within an aetiological framework, the ICF is focused on functioning and disability associated with health conditions. The ICIDH originally distinguished three levels of experiences and of consequences of disease or disorder for the individual: impairment (i.e. loss or abnormality of psychological, physiological or anatomical structure or function, representing the exteriorisation of the pathological state), disability (i.e. restriction or lack of ability to perform an activity, representing objectification of an impairment and reflecting the disturbances at the level of the person) and handicap, representing the disadvantages experienced by the individual as a result of the impairments and/or disabilities that limit or prevent the fulfilment of social roles. A linear causality was implied in the interrelationships between these concepts.

The ICF differs substantially from this scheme and does not model the 'process' of functioning and disability; it provides a means to map the different constructs and domains – the building blocks to create models and study different aspects of this process. The ICF has two parts, each with two components: Part 1, Functioning and Disability, (a) body functions and structures and (b) activities and participation; Part 2, Contextual Factors, (a) environmental factors and (b) personal factors. 'Impairments' are problems in body functioning or structure as a significant deviation or loss. 'Activity' is the execution of a task or action by an individual and participation is his/her involvement in a life situation. Disabilities are now defined as activity limitations or as participation restrictions. Since concepts are formulated in as neutral terms as possible, 'handicap' is no longer used; disability is used as a general term, but not in defining categories. This revision is a major improvement in conceptual clarity, structure and meaning (e.g. the distinction between the function and structure, much less overlap, description of environmental factors) although the number of detailed categories is greatly expanded, which may limit its practical use. Important here, in particular for people with mental disorders, are the nine domains of activities and participation, of which self-care (e.g. looking after one's health), domestic life (e.g. household tasks), interpersonal interactions and relationships (e.g. family, partner), major life areas (e.g. education, work) and community, social and civic life (e.g. recreation, religion, citizenship) have relevance to role performance. Difficulties or problems in these domains can arise when there is a qualitative or quantitative alteration in the way an individual carries out these domain functions. Limitations or restrictions have to be assessed against a generally accepted population standard; the standard or norm is that of an individual without a similar health condition. The limitation or restriction records the discordance between the observed and the expected performance, and are coded on a five-point scale as 'no', 'mild', 'moderate', 'severe' or 'complete difficulty'. The domains are qualified by two qualifiers of 'performance' and 'capacity'. The performance qualifier describes what an individual does in his/her current environment, while the capacity qualifier describes an individual's ability to execute a task or an action. This construct aims to indicate the highest probable level of functioning that a person may reach in a given domain at a given moment. It is assumed that assessment of the full ability is done in a 'standardised' environment (e.g. test setting), to neutralise the varying impact of different environments. Thus, 'capacity' reflects the environmentally adjusted ability of the individual. The gap between capacity and performance reflects the difference between the impacts of current and uniform environments. Both capacity and performance qualifiers can be further used, with or without assistive devices or personal assistance.

All in all, disability is characterised as the outcome or the result of a complex relationship between an individual's health condition and both personal (e.g. gender, race, age, life style, social background, life events) and environmental factors (e.g. natural environment, support, attitudes, services, policies). The ICF remains in the broad context of health and does not cover circumstances that are not health related, such as those brought about by socioeconomic factors. The ICF is stated to be to some extent an integration of the medical and the social models of disability, by incorporating the various perspectives of functioning and disability. The medical model stresses disability as a direct consequence of disease that requires medical care, individual treatment, adjustment, and on the political level health care policy. The social model, however, sees disability as a socially created problem – not an attribute of an individual, but rather a complex condition in a social environment that requires social and political action; disability is a political issue of social change (see for more discussion Bickenbach *et al.*, 1999).

The revised classification has to a large extent met the conceptual criticisms levelled at the ICIDH, e.g. because of the distinction between the concepts of impairments, disabilities and handicaps, of the lack of internal coherence as to how the concepts were defined (e.g. role disability and handicap) and of the role of environmental factors (Wiersma and Chapireau, 1991). The ICIDH was ambiguous and confusing with respect to social functioning, the use of the concepts of role, values and norms, and the issue of circumstances. In the ICF, the concept of social or 'survival' role has been abandoned in favour of more neutral activities and participation in life situations. Though distinctions between the two are unclear and not specified, both represent a broad perspective on functioning (from washing one's hands to engaging in political life) and a wider range of categories (55!). Nevertheless, an important aspect of a social role is maintained and strengthened: taking explicitly into account the normative, societal approach in the assessment of actual performance of an individual, what is expected from a healthy person in the same circumstances and to what extent the individual deviates from that. How to assess the performance and capacity remains as yet an unresolved major problem, although there is progress in the development of the WHODAS II (asking about limitations of activity with physical and mental health) (World Health Organization, 2001a) and in linking health status measures to the ICF (World Health Organization, 2001b; see Cieza *et al.*, 2002).

Another conceptual model has been developed by Nagi (1969, 1991) using the terms of: (a) active pathology (i.e. involving interruption of normal processes and simultaneous efforts of the organism to regain a normal state), (b) impairment (i.e. loss or abnormality of an anatomical, physiological, mental or emotional nature), (c) functional limitation (i.e. at the level of the organism as a whole) and (d) disability. This latter term is defined as the inability or limitation to perform socially defined roles and tasks that are expected within a sociocultural and physical environment, such as in the family, work, education, recreation and self-care. The word 'handicap' has been left out, mainly because it is felt to be a stigma. Disability in this model is explicitly focused on role functioning (Pope and Tarlov, 1991). Role functioning is central in both models or conceptual frameworks. It may therefore be helpful to delineate the theoretical structure and status of social role theory.

SOCIAL ROLE THEORY

Sociologists, psychologists and anthropologists have used the concept of 'role' to study both the individual and the collectivity within a single conceptual framework. Anthropologists such as Ralph Linton (1936) traditionally treated role as a culturally derived blueprint for behaviour. In this sense, it is an external constraint on an individual and a normative rather than a behavioural concept. 'Roles' are always linked to a status or position in a particular pattern or social structure, which consists of a network of social relations and communications. A 'role' represents the dynamic aspect of a status. These anthropologists, however, made no distinction between behavioural and normative aspects of role; both actual and ideal behaviour were used to describe the people studied, and a uniform mode of behaviour was assumed in regard to status. However, empirical research showed that these assumptions are not valid and that a consensus concerning status–role behaviour is lacking.

Psychologists such as Newcombe (see Gordon, 1966) have relied heavily on interactional theory and were interested in roles more in relation to the self and to personality. They treated role and status as a given, and not as a variable, defining role as the subjective perception of direct interaction. This comes close to the symbolic interactionism that regards self-consciousness and the continuous interpretation of the actions of others as the motive of human action. Their focus is on the individual response, based on the meaning attached to certain actions of other people. This interactionistic role concept, however, may not properly take into account the pathological changes in experience and behaviour that is due to mental disorders.

In contrast, sociologists such as Parsons (1958), described as the structural functionalists, considered the reciprocal relationship or the socially preconditioned interaction of two or more persons as the core of the analysis. Parsons regarded a role as the organised system of participation of an individual in a social system and defined it in terms of reciprocal orientations. Thus, status and role were the building blocks or means by which individuals are able to engage in a reciprocal relationship. Essential parts of such a relationship are expectations that, according to Dahrendorf (1965), could have the character of *kann* (can), *soll* (shall) or *muss* (must), implying the application of positive or negative sanctions in order to promote conformity to the prevailing norms and values. However, other people are important here, to define whether an individual is behaving in a 'normal', 'deviant' or 'maladjusted' way.

There is, unfortunately, no clear consensus as to how to define a social role (see Biddle, 1979). The following description, composed of common elements found in most of the definitions, may be helpful: 'a social role is a complex of expectations which people have as to the behaviour of a person who takes up a certain position in society'. A 'position' is a location in a social structure which is associated with a set of social norms or expectations, held in common by members of a social group. Such a group consists mainly of people with whom the individual frequently interacts, such as family members, friends and colleagues. There are many positions in the social structure of a group, an association, a profession, a community or society as a whole, with a corresponding number of social roles. Role performance therefore refers to the actual behaviour of the individual in the context of a particular role.

A social disability or role disability could now be defined as: 'a deficiency in the ability to perform activities and manifest behaviour, as these are expected in the context of a well-defined social role'. The deficiency can be inferred from violations of or deviations from norms and expectations, but it is important to understand that anyone's behaviour should always be assessed against the background of how other people expect the individual to behave. It also means that such an assessment pertains above all to the individual's capacity for interpersonal functioning.

CLASSIFICATION OF ROLE PERFORMANCE

Social role theory does not produce a standard classification of roles that can be taken into account to give an adequate description of the individual's overall functioning or integration in the community. We therefore rely on what researchers put into their scales, schedules and instruments, but the number and content of roles in existing instruments vary. There is an overwhelming number of schedules and instruments, reviewed by Weissman, (1975), Weissman, Sholomskas and John (1981), Katschnig

(1983), Wing (1989) and Tyrer and Casey (1993). Others have considered instruments for specific use: Hall (1980) with respect to ward behaviour, Wallace (1986), Rosen, Hadzi-Pavlovic and Parker (1989) and Scott and Lehman (1998) with respect to schizophrenia and Tyrer (1990) with respect to personality disorders. (See also Chapter 7 on instruments of quality of life that over the main life domains.) The instruments for measuring social function or role performance show a reasonable level of agreement on a number of roles (see Table 4.1).

These are all more or less well-known instruments, described with data on their reliability and validity, but it is striking that different terms are used to describe role behaviour; some instruments use terms with a negative connotation (maladjustment, disability) and others neutral terms (adjustment, performance). Nevertheless, the content of these terms and concepts is to a large extent similar, although great differences remain as to the precise wording, description, assessment, anchor points, scaling, etc. Most instruments also measure other concepts such as social support, psychiatric symptoms, burden of the illness on the family, satisfaction or attitudes. However, there seems to be a consensus of opinion on eight areas of role behaviour (see Table 4.2).

These areas describe general domains of roles and status that apply to every individual in the community. Each area could be subdivided into smaller behavioural domains, e.g. in instrumental tasks and affective or attitudinal aspects. The description of expected behaviour is of course different in various communities or cultures: e.g. doing nothing is highly undesirable in Western countries, but may be less so in Eastern countries; similarly, taking part in the household by doing some cooking or household chores has a quite different meaning for young men in various European countries. The

Table 4.1 Selection of scales for social role function

Scale	Authors
Social Role Performance (SRP)	Hurry and Sturt (1981)
Groningen Social Disabilities Schedule (GSDS)	Wiersma, De Jong, and Ormel (1988); Wiersma *et al.* (1990)
Psychiatric Disability Assessment Schedule (DAS)	World Health Organization (1988)
Role Activity Performance Scale (RAPS)	Good-Ellis *et al.* (1987)
Social Adjustment Scale (SAS)	Weissman and Paykel (1974)
Social Behaviour Assessment Schedule (SBAS)	Platt *et al.* (1990)
Social Role Adjustment Instrument (SRAI)	Cohler *et al.* (1968)
Standardised Interview to Assess Social Maladjustment	Clare and Cairns (1978)
Structured and Scaled Interview to Assess Maladjustment (SSIAM)	Gurland *et al.* 1972

Table 4.2 Description of eight roles and role behaviour

Role area	Role behaviour with respect to
Occupation	Performance and routine in work, education, household and other daily activities
Household	Participation in and contribution to the household and its economic independence
Partner and marriage	Emotional and sexual relationship with partner or spouse
Parenthood	Contacts and affective relationship with children, including their caring
Family or kinship	Contacts and affective relationship with parents and siblings
Social relationships	Contacts and relationships in the community: friends, acquaintances and neighbours
General interest and participation	Interest in society and participation in societal organizations, including spare-time activities
Self-care	Personal care and hygiene and self-presentation of appearance

applicability of the role concept seems to be culturally universal, but it is essential to establish that the norms and values of the local community or of the people with whom the individual is interacting are decisive in the assessment. We should not assume the existence of general norms and values that apply to everybody; there is no general or objective standard of behaviour. Norms and values vary from community to community, and the acceptability of particular behaviour will sometimes be the result of negotiations between those involved. Therefore, ideal norms with respect to what should be done are not relevant here; empirical research has shown that their applicability hardly exists in practice (cf. Platt, 1981). Neither statistical nor personal norms are sufficient and adequate: they do not take into account the sociocultural context of the individual and do not reflect the actual differences between social and cultural environments. On the other hand, reliance on individual norms runs the risk of measuring merely on the coping style, personality or symptomatology of a person. It is preferable to speak about the norms of the 'reference group'. This consists of people who are in social or other respects of great importance to the individual. These could be people in his/her close environment, such as the partner, members of the family and those with whom the individual comes into direct contact while performing the different roles: colleagues at work, friends, neighbours. The composition of the reference group will be dependent partly on the role to be assessed. It is important here that the concept of reference group is not defined in sociological terms. That would imply that the person strives to be a member of a group to which he does not yet belong (Dahrendorf, 1965).

ISSUES IN THE ASSESSMENT OF DISABILITY OF ROLE PERFORMANCE

The measurement of social function and social adjustment has been heavily criticised, not only because of its normative perspective but also with respect to independence of psychopathology, actual role behaviour, opportunities, criteria of assessment, source of information and method of measurement (Platt, 1981; Katschnig, 1983; Link et al., 1990). These crucial issues in the assessment of disability in role performance will now be briefly reviewed.

In the context of the models of disabilities of ICF and of Nagi (1969, 1991), it has been argued that a clear distinction between signs and symptoms of psychopathology or psychological functioning, on the one hand, and social functioning, on the other, is necessary for reasons of causal versus consequential reasoning and of evaluation of mental health intervention. Thus, hearing voices or feeling depressed should not automatically be linked to a social or role disability. Their measurement should be separated, and not mixed, as it is in the Global Assessment of Functioning Scale (GAFS) (Endicott et al., 1976) in the DSM-III-R. In the DSM-IV (American Psychiatric Association, 1994, pp. 758–761), a proposal is made for separate axes for relational functioning and social and occupational functioning to track progress in rehabilitation that is independent of the severity of psychological symptoms.

Health Related or Not

It should be stressed that a role disability has been caused, demonstrably or plausibly, by physical, psychological and/or psychopathological impairment or functional limitation. The assessment has to take place in the context of health experience – or a health problem. If there is no health problem, then there is no disability. It should be kept in mind that a person may not be working, not be married, could have a bad relationship with his/her family or have financial problems for other reasons than a mental disorder. The existence of a social problem does not in itself presuppose a mental health problem: such a relationship should be demonstrated or made plausible. Therefore, the assessment of role disability has to be based on the actual performance of activities, actual manifestation of behaviour or actual execution of tasks over a defined period (e.g. the last month). The focus is on observable phenomena and not on inferences from abstract concepts such as competence or abilities that are assumed to be present.

Criteria of Disability

Each community or society has developed more or less defined criteria for entering or exiting from social roles, such as marital, occupational or parental. The eligibility for sickness benefits, disability pensions, sheltered work or accommodation, social assistance, etc., is based on norms and regulations that define the individual's level and quality of functioning to a certain extent, and are thus a first guideline for the assessment. Other criteria are the frequency of contacts, number of completed tasks, degree of conflict, depth of involvement or strength of motivation. Decisive criteria for the assessment of a role disability are: (a) the frequency and duration of the deviations, (b) the damage inflicted to the person him/herself or to others and (c) the desirability or necessity of help. This means, for example, that not having a job or being divested of parental authority because of mental disorder – i.e. not fulfilling the occupational or parental role – implies a severe or maximum role disability.

Freedom of Action

The reduction in or lack of performance should not result from personal or social circumstances that are beyond the control of the individual. There must be a freedom of action at the disposal of the individual to make it possible for the expected behaviour to be displayed. This points to the possibility of deviations in role behaviour which do not result from the individual's physical and/or psychological impairments, but which are the consequences of external factors over which the individual has no control. Examples of such factors are lack of financial resources, unfavourable living conditions, geographical distance, behaviour of others, illness in the family, formal or informal rules precluding an (ex-)patient from normal role performance (such as civil rights or getting a driving licence), social stigma and the state of the labour market. All of these can influence the individual's role behaviour negatively. An example is the hospitalised patient who cannot demonstrate certain behaviours because of the rules prevailing on the ward (e.g. visiting friends or family). It is evident that these factors should not lead to a disability *per se*. The assessment has to take into account the influence of such circumstances or barriers in assessing role performance.

Source of Information

There are three main sources of information: the patient him/herself, an informant (the partner, a parent or other family member) and an expert or mental health professional. Each source has its advantages and disadvantages, which could influence the validity and reliability of the assessment. The assessment of role performance should preferably rely on several sources, and not only on one. The patient should always be interviewed, although the severity of symptoms may sometimes negatively influence the behavioural report. Patients' own opinions are important for the observer to become informed on their perceptions, feelings and satisfaction with social situations, as well as actual behaviour. The informant (partner, parent, or friend) is also influenced by the patient's symptoms to a certain extent. Information on (dis)agreements and on the evaluation of the patient's behaviour is of value, e.g. if an informant is mostly acquainted with only some roles. One has to find out the normative standards of the people with whom the patient is interacting, though that may be difficult for certain groups, such as those who live alone. An expert or a mental health professional has to be chosen as the informant if a (hospital) treatment or long stay in hospital is being evaluated, but there are disadvantages in using these as informants: the difference in education, lack of opportunity to observe the patient outside the treatment setting and conceptions of normal and abnormal social behaviour. For the assessment of social or role disabilities, the semi-structured investigator-based interview is to be preferred, because it is the most flexible method, although more costly (in training) and time-consuming. The advantages of this method are direct observation of the patient's behaviour, the possibility of getting more precise information (probing) and the possibility of taking into account the biographical and sociocultural context of the individual. Another implication of this method is that the investigator (or in some cases the clinician) and not the individual (patient or family member) decides the presence or absence of a disability. This method might therefore be called 'objective', in contrast to the 'subjective' approach of the patient's self-report or response to standardised scales.

SOME EMPIRICAL CONSIDERATIONS ON ROLE FUNCTIONING AND ON QUALITY OF LIFE

Platt (1981) and Katschnig (1983) were fairly pessimistic about the state of the art with respect to measuring social adjustment, because of the lack of agreed social norms, together with the unwarranted assumptions, variability of expectations, number of relevant roles and lack of validity. Much criticism can also be levelled towards the concept and measurement of QoL as to the objectivity, the dimensionality, the overlap with and inclusion of symptoms and the shift over time of the standard (see Katschnig, Chapter 1 in this volume). Our ongoing research on role functioning and QoL in schizophrenia over the last decade has provided some relevant data supporting a less pessimistic view on these issues. The Groningen Social Disabilities Schedule (GSDS) (Wiersma *et al.*, 1990; Kraaijkamp, 1992) has been developed on the basis of our experience with the WHO Psychiatric Disability Assessment Schedule (World Health Organization, 1988) and has taken into account the issues mentioned above: health-related role disabilities, explicit criteria, several sources of information, freedom of action, investigator-based assessment (on a four-point scale) of eight social roles in the area of self care, household role, family role, partner role, parental role, social role, citizen role and occupational role (see Table 4.2).

Reliability

Research using the GSDS among a stratified sample of 131 patients from various mental health services and 26 control persons from general practice (Kraaijkamp, 1992) showed a high level of agreement; the inter-rater (observation as well as audiotape) and test–retest reliability (observation) as measured by κ, intraclass correlation, Finn's r and proportion of agreement demonstrated that all role disabilities were rated as reliable (e.g. all $\kappa > 0.40$) and that these results were robust. The reliability of the ratings was independent of the source of information (patient versus partner or family member). Recently, it appeared that the GSDS could also be used reliably in a cross-national European study on day hospitals (Schützwohl *et al.*, 2003).

Source of Information

The influence of the informant on the ratings is substantial: an 8–29% change in the ratings, mostly in the direction of greater disability, compared to those based on the patient's report only. This occurred more often in the role areas of family, parenthood and social relationship with friends and acquaintances. It was felt that the use of an informant rectified socially desirable responses of the individual and made social expectations more explicit. The change in ratings was not influenced by such variables as age, sex, diagnosis or setting of care (hospital versus community). In several cases, disability ratings were reduced by the additional information.

Concept Validity

Factor analysis and (Mokken) hierarchical scaling methods (dichotomy and trichotomy) underlined the reliability and validity of one score, for overall role disability Mokken analysis yields $H = 0.48$, $\rho = 0.79$ and $\delta = 19.03$. This hierarchical scaling analysis also revealed that self-care and household disabilities predicted the existence of widespread disability over all social roles; on the contrary, a disability in the occupational role, although quite prevalent, was not predictive of any other disability. Furthermore, indicators of the biographical and sociocultural context of the individual, such as age, sex, education and occupation, were not related to role disabilities, with a few minor exceptions. Women function slightly better in the social role ($N = 157$, t-test, $p = 0.03$) and older ($r < -0.23$) and higher professional ($r < -0.18$) people appear to have less general (and some specific) role disabilities, which means that only a small part of the variance could be explained by age and profession. This also signifies that the patient's sociodemographic background has been adequately taken into account and that the assessment is not being biased by factors of intellect, gender or social class.

Diagnosis and Setting of Health Care

An important finding was that neither specific nor general role disabilities differentiated between four diagnostic groups (alcohol and drug dependency, affective and non-affective psychoses, neurosis and personality disorders), but did so between settings of care. The intensity of care ranged from a psychiatric hospital (most intensive) via a psychiatric department of a general hospital, a day hospital and out-patient care to general medical practice (for the control patients, as the least intensive). Disability scores decreased significantly in that order ($F = 20.1$, $p < 0.001$). This indicates that treatment is probably more related to social dysfunctioning than to diagnosis *per se*.

Changeability

These role disabilities are amenable to change due to treatment, as was shown in a randomised controlled trial on hallucination-focused integrative treatment (HIT) among 76 chronic schizophrenic patients whose role functioning indeed improved over a period of 1.5 years (Wiersma, *et al.*, 2004). However, it has also been demonstrated that for many patients, these disabilities are much more persistent than symptoms, and therefore typify their situation of disablement. This latter finding is obvious among patients with schizophrenia and affective psychoses (two-year follow-up; Wiersma, *et al.*, 1995) or with alcohol amnestic disorder (three-year follow-up; Blansjaar, Takens and Zwinderman, 1992), but also among patients with 'minor' psychiatric disorders in primary care (Ormel *et al.*, 1994).

Relation with Quality of Life

In the RCT on HIT (van de Willige *et al.*, 2005), as well as the GSDS we used the Positive and Negative Syndrome Scale (PANSS), a 30-item, semi-structured interview and also an investigator-based assessment of psychopathology (Kay, Opler and Lindenmayer, 1989) and a generic instrument for QoL, the WHOQOL-Bref (WHOQOL Group, 1998), a 26-item self-report questionnaire on four domains: physical health, psychological functioning, social relationships and environmental opportunities. In addition, there was one question about QoL in general and one about satisfaction with health in general (WHOQOL Group, 1998; O'Carroll *et al.*, 2000). The question at issue was whether changes in subjective assessment of QoL could be predicted from changes in objective ratings of psychopathology and/or role functioning. It appeared that improvement in subjective QoL was predicted by a decrease in positive symptoms (the most important factor) and further by improved daily (occupational) functioning, improved relationship with the partner and a decrease of negative symptoms ($R = 0.74$, $F = 17.26$, $p < 0.000$). Depression was not significantly related to QoL. Role functioning and psychopathology – as objectively identified by an independent observer – were both important in determining a person's feeling of the quality of his/her life.

CONCLUSION

Disability in social role functioning or role performance deserves its own place in a classification of diseases, for its significance in the study of the origins and course of psychiatric symptoms, in the choice of treatment and rehabilitation and in the evaluation of the use of mental health services. For the sake of clarity, it should not be mixed with other concepts such as symptoms, social support, adverse social circumstances, unemployment, homelessness or personality. Both diagnostic systems, DSM IV and ICD-10, have proposals for additional axes of social and occupational functioning. The DSM IV proposes two axes (see above) and the World Health Organization (1997) introduces an axis that covers four distinct areas: (a) personal care and survival, (b) occupational functioning (role of worker, student or homemaker), (c) functioning with family (interaction with spouse, parent, children, other relatives) and (d) broader social behaviour (other roles and activities). Essentially, this comprises all the areas listed in Table 4.2, but condensed into four categories.

About 20 years ago, social adjustment was considered an umbrella concept encompassing areas such as skills, competence, integration, impairment, disability and inadequacy. Now, it seems to have been replaced by the paradigm of QoL. In its measurement, there is the risk of a reliance on simple self-report questionnaires on well-being, psychological problems, satisfaction with social life, etc., reflecting to a large extent personality traits or general response tendencies. The WHOQOL instrument seems to be a culturally valid, conceptually distinguishing and reliable instrument to be used in practice. It is informative on an individual's subjective view on his/her physical health, psychological functioning, social relations and environmental opportunities. Role performance which, more than anything else, typifies the individual's integration and participation in the local community or society at large appears to be a key dimension in the assessment of QoL from the perspective of the person.

REFERENCES

American Psychiatric Association (1987). *Diagnostic and Statistical Manual of Mental Disorders*, American Psychiatric Association Press, Washington, DC.

American Psychiatric Association (1994). *Diagnostic and Statistical Manual of Mental Disorders*, Fourth Edition (*DSM-IV*), American Psychiatric Association Press, Washington, DC.

Bickenbach, J.E., Chatterji, S., Badley, E.M. & Üstün, T.B. (1999). Models of disablement, universalism and the international classification of impairments, disabilities and handicaps, *Social Sci. Med.*, **48**, 1173–1187.

Biddle, B. (1979). *Role Theory: Expectations, Identities and Behaviour*, Academic Press, New York, London.

Blansjaar, B.A., Takens, H. & Zwinderman, A.H. (1992). The course of alcohol amnestic disorder. A three-year follow-up study of clinical signs and social disabilities, *Acta Psychiatrica Scand.*, **86**, 240–246.

Casey, P.R., Tyrer, P. & Platt, S. (1985). The relationship between social functioning and psychiatric symptomatology in primary care, *Social Psychiatry*, **20**, 5–9.

Cieza, A., Brockow, T., Ewert, T., Amman, E., Kollerits, B., Chatterji, S., Üstün, T.B. & Stucki, G. (2002). Linking health-status measurements to the international classification of functioning, disability and health, *J. Rehabil. Med.*, **34**, 205–210.

Clare, A.W. & Cairns, V.E. (1978). Design, development and use of a standardised interview to assess social maladjustment and dysfunction in community studies, *Psychol. Med.*, **8**, 589–604.

Cohler, B., Woolsey, S., Weiss, J. & Grunbaum, H. (1968). Child rearing attitudes among mothers volunteering and revolunteering for a psychological study, *Psychol. Rep.*, **23**, 603–612.

Dahrendorf, D. (1965). *Homo Sociologicus. Ein Versuch zur Geschichte, Bedeutung und Kritik der Kategorie der sozialen Rolle*, Fünfte Auflage, Westdeutscher Verlag, Köln, Opladen.

De Jong, A., Giel, R., Slooff, C.J. & Wiersma, D. (1986). Relationship between symptomatology and social disability, *Social Psychiatry*, **21**, 200–205.

Endicott, J., Spitzer, R., Fleiss, J. & Cohen, J. (1976). The Global Assessment Scale: A procedure for measuring overall severity of psychiatric disturbance, *Arch. Gen. Psychiatry*, **33**, 766–771.

Freeman, H. & Henderson, J. (1991). *Evaluation of Comprehensive Care of the Mentally Ill*, Gaskell, London.

Glynn, S.M. (1998). Psychopathology and social functioning in schizophrenia, in *Handbook of Social Functioning in Schizophrenia* (Eds K.T. Mueser & N. Tarrier), pp. 66–78, Allyn and Bacon, Boston, Massachusetts.

Good-Ellis, M.A., Fine, S.B., Spencer, J.H. & Divittis, A. (1987). Developing a role activity scale, *Am. J. Occup. Therapy*, **41**, 232–241.

Gordon, G. (1966). *Role Theory and Illness. A Sociological Perspective*, College and University Press, New Haven, Connecticut.

Gurland, B.J., Yorkston, N.J., Stone, A.R., Frank, J.D. & Fleiss, J.L. (1972). The structured and scaled interview to assess maladjustment (SSIAM): Description, rationale and development, *Arch. Gen. Psychiatry*, **27**, 259–264.

Hall, J.N. (1980). Ward rating scales for long stay patients. A review, *Psychol. Med.*, **10**, 277–288.

Hurry, J. & Sturt, E. (1981). Social performance in a population sample: relation to psychiatric symptoms, in *What is a Case?* (Eds J.K.Wing, P. Bebbington & L.N. Robins), pp. 202–213, Grant McIntyre, London.

Katschnig, H. (1983). Methods for measuring social adjustment, in *Methodology in Evaluation of Psychiatric Treatment* (Ed. T. Helgason), pp. 205–218, Cambridge University Press, Cambridge.

Kay, S.R., Opler, L.A. & Lindenmayer, J.P. (1989). The Positive and Negative Syndrome Scale (PANSS): Rationale and standardization, *Br. J. Psychiatry*, **155**(Suppl. 7), 59–65.

Kraaijkamp, H.J.M. (1992). *Moeilijke rollen. Psychometrisch onderzoek naar de betrouwbaarheid en validiteit van de Groningse Sociale Beperkingenschaal bij psychiatrische Patiënten* (*Difficult roles. A study into the Reliability and Validity of the Mental Health Research Center*).

Link, B.G., Mesagno, F.P., Lubner, M.E. & Dohrenwend, P. (1990). Problems in measuring role strains and social functioning in relation to psychological symptoms, *J. Health Social Behaviour*, **31**, 354–369.

Linton, R. (1936). *The Study of Man*, D. Appleton-Century Company, New York.

Mueser, K.T. & Tarrier, N. (1998). *Handbook of Social Functioning in Schizophrenia*, Allyn and Bacon, Boston, Massachusetts.

Munk-Jorgensen, P. (1999). Has deinstitutionalization gone too far?, *Eur. Arch. Psychiatry Clin. Neurosci.*, **249**, 136–143.

Nagi, S.Z. (1969). *Disability and Rehabilitation*, Ohio State University Press, Columbus, Ohio.

Nagi, S.Z. (1991). Disability concepts revisited: implications for prevention, in *Disability in America. Toward a National Agenda for Prevention* (Eds A.M. Pope & A.R. Tarlov), pp. 309–327, Institute of Medicine, National Academy Press, Washington DC.

O'Carroll, R.E., Smith, K., Couston, M., Cossar, J.A. & Hayes, P.C. (2000). A comparison of the WHOQoL-100 and the WHOQoL-BREF in detecting change in quality of life following liver transplantation, *Quality of Life Res.*, **9**, 121–124.

Ormel, J., Von Korff, M., Üstün, T.B., Pini, S., Korten, A. & Oldehinkel, T. (1994). Common mental disorders and disability across cultures: Results from the WHO Collaborative Study on Psychological Problems in General Health Care, *J. Am. Med. Ass.*, **272**, 1741–1748.

Parsons, T. (1958). Definitions of health and illness in the light of American values and social structure, in *Patients, Physicians, Illnesses* (Ed. E.G. Jaco), Free Press, Glencoe, Illinois.

Platt, S. (1981). Social adjustment as a criterion of treatment success: just what are we measuring?', *Social Psychiatry*, **44**, 95–112.

Platt, S., Weyman, A, Hirsch, S.R. & Hewett, S. (1980). The social behaviour assessment schedule (SBAS): Rationale, contents, scoring and reliability of a new interview schedule, *Social Psychiatry*, **15**, 43–55.

Pope, A.M. & Tarlov, A.R. (1991). *Disability in America. Toward a National Agenda for Prevention*, Institute of Medicine, National Academy Press, Washington DC.

Rosen, A., Hadzi-Pavlovic, D. & Parker, G. (1989). The life skills profile: A measure assessing function and disability in schizophrenia, *Schizophrenia Bull.*, **15**, 325–337.

Schützwohl, M., Jarosz-Nowak, J., Briscoe, J., Szajowski, K., Kallert, T. & the EDEN Study Group (2003). Inter-rater reliability of the Brief Psychiatric Rating Scale (BPRS 4.0) and the Groningen Social Disabilities Schedule (GSDS-II) in a European multi-site randomised controlled trial on the effectiveness of acute psychiatric day hospitals, *Int. J. Meth. Psychiat. Res.*, **12**(4), 197–207.

Scott, J.R. & Lehman, A.F. (1998). Social functioning in the community, in *Handbook of Social Functioning in Schizophrenia* (Eds K.T. Mueser & N. Tarrier), pp. 1–19, Allyn and Bacon, Boston, Massachusetts.

Skodol, A.E., Link, B.G., Shrout, P.E. & Horwath, E. (1988). The revision of axis V in DSM-III-R: should symptoms have been included?, *Am. J. Psychiatry*, **145**, 825–829.

Sytema, S., Burgess, P. & Tansella, M. (2002). Does community care decrease length of stay and risk of rehospitalization in new patients with schizophrenia disorders? A comparative case register study in Groningen, The Netherlands; Victoria, Australia; and South-Verona, Italy, *Schizophrenia Bull.*, **28**, 273–281.

Tyrer, P.J. (1990). Personality disorder and social functioning, in *Measuring Human Problems. A Practical Guide* (Eds D.F Peck & C.M. Shapiro), pp. 119–142, John Wiley & Sons, Chichester.

Tyrer P.J. & Casey P. (1993). *Social Function in Psychiatry. The Hidden Axis of Classification Exposed*, Wrightson Biomedical.

van de Willige, G., Wiersma, D., Nienhuis, F.J. & Jenner, J.A. (2005). Changes in quality of life in chronic psychiatric patients: a comparison between EuroQoL (EQ-5D) and WHOQoL, *Quality of Life Res.*, **14**(2), 441–452.

Wallace, C.J. (1986). Functional assessment in rehabilitation, *Schizophrenia Bull.*, **12**, 604–630.

Weissman, M.M. (1975). The assessment of social adjustment. A review of techniques, *Arch. Gen. Psychiatry*, **32**, 357–365.

Weissman, M.M. & Paykel, E.S. (1974). *The Depressed Women: A Study of Social Relationships*, University of Chicago Press, Chicago, Illinois.

Weissman, M.M., Sholomskas, D., John, K. (1981). The assessment of social adjustment. An update, *Arch. Gen. Psychiatry*, **38**, 1250–1258.

WHOQOL Group (1998). Development of the World Health Organization WHOQoL-BREF Quality of Life Assessment, *Psycholog. Med.*, **28**, 551–558.

Wiersma, D., De Jong, A. & Ormel, J. (1988). The Groningen Social Disabilities Schedule: Development, relationship with the ICIDH and psychometric properties, *Int. J. Rehabit. Res.*, **3**, 213–224.

Wiersma, D., De Jong, A., Kraaijkamp, H.J.M. & Ormel, J. (1990). *GSDS-II. The Groningen Social Disabilities Schedule*, Second Version, *Manual, Questionnaire and Rating Form*, Department of Social Psychiatry, University of Groningen.

Wiersma, D. & Chapireau, F. (1991). *The Use of the International Classification of Impairments, Disabilities and Handicaps in Mental Health*, Council of Europe, Strasbourg.

Wiersma, D., Kluiter, H., Nienhuis, F.J. & Giel, R. (1995). Costs and benefits of hospital and day treatment with community care of affective and schizophrenic disorders. A randomized trial with a follow up of two years, *Br. J. Psychiatry*, **166**(Suppl. 27), 52–59.

Wiersma, D., Kluiter, H., Pijl, Y.J. & Sytema, S. (2002). Mental health care in the Netherlands. Community care with or without hospitals, *Int. J. Men. Health*, **31**, 50–65.

Wiersma, D., Jenner, J.A., van de Willige, G. & Nienhuis, F.J. (2004). Hallucination focused integrative treatment improves quality of life in schizophrenia patients, *Acta Psychiatrica Scand.*, **109**(3), 194–201.

Wing, J.K. (1989). The measurement of 'social disablement'. The MRC social behaviour and social role performance schedules, *Social Psychiatry Psychiat. Epidemiol.*, **24**, 173–178.

Wohlfarth, T.D., van den Brink, W., Ormel, J., Koeter, M.W.J. & Oldehinkel, A.J. (1993). The relationship between social dysfunctioning and psychopathology among primary care attenders, *Br. J. Psychiatry*, **163**, 37–44.

World Health Organization (1980). *International Classification of Impairments, Disabilities and Handicaps (ICIDH)*, WHO, Geneva.

World Health Organization (1988). *Psychiatric Disability Assessment Schedule (DAS)*, WHO, Geneva.

World Health Organization (1992a). *International Classification of Diseases and Related Health Problems, Tenth Revision (ICD-10)*, WHO, Geneva.

World Health Organization (1992b). *The ICD-10 Classification of Mental and Behavioral Disorders. Clinical Description and Diagnostic Guidelines*, WHO, Geneva.

World Health Organization. (1997). *The Multiaxial Presentation of the ICD–10 for use in Adult Psychiatry*. Cambridge University Press, Cambridge.

World Health Organization (2001a). *Disability Assessment Schedule II (WHODAS II)*, WHO, Geneva.

World Health Organization (2001b). *International Classification of Functioning, Disability and Health (ICF)*, WHO, Geneva.

5

'Standard of Living' and Environmental Factors as a Component of Quality of Life in Mental Disorders

Hugh L. Freeman

INTRODUCTION

Material environmental factors determine to a large degree the limits that can be achieved in the level of an individual's quality of life (QoL). With a few voluntary exceptions, such as religious orders, the fulfilment of a certain basic level of standards of environmental circumstances is necessary if an adequate QoL is to be attained. In addition to the physical environment, however, social support and social networks are also relevant to this question, as is the factor of autonomy in relation to social control. Institutional life inevitably involves the reduction of personal autonomy (though this need not be to a marked extent), but in the general community the only control on such autonomy is from the norms of society. The environmental aspects of QoL have been generally neglected, and very few studies have obtained objective data that could allow these matters to be reliably assessed.

Personal autonomy assumes that an individual will not just adapt to a particular environment or to constant environmental changes, but will sometimes seek to change these conditions. Angermeyer and Kilian (Chapter 2 in this volume) refer to the role-functioning model of QoL, in which happiness and satisfaction are related to the social and environmental conditions required to fill basic human needs. Using Maslow's well-known hierarchy of human needs, Bigelow *et al.* (1982) have developed a person–environment model of QoL in which the environment is seen as consisting of opportunities (both material and social) through which an individual's needs may be satisfied. The social opportunities are associated with requirements for performance, so that the degree to which an individual's needs can be satisfied may depend largely on his/her ability to meet the demands of different social roles. However, there are a number of problems about this model, which Angermeyer and Kilian discuss fully.

In the study of resettlement reported by Zissi and Barry (Chapter 3 in this volume), one of the biggest changes recorded in patients' lives was the increased freedom and autonomy resulting from their move from hospital to community settings. Constructs such as 'autonomy' and 'perceived control' were found to be important determinants of subjective well-being, and awareness of their importance seemed to have been triggered by the environmental change. The same point was made by Leff (1997) about the reprovision of accommodation for long-stay mental hospital patients in London: 'they were living under

Quality of Life in Mental Disorders, Second Edition   Edited by H. Katschnig, H. Freeman and N. Sartorius
© 2006 John Wiley & Sons, Ltd

much freer conditions and greatly appreciated the increased freedom'. It also appeared that this freedom has been appreciated by them even more with the passage of time.

There is, in fact, an interaction between the coping behaviour of individuals and environmental circumstances. The *International Pilot Study of Schizophrenia* (World Health Organization, 1992) found that affected people showed a better overall adjustment in developing than in industrialised countries. The reasons for this environmental effect remain unproven, but it is not difficult to accept that moderately handicapped individuals (who constitute at least one-third of those affected by schizophrenia) would adjust better to the extended families and simple employment of agrarian societies than to the complex and impersonal surroundings of an industrial city. However, as urbanisation increases rapidly in developing countries, this advantage may be gradually lost. Where the social environment is fragmented by suspicion and hostility, as in many Western public housing developments, social support is lost and the opportunities for adaptive behaviour are greatly reduced. Newman (1972) showed that where a single entrance was used by a large number of people, social behaviour deteriorated, whereas semi-public spaces – used by a limited number of residents – had the opposite effect.

The influence of environmental factors on mental health in general is also a much neglected issue, in spite of the salience of the environment as a political and social issue for several decades past. Although an attempt has been made to examine and summarise existing knowledge of the subject (Freeman, 1984), there is still a marked shortage, not only of empirical data but also of well-defined concepts for it. Yet this is surprising, considering that psychiatry operates on the basis of a multifactorial model in which genetic factors interact with those of an environmental origin. If these caveats apply to the attempts to relate specific psychiatric disorders to environmental factors, they would apply even more to the rather 'softer' phenomena that make up 'quality of life'. Neither 'mental health' nor 'the environment' is a unitary factor; both are often discussed in vague terms which may apply more to an ideal than to reality, and the same tends to be true of QoL. Scientific study, however, can only make progress through the deconstruction of all these categories into discrete items that are capable of measurement. There also has to be concern with social values, since what is seen as a 'good' environment by any population may depend as much on cultural or aesthetic values as on the extent to which it promotes physical or mental health.

Halpern (1995) distinguishes four channels of environmental influence through which mental health may be affected. The first of these is environmental stress (pollution, noise, heat, adverse weather, high social densities), which may lead to annoyance or overt symptoms. The second is social support, which is not necessarily gained from the proximity of others; the quality of neighbouring relationships may be strongly influenced by the physical environment (e.g. the presence of many strangers makes positive relationships less likely). Thirdly, there are symbolic aspects of the environment, whereby residents may be affected by social labelling, e.g. of a 'respectable' or a 'bad' area. Fourthly, planning or redevelopment may cause forced relocation with adverse effects on mental health (Fried, 1963), or it may separate people geographically from employment or essential services. An example of the last of these influences is that long-stay patients being discharged from mental hospitals may have to take whatever accommodation is available in public housing, which may well be the least desirable; exposure to harassment, crime or social isolation may then worsen their psychiatric condition.

The question of social roles deserves some attention at this point; it is dealt with at length elsewhere in this volume (Wiersma, Chapter 4 in this volume). Though there is no clear consensus about the meaning, Wiersma defines it as 'a complex of expectations that people have as to the behaviour of a person who occupies a certain position in society'. Such expectations depend on the norms of the individual's reference group, particularly those present in the close environment. While some deviations in role behaviour result from the individual's own impairment (physical or mental), others are the consequence of external factors that the individual cannot control. These environmental circumstances include unfavourable living conditions, geographical distance from social support and the availability of employment. Wiersma refers to the development of an extended model of disability which assumes the presence of risk factors including biological, environmental and those relating to lifestyle. The use of such a model should result in environmental factors being more widely recognised than in the past.

COMPARISON OF ENVIRONMENTS

A landmark study by Wing and Brown (1970) examined the adverse effects on schizophrenic patients of a prolonged stay in three varying British mental hospitals, with the object of finding ways in which these effects could be counteracted and prevented. They concluded that a substantial proportion of the morbidity shown by such patients was a product of their environment, and that the social pressures which acted to produce this extra morbidity could be counteracted to some extent by the efforts of the hospital staff. 'Environmental poverty' (e.g. lack of personal possessions, interesting activities and contacts with the outside world) was very highly correlated with the 'clinical poverty syndrome' of social withdrawal, flatness of affect and poverty of speech. Both types of poverty became more intense with increased length of stay, while the longer a patient had been in hospital, the more likely it was that he/she would wish to remain there or be indifferent about leaving.

These authors defined 'institutionalism' as the gradual acceptance of and contentment with the values and routine of an institution, so that the person no longer wishes to live any other sort of life. While this can sometimes be an adaptive attitude, it can also prevent individuals from improving their level of functioning and could cause them to remain more dependent than is really necessary. In principle, institutionalism in mental hospitals is no different from that in other institutions, such as hostels or group homes, but it might be seen in its most severe form in long-stay schizophrenic patients, because of their vulnerability to social understimulation. If they are living in wards containing large numbers, this process is likely to be reinforced, because it becomes very difficult for staff to care for them in an individual way.

Brown, Birley and Wing (1972) then extended this research to community settings, concluding that the optimal social environment for chronically handicapped schizophrenic patients was one that was structured and mentally stimulating, but without situations requiring complex decision-making. However, if the patient was living with relatives, emotional over-involvement, critical comments and hostility were strongly associated with symptomatic relapse.

In most countries, long-term residence in mental hospitals by patients with chronic psychoses is now relatively uncommon, but it cannot be assumed that this environmental change is necessarily a favourable one. Smaller institutions, such as 'nursing homes', may offer even greater environmental poverty than many mental hospitals, while patients discharged to live on their own may be equally deprived of social support and stimulation. Rather than being concerned primarily with the run-down of psychiatric hospitals, true 'deinstitutionalisation' should have as its major objectives the improvement of patients' clinical state and QoL, through resettlement in the community. One of the unfortunate results of these changes, with the loss of long-stay or medium-stay accommodation, is that chronically handicapped patients may remain for long periods on admission wards. As Bridges, Davenport and Goldberg (1994) point out, this is a very unsuitable environment for such people: the ward atmosphere will often be too arousing and disruptive, so that relapse may be provoked; ward staff may concentrate their time and interest on the acute patients; and the maintenance of a consistent rehabilitation programme may be impossible. However, 'deinstitutionalisation' has been an expression of major cultural and political processes, and is unlikely to be influenced by any evidence that it is often working badly.

Shepherd et al. (1996) point out that over the past 30 years, there have been profound changes in the pattern of residential care for people with long-term psychiatric problems. These changes have been mainly associated with the reduction of beds in mental hospitals, which usually results in the less disabled patients leaving hospital first, so that those with the most severe difficulties fill the remaining accommodation. At the same time, in Britain and most other industrialised countries, there has been a considerable expansion of residential care in the community, though in a great variety of settings. While it has been argued (Davidge et al., 1993) that the overall result of these changes is to leave the number of beds available to the mentally ill unaltered, this assumes that a bed in a fully staffed hospital is equivalent to one in a home operated for profit by unqualified persons. Any such assumption is clearly wrong, but in most countries little systematic information is available about the range of alternative accommodation for the mentally ill outside hospitals.

Shepherd et al. (1996) compared a random sample of community residential homes with a sample of hospital rehabilitation wards, both in outer London; the 'general acceptability of the environment' was assessed in each case. The hospital wards were all in old buildings, which had mostly been neglected;

basic provision for privacy and the care of personal possessions was generally absent. In the community homes, standards were variable, but they were generally clean and pleasant, with a more 'homely' atmosphere than any of the hospital wards. Overall, the most disabled residents were still living in hospital, in the worst accommodation, receiving the poorest quality of care and often expressing the most dissatisfaction with their living situation. Those who had recently moved from long-stay hospitals particularly appreciated the improved quality of their new accommodation, especially in non-private sector homes. The usual restrictions of hospital settings may result partly from their having to look after a very disabled group of residents, but may also be related to the training and attitudes of staff. Therefore, better training could result in an improved QoL for the patients in their care.

Among those affected by chronic mental illness in every population, there is a relatively small number of people who are disabled by chronic psychosis or organic brain syndromes and who cannot be safely managed in any community setting. They need 24-hour nursing care for prolonged periods, as well as an appropriate rehabilitation programme, but do not need to be resident within a hospital. Some will be long-stay patients from mental hospitals, some may come directly from the community and others will have failed to settle in sheltered accommodation. It is necessary for these people to remain in a hospital unit, where they can receive intensive rehabilitation and where disturbed or violent behaviour can be controlled without danger to other patients, staff or the general community. Here, extra nursing or medical help can be obtained quickly, some secure accommodation is available and there is spatial separation from the local community (which benefits both them and the patients).

One facility designed to meet this need in Britain is the 'hospital-hostel'. These units have been developed in domestic settings within the community – usually a large old house – and may be operated by health services alone or in partnership with voluntary organisations. No time limit is specified for a resident to remain, but if any shows severe behavioural problems that cannot be safely managed there, a return to hospital may be unavoidable. Oliver (1991) compared the QoL of 'hospital-hostel' residents with that of similar people residing in group homes, conventional hostels or supervised lodgings. As people moved from hospital to a less restrictive setting, there was a trend for aspects of their QoL to improve; most residents were generally satisfied with their current living conditions. It was concluded that all these forms of residential support should be seen as elements in a spectrum of provision for patients with varying needs.

As mentioned above, it is undesirable for patients of this kind to be housed on acute psychiatric wards, but a long-stay unit of this kind can still show special concern for their QoL. Space around the unit should allow some freedom of movement, without risk to people outside the hospital, and the accommodation should be more of a domestic than an institutional type. There should be ready access to the occupational and recreational activities of a rehabilitation service, as well as to community accommodation (e.g. a hospital-hostel), when any patient is ready to try resettlement outside. Unfortunately, in Britain, hospital hostels have proved to be unpopular with managers and funding bodies because of their staff costs, even though they have been shown to be the optimum setting for an important group of psychiatric patients.

Simpson, Hyde and Faragher (1989) point out that when the populations of different kinds of facilities are being compared, there must be control for their levels of severe psychopathology; otherwise, apparent benefits from living in one or another 'may be illusory, reflecting only differing population characteristics'. Also, 'very severe forms of psychopathology affect the cognitive processes involved in the perception and evaluation of personal experiences' (Oliver *et al.*, 1996), so that in these cases, greater importance may have to be given to the objective assessments of staff or independent observers than to patients' subjective ratings. Nevertheless, some interesting findings emerged from a comparison of patients' assessments of their QoL in a general hospital based service in Manchester (UK) with those of patients treated by the community mental health service in Boulder (USA). The significant differences (at the 0.05 level) were that hospital patients in Manchester were significantly less happy about their personal safety than those in the acute treatment unit in Boulder, which is a converted house. These Manchester patients were also less happy about their living situation than those receiving out-patient case management in Boulder, as well as group home residents in Manchester (Warner and Huxley, 1993). It seems that the most appropriate form of hospital accommodation for acute psychiatric patients has yet to be found in most countries.

ENVIRONMENT OF DISCHARGED PATIENTS

Until the 1970s, there had been little research on the effects of either physical characteristics of the environment or of the conditions within different living settings on discharged patients' level of functioning and length of stay within the community. However, it is now widely recognised that these latter have been found to be influenced by the social–emotional circumstances of the home, such as social support and interpersonal stress. Wing (1986) has emphasised that the QoL of those affected by chronic psychoses is often undermined by material disadvantages, which tend to accumulate over time. These can include poverty, poor housing, homelessness, unemployment, or poor opportunities for meaningful activities (work-related or recreational), as well as lack of a supportive social network and appropriate services. A study of discharged patients from the psychiatric hospitals in York, in the north of England, found that different kinds of facilities fulfilled different needs for these individuals. Mental hospitals were the best at providing for patients' basic survival needs, for their health care and for their general activities (Jones, Robinson and Golightly, 1986). However, by 2004, very little mental hospital accommodation was still in use in England.

Focusing on the question of living environments, Oliver *et al.* (1996) point out that people who suffer from schizophrenia over a long period have a range of needs for accommodation, which arise in various ways: 'There are those who are actually homeless; those who are inappropriately hospitalised; those lodging in inappropriate residential settings; and some who are at risk of eviction because of the consequences of intolerable and persistent forms of psychopathology and disability.' While it may be generally agreed that any given area covered by a psychiatric service should have a spectrum of residential provision for those suffering from chronic mental illness, the degree to which this actually exists anywhere will clearly depend on many factors, both local and national.

However, the residential accommodation will be unable to function effectively for long unless closely linked to a clinical service that also has a range of facilities, capable of dealing with even the most severely disabled and disturbed patients. These will include acute admission and long-term, high-dependency units in hospital, while in the community there should be 'hospital-hostels', conventional hostels, group homes, supervised lodgings and residential units with only part-time support staff (Oliver and Mohamad, 1992). Provision on that scale, however, is rarely to be found in any country.

It was pointed out earlier that the community-based accommodation available to many severely disabled people is usually sited in inner-city areas. Oliver *et al.* (1996) comment that the advantages of this policy may include cheaper rents and lower costs for travelling to various amenities and services. However, the disadvantages may include having to live in poorly maintained and substandard buildings, coping with neighbourhood problems and difficulties in getting household insurance. Even when residential units are available, their design, size, operational policies and forms of care may not be appropriate for the needs of their residents. In Britain, their management has moved steadily from the public to the private sector since the 1980s.

A linkage between social support and the course of serious psychiatric disorder is proposed by Goldstein and Caton (1983), who followed up for one year 119 schizophrenic individuals with a history of multiple admissions, returning to a variety of living arrangements in poor areas of New York City. In this study, patients' living arrangements were separated into six categories (e.g. with parents or alone in the patient's own flat), but these categories were found to have no significant differential effect on the rate of readmission, level of clinical functioning or degree of adjustment in the community. Similarly, no major social or clinical differences were found between those living with their families and those who had a solitary domestic environment; the latter experienced less interpersonal stress, but clearly had poorer social support. Although some patients changed their home during the course of the year, the new environments tended to be quite similar to the old ones.

In this study, outcome over the year was more strongly predicted by social support and interpersonal stress within the home than by the use of available treatment service. Those patients who were in high stress/poor social support environments had the highest risk of readmission. Goldstein and Caton concluded that since interpersonal stress and degree of social support are strong predictors of rehospitalisation, regardless of the patient's type of living arrangement, the most valuable community care resource might be natural support environments such as families. In that case, help to improve these family situations should perhaps have more priority for resources than is usually the case. These results were open to some selection bias, for instance through living arrangements not being randomly assigned, and it is possible that more effective treatment services than the ones available to these particular patients would have shown a stronger effect on outcome. Nevertheless, this New York study does indicate an important direction for further research.

Also in New York, Cohen and Sokolovsky (1978) found that for schizophrenic patients with few manifest symptoms, small social network size predicted readmissions, but this was not so for those with severe symptoms. This may be because in a small network, the patient depends on one person both for medication and other needs, and will deteriorate if that person becomes dysfunctional. Also, readmission was more frequent for patients with few instrumental relationships (i.e. doing things for other people) but many dependent ones.

Discharged schizophrenic patients in the English industrial city of Salford (Cotterill, 1993) were found to have impoverished social networks (in terms of size and density), which also varied significantly with gender and age. Elderly males tended to be socially isolated, whereas females were not. On average, females had larger, denser networks, which were composed of a higher proportion of kin, and younger patients had larger, slightly less dense networks, composed of a higher proportion of non-kin.

Also in the north of England, Oliver and Mohamad (1992) undertook a pilot survey comparing three types of resettlement facility for chronic psychiatric patients – publicly provided hostel, private boarding-out and voluntary group-home. Social relations were greatest in the first and least in the third, so far as total and within-residence contacts were concerned, whereas for outside the residence, the ratio was 1:3:2. However, these findings were complicated by the fact that personal characteristics of the residents varied considerably between the three settings. For most of these people with severe, long-standing psychiatric disabilities, global well-being or QoL was essentially positive across all forms of accommodation. However, the life satisfactions of this sample could not be explained simply by their underlying mental health, since some dimensions of it showed marked differences between the residential settings.

Hamilton and Hoenig (1966) investigated social isolation in a selected group of new patients of two district services in the north of England, followed up over four years. At inception, 84.7% were more or less confined to the home; 16.8% died during the four years. At follow-up, 53% were still partly or wholly confined to the home. The over-65 age group, in which, not unexpectedly, organic psychosyndromes and concomitant physical illness were over-represented, was most vulnerable to isolation. It was concluded that mental health services needed to do more to counteract the socially isolating results of psychiatric illness, particularly the severe, chronic forms.

Very few studies have attempted to relate the quality of care provided in residential homes or hostels for the mentally ill to the QoL, as experienced there by residents. However, Lehman, Possidente and Hawker (1986) in the United States investigated the QoL of four groups of chronic patients. These were divided along the following two dimensions: (a) in-patients of a state mental hospital or residents of a supervised community home; (b) those with a current length of stay that had been greater or less than six months. Irrespective of length of stay, the community residents perceived their living conditions more favourably than the hospital patients, had more financial resources and were less likely to have been assaulted in the past year.

Similarly, Simpson, Hyde and Faragher (1989) compared patients in three different living situations in Manchester – general hospital ward, hospital-hostel, and group home – for both QoL and psychopathology. Their placement within the spectrum of care was found to correspond well to the severity of their psychopathology. There was an overall tendency for QoL to be better in the group homes, with higher levels of general well-being, subjective satisfaction with the living situation and social contacts, and greater comfort. Residents of the hospital-hostel occupied an intermediate position for QoL, while those in the acute ward complained particularly about lack of safety (from disturbed patients) and lack of comfort.

The role of a hospital-hostel in a rural community was evaluated by Simpson (1996), who surveyed the ten patients admitted to a new, five-bed unit. There was particular concern as to whether such a small hostel, with care assistants sleeping in at night (but no awake staff), could manage a group of severely mentally ill patients. Assessment was made of QoL (Lehman, 1983), mental state and behaviour, and staff attitudes and practices. Despite this being a 'hospital' unit, staff were found to be geared towards individual care of the residents, rather than the running of the facility. There was a general trend in improvement of the QoL scores, compared with the patients' previous circumstances, particularly in respect of comfort and residents' cohesion. The hostel was shown to be taking a very disturbed group of patients, similar to those described in 1989 by Simpson, Hyde and Faragher, and their QoL in the two units was similar. The residents were also thought to be similar to patients treated in the United States in a form of case management programme (Warner and Huxley, 1993) in one urban area.

In the very different setting of pre-communist Laos, Westermeyer (1980) found that the chronic mentally ill had social networks that were reduced in size, in spite of the fact that they had generally lived in the same agrarian village all their lives. Without the ability to exchange goods or labour, they mostly became dependent on a few family members or altruistic others to care for them.

Although schizophrenia is usually considered to run a generally benign course in non-industrialised societies (World Health Organization, 1979), these important findings show that the more severe forms can be as disabling there as in communities with a modern way of life.

Discussing the economic aspects of this question, Baines *et al.* (1995) report on the reprovision of services from two mental hospitals in London, which they had studied since 1985 through the Team for Assessment of Psychiatric Services (TAPS) project. They had found an upward trend in the costs of providing care for each successive group of leavers over time, since each one had a wider range of problems than its predecessors. Out of 751 former long-stay patients, 72 eventually had to be accommodated either in other hospitals or in purpose-built facilities in or near the hospital grounds. Accommodation dominates the cost of reproviding care in the community, and in Britain this cost has been shifted from being mainly borne by the National Health Service to become the responsibility of local authority social services, acting as purchasers. However, this study has shown that a comprehensive and unusually well-financed programme of reprovision has by no means eliminated the need for hospital services among the complete cohort of in-patients – quite apart from new and relapsed patients who will emerge from the local population year by year.

Baines *et al.* (1995) state that:

> The variety of accommodation types used by former hospital residents reflects their different demands and needs but, over and above the care offered in these facilities, a range of other services is required to provide comprehensive support. Even were it desirable, the most highly staffed accommodation units cannot provide all the components of care packages in-house: psychiatry, psychology, chiropody, and social work services are usually supplied on a peripatetic basis; and recreational and leisure activities are still required.

Emphasising that a first-class service cannot be provided on the cheap, Baines *et al.* conclude that: 'higher-cost care packages are significantly correlated with improvements in mental health and quality of life in a number of dimensions'. In other words, one gets what one pays for, and no more than that.

METHODOLOGICAL ISSUES

Awad (1994) states that not much attention has been given to systematic evaluation of the QoL of schizophrenic patients taking neuroleptics. Thus, the lack of an integrative conceptual model for QoL when medication is being taken on a long-term basis may have slowed the progress of research in this important area. As in other chronic illnesses, a serious problem in assessing the QoL of schizophrenic patients is to define the critical factors that compose the QoL profile. It is important that only significant factors that make clinical sense or are supported by research evidence should be incorporated in such conceptual models. On the other hand, evaluating QoL has to be more than merely the assessment of symptomatic improvement or deterioration. In Awad's view, the three major determinants of the QoL of schizophrenic patients on continuous medication are the number and severity of schizophrenic symptoms, the number and severity of side-effects of the medication and patients' psychosocial performance. Such determinants are not merely baseline conceptual factors for judging the QoL; these are also factors influencing therapeutic outcome. Symptoms may improve with neuroleptic therapy, but even dramatic symptomatic improvement may not necessarily allow the patient to become self-sufficient or productive.

Discussing the relationship of neuroleptics to QoL, Weiden (1994) states that compared to self-report by the patient, family report of extra-pyramidal symptoms (EPSs) seems to be a better indicator of the impact EPSs have on global distress. This paper proposed, therefore, that family observation should be used when studying the adverse impact of neuroleptics on QoL, though of course not all patients have available relatives. It adds to the widespread view that more objective data are needed to assess various aspects of the QoL of patients with severe mental illness. With the increasing use of 'atypical' antipsychotic drugs, EPSs are likely to become less significant as a problem in cases of this kind.

So far as the relationship between psychopathology and QoL in schizophrenia is concerned, Packer (1994) states that in addition to medication, other methods that may lessen symptoms must be explored. These include psychosocial and psychoeducational interventions. Improved housing, for example, while objectively enhancing QoL, may also positively influence the individual's sense of satisfaction and well-being. Family psychoeducational approaches may help to enrich these relationships, while supportive psychotherapy may enhance self-esteem. Though symptoms may recur or become exacerbated even under the most supportive and positive circumstances, intervention of this sort may indirectly modify symptoms by decreasing stress, and so further improve QoL.

Considering problems in assessing QoL in clinical trials, Lehman (1994) proposed that: (a) psychiatric symptoms are significantly correlated with QoL experiences; (b) changes in psychiatric symptoms correlate with changes in QoL; (c) in the United States, QoL experiences are correlated with patients' gender and race; (d) symptoms and QoL experiences are both significant and are predictors of hospital readmission; and (e) 'objective' life conditions and life satisfaction are at best only modestly correlated. The QoL interview of Lehman, Ward and Linn (1982) seeks data on nine life domains, including 'living situation'. The data are divided into 'objective' (i.e. obtained by asking direct questions) and 'subjective' (from patients rating their satisfaction with any of these domains). However, the degree of 'objectivity' is very limited, since it may be influenced by the individual's mental state, so that the description 'objective' is better kept for information from other people or from documents. Alternatively, Sainfort, Becker and Diamond (1996) contrast 'subjective' perceptions of life satisfaction, happiness, social relations, physical health and psychological well-being with 'objective' indicators such as income, quality of housing and physical functioning.

In Britain, Oyebode (1994) stated that there are problems with the application of QoL measurements such as Quality-Adjusted Life Years (QALYs) to psychiatry. For instance, the emphasis on the extension of life as one of the major components of outcome is probably not appropriate to psychiatry (Wilkinson et al., 1990; Oyebode et al., 1992). As a method, QALY is likely to favour treatment of acute fatal conditions that effect a full recovery characterised by a good QoL. On the other hand, treatment for either fatal or non-fatal conditions that produce only minimal or no extension of life and only moderate improvement in QoL may be unjustifiably disfavoured. Treatments for conditions such as schizophrenia may fall into this category, although those for the major mood disorders that can be shown to prevent fatality (suicide), such as long-term lithium treatment, may be favoured (Boyle and Callaghan, 1993). Nonetheless, there may still be a formalised structural disadvantage for psychiatric treatment if the QALY were to be accepted as a principal method for allocating resources.

Rather similarly, McGill (1995) claimed that most measurements of QoL seem to aim at the wrong target; i.e. most investigators, while professing to measure QoL, are in fact measuring various aspects of health status. What distinguishes QoL from all other measures of health is the need to obtain and incorporate patients' values and preferences into the final assessment. McGill also stated that the absence of instruments suitable for measuring QoL can be explained, in part, by two distinct but related phenomena: the use of psychometric, as opposed to clinical, measurement techniques and a failure to recognise the fundamental importance of patients' individual values and preferences.

Emphasising that most of the instruments for assessing QoL that are used in mental health rely on a single respondent, Sainfort, Becker and Diamond (1996) gave two QoL instruments to both 37 schizophrenic patients and their primary clinicians. The judgements of the two groups coincided more on clinical aspects, such as symptoms, than on social aspects. There was in fact little agreement between the two on patients' social relationships and the occupational aspects of their QoL.

As QoL may encompass not only health-related factors but also many non-medical phenomena, such as work, religion and interpersonal relationships, investigators could ask patients to give two global ratings – one for overall QoL and the other for 'health-related' QoL. In McGill's view, multiple-term indices that measure QoL may differ substantially in content among themselves, but their design should be guided by three general principles. Firstly, patients should be allowed to identify the items that affect their QoL. Secondly, the severity of the identified items should be rated. Thirdly, patients should be invited to rate the relative importance of these items to their QoL. McGill maintains that only after investigators acknowledge the fundamental importance of patients' values and preferences will QoL be measured, not just with statistical elegance but with convincing face validity.

Keilen *et al.* (1994) proposed that inferences about overall quality cannot be drawn without actually measuring the health profile with a generic QoL instrument. In the Rosser–Kind Index, which has been used for the calculation of QALYs, all the data for an individual and then for a set of individuals are collapsed to form a single measure to be used in comparative calculations.

Oliver *et al.* (1996) have developed the Lancashire Quality of Life Profile (LQOLP), which includes a number of well-known indicators or QoL. When used to assess chronically mentally ill people, this has appeared to be useful under a variety of conditions. The profile's internal reliability coefficients for multi-item scales have been consistently above 0.5, which is regarded as acceptable for group comparisons, though specific mental symptoms such as loneliness or boredom can be associated with inaccuracy. The validity of the profile has also appeared to be satisfactory, though it is still in an extended process of development. Among the operational uses to which QoL assessment is well suited, Oliver *et al.* mention the monitoring of patients' life conditions, which are related to the outcomes of medical and social services.

CONCLUSION

As both the opportunities and the costs of medicine grow, society is being asked to provide ever more resources for it, and in turn is demanding that health care professionals become more accountable in the way they work. Swales (1995) stated that the medical 'issues of the day' are in fact largely social issues – areas of activity where the doctor or other health professional meets those of the society in which he/she works. Conflict under such circumstances often results from a failure of understanding between the health professional and those responsible for public policies. Sainfort, Becker and Diamond (1996) emphasised that, whatever the difficulties of definition and measurement, QoL has become an important feature of outcome in mental health care. However, not only do patients differ from professionals in their views on the different aspects of QoL, but individual patients vary between themselves. Therefore, mental health services and treatment strategies should be concerned with a wide range of needs, reflecting different domains of QoL, which are perceived as being important by individual patients. Ultimately, 'Quality of Life is a personal and subjective value' (Sainfort, Becker and Diamond, 1996).

The question of resources is clearly a key issue in relation to the environment of those affected by mental illness. This chapter has illustrated ways in which individuals can be matched to appropriate environmental settings, with a view to encouraging the optimal result that is possible in view of the clinical and social handicaps that may affect them. To provide the required range of these settings will make large demands on the resources of any community, but it is a necessary expenditure if there is genuine concern for the QoL of the mentally ill.

REFERENCES

Awad, A.G. (1994). Quality of life of schizophrenic patients on medications – implications for clinical trials, *Neuropsychopharmacology*, **10**(3S), 2385.

Baines, B., Beecham, J., Hallam, A. & Knapp, M. (1995). Community reprovision: Is it cost-effective?, in *Summary of Proceedings of Tenth Annual Conference*, TAPS Research Unit, London.

Bigelow, D.A., Brodsky, G., Stewart, L. & Olson, M.M. (1982). The concept and measurement of quality of life as a dependent variable in evaluation of mental health services, in *Innovative Approaches to Mental Health Evaluation* (Eds G.J. Stahler & W.R. Tash), pp. 345–366, Academic Press Inc., New York.

Boyle, P.J. & Callaghan, D. (1993). Minds and hearts: priorities in mental health services, Hastings Centre Report 23, no. 5, Special Supplement.

Bridges, K., Davenport, S. & Goldberg, D. (1994). The need for hospital-based rehabilitation services, *J. Ment. Health*, **3**, 205–212.

Brown, G.W., Birley, J.L.T. & Wing, J.K. (1972). Influence of family life on the course of schizophrenic disorders: A replication, *Br. J. Psychiatry*, **121**, 241–258.

Cohen, C.J. & Sokolovsky, J. (1978). Schizophrenia and social networks: ex-patients in the inner city, *Schizophrenia Bull.*, **4**, 546–560.

Cotterill, L. (1993). Schizophrenia and social networks, PhD Thesis, University of Manchester.

Davidge, M., Elias, S., Jayes, B. *et al* (1993). *Survey of English Mental Illness Hospitals*, Health Services Management Centre, Birmingham.

Freeman, H.L. (1984). *Mental Health and the Environment*, Churchill Livingstone, London.

Fried, M. (1963). Grieving for a lost home, in *The Urban Condition* (Ed. L.J. Duhl), Basic Books, New York.

Goldstein, J.M. & Caton, C.L.M. (1983). The effects of the community environment on chronic psychiatric patients, *Psychol. Med.*, **13**, 193–199.

Halpern, D. (1995). *Mental Health and the Built Environment*, Taylor and Francis, London.

Hamilton, M. & Hoenig, J. (1966). *The Desegregation of the Mentally Ill*, Routledge and Kegan Paul, London.

Jones, K., Robinson, M. & Golightly, M. (1986). Long-term psychiatric patients in the community, *Br. J. Psychiatry*, **149**, 537–540.

Keilen, M., Treasure, T., Schmidt, U. & Treasure, J. (1994). Quality of life measurements in eating disorders, angina and transplant candidates: are they comparable?, *J. Ry. Soc. Med.*, **87**, 441–444.

Leff, J. (1997). Whose life is it anyway? Quality of life for long-stay patients discharged from psychiatric hospitals, in *Quality of Life in Mental Disorders* (Eds H. Katschnig, H. Freeman & N. Sartorius), John Wiley & Sons, Chichester.

Lehman, A.F. (1983). The well-being of chronic mental patients: Assessing their quality of life, *Arch. Gen. Psychiatry*, **40**, 369–373.

Lehman, A.F. (1994). Continuity of care and client outcomes in the R.W. Johnson Programme on chronic mental illness, *Milbank Q.*, **72**, 105–122.

Lehman, A.F., Ward, N.C. & Linn, L.S. (1982). Chronic mental patients: The quality of life issue, *Am. J. Psychiatry*, **139**, 1271–1276.

Lehman, A.F., Possidente, S. & Hawker, F. (1986). The quality of life of chronic patients in a State hospital and in community residences, *Hosp. Community Psychiatry*, **37**, 901–907.

McGill, T.M. (1995). Quality of life assessment: values and pitfalls, *J. Ry. Soc. Med.*, **88**, 680–683.

Newman, O. (1972). *Defensible Space*, Macmillan, New York.

Oliver, J.P.J. (1991). The quality of life in community care, in *Residential Needs for Severely Disabled Psychiatric Patients: The Case for Hospital Hostels* (Ed. R. Young), HMSO, London.

Oliver, J. & Mohamad, H. (1992). The quality of life of the chronically mentally ill: A comparison of public, private and voluntary residential provisions, *Br. J. Social Work*, **22**, 391–404.

Oliver, J., Huxley, P., Bridges, K. & Mohamad, H. (1996). *Quality of Life and Mental Health Services*, Routledge, London.

Oyebode, F. (1994). Ethics and resource allocation: Can health care customers be qualified?, *Psychiat. Bull.*, **18**, 395–398.

Oyebode, F., Cumella, S., Garden, G. & Nicholls, J. (1992). Development of outcome measures in acute psychiatry, *Psychiat. Bull.*, **16**, 618–619.

Packer, S. (1994). Psychopathology and quality of life in schizophrenia, *Neuropsychopharmacology.*, **10**(35, Suppl.), 2405.

Sainfort, F., Becker, M. & Diamond, R. (1996). Judgments of quality of life of individuals with severe mental disorders, *Am. J. Psychiatry*, **153**, 497–502.

Shepherd, G., Muijen, M., Dean, R. & Cooney, M. (1996). Residential care in hospital and in the community – quality of care and quality of life, *Br. J. Psychiatry*, **168**, 448–456.

Simpson, C.J. (1996). Quality of life in a new hospital hostel, *Psychiat. Bull.*, **20**, 275–276.

Simpson, C.J., Hyde, C.E. & Faragher, E.B. (1989). The chronically mentally ill in community facilities – a study of quality of life, *Br. J. Psychiatry*, **154**, 77–82.

Swales, J.D. (1995). Quality of life data: How can we get the best quality of them?, *J. Ry. Soc. Med.*, **88**, 125.

Warner, R. & Huxley, P. (1993). Psychopathology and quality of life among mentally ill patients in the community, British and US samples compared, *Br. J. Psychiatry*, **163**, 505–509.

Weiden, P. (1994). Neuroleptics and quality of life – the patient's perspective, *Neuropsychopharmacology.*, **10**(35), 241–244

Westermeyer, J. (1980). Psychosis in a peasant society: Social outcomes, *Am. J. Psychiatry*, **137**, 1390–1394.

Wilkinson, G., Croft-Jeffreys, C., Krekorian, H. *et al* (1990). QALYs in psychiatric care, *Psychiat. Bull.*, **14**, 582–585.

Wing, J.K. (1986). Psychosocial factors affecting the long-term course of schizophrenia, in *Psychosocial Treatment of Schizophrenia* (Eds J.S. Strauss, W. Boker & H.D. Brenner), Hans Huber, Bern.

Wing, J.K. & Brown, G.W. (1970). *Institutionalism and Schizophrenia: A Comparative Study of Three Mental Hospitals 1960–68*, Cambridge University Press, London.

World Health Organization (1979). *Schizophrenia: A Two-Year Follow-up Study*, John Wiley & Sons, New York.

World Health Organization (1992). *The International Pilot Study of Schizophrenia*: Five-Year Follow-up Findings, WHO, Geneva.

Section III
ASSESSMENT AND MEASUREMENT

6

Instruments for Measuring Quality of Life in Mental Disorders. I: up to 1996

Anthony F. Lehman

INTRODUCTION

Mental illnesses exert a wide range of effects on persons' lives, which include psychiatric symptoms as well as changes in functional status, access to resources and opportunities, subjective well-being, family burden and sometimes community safety (Attkisson et al., 1991). Because of this broad array of relevant outcomes and a prevailing concern that assessments of these should include the patient's perspective, increased attention has been paid to the development of measures of their 'quality of life' (QoL).

Over the past decade, several measures have been developed to assess the QoL experiences of persons with mental illnesses, in particular severe and persistent psychoses, but more recently also depression and anxiety disorders. These are in addition to the more generic QoL measures that have been developed in general health care and which, to a limited extent, have been applied to persons with psychiatric disorders (Revicki and Murray, 1994).

This chapter reviews the published instruments available to assess QoL for persons with mental disorders. It is based on a computerised search of MEDLINE and PSYCLIT for the years 1984–1995 which crossed 'quality of life' with 'depression,' 'bipolar disorder,' 'anxiety disorders,' 'mental disorders,' 'schizophrenia,' 'neurotic disorders,' 'adjustment disorders,' 'personality disorders' and 'paranoid disorders.' Citations were restricted to the English language, due to the author's limitations. Additional citations were identified through a review of bibliographies of articles and the author's prior reviews of the topic.

Although definitions vary, the 'quality of life' concept encompasses three overarching dimensions: (a) what a person is capable of doing (functional status), (b) access to resources and opportunities to use these abilities to pursue interests, and (c) sense of well-being. The former two dimensions are often referred to as the objective quality of life and the latter as the subjective quality of life. Within these overarching dimensions, certain life domains have been identified, e.g. health, family, social relations, work, financial status and living situation. Quality of life is thus a complex notion. Three perspectives can be identified to frame core issues regarding QoL assessment in health care: (a) the general QoL framework; (b) the health-related QoL framework; and (c) the disease-specific QoL framework.

The general QoL framework underlies the considerable research that has been done in the general population – work which for the most part preceded the more recent development of such research in

Quality of Life in Mental Disorders, Second Edition   Edited by H. Katschnig, H. Freeman and N. Sartorius
© 2006 John Wiley & Sons, Ltd

the health care context (Andrews and Withey, 1976; Campbell, Converse and Rodgers, 1976). The intent of this line of research has been to derive a social perspective about the status and well-being of various groups of people, and the values that they and their societies place upon various aspects of life experience. Such a perspective may provide insights into what people strive for, why they choose as they do and how different societies and subgroups within a society fare, relative to others, in their life aspirations. These insights may help to guide decisions about how to improve QoL. Measures based on this approach typically cover functional status, access to resources and opportunities, and sense of well-being across multiple aspects of life domains, necessarily directly affected by health care (e.g. housing).

The health-related QoL (HRQL) framework emphasises the specific impacts that the prevention and treatment of disease and injury have on the value of survival (Patrick and Erickson, 1993). The concept of HRQL acknowledges the limited, but often vital, influences that disease and health care have on QoL, and holds health care accountable only for those aspects that it may directly affect. The health-related QoL framework focuses on functional status and sense of well-being but, within these dimensions, covers only those aspects directly related to health (e.g. functional role limitations owing to emotional or physical illness, as opposed to limitations owing to poverty or limited social opportunities). Such HRQL measures offer generic health-related QoL assessments that can be used across most medical conditions.

The disease-specific QoL framework presses for an even narrower definition of QoL in health care evaluations, tailored to the potential impacts or QoL of a specific disorder and its treatment.

SPECIFIC MEASURES

The vast majority of QoL measures that were identified in this survey were designed for mixed diagnostic groups of persons with severe and persistent mental illnesses, primarily schizophrenia, but also including chronic and disabling affective disorders and a variety of other seriously disabling mental disorders in the DSM (*Diagnostic and Statistical Manual of Mental Disorders*) system. More recently, QoL measures for less disabling, common psychiatric disorders, particularly acute depression and anxiety disorders, have been developed. These measures will be discussed according to the illness(es) they target: (a) severe and persistent mental illnesses, (b) schizophrenia and (c) depression and anxiety disorders. Most include the general QoL framework, but a few disease-specific measures are becoming available. Each measure is summarised in terms of its name, key reference(s), original purpose, types of patients studied, type of instrument, number of items, length of administration, summary content and data on reliability and validity.

Severe and Persistent Mental Illnesses

Quality of life assessments for persons with chronic mental illnesses have typically assumed a general QoL perspective, assessing multiple life domains and including measures of functional status, access to resources and opportunities, and sense of well-being (Lehman and Burns, 1990). The fact that QoL assessments for the chronic disorders have taken this direction reflects the social and economic impacts that these disabling conditions have on patients, as well as the policy context in which they evolved. Assessments for persons with chronic mental illnesses arose in the era of deinstitutionalisation and the need to develop strategies to care for these persons in the community. In this regard, it was not only the patients' medical needs that were of concern (pharmacotherapy, psychiatric care and medical care) but also social support needs (housing, income support, safety and integration into families and communities) (Schulberg and Bromet, 1981). Therefore, a wider social perspective was chosen to assess these broader issues and to inform policy makers and service providers about how well comprehensive service programmes, not just treatments, were meeting these needs.

Community Adjustment Form (CAF) (Stein and Test, 1980; Hoult and Reynolds, 1984)

This semi-structured self-report interview was developed to assess life satisfaction and other QoL outcomes in a randomised study of an experimental system of community-based care for the severely mentally ill versus standard care in Dane County, Wisconsin. It consists of 140 items, and requires approximately 45 minutes to complete. The areas assessed include: leisure activities, quality of living situation, employment history and status, income sources and amounts, free lodging and/or meals, contact with friends, family contact, legal problems, life satisfaction (21 items), self-esteem, medical care, and agency utilisation. No psychometric data have been reported. The original sample that was studied consisted of 130 patients seeking admission to a state mental hospital; over half were men (55%) and their mean age was 31 years. Half carried a diagnosis of schizophrenia. They were treated both in the state hospital and in a community-based assertive community treatment programme. The results of the original Wisconsin study were replicated in Australia, using the same measures (Hoult and Reynolds, 1984).

Quality of Life Checklist (QLC) (Malm, May and Dencker, 1981)

This checklist was developed to provide information about which aspects of QoL are particularly important to both patients and clinician raters, to assist in therapeutic planning. It is a 93-item rating scale, completed by a trained interviewer after a one-hour semi-structured interview. Scoring for all areas assessed is dichotomized as 'satisfactory' or 'unsatisfactory.' The areas assessed include: leisure activities, work, vocational rehabilitation, economic dependency, social relationships, knowledge and education, psychological dependency, inner experience, housing standard, medical care (psychiatric and general) and religion. No psychometric data are collected, but analyses report simple frequencies of 'satisfactory' versus 'unsatisfactory' by items. The patients studied included 40 with chronic schizophrenia from a Swedish outpatient clinic; they ranged in age from 18 to 50 and 68% were men.

Satisfaction with Life Domains Scale (SLDS) (Baker and Intagliata, 1982; Johnson, 1991)

This instrument was developed to evaluate the impact on the QoL of chronically mentally ill patients of the Community Support Program (CSP) in New York State. It is administered to the subject by a trained interviewer, consists of 15 items and requires approximately 10 minutes. Its individual items cover: satisfaction with housing, neighbourhood, food, clothing, health, people lived with, friends, family, relations with other people, work/day programming, spare time, leisure, local services and facilities, economic situation and the place lived in now compared to the state hospital. These can be summed into a total life satisfaction score, which correlates at $r=0.64$ with the Bradburn Affect Balance Scale (Bradburn, 1969) and at $r=0.29$ with the Global Assessment Scale (Endicott et al., 1976). No other psychometric data are provided. The frequencies and means on these items can be compared with item scores in a national QoL survey of the general population (Andrews and Withey, 1976). The patients studied were 118 chronically mentally ill outpatients, aged 18–86, in two community support programmes. They had a mean age of 53.3 years, 61% were women and 84% lived in supervised residential settings. Diagnoses included 56% schizophrenia, 14% affective disorders 5% substance use disorders, and 3% organic mental syndromes.

Oregon Quality of Life Questionnaire (OQLQ) (Bigelow, Gareau and Young, 1982; Bigelow et al., 1982, 1991; Bigelow, McFarland and Olson, 1991; Bigelow and Young, 1991)

The OQLQ was originally based on the Denver Community Mental Health Scale, but has undergone a series of developments since 1981. The original purpose was to assess QoL outcomes among clients served by community mental health programmes, especially those developed under the National Institute of Mental Health Community Support Program (NIMH CSP) initiative. The OQLQ has been updated with more recent psychometric data, alternative versions and further programme applications.

This instrument exists in two versions: a structured self-report interview (263 items) and a semi-structured interviewer-rated interview (146 items). Both are administered by a trained (not necessarily clinical) interviewer. The underlying theory states that QoL derives from the social contract between an individual and society: individuals' needs are met to the extent that persons fulfil the demands placed upon them by society. Most of the items use fixed, ordinal response categories, and the interview requires approximately 45 minutes to administer. The OQLQ yields 14 scale scores: psychological distress, psychological well-being, tolerance of stress, total basic need satisfaction, independence, interpersonal interactions, spouse role, social support, work at home, employability, work on the job, meaningful use of time, negative consequences of alcohol use and negative consequences of drug use.

The data on reliability and validity of the OQLQ have been evaluated extensively. Cronbach's alpha for the 14 scales on the self-report interview versions range from 0.05 to 0.98, with a median of 0.84. Eight of the scales have excellent reliability (alpha > 0.8), two have intermediate reliability (alpha between 0.8 and 0.4) and four have poor reliability (<0.4). Test–retest reliabilities (interval not specified) ranged from 0.37 to 0.64, with a median of 0.50. The interrater reliability for the interviewer-rated version has been assessed in a small sample study ($N = 6$) and produced interrater agreement levels between 58 and 100% on the interviewer judgements. More than half of the items showed greater than 90% agreement, and Cronbach's alpha ranged from 0.32 to over 0.80 (more than half over 0.80). The predictive validity of the OQLQ has been evaluated by comparing: (a) clients in different types of community mental health programmes (CSP, drug, alcohol and general psychiatric clinics), (b) general community respondents from economically distressed and non-distressed communities and (c) changes in community mental health clients over time. Results of these analyses support the overall predictive validity of the questionnaire.

The OQLQ has been applied to both outpatients of mental health programmes and samples of the general population. The outpatient samples included patients at intake to community mental health programmes in Oregon (including chronically mentally ill, drug abusers, alcoholics and general psychiatric patients); their mean age was 33.8 years (range 18–85) and there were 60% men and 96% 'non-Hispanics'. The community sample had 43% men, with a mean age of 36.8, and was 92% non-Hispanic.

Lehman Quality of Life Interview (QOLI) (Lehman, Ward and Linn, 1982; Lehman, 1983a, 1983b, 1988; Lehman, Possidente and Hawker, 1986; Franklin *et al.*, 1987; Simpson, Hyde and Faragher, 1989; Levitt, Hogan and Bucosky, 1990; Lehman, Slaughter and Meyers 1991; Huxley and Warner, 1992; Rosenfield, 1992; Sullivan, Wells and Leake, 1992; Rosenfield and Neese-Todd, 1993; Mechanic *et al.*, 1994; Lehman, Rachuba and Postrado, 1995)

The QOLI assesses the life circumstances of persons with severe mental illnesses, both in terms of what they actually do and experience ('objective' QoL) and their feelings about these experiences ('subjective' QoL). This interview provides a broad-based assessment of the recent and current life experiences of the respondent in a wide variety of life areas of potential interest, including living situation, family relations, social relations, leisure activities, finances, safety and legal problems, work and school, and health (as well as religion and neighbourhood in some versions).

The QOLI is a structured self-report interview, administered by trained lay interviewers. Its original version consists of 143 items and requires approximately 45 minutes to administer, but it has undergone a variety of revisions over the past ten years, primarily to improve its data on reliability and validity and to shorten it. The core version contains a global measure of life satisfaction, as well as measures of objective and subjective QOL in eight life domains: living situation, daily activities and functioning, family relations, social relations, finances, work and school, legal and safety issues, and health. Each section is organised such that information is obtained first about the objective QoL and then about the level of life satisfaction in that area. This pairing of objective and subjective QoL indicators is essential to the QoL assessment model (Lehman, 1988).

All the life satisfaction items in the interview use a fixed interval scale, which was originally developed in a national survey of the quality of American life (Andrews and Withey, 1976). The types of objective QoL indicators used vary considerably across the different aspects. In general, they can be viewed as of two types: measures of functioning (e.g. frequency of social contacts or daily activities) and measures of access to resources and opportunities (e.g. income support or housing type). The QoL indicators include both individual items (e.g. monthly income support) and scales (e.g. frequency of social contacts).

The variables generated by the QOLI include: (a) *objective QoL indicators*: residential stability, homelessness, daily activities, frequency of family contacts, frequency of social contacts, total monthly spending money, adequacy of financial supports, current employment status, number of arrests during the past year, victim of violent crime during the past year, victim of non-violent crime during the past year, general health status; and (b) *subjective QoL indicators*: satisfaction with: living situation, leisure activities, family relations, social relations, finances, work and school, legal and safety, and health.

The data on reliability and validity of the QOLI have been extensively assessed. Internal consistency reliabilities range from 0.79 to 0.88 (median = 0.85) for the life satisfaction scales and from 0.44 to 0.82 (median = 0.68) for the objective QoL scales. These reliabilities have been replicated in two separate studies of persons with severe mental illness. Test–retest reliabilities (one week) have also been assessed for the QOLI: life satisfaction scales are 0.41–0.95 (median = 0.72) and objective QoL scales are 0.29–0.98 (median = 0.65). Construct and predictive validity have been assessed as good by confirmatory factor analyses and multivariate predictive models. The QOLI also differentiates between patients living in hospitals and supervised community residential programmes in both the United States and Britain (Lehman, Possidente and Hawker, 1986; Simpson, Hyde and Faragher, 1989). Individual life satisfaction items clearly discriminate between persons with severe mental illness and the general population (Lehman, Ward and Linn, 1982). Further construct validation has been assessed in studies of the predictors of QoL among day-treatment patients in Britain (Levitt, Hogan and Bucosky, 1990) and the relationship between QoL and feelings of empowerment among persons with severe mental illness in the United States (Rosenfield and Neese-Todd, 1993). A variety of methodological papers have explored such other issues as the relationship between QoL and clinical symptoms (Lehman, 1983b), gender, race, and age (Lehman, Slaughter and Meyers 1992; Lehman, Rachuba and Postrado, 1995), and housing type (Slaughter and Lehman, 1991; Lehman, Slaughter and Meyers, 1991).

The QOLI has been used almost exclusively with persons with severe mental disorders. The samples in published studies have included approximately equal numbers of men and women, about 75% Caucasian, ranging in age from 18 to 65. The predominant diagnosis in these studies, ranging from 57 to 76% of patients, has been schizophrenia. General population norms for individual life satisfaction items are available (Andrews and Withey, 1976).

A brief version of the QOLI is now available (Health Services Research Institute, 1995). As with the core version, this provides a broad-based QoL assessment and consists of 78 questions, taken from the full version. It too is a self-report interview, administered by trained lay interviewers. It requires an average of 16 minutes and measures the same life domains as the core version, including the global measure of life satisfaction as well as measures of objective and subjective QoL in the eight life domains.

This brief QOLI has been tested on a sample of 50 individuals with severe and persistent mental illness from a local psychosocial rehabilitation programme participated in this pilot study. Diagnoses included schizophrenia ($N = 17$), major depression ($N = 17$) and other severe and persistent mental illness ($N = 16$). Internal consistency reliabilities for the brief QOLI life satisfaction are comparable to those for the full version, ranging from 0.70 to 0.87 (median = 0.83). Internal consistency reliabilities for the objective brief QOLI scales range from 0.56 to 0.82 (median = 0.65).

Client Quality of Life Interview (CQLI) (Mulkern *et al.*, 1986; Goldstrom and Manderscheid, 1986)

The CQLI was developed as part of a battery of instruments to assess outcomes among persons with severe mental disorders who were served by the NIMH Community Support Program (CSP). These instruments include the Uniform Client Data Instrument (UCDI), the UCDI-Short Form, the CSP Participant Follow-up Form and the CQLI, the contents of which overlap to a considerable degree. All but the CQLI are completed by case managers or other professionals serving the clients and generally focus on functioning, services and clinical outcomes. Only the CQLI asks clients directly about the quality of their lives and therefore it is only reviewed here. The conceptual model underlying the CQLI assumes that certain life essentials are necessary precursors to a QoL. One major purpose of the CSP was to provide these essentials, and thus to enhance QoL.

The CQLI is a structured self-report interview, administered by a trained lay interviewer. It consists of 46 items rated by the respondent, as well as 19 interviewer ratings; ratings are done on fixed, ordinal scales. The content areas covered include: essentials of life (food, clothing, shelter, health and hygiene, money and safety), job training and education, daily activities and recreation, privacy, social support, social time, self-reliance and peace of mind. In each area, questions generally cover both the quantity of resources or activity, as well as the respondent's subjective feelings about these resources and activities. Many of the item sets lend themselves readily to composite scales, although their development or scoring is not available for the CQLI. Some of the scales parallel the UCDI, for which both scale computation guidelines and data on reliability and validity are available.

No formal psychometric analyses of the CQLI are available; correlations of items rated by the clients with comparable items from the UCDI rated by the case manager were quite low. The CQLI ratings remained stable over a 14-month follow-up period. The subsample in the CSP study who completed the CQLI were 109 severely mentally ill clients from six exemplary CSPs. They comprised 51% men, 82% Caucasian, 11% black, 6% Hispanic and 1% other, and had a mean age of 41.5. All were severely mentally ill, though detailed diagnoses were given.

California Well-Being Project Client Interview (CWBPCI) (Campbell *et al.*, 1989)

The California Well-Being Project was a three-year initiative, funded by the California Department of Mental Health, to develop a better understanding of the health and well-being concerns of persons who have been treated for mental illness (the 'psychiatrically labelled'). The most unique aspect of this initiative is that it was designed and conducted entirely by consumers of mental health care. It consisted of three components: (a) research and analysis of well-being factors for individuals assessed through a structured survey of consumers, family members and professionals, (b) production of educational materials based upon this survey and (c) dissemination of these educational materials to consumers, family members and mental health providers.

Three versions of the survey questionnaire on well-being were developed for consumers (151 items), family members (76 items) and mental health professionals (77 items). The time required for its administration has not been indicated. The questionnaires consist predominantly of Likert-scaled questions, but with some open-ended items interspersed. The questionnaires are designed to be either administered in face-to-face interviews (conducted by trained consumers), self-administered by mail or self-administered in groups, with an interviewer available to answer questions. The instrument is thus designed for flexibility in administration to provide the multiple perspectives of consumers, family members and professionals.

In the California survey, the CWBPCI was administered to 331 persons who were 'psychiatrically labelled' and living in various settings, including psychiatric hospitals (non-state), skilled nursing facilities, board-and-care homes, satellite houses, single occupancy hotels, community residential treatment centres, drop-in centres, client self-help groups, organisations serving people identified as 'homeless mentally ill', and on the streets. The final sample consisted of 61 randomly selected members of the California Network of Mental Health Consumers (surveyed by mail), 249 volunteer respondents from various facilities in California (face-to-face interviews, not randomly selected) and 21 randomly selected project return clients. Project return was a programme designed to help ease the transition of clients from the hospital to the community. The sample was 52% men, 67.5% Caucasian, 14.7% black and 4.6% Hispanic. They were predominantly young, with 41% below the age of 35 and 75% below the age of 45; the authors describe them as predominantly chronically mentally ill, but no further clinical details are given.

No information is provided on the instrument's data on reliability and validity, most data from individual items having been reported as frequencies (or percentages) in a narrative section about the concerns of the respondents. The instrument covered a broad range of topics; a few examples include adequate resources, aspirations, children, family relationships, freedom, homelessness, income, patients' rights, stigma, and warmth and intimacy.

A key measure derived from the interview is the Well-Being Quotient. This is derived from two questions providing information about the relative importance assigned to various factors that may affect well-being, and whether the respondent currently lacks these factors. The questions read:

(a) 'Below is a list of things that some people have said are essential for their well-being. Please mark all of those things that you believe are *essential* for your well-being.' (b) 'Of the things that people have mentioned that are essential for well-being, which of the following, if any, do you lack in your everyday life?' The response factors include happiness, health, adequate income, meaningful work or achievement, comfort, satisfying social life, satisfying spiritual life, adequate resources, good food and a decent place to live, satisfying sexual life, creativity, basic human freedoms, warmth and intimacy, and safety. Besides rank-ordering these factors according to the percentages of respondents who identify each factor in each of the questions, four well-being profiles are computed: (a) for each factor, the proportion of respondents who indicate that they lack a well-being factor that they consider essential; (b) the proportion of respondents who do not lack a factor they consider essential; (c) the proportion of clients who consider a factor essential, regardless of whether they have it; (iv) the proportion of respondents who lack a given factor regardless of its essentialness.

The most noteworthy aspect of this instrument is that it was entirely consumer generated. This fact enhances its face validity, even though no formal psychometric analyses were conducted. However, the researchers consider this instrument to be still in a developmental stage.

Lancashire Quality of Life Profile (LQOLP) (Oliver, 1992; Oliver and Mohamad, 1992)

The LQOLP was developed in the United Kingdom during the late 1980s by Oliver and co-workers in response to a request by the British government for community care programmes serving persons with severe mental disorders to assess the impact of their services on patients' QoL. The LQOLP is based on the Lehman QOLI and uses the same underlying theory, but is modified to reflect cultural variations and the broader wish for a service-based evaluation of QoL.

The LQOLP is a structured self-report patient interview, designed for administration by clinical staff in community settings. It consists of 100 items and requires approximately one hour to administer. It assesses objective QoL and life satisfaction in nine life domains: work/education, leisure/participation, religion, finances, living situation, legal and safety, family relations, social relations and health. It also includes a measure of general well-being and self-concept. Objective QoL information is collected by means of categorical or continuous measures, depending on the content area. Life satisfaction ratings are on a seven-point Likert scale.

Data on reliability and validity of life satisfaction have been evaluated in a series of pilot studies (Oliver, 1992). Test–retest reliabilities for life satisfaction scores range from 0.49 to 0.78, depending upon the patient sample, while internal consistency reliabilities (Cronbach's alpha) of these scales range from 0.84 to 0.86. Content, construct and criterion validities were also assessed using a variety of techniques and judged to be adequate.

The LQOLP has been used with chronically mentally ill patients in a variety of community care settings in both the United Kingdom and Colorado, but details of the sample characteristics are not available. A briefer version of the LQOLP is currently being piloted in 12 European countries and is being considered by the World Health Organization in conjunction with their broader studies of QoL.

Quality of Life Self-Assessment Inventory (QLSAI) (Skantze, 1993)

The QLSAI provides information about which aspects of QoL are particularly important to patients and natural raters to assist in therapeutic planning. It is an updated version of the QoL checklist (Malm, May and Dencker, 1981) and has been used with out-patients with chronic schizophrenia ($N=66$). The QLSAI is a 100-item self-report inventory completed by the patient, followed by a semi-structured interview with a clinician to check the patient's ratings of satisfaction and dissatisfaction and to discuss the implications for treatment planning. It requires approximately ten minutes for the patient to complete the self-rated inventory, plus 40–50 minutes for the semi-structured clinical interview.

The aspects assessed include: physical health, finances, household and self-care, contacts, dependence, work and leisure, knowledge and education, inner experiences, mental health, housing, housing environment, community services and religion. For all these, ratings are either 'satisfactory' or 'unsatisfactory'. The test–retest (7–10 days) correlation for the overall scale is 0.88. Comparative data are available from healthy university students.

Quality of Life Index for Mental Health (QLI-MH) (Becker, Diamond and Sainfort, 1993)

The QLI-MH provides a patient-focused assessment of QoL that is intended to be responsive to the needs and constraints of clinical practice and research, and which incorporates the multiple perspectives of patients, families and clinicians. It is designed as a self-administered questionnaire, with which assistance may be given to more severely impaired patients. Versions exist for patients, families and clinicians.

It consists of 113 items; the patient version requires about 20–30 minutes and the provider version 10–20 minutes. It has been tested with a sample of 40 out-patients meeting DSM-III-R criteria for schizophrenia.

The QLI-MH produces eight scaled scores on the following aspects: life satisfaction (using 15 items from Andrews and Withey (1976), occupational activities, psychological well-being (using the Bradburn Affect Balance Scale) (Bradburn, 1969), physical health, activities of daily living (using the Life Skills Profile) (Rosen, Hadzi-Pavlovic and Packer, 1989) and the QLI (Spitzer *et al.*, 1981), social relationships (using items from the International Pilot Study of Schizophrenia) (Strauss and Carpenter, 1974), economics (adequacy and satisfaction with finances) and symptoms (using the Brief Psychiatric Rating Scale) (Overall and Gorham, 1962). The QLI-MH also includes some open-ended questions to generate individual goals for improvement with treatment. Finally, the instrument includes ratings of the importance of each aspect in relation to subjects' overall QoL.

Test–retest reliabilities have been assessed on a subsample of 10 patients with schizophrenia over 3–10 days. The 'percentage match' for the various aspects ranged from 0.82 to 0.87. Content validity is supported by some previously developed scales and a scale development process that uses key informants, including patients, family members and providers. Criterion validity has been assessed through correlations between patient QLI-MH scores and provider ratings on the Uniscale and the Spitzer QLI (0.68 and 0.58, respectively).

Quality of Life Interview Scale (QOLIS) (Holcomb *et al.*, 1993)

The QOLIS is designed as a QoL measure for assessing severely mentally ill persons. It is a semi-structured interview, administered by trained clinical interviewers, and consists of 87 items. The length of time required to administer is not reported. The QOLIS was used with 201 patients, including 100 long-term in-patients and 101 in surrounding community residences. Diagnoses were: 45% schizophrenia, 16% organic mental disorders, 11% major affective disorders and 16% other. QOLIS items are rated on a Likert scale from 'strongly agree' to 'strongly disagree' and generate eight factors: autonomy, self-esteem, social support, physical health, anger/hostility, emotional autonomy and personal fulfillment.

Factor analysis of an initial pool of 148 items yielded the proposed eight factors, with 87 items. Coefficient alphas for these factors range from 0.72 to 0.93 (median = 0.77). Stepwise multiple regression analyses were used to predict self-reported life satisfaction using the Baker and Intagliata SLDS (Baker and Intagliata, 1982) and the Global Assessment of Functioning Scale (GAF) (Endicott *et al.*, 1976) ($p < 0.0001$ for both analyses). All of the QOLIS scales significantly discriminated between the in-patient and community-based samples. Canonical analysis of the QOLIS scales and the scales from the Heinrichs–Carpenter QLS (Heinrichs, Hanlon and Carpenter, 1984) showed substantial correlation.

Schizophrenia

Although all the QoL measures reviewed above have been used with samples that had a predominance of schizophrenic patients, none was specifically developed as a disease-specific QoL measure. Only one schizophrenia-specific QoL measures exists.

Quality of Life Scale (QLS) (Heinrichs, Hanlon and Carpenter, 1984)

The QLS was developed to assess the deficit syndrome in patients with schizophrenia; it is a semi-structured interview rated by trained clinicians. Its 21 items are rated on fixed interval scales, based on the interviewer's judgement of the patient's functioning in each of the 21 areas. The interview requires approximately 45 minutes. The 21 items of the QLS cover: commonplace activities, occupational role, work functioning, work level, possession of commonplace objects, interpersonal relations (household, friends, acquaintances, social activity, social network, social initiative, social withdrawal, sociosexual functioning), sense of purpose, motivation, curiosity, anhedonia, aimless inactivity, empathy, emotional interaction and work satisfaction. These items reduce to four scales: intrapsychic foundations, interpersonal relations, instrumental role and total score.

The interrater reliabilities on conjointly conducted interviews range from 0.84 to 0.97 on summary scales. Individual item intraclass correlations range from 0.5 to 0.9, and a confirmatory factor analysis has been undertaken. This scale is widely used in the evaluation of psychopharmacological treatments for schizophrenia, but predominantly in out-patients (e.g. see Meltzer *et al.*, 1990).

Affective and Anxiety Disorders

Work on QoL measures for use with persons with mental illnesses that do not fall into the traditional definition of 'severe and persistent' has been quite recent. This has been stimulated by current pressures to assess the QoL impacts of pharmaceuticals, as well as by a broadening general interest in such outcomes, paralleling the earlier work on severe and persistent mental illnesses. These newer measures are closer to being 'disease-specific' or 'health-related' than the measures developed for severe and persistent mental illnesses, which follow the 'general' QoL framework. This trend probably reflects both the focus on short-term pharmacological effects and the less disabling nature of these disorders over the long run.

Quality of Life Enjoyment and Satisfaction Questionnaire (Q-LES-Q) (Endicott *et al.*, 1993)

The intent of the Q-LES-Q is to provide an easy-to-use assessment of patients' enjoyment and satisfaction with their lives. It is a self-administered, 93-item questionnaire; the length of time to complete it has not been reported. The Q-LES-Q has been used with 95 out-patients meeting DSM-III-R criteria for major depression. It yields eight summary scale scores. Five of these are relevant to all subjects: physical health, subjective feelings, leisure time activities, social relationships and general activities. Three can be scored for appropriate subgroups: work, household duties, and school/course work. Items are posed as questions, and respondents rate their degree of enjoyment or satisfaction on a five-point scale. The Q-LES-Q also includes single items assessing satisfaction with medication and overall life satisfaction.

Test–retest reliabilities (interval not specified) were assessed on 54 stable out-patients; these intraclass correlations ranged from 0.63 to 0.89 (median = 0.74) on the various scales. Internal consistency reliabilities all exceeded 0.90 (median = 0.92). Validity has been assessed with correlations of the Q-LES-Q scales with illness severity and depression measures. The correlations of the Q-LES-Q scales ranged from −0.34 to −0.68 (median = −0.54) with the Clinical Global Impressions (CGI) scale (National Institute of Mental Health, 1985) and showed comparable correlations with the Hamilton Rating Scale for Depression (HAM-D)(Hamilton, 1960), the Beck Depression Inventory (Beck and Beamesderfer, 1974) and the Symptom Checklist-90 (Derogatis, Lipman and Covi, 1973). Changes in the Q-LES-Q correlated with changes in the CGI scale and the HAM-D (correlations of change scores ranged from −0.30 to −0.54; median = −0.46).

SmithKline Beecham Quality of Life (SBQOL) Scale (Stoker, Dunbar and Beaumont, 1992)

The SBQOL scale was specifically designed to provide a method for assessing QoL in patients with affective disorders. It is a 28-item self-report questionnaire (time to complete has not been specified). It was developed with data from 129 out-patients who presented in general practice and met criteria for either DSM-III-R major depression or generalised anxiety disorder. The items in the SBQOL scale are rated on a ten-point scale, anchored by positive and negative extremes of the various constructs. Aspects covered include: psychic well-being, physical well-being, social relationships, activities/interests/hobbies, mood, locus of control, sexual function, work/employment, religion and finances. To provide an idiographic component, the respondent is asked to rate themselves on these constructs from three perspectives: self now, ideal self and sick self. A summary score is then generated across the aspects for the differences between self now and either ideal self or sick self.

Changes in the self now/sick self and self now/ideal self paralleled improvements in clinical depression (measured by the Hamilton Depression Rating Scale) over a 12-week therapeutic period. The self now/sick self and self now/ideal self 'distances' correlated with the Sickness Impact Profile (Bergner *et al.*, 1981) and the General Health Questionnaire (Goldberg, 1979) – two generic health-related QoL measures. One-day test–retest reliabilities for the self now, sick self, ideal self, self now/sick self and self now/ideal self scores ranged from 0.66 to 0.83 (median = 0.70). Internal consistency reliabilities for these scores ranged from 0.85 to 0.95 (median = 0.90).

Quality of Life in Depression Scale (QLDS) (Hunt and McKenna, 1992a, 1992b; Gregoire *et al.*, 1994)

The QLDS was designed to assess the impact of depression on QoL of patients. It is a 34-item, self-report questionnaire (time to complete has not been specified). It has been used in a study of 74 patients with depression in the United Kingdom. The QLDS generates a summary score encompassing six dimensions: domestic activities, interpersonal relationships, social life, cognition, personal hygiene, leisure activities and relaxation. The two-week test–retest reliability coefficient was 0.81 and the internal consistency reliability 0.93. The QLDS score had a correlation of 0.79 with the General Well-Being Index (DuPuy, 1984). These results have been replicated on samples of both non-elderly and elderly Dutch patients with major depression (Gregoire *et al.*, 1994).

DISCUSSION

Measurement of QoL among persons with mental disorders is currently a very active and fertile field of assessment research. Several of the measures reviewed here are reasonably well developed from a psychometric standpoint and have been used in various types of clinical studies. However, the apparent proliferation of newer measures suggests that no current one fulfills the needs of most researchers and clinicians.

The choice of a QoL measure should be determined by the intended application and in turn by the framework (general, health-related or disease-specific) appropriate for the task. In developing an assessment of QoL in a mental health care context, one must consider both the breadth and specificity of the measures. No single QoL measure will meet all needs. A general QoL approach may raise QoL issues that mental health care cannot reasonably be expected to address (e.g. decent and affordable housing or access to good jobs), and hence may be insensitive to the effects of treatment on QoL. A disease-specific approach, while sensitive to the QoL issues of concern to patients with a specific diagnosis, lacks generalisability and comparability to other patient groups. General HRQL measures, such as the Duke Health Profile (Parkerson, Broadhead and Tse, 1990) and the Medical Outcome Study Short Form-36 (Ware and Sherbourne, 1992), permit fruitful comparisons across conditions (Wells *et al.*, 1988), but may lack sufficient specificity to guide improvements in care for persons with specific mental disorders. The information derived from HRQL measures may be too narrow to reflect adequately the needs of persons who are chronically disabled and socially disadvantaged due to medical problems.

QoL assessments can prove useful in assessing needs, developing intervention strategies and evaluating outcomes of interventions at both the system and individual patient levels. At the system or policy level, the development of services and the deployment of resources must derive from a clear understanding of the needs of those being served and the priorities of these needs. Regarding system planning for persons with chronic mental illnesses, QoL assessment provides important information about how patients are experiencing their current life circumstances (not just their health status) and permits some estimation about the priorities that they place on these needs. Such information may be vital for allocating resources within service systems that are based on patients' priorities. Although the ultimate allocation of resources must take into account the needs and perceptions of multiple constituencies (e.g. families, providers and communities), a patient-based QoL assessment provides the opportunity for systematic input from service recipients who often lack access to this decision-making process. Also at the system level, QoL assessment can provide continuous feedback from these recipients about the outcomes of services, and thus influence the further development of services and resource allocation.

At the individual patient level, QoL assessment can similarly be used to assess needs and to monitor the impact of treatment interventions and services. Malm, May and Dencker (1981) used a QoL assessment to guide treatment planning in a mental health clinic. Diamond (1985), Awad (1992) and Revicki and Murray (1994) have discussed the use of QoL assessment in the context of psychopharmacology for patients with mental illnesses. Liberman (1988) has proposed that in a rehabilitation context, QoL assessments can be used to identify those life areas with which a patient is most dissatisfied and which therefore may be most fruitful to address in a behavioural treatment programme. Finally, Oliver and co-workers in Great Britain have used QoL assessments in developing and assessing a national policy that includes case management services (renamed 'care management') (Oliver, 1992).

In summary, the development of QoL assessment procedures that are appropriate for various subgroups of persons with mental disorders in various contexts remains a worthwhile endeavour. Considerable progress towards this objective has already occurred. There have been thoughtful adaptations of currently available measures, as well as development of new ones to fill certain gaps in order to meet the growing demand for efficient, reliable, valid and sensitive QoL information for research, clinical decision-making and policy development.

ACKNOWLEDGEMENT

Preparation of this paper was supported by a National Institute of Mental Health Grant MH43703.

REFERENCES

Andrews, F.M. & Withey, S.B. (1976). *Social Indicators of Well-Being*, Plenum Press, New York.

Attkisson, C., Cook, J., Karno, M., Lehman, A., McGlashan, T.H., Meltzer, H.Y., O'Connor, M., Richardson, D., Rosenblatt, A., Wells, K. & Williams, J. (1991). Clinical services research, *Schizophrenia Bull.*, **18**, 561–626.

Awad, A.G. (1992). Quality of life of schizophrenic patients on medications and implications for new drug trials, *Hosp. Community Psychiatry*, **43**, 262–265.

Baker, F. & Intagliata, J. (1982). Quality of life in the evaluation of community support systems, *Evaluation and Progm. Planning*, **5**, 69–79.

Beck, A.T. & Beamesderfer, A. (1974). Assessment of depression: the depression inventory, *Modern Problems in Pharmacopsychiatry* (Ed. P. Pichot), pp. 151–169, S. Karger, Basel, Switzerland.

Becker, M., Diamond, R. & Sainfort, F. (1993). A new patient focused index for measuring quality of life in persons with severe and persistent mental illness, *Quality of Life Res.*, **2**, 239–251.

Bergner, M., Bobbit, R.A., Canter, W.B., & Gilson, B.S. (1981). The Sickness Impact Profile: Development and final revision of a health status measure, *Med. Care*, **19**, 787–805.

Bigelow, D.A., Gareau, M.J. & Young, D.J. (1982). A quality of life interview, *Psychosocial Rehabil. J.*, **14**, 94–98.

Bigelow, D.A., McFarland, B.H. & Olson, M.M. (1991): Quality of life of community mental health program clients: validating a measure, *Community Ment. Health J.*, **27**, 43–55.

Bigelow, D.A. & Young, D.J. (1991). Effectiveness of a case management program, *Community Ment. Health J.*, **27**, 115–123.

Bigelow, D.A., Brodsky, G., Steward, L. & Olson, M. (1982). The concept and measurement of quality of life as a dependent variable in evaluation of mental health services, in *Innovative Approaches to Mental Health Evaluation*, (Eds G. Stahler & W. Tash), pp. 345–366, Academic Press, New York.

Bigelow, D.A., McFarland, B.H., Gareau, M.J. & Young, D.J. (1991) Implementation and effectiveness of a bed reduction project, *Community Ment. Health J.*, **27**, 125–133.

Bradburn, N.M. (1969). *The Structure of Psychological Well-Being*, Aldine, Chicago, Illinois.

Campbell, A., Converse, P.E. & Rodgers, W.L. (1976). *The Quality of American Life*, Russell Sage Foundation, New York.

Campbell, J., Schraiber, R., Temkin, T. & Tusscher, T. (1989). The Well-Being Project: mental health clients speak for themselves, Report to the California Department of Mental Health.

Derogatis, D.A., Lipman, R.S. & Covi, L. (1973). SCL-90: an outpatient psychiatric rating scale: Preliminary report, *Psychopharmacol. Bull.*, **9**, 13–28.

Diamond, R. (1985). Drugs and quality of life: the patient's point of view, *J. Clin. Psychiatry*, **46**, 29–39.

DuPuy, H. (1984). The Psychological General Well-Being Index, in *Assessment of Quality of Life in Clinical Trials of Cardiovascular Therapies*, (Ed. N. Wenger), pp. 170–183, Le Jacq, New York.

Endicott, J., Spitzer, R., Fleiss, J. & Cohen, J. (1976). The global assessment scale: A procedure for measuring overall severity of psychiatric disturbance, *Arch. Gen. Psychiatry*, **33**, 766–771.

Endicott, J., Nee, J., Harrison, W. & Blumenthal, R. (1993). Quality of life enjoyment and satisfaction questionnaire: A new measure, *Psychopharm. Bull.*, **29**, 321–326.

Franklin, J.L., Solovitz, B., Mason, M., Clemons, J.R. & Miller, G.E. (1987). An evaluation of case management, *Am. J. Psychiatry*, **77**, 674–678.

Goldberg, D. (1979). *Manual of the General Health Questionnaire*, NFER Publishing, Windsor, England.

Goldstrom, I.D. & Manderscheid, R.W. (1986). The chronically mentally ill: A descriptive analysis from the Uniform Client Data Instrument, *Community Supply Serv. J.*, **2**, 4–9.

Gregoire, J., de Leval, N., Mesters, P. & Czarka, M. (1994). Validation of the quality of life in depression scale in a population of adult depressive patients aged 60 and above, *Quality of Life Res.*, **3**, 13–19.

Hamilton, M. (1960). A rating scale for depression, *J. Neurol. Neurosurg. Psychiatry*, **23**, 56–62.

Health Services Research Institute (1995). *Quality of Life Toolkit*, Boston, Massachusetts.

Heinrichs, D.W., Hanlon, T.E. & Carpenter, W.T. (1984). The quality of life scale: An instrument for rating the schizophrenic deficit syndrome, *Schizophrenia Bull.*, **10**, 388–398.

Holcomb, W.R., Morgan, P., Adams, N.A., Ponder, H. & Farrel, M. (1993). Development of a structured interview scale for measuring quality of life of the severely mentally ill, *J. Clin. Psychology*, **49**, 830–840.

Hoult, J. & Reynolds, J. (1984). Schizophrenia: A comparative trial of community oriented and hospital oriented psychiatric care. *Acta Psychiatrica Scand.*, **69**, 359–372.

Hunt, S.M. & McKenna, S.P. (1992a). The QLDS: A scale for measurement of quality of life in depression, *Health Policy*, **22**, 307–319.

Hunt, S.M. & McKenna, S.P. (1992b). A new measure of quality of life in depression: Testing the reliability and construct validity of the QLDS, *Health Policy*, **22**, 321–330.

Huxley, P. & Warner, R. (1992). Case management, quality of life, and satisfaction with services of long-term psychiatric patients, *Hosp. Community Psychiatry*, **43**, 799–802.

Johnson, P.J. (1991). Emphasis on quality of life of people with severe mental illness in community-based care in Sweden, *Psychosocial Rehabil. J.*, **14**, 23–37.

Lehman, A.F. (1983a). The well-being of chronic mental patients: Assessing their quality of life, *Arch. Gen. Psychiatry*, **40**, 369–373.

Lehman, A.F. (1983b). The effects of psychiatric symptoms on quality of life assessments among the chronic mentally ill, *Evaluation and Progm. Plann.*, **6**, 143–151.

Lehman, A.F. (1988). A quality of life interview for the chronically mentally ill, *Evaluation and Progm. Plann.*, **11**, 51–62.

Lehman, A.F. & Burns, B. (1990). Severe mental illness in the community, in *Quality of Life Assessments in Clinical Trials*, (Ed. B. Spilker), pp. 357–366, Plenum Press, New York.

Lehman, A.F., Possidente, S. & Hawker, F. (1986). The quality of life of chronic mental patients in a state hospital and community residences, *Hosp. Community Psychiatry*, **37**, 901–907.

Lehman, A.F., Rachuba, L.T. & Postrado, L.T. (1995). Demographic influences on quality of life among persons with chronic mental illnesses, *Evaluation and Progm. Plann.*, **18**, 155–164.

Lehman, A.F., Slaughter, J.C. & Myers, C.P. (1991). The quality of life of chronically mentally ill persons in alternative residential settings, *Psychiat. Q.*, **62**, 35–49.

Lehman, A.F., Slaughter, J.C. & Myers, C.P. (1992). Quality of life of the chronically mentally ill: Gender and decade of life effects, *Evaluation Progm. Plann.*, **15**, 7–12.

Lehman, A.F., Ward, N. & Linn, L. (1982). Chronic mental patients: The quality of life issue, *Am. J. Psychiatry*, **10**, 1271–1276.

Levitt, A.J., Hogan, T.P. & Bucosky, C.M. (1990). Quality of life in chronically mentally ill patients in day treatment, *Psychol. Med.*, **20**, 703–710.

Liberman, R.P. (Ed.) (1988). *Psychiatric Rehabilitation of Chronic Mental Patients*, American Psychiatric Press, Washington, DC.

Malm, U., May, P.R.A. & Dencker, S.J. (1981). Evaluation of the quality of life of the schizophrenic outpatient: A checklist, *Schizophrenia Bull.*, **7**, 477–487.

Mechanic, D., McAlpine, D., Rosenfield, S. & Davis, D. (1994). Effects of illness attribution and depression on the quality of life among persons with serious mental illness, *Social Sci. Med.*, **39**, 155–164.

Meltzer, H.Y., Burnett, S., Bastani, B. & Ramirez, L.F. (1990). Effects of six months of clozapine treatment on the quality of life of chronic schizophrenic patients, *Hosp. Community Psychiatry*, **41**, 892–897.

Mulkern, V., Agosta, J.M., Ashbaugh, J.W., Bradley, V.J., Spence, R.A., Allein, S., Nurczynski, P. & Houlihan, J. (1986). Community Support Program Client Follow-up Study, Report to National Institute of Mental Health.

National Institute of Mental Health (1985). Special feature: rating scales and assessment instruments for use in pediatric psychopharmacology research, *Psychopharmical Bull.*, **21**, 839–843.

Oliver, J.P.J (1992). The social care directive: Development of a quality of life profile for use in community services for the mentally ill, *Social Work and Social Sci. Rev.*, **3**, 5–45.

Oliver, J.P.J. & Mohamad, H. (1992). The quality of life of the chronically mentally ill: A comparison of public, private, and voluntary residential provisions, *Br. J. Social Work*, **22**, 391–404.

Overall, J.E. & Gorham, D.R. (1962). The brief psychiatric rating scale, *Psychol. Rep.*, **10**, 799–812.

Parkerson, G.R., Broadhead, W.E. & Tse, C.K.J. (1990). The Duke Health Profile, *Med. Care*, **28**, 1056–1072.

Patrick, D. & Erickson, P. (1993). *Health Status and Health Policy: Allocating Resources to Health Care*, Oxford University Press, New York.

Revicki, D.A. & Murray, M. (1994). Assessing health-related quality of life outcomes of drug treatments for psychiatric disorders, *CNS Drugs*, **1**, 465–476.

Rosen, A., Hadzi-Pavlovic, D. & Parker, G. (1989). The life skills profile: a measure assessing function and disability in schizophrenia, *Schizophrenia Bull.*, **15**, 325–337.

Rosenfield, S. (1992). Factors contributing to the subjective quality of life of the chronically mentally ill, *J. Health Social Behaviour*, **33**, 299–315.

Rosenfield, S. & Neese-Todd, S. (1993). Elements of a psychosocial clubhouse program associated with a satisfying quality of life, *Hosp. Community Psychiatry*, **44**, 76–78.

Schulberg, H. & Bromet, E. (1981). Strategies for evaluating the outcome of community services for the chronically mentally ill, *Am. J. Psychiatry*, **138**, 930–935.

Skantze, K. (1993). Defining subjective quality of life goals in schizophrenia: The Quality of Life Self-Assessment Inventory, QLS-100, a new approach to successful alliance and service development, Department of Psychiatry, Sahlgrenska Hospital, University of Gothenburg, Goteborg, Sweden.

Simpson, C.J., Hyde, C.E. & Faragher, E.B. (1989). The chronically mentally ill in community facilities: A study of quality of life, *Br. J. Psychiatry*, **154**, 77–82.

Slaughter, J.C. & Lehman, A.F. (1991). Quality of life of severely mentally ill adults in residential care facilities, *Adult Residential Care J.*, **5**, 97–111.

Spitzer, W.O., Dobson, A., Hall, J., Chesterman, E., Levi, J., Sheperd, R., Battista, R.N. & Catchlove, B.R. (1981). Measuring the quality of life in cancer patients: A concise Q/L index for use by physicians, *J. Chronic Dis.*, **34**, 585–597.

Stein, L.I. & Test, M.A. (1980). Alternative to mental hospital treatment: I. Conceptual model, treatment program and clinical evaluation, *Arch. Gen. Psychiatry*, **37**, 392–397.

Stoker, M.J., Dunbar, G.C. & Beaumont, G. (1992). The SmithKline Beecham 'quality of life' scale: a validation and reliability study in patients with affective disorder, *Quality of Life Res.*, **1**, 385–395.

Strauss, J.S. & Carpenter, W.T. (1974). The prediction of outcome in schizophrenia: II. Relationships between predictor and outcome variables: A report from the WHO international pilot study of schizophrenia, *Arch. Gen. Psychiatry*, **31**, 37–42.

Sullivan, G.S., Wells, K.B. & Leake, B. (1992). Clinical factors associated with better quality of life in a seriously mentally ill population, *Hosp. Community Psychiatry*, **43**, 794–798.

Ware, J.E. & Sherbourne, C.D. (1992). The MOS 36 Item Short-Form Health Survey (SF-36), *Med. Care*, **30**, 473–483.

Wells, K.B., Stewart, A., Hays, R.D., Burnam, A., Rogers, W., Daniels, M., Berry, S., Greenfield, S. & Ware, J. (1988). The functioning and well-being of depressed patients, *J. Am. Med. Ass.*, **262**, 914–919.

7

Instruments for Measuring Quality of Life in Mental Disorders II: Some New Developments

Chijs van Nieuwenhuizen

INTRODUCTION

Over the last decade, several reviews have been published describing the instruments for measuring quality of life (QoL) in mental disorders and their psychometric properties (Lehman, 1996; Awad, Voruganti and Heslegrave, 1997; Lehman, 1997; McKenna, 1997; van Nieuwenhuizen et al., 1997; van Nieuwenhuizen, Schene and Koeter, 2001; Simeoni et al., 2000). These reviews show that QoL is measured for a number of reasons: to assess an individual's life circumstances and his/her satisfaction with them, to gain an insight into the specific consequences of a psychiatric disability, as well as to be used as an outcome measure and to evaluate different mental health care programmes.

This chapter reviews new developments in measuring QoL in mental disorders from 1997 to the autumn of 2003. In the last six or seven years, the focus in QoL literature has made a substantial change: from emphasising the development of instruments to new aspects of QoL measurement, e.g. shortening and evaluating existing instruments as well as translating and validating them for other than the original language. Therefore, the content of this chapter, instead of describing QoL instruments and their psychometric qualities extensively, will refer generally to those developed since 1997 and will also discuss other aspects.

To identify QoL instruments and gain an insight into new developments for the period 1997–2003, a computerised search was undertaken in Pubmed and other computer databases, using the same keywords as Lehman (1997): 'quality of life', 'mental disorders', 'schizophrenia', 'depression', 'bipolar disorders', 'anxiety disorders', neurotic disorders', 'adjustment disorders', 'personality disorders' and 'paranoid disorders'. Added to these were: 'instrument development', 'questionnaire', 'scale', 'interview', 'assessment', 'overview' and 'review'.

INSTRUMENTS DEVELOPED SINCE 1997

Since the publication of Lehman (1997) and other review articles, several new instruments have been developed. Korr and Ford (2003) mention three new ones to measure the QoL of mentally ill patients. Greenley, Greenberg and Brown (1997) developed a 24-item self-report measure they have called the Quality of Life Questionnaire (QLQ). This has good psychometric properties and takes a patient

Quality of Life in Mental Disorders, Second Edition Edited by H. Katschnig, H. Freeman and N. Sartorius
© 2006 John Wiley & Sons, Ltd

10–15 minutes to complete. Dazord *et al*. (1998) have developed a French 36-item self-report instrument and applied it to different populations: psychotic, depressed and substance-abuse patients respectively. Katsavdakis *et al*. (1999) developed a 55-item scale that stresses the consumer's perspective. It is specially designed to be used repeatedly during clinical practice and its psychometric properties seem promising.

Another questionnaire published since 1997 is the World Health Organization (WHO) Quality of Life Assessment Instrument (WHOQOL-100) (WHOQOL Group, 1998a). This was constructed to facilitate investigation into the individual's perception of his/her own position in life in the context of the culture and value systems in which he/she lives, and in relation to the individual's goals, expectations, standards and concerns. The development of the WHOQOL was started in 1991 and a pilot version comprising 276 items was tested in February 1994 in centres all over the world (De Vries, 1996). It has been developed in such a way that it reflects six domains that both scientific experts and lay people felt were important to QoL, namely physical health, psychological health, level of independence, social relationships, environment and spirituality/religion/personal beliefs (Sartorius and Orley, 1992; see also Sartorius and Janca, 1996). These six domains contain altogether 23 subcategories, named 'facets' (e.g. 'pain and discomfort' under the domain 'physical health', 'positive feelings'under 'psychological health', 'mobility' under 'level of independence', etc.). This instrument is still being improved and critically reviewed by the WHOQOL Group (Skevington, Bradshaw and Saxena, 1999; Skevington and Wright, 2001; see also below).

In 2001, Welham *et al*. published the QoL-GAP – an instrument based on self-appraised items within various life domains. In contrast to previous instruments, the authors tried to measure the weighted gap between actual and ideal life. Among its merits is the fact that it illustrates that the 'gap' approach can help consumers state their own goals and opinions. Also in the year 2001, two articles were published introducing instruments that allow the patient to identify his/her own life domains and to give individual weightings to each of these (Prince and Gerber, 2001: the Schedule for the Evaluation of Individual Quality of Life; Noerholm, Svensson and Bech, 2001: the GRIDQoL).

Finally, Condello *et al*. (2003) describe the use of a questionnaire called the LEIPAD. This was specifically designed to assess QoL in the elderly population. It includes seven subscales and five 'moderator' scales (e.g. perceived personality disorder and self-esteem).

OTHER DEVELOPMENTS

A number of short versions have been developed, e.g. the WHOQOL-BREF (WHOQOL Group, 1998b) and the Manchester Short Assessment of Quality of Life (MANSA) (Priebe *et al*., 1999). The former was derived from data collected using the WHOQOL-100 (see above) and consists of 26 items. It is a valid and reliable alternative to the WHOQOL-100. This is especially the case in studies that require a brief assessment of QoL, e.g. in routine clinical work, large-scale epidemiological studies and clinical trials. The WHOQOL-BREF, however, does not allow assessment of individual facets within the six domains. The MANSA has been developed as a condensed and slightly modified version of the Lancashire Quality of Life Profile (LQOLP). The psychometric properties of the MANSA are satisfactory and its high correlations with the LQOLP suggest concurrent validity (see Priebe *et al*., 1999).

Furthermore, instruments have been translated and validated for other than the original language. From the start, the WHOQOL-100 has been available in many languages and as such has taken a leading position in cross-cultural research. Recently, a Korean version was developed, in addition to one of the WHOQOL-BREF (Min *et al*., 2002). The LQOLP has been translated and used in other European countries such as Austria, Italy, Germany, Poland, the Netherlands, Spain and Scandinavia (Priebe *et al*., 1995; Kaiser *et al*., 1996; Heinze *et al*., 1997; Kemmler *et al*., 1997; Oliver *et al*., 1997; Becker *et al*., 1999; van Nieuwenhuizen *et al*., 2001) and is also used in the United States (see Warner *et al*., 1998) and Taiwan. The short version of the LQOLP, the MANSA, has been translated into Dutch and German (for the German version see Kaiser *et al*., 1999). The Wisconsin Quality of Life Index is also used in a French version (Diaz *et al*., 1999), the Quality of Life Index is available in Spanish (Mezzich *et al*., 2000) and the French version of the Satisfaction with Life Domains Scale has been validated

(Caron, Mercier and Tempeir, 1997). Finally, a short version of the Quality of Life Interview has been validated in French (Lancon *et al.*, 2000).

Recently, a number of articles have been published in which instruments have been used in psychiatry that were originally developed for general medicine. Examples are the use of the RAND-36 in depressed patients (Hays and Morales, 2001) and the EURO-QoL-5D with psychotic patients (Prieto *et al.*, 2003). Moreover, in the development of a number of new health-related instruments, the process included samples of mentally ill patients (see Hawthorne, Richardson and Osborne, 1999; Hawthorne, Richardson and Day, 2001; Sintonen, 2001; Herrman, Hawthorne and Thomas, 2002; Pedersen, Pallay and Rudolph, 2002). Additionally, there have been studies comparing disease-specific, general and health-related QoL instruments. Recent examples are the comparison of the LQOLP with the Medical Outcome Study Short Form (MOS SF-36) (Meijer, Schene and Koeter, 2002) and the QoL Enjoyment and Satisfaction Questionnaire with self-report items of the LQOLP (Ritsner *et al.*, 2002).

Finally, more and more, QoL instruments are also being used to gain insight into their relationships with other patient-related measures. In mentioning a number of studies in which a standardised QoL assessment was carried out, two specific subjects will be emphasised. There have been a number of interesting studies on the relationship between needs and quality of life (Bengtsson-Tops and Hansson, 1999; Wiersma and van Busschbach, 2001). It was found that QoL is not related to satisfaction with services, but is strongly associated with unmet needs in the areas of mental and physical health and rehabilitation (Wiersma and van Busschbach, 2001). In addition, a greater need for care and support is associated with a worse total QoL (Bengtsson-Tops and Hansson, 1999; see also Wolf, 1997, for the more theoretical background). Becker *et al.* (1998) and Dufort, Dallaire and Lavoie (1997) investigated the links between social networks and QoL, finding that the size of the social network is related to overall QoL and that the social support network is also associated with separate QoL components.

CONCLUSION

This chapter has shown that QoL research has been evolving in a positive direction. At first, attention was focused on the development of one instrument after another. More recently, however, other developments have taken place. These have included: (a) the introduction of short versions that have different purposes from the original extended ones, (b) the translation and validation of instruments for other than the original language and (c) a deepening of the definition and operationalisation of life quality by looking at its relationship with other constructs.

Nevertheless, it is always necessary to remain critical of the use of the QoL concept because of its indefinable and elusive nature. QoL is 'a winner of a title' because, in spite of all the problems surrounding it, researchers and clinicians alike still cling to its use. In fact, health status or functioning are being increasingly regarded as QoL equivalents (see also de Vries, 1996). Oliver *et al.* (1996) expressed their concern about this trend:

> While it is reasonable to wish to target quality of life measures on areas of health which medicine is most likely to be able to treat effectively, such a narrow focus may do a disservice to services designed for chronic patients whose needs can be seen to range more widely than their health status alone.

Conceiving health status as equivalent to QoL does no justice to the large group of people for whom the concept in the first place was devised and 'discovered'. Gill and Feinstein (1994) noted in their critical appraisal of QoL measurements in medicine in general that it was all too often ill-conceptualised and included domains that denote health status, rather than QoL. They emphasised that QoL measurements are likely to be aimed at the wrong target, unless individuals are given the opportunity to express their own opinions and reactions. Leplège and Hunt (1997) – in general agreement with Gill and Feinstein (1994) – have suggested that QoL be replaced by a more easily handled and more rigorously defined notion, e.g. that of subjective health status, which in their view says little or nothing about what patients perceive as QoL.

The suggestions of those authors, in terms of medicine in general, as well as Gill and Feinstein's view (1994) that patients should be given the opportunity to express their own opinions and reactions, deserve to be supported. For psychiatry, therefore, we suggest: (a) that there should be support for research aimed at defining a theoretical QoL foundation and (b) that health status and functioning are not to be seen as equivalents of QoL.

REFERENCES

Awad, A.G., Voruganti, L.N.P. & Heslegrave, R.J. (1997). Measuring quality of life in patients with schizophrenia, *Pharmacoeconomics*, **11**(1), 32–47.

Becker, T., Leese, M., Clarkson, P., Taylor, R.E., Turner, D., Kleckham, J. & Thornicroft, G. (1998). Links between social networks and quality of life: An epidemiologically representative study of psychotic patients in South London, *Social Psychiatry & Psychiat. Epidemiol.*, **33**, 299–304.

Becker, T., Knapp, M., Knudsen, H., Schene, A., Tansella, M., Thornicroft, G., Vázquez-Barquero, J.L. & the EPSILON Study Group (1999). The EPSILON study of schizophrenia in five European countries, *Br. J. Psychiatry*, **173**, 511–521.

Bengtsson-Tops, A. & Hansson, L. (1999). Clinical and social needs of schizophrenic outpatients living in the community: The relationship between needs and subjective quality of life, *Social Psychiatry & Psychiat. Epidemiol.*, **34**, 513–518.

Caron, J., Mercier, C. & Tempier, R. (1997). Une validation québécoise du Satisfaction with Life Domains Scale, *Santé mentale au Québec*, **XXII**(2), 195–217.

Condello, C., Padoani, W., Uguzzoni, U., Caon, F. & De Leo, D. (2003). Personality disorders and self-perceived quality of life in an elderly psychiatric outpatient population, *Psychopathology*, **36**, 78–83.

Dazord, A., Astolfl, F., Guisti, P., Rebetez, M., Mino, A., Terra, J. & Brochier, C. (1998). Quality of life assessment in psychiatry: the Subjective Quality of Life Profile (SQLP) – first results of a new instrument, *Community Ment. Health J.*, **34**(5), 525–536.

de Vries, J. (1996). Beyond health status. Construction and validation of the Dutch WHO quality of life assessment instrument, Academic Thesis, Catholic University, Brabant, The Netherlands.

Diaz, P., Mercier, C., Hachey, R., Caron, J. & Boyer, G. (1999). An evaluation of psychometric properties of the client's questionnaire of the Wisconsin Quality of Life Index-Canadian version (CaW-QLI), *Quality of Life Res.*, **8**, 509–514.

Dufort, F., Dallaire, L. & Lavoie, F. (1997). Factors contributing to the perceived quality of life of people with mental disorders, *Social Work & Social Sci. Rev.*, **7**(2), 89–100.

Gill, T.M. & Feinstein, A.R. (1994). A critical appraisal of the quality of quality-of-life measurements, *J. Am. Med. Ass.*, **272**(8), 619–626.

Greenley, J.R., Greenberg, J.S. & Brown, R. (1997). Measuring quality of life: A new and practical survey instrument, *Social Work*, **42**(3), 244–254.

Hawthorne, G., Richardson, J. & Day, N. (2001). A comparison of the Assessment of Quality of Life (AQoL) with four other generic utility instruments, *Ann. Med.*, **33**, 358–370.

Hawthorne, G., Richardson, J. & Osborne, R. (1999). The Assessment of Quality of Life (AQoL) instrument: A psychometric measure of health-related quality of life, *Quality of Life Res.*, **8**, 209–224.

Hays, R.D. & Morales, L.S. (2001). The RAND-36 measure of health-related quality of life, *Ann. Med.*, **33**, 350–357.

Heinze, M., Taylor, R.E., Priebe, S. & Thornicroft, G. (1997). The quality of life of patients with paranoid schizophrenia in London and Berlin, *Social Psychiatry Psychiat. Epidemiol.*, **32**, 292–297.

Herrman, H., Hawthorne, G. & Thomas, R. (2002). Quality of life assessment in people living with psychosis, *Social Psychiatry Psychiat. Epidemiol.*, **37**, 510–518.

Kaiser, W., Priebe, S., Hoffmann, K. & Isermann, M. (1996). Subjektive Lebensqualität bei Patienten mit chronischer Schizophrenie, *Nervenarzt*, **67**(7), 572–582.

Kaiser, W., Isermann, M., Hoffmann, K., Huxley, P. & Priebe, S. (1999). A short assessment of subjective quality of life. Application and results of short form of the Berliner Lebensqualitätsprofil (BELP-KF), *Fortschritte der Neurologie und Psychiatrie*, **67**(9), 413–425.

Katsavdakis, K.A., Clifford, P.I., Evans, R.B., Graham, P., Allen, J.G., Sargent, J., Lyle, J. & Frager, D.C. (1999). The how are you? scale. A quality-of-life outcomes measure for routine practice, *Bull. Menninger Clinic*, **63**, 366–387.

Kemmler, G., Holzner, B., Neudorfer, C., Meise, U. & Hinterhuber, H. (1997). General life satisfaction and domain-specific quality of life in chronic schizophrenic patients, *Quality of Life Res.*, **6**, 265–273.

Korr, W.S. & Ford, B.C. (2003). Measuring quality of life in the mentally ill, *Quality of Life Res.*, **12**(Suppl. 1), 17–23.

Lancon, C., Auquier, P., Launois, R., Toumi, M., Llorca, P., Bebbington, P. & Lehman, A. (2000). Evaluation de la qualité de vie dans des patients schizophrènes: Validation de la version courte de la QoLI, *L'Encéphale*, **XXVI**, 11–16.

Lehman, A.F. (1996). Measures of quality of life among persons with severe and persistent mental disorders, *Social Psychiatry Psychiat. Epidemiol.*, **31**, 78–88.

Lehman, A.F. (1997). Instruments for measuring quality of life in mental illnesses, in *Quality of Life in Mental Disorders* (Eds H. Katschnig, H. Freeman & N. Sartorius), pp. 79–94, John Wiley & Sons, Chichester.

Leplège, A. & Hunt, S. (1997). The problem of quality of life in medicine, *J. Am. Med. Ass.*, **278**(1), 47–50.

McKenna, S.P. (1997). Measuring quality of life in schizophrenia, *Eur. Psychiatry*, **12**(Suppl. 3), 267s–274s.

Mezzich, J.E., Ruipérez, M.A., Pérez. C., Yoon, G., Liu, J. & Mahmud, S. (2000). The Spanish version of the Quality of Life Index – Presentation and validation, *J. Nerv. Ment. Dis.*, **188**(5), 301–305.

Meijer, C.J., Schene, A.H. & Koeter, M.W.J. (2002). Quality of life in schizophrenia measured by the MOS SF-36 and the Lancashire Quality of Life Profile: A comparison, *Acta Psychiatrica Scand.*, **105**, 293–300.

Min, S.K., Kim, K.I., Lee, C.I., Jung, Y.C., Suh, S.Y. & Kim, D.K. (2002). Development of the Korean versions of the WHO Quality of Life Scale and WHOQOL-BREF, *Quality of Life Res.*, **11**, 593–600.

Noerholm, V., Svensson, L. & Bech. P. (2001). Individual quality of life in schizophrenic patients – description and applicability of GRIDQoL in a computer-based version, *Int. J. Meth. Psychiatry*, **10**, 134–139.

Oliver, J., Huxley, P., Bridges, K. & Mohamad, H. (1996). *Quality of Life and Mental Health Services*, Routledge, London, New York.

Oliver, J.P.J., Huxley, P.J., Priebe, S. & Kaiser, W. (1997). Measuring the quality of life of severely mentally ill people using the Lancashire Quality of Life Profile, *Social Psychiatry Psychiat. Epidemiol.*, **32**, 76–83.

Pedersen, R.D., Pallay, A.G. & Rudolph, R.L. (2002). Can improvement in well-being and functioning be distinguished from depression improvement in antidepressant clinical trials?, *Quality of Life Res.*, **11**, 9–17.

Priebe, S., Gruyters, T., Heinze, M., Hoffmann, C. & Jäkel, A. (1995). Subjektive Evaluationskriterien in der psychiatrischen Versorgung – Erhebungsmethoden für Forschung und Praxis, *Psychiatrische Praxis*, **22**, 140–144.

Priebe, S., Huxley, P., Knight, S. & Evans, S. (1999). Application and results of the Manchester Short Assessment of Quality of Life (MANSA), *Int. J. Social Psychiatry*, **45**(1), 7–12.

Prieto, L. Novick, D., Sacristán, J.A., Edgell, E.T. & Alonso, J. on behalf of the SOHO Study Group (2003). A Rasch model analysis to test the cross-cultural validity of the EuroQoL-5D in the Schizophrenia Outpatient Health Outcomes Study, *Acta Psychiatrica Scand.*, **107**(Suppl. 416), 24–29.

Prince, P.N. & Gerber, G.J. (2001). Measuring subjective quality of life in people with serious mental illness, *Quality of Life Res.*, **10**, 117–122.

Ritsner, M., Kurs, R., Kostizky, H., Ponizovsky, A. & Modai, I. (2002). Subjective quality of life in severely mentally ill patients: A comparison of two instruments, *Quality of Life Res.*, **11**, 553–561.

Sartorius, N. & Janca, A. (1996). Psychiatric assessment instruments developed by the World Health Organization, *Social Psychiatry Psychiat. Epidemiol.*, **31**, 55–69.

Sartorius, N. & Orley, J. (1992). Quality of life assessment, *The Int. Monitor*, **4**(September), 61–63.

Simeoni, M., Auquier, P., Lançon, C., LePlège, A., Simon-Abbadi, S. & Guelfi, J. (2000). Revue critique des instruments de mesure de la qualité de vie dans la schizophrénie, *L'Encéphale*, **XXVI**, 35–41.

Sintonen, H. (2001). The 15D instrument of health-related quality of life: Properties and applications, *Ann. Med.*, **33**, 328–336.

Skevington, S.M., Bradshaw, J. & Saxena, S. (1999). Selecting national items for the WHOQOL: Conceptual and psychometric considerations, *Social Sci. Med.*, **48**, 473–487.

Skevington, S.M. & Wright, A. (2001). Changes in the quality of life of patients receiving antidepressant medication in primary care: Validation of the WHOQOL-100, *Br. J. Psychiatry*, **178**, 261–267.

van Nieuwenhuizen, Ch., Schene, A.H., Boevink, W.A. & Wolf, J.R.L.M. (1997). Measuring the quality of life of clients with severe mental illness. A review of instruments, *Psychiat. Rehabil. J.*, **20**(4), 33–41.

van Nieuwenhuizen, Ch., Schene, A.H. & Koeter, M.W.J. (2001). Review of quality of life instruments, in *Commissioned Reviews of 250 Psychological Tests* (Eds J. Maltby, C.A. Lewis & A. Hill), pp. 641–647, The Edwin Mellen Press, Wales, UK.

van Nieuwenhuizen, Ch., Schene, A.H., Koeter, M.W.J. & Huxley, P.J. (2001). The Lancashire Quality of Life Profile: Modification and psychometric evaluation, *Social Psychiatry Psychiat. Epidemiol.*, **36**, 36–44.

Warner, R., De Girolamo, G., Belelli, G., Bologna, C., Fioritti, A. & Rosini, G. (1998). The quality of life of people with schizophrenia in Boulder, Colorado, and Bologna, Italy, *Schizophrenia Bull.*, **24**(4), 559–568.

Welham, J., Haire, M., Mercer, D. & Stedman, T. (2001). A gap approach to exploring quality of life in mental health, *Quality of Life Res.*, **10**, 421–429.

WHOQOL Group (1998a). The World Health Organization Quality of Life Assessment (WHOQOL): development and general psychometric properties, *Social Sci. Med.*, **46**(12), 1569–1585.

WHOQOL Group (1998b). Development of the World Health Organization WHOQOL-BREF Quality of Life Assessment, *Psycholog. Med.*, **28**, 551–558.

Wiersma, D. & van Busschbach, J. (2001). Are needs and satisfaction of care associated with quality of life? An epidemiological survey among the severely mentally ill in the Netherlands, *Eur. Arch. Psychiatry and Neurosci.*, **251**, 239–246.

Wolf, J.R.L.M. (1997). Clients needs and quality of life, *Psychiat. Rehabil. J.*, **20**(4), 16–24.

8

Assessing Daily Quality of Life with the Experience Sampling Method

Daniela Q.C.M. Barge-Schaapveld,
Nancy A. Nicolson, Philippe A.E.G. Delespaul
and Marten W. deVries

INTRODUCTION

Over the second half of the twentieth century, evolving medical, governmental and industrial perspectives on health care have urged the need for treatment optimisation that would reach beyond standard medical outcome variables. Traditional indicators of the severity of illness have helped clarify both disease pathophysiology and the effects of treatment, but they do not provide insight into whether or not a therapy helps from the patient's perspective (Read, Quinn and Hoefer, 1987). To meet these needs, a new concept has emerged in medicine: 'quality of life' (QoL).

Current methods of assessing QoL have developed out of three main research traditions: 'happiness', 'social indicators' and 'health status'. Each tradition has placed a different emphasis on affective, cognitive appraisal and behavioural dimensions (Wilson, 1967; Diener, 1984) and has influenced to some extent the use of QoL in clinical research. Patient's QoL, defined as a sense of well-being and ability to function in important life domains, is now commonly accepted as a secondary outcome measure in clinical trials. In this paper, the rationale for investigating QoL at the level of daily life experience is discussed, and QoL approaches are described derived from the three research traditions and operationalised within dynamic models of daily life experience. Time-sampling techniques such as the Experience Sampling Method (ESM) are illustrated with examples of how this method has been applied in research on QoL in mental disorders.

THE QUALITY OF DAILY LIFE EXPERIENCE

Across the three research traditions that have played an important role in the operationalisation of the QoL concept, a number of issues appear to be still unresolved or unaddressed. The first controversy concerns the stability of QoL over time – more specifically, whether QoL reflects a top-down or a bottom-up process (Lance *et al.*, 1989; Headey, Veenhoven and Wearing, 1991; Feist *et al.*, 1995). If we

Quality of Life in Mental Disorders, Second Edition Edited by H. Katschnig, H. Freeman and N. Sartorius
© 2006 John Wiley & Sons, Ltd

are interested in changes in QoL resulting from either the natural course or the treatment of an illness, we would like to understand, for example, how the illness impinges on daily experiences of positive emotions, rewarding situations and the satisfying use of productive and leisure time – inherently a bottom-up approach. However, while such daily experiences are made up of states that vary from moment to moment, it seems evident that a QoL index should be a summary measure of experiences over some representative period of time.

A second issue concerns the reliability of available QoL measures. In 'health status' studies, individuals are asked to evaluate how an illness and its treatment affect their lives. However, traditional retrospective assessments of both objective and subjective QoL dimensions are prone to a number of potential biases. Prospective monitoring of behaviours in time-budget research allows more accurate measures of the frequency and duration of activities than is possible with retrospective questionnaires (Juster, 1985). For emotional states, retrospective bias has been well documented, while effects of social desirability (Milbrath, 1982; Diener *et al.*, 1991; Veenhoven, 1991) and of recall errors (Lehman and Burns, 1990) have been reported.

The third issue is ecological validity (Bronfenbrenner, 1979). Beyond the reliability issues involved, the emotional states elicited during traditional assessment situations such as clinical interviews are not necessarily the same as those occurring in natural environments. Lack of ecological validity may occur as a consequence of clinically based reports bias (e.g. 'white coat' hypertension), subject manipulation (e.g. pain reports biased by desire to influence the treating doctor) or failure to sample patients' typical roles, activities and settings (e.g. symptom reports influenced by whether the patient is at work or at home) (Stone, Shiffman and deVries, 1999).

Models of Daily QoL

The problems described in the previous section have stimulated a search for new models and methods for assessing daily QoL. For example, parameters of daily life experience, such as the diversity of an individual's activities or social contexts, have been related to QoL (Delespaul, 1995). According to this hypothesis, QoL will be higher when individuals have contact with a variety of different persons and carry out a wider variety of activities. QoL is also expected to be higher when social contacts are distributed over time, instead of being, for example, concentrated all in one day, with social isolation the rest of the week. Similarly, QoL is hypothesised to be low when the same activities have to be performed for extended periods of time without a break.

However, QoL is not an objective state. While it might be true that most people prefer variability to continuously performing the same task, the concept of QoL points to the crucial role of subjective experience. Daily QoL is not then restricted to what individuals actually do in reference to some absolute norm, but incorporates the concurrent assessment of the individual's mood state. For example, 'being alone' most of the time may be a particular problem if a person experiences his/her worst mental states in that context. On the other hand, being in social contexts will not improve QoL if these contexts are experienced as negative. Knowledge of individual preferences and experiences is thus vital for understanding QoL.

'Objective happiness' was introduced by Kahneman (1999) as a bottom-up approach to the analysis of well-being, derived from a record of the quality of experience at each 'point-instant utility'. Instant utility is conceptualised as an attribute of experience (being pleased or distressed) at a particular moment, and is more specifically defined as the strength of the disposition to continue or to interrupt the current experience. Objective happiness is therefore the average of utility over a period of time and contrasts with 'subjective happiness', which is assessed by asking respondents to state (retrospectively) how happy they have been throughout that same period of time.

The 'flow' model conceptualises optimal experience as a state in which positive mood, motivation, alertness, concentration and control are high, while negative mood is low. According to the model's theory, this state is most likely to be attained in the context of activities that are challenging and in which the individual is skilled (Massimini and Carli, 1988; Csikszentmihalyi, 1990). The subjects of studies contributing to the development of 'flow' theory included artists, mountain climbers and high achievers at school. One might question, though, whether individuals with a psychiatric disorder pursue optimal experience by maximising 'flow'. Escaping stagnation, boredom and negative feelings may represent an equally great improvement in daily QoL (Massimini, Csikszentmihalyi and Carli, 1992).

Bringing daily life in line with personal tasks, as suggested by Cantor *et al.* (1991), may also be regarded as a daily QoL model. Indeed, individuals who find ways to work on their most important or rewarding tasks in their day-to-day life may well experience increased emotional involvement, positive affect and satisfaction in daily life.

Finally, according to a daily QoL model formulated by Brandstätter (1994), an important determinant of well-being may be the adequacy of the fit between the person and environment. Here, states of well-being are hypothesised to be dependent on the correspondence between an individual's goals, or motives, and the gratification provided by the environment in terms of the settings of specific behaviour.

In summary, we propose that the QoL approaches derived from the 'happiness', 'social indicators' and 'health status' traditions may be operationalised within dynamic models of daily life experience. New data and models that include the frequency of and variability in doing activities one likes, the experience of well-being that comes about when challenges and skills are in optimal balance and the goodness of fit between an individual and his/her environment form a starting point for operationalising and further exploring QoL in real-life settings.

Experience Sampling Method

Time-sampling methods offer a strategy for obtaining reliable, quantitative estimates of frequencies and durations of various behaviours or contexts. They have long been used in ethological studies of animal and human behaviours (Altmann, 1974; Whiting and Whiting, 1975; Wheeler and Reis, 1991). When self-assessments of emotional states are added, time-sampling methods allow us to investigate subjective as well as objective (behavioural) states in daily life.

The Experience Sampling Method (ESM) is a time-sampling approach in which subjects are signalled by an electronic device at random intervals throughout the day to complete a self-report form concerning aspects of their current situation, such as activity, physical location, social context, thoughts, motivation and mood. Because data collection takes place in the context and time-frame of daily life, retrospective bias is reduced and ecological validity is increased. Information concerning the compliance, reliability and validity of the ESM have been reported elsewhere (Csikszentmihalyi and Larson, 1987; deVries, 1987; deVries and Delespaul, 1989; Delespaul, 1995). It is interesting to note that QoL theories were a driving force behind the development of the ESM. Csikszentmihalyi and colleagues saw the advantage of time-sampling methods to investigate optimal states or 'flow' (Csikszentmihalyi and Csikszentmihalyi, 1988), while deVries (1987) and colleagues believed that making repeated assessments in daily life might help to identify situations conducive to positive mental states, as well as determinants of symptom variability, in individuals with a mental disorder.

Researchers have used ESM in studies of different psychiatric and psychosomatic disorders, examining a wide range of hypotheses (e.g. deVries, 1992a; Affleck *et al.*, 1998; Steiger *et al.*, 1999; Myin-Germeys, Nicolson and Delespaul, 2001; Peeters *et al.*, 2003). In Maastricht, data from a large number of studies have been combined in an archive that allows secondary analyses spanning a range of disorders to be performed. The first examples, described below, entail a comparison of time use and patterns of concurrent emotions in everyday activities; this will allow some basic insights to be obtained into the effects of an illness on objective and subjective aspects of daily life functioning. Next, illustrations of how aspects of daily QoL measured with ESM can be used to evaluate the side-effects of pharmacological treatments will be presented. Finally, an example will be given of the use of ESM data in planning interventions with the specific goal of improving an individual's QoL.

TIME USE AND AFFECTIVE STATES IN ILLNESS AND HEALTH

What effects does illness have on time use and emotional experience during daily activities? Are these effects related to the diagnosis or severity of the disorder?

Example 1

As a first step, we compared five groups of subjects, selected from the Maastricht data archive: (a) healthy controls ($n=84$), (b) patients with respectively acute or chronic backpain ($n=49$), (c) anxiety disorders ($n=77$), (d) major, unipolar depression ($n=63$) and (e) schizophrenia ($n=55$). Subjects were signalled randomly, using a pre-programmed watch, to fill in ESM forms 10 times a day for six days. The forms included seven-point Likert scales for the evaluation of current thoughts, mood, motivation with respect to the current activity, physical well-being and symptoms. The forms also contained open-ended questions assessing what the individual was doing and the social context when signalled. For this analysis, the 45 activity codes were combined into the categories: work, chores, social interactions, active leisure (e.g. hobbies or sports), passive leisure (e.g. watching television) and doing nothing. (A small percentage of activities not fitting into one of the above categories (e.g. meals, transportation, personal hygiene) were excluded from subsequent analyses.) With respect to patterns of time use, differences between the diagnostic groups were statistically significant only for the activities 'work' and 'doing nothing'. As might be expected, control subjects spent the most time (22.1%) and schizophrenics the least time (4.9%) in work activities, with the other groups being intermediate in this respect (pain, 10.5%; anxiety, 7.8%; depression, 8.6%). Time spent 'doing nothing' mirrored work: it was lowest in controls (6.1%) and highest in schizophrenics, who spent 25% of their time in this context.

To gain further insights into the subjective experience of individuals in the five groups during different activities, mean ratings for the ESM item 'happy' were computed first for each subject and then for each group, for each category of activity. There were both similarities and differences among the groups in how these common activities were experienced. Firstly, there were pronounced differences in mean ratings, with controls, pain patients and schizophrenics reporting more positive emotional states (with means for 'happy' of 4.98, 4.54 and 4.35, respectively, on the seven-point scale), while anxiety and especially depressed patients reported lower scores of happiness (means of 3.46 and 2.81, respectively). At the same time, the groups showed striking similarities both in the range of happiness ratings over different activities and in the ranking of activities according to how happy subjects were while doing them. Taking each subject's mean happiness level across all activities as a baseline, within-subject z-scores were computed for each ESM report. Figure 8.1 shows the mean deviations in

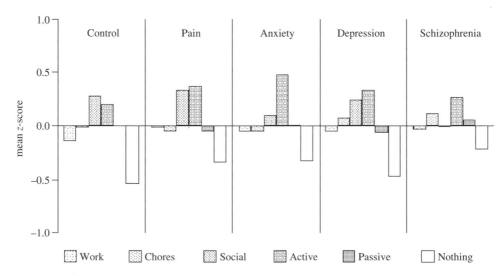

Figure 8.1 Within-subject variability in happiness, by current activity. Ratings for the ESM item 'happy' were first standardised relative to each subject's mean level over all reports. Mean z-scores were then calculated for each diagnostic group. The total sample included 84 healthy control subjects, 49 patients diagnosed with pain, 77 patients with an anxiety disorder, 63 patients with depression and 55 patients with schizophenia. As not every subject reported occurrences of all six activities, sample sizes for the diagnostic groups were lower for certain activity categories (in particular, work and active leisure)

happiness experienced in each activity context, by group. Happiness was lowest when 'doing nothing' and was highest during active leisure. Passive leisure occupied a neutral position, with ratings close to individual mean levels. While social interactions were accompanied by positive mood in the control, pain and depression groups, they were neutral in anxiety patients and even slightly negative in schizophrenics.

As mentioned earlier, QoL is thought to reflect both positive and negative emotional states. Repeating this analysis for the negative mood scale (including the items 'angry', 'anxious' and 'lonely'), significant differences were found among the groups in mean levels, with schizophrenics reporting the most negative mood (2.61), followed by anxiety (2.26) and depression (2.11), with pain patients (1.29) and controls (1.32) scoring lowest. In contrast to happiness, however, negative mood was not highly dependent on the activity context. Only 'doing nothing' was accompanied by worse than average negative mood in the control, anxiety and depression groups, and negative mood tended to be slightly lower than average during social and active leisure activities in all groups except schizophrenics. Negative mood in schizophrenia and anxiety disorders tended to be lowest during work.

Example 2

In the context of a study on the general impact of depression on daily QoL (Barge-Schaapveld *et al.*, 1999), 63 depressed patients and 22 controls were asked to fill in ESM forms 10 times a day for six days (in a similar manner to that described above). The recruitment procedure for control subjects was designed so that there were no significant differences between the two groups in age, sex distribution, living situation (alone or not) or work status.

With regard to reported activities, more depressed than control subjects stated that they were doing nothing at times and fewer depressed patients were engaged in work activities, even though the two groups did not differ in employment status. As shown in Fig 8.2, there were few differences between

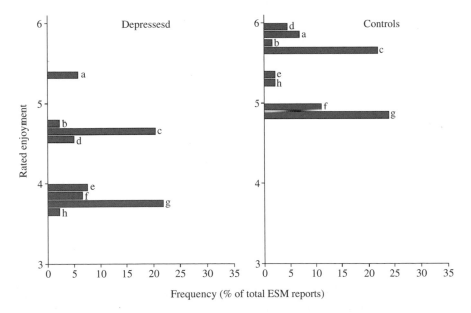

Figure 8.2   Frequency and enjoyment of each category of activity: a = active leisure; b = child care; c = passive leisure; d = social activities; e = doing nothing; f = work or study; g = chores; h = shopping. *X* axis: frequency of ESM reports mentioning each activity, expressed as a percentage of total valid reports, was first calculated for each subject. Length of the bars represents the mean frequency over all subjects in each group. Depressed *N* = 63; control subjects *N* = 22. *Y* axis: a mean enjoyment rating was first calculated for each subject's activities, including only those ESM reports in which the specific activity was recorded. Placement of the bars indicates the mean enjoyment rating for each activity in the subset of subjects who reported that activity. (From Barge-Schaapveld *et al.*, 1999. Reproduced by permission of Elsevier)

the two groups in the frequency of performing various activities, though depressed subjects spent a greater percentage of time in doing nothing than controls. In contrast to the small differences in use of time, the groups differed markedly in the level of enjoyment experienced in daily activities, with depressed individuals reporting significantly less enjoyment than controls in all activities except child care and active leisure.

The implications of these results for daily QoL can be summarised as follows:

1. The finding that subjects experienced their least positive and most negative moods in the context of doing nothing suggests that this context, which was more frequent the more severe the disorder, may be a behavioural indicator of poor QoL at the daily level.
2. While subjects in all groups spent more time in passive leisure (such as watching television), active leisure (such as hobbies or sports) was associated with a much more positive experience.
3. Time spent doing nothing was inversely correlated with time spent in productive activities. Work and household chores, although not highly preferred activities, were associated with average happiness and, especially in the psychiatric disorders, with relatively low negative mood. A shift in use of time from inactivity to productive activity is likely to bring about improvements in mental state and can be interpreted as a sign of improved QoL.

One of the limitations of aggregating data over diagnostic groups, as well as over broad activity categories, is that this may obscure clinically important individual differences. The following applications of the ESM go beyond general patterns in monitoring change and in evaluating daily QoL in individual patients.

MONITORING THE (SIDE) EFFECTS OF TREATMENT ON DAILY QUALITY OF LIFE

In general, patients with a mental disorder have a lower QoL, compared with the general population (Franklin et al., 1986), and have been reported to be even less satisfied with life than patients with chronic somatic disorders (Huber et al., 1988). In particular, depressed patients have impaired social functioning (De Lisio et al., 1986; Gotlib, 1990; Agosti, Stewart and Quitkin, 1991) and pronounced work disabilities (De Lisio et al., 1986; Broadhead et al., 1990). Impairments in the performance of household roles and leisure activities have also been noted (De Lisio et al., 1986). Although several studies have evaluated the effects of antidepressants on QoL (Kocsis et al., 1988; Revicki et al., 1992; Rost et al., 1992; Lonnqvist et al., 1994; Turner et al., 1994), little is known about the effects of such interventions on daily QoL. However, the ESM has been used to assess changes in the quality of daily life associated with pharmacological treatment for depression.

Example 1

A pilot study (Barge-Schaapveld et al., 1995) was carried out in five primary care practices in South Limburg, the Netherlands. Twenty-one patients completed the study. They ranged in age from 18 to 65 years, met DSM-III-R criteria for major depressive disorder and scored at least 18 on the 17-item version of the Hamilton Depression Rating Scale (HDRS). Patients were randomised to either fluvoxamine (100 mg) or amitriptyline (150 mg), which they received for six weeks. Subjects were sampled 10 times each day for two periods of six days, both pre- and post-treatment.

ESM measures of subjective experience in daily contexts changed following six weeks of antidepressant treatment, especially in responders (post-treatment HDRS ≤ 7; $n = 12$), compared with non-responders ($n=9$). Treatment responders increased the time spent doing household chores and reduced their passive leisure time. They also experienced greater increases in average positive mood and greater decreases in average negative mood during chores, passive leisure and social activities than non-responders.

Example 2

In another ESM study of depressed primary care patients, subjects received either imipramine (200 mg/day) or placebo for 6 weeks with a possible extension for another 12 weeks (Barge-Schaapveld and

Nicolson, 2002). ESM sampling periods took place pre-treatment, in the first week of treatment and again in the sixth week of treatment. Finally, patients who remained in the treatment prolongation phase again completed six consecutive days of ESM measures in week 18. A control group of 22 healthy individuals, similar to the patient group in sociodemographic characteristics, was recruited to provide normal reference values for ESM measures.

The ESM forms included a seven-point Likert scale asking 'In general, how is it going with you right now?', referred to as the momentary QoL (mQoL), with responses ranging from −3 ('very bad') to 3 ('very good'). For physical complaints, the ESM forms also included three common side-effects of imipramine (i.e. dry mouth, dizziness and nausea). The mean severity of each ESM complaint was obtained by averaging across all ESM records for each subject per sampling week. The frequency of each ESM complaint was defined as the percentage of records in which the complaint was reported to be present. Patients who showed an increase from the pre-treatment baseline in either the mean severity or the frequency of a complaint were considered to have experienced a side-effect of treatment.

To clarify the clinical relevance of side-effects, as reported by the ESM in the first week of treatment we examined their relationship to subsequent drop-out from treatment. Associations between mQoL and both frequency and severity of complaints were greater in the drop-outs ($n = 10$) than in completers ($n = 49$). In addition, drop-outs tended to report greater decreases in mQoL from pre-treatment to the first week than patients who subsequently completed six weeks of treatment. This suggests that the impact of side-effects on mQoL led some patients to withdraw from treatment.

Of the 28 patients who completed treatment, 23 were considered to be clinically remitted at 18 weeks (HDRS ≤ 7). To determine whether QoL measures achieve normal levels, ESM measures in the remitted patients were contrasted with those in the healthy control group. Remitted patients still had a significantly lower mQoL. Moreover, physical complaints, such as dry mouth and dizziness, also occurred with a higher frequency and were rated as more severe in the remitted than in the control group. In summary, despite normalised HDRS scores, remitted patients still differed from healthy controls in most aspects of daily QoL.

These studies illustrate the sensitivity of the ESM for evaluating the effects of pharmacological interventions at the level of daily life. By providing a means for obtaining more descriptive information on the experience of side-effects in daily life, ESM data potentially provide a better understanding of patients' difficulties with and expectation of treatment.

USING ESM ASSESSMENTS TO OPTIMISE INDIVIDUAL QUALITY OF LIFE

QoL is a subjective assessment of an individual's condition of living and is directly influenced by the manifestations of illness. Since suffering is a personal appraisal, strategies to alleviate this suffering should take into account the specific daily life conditions and experiences of each individual. Differences in daily experience reflect the multitude of possible living situations and developmental histories. As a result, universal intervention strategies that disregard individual circumstances will have only marginal effects on QoL.

Several reports describe more personalised assessments and applications of ESM in clinical situations. These include: (a) a self-help strategy (Donner, 1992), (b) evaluating responses to therapeutic interventions for use in individualised case management (van der Poel and Delespaul, 1992), (c) examining the role of self-awareness in psychopathology and therapy (Figurski, 1992), (d) increasing the opportunities for optimal experience (Massimini, Csikszentmihalyi and Carli, 1992) and (e) facilitating activities that promote optimal experience (Delle Fave and Massimini, 1992). Optimising the individual QoL entails first determining the contexts in which the patient feels best and then determining whether it is opportune to pursue those contexts. For example, although someone may enjoy fishing, increasing the frequency of this activity could result in marital discord or neglect of work, leading to emotional and financial problems that will subsequently reduce QoL. In this paradigm, the person (and the family) may be taught to evaluate trade-offs in daily activities, with the aim of reducing the occurrence of symptoms and optimising general well-being. In this personalised strategy, ESM can be incorporated in a dynamic process of recurrent assessment periods, intervention and evaluation to further optimise QoL over time.

Sampling daily life experience using the ESM generates useful treatment-related information that is not available to mental health professionals when only traditional assessment instruments such as clinical interviews, observations and standardised questionnaires are used. Since in real life neither mental states nor salient aspects of the environment are well-defined and their impact cannot be easily determined in the continuous flow of experience, patients are generally unable to formulate a strategy for behavioural change. Some individuals may be able to assess their mental state in one situation and contrast it to all others, e.g. 'I am more unhappy when I am alone', but for most people, aggregating a picture of their experience over different contexts yields poor results. Indeed, if the behavioural changes needed to optimise well-being were so obvious, patients would be able to find solutions to their problems themselves, and professional intervention would not be required.

In therapy, ESM data may function like a videotape of daily life, which the therapist and patient can view together. Reconstructing the week together fosters mutual respect and partnership. The detailed dimensions of a person's experience, visualised from the plots and frequency counts, situational correlations, time budgets, variability, stability and other patterns in their self-reports, provide the material for a script immediately available for clinical use (deVries, 1992b). One such use of ESM is in directive therapy or case management approaches, where the specific information provided by time sampling may be used to guide changes in behaviour and activities in patients' lives. The case of Peter provides an example:

At the time of the initial study, Peter was a 36-year-old man diagnosed as having chronic disorganised schizophrenia, with acute exacerbations. The psychopathology was severe, as shown by a mean Brief Psychiatric Rating Scale (BPRS) item score of 2.83. BPRS items such as anxiety, guilt, hostility, distrust, aberrant thought content and hallucinations were rated high (score > 3). Clinically, he appeared tense and hyperactive. Social functioning was reasonably high: 4.6 on a scale from 1 to 7. Ambulatory supervision was carried out weekly by a psychiatrist from the Social Psychiatric Service. Peter lived with his 28-year-old girlfriend, a schizophrenic woman showing primarily negative symptoms. They had a 5-month-old son and were living in a one-room studio apartment. Given that both parents wanted to raise the child themselves, how could we help to improve their QoL and create the best possible environment for the baby?

The ESM time budget assessments, clinical evaluations and observation convinced us that the baby was being taken care of adequately. The parents shared responsibility for household chores and devoted much time to playing with the baby. Emotional states measured in different social contexts demonstrated that Peter experienced optimal states when he was alone with his son (see Fig. 8.3). Unfortunately, this situation was infrequent, occurring only 3% of the time. In contrast, in the company of his wife (26% of the time) he experienced the worst mental states, a situation that appeared to be neutralised if the child

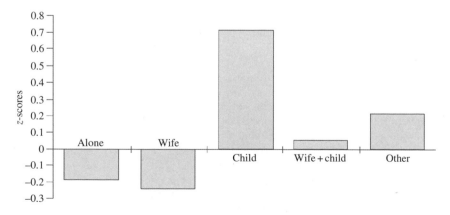

Figure 8.3   The breakdown of 'feeling happy' (z-scores) by 'persons present' shows clear differences in emotional state according to the social context. These patterns were used to plan interventions to optimise Peter's QoL

happened to be present (an additional 24% of the time). These data suggested that a more optimal experience could be reached if the couple reallocated the household chores, giving Peter more time alone with his son. Peter was also encouraged to spend more time with his friends (also a positive state) and less time with his wife. Since the need for living quarters with more room for individual privacy was clear, an attempt was made to get them a larger apartment. We decided not to try to influence Peter's 'alone' time, assuming that he needed that time to compensate for social stress in the living situation.

A reassessment in their new apartment, three months later, showed that although the couple had not been successful in reallocating household chores, Peter had been able to reduce the amount of time spent alone and with his wife (the contexts in which negative mental states had been the worst). Peter's overall mental state improved accordingly and living conditions stabilised, giving the couple a better environment in which to raise their son (Delespaul, 1995).

DISCUSSION

In contrast to the standardised questionnaire and clinical interview measures of QoL, the ESM shifts the assessment strategy from a one-time retrospective measure towards an aggregation of subjective and objective ratings of well-being, sampled repeatedly in the subject's normal daily environment. We have presented three applications of the ESM in QoL research. In the first application, ESM measures of behaviour and affect in daily life were able to discriminate between different diagnostic groups. Such measures are also sensitive to longitudinal clinical change, as illustrated by changes in daily activities and emotions in responders to treatment with an antidepressant and by the results of a personalised intervention to change the amount of time spent in specific social contexts by a schizophrenic man.

In the future, the ESM could be used to gain insight into a variety of treatment-related processes, e.g. decreases in daily QoL due to the side-effects of long-term neuroleptic treatment. We have proposed that ESM assessments of QoL in daily life will enhance reliability, validity and sensitivity, but additional studies will be necessary to evaluate this claim and clarify the areas in which this approach will be most fruitful. Such studies can be expected to add to QoL research a deeper understanding of the dimensions that make up the concept, possibly leading to innovative assessment instruments for use in medical outcome research. The ESM is proving to be a valuable tool in clinical practice, yielding information that can be used to design intervention strategies to optimise QoL in individual patients. Thus, ESM can provide new insights into the effects of mental disorders and their treatments. It should be added to the armamentarium of methods in this new area of medical research, which ultimately aims to improve the quality of life in both sickness and health.

ACKNOWLEDGEMENTS

ESM research on quality of life in mental disorders has been supported by research grants from Solvay Duphar (the Netherlands), the L.F. Saugstad Foundation and Maastricht University. The authors thank the patients and treatment staff of the Vijverdal Regional Psychiatric Hospital, the Maastricht Community Mental Health Center (RIAGG) and collaborating primary care practices in Hoensbroek. They gratefully acknowledge the assistance of T. Driesen, C. Dijkman and F. Van Goethem in various aspects of the research, and the generosity of colleagues who contributed data to the ESM data archive. Some of the unpublished results were presented by the co-authors in separate papers at the Association of European Psychiatrists Symposium on *Quality of Life and Disabilities in Mental Disorders*, Vienna, Austria, 4–7 April 1994.

REFERENCES

Affleck, G., Tennen, H., Urrows, S., Higgins, P., Abeles, M., Hall, C., Karoly, P. & Newton, C. (1998). Fibromyalgia and women's pursuit of personal goals: A daily process analysis, *Health Psychol.*, **17**, 40–47.

Agosti, V., Stewart, J.W. & Quitkin, F.M. (1991). Life satisfaction and psychosocial functioning in chronic depression: Effect of acute treatment with antidepressants, *J. Affect. Disord.*, **23**, 35–41.

Altmann, J. (1974). Observational study of behavior: Sampling methods, *Behaviour*, **49**, 227–267.

Barge-Schaapveld, D.Q.C.M. & Nicolson, N.A. (2002). Effects of antidepressant treatment on the quality of daily life: An experience sampling study, *J. Clin. Psychiatry*, **63**, 477–485.

Barge-Schaapveld, D.Q.C.M., Nicolson, N.A., Gerritsen van der Hoop, R. & deVries, M.W. (1995). Changes in daily life experience associated with clinical improvement in depression, *J. Affect. Disord.*, **34**, 139–154.

Barge-Schaapveld, D.Q.C.M., Nicolson, N.A., Berkhof, J. & deVries, M.W. (1999). Quality of life in depression: Daily life determinants and variability, *Psychiatry Res.*, **88**, 173–189.

Brandstätter, H. (1994). Well-being and motivational person–environment fit: A time-sampling study of emotions, *Eur. J. Personality.*, **8**, 75–93.

Broadhead, W.E., Blazer, D.G., George, L.K. & Tse, C.K. (1990). Depression, disability days, and days lost from work in a prospective epidemiologic survey, *J. Am. Med. Ass.*, **264**, 2524–2528.

Bronfenbrenner, U. (1979). *The Ecology of Human Development*, Harvard University Press, Cambridge, Massachusetts.

Cantor, N., Norem, J., Langston, C., Zirkel, S., Fleeson, W. & Cook-Flannagan, C. (1991). Life tasks and daily life experience, *J. Personality*, **59**, 425–451.

Csikszentmihalyi, M. (1990). *Flow: The Psychology of Optimal Experience. Steps Toward Enhancing the Quality of Life*, Harper Perennial, New York.

Csikszentmihalyi, M. & Csikszentmihalyi, I. (1988). *Optimal Experience. Psychological Studies of Flow in Consciousness*, Cambridge University Press, Cambridge.

Csikszentmihalyi, M. & Larson, R. (1987). Validity and reliability of the Experience-Sampling Method, *J. Nerv. Ment. Dis.*, **175**, 526–537.

Delespaul, P.A.E.G. (1995). *Assessing Schizophrenia in Daily Life: The Experience Sampling Method*, Universitaire Pers, Maastricht.

De Lisio, G., Maremmani, I., Perugi, G., Cassano, G.B., Deltito, J. & Akiskal, H.S. (1986). Impairment of work and leisure in depressed outpatients: A preliminary communication, *J. Affect. Disord.*, **10**, 79–84.

Delle Fave, A. & Massimini, F. (1992). The ESM and the measurement of clinical change: A case of anxiety disorder, in *The Experience of Psychopathology: Investigating Mental Disorders in Their Natural Settings* (Ed. M.W. deVries), Cambridge University Press, Cambridge.

deVries, M.W. (1987). Investigating mental disorders in their natural settings, *J. Nerv. Ment. Dis.*, **175**, 509–513.

deVries, M.W. (Ed.) (1992a). *The Experience of Psychopathology: Investigating Mental Disorders in Their Natural Settings*, Cambridge University Press, Cambridge.

deVries, M.W. (1992b). The uses of the ESM in psychotherapy, in *The Experience of Psychopathology: Investigating Mental Disorders in Their Natural Settings* (Ed. M. W. deVries), Cambridge University Press, Cambridge.

deVries, M.W. & Delespaul, P.A. (1989). Time, context, and subjective experiences in schizophrenia, *Schizophrenia Bull.*, **15**, 233–244.

Diener, E. (1984). Subjective well-being, *Psychol. Bull.*, **95**, 542–575.

Diener, E., Sandvik, E., Pavot, W. & Gallagher, D. (1991). Response artifacts in the measurement of subjective well-being, *Social Indications Res.*, **24**, 35–56.

Donner, E. (1992). Expanding the experiential parameters of cognitive therapy, in *The Experience of Psychopathology: Investigating Mental Disorders in Their Natural Settings* (Ed. M.W. deVries), Cambridge University Press, Cambridge.

Feist, G.J., Bodner, T.E., Jacobs, J.F., Miles, M. & Tan, V. (1995). Integrating top-down and bottom-up structural models of subjective well-being: A longitudinal investigation, *J. Personal Social Psychol.*, **68**, 138–150.

Figurski, T.J. (1992). Everyday self-awareness: Implications for self-esteem, depression and resistance to therapy, in *The Experience of Psychopathology: Investigating Mental Disorders in Their Natural Settings* (Ed. M.W. deVries), Cambridge University Press, Cambridge.

Franklin, J.L., Simmons, J., Solovitz, B., Clemons, J.R. & Miller, G.E. (1986). Assessing quality of life of the mentally ill, *Evaluation of Health Prof.*, **9**, 376–388.

Gotlib, I.H. (1990). An interpersonal systems approach to the conceptualization and treatment of depression, in *Contemporary Psychological Approaches to Depression* (Ed. R.E. Ingram), Plenum Press, New York.

Headey, B., Veenhoven, R. & Wearing, A. (1991). Top-down versus bottom-up theories of subjective well-being, *Social Indications Res.*, **24**, 81–100.

Juster, F.T. (1985). The validity and quality of time use estimates obtained from recall diaries, in *Time, Goods, and Well-being* (Eds F.T. Juster & F.P. Stafford), Institute for Social Research, University of Michigan, Ann Arbor, Michigan.

Kahneman, D. (1999). Objective happiness, in *Well-Being: The Foundations of Hedonic Psychology* (Eds D. Kahneman, E. Diener & N. Schwarz), Russell Sage Foundation, New York.

Kocsis, J.H., Frances, A.J., Voss, C., Mann, J.J., Mason, B.J. & Sweeney, J. (1988). Imipramine treatment for chronic depression, *Arch. Gen. Psychiatry*, **45**, 253–257.

Lance, C.E., Lautenschlager, G.J., Sloan, C.E. & Varca, P.E. (1989). A comparison between bottom-up, top-down, and bidirectional models of relationships between global and life facet satisfaction, *J. Personality*, **57**, 601–624.

Lehman, A.F. & Burns, B. (1990). Severe mental illness in the community, in *Quality of Life Assessments in Clinical Trials* (Ed. B. Spilker), Raven Press, New York.

Lonnqvist, J., Sintonen, H., Syvalahti, E., Appelberg, B., Koskinen, T., Mannikko, T., Mehtonen, O.P., Naarala, M., Sihvo, S., Auvinen, J. & Pitkanen, H. (1994). Antidepressant efficacy and quality of life in depression: A double-blind study with moclobemide and fluoxetine, *Acta Psychiatrica Scand.*, **89**, 363–369.

Massimini, F. & Carli, M. (1988). The systematic assessment of flow in daily life experience, in *Optimal Experience: Psychological Studies of Flow in Consciousness* (Eds M. Csikszentmihalyi & I. Csikszentmihalyi), Cambridge University Press, New York.

Massimini, F., Csikszentmihalyi, M. & Carli, M. (1987). The monitoring of optimal experience. A tool for psychiatric rehabilitation, *J. Nerv. Ment. Dis.*, **175**, 545–549.

Massimini, F., Csikszentmihalyi, M. & Carli, M. (1992). The monitoring of optimal experience: a tool for psychiatric rehabilitation, in *The Experience of Psychopathology: Investigating Mental Disorders in Their Natural Settings* (Ed. M.W. deVries), Cambridge University Press, Cambridge.

Milbrath, L.W. (1982). A conceptualization and research strategy for the study of ecological aspects of the quality of life, *Social Indications Res.*, **10**, 133–157.

Myin-Germeys, I., Nicolson, N.A. & Delespaul, P.A.E.G. (2001). The context of delusional experiences in the daily life of patients with schizophrenia, *Psychol. Med.*, **31**, 489–498.

Peeters, F., Nicolson, N.A., Berkhof, J., Delespaul, P. & deVries, M.W. (2003). Effects of daily events on mood states in major depressive disorder, *J. Abnorm. Psychol.*, **112**, 203–211.

Read, J.L., Quinn, R.J. & Hoefer, M.A. (1987). Measuring overall health: An evaluation of three important approaches, *J. Chronic Dis.*, **40**, 7S–21S.

Revicki, D.A., Turner, R., Brown, R. & Martindale, J.J. (1992). Reliability and validity of a health-related quality of life battery for evaluating outpatient antidepressant treatment, *Quality of Life Res.*, **1**, 257–266.

Rost, K., Smith, G.R., Burnman, M.A. & Burns, B.J. (1992). Measuring the outcomes of care for mental health problems: The case of depressive disorders, *Med. Care*, **30**, S266–S273.

Steiger, H., Gauvin, L., Jabalpurwala, S., Séguin, J.R. & Stotland, S. (1999). Hypersensitivity to social interactions in bulimic syndromes: Relationship to binge eating, *J. Consult. Clin. Psychol.*, **67**, 765–775.

Stone, A.A., Shiffman, S.S. & deVries, M.W. (1999). Ecological momentary assessment, in *Well-Being: The Foundations of Hedonic Psychology* (Eds D. Kahneman, E. Diener & N. Schwarz), Russell Sage Foundation, New York.

Turner, J.A., Deyo, R.A., Loeser, J.D., Von Korff, M. & Fordyce, W.E. (1994). The importance of placebo effects in pain treatment and research, *J. Am. Med. Ass.*, **271**, 1609–1614.

van der Poel, E.G.T. & Delespaul, P.A.E.G. (1992). The applicability of ESM in personalized rehabilitation, in *The Experience of Psychopathology: Investigating Mental Disorders in Their Natural Settings* (Ed. M.W. deVries), Cambridge University Press, Cambridge.

Veenhoven, R. (1991). Is happiness relative?, *Social Indications Res.*, **24**, 1–34.

Wheeler, L. & Reis, H.T. (1991). Self-recording of everyday life events: Origins, types, and uses, *J. Personality*, **59**, 339–354.

Whiting, B.B. & Whiting, J.W.M. (1975). *Children of Six Cultures: A Psychocultural Analysis*, Harvard University Press, Cambridge, Massachusetts.

Wilson, W. (1967). Correlates of avowed happiness, *Psychol. Bull.*, **67**, 294–306.

9

Quality of Life and Positive Health: Their Place in Comprehensive Clinical Diagnosis

Juan E. Mezzich and Margit M. Schmolke

INTRODUCTION

The main meanings of diagnosis emerging in recent times are to provide the informational bases for clinical care and to represent a process of engagement among patients, families and health professionals involved in clinical care. To fulfil these demands, a diagnostic formulation must encompass not only syndromes and illnesses but also an indication of the patient's whole clinical condition, including non-pathological and positive aspects of health. Likewise, diagnosis as a process must organise and energise the various key players in the clinical setting for joint understanding of an individual's health status and joint commitment to a programme of clinical care (Mezzich, 2003).

Among the positive aspects of health to be considered and covered in comprehensive diagnostic models, the concept of quality of life (QoL) is gaining considerable attention. This may be related to a broad range of elements, commensurate with those of a broader concept of health, and also because of the emphasis the assessment of such domain places on the role of the person as an appraiser of the quality of his own life.

Recent studies on patients' self-report versus clinicians' perspectives on QoL (e.g. Sainfort, Becker and Diamond, 1996) suggest that there is often a discrepancy between these paradigmatic evaluators on different aspects of health assessment, particularly those involving social domains. This calls for engaging the patient more fully in the process of such assessment.

Interest in broader conceptualisations of clinical diagnosis can be found in ancient notions of disease and classification, yet it has been only in recent decades that extended and worldwide models of comprehensive diagnosis have emerged. Such models encompass a number of elements and structures (e.g. disease categories, levels of disability, idiographic or personalised statements) which are relevant to several aspects of health as well as to a multidimensional concept of QoL. It should be helpful to elucidate specific structural levels within a comprehensive diagnostic model, where aspects of QoL and other aspects of positive health and approaches to their assessment could be incorporated. The content and form of the instruments for such incorporation would also need to be determined.

The process of this discourse may illuminate our understanding of the concepts of comprehensive diagnosis, QoL and positive health. It may also provide useful perspectives for their joint contribution to the advancement of effective clinical care.

Quality of Life in Mental Disorders, Second Edition   Edited by H. Katschnig, H. Freeman and N. Sartorius
© 2006 John Wiley & Sons, Ltd

COMPREHENSIVE CLINICAL DIAGNOSIS

Feinstein (1967) noted that the basic role of diagnosis is to establish the patterns according to which clinicians observe, think, remember and act. This points out the critical importance of diagnosis for defining the field and articulating clinical care.

What is diagnosis from a formal viewpoint? A fresh conceptualisation suggests that it is a synoptic representation of the clinical condition that is efficient, informative and useful for care. These key attitudes represent:

1. Efficiency is a requirement of the summarising nature of a diagnostic statement, necessary for agility in a clinician's cognitive processing and for its effective handling (storage, processing, and retrieval) through modern informational technologies.
2. The exigency of informativeness refers to the need for sufficient grounds for understanding the patient's condition as profoundly and thoroughly as possible.
3. The third requirement, usefulness for care, refers to the central role of diagnosis for treatment planning in terms of both interventional techniques and professionals involved.

From a scaling viewpoint, while diagnosis has traditionally been framed typologically, in principle both typological and dimensional instruments can be used to describe the domains of interest.

From a content or domain point of view, several contrasting concepts of diagnosis have been offered. Most traditionally, although not without current endorsers, diagnosis has been equated with disorder or disease. Various levels of discourse for analysing a disease concept have led to corresponding forms of diagnosis, e.g. physicochemical, clinical, etc. Some other concepts of disease such as that of Seguin (1946) posit that disease represents a response of the whole person to both external and internal stimuli and as such they argue for the need to contextualise the concept of disease and to articulate a number of domains beyond a biomedical formulation.

Broader concepts of diagnosis transcend the description or identification of a disease to consider elements of the patient's whole clinical condition, such as the psychosocial environment where the patient lives and illness emerges, as well as the consequences or impact of illness on his/her ability to perform basic social roles. For example, Meyer (1907) argued that psychiatrists should be concerned with understanding the sick person in terms of life experiences, rather than with fitting his symptoms into a classificatory schema. Furthermore, the eminent historian and philosopher of medicine Lain Entralgo (1982) pointed out that the purpose of diagnosis, more than identifying disorders (nosological) or distinguishing one disorder from another (differential), is to understand what happens in the mind and body of the person who presents for care.

The contrast outlined above between restricted and contextualised concepts of diagnosis can be illustrated further through etymological analyses. The two principal meanings of the New Latin and Greek term *dia-gignoskein*, discernible from the etymological presentations made in several dictionaries (*Random House Dictionary*, 1971; *Dorland's Dictionary*, 1974; *Webster's Dictionary*, 1976), are the following: (a) to identify and differentiate and (b) to know thoroughly. It can be argued that the first meaning corresponds to the medical concept of nosological and differential diagnosis and that the second involves understanding deeply the nature and context of a problem or situation. The latter appears to correspond to the concept of comprehensive diagnosis.

On Structurally Advancing Diagnostic Systems

One of the major recent advances in diagnostic methodology (Maser and Kaelber, 1991; Mezzich and Jorge, 1993) has been the systematisation of psychiatric nosology. This thrust has principally encompassed a syndromic, principally phenomenological organisation of the nosological classification, as well as the use of explicit or specific definitions of diagnostic categories. Both developments appear to have contributed to the achievement of higher levels of diagnostic reliability.

Advances in diagnostic validity (i.e. greater fulfilment of the purposes of diagnosis in regard to communication, understanding of the case, treatment planning and prognosis) would require work in the following directions:

1. One area for advancing diagnostic validity would be the refinement of pathology description. For this, attentiveness to the results of empirical (biological, psychological and social) research would be important. For example, new aetiological explorations could in due course lead to the formulation of illness on genetic–environmental terms, as suggested by Charney *et al.* (2002). Concerning measurement, the instruments for the description of pathology may be categorical – not only classical, but also prototypical (Cantor *et al.*, 1980) – as well as dimensional (as has been experimented with for describing personality and schizophrenic pathology during the development of DSM-IV).
2. The further development of standardised multiaxial formulations offers another opportunity for upgrading diagnostic validity. Important here would be refining the concepts underlying the axial description of the patient's whole clinical condition and of the categorical and dimensional standardised instruments for appraising each of the axes.
3. The inclusion of an idiographic formulation as an important component of a comprehensive diagnostic model (complementary rather than a confrontational alternative to standardised diagnosis) is another promising approach to advancing diagnostic validity. A major challenge in this development is the determination of the key elements of the clinician's explanatory models (e.g. biological, psychodynamic, cognitive–behavioural, sociocultural) and the principal thrusts to organise the patient's perspectives (e.g. biographical, QoL). Another challenge would be to develop efficient assessment procedures and recording formats to minimise cumbersomeness and to facilitate the use of an idiographic formulation in regular clinical care.

Conceptually supportive of the comprehensive diagnostic model outlined above is the ongoing development of assessment instruments of health status characterised by a broad outlook and an emphasis on the positive aspects of health.

Pradigmatic of this approach is the definition of health embodied in the constitution of the World Health Organization (WHO). It proclaims that health is a state of complete physical, mental and social well being and not merely the absence of disease. To illustrate efforts at operationalising the assessment of health status one can mention the broad health inventories designed as part of the Medical Outcomes Study (MOS) (Stewart, Hays and Ware, 1988). The 20 items of the MOS Short-Form General Health Survey were selected to represent six health concepts: physical functioning (limitations of physical activities), role or occupational functioning, social functioning (interpersonal contacts), mental health (psychological distress and well-being), health perceptions (patients' own ratings of current general health) and pain (as distinguished from physical discomfort) (Stewart, Hays and Ware, 1994).

INCORPORATING QUALITY OF LIFE IN COMPREHENSIVE DIAGNOSTIC MODELS

Quality of life has been accorded a special place in health care (e.g. Spilker, 1990; Kuyken and Orley, 1994) as it is becoming clear that the purpose of such care cannot be only to eliminate symptoms or restore functioning but also to help the individual to achieve fuller levels of health and satisfaction of personal life aspirations. A number of facets have been proposed to delineate the range of domains relevant to QoL. Among the most frequently endorsed are the following: physical, psychological, independent functioning, social relationships, environmental factors and higher personal aspiration. The World Health Organization's Quality of Life Instrument WHOQOL (Kuyken and Orley, 1994) has adopted these particular facets as constituent domains.

To assess all or a fraction of these facets of QoL, a number of distinct instruments have been proposed. They vary in terms of the domains they actually cover as well as in regard to the scaling or measurement approaches they use, which range from typological to dimensional procedures and from extensive instruments to one-item scales.

Different levels and structures in diagnostic systems where QoL concepts can be incorporated are briefly described below:

1. *Disorder-specific scales as ad hoc assessment.* Considered here are QoL instruments specifically developed for individuals afflicted by a particular illness or condition. Examples include the AIDS Health Assessment Questionnaire (Lubeck and Fries, 1991), the Arthritis Impact Measurement Scales

(Meenan, Gertman and Mason, 1980) and the Diabetes QoL instrument (Diabetes Control and Complications Trial Research Group, 1985). Here, QoL is assessed not as an intrinsic part of a diagnostic system but as a further evaluative study of individuals classified with a standard diagnostic schema (e.g. the International Classification of Diseases) as being affected by a particular disorder or condition.

2. *Generic instruments as specific axes.* Quality of life can also be assessed in a way generalisable to all patients or subjects, regardless of the specific diseases they may be experiencing. Examples include the World Health Organization Quality of Life Instrument WHOQOL (WHOQOL Group, 1998), the Quality of Well-being Scale (Bush, 1984) and the Sickness Impact Profile (Bergner *et al.*, 1981). More recently, a multicultural QoL index has been designed in several languages, allowing for a cultural-informed self-rating of key dimensions of QoL, from physical well-being to spiritual fulfilment (Mezzich *et al.*, 2000; Lorente *et al.*, 2002; Mezzich *et al.*, 2003a, 2003b, 2003c). Such generic instruments could be used to evaluate a QoL axis in a multiaxial diagnostic schema. In this way, generic measures of QoL may have the place that, for instance, social and occupational functioning scales have as optional axes in DSM-IV.

3. *Health status and QoL assessments as multiaxial schemas.* Health status is a complex subject, as pointed out by a consensus conference (Walker and Ascher, 1986), which identified physical, cognitive, affective, social and economic as its key aspects. Quality of life is also a pluralistic concept. The WHO Quality of Life Instrument encompasses the following six domains: physical, psychological, level of independence, social relationships, environment and spirituality/religion/personal beliefs. Joyce (1987) noticed the significant thematic similarities between complex health status and QoL concepts. In both cases, the assessment of thematic complexity may be profitably approached through a multiaxial procedure. Such a procedure provides architectural coherence to the protean and heterogeneous content of these concepts and ensures their systematic assessment.

4. *Complementary idiographic formulation.* The intricate, subjective, and not always standardisable information pertinent to QoL, makes it appropriate and promising to consider an idiographic or personalised formulation as one vehicle for the inclusion of QoL in comprehensive diagnostic systems. Qualitative research methods are very relevant here (World Health Organization, 1994). The relevance of idiographic formulations is predicated on the grounds of both the flexibility of such formulation and its prominent concern with the perspectives of the patient. Assessment of a subject in an idiographic formulation typically involves the use of flexible guidelines or suggested questions rather than standardised or rigidly scheduled procedures.

The analysis presented above on the possible ways of incorporating QoL concepts in comprehensive diagnostic models has been undertaken in a largely architectural way in order to understand pertinent thematic relationships more clearly and heuristically. In line with this strategy, it should be illuminating to compare the contents covered by two major assessment instruments developed by the World Health Organization. One, the ICD-10 multiaxial schema (Mezzich, 1994; Sartorius, 1994), is focused on pathology and clinical concerns, while the other, the WHO Quality of Life Instrument (WHOQOL), has a broader field of interest. As the comparative Table 9.1 shows, the first axis (clinical diagnoses, encompassing both mental and non-mental disorders) of the ICD-10 multiaxial schema corresponds to the first two domains (physical and psychological) of the WHOQOL. The second ICD-10 axis (disablements in four areas: personal care, occupational functioning, functioning with family and broader social functioning) roughly corresponds to the third WHOQOL domain (level of independence). The third and

Table 9.1   Structural comparison of WHO's encompassing assessment schemas

ICD-10 multiaxial schema	WHO quality of life instrument
I. Clinical diagnoses	I. Physical domain
	II. Psychological domain
II. Disablements	III. Level of independence
III. Contextual problems	IV. Social relationships
	V. Environment
	VI. Spiritual/personal beliefs

final ICD-10 axis (contextual problems, including psychosocial environmental and personal lifestyle and management difficulties) overlaps thematically to some extent with the fourth and fifth WHOQOL domains (social relationships and environment). The sixth WHOQOL domain (spirituality, religion and personal beliefs) is the only one without correspondence within the ICD-10 multiaxial schema.

There are some important differential characteristics of QoL assessment, compared with the assessment of psychopathology and related health problems. These characteristics are:

1. *Focus on the person.* While the assessment of health problems should be made while paying attention to the complexity of the patient's clinical condition by considering not only illnesses but also other problems and their context, QoL assessment is even more squarely focused on the individual examined.
2. *Subjective perspective.* The assessment of health problems is typically based on the clinician's judgement of the patient's condition. In contrast, QoL assessment fundamentally displays the subjective viewpoint of the person whose life is being evaluated.
3. *Emphasis on positive health.* While the assessment of health problems is focused on disease, disabilities and psychosocial problems, QoL assessment preferentially looks for assets and strengths, i.e. the more positive polarity of the health dimension.
4. *Greater cultural sensitivity.* While substantial attention is being paid to cultural factors influencing the experience and formulation of health problems, their context and consequences, there is an even greater need to frame the assessment of QoL culturally, given the culture-boundness of the broad range of aspects of life.
5. *Holistic approach.* The assessment of health problems covers much of what is considered characteristic of the patient's condition. Quality of life assessment is even more encompassing of the totality of the individual involved. As shown in Table 9.1, it includes a domain involving spirituality and personal values and beliefs that are not covered in a pathology-focused clinical diagnosis.

INCLUDING POSITIVE HEALTH IN COMPREHENSIVE CLINICAL DIAGNOSIS

A positive health or 'salutogenetic' (Antonovsky, 1987) approach has become increasingly important for psychiatry as a complementary element to the traditional pathogenetic perspective. Recently, empirical data have been published in clinical psychiatry and psychology focusing on positive aspects of health (e.g. Friborg *et al.*, 2003; Schmolke, 2003; Seligman and Peterson, 2003). According to the Ottawa Charter of Health Promotion (World Health Organization, 1986), five strategies have been conceptualised: (a) building healthy public policy, (b) creating supportive environments, (c) strengthening community action, (d) developing personal skills and (e) reorientating health services. 'Mental health promotion' is an umbrella term that covers a variety of strategies, all aimed at having positive effects on mental health. Among them are the encouragement of individual resources and skills as well as improvements in the socioeconomic environment (World Health Organization, 1999).

The most frequently considered elements of positive health are adaptive functioning, social supports and QoL. Salutogenic or positive health-orientated clinical care focuses on lifting the level of health status and well-being of a given person as much as possible, instead of being restricted to minimising or resolving illnesses and disabilities. These positive health-orientated activities are now often mentioned as examples of health promotion. Characteristically, health promotion involves a creative and empowering process leading to higher stages of health status and the greater fulfilment of a person's life project. Critical players in health promotion are, first and foremost, the patient or consulting person as well as families and a broad range of health and social professionals.

Comprehensive diagnosis, by yielding organised data on critical aspects of clinical conditions and health status, may provide a rich informational basis for constructing an effective plan for clinical care, including health promotion. Comprehensive diagnosis as a process engaging and energising clinicians, consulting persons and families also facilitates the establishment of a social matrix propitious to the empowering and creative features of health promotion. Table 9.2 illustrates some of the useful connections between the informational areas of a comprehensive diagnosis and a broad profile of health care activities.

Table 9.2 Illustrating the connections between comprehensive diagnosis and broadly based clinical care, including health promotion

Components of comprehensive diagnosis	Illustrative health care activities[a]
Multiaxial formulation	
I. Illness (mental and non-mental)	• Early identification of illness (2nd Pv)
II. Disabilities	• Skills development (4th Pv, HP)
III. Contextual factors	• Activating social supports (4th Pv, HP)
IV. Quality of life	• Spiritual counselling (HP)
Idiographic formulation (perspectives of clinician, patient and family, and discrepancy resolution)	
• Contextualised clinical problems	• Affirmation of cultural identity (HP)
• Positive factors or assets	• Engagement of special talents (HP)
• Expectations on health restoration and promotion	• Integration of services (3rd Pv, HP)

[a]2nd Pv = secondary prevention, 3rd Pv = tertiary prevention, 4th Pv = quaternary prevention, HP = health promotion.

QUALITY OF LIFE AND POSITIVE HEALTH IN THE INTERNATIONAL GUIDELINES FOR DIAGNOSTIC ASSESSMENT (IGDA)

An emerging diagnostic model that may be useful for the assessment of QoL and other aspects of positive health as well as for standard treatment is that at the core of the new World Psychiatric Association (WPA) International Guidelines of Diagnostic Assessment (IGDA) (Mezzich *et al.*, 2003d). It includes a standardised multiaxial formulation composed of the following domains: I. Clinical disorders, II. Disabilities, III. Contextual factors and IV. Quality of life. It also incorporates an idiographic personalised formulation integrating the perspectives of the clinician, the patient and the family on the following areas: contextualised clinical problems, patient's positive factors for care and expectations on restoration and promotion of health. In the recently published Essentials of WPA's IGDA an illustrative clinical case shows the concrete application of the diagnostic formulation with the standardised and idiographic parts as well as the treatment plan including health promotion activities.

CONCLUSION

An emerging comprehensive diagnostic model involving a standardised multiaxial formulation of illnesses, their context and consequences, together with a complementary idiographic formulation, offers an opportunity to upgrade the validity and usefulness of diagnosis. Furthermore, such a model furnishes structures that can accommodate QoL and other positive health concepts and measures. In effect, disorder-specific scales may be helpful for additional post-diagnostic evaluation, generic scales may be used as additional or optional axes, the set of domains underlying QoL may be arranged as a whole multiaxial schema and, finally, QoL and positive health may be assessed as part of a complementary idiographic formulation.

The innovative ferment connected to the recently emerging concepts of comprehensive diagnosis, QoL and positive health is being anchored by and nurtured through significant international efforts. In the diagnosis field, this is illustrated by the WPA–WHO ongoing collaborative effort towards the development of new international classification and diagnostic systems (Mezzich and Üstün, 2002). In the field of positive health and health promotion, there is a major publication project in preparation on 'Promotion Mental Health: Concepts, Evidence and Practice', directed by Herrman, Shekhar and Moodie on behalf of WHO in collaboration with the Victorian Health Promotion Foundation and the University of Melbourne.

Enriching diagnosis with QoL and other positive health concepts may advance deeper understanding of the patient's condition, designing a more adequate treatment strategy, fostering effective communication between clinician and patient, and the active engagement of the patient in the process of treatment and of achieving higher levels of health. Such integration may be maximised through a process of deliberate interactions among all key players.

REFERENCES

Antonovsky, A. (1987). *Unraveling the Mystery of Health. How People Manage Stress and Stay Well*, Jossey-Bass, San Francisco, California.

Bergner, M., Bobbitt, R.A., Carter, W.B. & Gilson, B.S. (1981). The Sickness Impact Profile: developmental and final revision of a health status measure, *Med. Care*, **19**, 787–805.

Bush, J.W. (1984). General Health Policy Model/Quality of Well-being (QWB) scale, in *Assessment of Quality of Life in Clinical Trials of Cardiovascular Therapies* (Eds N.K. Wenger, M.F. Mattson & C.D. Furber), LeJacq, New York.

Cantor, N., Smith, E.E., French de Salles, R. & Mezzich, J.E. (1980). Psychiatric diagnosis of prototype categorization, *J. Abnormal Psychol.*, **89**, 181–193.

Charney, D.S., Barlow D.H., Botteron, K., *et al* (2002). Neuroscience research agenda to guide development of a pathophysiologically based classification system, in *A Research Agenda for DSM-V* (Eds D.J. Kupfer, M.B.First & D.A. Regier), pp. 31–83, American Psychiatric Association, Washington, DC.

Diabetes Control and Complications Trial Research Group (1985). The DCCT Quality of Life Measure: A preliminary study of reliability and validity, Technical Report, DCCT Coordinating Center, Bethesda, Maryland.

Dorland's Illustrated Medical Dictionary (1974). W.B. Saunders, Philadelphia, Pennsylvania.

Feinstein, A.R. (1967). *Clinical Judgement*, Robert E. Krieger, Huntington, New York.

Friborg, O., Hjemdal, O., Rosenvinge, J.H. & Martinussen, M. (2003). A new rating scale for adult resilience: What are the central protective resources behind healthy adjustment?, *Int. J. Meth. Psychiatr. Res.*, **12**, 65–76.

Joyce, C.R.B. (1987). Quality of life. The state of the art in clinical assessment, in *Quality of Life: Assessment and Application* (Eds S.R. Walker & R.M. Rosser), MTP Press, Lancaster, England.

Kuyken, W. & Orley, J. (1994). The development of the World Health Organization Quality of Life Assessment Instrument (the WHOQOL), in *International Quality of Life Assessment* (Eds J. Orley & W. Kuyken), Springer, Heidelberg.

Lain Entralgo, P. (1982). *El Diagnóstico Médico*, Salvat, Barcelona.

Lorente, E., Ibáñez, M.I., Moro, M. & Ruipérez, M.A. (2002). Índice de Calidad de Vida: estandarización y características psicométricas en una muestra española, *Psiquiatría y Salud Integral*, **2**(2), 45–50.

Lubeck, D.P. & Fries, J.F. (1991). Health status among persons with HIV infection: A community-based study, American Public Health Association, Annual Meeting, Atlanta (Abstract).

Maser, J.D. & Kaelber, C. (1991). International use and attitude towards DSM-III and DSM-III-R: Growing consensus in psychiatric classification. Special Issue: Diagnosis, dimensions, and DSM-IV: The science of classification, *J. Abnormal Psychol.*, **100**, 271–279.

Meenan, R.F., Gertman, P.M. & Mason, J.M. (1980). Measurement of health status in arthritis: the Arthritis Impact Measurement Scales, *Arthritis Rheum.*, **23**, 146.

Meyer, A. (1907). Fundamental conceptions of dementia praecox, *J. Nerv. Ment. Dis.*, **34**, 331–336.

Mezzich, J.E. (1994). Multiaxial diagnosis: Purposes and challenges, in *Psychiatric Diagnosis. A World Perspective* (Eds J.E. Mezzich, Y. Honda & M.C. Kastrup), Springer, New York.

Mezzich, J.E. (2003). Comprehensive diagnosis as formulation and process towards health promotion, *Dynamic Psychiatry*, **36**, 247–253.

Mezzich, J.E. & Jorge, M.R. (1993). Psychiatric nosology: Achievements and challenges, in *International Review of Psychiatry*, Vol. 1, (Eds J.A. Costa e Silva & C.C. Nadelson), American Psychiatric Press, Washington, DC.

Mezzich, J.E., Ruiperez, M.A., Perez, C., Yoon, G., Liu, J. & Mahmud, S. (2000). The Spanish version of the quality of life index: presentation and validation, *J. Nerv. Ment. Dis.*, **188**(5), 301–305.

Mezzich, J.E. & Üstün, T.B. (Eds)(2002). International classification and diagnosis: Critical experience and future directions, *Psychopathology*, **35**, 55–202.

Mezzich, J.E., Cohen, N., Ruiperez, M., Zapata-Vega, M.I. & Hyzak, S.R. (2003a). Multicultural Quality of Life Index: Presentation and validation of an efficient and culture-informed model, Presented at the WPA International Congress, Caracas, pp. 108–109.

Mezzich, J.E., Yoon, G., Sun-Kyung, S., Ruiperez, M. & Zapata-Vega, M.I. (2003b). The Korean Version of the Multicultural Quality of Life Index (MQLI-Kr): Presentation and validation, Presented at the WPA International Congress, Caracas, p. 133.

Mezzich, J.E., Liu, J., Ruiperez, M., Zapata-Vega, M.I. & Rahman, A. (2003c). Multicultural Quality of Life Index, Chinese version (MQLI-Ch): Presentation and validation, Presented at the WPA International Congress, Caracas, pp. 133–134.

Mezzich, J.E., Berganza, C.E., Von Cranach, M., Jorge, M.R., Kastrup, M.C., Murthy, R.S., Okasha, A., Pull, C., Sartorius, N., Skodol, A. & Zaudig, M. (2003d). Essentials of the World Psychiatric Association's International Guidelines for Diagnostic Assessment (IGDA), *Br. J. Psychiatry*, **182**(Suppl. 45), 37–66.

Random House Dictionary for the English Language, The Unabridged Edition (1971). Random House, New York.

Sainfort, F., Becker, M. & Diamond, R. (1996). Judgements of quality of life of individuals with severe mental disorders: Patient self-report versus provider perspectives, *Am. J. Psychiatry*, **153**, 497–502.

Sartorius, N. (1994). Progress in the development of the classification of mental disorders in the ICD-10, in *Psychiatric Diagnosis: A World Perspective* (Eds J.E. Mezzich, Y. Honda & M.C. Kastrup), Springer, New York.

Schmolke, M. (2003). Das Gesunde im Patienten entdecken. Eine salutogenetisch orientierte Untersuchung mit schizophrenen Patienten (Discovering positive health in the schizophrenic patient: a salutogenetic-oriented study), *Verhaltenstherapie*, **13**, 102–109.

Seguin, C.A. (1946). The concept of disease, *Psychosomatic Med.*, **8**, 252–257.

Seligman, M.E.P. & Peterson, C. (2003). Positive clinical psychology, in *A Psychology of Human Strengths. Fundamental Questions and Future Directions for a Positive Psychology* (Eds L.G. Aspinwall & U.M. Staudinger), pp. 305–317, American Psychological Association, Washington, DC.

Spilker, B. (Ed.) (1990). *Quality of Life Assessments in Clinical Trials*, Raven Press, New York.

Stewart, A.L., Hays, R.D. & Ware, J.E. (1988). The MOS Short-Form General Health Survey: Reliability and validity in a patient population, *Med. Care*, **26**, 724.

Stewart, A.L., Hays, R.D. & Ware, J.E. (1994). The Medical Outcome Study Short-Form General Health Survey, in *Psychiatric Epidemiology, Assessment Concepts and Methods* (Eds J.E. Mezzich, M.R. Jorge & I.M. Salloum), John Hopkins University Press, Baltimore, Maryland.

Walker, S.R. & Ascher, W. (Eds) (1986). *Medicine and Risk/Benefit Decisions*, MTP Press, Lancaster, England.

Webster's Seventh New Collegiate Dictionary (1976). G. & R. Merriam, Springfield, Massachusetts.

WHOQOL Group (1998). The World Health Organization Quality of Life Assessment (WHOQOL): Development and general psychometric properties. The WHOQOL Group, *Social Sci. Med.*, **46**(12), 1569–1585.

World Health Organization (1986). *Ottawa Charter of Health Promotion*, WHO, Geneva.

World Health Organization (1994). *Qualitative Research for Health Programmes*, Division of Mental Health, WHO, Geneva.

World Health Organization (1999). Strengthening mental health promotion, Fact Sheet no. 220, April 1999, revised November 2001.

10

Quality of Life Measurement in Persons with Schizophrenia: Are We Measuring What's Important?

Marion A. Becker and Ronald J. Diamond

INTRODUCTION

Quality of life measurement for people with schizophrenia has become increasingly important for both clinical practice and evaluation research. The goals for treating individuals with schizophrenia have changed radically as treatment has shifted from a hospital-based to a community-based system. In traditional systems, symptom reduction was considered the major goal. While this objective remains important in community-based systems, the ability to live a stable life in the community has become a primary goal. For people with schizophrenia, achieving a good quality of life (QoL) is often their most important goal. Furthermore, improving QoL has achieved a second role as an important indicator of treatment outcome (Baker, 1995; Lehman, 1995; Cheung, 1997; Durbin et al., 2003). In tandem with a shift in treatment goals within mental health and increasing pressures for greater system accountability, there has been an exponential increase in the use of QoL outcome evaluation. Nonetheless, confusion continues over its definition and measurement. There remains no 'gold standard' for QoL measurement in psychiatry and little information exists about what changes in scores mean in terms of clinical improvement or deterioration, or what relevance they hold for consumers or service managers (Juniper et al., 1994; Cramer et al., 2000; Moos, Nichol and Moos, 2002). In addition, QoL researchers have been criticised, when purporting to assess the impact of treatment, for their failure to use appropriate measures that incorporate concerns of consumers and their families (Awad et al., 1995; Lefley, 1996; Fischer, Shumway and Owen, 2002). There is now growing interest in having standards for measurement and using QoL questionnaires, both to improve clinical practice and provide accurate evidence of outcomes from the consumer's point of view (Gill and Feinstein, 1994; Becker, 1998; Garratt et al., 2002).

After reviewing concerns about QoL measurement and treatment outcomes for persons with schizophrenia, this chapter presents a new approach to QoL assessment.

SCHIZOPHRENIA

Schizophrenia is a prolonged mental disorder that usually begins before the age of 25 and persists throughout life. Research demonstrates that the eventual course and outcome are much more heterogeneous

Quality of Life in Mental Disorders, Second Edition   Edited by H. Katschnig, H. Freeman and N. Sartorius
© 2006 John Wiley & Sons, Ltd

than was previously thought (Harding, Zubin and Strauss, 1987; Leff *et al.*, 1992; Bermanzohn *et al.*, 2001). The traditional view was that this disorder led to a persistent, downhill course of increasing disability and decreasing QoL, but we know now that the course is often erratic, with periods of relatively good functioning mixed with relapses and decreased function. Often, the pattern is unpredictable. Recent research shows that associated psychiatric syndromes (depression, substance abuse, obsessive–compulsive disorder and panic disorder) co-occur with schizophrenia at significant rates. Unfortunately, these syndromes frequently go unrecognised, undiagnosed and untreated. Their presence may contribute to and help to explain the heterogeneous levels of recompensation and change reported in outcome studies (Siris, Bermanzohn and Kessler 1997). Although the reported prevalence rates of associated psychiatric syndromes (APS) in persons with schizophrenia have varied considerably, estimates have all been substantial. Bermanzohn, Porto and Siris (2000), as well as Harvey (2005), found that the lifetime rates of depression, obsessive–compulsive disorder and panic disorder in persons diagnosed with schizophrenia were 54.2, 59.2, and 29.5%, respectively. Soni *et al.* (1992) found that persons with schizophrenia living in the community had more depression and anxiety than those living in the hospital and attributed this to the greater stress and lowered QoL reported for this vulnerable population.

While a cure is not now a realistic goal for most persons (Hegarty *et al.*, 1994), long-term outcome studies show that a substantial proportion of people with schizophrenia have a good to excellent long-term prognosis (Carpenter and Strauss, 1991; Musser *et al.*, 1997; Siris, 2000). Research also suggests that some people recover and become symptom free, no longer needing medication or other treatment, although we know little about what promotes this recovery (Ciompi, 1980; Warner, 1985; Strauss, 1994). As with many chronic illnesses, the main treatment goals are to maintain function, promote recovery and maximise QoL.

Given the prolonged nature of the illness, the complexity of treatment and its cost to society, to determine which individuals are improving and which are not, it is critical to use appropriate outcome measurements that incorporate the concerns of consumers. To develop better treatment programmes, it is necessary to know which are effective and what circumstances are required to assure their effectiveness.

QUALITY OF LIFE AND DEINSTITUTIONALISATION

In the United States, interest in QoL and the social disabilities associated with schizophrenia intensified in the wake of the deinstitutionalisation of the late 1960s and early 1970s, with the wholesale transfer of psychiatric patients into the community, where they have become increasingly visible.

In support of deinstitutionalisation, a number of research projects demonstrated that appropriate community-based treatment and support could increase QoL (Stein and Test, 1987; Levitt, Hogan and Bocosky, 1990; Lehman, Slaughter and Myers, 1991; Sullivan, Wells and Leake, 1991). Too often, however, appropriate supports were not provided and people with schizophrenia were ejected from hospitals and abandoned in communities (Shadish and Bootzin, 1981; Mechanic, 1986). Although this transfer out of hospitals was claimed to be partly justified as improving peoples' lives, over time it became apparent that it did not automatically improve anyone's life.

Research shows that community-dwelling persons with schizophrenia are among the psychiatric patients with the lowest overall life satisfaction scores in the general population (Lehman, Possidente and Hawker, 1986; Rosenfield, 1992). Quality of life, at least for some persons, was worse in the community than in long-stay hospitals (Schmidt *et al.*, 1977; Lamb, 1979, 1981). Research shows that deinstitutionalised individuals often live in substandard housing (Bachrach, 1982; Uehara, 1994), are dissatisfied with their finances, employment, social relationships and personal safety (Lehman, 1992), and are over-represented in the homeless population (Bassuk and Lamb, 1986; Rossi and Wright, 1987; Drake, Wallach and Hoffman, 1989; Rosenheck, Bassuk and Salomon, 1999).

During the early phase of deinstitutionalisation, the primary concern was hospital recidivism. How could tenure in the community be extended and stabilised? Over time, it became increasingly evident that just being out of the hospital was not enough (Bachrach, 1982, 1987; Solomon, 1992). Living situations and levels of despair that had been accepted in hospitals were less tolerable in the community. Reported poor QoL conditions and marked social disabilities caused alarm, generating a sustained interest in targeting treatment towards these issues and developing guidelines for treatment (Stein and Test, 1985; Hadorn, 1993; Stein and Santos, 1998; Milner and Valenstein, 2002; Ridgely *et al.*, 2002). Concerns about the effects of deinstitutionalisation stimulated a substantial body of research on the correlates of successful adaptation and psychiatric rehabilitation (Anthony and Farkas, 1982; Avison and Speechley, 1987; Carpenter and Strauss, 1991; Strauss, 1994; McGrew, Wilson and Bond, 2002).

Over time, clinicians working in the community gained a better understanding of the centrality of QoL concerns. They began to recognise that an individual's subjective experience of QoL affects motivation to seek treatment and to continue with medication and rehabilitation (Hogan, Awad and Eastwood, 1983; Diamond, 1985; Diamond and Becker, 1999; Awad *et al.*, 1995). Some have even speculated that an individual's perception of his/her life quality may influence the phases and course of the illness (Strauss, 1989).

As a consequence of the profound shift in thinking about the abilities, needs and aspirations of community-living persons with schizophrenia, improving their QoL emerged as the major goal of community treatment (Baker and Intagliata, 1982; Rosenfield, 1992; Becker, 1995; Cramer *et al.*, 2000). Fuelled by a rise in the consumer movement and by the growing importance of giving individuals and their families a voice in treatment decisions, QoL assessments that incorporate these perspectives have gained a place in the processes of quality assurance and the difficult task of improving services for persons with schizophrenia (Llewellyn-Thomas, Sutherland and Tibshirani, 1982; Levine, 1987; Ellwood, 1988; Geigle and Jones, 1990; Lehman and Burns, 1990; Struening *et al.*, 2001).

QUALITY OF LIFE AS AN OUTCOME MEASURE IN MENTAL HEALTH

In the wake of deinstitutionalisation, clinicians working in the community began questioning the value of such traditional, common outcome measures as hospital readmission rates and symptoms (Schmidt *et al.*, 1977; Lamb, 1979), seeing these hallowed measures as inadequate and simplistic. Hospital readmission, for example, may reveal more about the mental health system and economic conditions than about the clinical status of the person evaluated. Many admissions are precipitated by a concrete need, such as housing, that has little relation to the person's illness. The same individual who is hospitalised in one treatment system might be treated as an out-patient in another, where effective community-based crisis services can meet their needs (Stein, Diamond and Factor, 1990).

Likewise, positive symptoms of psychosis, such as delusions, hallucinations and cognitive disorganisation, were another traditional measure of severity of illness, and change in these symptoms has frequently been used as the primary indication of improvement (Revicki and Maranda, 1994). While reliance on symptoms appeals to common sense, they are actually important only as markers for the severity of the underlying disease process, or if they directly interfere with the person's life. The primacy of symptom outcomes is being questioned in the light of research which shows that symptoms can have a relatively low correlation with ability to function, satisfaction with treatment or self-reported QoL (Anthony and Rogers, 1995; Sainfort, Becker and Diamond, 1996). Symptoms may indicate little about treatment outcome from the consumer's point of viewpoint. Furthermore, because symptoms are an unreliable predictor of function, they can be a misleading outcome indicator. Two people whose symptoms suggest a similarly severe illness may actually have quite different capacities to function in the community and different perspectives on the value of their treatment.

The main advantage of symptoms as an outcome measure is that they can be measured easily and with reasonable reliability (Patrick and Erickson, 1993; Revicki and Maranda, 1994; Fitzpatrick *et al.*, 2001). Without a practical alternative, symptom measures continue as the primary tool for assessing improvement. A published review of therapeutic responses in schizophrenia found that most clinical trials evaluated psychopathology and positive symptoms (Collins, Hogan and Himansu, 1991). Recent studies have expanded their outcome focus to include negative symptoms, but the family or individual's perspective about their experience of the disease or the outcome of treatment is not routinely collected (Lefley, 1990, 1996; Kuck *et al.*, 1992; Siris, 2000). As QoL gains importance as a focus of treatment and outcome research, the development of instruments to measure changes in this area easily and reliably gains urgency (Feinstein, 1992; Lehman, 1992; Patrick, 1992; Gill and Feinstein, 1994; Becker and

Diamond, 2000). The publication of several large clinical trials showing that QoL measures are respon-sive to important changes has further encouraged their use (Wilson and Cleary, 1995).

The emphasis on using QoL (especially as perceived by consumers themselves) as a goal of treatment has gained support from the consumer movement. Indeed, modern treatment of mental disorders gives increased weight to the values and goals of consumers and their families, since all of us have the right to set, as much as possible, the direction and goals for our lives (McCabe and Unzicker, 1995; Leff, 1997). There is also a growing belief that involving people in their treatment produces better outcomes. Meas-uring an individual's subjective evaluation of various life domains is one approach to assessing how mental health services are meeting their needs (Becker, Diamond and Sainfort, 1994).

Concern for the welfare of psychiatric patients in the community has also enlivened the debate over defining and measuring treatment effectiveness (Rosenfield and Neese-Todd, 1993). This concern has challenged professionals to learn to measure QoL accurately in schizophrenia and tease out factors and remedies associated with an improved quality for persons who suffer with mental illness or other perceived disabilities (Edwards, Patrick and Topolski, 2003). Doubtless, future research on QoL both as a concept and an indicator of outcome will fundamentally change policies and programmes from governmental perspectives. Quality of life concerns slowly replaced deinstitutionalisation and community adjustment as the mental health issue of the 1990s (Schalock et al, 1989).

CHALLENGES TO DEFINITION OF QUALITY OF LIFE

Defining and measuring QoL in the context of schizophrenia is extremely complex. Disagreements about its definition abound, despite a growing body of research (Mor and Guadogoli, 1988; Deyo, 1991; Spilker, 1992; McHorney, 1997; Garratt et al., 2002). As noted by Gill and Feinstein (1994), 'Despite the proliferation of instruments and the burgeoning theoretical literature devoted to the measurement of quality of life, no unified approach has yet been devised for its measurement, and little agreement has been attained on what it means' (page 619). Although the field lacks a consistent definition and measurement approach, consistent trends, ideas and propositions unite the diversity of opinion about QoL measurement. For example, there is general agreement about the essentially subjective nature of QoL and an emerging consensus regarding its major component domains (Bergner, 1985, 1989; Diener et al., 1999; Spilker, 1990).

Most definitions consider: (a) physical health status, (b) functional ability, (c) psychological status and well-being, (d) social interactions and (e) economic status (Spilker, 1990). QoL instruments used in mental health generally include one or more of these domains, often using Lehman's structured interview as the model for collecting data. However, there is little discussion, let alone agreement in the literature, about a standard rule for criteria as to which domains are essential for assessing validly a clinical programme or a person's improvement with treatment. These limitations extend to the problem of weighting and scoring domains, which has been done only arbitrarily. This lack of conceptual clarity, as well as the absence of standardisation, have exacerbated the problem of developing useful instruments, preventing generalisation between studies, and so adding to conceptual confusion and ethical concerns (Mor and Guadogoli, 1988; Guyatt et al., 1989; Mike, 1992; McHorney, 1997).

METHODS OF MEASUREMENT

While there are currently no agreed standards for defining or measuring QoL for persons with schizo-phrenia, many instruments and scoring methods have been developed. For example, Van Dam, Somers and Van Beek-Couzijn (1981) estimated that more than 250 methods had been used to assess QoL in medicine; in 1990, Spilker and colleagues reviewed more than 300 QoL indices, with a diversity of meas-urement strategies and scaling approaches, ranging from disease-specific to generic. Existing instruments cover an array of domains, use several methods of aggregation and ascribe various 'weights' to different items and domains (Deyo, 1991; Berzon et al., 1995; Delespaul, 1995). A diversity of QoL instruments and measurement methods have been developed for schizophrenia (see, for example, Becker, Diamond and Sainfort, 1993; Bigelow, McFarland and Olson, 1991; Heinrichs, Hanlon and Carpenter, 1984; Lehman,

1996; Cramer *et al.*, 2000). Many of these instruments and measurement methods have limitations in their general strategy and application. Disagreement about measuring methods in schizophrenia are generally attributed to differing views about the importance of preferences and varying goals, the goals of researchers and clinicians, and different views of the appropriate roles of consumers and their families (Baker and Intagliata, 1982; Becker, 1995; Cramer *et al.*, 2001).

Much discussion has focused on the role of self-report questionnaires and individual preferences in evaluating and scoring QoL data (Pickney, Gerber and Lafave, 1991; Pavot and Deiner, 1993; Thepa and Rowland, 1995; Atkinson, Zibin and Chuang, 1997). It is well known that subjective and objective assessments of QoL domains do not necessarily coincide, further complicating the measurement process (Heady, Veenhoven and Wearing, 1991; Rosen, Simon and Mckinsey, 1995; Diener *et al.*, 1999). Furthermore, some studies show that biological and psychosocial factors influence each other and that measures of subjective QoL are affected by the clinical status of the individual (Lehman, 1992; Becker, Diamond and Sainfort, 1994; Mechanic *et al.*, 1994; Diener, 1996; Becker, 2003). Although a few studies have looked at the correlations between distinct domains of QoL, researchers have not studied their interaction, and there is little information about how outcomes in different domains are related to treatments received.

Nevertheless, the importance of consumers' perceptions is underscored by evidence that individuals' perceptions of their QoL (which include how they see their own health) reliably predict loss of function, morbidity, mortality and functioning in physical, psychological and social terms (Gill and Feinstein, 1994; Smith, Avis and Assmann, 1999). The interrelatedness of different aspects of peoples' lives is illustrated by data showing that both psychopathology and environmental factors affect QoL; however, the exact nature of the interaction is undetermined (Meltzer *et al.*, 1990; Lehman, 1992; Becker, Diamond and Sainfort, 1994; Ryff and Keyes, 1995). While an outside observer can verify objective aspects independently, this is not possible for subjective assessments.

Until the complex relationship between subjective and objective dimensions of QoL are better understood, global assessment of it will not be a useful or sufficient outcome measure for clinical trials or for evaluating mental health services. New reliable instruments must be developed to measure individual perceptions and specific elements that affect QoL in schizophrenia, so that important interactions between objective and subjective factors can be studied. While several conceptual models for relationships among domains of QoL have been proposed, these models often exclude domains identified as important to consumers and their families. Typically, such proposed models have not been empirically tested (Wilson and Cleary, 1995). The chief goal of existing studies has been that of describing and measuring QoL outcomes in clinical trials and programme evaluation. Relatively unstudied are the relationships between QoL and other outcome measures, and the correlations between separate domains in global QoL. In the short run, rather than limit domains by standard definitional inclusion or exclusion criteria, we might do well to view QoL as a causal network of interrelated domains that require further study so as to determine the entities that determine this multidimensional construct.

SELECTING AN INSTRUMENT FOR MENTAL HEALTH SETTINGS

To be useful, an instrument for measuring QoL in schizophrenia must be appropriate for the setting and reflect the aims of the researcher or practitioner using it. Any instrument designed for use in a (typically overburdened) mental health treatment setting must be fast to administer and easy to understand and score. Its questions must fit categories that both consumers and clinicians feel are important. Since clinical charts are often incomplete, disorganised or illegible, in order to minimise the clinician's time investment the instrument must seek a minimum of information from there or elsewhere. All information sought must be directly relevant to the clinical work. Consumers and staff will willingly complete an instrument only if the information is relevant and useful to both. Ideally, the information will also be directly useful to planning, implementation and evaluation of care as well.

Along with Feinstein (1992), we believe that in clinical practice the most important domains of QoL are those that the consumer wants to improve in the clinical setting. An appropriate instrument would also consider the unique characteristics of the illness and what problems might be encountered in data collection. Assessment can be complicated by problems associated with decreased attention span, cognition, energy and mood. Additionally, poor communication ability and reality testing may present obstacles to assessment, as can limited educational background.

The mental health field is witnessing an ongoing debate about the value of self-report and interview methods for measurement of QoL (Atkinson, Zibin and Chuang, 1997). Because of an untested assumption that persons with schizophrenia cannot reliably complete paper-and-pencil self-report questionnaires, most investigators have developed interview administered questionnaires, which are expensive. This practice has limited the use of QoL as a routine measure for use in clinical practice. There is, however, growing empirical support for using shorter, self-administered instruments. Self-report paper-and-pencil QoL instruments for mental health have passed internal consistency and test–retest reliability standards (Revicki and Maranda, 1994; Becker, 1995).

Data suggest that a brief, self-administered QoL measure can yield results consistent with in-depth interviews (Greenley and Greenberg, 1994). Furthermore, evidence from research with physically ill persons suggests that self-administered instruments might suffer less contamination from social desirability concerns, which are stronger in interviews. In some studies, self-administered questionnaires have shown a lower subjective QoL rating than interviews (Bremer and McCauley, 1986). Because people may be more honest about their feelings without the pressures of the face-to-face interview, self-administered assessments of QoL could be more valid than interview assessments. Finally, self-report data collection is cost-effective. Research shows that personal interviews cost 3 to 10 times as much as self-report paper-and-pencil approaches (Anderson, Bush and Berry, 1986).

NEW DIRECTIONS IN QUALITY OF LIFE MEASUREMENT

In the United States, there have been enormous changes in recent decades in the organisation financing and culture of the mental health delivery system and in the roles of its participants (Mechanic 1991, 1997; Fischer, Shumway and Owen, 2002; Ridgley et al., 2002). For example, the psychiatric professional's relationship has moved away from one characterised by paternalism to another in which consumers take an active role in their care and are more fully engaged in self-management of their illness (Eckman et al., 1992; Smith et al., 1997; Tauber, Wallace and Lecomte, 2000). Along with the development of consumer-run services and a shift towards their increasing autonomy and responsibility has come a rising demand for a more participatory approach to outcome measurement and psychiatric research. A confluence of forces, including changes in the focus of disability policy from dependence to independence, the growing strength of the consumer movement and emphasis on self-management, has raised professionals' awareness of the importance of participation of consumers and families in both health care and research. These events have sparked a demand for the incorporation of consumer preferences in health care decision making and the development of new, more consumer-centred approaches to QoL and other measurements of outcome. The Wisconsin Quality of Life Index W-QLI (Becker, Diamond and Sainfort, 1993) exemplifies this new approach to measurement.

Development of the W-QLI, initially called the Quality of Life Index for Mental Health (QLI-MH), began in 1991 when a state Medicaid agency approached Becker to help with a cost–benefit assessment for clozapine, a new and very expensive antipsychotic. The agency wanted to develop authorisation criteria and assess which individuals showed enough improvement with the drug to justify its continued use at the high cost. It quickly became apparent that there was no easy way to assess 'improvement' in a largely community-based sample of individuals throughout the state. A significant number of people did not seem improved, based on their change scores for the required Brief Psychiatric Rating Scale (BPRS), yet they were reported by treating clinicians as improved enough to warrant staying on clozapine, despite its high cost, risks and need for weekly blood tests. An outcome measure was required that would capture the complexity of 'improvement' from the perspectives of the consumer, clinician and later the family. It was also important to consider the complexity of change: one person may have significant improvement in one area, while someone else might improve very differently. A consensus developed that QoL, with all its complexity, was the best outcome for measuring meaningful change in persons with treatment-resistant schizophrenia.

Since the literature at that time did not reveal an instrument that would be easy to use, capture client values and preferences, and include provider, client and family perspectives, we undertook to develop a new instrument. Our approach was influenced by a desire for a practical measure that clinicians would willingly use, and that would encompass what both clinicians and consumers considered most important in their common-sense notion of 'improvement'. The final definition for QoL was influenced by many other definitions, including the work of Andrews and Withey (1976), Campbell, Converse and Rogers (1976) and Ferrans and Powers (1992). Along with Ferrans (1990), we defined QoL as 'a person's sense of well-being that stems from satisfaction or dissatisfaction with the areas of life that are important to him/her'. Since, according to this definition, QoL is determined by the patient's values and perceptions of what is important, it followed that the instrument would have to allow for individual preference weighting.

Decisions on scoring are an integral part of instrument development. For example, there is no obvious way to decide whether the domain of health status is more or less important than that of interpersonal relationships. Allowing multiple responders to rate the importance of different areas allows investigators to analyse whether the consumer, clinician and family agree on the relative importance of different areas of the consumer' s life. Developing the new instrument was complicated by the complexity of the construct and by the number of possible methods of aggregation and scoring of each domain. The most common scoring approach has been the multifaceted one, which provides a global score for QoL by aggregating across items and domains. However, this would lose important information about specific domains that: (a) decrease the clinical utility of the instrument and (b) limit information about causation, which operate on specific outcomes, not on aggregations of domains. Thus, in the W-QLI, we decided to score and analyse the different QoL domains separately, so that the outcome of each domain could be evaluated and the causal processes for both negative and positive outcomes could be studied.

While aggregated or single-score measures of QoL may be useful for economic decision making, they are not very helpful for clinical work. The objectives of improving clinical practice and QoL outcomes requires discrete knowledge of the impact of treatment on specific domains and of the processes which bring about that improvement. Domain-specific information allows clinicians and researchers to better understand the process by which individuals judge their overall QoL, and how different domains are perceived and valued. Such data help to discriminate between the long-term effects of competing therapies and can be used in making resource-allocation decisions and treatment planning.

The conceptual framework for the W-QLI included eight semi-independent domains: life satisfaction, occupational activities, psychological well-being, physical health, social relations, economics, activities of daily living and symptoms. Each is independently assessed by the consumer, the primary clinician and a family member (if available). Goal attainment is included as a ninth domain, with its own scoring strategy (see Fig. 10.1). The instrument represents a new approach to measurement, which is inclusive

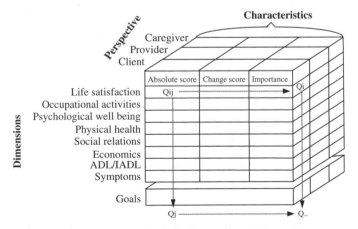

Q_{ij} = Evaluation of a particular dimension with respect to a particular characteristic.
Q_i = Evaluation of dimension across characteristics.
Q_j = Evaluation across dimensions.
$Q_{..}$ = Evaluation of quality of life as a whole (perceived QoL)

Figure 10.1   Wisconsin Quality of Life Index, a multidimensional conceptual model for evaluating quality of life

of both the consumer and the family. Although intended for people with schizophrenia, it can be used for other community-dwelling individuals with severe and prolonged mental disorders.

MULTIDIMENSIONALITY OF THE CONSTRUCT

In developing the Wisconsin Quality of Life Index, we conceptualised QoL as a complex, multidimensional construct that includes subjective or perceived (consumer-rated) as well as objective assessment of each domain. In this conceptual model, the greater the discrepancy between what is desired and what is achieved, the poorer the outcome. Thus, QoL is a reflection of how patients perceive and react to important aspects of their lives, including both their health status and important aspects of non-medical status. An individually preference-weighted measure is assumed to be more accurate in reflecting consumer values. If, as suggested by Diamond (1985) and others, consumers' subjective experiences influence the phases, course and outcome of schizophrenia, then it is particularly important that QoL measurements reflect their points of view (Strauss, 1989, Weiden, Dixon and Frances, 1991; Awad, 1993, 1994, 1995).

Since the W-QLI domains are all facets of a person's underlying QoL, moderate correlations were found between and among them. However, the observed correlations between domain scores were not strong enough to raise the possibility that the domains were not empirically distinct from one another. For example, in keeping with clinician descriptions, we found that activity of daily living (ADL) functioning was only weakly associated (0.33) with psychiatric symptoms. Our data show that patients with similar levels of ADL functioning can experience mild or severe psychiatric symptoms. Psychiatric symptoms and consumers' global ratings of their life quality were only modestly correlated, suggesting that perceived QoL is not well predicted by psychopathology. In our validation study of the W-QLI, the domain most strongly correlated with global QoL was social relations (0.58).

ISSUES OF SENSITIVITY

Although most QoL measures give equal weight to the separate domains assessed, it is unlikely that each domain would have the same significance to persons of different ages, genders and ethnicities. Despite concern expressed about the cultural sensitivity of QoL instruments, few have attempted to validate existing measures with diverse populations. Since subjective assessment of QoL is inherently based on one's values, attitudes and conceptual framework, it is very likely that significant differences in culture will affect the measurements. Despite the current emphasis on cultural sensitivity, consumer values, empowerment and choice in mental health, few of the commonly used instruments allow responders to evaluate separately the importance of different domains or to add information about their desired goals for improvement with treatment.

It is very likely that different cultural groups will weight the domains differently. Unfortunately, initial data from the W-QLI did not include enough culturally diverse subjects to analyse this issue, though preliminary data suggest that men and women with schizophrenia use different importance weightings. These observed gender differences are in the same direction as would be expected in the general population. For example, women rank interpersonal relationships as more important to their QoL than men, while men rank the importance of occupational activities higher than women (Becker, Diamond and Sainfort, 1994). As anticipated, we found differences between clinicians and consumers in their weighting of domains: clinicians placed more importance on symptoms, while consumers rated social relations as more important.

GOAL ATTAINMENT AS PART OF A QUALITY OF LIFE MEASUREMENT

If, as has been suggested by Ryff (1995), QoL is 'in the eyes of the beholder,' then measurement of it must be based on the individual's evaluation of the distance to the desired quality and on personal goals for improvement with treatment. Surprisingly, despite ample evidence about the importance of consumers' preferences and goals to QoL assessment, existing measures rarely ask about goals or the degree to which consumers believe these are being achieved. While one person may stress ability to work as a primary goal of treatment, another may stress the absence of medication side-effects or improved personal relationships. Goal attainment information can have many uses in psychiatry. Diamond (1985) and others have argued that attention to personal goals, along with the subjective effects of medication, can positively affect adherence to prescribed medication and thus influence treatment outcomes (Weiden, Dixon and Frances, 1991; Awad *et al.*, 1995; Awad and Voruganti, 1999). Attention to an individual's desired goals for improvement can also help in planning rehabilitation approaches and can inform decisions on vocational or residential placements (Anthony, Cohen and Marianne, 1990). The Wisconsin Index asks individuals to state their goals for improvement with treatment, as well as ranking the importance of the goals and the degree to which they feel they have achieved them. Documenting a person's important goals and unmet needs may help clinicians to improve their clinical practice by targeting interventions to the areas of greatest need. Information from the W-QLI goals domain can be used to create a matrix of client needs; it also allows consumers and staff to track progress towards goals that have been selected as most important.

A taxonomy of the goals for improvement with treatment, as proposed by clients, clinicians and families, was developed by Becker and Feinstein (1994) from the verbatim data provided by the W-QLI (Table 10.1). The outline of categories proposed by responders indicates that clients desire the very things that make up a good QoL. The dimensions of the taxonomy of responders' goals for improvement with treatment bear a striking resemblance to the conceptual model of QoL that was used to develop the W-QLI and to the dimensions identified by a factor analytical study of W-QLI data. The results of the factor analysis, based on data from 397 persons with schizophrenia, indicate that the underlying factor structure of the W-QLI is composed of three core constructs: (a) perceived life satisfaction (alpha = 0.83), (b) psychological symptoms/outlook (alpha = 0.80) and (c) social relations (alpha = 0.68) (Becker, Thorton and Banks, 2000). Both these findings and our experience with this measure argue that QoL for persons with schizophrenia is a multidimensional construct that can be measured quantitatively with a self-administered questionnaire. Most but not all persons can complete the paper-and-pencil form with a minimum of difficulty, though some require the help of a peer coach or professional interviewer and a few may be too ill to respond sensibly. These findings support the sensibility of a conceptual approach to QoL measurement that incorporates the individual's perspective instead of imposing a socially prescriptive definition. Preliminary data collected with the W-QLI

Table 10.1   Outline of categories: taxonomy of treatment goals for improvement of persons with schizophrenia proposed by clients, clinicians and families

1. *Control of disease*
   1.1 Manifestation of illness
   1.2 Therapy
   1.3 Side-effects of therapy
   1.4 Co-morbidity

2. *Personal status*
   2.1 Self-care
   2.2 Independence
   2.3 Sense of well-being

3. *Interpersonal status*
   3.1 Family relationships
   3.2 Non-family relationships
   3.3 Social functioning

4. *Care giver relief*
   4.1 Less dependence on parent
   4.2 Less dependence on spouse
   4.3 Less dependence on professional staff

5. *Miscellaneous treatment goals*
   5.1 Main hope for the future

indicate that both families and consumers more frequently stress the importance of goals related to desires for improved social relations and interpersonal functioning, while clinicians more frequently stress goals related to symptom reduction and compliance with treatment.

DIRECTIONS FOR FUTURE RESEARCH

Despite extensive investigation in medicine, we still know relatively little about the causal sequence of quality of life or the important interaction between objective and subjective factors in it. The situation is further complicated by empirical evidence showing that positive QoL evaluations represent different causal processes from negative evaluations (Heady and Wearing, 1989) and that subjective and objective evaluations do not necessarily coincide. For example, depending on the study, an individual's mood can account for up to 40% of the variance in QoL outcomes (Moum, 1988; Becker, Diamond and Sainfort, 1994). While it is clear that QoL is not independent of morbidity, the exact nature of the connection is unclear (Smith, Avis and Assmann, 1999). Since research has not examined the interaction of symptoms with occupational and functional outcomes in schizophrenia over time, we remain uncertain about the relative importance of these factors to the course and outcome of the disease. Although many of the studies dealing with chronic mental illness have focused on schizophrenia, they have mostly considered psychopathology and have been focused on positive and negative symptoms, rather than on functional or subjective outcomes (PogueGeile and Harrow, 1984; Lehman and Burns, 1990; Fenton and McGlashan, 1991). Thus, additional research is needed on the relationships between relevant domains, but until the necessary theoretical work is accomplished, definitional confusion is likely to remain.

Additional research is also needed to validate the applicability of the numerous measures to diverse social–cultural groups and across the developmental and chronological age span. Further, we need studies to understand the psychological reaction of patients to their illness and to examine QoL as several different causal sequences, rather than a single outcome. Comparative studies should determine which instruments or combination of instruments and measurement approaches are most useful, reliable and valid for measuring QoL in persons with schizophrenia.

To understand the complex dynamics of QoL in schizophrenia, the interrelationships of important factors such as coping style, mood, hopefulness and economic–employment status need further study. These factors have been shown to have an importance influence on QoL (Evans, 1981, 1991; Moum, 1988; Jenkins et al., 1990; Farran, Herth and Popovich, 1994). For example, one possible way of coping with schizophrenia is for people to reduce substantially their goals and expectations. However, while an avoidant style of coping may reduce negative QoL, it also reduces positive events and therefore may reduce life quality. We propose that future research should concentrate on investigating the causal sequence of QoL and important interactions between psychiatric morbidity and other quality factors. Future studies with the W-QLI will include investigations of the links and interactions between separate domains, goal attainment and the importance of culture, gender, economics and treatment setting to QoL outcomes in schizophrenia.

CONCLUSION

Results from the validation studies of instruments that document QoL measures can be sensitive to population differences and treatment effects (Malm, May and Dencher, 1981; Levitt, Hogan and Bocosky, 1990; Bigelow, McFarland and Olson, 1991; Lehman, Slaughter and Myers, 1991; Revicki et al., 1992; Lehman, 1996, 1997; Becker, Martin and Thornton, 2001). Hence, they can be used to evaluate the effect of drug therapy and to measure the cost /benefits of the mental health service (Hogan, Awad and Eastwood, 1983; Patrick, 1992; Revicki and Maranda, 1994). However, due to the variety of definitions and approaches used in existing research, interpreting and generalising from it is difficult.

It is premature to make recommendations about specific instruments or to generalise from initial results. Our challenge now is to develop consistent definitions, scoring and concepts. Use of a standardised approach and instruments would allow meta-analysis of divergent studies and so increase our understanding of QoL as a treatment outcome and causal sequence in schizophrenia. To ensure that instruments are measuring what is important, we need to develop a comprehensive and coherent theoretical model to inform the research methodology, to guide the construction of new instruments and clinical practices, and to improve the life quality of people who are being treated and living in the community. Finally, every effort must be made to incorporate consumers' and families' points of view in QoL assessment. Additionally, researchers need to create a forum to bring innovations in this research into the mainstream of professional dialogue.

REFERENCES

Anderson, J.P., Bush, J.W. & Berry, C.C. (1986). Classifying function for health outcome and quality-of-life evaluation: Self versus interview modes, *Med. Care*, **24**, 454–469.

Andrews, F. & Withey, S. (1976). *Social Indicators of Well Being: American Perceptions of Quality of Life*, Plenum Press, New York.

Anthony, W.A., Cohen, M.R. & Marianne, F.D. (1990). *Psychiatric Rehabilitation*, Boston University, Sargent College of Allied Health Professionals, Center for Psychiatric Rehabilitation, Boston, Massachusetts.

Anthony, W.A. & Farkas, M.A. (1982). A client outcome planning model for assessing psychiatric rehabilitation interventions, *Schizophrenia Bull.*, **8**(1), 13–38.

Anthony, W. & Rogers, S. (1995). Relationships between psychiatric symptomatology, *Psychiat. Serv.*, **46**(4), 353–358.

Atkinson, M., Zibin, S. & Chuang, H. (1997). Characterizing quality of life among patients with chronic mental illness: A critical examination of the self-report methodology, *Am. J. Psychiatry*, **154**, 99–105.

Avison, W.R. & Speechley, K.N. (1987). The discharged psychiatric patient: A review of social, social-psychological and psychiatric correlates of outcome, *Am. J. Psychiatry*, **144**, 10–18.

Awad, A.G. (1993). Subjective response to neuroleptics in schizophrenia, *Schizophrenia Bull.*, **19**, 609–618.

Awad, A.G. (1994). Prediction research of neuroleptics in schizophrenia: State of the art 1978–1993, in *Prediction of Neuroleptic Treatment Outcome in Schizophrenia: Concepts and Methods* (Eds W. Gabel & A.G. Awad), pp.1–4, Springer-Verlag, Heidelberg.

Awad, A.G. (1995). Quality of life issues in medicated schizophrenic patients, in *Contemporary Issues in the Treatment of Schizophrenia* (Eds C. Shirqui & H. Nasrallah), pp. 833–846, American Psychiatric Association Press, Washington, DC.

Awad, A.G. & Voruganti, L.N. (1999). Quality of life and new antipsychotics in schizophrenia: Are patients better off?, *Int. J. Social Psychiatry*, **45**, 268–274.

Awad, A.G., Hogan, T.P., Vorganti, L.N.P. & Heslegrave, R.J. (1995). Patients' subjective experiences on antipsychotic medications: Implications for outcome and quality of life, *Int. Clin. Psychopharmacol.*, Suppl. 3, 123–132.

Bachrach, L.L. (1982). Assessment of outcomes in community support systems: Results, problems and limitations, *Schizophrenia Bull.*, **8**, 39–61.

Bachrach, L.L. (1987). The homeless mentally ill, in *The Chronic Mental Patient/II*, pp. 65–92, American Psychiatric Association Press, Washington, DC.

Baker, F. & Intagliata, J. (1982). Quality of life in the evaluation of community support system, *Evaluation and Prog. Plann.*, **7**(5), 69–79.

Baker, G.A. (1995). Health-related quality-of-life issues: Optimizing patient outcomes, *Neurology*, **45**(Suppl. 2), S29-S34

Bassuk, E.L. & Lamb, H.R. (1986). Homelessness and the implementation of deinstitutionalization. The mental health needs of homeless persons, *New Directions for Mental Health*, pp. 7–14, No. 30, Jossey-Bass, San Francisco, California.

Becker, M. (1995). Quality-of-life instruments for severe chronic mental illness: Implications for pharmacotherapy, *PharmacoEconomics*, **7**(3), 229–237.

Becker, M. (1998). A U.S. experience: Consumer responsive quality of life measurement, *Can. J. of Mental Health*, **1**(1, Suppl. 3), 41–52.

Becker, M.A. (2003). The mentally ill chemical abuser, *Advance for Nurses*, **4**(14), 13–17.

Becker, M. & Diamond, R. (2000). Wisconsin Quality of Life Index (W-QLI), in *Handbook of Psychiatric Measures* (Eds A.J. Rush *et al*), pp. 141–142, American Psychiatric Association Press, Washington, DC.

Becker, M., Diamond, R. & Sainfort, F. (1993). A new client centered index for measuring quality of life in persons with severe and persistent mental illness, *Quality of Life Res.*, **2**, 239–251.

Becker M., Diamond R. & Sainfort F. (1994). Factors affecting quality of life among people with severe and persistent mental illness, Paper Series 33, Mental Health Research Center, Madison, Wisconsin.

Becker, M. & Feinstein, A.R. (1994). Consumer values and quality of life evaluations, Paper presented at Faculty Residents and Staff Research Division Seminar, University of Wisconsin Medical School, Madison, Wisconsin.

Becker, M., Martin, L. & Thornton, D. (2001) Assessment of quality of life in women receiving outpatient mental health services, Paper presented at the Annual Meeting of the International Society for Quality of Life Studies, Washington, DC, December 2001.

Becker, M., Thorton, D. & Banks, S. (2000). Quality of life in mental health: How many factors are there?, Paper presented at the Annual Meeting of the International Society for Quality of Life Research, Vancouver, Canada.

Bergner, M. (1985). Measurement of health status, *Med. Care*, **23**, 696–704.

Bergner, M. (1989). Quality of care, health status, and clinical research, *Med. Care*, **27**(Suppl.), S148-S156.

Bermanzohn, P.C., Porto, L. & Siris, S.G. (2000). Hierarchical diagnosis in chronic schizophrenia: A clinical study of co-occurring syndromes, *Schizophrenia Bull.*, **26**, 519–527.

Bermanzohn, P.C., Porto, L., Siris, S., Stronger, R., Hwang, M.Y. & Pollack, S. (2001). Hierarchy, reductionism, and 'comorbidity' in the diagnosis of schizophrenia, in *Schizophrenia and Comorbid Conditions, Diagnosis and Treatment* (Eds M.Y. Hwang & P.C. Bermanzohn), pp. 1–29, American Psychiatric Association Press, Washington DC.

Berzon, R.A., Simeon, G.P., Simpson Jr, R.L., Donnelly, M.A. & Tilson, H.H. (1995). Quality of life bibliography and indexes: 1993 update, *Quality of Life Res.*, **1**, 53–73.

Bigelow, D.A., McFarland, B.H. & Olson, M.M. (1991). Quality of life of community mental health program clients: Validating a measure, *Community Ment. Health J.*, **27**(1), 34–55.

Bremer, B.A. & McCauley, C.R. (1986). Quality-of-life measures: Hospital interview versus home questionnaire, *Health Psychol.*, **5**, 171–177.

Campbell, A., Converse, P.E. & Rogers, W.L. (1976). *The Quality of American Life*, Russell Sage Foundation, New York.

Carpenter, W.T. & Strauss, J.S. (l991). The prediction of outcome in schizophrenia: Eleven year followup of the Washington IPSS Cohort, *J. Nerv. Ment. Dis.*, **179**, 517–525.

Cheung, C.K. (1997) Toward a theoretically based measurement model of the good life, *J. Genet. Psychol.*, **158**(2), 2200–2215.

Ciompi, I. (1980). Catamnestic long term study on the course of life and aging of schizophrenics, *Schizophrenia Bull.*, **6**, 606–618.

Collins, E.J., Hogan, T.P. & Himansu, D. (1991). Measurement of therapeutic response in schizophrenia: A critical survey, *Schizophrenia Res.*, **5**, 249–253.

Cramer, J.A., Rosenheck, R., Xu, W., Henderson, W., Thomas, J. & Charney, D. (2000). For the Dept. of Veterans Affairs Cooperative Study on Clozapine in Refractory Schizophrenia: Detecting improvement in symptomatology and quality of life in schizophrenia, *Schizophrenia Bull.*, **26**, 659–666.

Cramer, J., Rosenheck, R., Xu, W., Henderson, W., Thomas, J. & Charney, D. (2001). Detecting improvement in quality of life and symptomatology in schizophrenia, *Schizophrenia Bull.*, **17**(2), 227–234.

Delespaul, P. (1995). Assessing 'quality of life' in schizophrenia, in *Assessing Schizophrenia in Daily Life: The Experience Sampling Method*, Universitaire Pers Maastricht.

Deyo, R.A. (1991). The quality of life, research and care, *Ann. Internal Med.*, **114**, 695–696.

Diamond, R. (1985). Drugs and the quality of life: The patient's point of view, *J. Clin. Psychiatry*, **46**, 29–35.

Diamond, R. & Becker, M. (1999). The Wisconsin Quality of Life Index: A multidimensional model for measuring quality of life, *J. Clin. Psychiatry*, Suppl. 3, 29–31.

Diener, E. (1996). Traits can be powerful, but are not enough. Lessons from subjective well-being, *J. Res. on Personality*, **30**, 388–399

Diener, E., Suh, E.M., Lucas, R.E. & Smith, H.L. (1999). Subjective well-being. Three decades of progress, *Psycholog. Bull.*, **125**(2), 276–302.

Drake, R.E., Wallach, M. A. & Hoffman, J.S. (1989). Housing instability and homelessness among aftercare patients of an urban state hospital, *Hosp. Community Psychiatry*, **33**, 225–227.

Eckman, T.A.,Wirshing, W.C., Marder, S.R., *et al* (1992). Technique for training schizophrenic patients in illness self-management: A controlled trial, *Am. J. Psychiatry*, **149**, 1549–1555.

Edwards, T.C., Patrick, D.L. & Topolski, T.D. (2003). Quality of life of adolescents with perceived disabilities, *J. Pediat. Psychol.*, **28**(4), 233–241.

Ellwood, P.M. (1988). Outcomes management: A technology of patient experience, *New Engl. J. Med.*, **318**, 1549–1552.

Evans, R. (1981). The relationship of two measures of perceived control to depression, *J. Personality Assessment*, **45**, 66–70.

Evans, R.W. (1991). Quality of life, *Lancet*, **319**(7614), 338–363.

Farran, C.J., Herth, K.A. & Popovich, J.M. (1994). Hope and hopelessness, in *Critical Clinical Constructs*, Sage Publications, Newbury Park, California.

Feinstein, A.R. (1992). Benefits and obstacles for development of health status assessment measures in clinical settings, *Med. Care*, **30**(5), MS50-MS56.

Fenton, W.S. & McGlashan, T.H. (1991). Natural history of schizophrenia subtypes: Positive and negative symptoms and long-term course, *Arch. Gen. Psychiatry*, **48**, 978–986.

Ferrans, C.E. (1990). Quality of life: Conceptual issues, *Semin. Oncol. Nurs.*, **6**, 248–254.

Ferrans, C.E. & Powers, M.J. (1992). Psychometric assessment of the quality of life index, *Res. Nurs. Health*, **15**, 29–38.

Fische, E.P., Shumway, M. & Owen, R.R. (2002). Priorities of consumers, providers, and family members in the treatment of schizophrenia, *Psychiat. Serv.*, **53**(6), 724–729.

Fitzpatrick, R., Davey, C., Buston, M. & Jones, D.R. (2001). Criteria for assessing patient based outcome measures for use in clinical trials, in *The Advanced Handbook of Methods in Evidence Based Healthcare* (Eds A. Stevens, K. Abrams, J. Brazier, R. Fitzpatraick & R. Lilford), pp. 181–194, Sage, London.

Garratt, A., Schmidt, L., Mackintosh, A. & Fitzpatrick, R. (2002). Quality of life measurement: Bibliographic study of patient assessed health outcome measures, *Br. Med. J.*, **324**, 1–5.

Geigle, R. & Jones, S.B. (1990). Outcomes measurement: A report from the front, *Inquiry*, **27**, 7–13.

Gill, T. & Feinstein, A.R. (1994). A critical appraisal of the quality of quality-of-life measurements, *J. Am. Med. Ass.*, **272**(8), 619–626.

Greenley, J.R. & Greenberg, J. (1994). Measuring quality of life: A new and practical survey instrument, Paper Series 38, Mental Health Research Center, Madison, Wisconsin.

Guyatt, G.H., Veldhuyzen Van Zanten, S.J., Feeny, D.H. & Patrick, D.L. (1989). Measuring quality of life in clinical trails; A taxonomy and review, *Can. Med. Ass. J.*, **140**, 1441–1448.

Hadorn, D.C. (1993). Outcomes management and resource allocation: How should quality of life be measured?, Health Policy Research Unit Discussion Paper HPRU93, Vol. 7D, pp. 1–56.

Harding, C.M., Zubin, J. & Strauss, J.S. (1987). Chronicity in schizophrenia: Fact, partial fact, or artifact?, *Hosp. Community Psychiatry*, **18**(5), 480–484.

Harvey, P.D. (2005). *Schizophrenia in Late Life*, United Booj Press, Baltimore, Maryland.

Heady, B., Veenhoven, R. & Wearing, A. (1991). Top-down versus bottom-up theories of subjective well-being, *Social Indicators Res.*, **24**, 81–100.

Heady, B. & Wearing, A. (1989). Personality, life events, and subjective well-being: Toward a dynamic equilibrium model, *J. Personal Social Psychol.*, **57**, 731–739.

Hegarty, J.D., Baldessarini, R.J., Tohen, M., Waternaux, C. & Oepen, G. (1994). One hundred years of schizophrenia: A meta-analysis of the outcome literature, *Am. J. Psychiatry*, **151**, 1409–1416.

Heinrichs, D.W., Hanlon, T.E. & Carpenter, W.T. (1984). The quality of life scale: An instrument for rating the schizophrenic deficit syndrome, *Schizophrenia Bull.*, **10**, 388–398.

Hogan, T.P., Awad, A.G. & Eastwood, M.R. (1983). A self-report scale predictive of drug compliance in schizophrenics: Reliability and discriminative validity, *Psycholo. Med.*, **13**, 177–183.

Jenkins, C.D., Jono, R.T., Stanton, B.A. & Stroup-Benham, C.A. (1990). The measurements of health-related quality of life: Major dimensions identified by factor analysis, *Social Sci. Med.*, **31**, 25–33.

Juniper, E.F., Guyatt, G.H., Wiland, A. & Griffith, L.E. (1994) Determining a minimal important change in a disease-specific quality of life questionnaire, *J. Epidemol.*, **47**(1), 81–87.

Kuck, J., Zisook, S., Moranville, J.T., *et al* (1992). Negative symptomatology in schizophrenic outpatients, *J. Nerv. Ment. Dis.*, **180**, 510–515.

Lamb, H. (1979). The new asylums in the community, *Arch. Gen. Psvchiatry*, **36**, 129–134.

Lamb, H. R. (1981). What did we really expect from deinstitutionalization?, *Hosp. Community Psychol.*, **32**, 105–109.

Leff, J. (1997). Whose life is it anyway? Quality of life for long-stay patients discharged from psychiatric hospitals, in *Quality of Life in Mental Disorders*, (Eds H. Katschnig, H. Freeman & N. Sartorius), pp. 241–252, John Wiley & Sons, New York.

Leff, J., Sartorius, N., Jablensky, A., Korten, A. & Ernberg, G. (1992). The international pilot study of schizophrenia: Five-year follow-up findings, *Psycholog. Med.*, **22**, 131–145.

Lefley, H.P. (1990). Culture and chronic mental illness, *Hosp. Community Psychiatry*, **41**, 277–286.

Lefley, H.P. (1996). *Family Caregiving in Mental Illness*, Sage, Thousand Oaks, California.

Lehman, A.F. (1992). The effects of psychiatric symptoms on quality of life, *J. Health and Social Behaviour*, **33**, 299–315.

Lehman, A.F. (1995). Promises and problems in assessing quality of life in clinical trials, *Neuropsychopharmacy*, **10**(35), 23–95.

Lehman, A.F. (1996). Measures of quality of life among persons with severe and persistent mental disorders, *Social Psychiatry Psychiat. Epidemiol.*, **31**, 78–88.

Lehman A.F. (1997). Instruments for measuring quality of life in mental disorders, in *Quality of Life in Mental Disorders*, (Eds H. Katschnig, H. Freeman, S.N. Sartorius), John Wiley & Sons, Chichester.

Lehman, A.F. & Burns, B.J. (1990). Severe mental illness in the community, in *Quality of Life Assessments in Clinical Trials*, pp. 357–366, Raven Press, New York.

Lehman, A.F., Possidente, S. & Hawker, F. (1986). The quality of life of chronic mental patients in a state hospital and community residents, *Hosp. Community Psychiatry*, **37**, 901–907.

Lehman, A.F., Slaughter, J.G. & Myers, C.P. (1991). Quality of life in alternative residential settings, *Psychiat. Q.*, **62**, 35–49.

Levine, S. (1987). The changing terrains in medical sociology: Emergent concerns with quality of life, *J. Health and Social Behaviour*, **28**, 1–6.

Levitt, A.J., Hogan, T.P. & Bocosky, C.M. (1990). Quality of life in chronically mentally ill patients in day treatment, *Psycholog. Med.*, **20**, 703–710.

Llewellyn-Thomas, H., Sutherland, H.J. & Tibshirani, R. (1982). The measurement of patients values in medicine, *Med. Decision Making*, **2**(4), 449.

McCabe, S. & Unzicker, R. (1995). Changing roles of consumer/survivors in mature mental health systems, *New Directions in Ment. Health Serv.*, **66**, 61–73.

McGrew, J.H., Wilson, R.G. & Bond, G.R. (2002). An exploratory study of what clients like least about assertive community treatment, *Psychiat. Serv.*, **53**(6), 761–763.

McHorney, C.A. (1997). Generic health measurement: Past accomplishments and a measurement paradigm for the 21st century, *Ann. Internal Med.*, **127**(8), 743–750.

Malm, U., May, P.B.R. & Dencher, S. L. (1981). Evaluation of the quality of life of the chronic schizophrenic outpatient: A checklist, *Schizophrenia Bull.*, **7**(3), 477–487.

Mechanic, D. (1986). The challenge of chronic mental illness: A retrospective and prospective view, *Hosp. Community Psychiatry*, **37**, 891–896.

Mechanic, D. (1991). Strategies for integrating public mental health services, *Hosp. Community Psychiatry*, **42**, 797–801.

Mechanic, D. (1997). Organisation of care and quality of life of persons with serious and persistent mental illness, in *Quality of Life in Mental Disorders*, (Eds H. Katschnig, H. Freeman & N. Sartorius) pp. 305–317, John Wiley & Sons, New York.

Mechanic, D., McAlpine, D., McAlpine, D., Rosenfield, S. & Davis, D. (1994). Effects of illness attribution and depression on the quality of life among persons with serious mental illness, *Social Sci. Med.*, **39**, 155–164.

Meltzer, H.Y., Burnett, S., Bastani, B. & Ramerez, L. F. (1990). Effects of six months of clozapine treatment on the quality of life of chronic schizophrenic patients, *Hosp. Community Psychiatry*, **41**, 892–897.

Mike, V. (1992). Quality of life research and the ethics of evidence, *Quality of Life Res.*, **1**, 273–276.

Milner, K.K. & Valenstein, M. (2002). A comparison of guidelines for the treatment of schizophrenia, *Psychiat. Serv.*, **53**(7), 888–890.

Moos, R., Nichol, A.C. & Moos, B.S. (2002). Global assessment of functioning ratings and the allocation and outcomes of mental health services, *Psychiat. Serv.*, **53**(6), 730–737.

Mor, V. & Guadogoli, E. (1988). Quality of life measurement: A psychometric Tower of Babel, *J. Clin. Epidemiol.*, **41**, 1055–1058.

Moum, T. (1988). Yea-saying and mood-reporting quality of life, *Social Indicators Res.*, **20**, 117–139.

Musser, K.T., Becker, D.T., Torrey, E.F. *et al* (1997). Work and nonvocational domains of functioning in persons with severe mental illness: A longitudinal analysis, *J. Nerv. Ment. Dis.*, **185**, 419–426.

Patrick, D.L. (1992). Health-related quality of life in pharmaceutical evaluation: Forging progress and avoiding pitfalls, *PharmacoEconomics*, **1**(2), 76–78.

Patrick, D.L. & Erickson, P. (1993). *Health Status and Health Policy: Quality of Life in Health Care Evaluation and Resource Allocation*, Oxford University Press, New York.

Pavot, W. & Deiner, E. (1993). The affective and cognitive context of self-reported measures of subjective well-being, *Social Indicators Res.*, **28**, 1–20.

Pickney, A.A., Gerber, G.J. & Lafave, H.G. (1991). Quality of life after psychiatric rehabilitation: The client's perspective, *Acta Psychiatrica Scand.*, **83**, 86–91.

Pogue-Geile, M.F. & Harrow, M. (1984). Negative and positive symptoms in schizophrenia and depression: A followup, *Schizophrenia Bull.*, **10**, 371–376.

Revicki, D.A. & Maranda, M. (1994). Assessing health-related quality of life outcomes of drug treatments for psychiatric disorders, *CNS Drugs*, **1**(6), 465–476.

Revicki, D.A., Turner, R., Brown, R. & Martindale, A. (1992). Reliability and validity of health related quality of life battery for evaluating outpatient antidepressant treatment, *Quality of Life Res.*, **1**, 257–266.

Ridgley, S.M., Mulkern, V.M., Giard, J. & Shern, D. (2002). Critical elements of public-sector managed behavioral health programs for severe mental illness in five states, *Psychiat. Serv.*, **53**(4), 397–399.

Rosen, M., Simon, E. & McKinsey, L. (1995). Subjective measure of quality of life, *Ment. Retardation*, **33**, 31–34.

Rosenfield, S. (1992). Factors contributing to the subjective quality of life of the chronic mentally ill, *J. Health and Social Behaviour*, **33**, 299–315.

Rosenfield, S. & Neese-Todd, S. (1995). Elements of a psychosocial clubhouse programme associated with a satisfactory quality of life, *Hosp. Community Psychiatry*, **44**, 76–78.

Rosenheck, R., Bassuk, E. & Salomon, A. (1999). Social populations of homeless Americans, in *Practical Lessons. The 1998 National Symposium on Homeless Research* (Eds L.B. Fosberg & D.L. Dennis), On-line: http//aspe.os.dhhs.gov/progsys/homeless/symposium/Toc.htm.

Rossi, H. & Wright, J.D. (1987). The determinants of homelessness, *Health Affairs*, **6**, 19–32.

Ryff, C.D. (1995). Psychological well-being in adult life, *Current Directions in Psycholog. Sci.*, **4**, 99–104.

Ryff, C.D. & Keyes, C.L.M. (1995). The structure of psychological well-being revisited, *J. Personality Social Psychol.*, **69**, 719–727.

Sainfort, F., Becker, M. & Diamond, R. (1996). Judgements of quality of life of individuals with severe mental disorders: Client self-report versus provider perspectives, *Am. J. Psychiatry*, **153**(4), 497–502.

Schalock, R.L., Keith, K.D., Hoffman, K. & Karan, U.D. (1989). Quality of life: Its measurement and use, *Ment. Retardation*, **27**, 25–31.

Schmidt, L., Reinhardt, A., Kane, R. & Olsen, M. (1977). The mentally ill in nursing homes: New backwards in the community, *Arch. Gen. Psychiatry*, **34**, 687–691.

Shadish, W. & Bootzin, R. (1981). Nursing homes and chronic mental patients, *Schizophrenia Bull.*, **7**, 488–498.

Siris, S.G. (2000). Depression in schizophrenia: Perspective in the era of 'atypical' antipsychotic agents, *Am. J. Psychiatry*, **157**, 1379–1389.

Siris, S.G., Bermanzohn, P.C. & Kessler, R.J. (1997). Drug treatment of schizophrenia with comorbidity, in *Treatment Strategies for Patients With Psychiatric Comorbidity* (Eds S. Swetzler & W.C. Sanderson), pp. 219–252, John Wiley & Sons, New York.

Smith, K., Avis, N. & Assmann, S. (1999). Distinguishing between quality of life and health status in quality of life research: A meta-analysis, *Quality of Life Res. An Int. J. Quality of Life Aspects of Treatment, Care and Rehabil.*, **8**(5), 447–459.

Smith, T.E, Hull, J.W., Anthony, D.T., *et al.*, (1997). Post-hospitalization treatment adherence of schizophrenic patients, *Psychiatry Res.*, **69**, 123–129.

Solomon, P. (1992). The closing of a state hospital: What is the quality of patient's lives one year post release?, *Psychiatry Q.*, **63**, 279–296.

Soni, S.D., Mallik, A., Reed, P., *et al* (1992). Differences between chronic schizophrenic patients in the hospital and in the community, *Hosp. Community Psychiatry*, **43**, 1233–1238.

Spilker, B. (1990). *Quality of Life Assessments in Clinical Trials*, Raven Press, New York.

Spilker, B. (1992). Standardization of quality of life trials: An industry perspective, *PharmacoEconomics*, **1**(2), 73–75.

Stein, L.I., Diamond, R.J. & Factor, R.M. (1990). A system approach to the care of persons with schizophrenia, in *Handbook of Schizophrenia: Psychosocial Therapies* (Eds M.I. Herz, S.J. Keith & J.P. Docherty), Vol. 5, pp. 213–246, Elsevier Science, Amsterdam, The Netherlands.

Stein, L.I. & Santos, A.B. (1998). *Assertive Community Treatment of Persons with Severe Mental Illness*, W.W. Norton & Company Inc., New York.

Stein, L.I. & Test, M.A. (1985). *The Training in Community Living Model: A Decade of Experience*, Josey Bass, San Francisco, California.

Stein, L.I. & Test, M.A. (1987). Training in community living: Research design and results, in *Alternatives to Mental Hospital Treatment* (Eds L.I. Stein & M.A. Test), pp. 57–74, Plenum Press, New York.

Strauss, J. S. (1989). Subjective experiences of schizophrenia: Toward a new dynamic psychiatry – II, *Schizophrenia Bull.*, **15**, 179–187.

Strauss, J. S. (1994). Is biological psychiatry building on an adequate base? Clinical realities and underlying processes in schizophrenic disorders, in *Schizophrenia: From Mind to Molecule* (Ed. N.C. Andreasen), pp. 31–44, American Psychiatric Association Press, Washington, DC.

Struening, E.L., Perlick, D., Link, B., Hellman, F., Herman, D. & Stirey, J. (2001). The extent to which caregivers believe most people devalue consumers and their familes, *Psychiat. Serv.*, **52**(12), 1633–1638.

Sullivan, G., Wells, K.B. & Leake, B. (1991). Quality of life of seriously mentally ill persons in Mississippi, *Hosp. Community Psychiatry*, **4**, 752–755.

Tauber, R., Wallace, C.J. & Lecomte, T. (2000). Enlisting indigenous community supporters in skills training programs for persons with severe mental illness, *Psychiat. Serv.*, **51**, 1428–1432.

Thepa, K. & Rowland, L. (1995). Quality of life perspectives in long-term care: Staff and patient perceptions, *Acta Psychiatrica Scand.*, **80**, 267–271.

Uehara, E.A. (1994). Race, gender and housing inequality; An exploration of the correlates of low-quality housing among clients diagnosed with severe and persistent mental illness, *J. Health and Social Behaviour*, **35**, 309–321.

Van Dam, F.S.A.M., Somers, R. & Van Beek-Couzijn, A.L. (1981). Quality of life: Some theoretical issues, *J. Clin. Pharmacol.*, **21**, 166–168.

Warner, R. (1985). *Recovery from Schizophrenia Psychiatry and Political Economy*, Routledge and Kegan Paul, London, New York.

Weiden, P. J., Dixon & Frances (1991). Neuroleptic non-compliance in schizophrenia, in *Advances in Neuropsychiatry and Psychopharmacology* (Eds C. Tammings & S.C. Schulz), pp. 285–295, Vol. 1. Raven Press, New York.

Wilson, I.B. & Cleary, P.D. (1995). Linking clinical variables with health-related quality of life: A conceptual model of patient outcomes, *J. Am. Med. Ass.*, **273**, 59–65.

Section IV
QUALITY OF LIFE IN SPECIFIC MENTAL DISORDERS

11

Quality of Life in Depression

Heinz Katschnig, Monika Krautgartner, Beate
Schrank and Matthias C. Angermeyer

INTRODUCTION

Suppose that you have experienced a depressed mood most of the day for the last two weeks, have markedly diminished interest or pleasure in all or almost all activities, feel worthless and tired all the time, and have recurrent thoughts of death (i.e. you suffer from major depression according to DSM-IV). How would you evaluate your quality of life (QoL)? This would, of course, depend on how QoL is defined. If it is equated with subjective well-being, happiness and life satisfaction – as is the case in most QoL studies in medicine, using subjective measures – you would certainly judge your QoL as reduced. If a judgement about satisfaction with various life domains is added, it would most probably reflect the typically bleak way in which depressed persons look at themselves, the world and the future (Beck, 1976).

As defined by operational criteria, depression is a highly prevalent disorder in the general population. At least one in six Americans suffers from a major depressive episode at some stage of their lives (Kessler *et al.*, 2005). Comorbidity with other psychiatric disorders, especially substance abuse and anxiety disorders, is high (Weissman, Bland and Canino, 1996). Depression is also highly prevalent among medical patients, especially in those suffering from chronic conditions (Friedmann and Booth-Kewley, 1987; Katon *et al.*, 1990; von Korff *et al.*, 1992) – a fact that is seemingly not yet well understood in QoL research on somatic disorders (Jacobson, de Groot and Samson, 1997, see below).

A number of overviews have been published in recent years on QoL in unipolar, bipolar and seasonal depression (Namjoshi and Buesching, 2001; Papakostas *et al.*, 2003; Ritsner and Kurs, 2003; Dean, Gerner and Gerner, 2004; Michalak *et al.*, 2004). Usually, the reduction of QoL is quite significant, especially if compared to that of patients suffering from somatic disorders. Little attention has been given, however, to the problems of measuring QoL, which are especially large when assessing depression. The present article deals mainly with these issues.

Today's QoL research in medicine is heavily influenced by both long-lasting neglect of the patient's subjective experience of the disease and by consumer dissatisfaction with medical services (Albrecht and Fitzpatrick, 1994). The rising awareness of this neglect has, over recent decades, led to two developments. Firstly, well-being scales were applied in medicine. Examples are the Affect Balance Scale (ABS) by Bradburn (1969), the Quality of Well-Being Scale (QWBS) by Kaplan, Bush and Berry (1976) and the Psychological General Well-Being (PGWB) Index by DuPuy (1984). Secondly, disease-specific instruments for measuring QoL in somatically ill patients, which focus on the subjective view of the patient, were developed.

Quality of Life in Mental Disorders, Second Edition   Edited by H. Katschnig, H. Freeman and N. Sartorius
© 2006 John Wiley & Sons, Ltd

Of the literally hundreds of QoL instruments developed in this period, virtually all put the emphasis on psychological well-being and subjective life satisfaction. Certainly, with a more and more technically determined medicine, assessing 'quality of life' in terms of psychological well-being and satisfaction provides the basis for a more humanistic and holistic approach to the somatically ill patient. Today, it seems to be generally agreed that health-related QoL (HRQL) refers to the ways in which health, illness and medical treatment influence an individual's perception of functioning and well-being (Jacobson, de Groot and Samson, 1997).

In consequence, most QoL instruments used today in medicine: (a) measure subjective well-being, (b) elicit the patient's subjective satisfaction with various aspects of life and (c) are self-rating instruments. However, it will be argued below that relying on this 'subjectivity' approach in assessing QoL in depression is tautological. This is because of the overlap of the concepts of 'well-being' and 'satisfaction' with depression, because of the negative influence of depressed mood on the perception of oneself and the environment, and because of the overlap of items between QoL instruments and psychopathological depression rating scales. The following section of this chapter will discuss these problems, before we go on to advocate a broader and multidimensional concept of QoL that includes social functioning and environmental living conditions.

DEPRESSION AND PSYCHOLOGICAL WELL-BEING: THE INDIVIDUAL'S PERSPECTIVE

In their frequently quoted paper, 'The functioning and well-being of depressed patients: Results from the medical outcomes study', Wells *et al.* (1989) reported that a group of 2476 depressed patients (defined by a specific cut-off score on an eight-item depression symptom scale) scored below patients with chronic medical conditions on a well-being measure, defined as 'perception of current health, such as feeling well or ill' and measured by five items. They used an earlier version of the now well-known SF-36 (Ware and Sherbourne, 1992). Pyne *et al.* (1997) applied the Quality of Well-Being Scale (QWBS) by Kaplan, Bush and Berry (1976) to assess the QoL of patients with major depression. The quality of well-being index includes four subscales: symptom or problem complex, mobility, physical activity and social activity, but produces a single figure between 0 ('death') and 1 ('asymptomatic optimal functioning'). Measured with this index, the reduction in QoL associated with psychiatric symptoms of depression was found comparable to that observed among physically ill patients – a finding which is similar to that reported by Wells *et al.* (1989).

Both studies use the term 'well-being' and report that this is reduced in depressed persons, but it is doubtful whether they measured the same phenomenon. What does 'well-being' mean? The literature on the meaning and measurement of psychological well-being – especially on the numbers and kinds of its subdimensions – is controversial. For instance, Ryff (1995) argues that 'well-being' should be assessed on the following six theory-derived dimensions: personal growth and purpose in life, environmental mastery and autonomy, positive relations with others and self-acceptance. She criticises the way in which the issue is often simplified so that it just distinguishes two dimensions: happiness (the affective component of well-being) and satisfaction (the cognitive component); she also says that the theoretical foundation of this distinction is weak (see also Zissi and Barry, Chapter 3 in this volume).

The discussion whether positive affect ('joy', 'happiness') and negative affect ('joylessness', 'unhappiness') should be regarded as independent dimensions, or just as opposite ends of one single dimension, is complex (see Ryff and Keyes, 1995; Bech, 1996). While it is justifiably argued by psychologists that 'to be well psychologically is more than to be free of distress or other mental problems' (Ryff, 1995), i.e. that a person who is free of distress may or may not experience positive well-being in several domains, it is quite evident that depression excludes the experience of positive well-being. If joy and happiness are a component of psychological well-being, then 'joylessness' in a depressive state necessarily means that well-being is reduced. The old term 'anhedonia' captures this characteristic feature of depression in a telling way.

Given this relationship, it is only logical that depression items, as representing negative affect, were included in virtually all of the several hundred published QoL instruments. Examples are the QLQ-C30 (Aaronson *et al.*, 1993) developed by the EORTC (European Organization for Research and Treatment of Cancer), the EUROQOL (EuroQoL Group, 1990) and the FACT (Functional Assessment of Cancer Therapy) developed by Cella *et al.* (1993). In many QoL studies on somatic disorders, explicit psycho-pathological rating scales, such as the Hospital Anxiety and Depression Scale (HADS) (Zigmond and Snaith, 1983), are explicitly used as measures for 'quality of life' (e.g. Hopwood *et al.*, 1994).

Following the general trend of developing disease-specific QoL instruments, depression-specific QoL inventories were developed, e.g. the Quality of Life in Depression Scale (QLDS) by McKenna and Hunt (1992) and the SmithKline Beecham Quality of Life (SBQOL) scale by Stoker, Dunbar and Beaumont (1992). Both were primarily constructed for measuring change in clinical trials of antidepressants and are self-rating instruments. A closer look at the items of these inventories suggests that the resulting measure for QoL should be closely correlated with the severity of depression, since many items correspond to depression items in the usual rating scales for depression (e.g. I have lost all pleasure in life; it is difficult for me to make even simple decisions; I feel useless; I do not enjoy life). A study by Katschnig *et al.* (1996) confirmed this assumption. In 100 depressed and anxious patients, the total score of the Beck Depression Inventory (BDI), a self-rating instrument for assessing the severity of depression (Beck *et al.*, 1961), correlated significantly both with the total scores of the QLDS (0.69) and with that of the SBQOL scale (0.70).

In addition to affective psychological well-being, subjective satisfaction with various life domains is often assessed separately in health-related QoL research. The Quality of Life Enjoyment and Satisfaction Questionnaire (Q-LES-Q) by Endicott *et al.* (1993) already captures this distinction in its title. However, how independent are such satisfaction judgements from a state of depression? Cognitive theories of depression suggest that they are not (Beck, 1976). Similar evidence comes from psychological research, which indicates that people use their momentary affective state as information in making judgements of how happy and satisfied they are with their lives (Schwarz and Clore, 1983). In order to check whether this assumption is correct in a clinically depressed population, we also used the Q-LES-Q in the above-mentioned sample (Katschnig *et al.*, 1996). We not only found a high correlation between the BDI score and the 'enjoyment dimension' of this questionnaire (0.62), but also with the aggregate satisfaction rating (0.62).

Koivumaa-Honkanen *et al.* (1996) showed that the BDI depression score explained 48% of the variance in subjective life satisfaction among psychiatric patients. Pukrop *et al.* (2003) arrived at similar conclusions.

Thus, the use of these and most other QoL inventories as self-rating instruments is highly problematic. It is difficult to know what a patient means when making the rating (Williams and Wilkinson, 1995), and the influence of negative affect and cognition on ratings is even less controllable than it is in an interview (Atkinson, Zibin and Chuang, 1997).

Thus, subjective assessment of one's well-being, ratings of subjective satisfaction with different life domains and the application of self-rating scales are all of doubtful value when assessing the QoL of depressed patients. Evidence is accumulating that the scores obtained in this way are closely correlated with the severity of depression and do not provide any useful additional information, especially if QoL is to be assessed in a clinical setting, where therapeutic action is the aim of the assessment (Atkinson, Zibin and Chuang, 1997). It seems that depression and reduced QoL – as measured by the inventories discussed above – are tautological concepts, so that measuring both with similar instruments is a clear case of measurement redundancy leading to spurious correlations (Monroe and Steiner, 1986). It is not much more than sticking the new label 'quality of life' on the old bottle 'depression'. Thus, the finding that psychological well-being is impaired in depression must be regarded as at least trivial – if not problematic – since concentrating on assessing QoL instead of on depression might lead to overlooking the presence of a treatable comorbid depression in somatically ill patients (Jacobson, de Groot and Samson, 1997). Also, statements that antidepressant drugs not only improve symptoms but also QoL may be wrong, if both domains are measured by an overlapping item pool.

DEPRESSION, FUNCTIONING IN EVERYDAY LIFE AND LIVING CONDITIONS: THE CONTEXTUAL PERSPECTIVE

We contend that there is no way around a multidimensional concept of QoL for depressed persons. In this connection, it is useful to stress the sociological perspective coming from the tradition of social indicators and health status research, which is a multidimensional one (Siegrist and Junge, 1989; Albrecht and Fitzpatrick, 1994).

In a study on the relocation of chronic psychiatric patients into the community, Barry and Crosby (1996) found a dissociation between the patients' subjective assessment of life satisfaction – which had not improved – and objective indices, e.g. improved living conditions, higher levels of social contact and increased leisure activities. In chronic depression, such a dissociation might be observed the other way round: patients might be subjectively dissatisfied and complain about reduced well-being, while their objective functioning and/or actual living conditions, including social support, might be appropriate. Kay, Beamisch and Roth (1964) observed that complaints of loneliness in elderly depressed patients proved to have little association with actual isolation, while Morgado *et al.* (1991) found that depressed patients unwittingly over-report poor social adjustment, which they reappraise when recovered.

Albrecht and Fitzpatrick (1994) have criticised the fact that such conceptual issues as the multi-dimensional nature of QoL, as opposed to a unidimensional assessment of well-being, have been neglected so far in relevant research and that psychometric considerations have unduly dominated conceptual thinking. Similarly, Romney and Evans (1996) have argued for a multidimensional model of QoL and have demonstrated the usefulness of including domains other than psychological well-being and life satisfaction.

At least two additional domains – functioning in daily life or disability, on the one hand, and environmental living conditions, both material and social, on the other – should be included in a broader QoL concept. This approach is being pursued in psychiatry, both by new multiaxial diagnostic systems (e.g. the multiaxial version of the ICD-10 by Janca *et al.*, 1996; World Health Organization, 1997) and by more complex assessment instruments, which have been available for some time (e.g. the Standardised Interview to Assess Social Maladjustment and Dysfunction by Clare and Cairns, 1978; Katschnig, 1983). They are so far not used extensively in QoL research, although social functioning is often assessed (but mostly as a self-report measure), while environmental living conditions are rarely included. Bech (1994) has stressed this multidimensional perspective by introducing the PCASEE model, where P stands for physical indicators, C for cognitive indicators, A for affective indicators, S for social indicators, E for economic–social stressors and the second E for ego functions (see also Bech, 1997).

There is abundant evidence that both acute and chronic depression are associated with social dysfunction. Depression seems to impair the individual's ability to interact appropriately with the social environment, in terms of the fulfilment of more formal roles and of interacting with the immediate social environment. Depressed persons thereby undermine positive feedback from others (Lewinsohn, 1974), which in turn prevents them from interacting properly, and so on. In psychological research, rejection of depressed persons by others is a consistent finding (Coyne, 1976; Gurtman, 1986).

One of the earliest methods used for assessing functioning in social roles is the Social Adjustment Scale (SAS) by Weissman and Paykel (1974). These authors demonstrated reduced functioning in social roles (such as parental, housewife, leisure) in depressed women; later, the same findings were reported for men (Weissman *et al.*, 1978). Wells *et al.* (1989) found that the extent to which depression interfered with work, housework or schoolwork, on the one hand, and with social activities such as visiting friends or relatives, on the other, was significantly higher than for chronic medical conditions. Also, the number of days in bed due to depression in the last 30 days was higher than in most other chronic conditions. Similarly, a large number of studies have documented the fact that depression is accompanied by impairment and disabilities in role functioning (Blumenthal and Dielman, 1975; Fredrichs *et al.*, 1982; Craig and Van Natta, 1983; Puig-Antick *et al.*, 1985a; Klerman, 1989; Broadhead *et al.*, 1990; Dew *et al.*, 1991; Mintz *et al.*, 1992; Lyness *et al.*, 1993; Rogers *et al.*, 1993; Tweed, 1993; Goethe and Fischer, 1995; Alexopoulos *et al.*, 1996; Mauskopf *et al.*, 1996; Lépine *et al.*, 1997). It is beyond the scope of this chapter to analyse factors that affect the impairment associated with a depressive episode. Akiskal (1988) and Hirschfeld *et al.* (1989) have suggested that pre-morbid personality factors may be important mediators of such impairment.

The extent of impairment of social functioning seems to be not so much dependent on the severity of depression but on its duration. Several studies have found that dysthymia, a milder but longer lasting form of a depressive disorder, is associated with greater impairment in both social and occupational functioning than is episodic major depression (Stewart, Hays and Ware, 1988; Cassano *et al.*,

1989; Wells *et al.*, 1989; Johnson, Weissman and Klerman, 1992; Leader and Klein, 1996). In contrast to these findings and contrary to clinical experience, Spijker *et al.* (2004) did not detect such a relationship between the duration of depression and functional disability in subjects from the general population with newly originated episodes of major depression.

Bothwell and Weissman (1977) and Paykel, Weissman and Prusoff (1978) found evidence of persisting social maladjustment after the ending of depression. This led Weissman and Klerman to develop interpersonal psychotherapy for depression, which was aimed at restoring social functioning in the same way as antidepressants are regarded as targeting symptoms (Weissman, Markowitz and Klerman, 2000). Similar effects on social functioning have been reported by Goering *et al.* (1983) and Puig-Antick *et al.* (1985b), though some studies have failed to find persisting effects (Carson and Carson, 1984; Zeiss and Lewinsohn, 1988; Rhode, Lewinsohn and Seeley, 1990). Tweed (1993) confirmed persisting effects, identifying certain symptoms (mood, an extended dysphoric period, fatigue, sexual disinterest, cognitive problems and suicidal ideation/behaviour) as being associated with both concurrent and lingering impairment. Why social disabilities persist even after the remission of depression is not quite clear. It might be that unrecognised subdepressive residual symptoms are responsible for this ongoing malfunctioning. Ormel *et al.* (1993a) observed among depressed general practice attenders that 38% of patients were still at least mildly impaired in social role functioning three and a half years after baseline, while most other disabilities (self-care, family role, occupational role) had practically disappeared. In that study, improvements in symptoms and disabilities were largely synchronous, and patients with unimproved or residual symptoms continued to be dysfunctional (Ormel *et al.*, 1993b). Wells *et al.* (1992) carried out a longitudinal follow-up study on a subsample of their depressed patients of the Medical Outcomes Study (MOS) (Wells *et al.*, 1989) and found that social functioning had only partially improved after two years (see also Hays *et al.*, 1995).

In an attempt to assess the improvement of social functioning differentially in depressed patients after the use of different types of antidepressants Bosc, Dubini and Polin (1997) developed the Social Adaptation Self-evaluation Scale (SASS), which has, however, been criticised as measuring well-being rather than social functioning (Healy, 2000).

In order to appreciate more fully the implications of the QoL of depressed patients, one further step seems to be necessary: assessment of the depressed patient's living conditions, which may influence his/her well-being and functioning and may contribute to chronicity or relapse. By impairing functioning in social roles and at work, depression may eventually lead to depriving the depressed person of both material and social support (see also Freeman, Chapter 5 in this volume).

Several epidemiological studies show that depressed persons are disadvantaged in many respects. In the *OPCS Surveys of Psychiatric Morbidity in Great Britain*, Meltzer *et al.* (1996) reported that persons with depressive episodes have a significantly increased risk of living as a 'lone person with child(ren)' or in a 'one person only' household, and being unemployed or economically inactive. Men with a depressive episode had the highest percentage (25%) of all neurotic disorders for being 'permanently unable to work', as opposed to only 3% of those without neurotic disorders. In the US National Comorbidity Survey, Blazer *et al.* (1994) found that major depression was significantly correlated with 'separated/widowed/divorced and never married' status and with employment classification as homemaker. In the Epidemiologic Catchment Area (ECA) study, men and women with a history of affective disorders were found to have greater difficulty obtaining and maintaining employment; those with a major depressive disorder in the last year were significantly more often financially dependent on others than were non-depressed subjects (Robins and Regier, 1991).

As a rule, it is impossible to distinguish between cause and effect in such cross-sectional studies; nevertheless, it is remarkable that the social factors described above are usually discussed only under the topic of causative and not outcome aspects of depression (e.g. Smith and Weissman, 1992). Prospective longitudinal studies would be necessary to clarify this relationship. There are only a few such studies about the effect of depression on environmental living conditions. Merikangas (1984) reported the divorce rate among previously depressed patients to be nine times that of the general population, two years after discharge, while Coyne *et al.* (1987), Coyne, Wortman and Lehman (1988) and Hammen (1990) stressed that depression leads to life disruptions (relational disruption, career setbacks, etc.). Wittchen and von Zerssen (1987) found an increased proportion of divorced persons among depressed patients seven years after intake into their follow-up study, and nearly 10% prematurely in receipt of pensions. In an ECA panel study, Coryell *et al.* (1993) demonstrated a decline in job status and income in a five-year follow-up study of patients with bipolar or unipolar affective disorder. In contrast, Catalano, Dooley and Wilson (1994) did not find an effect of clinical depression on unemployment.

As a whole, these results suggest that the relationship between depression and disadvantaged social and material status might be a circular one. Depression may lead to disadvantage and disadvantage may lead to depression. Future studies should consider both possibilities (Katschnig and Nutzinger, 1988).

AN ACTION-ORIENTATED MULTIDIMENSIONAL FRAMEWORK FOR ASSESSING QUALITY OF LIFE IN DEPRESSION

Even if 'quality of life' in the narrow sense of psychological well-being and satisfaction with one's life is the focus of interest, both functioning in everyday life and social and material environmental living conditions have to be considered, since they may influence both psychological well-being and satisfaction in various life domains. A further reason for going beyond well-being and satisfaction is the high correlation of these concepts with depression, which implies that QoL information which relies on psychological well-being and satisfaction measures is redundant. Finally, if assessment of QoL is to have management implications, the functioning and environmental living conditions of individuals should be assessed as possible targets of therapeutic action.

While the number of variables and dimensions to be considered in a multidimensional model of QoL in depression is arbitrary, we would like to suggest a framework including four dimensions, two psychological and two sociological (Fig. 11.1). Our main motive for this choice is the theoretical

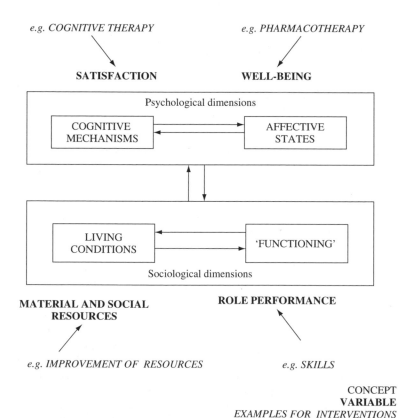

Figure 11.1   An action-orientated multidimensional framework for assessing quality of life

importance of these dimensions (at least in some contemporary thinking), the possibility of measuring at least some aspects of these dimensions in a valid and reliable way and – the main motive – the availability of therapeutic and management strategies that can be conceived as acting specifically on each of these dimensions.

The psychological dimensions comprise cognitive mechanisms ('self-esteem', 'satisfaction') and the affective state ('well-being'). If disturbed, the specific corresponding treatments of cognitive therapy (for negative cognitions) and pharmacotherapy or non-cognitive psychotherapy (for negative affect) may be introduced. Of course, many different concepts can be subsumed under 'cognitive' and 'affective'. Since cognitive and affective factors are closely interrelated – according to cognitive theory, cognitions influence emotions, whereas according to psychodynamic theories it is the other way round – they are subsumed here under the common heading 'psychological dimensions'. The two sociological dimensions are 'functioning in daily life' and 'environmental living conditions', each with many possible subdimensions according to the life domains concerned and differentiated according to both material and social aspects. Again, since both dimensions are closely interrelated (e.g. malfunctioning in social roles may lead to a break-up of relationships, with ensuing loneliness; lack of social support may lead to dysfunction in work roles), they are subsumed under one broad sociological heading. Management actions could comprise skills training or role play for social dysfunction, as well as interventions aimed at the improvement of environmental resources (housing, jobs, social support).

In addition to the interrelations within each category, the psychological and sociological domains may influence each other. In this framework, it is assumed that practically all the causal relationships depicted are possible. Thus, social disadvantage may be the cause of psychological ill-health ('depression'), as well as its consequence. The same is true for therapeutic interventions. Both cognitive therapy and pharmacotherapy may eventually lead to better role functioning, while correcting social disadvantage (e.g. unemployment) may be conducive to the improvement of depression.

The main purpose of providing this framework is to demonstrate possible pathways for the origin of depression, its consequences, and possible interventions. These pathways have, to a large extent, still to be explored by empirical research, both descriptive and interventional. What is urgently needed are longitudinal studies that test the possible vicious circles in terms of such different pathways: 'negative cognitions → depression → social malfunctioning → social disadvantage → negative cognitions' or 'social disadvantage → social dysfunction → negative cognitions → depression', etc. In addition, intervention studies would have to show at which points these circles can be interrupted. An example is a study by Kocsis et al. (1997), where it was shown that antidepressant pharmacotherapy can improve social functioning in dysthymic patients.

However, such research requires the relevant variables to be measurable in a valid and reliable way. Here, substantial work remains to be done. It is at least as difficult to assess a person's satisfaction with a specific aspect of life or the social support available to him/her as it is to elicit the presence of a specific psychopathological phenomenon. The traps in collecting these data are manifold. Self-rating procedures have no control over how a patient understands a specific item; self-reports (obtained either by self-rating or by interview) about functioning and living conditions may be heavily influenced by the emotional state of the respondent (see Katschnig, Chapter 1 in this volume). Different measurement inventories may contain identical or very similar items, but nevertheless be labelled differently (in one instance a 'depression rating scale', in the other a 'well-being scale').

One of the main problems in this field is measurement redundancy; i.e. inventories or measures purporting to measure a specific phenomenon unwittingly also measure a different phenomenon (Monroe and Steiner, 1986). If a study aims at checking the relationship between such phenomena and uses redundant measurements, an identified correlation might be spurious.

For instance, many measures used in the QoL field contain symptoms. This is obvious for the psychological well-being scales and also for most of the more complex QoL measures, which contain depression items. Also, the well-known Social Adjustment Scale (SAS) (Weissman, 1975) contains symptoms, which has led Stewart, Hays and Ware (1988) to remove these symptoms from the scale, in order to assess properly the improvement of social functioning in a clinical trial of antidepressants. The most notable example of such a symptom-contaminated measure is the Global Assessment of Functioning (GAF), contained as Axis V in DSM-IV (American Psychiatric Association, 1994).

A more indirect kind of measurement redundancy takes place if the affective state of the respondent is not controlled for. Thus, depressed or manic patients might underestimate or overestimate their social support (Kay, Beamisch and Roth, 1964), and it is well-known that satisfaction judgements are clearly influenced by actual mood state (Schwarz and Clore, 1983). One way out of this dilemma would be to use third-party ratings (professionals or relatives), but few QoL instruments (e.g. Spitzer *et al.*, 1981; Becker, Diamond and Sainfort, 1993) provide this possibility in addition to the usual self-reports. If such additional assessments by external observers are carried out, the results might be quite discrepant (Sainfort, Becker and Diamond, 1996). An in-between strategy which at least reduces the influence of emotions on recall is the Experience Sampling Method (ESM), whereby patients are prompted by a wristwatch tone, several times a day, to report their thoughts, current activity and the physical and social context (Barge-Schaapveld *et al.*, 1995; Barge-Schaapveld *et al.*, Chapter 8 in this volume). A special case of measurement redundancy is the use of global indices, which is quite popular in QoL research. Such inidices might be convenient for statistical purposes, but they are not useful either for planning clinical intervention or for correlational research, since they may contain unknown portions of other variables that they are finally correlated with.

In conclusion, there is no way round a multidimensional and differentiated assessment of QoL in psychiatric, especially in emotional disorders. As far as QoL in depression is concerned, many questions remain open. Self-rating measures that are easy to use might be deceptive, especially when employed in clinical trials. Life is complicated, and there is no reason why society should not invest as much into properly assessing QoL as into brain imaging.

REFERENCES

Aaronson, N.K., Ahmedzai, S., Bergman, B. *et al* (1993). The European Organization for Research and Treatment for Cancer QLQ-C30: A quality-of-life instrument for use in international clinical trials in oncology, *J. Natl Cancer Inst.*, **85**, 365–376.

Akiskal, H. (1988). Personality as a mediating variable in the pathogenesis of mood disorders: Implications for theory, research and prevention, in *Depressive Illness: Prediction of Course and Outcome* (Eds T. Helgason & R. Daly), pp. 131–146, Springer-Verlag, Berlin.

Albrecht, G.L. & Fitzpatrick, R. (1994). A sociological perspective on health-related quality of life research, in *Advances in Medical Sociology*, Vol. 5, *Quality of Life in Health Care* (Eds G.L. Albrecht & R. Fitzpatrick), pp. 1–21, Jai Press Inc., Greenwich, Connecticut, London, England.

Alexopoulos, G.S., Vrontou, C., Kakuma, T., Meyers, B.S., Young, R.C., Klausner, E. & Clarkin, J. (1996). Disability in geriatric depression, *Am. J. Psychiatry*, **153**, 877–885.

American Psychiatric Association (1994). *Diagnostic and Statistical Manual of Mental Disorders*, Fourth Edition, *(DSM-IV)*, American Psychiatric Association, Washington, DC.

Atkinson, M., Zibin, S.H. & Chuang, H. (1997). Characterizing quality of life among patients with chronic mental illness: A critical examination of the self-report methodology, *Am. J. Psychiatry*, **105**, 99–105.

Barge-Schaapveld, D.Q.C.M., Nicolson, N.A., Gerritsen van der Hoop, R. & deVries, M.W. (1995). Changes in daily life experience associated with clinical improvement in depression, *J. Affect. Disord.*, **34**, 139–154.

Barry, M. & Crosby, C. (1996). Quality of life as an evaluative measure in assessing the impact of community care on people with long term psychiatric disorders, *Br. J. Psychiatry*, **168**, 210–216.

Bech, P. (1994). The PCASEE model: An approach to subjective well-being, in *Quality of Life Assessment: International Perspectives* (Eds J. Orley & J. Kuyken), pp. 75–79, Springer-Verlag, Berlin.

Bech, P. (1996). Quality of life measurements in major depression, *Eur. Psychiatry*, **11**, 123–126.

Bech, P. (1997). Quality of life instruments in depression, *Eur Psychiatry*, **12**, 194–198.

Beck, A.T. (1976). *Cognitive Therapy and the Emotional Disorders*, International University Press, New York.

Beck, A.T., Ward, C.H., Mendelson, M., Mock, J. & Erbaugh, J. (1961). An inventory for measuring depression, *Arch. Gen. Psychiatry*, **4**, 561–571.

Becker, M., Diamond, R. & Sainfort, F. (1993). A new patient focused index for measuring quality of life in persons with severe and persistent mental illness, *Quality of Life Res.*, **2**, 239–251.

Blazer, D.G., Kessler, R.C., McGonagle, K.A. & Swartz, M.S. (1994). The prevalence and distribution of major depression in a national community sample: The national comorbidity survey, *Am. J. Psychiatry*, **151**, 979–986.

Blumenthal, M. & Dielman, T. (1975). Depressive symptomatology and role function in the general population, *Arch. Gen. Psychiatry*, **32**, 985–991.

Bosc, M., Dubini, A. & Polin, V. (1997). Development and validation of a social functioning scale, the social adaptation self-evaluation scale, *Eur. Neuropsychopharmacol.*, **7**, 57–70.

Bothwell, S. & Weissman, M. (1977). Social impairments four years after an acute depressive episode, *Am. J. Orthopsychiatry*, **47**, 231–237.

Bradburn, N.M. (1969). *The Structure of Psychological Well-Being*, Aldine, Chicago, Illinois.

Broadhead, W.E., Blazer, D.G., George, L.K. & Tse, C.K. (1990). Depression, disability days, and days lost from work in a prospective epidemiologic survey, *J. Am. Med. Ass*, **264**, 2524–2528.

Carson, T. & Carson, R. (1984). The affective disorders, in *Comprehensive Handbook of Psychopathology* (Eds H. Adams & P. Sucker), pp. 349–381, Plenum Press, New York.

Cassano, G.B., Perugi, G., Musetti, L. & Akiskal, H.S. (1989). The nature of depression presenting concomitantly with panic disorder, *Comp. Psychiatry*, **30**, 473–482.

Catalano, R., Dooley, D. & Wilson, G. (1994). Depression and unemployment: Panel findings from the epidemiologic catchment area study, *Am. J. Community Psychol.*, **22**, 745–765.

Cella, D.F., Tulsley, D.S., Gray, G. *et al* (1993). Functional assessment of cancer therapy scale: Development and validation of the general measure, *J. Clin. Oncol.*, **11**, 570–579.

Clare, A.W. & Cairns, V.E. (1978). Design, development and use of a standardised interview to assess social maladjustment and dysfunction in community studies, *Psychol. Med.*, **8**, 589–604.

Coryell, W., Endicott, J., Keller, M., Klerman, G.L., Maser, J. & Scheftner, W. (1993). The enduring psychosocial consequence of mania and depression, *Am. J. Psychiatry*, **150**, 720–727.

Coyne, J.C. (1976). Depression and the response of others, *J. Abnormal Psychol.*, **85**, 186–193.

Coyne, J., Wortman, C. & Lehman, D. (1988). The other side of support: Emotional overinvolvement and miscarried helping, in *Social Support: Formats, Processes, and Effects* (Ed. B. Gottlieb), pp. 137–154, Sage, New York.

Coyne, J., Kessler, T., Tal, M., Turnbull, J., Wortman, C. & Greden, J. (1987). Living with a depressed person, *J. Cons. Clin. Psychol.*, **55**, 347–352.

Craig, T. & Van Natta, P. (1983). Disability and depressive symptoms in two communities, *Am. J. Psychiatry*, **140**, 598–601.

Dean, B.B., Gerner, D. & Gerner, R.H. (2004). A systematic review evaluating health-related quality of life, work impairment, and health-care cost and utilisation in bipolar disorder, *Curr. Med. Res. Opinion*, **20**(2), 139–154.

Dew, M.A., Bromet, E.J., Schulberg, H.C., Parkinson, D.K. & Curtis, E.C. (1991). Factors affecting service utilization for depression in a white collar population, *Social Psychiatry Psychiatr. Epidemiol.*, **26**, 230–237.

DuPuy, H.J. (1984). The psychological general well-being index, in *Assessment of Quality of Life in Clinical Trials of Cardiovascular Therapies* (Eds N.K. Wenger, M.E. Mattson, C.D. Furberg & J. Elinson), Le Jacq, New York.

Endicott, J., Nee, J., Harrison, W. & Blumenthal, R. (1993). Quality of life enjoyment and satisfaction questionnaire: A new measure, *Psychopharmacol. Bull.*, **29**, 321–326.

EuroQol Group (1990). EuroQol – A new faculty for the measurement of health-related quality of life, *Health Policy*, **16**, 199–208.

Fredrichs, R., Aneshensel, C., Yokopenic, P. & Clark, V. (1982). Physical health and depression: An epidemic survey, *Preventative Med.*, **11**, 639–646.

Friedman, H.S. & Booth-Kewley, S. (1987). The 'disease-prone personality': A meta-analytic view of the construct, *Am. Psychol.*, **42**, 539–555.

Goering, P., Wasylenki, D., Lancee, W. & Freeman, S.J.J. (1983). Social support and post-hospital outcome for depressed women, *Can. J. Psychiatry*, **28**, 612–618.

Goethe, J.W. & Fischer, E.H.(1995). Functional impairment in depressed inpatients, *J. Affect. Disord.*, **33**, 23–29.

Gurtman, M.B. (1986). Depression and the response of others: Reevaluating the reevaluation, *J. Abnormal. Psychol.*, **95**, 99–101.

Hammen, C. (1990). Vulnerability to depression: Personal, situational and family aspects, in *Contemporary Psychological Approaches to Depression* (Ed. R. Ingram), pp. 59–70, Plenum Press, New York.

Hays, R.D., Wells, K.B., Sherbourne, M.P.H., Donald, C., Rogers, W. & Spritzer, K. (1995). Functioning and well-being outcomes of patients with depression compared with chronic general medical illnesses, *Arch. Gen. Psychiatry*, **52**, 11–19.

Healy, D. (2000). The assessment of outcomes in depression the place for measures of social functioning, *Rev. Contemporary Pharmacotherapy*, **11**, 295–301.

Hirschfeld, R., Klerman, G., Lavori, P., Keller, M., Griffith, P. & Coryell, W. (1989). Premorbid personality assessment of first onset of major depression, *Arch. Gen. Psychiatry*, **46**, 345–350.

Hopwood, P., Stephens, R.J., Machin, D., for the MRC Lung Cancer Working Party (1994). Approaches to the analysis of quality of life data: Experiences gained from a Medical Research Council Lung Cancer Working Party palliative chemotherapy trial, *Quality of Life Res.*, **3**, 339–352.

Jacobson, A.M., de Groot, M. & Samson, J.A. (1997). The effect of psychiatric disorders and symptoms on quality of life in patients with Type I and Type II diabetes mellitus, *Quality of Life Res.*, **6**, 11–20.

Janca, A., Kastrup, M., Katschnig, H., Lopez-Ibor, J.J., Mezzich, J.E. & Sartorius, N. (1996). The ICD-10 multiaxial system for use in adult psychiatry: Structure and application, *J. Nerv. Ment. Dis.*, **184**, 191–192.

Johnson, J., Weissman, M.M. & Klerman, G.L. (1992). Service utilization and social morbidity associated with depressive symptoms in the community, *J. Am. Med. Ass.*, **267**, 1378–1483.

Kaplan, R., Bush, J. & Berry, C. (1976). Health status: Types of validity and the index of well-being, *Health Serv. Res.*, **11**, 478–507.

Katon, W., von Korff, M., Lin, E., Lipscomb, P., Russo, J., Wagner, E. & Polk, E. (1990). Distressed high utilizers of medical care: DSM-III-R diagnoses and treatment needs, *Gen. Hosp. Psychiatry*, **12**, 355–362.

Katschnig, H. (1983). Methods for measuring social adjustment, in *Methodology in Evaluation of Psychiatric Treatment* (Ed. T. Helgason), pp. 205–218, Cambridge University Press, Cambridge.

Katschnig, H. & Nutzinger, D.O. (1988). Psychosocial aspects of course and outcome in depressive illness, in *Depressive Illness: Prediction of Course and Outcome* (Eds T. Helgason & R.J. Daly), pp. 63–75, Springer-Verlag, Berlin.

Katschnig, H., Simhandl, C., Serim, M., Subasi, B., Zoghlami, A. & Jaidhauser, K. (1996). Depression-specific quality of life scales are flawed, in *New Research Abstracts,* APA Annual Meeting, New York, 4–9 May 1996.

Kay, D.W.K., Beamisch, P. & Roth, M. (1964). Old age mental disorders in Newcastle-upon-Tyne, II. A study of possible social and medical causes, *Br. J. Psychiatry*, **110**, 668–682.

Kessler, R.C., Berglund, P., Demler, O., Jin, R. & Walters, E.E. (2005). Lifetime prevalence and age-of-onset distributions of DSM-IV disorders in the national comorbidity survey replication, Arch. Gen. Psychiatry, **62**, 593–602.

Klerman, G. (1989). Depressive disorders: Further evidence for increased medical morbidity and impairment of social functioning, *Arch. Gen. Psychiatry*, **46**, 856–858.

Kocsis, J.H., Zisook, S., Davidson, J., Shelton, R., Yonkers, K., Hellerstein, D.J., Rosenbaum, J. & Halbreich, U. (1997). Double-blind comparison of sertraline, imipramine, and placebo in the treatment of dysthymia: Psychosocial outcomes, *Am. J. Psychiatry*, **154**, 390–395.

Koivumaa-Honkanen, H.T., Viinamaki, H., Honkanen, R. *et al* (1996). Correlates of life satisfaction among psychiatric patients, *Acta Psychiatrica Scand.*, **94**, 372–378.

Leader, J.B. & Klein, D.N. (1996). Social adjustment in dysthymia, double depression and episodic major depression, *J. Affect. Disord.*, **37**, 91–101.

Lépine, J.-P., Gastpar, M., Mendlewicz, J., Tylee, A., and on behalf of the DEPRES Steering Committee (1997). Depression in the community: The first pan-European study DEPRES (Depression Research in European Society), *Int. Clin. Psychiatry*, **12**, 19–29.

Lewinsohn, P.M. (1974). A behavioral approach to depression, in *The Psychology of Depression: Contemporary Theory and Research* (Eds R.J. Friedman & M.M. Katz), pp. 157–178, Winston–Wiley, New York.

Lyness, J.M., Caine, E.D., Conwell, Y., King, D.A. & Cox, C. (1993). Depressive symptoms, medical illness, and functional status in depressed psychiatric inpatients, *Am. J. Psychiatry*, **150**, 910–915.

McKenna, S.P. & Hunt, S.M. (1992). A new measure of quality of life in depression: Testing the reliability and construct validity of the QLDS, *Health Policy*, **22**, 321–330.

Mauskopf, J.A., Simeon, G.P., Miles, M.A., Westlund, R.E. & Davidson, J.R.T. (1996). Functional status in depressed patients: the relationship to disease severity and disease resolution, *J. Clin. Psychiatry*, **57**, 588–592.

Meltzer, H., Gill, B., Petticrew, M. & Hinds, K. (1996). *OPCS Survey of Psychiatric Morbidity in Great Britain*, Report 1: The prevalence of psychiatric morbidity among adults living in private households, Report 3: Economic activity and social functioning of adults with psychiatric disorders, HMSO, London.

Merikangas, K. (1984). Divorce and assertive mating among depressed patients, *Am. J. Psychiatry*, **141**, 74–76.

Michalak, E.E., Tam, E.M., Manjunath, C.V., Solomons, K., Levitt, A.J., Levitan, R., Enns, M., Morehouse, R., Yatham, L.N. & Lam, R.W. (2004). Generic and health-related quality of life in patients with seasonal and nonseasonal depression, *Psychiatry Res.*, **128**(3), 245–251.

Mintz, J., Mintz, L.I., Arruda, M.J. & Hwang, S.S. (1992). Treatment of depression and the functional capacity to work, *Arch. Gen. Psychiatry*, **49**, 761–768.

Monroe, S.M. & Steiner, S.S. (1986). Social support and psychopathology: Interrelations with preexisting disorders, stress, and personality, *J. Abnormal Psychol.*, **95**, 29–39.

Morgado, A., Smith, M., Lecrubier, Y. & Widlocher, D. (1991). Depressed subjects unwittingly overreport poor social adjustment which they reappraise when recovered, *J. Nerv. Ment. Dis.*, **179**, 614–619.

Namjoshi, M.A. & Buesching, D.P. (2001). A review of the health-related quality of life literature in bipolar disorder, *Quality of Life Res.*, **2**, 105–115.

Ormel, J., Oldehinkel, T., Brilman, E. & van den Brink, W. (1993a). Outcome of depression and anxiety in primary care, *Arch. Gen. Psychiatry*, **50**, 759–766.

Ormel, J., Von Korff, M., van den Brink, W., Katon, W., Brilman, E. & Oldehinkel, T. (1993b). Depression, anxiety and social disability show synchrony of change in primary care patients, *Am. J. Public Health*, **83**, 385–390.

Papakostas, G.I., Peterson, T., Mahal, Y., Mischoulon, D., Nierenberg, A.A. & Fava, M. (2003). Quality of life assessments in major depressive disorder: A review of the literature, *Gen. Hosp. Psychiatry*, **26**, 13–17.

Paykel, E.S., Weissman, M.M. & Prusoff, B. (1978). Social maladjustment and severity of depression, *Comp. Psychiatry*, **19**, 121–128.

Puig-Antick, J. & Lukens, E., Davies, M., Goetz, C., Brennan-Quattrock, J. & Todak, G. (1985a). Psychosocial functioning in prepubertal major depressive disorders. I. Interpersonal relationships during the depressive episode, *Arch. Gen. Psychiatry*, **42**, 500–507.

Puig-Antick, J., Lukens, E., Davies, M., Goetz, C., Brennan-Quattrock, J. & Todak, G. (1985b). Psychosocial functioning in prepubertal major depressive disorders: 2. Interpersonal relationships after sustained recovery from affective episode, *Arch. Gen. Psychiatry*, **42**, 511–517.

Pukrop, R., Schlaak, V., Moller-Leimkuhler, A.M., Albus, M., Czernik, A., Klosterkotter, J. & Moller, H.J. (2003). Reliability and validity of quality of life assessed by the short-form 36 and the modular system for quality of life in patients with schizophrenia and patients with depression, *Psychiat. Res.*, **11**, 63–79.

Pyne, J.M., Patterson, T.L., Kaplan, R.M., Gillin, J.C., Koch, W.L. & Grant, I. (1997). Assessment of the quality of life of patients with major depression, *Psychiat. Serv.*, **48**, 224–230.

Rhode, P., Lewinsohn, P. & Seeley, J. (1990). Are people changed by the experience of having an episode of depression? A further test of the scar hypothesis, *J. Abnormal Psychol.*, **99**, 264–271.

Ritsner, M. & Kurs, R. (2003). Quality of life outcomes in mental illness: Schizophrenia, mood and anxiety disorders, *Expl Rev. Pharmacoeconomics Outcome Res.*, **3**(2), 189–199.

Robins, L.N. & Regier, D.A. (1991). *Psychiatric Disorders in America. The Epidemiologic Catchment Area Study*, The Free Press, Maxwell Macmillan International, New York, Oxford, Singapore, Sydney.

Rogers, W.H., Wells, K.B., Meredith, L.S., Sturm, R. & Burnam, M. (1993). Outcomes for adult outpatients with depression under prepaid or fee-for-service financing, *Arch. Gen. Psychiatry*, **50**, 517–525.

Romney, D.M. & Evans, D.R. (1996). Toward a general model of health-related quality of life, *Quality of Life Res.*, **5**, 235–241.

Ryff, C.D. (1995). Psychological well-being in adult life, *Current Directions in Psycholog. Sci.*, **4**, 99–104.

Ryff, C.D. & Keyes, C.L.M. (1995). The structure of psychological well-being revisited *J. Personality Social Psychol.*, **69**, 719–727.

Sainfort, F., Becker, M. & Diamond, R. (1996). Judgments of quality of life of individuals with severe mental disorders, *Am. J. Psychiatry*, **153**, 497–502.

Schwarz, N. & Clore, G.L. (1983). Mood, misattribution, and judgments of well-being: Informative and directive functions of affective states, *J. Personality Social Psychol.*, **45**, 513–523.

Siegrist, J. & Junge, A. (1989). Conceptual and methodological problems in research on the quality of life in clinical medicine, *Soc. Sci. Med.*, **29**, 463–468.

Smith, A.L. & Weissman, M.M. (1992). Epidemiology, in *Handbook of Affective Disorders* (Ed. E.S. Paykel), pp. 111–129, Churchill Livingston, Edinburgh.

Spijker, J., de Graf, R., Bijl, R.V., Beekman, A.T.F., Ormel, J. & Nolen, W.A. (2004). Functional disability and depression in the general population, Results from the Netherlands Mental Health Survey and Incidence Study (NEMESIS), *Acta Psychiatrica Scand.*, **110**, 208–214.

Spitzer, W.O., Dobson, A., Hall, J., Chesterman, E., Levi, J., Sheperd, R., Battista, R.N. & Catchlove, B.R. (1981). Measuring the quality of life in cancer patients: A concise Q/L index for use by physicians, *J. Chronic Dis.*, **34**, 585–597.

Stewart, A.L., Hays, R.D. & Ware, J.E. (1988). The MOS short-form general health survey: Reliability and validity in a patient population, *Med. Care*, **26**, 724–735.

Stoker, M.J., Dunbar, G.C. & Beaumont, G. (1992). The SmithKline Beecham 'Quality of Life' Scale: A validation and reliability study in patients with affective disorder, *Quality of Life Res.*, **1**, 385–395.

Tweed, D.L. (1993). Depression-related impairment: Estimating concurrent and lingering effects, *Psychol. Med.*, **23**, 373–386.

von Korff, M., Ormel, J., Katon, W. & Lin, E. (1992). Disability and depression among high utilizers of health care: A longitudinal analysis, *Arch. Gen. Psychiatry*, **49**, 91–100.

Ware, J.E. & Sherbourne, C.D. (1992). The MOS 36-item short-form health survey (SF-36), *Med. Care*, **30**, 473–483.

Weissman, M.M. (1975). The assessment of social adjustment. A review of techniques, *Arch. Gen. Psychiatry*, **32**, 357–365.

Weissman, M.M., Markowitz, J.C. & Klerman, G.L. (2000). *Comprehensive Guide to Interpersonal Psychotherapy*, Basic Books, New York.

Weissman, M.M. & Paykel, E.S. (1974). *The Depressed Women: A Study of Social Relationships*, University of Chicago Press, Chicago, Illinois.

Weissmann, M.M., Prusoff, B.A., Thompson, W.D., Harding, P.S. & Myers, J.K. (1978) Social adjustment by self-report in a community sample and in psychiatric outpatients, *J. Nerv. Ment. Dis.*, **166**, 317–326.

Weissman, M.M., Bland, R.C., Canino, G.J. *et al* (1996). Cross-national epidemiology of major depression and bipolar disorder, *J. Am. Med. Ass.*, **276**, 293–299.

Wells, K.B., Stewart, A., Hays, R.D., Burnam, A., Rogers, W., Daniels, M., Berry, S., Greenfield, S. & Ware, J. (1989). The functioning and well-being of depressed patients: Results from the medical outcomes study, *J. Am. Med. Ass.*, **262**, 914–919.

Wells, K.B., Burnam, M.A., Rogers, W., Hays, R. & Camp, P. (1992). The course of depression in adult outpatients. Results from the medical outcomes study, *Arch. Gen. Psychiatry*, **49**, 788–794.

Williams, B. & Wilkinson, G. (1995). Patient satisfaction in mental health care. Evaluating and evaluative method, *Br. J. Psychiatry*, **166**, 559–562.

Wittchen, H.-U. & von Zerssen, D. (1987). *Verläufe behandelter und unbehandelter Depressionen und Angststörungen. Eine klinisch-psychiatrische und epidemiologische Verlaufsuntersuchung*, Springer-Verlag, Berlin, Heidelberg, New York, London, Paris, Tokyo.

World Health Organization (1997). *The Multiaxial Presentation of the ICD-10 for Use in Adult Psychiatry*, Cambridge University Press, Cambridge.

Zeiss, A. & Lewinsohn, P. (1988). Enduring deficits after remission of depression: A test of the 'scar' hypothesis, *Behaviour Res. Therapy*, **26**, 151–158.

Zigmond, A.S. & Snaith, R.P. (1983). The Hospital Anxiety and Depression Scale, *Acta Psychiatrica Scand.*, **67**, 361–370.

12

Quality of Life in Anxiety Disorders

Franklin R. Schneier and Gabriel Pantol

INTRODUCTION

Anxiety disorders are among the most common mental disorders, and their familiarity may contribute to the perception that they are relatively mild forms of psychopathology. Yet anxiety disorder sufferers and the clinicians who treat them recognise that these conditions have enormous effects on quality of life (QoL). Until recently, most attempts to assess QoL in anxiety disorders focused on disability or impairment in role functioning. However, the past decade has seen tremendous growth primarily in attempts to assess subjective well-being and satisfaction. A few studies have attempted to discern the relationship between symptoms, disability and subjective QoL.

Clinical experience suggests that different anxiety disorders may affect QoL in both shared and specific ways. Sufferers may be distracted from work, relationships and recreation by cognitive symptoms of fear, worry and obsession, distressed by the physiological arousal symptoms prominent in panic disorder (PD), social phobia, post-traumatic stress disorder (PTSD) and generalised anxiety disorder (GAD), limited by the avoidance intrinsic to the phobias and PTSD, and burdened by the secondary shame and demoralisation that sufferers of each of these disorders share. Comorbidity with other anxiety disorders, or commonly with depression or substance abuse occurring secondarily, adds to the strain.

A number of factors should be considered in reviewing the variety of reports in this field. Studies of patients in primary care or psychiatric treatment settings tend to demonstrate greater severity of symptoms and impairment. Reports that control for comorbidity help to disentangle effects attributable to a specific anxiety disorder, although including comorbid patients may better approximate the clinical norm. As the literature has grown too large to allow a description of all studies of QoL in anxiety disorders in this format, this chapter will emphasise larger and more recent studies, and those assessing subjective QoL.

PANIC DISORDER AND AGORAPHOBIA

Panic disorder (PD), commonly occurring with agoraphobia, was among the first anxiety disorders to be studied in respect to QoL, and a large literature now exists on this topic. In community samples, PD is associated with pervasive general health consequences, as well as with impairment of occupational and social function.

Quality of Life in Mental Disorders, Second Edition   Edited by H. Katschnig, H. Freeman and N. Sartorius
© 2006 John Wiley & Sons, Ltd

Community Settings

The US Epidemiologic Catchment Area (ECA) study provided one of the first views of QoL in PD from a large community sample. Klerman *et al.* (1991) found that after controlling for comorbidity, PD subjects ($N=254$) reported elevated rates of fair or poor physical health (35%) and emotional health (38%), increased medical and psychiatric care, and increased receipt of public assistance. Markowitz *et al.* (1989) found that PD subjects did not differ in social activities during the prior two weeks, but were more likely to have spent no time on hobbies and to report not getting along with their spouse.

More recent studies using community data from the National Comorbidity Survey (NCS) have yielded largely similar findings (Kessler *et al.*, 1994). Subjects with PD ($N=274$) had less education and were less likely to be working, but they did not have lower income. Magee *et al.* (1996) reported that agoraphobia was more common among persons who were not working, not receiving education, not living alone and not being a homemaker. Serious interference with life and activities was reported by 27% of agoraphobics, but by only 3% of agoraphobics without comorbid disorders. Agoraphobia was not associated with low social support.

A series of small community studies have provided additional information on the nature of QoL impairment in PD. QoL in PD sufferers was associated with comorbid depression, social support, worry and severity of chest pain, whereas work disability was associated with frequency of panic, illness attitudes, family dissatisfaction and gender (Katerndahl and Realini, 1997). In a comparison of persons with PD and those with infrequent panic (subsyndromal), both groups manifested impaired QoL, but only the PD subjects had panic-related work disability (Katerndahl and Realini, 1998).

Clinical Settings

More than a dozen studies have demonstrated impaired QoL and associated functioning in patients with PD. Studies utilising the Medical Outcomes Study Short Form-36 (SF-36) have consistently demonstrated impairment in mental health, role functioning and social functioning. Sherbourne, Wells and Judd (1996) found that this impairment in out-patients with PD ($N=433$), after controlling for comorbidity, was substantially worse than that of out-patients with hypertension, diabetes, heart disease, arthritis or asthma, but better than or comparable to that of patients with depression. Physical impairment in PD, however, did not differ from population norms. Others have reported both mental *and physical* health to be impaired in PD (Ettigi *et al.*, 1997; Candilis *et al.*, 1999; Simon *et al.*, 2002). Patients with PD lost 39 quality-adjusted days for each year that they lived with the disorder, similar to that reported by patients with non-insulin-dependent diabetes (Rubin *et al.*, 2000). In primary care settings, patients with PD and agoraphobia reported increased dysfunction in occupational role and physical disability (Ormel *et al.*, 1994), as well as more medical utilisation (Barsky, Delamater and Orav, 1999).

In respect to work disability, most of a group of 30 PD out-patients reported a decline in the quality of their work and lost jobs or income (Edlund and Swann, 1987). Of 84 PD patients 25% were unemployed or less productive (Ettigi *et al.*, 1997). Among 65 individuals with PD, work missed due to illness averaged one day per month, and life events frequently attributed to their panic attack were: losing a job (5%), leaving a job (17%) and marital conflicts (9%) (Siegel, Jones and Wilson, 1990). Another study did not find impairment in marital adjustment (Arrindell and Emmelkamp, 1986).

Comorbid MDD has been associated with further impairment in QoL in most studies of PD patients (Hollifield *et al.*, 1997; Candilis *et al.*, 1999). PD patients with comorbid MDD ($N=113$) exhibited increased morbidity and decreased psychosocial functioning as compared to PD patients ($N=324$) (Vasile *et al.*, 1997). Perugi *et al.* (1994) found that 48 patients with PD, agoraphobia and secondary major depression, compared to 35 patients with depression alone, had *less* impairment in four of the nine areas of social adjustment examined. Besides comorbidity, other factors associated with impairment in PD patients include the personality dimension of neuroticism and lower education level (Hollifield *et al.*, 1997), number of panic attacks, state anxiety and depressive symptoms (Rubin *et al.*, 2000).

Effects of Treatment

Improvement in panic attacks and related symptoms that constitute the standard diagnostic criteria for PD accounted for less than half of the overall improvement associated with recovery from PD in one report (Leon *et al.*, 1993), suggesting that factors related to QoL may be important. QoL improvement during treatment has generally been weakly associated with improvement in panic attacks (Telch *et al.*, 1995), but more so with improvement in anxiety and phobic avoidance (Telch *et al.*,1995; Jacobs *et al.*, 1997). Improvement in QoL measures has been demonstrated with acute treatment with serotonin reuptake inhibitors (e.g. Pohl, Wolkow and Clary, 1998), benzodiazepines (Jacobs *et al.*, 1997) and cognitive–behavioural therapy (Telch *et al.*, 1995). It has been suggested that QoL measures may help to distinguish a true medication response from a placebo response (Rapaport, Endicott and Clary, 2002). Placebo responders differed from drug responders in that they exhibited less improvement in QoL, despite similar symptomatic improvement.

QoL improvement with cognitive–behavioural therapy was maintained at a six-month follow-up (Telch *et al.*, 1995). Other follow-up studies of QoL in treated patients, however, suggest that impairment persists. Thirty patients whose PD remitted in response to behaviour therapy were found to have less environmental mastery, personal growth, purpose in life, self-acceptance and physical well-being than healthy control subjects (Fava *et al.*, 2001). In a prospective four-year follow-up of drug treatment, 20% of patients remained disabled. A naturalistic follow-up of PD outpatients 40 months after outpatient clinic evaluation found that 60% reported significant difficulty in performing daily activities and 40% expressed dissatisfaction in at least 50% of life domains (Carpiniello *et al.*, 2002).

Summary

A growing database on QoL in PD and agoraphobia demonstrates substantial impairment, which is at least partially reversible through treatment. While PD shares with other anxiety disorders a principal impact on emotional QoL, it differs in that it may often also impact physical QoL. This is consistent with clinical observations of high levels of health concerns and treatment seeking among PD patients. Employment problems are frequent, but social relationships may be relatively spared. Excessive dependence on a companion to protect the sufferer, however, may strain a relationship. Treatment data suggests that QoL may fill a void in describing outcome beyond symptom relief. While diagnostic criteria of PD emphasise panic attacks, QoL may be more impacted by anticipatory anxiety and agoraphobic avoidance.

SPECIFIC PHOBIAS

Because of their circumscribed nature, specific phobias have been believed to result rarely in marked impairment or diminution of QoL. The small amount of research that does exist on specific phobias, however, does not support this assumption.

Magee *et al.* (1996) found in the national comorbidity survey that serious interference with life and activities was reported by 25% of specific phobics without comorbid disorders and 30% sought professional help. Employed persons who had simple phobia in the past 30 days reported missing a mean of 0.7 days of work per month. In this community survey, simple phobias, even in the absence of comorbidity, appeared to impair QoL to at least as great an extent as agoraphobia and social phobia. A clinical study suggests that specific phobias occurring with comorbid disorders are more impairing than those that occur alone. Of 73 subjects attending a dental fears research clinic, subjects with a comorbid diagnosis self-reported more severe impairment in role function, social function, mental health and health perceptions than persons with a dental phobia alone (Roy-Byrne *et al.*, 1994).

The limited data on QoL in persons with specific phobias suggest that the impact of this disorder may have been underestimated. The nature of the particular specific phobia and the sufferer's life circumstances may influence the impairment it causes. Dental or blood/injection/injury phobias, for example, may lead to avoidance of preventive treatment or failure to address serious medical conditions early, when treatment may be most effective. Situational phobias of public transportation, flying, driving or enclosed spaces may lead to life constrictions similar to those seen in agoraphobia.

SOCIAL PHOBIA (SOCIAL ANXIETY DISORDER)

QoL has been fairly well studied in social phobia (SP), relative to other anxiety disorders, partially in response to early scepticism about the disorder's severity and impairment.

Community Settings

In the ECA study, persons with SP ($N=361$), after controlling for comorbidity, were less likely to be married, had elevated rates of suicidal ideation and were also more likely to be dependent on welfare or disability benefits (Schneier et al., 1992). Davidson et al. (1994) found that subjects who reported social fear but denied interference with life or activities ($N=248$) resembled the SP group in respect of having less income, being less likely to be married or to have at least one close friend, and more likely report 'no confidence in handling problems'. In the NCS (Magee et al., 1996), serious interference with life and activities was reported by 34% of social phobics and by 14% of social phobics without comorbidity. SP was also associated with low social support.

Wittchen and Beloch (1996) assessed a non-clinical sample with SP and no cormorbidity ($N=65$). On the SF-36, 23.1% were severely impaired and 24.6% were significantly impaired. Work productivity was decreased, with a threefold higher rate of unemployment, increased work hours missed and higher rates of self-reported impairment in work performance. Katzelnick et al. (2001) also used the SF-36 to assess QoL in 195 generalised social phobics screened from a large population of Health Maintenance Organisation enrollees. The generalised subtype of SP, after controlling for comorbidity, was associated with lower QoL on all emotional health subscales and some physical health subscales, lower work productivity and earnings, as well as increased health services and increased rates of attempted suicide.

In a large Canadian survey (Stein and Kean, 2000), SP ($N=566$) was associated with impairment in usual activities assessed by several measures (adjusted odds ratios $=4$ to 9). Comorbid major depressive disorder had no significant impact on these outcomes. SP was associated with dissatisfaction with one's main activity, family life, friends, leisure activities and income (adjusted odds ratios 1.8 to 6.0), and with poor quality of well-being (odds ratio$=4.4$), after adjustment for demographic factors and major depression. The magnitude of impairment in usual activities was several-fold stronger for a complex-fears subtype of SP than for persons with only public speaking fears, confirming earlier findings (Stein, Walker and Forde, 1994).

Clinical Settings

An early study (Turner et al., 1986) reported rates of significant impairment in SP patients of 85% for academic functioning, 92% for occupational performance and 69% for general social functioning. Schneier et al. (1994) used scales designed for SP to assess disability in 32 outpatients with SP. Mean scores suggested that these patients were able to work at a job appropriate to their abilities, but performed beneath their abilities; they had impairment in dating activities or minor marital problems; they were able to have a few close friends, but friendships were fewer than desired; and they were able to participate in some non-work-related activities (e.g. hobbies), but avoided some due to SP symptoms. Safren et al. (1996) also found that patients with SP ($N=44$) perceived their QoL to be relatively poor and that QoL was inversely related to the severity of symptoms.

Hambrick et al. (2003) compared disability and QoL measures in 96 patients with SP. Although symptoms, disability and QoL were all moderately related, a significant amount of the variance in QoL was not accounted for by disability. They concluded that disability may only partially mediate the relationship between symptoms and self-perceived QoL.

Clinical trials in SP have generally found symptomatic improvement to be associated with decreases in social and occupational disability (e.g. Stein et al., 1998). Recent treatment studies in SP have begun to incorporate QoL assessments. In a study of maintenance treatment of SP, paroxetine responders who were subsequently maintained on this drug for 24 weeks showed significantly more improvement on QoL than patients switched to placebo, who demonstrated a decline in QoL (Stein et al., 2002).

Summary

Patients with SP evidence major impairment in QoL, and a lesser degree of impairment is still present among persons with SP, even in subsyndromal forms. Because of its early age of onset, typically in the early teens, SP becomes a way of life for many sufferers, as they avoid jobs that require public speaking and limit socialisation to a small group of familiar friends. In this context, persons with SP may tend to underestimate their own limitations in functioning. Impairment among social phobics whose fears are limited to performance depends heavily on their life situation; a performance phobia that would end the career of a musical performer might be trivial for a homemaker.

QoL may be impaired directly by SP symptoms of anticipatory anxiety, avoidance of or anxiety in feared situations and demoralisation after leaving feared situations. Persons with generalised SP appear more likely to be impaired secondarily via secondary depression, alcohol abuse or other comorbid disorders. Other secondary effects are apparent from consistent data showing that persons with SP are more likely to be unmarried and to have problems in areas of education, work function and social life, though activities of daily living are less likely to be impaired. More subtle forms of impairment, such as failing to achieve one's potential in work or settling for less satisfying social relationships due to social fears, are present, although difficult to measure.

POST-TRAUMATIC STRESS DISORDER

An increase in studies of post-traumatic stress disorder (PTSD) in recent years has generated substantial data on the influence of PTSD on QoL, primarily in high-risk samples of persons exposed to trauma of various kinds, but also in PTSD patients and in the community at large.

Community Settings

Persons with PTSD in the community manifest multiple impairments associated with QoL, including greater job instability, attempted suicide and impaired social support (Davidson et al., 1991). PTSD is associated with significant impairment in occupational, social and home functioning (Stein et al., 1997), and subsyndromal PTSD may be associated with similar impairment in social and home functioning. Similarity between full and subthreshold PTSD in respect to social and work impairment has been noted in a clinical sample of treatment-seeking patients (Zlotnick, Franklin and Zimmerman, 2002) and in an Anxiety Disorders Screening Day sample (Marshall et al., 2001).

High-Risk Samples

PTSD has been associated with lower QoL within high-risk samples exposed to trauma of various kinds. Nine months after exposure to an earthquake, subjects with current PTSD ($N=28$) manifested worse QoL in physical, social and environmental domains (Wang et al., 2000). Motor vehicle accident survivors with PTSD showed poorer psychosocial functioning than survivors without PTSD, and emotional numbing best predicted psychosocial impairment (Kuhn, Blanchard and Hickling, 2003).

PTSD has been associated with poorer QoL in young adult survivors of childhood cancer (Meeske et al., 2001), cardiac surgical patients (Schelling et al., 2003) and heart or lung transplant patients (Kollner et al., 2002). Two studies have shown that among victims of physical trauma, those who had PTSD 6–12 months later reported lower QoL (Holbrook et al., 2002; Zatzick et al., 2002), and this impairment persisted up to18-month follow-ups (Holbrook et al., 2002). After controlling for other variables, PTSD remained the strongest predictor of adverse outcome (Zatzick et al., 2002). The severity of PTSD symptoms has been associated with poorer perceived physical well-being in a treatment-seeking sample of adult women with childhood abuse history ($N=67$) (Cloitre et al., 2001) and with lower mental health composite scores on the SF-36 among female victims of intimate partner violence ($N=40$) (Lafaye, Kennedy and Stein, 2003).

The National Vietnam Veterans Readjustment Study assessed QoL in 1200 veterans, 15% of whom had PTSD (Zatzick et al., 1997). Level of impairment, including bed days in the past 2 weeks, working status, subjective well-being, self-reported physical health and functioning, and perpetration of violence in the past year, were associated with the severity of PTSD symptoms. Most associations persisted after controlling for comorbidity. PTSD in Vietnam veterans has also been associated with decreased employment more than a decade after military service, decreased wages (Savoca and Rosenheck, 2000) and increased distress in intimate relationships (Gallagher *et al.*, 1998). US veterans of the Gulf War who reported PTSD in a telephone survey also reported lower levels of health-related QoL (Barrett *et al.*, 2002). The persistence of impairment can be life-long for some traumas. Forty-four adults who had survived the Holocaust as children were found 55 years later to have elevated PTSD symptom scores and lower physical, psychological and social QoL (Amir and Lev-Wiesel, 2003).

Psychiatric Clinic Settings

Warshaw *et al.* (1993) found that within an anxiety disorder clinic, PTSD ($N=63$) was associated with receipt of public assistance, and worse health, role functioning and emotional health. Improvement in measures of QoL has been shown to accompany symptomatic improvement in studies of PTSD treatment with selective serotonin reuptake inhibitors (SSRIs). One study showed improvement in vitality, social functioning and mental health on the SF-36 with fluoxetine versus placebo treatment (Malik *et al.*, 1999). In a multicentre placebo-controlled trial of 359 patients with PTSD treated for 12 weeks, sertraline was associated with marked improvement on all QoL measures. Within the subset of patients who were judged to be responders to sertraline, 58% achieved Quality of Life Enjoyment and Satisfaction Questionnaire (Q-LES-Q) total scores within 10% of community norms. Further improvement (20%) occurred after 24 weeks of maintenance treatment (Rapaport, Endicott and Clary, 2002).

Summary

Recent findings have documented a clear, long-lasting impact of PTSD on QoL among persons exposed to a wide variety of traumas. Subsyndromal PTSD appears to exert similar effects. Persons with PTSD experience broad impairments including difficulties in work, social relationships and intimacy, and somatic complaints, but with effective treatment, QoL may improve to normal levels.

PTSD may affect QoL via persistent arousal symptoms, avoidance of stimuli associated with a traumatic event or numbing of emotional responsiveness. Impairment in QoL has generally been shown to be associated more directly with PTSD than with severity of exposure to the trauma per se. Athough impairment in QoL has been noted across the whole spectrum of traumas known to induce PTSD, it is also likely that the nature and timing of the traumatic event (e.g. military trauma versus childhood sexual abuse) may yield different patterns of impairment in QoL. For example, childhood sexual abuse has been associated with lower self-assessed health and sexual attractiveness (Wenninger and Heiman, 1998). Commonly used QoL assessment instruments may not be designed to detect such specific differences.

GENERALISED ANXIETY DISORDER

Although generalised anxiety disorder (GAD) is highly prevalent, its specific contribution to impairment of QoL has been questioned in the past, due to its high comorbidity with other psychiatric conditions. Several large epidemiological and clinical studies in recent years have clarified this issue.

Community Settings

In the NCS and another large community study, the Midlife Development in the United States Survey, role impairment due to GAD was elevated and comparable to that due to MDD, even after adjusting for comorbid disorders (Kessler *et al.*, 1999). For example, in the NCS group with GAD only ($N=92$), 15.8% perceived their mental health as excellent, compared with 33.2% of the normal group, while 29.3% of the GAD patients perceived it as fair or poor, compared with only 4.7% of the control group. High impairment in social role was reported by 24% of GAD patients and by 8.4% of the control group.

Clinical Settings

Massion, Warshaw and Keller (1993) found outpatients with GAD (N=63) comparable to PD out-patients in overall satisfaction and functioning. Some recent treatment trials in GAD have incorporated disability assessments. Treatment with the SSRI paroxetine was associated with significant improvement in overall disability (Rickels et al., 2003). In primary care samples, Schonfeld et al. (1997) found decreased QoL in GAD patients assessed with the SF-36, even among those patients with no comorbidity; Olfson et al. (1997) reported elevated levels of disability in GAD patients, most of whom had comorbidity. In a German national survey, Wittchen et al. (2000) reported that GAD, after controlling for comorbidity, was associated with poor self-perceived health and low QoL scores on the SF-36.

Summary

These studies demonstrate that persons with GAD do suffer significant impairment, even in the absence of comorbidity. Persons with GAD experience chronic worry, physical symptoms of tension and insomnia, leading to work and social disabilities and high utilisation of medical resources.

OBSESSIVE–COMPULSIVE DISORDER

While obsessive–compulsive disorder (OCD) is generally believed to be one of the most impairing of anxiety disorders, until recently there were surprisingly few data on this subject.

Community Samples

In the ECA study (Karno et al., 1988), OCD was found to be more prevalent among divorced or separated and unemployed persons. There was also a significant association with lower socioeconomic status. A German study (Grabe et al., 2000) also found impaired social function and QoL in OCD and subclinical OCD.

Clinical Samples

Koran, Thienemann and Davenport (1996) studied 60 adult out-patients with OCD who were entering a pharmacological treatment trial. SF-36 scores for role limitation due to emotional problems were nearly one standard deviation below the average for the general US population. OCD patients were impaired in mental but not physical health domains, and the severity of OCD symptoms was correlated with worse social functioning. Among 43 out-patients with OCD, severity of depression and obsessions, but not severity of compulsions, predicted interference in QoL (Masellis, Rector and Richter, 2003). An in-patient study showed that patients with severe OCD (N = 17) had more functional impairment than hospitalised depressed patients, and they did not differ from patients with schizophrenia in functional impairment, quality of friendships, employment history or activities of daily living (Bystritsky et al., 1999).

A questionnaire study of Obsessive Compulsive Foundation members found that more than half of persons with OCD reported interference with social and work functioning, and nearly two-thirds reported interference with socialising or making friends. Difficulties in family relationships were reported by 70% and decreased self-esteem by 90%. Moderate to severe distress from obsessions occurred in 59% and from compulsions in 51% (Hollander et al., 1996). Similar findings emerged from a South African OCD organisation (Stein et al., 1996).

An additional source of impairment is the disruption in family relationships due to family conflict over OCD rituals. Calvocoressi et al. (1995) assessed a spouse or parent of 34 patients with OCD. Overall, 88% of the relatives reported accommodating the patient by modification of: family routine (35%), work schedule (22%) and leisure activities (53%). Fallon et al. (1996) found that among key relatives of OCD patients (N = 32), more than one-third reported a moderate or severe burden, including difficulty taking trips, poor social relationships and neglect of hobbies.

OCD patients ($N=649$) manifested improvement in QoL during 52 weeks of single-blind treatment with sertraline. Among patients ($N=225$) entering a subsequent placebo-controlled 28-week continuation phase, those randomised to sertraline showed further improvement and were significantly better than the placebo group (Koran *et al.*, 2002). In a smaller study in a partial hospitalisation programme, six months of open treatment led to improvement in three out of eight subjective QoL measures (activities, social and health dimensions) but not in respect to work, disability, employment and family support (Bystritsky *et al.*, 1999).

Summary

Zapotoczky (1994) has suggested that there are several aspects to the impairment of QoL among persons with OCD. These include direct impairment of QoL by such means as loss of time to compulsive behaviours, impairment related to the social isolation that may accompany OCD and impairment related to comorbid depression. Among severe patients, poor concentration and the need to engage in compulsive, repetitive behaviours may significantly hamper work performance. Social relationships frequently suffer due to the overriding focus on completion of rituals, while the ability to attend to personal hygiene, eat, dress, perform household chores, manage money and use the telephone are also often compromised.

More difficult to measure is the subjective toll OCD sufferers pay of feeling enslaved to unwanted obsessions and rituals. Some persons with OCD are able to suppress their rituals in public, but they continue to be distracted by frequent obsessive thoughts. The bizarre quality of some compulsive behaviours also results in a deep sense of shame for many patients, which may lead to social isolation and depression. Further study of the QoL in OCD is much needed.

CONCLUSIONS

While systematic study of QoL in persons with anxiety disorders has only recently begun, there is growing evidence of substantial impairment in subjective QoL, objective functioning and socioeconomic status. All anxiety disorders seem to impair QoL through the distress of the anxiety experience itself, the avoidance behaviour that often accompanies the anxiety and the stigma attached to having emotional problems. The nature of the impairment in QoL, however, shows some variation, depending on the particular disorder. For example, social functioning may be relatively spared in PD, whereas persons with SP may be less impaired in respect to ability to travel.

Existing data have focused on simple objective measures of functional impairment (e.g. unemployment) and global subjective reports of impairment and QoL. One area that remains lacking is richer description of the ways QoL is impaired in these disorders. Within disorders, are some symptoms particularly disabling or protective? Across disorders, is age of onset or absence of social support a crucial factor in the effect on QoL? The mechanisms leading to impairment remain unclear. The impact of treatment (and its limitations) on improving QoL, which is already apparent to both clinicians and patients, also needs to be clarified. Novel approaches may need to be developed to address deficits in QoL that persist despite symptomatic improvement.

REFERENCES

Amir, M. & Lev-Wiesel, R. (2003). Time does not heal all wounds: Quality of life and psychological distress of people who survived the Holocaust as children 55 years later, *J. Trauma Stress*, **16**, 95–99.

Arrindell, W.A. & Emmelkamp, P.M. (1986). Marital adjustment, intimacy and needs in female agoraphobics and their partners: A controlled study, *Br. J. Psychiatry*, **149**, 592–602.

Barrett, D.H., Doebling, C.C., Schwartz, D.A., Voelker, M.D., Falter, K.H., Woolson, R.F. & Doebbling, B.N. (2002). Posttraumatic stress disorder and self-reported physical health status among U.S. military personnel serving during the Gulf War period: a population-based study, *Psychosomatics*, **43**, 195–205.

Barsky, A.J., Delamater, B.A. & Orav, J.E. (1999). Panic disorder patients and their medical care, *Psychosomatics*, **40**, 50–56.

Bystritsky, A., Saxena, S., Maidment, K., Vapnik, T., Tarlow, G. & Rosen, R. (1999). Quality-of-life changes among patients with obsessive–compulsive disorder in a partial hospitalization program, *Psychiat. Serv.*, **50**, 412–414.

Calvocoressi, L., Lewis, B., Harris, M., Trufan, S.J., Goodman, W.K., McDougle, C.J. & Price, L.H. (1995). Family accommodation in obsessive–compulsive disorder, *Am. J. Psychiatry*, **152**, 441–443.

Candilis, P.J., McLean, R.Y., Otto, M.W., Manfro, G.G., Worthington 3rd, J.J. Penava, S.J., Marzol, P.C. & Pollack, M.H. (1999). Quality of life in patients with panic disorder, *J. Nerv. Ment. Dis.*, **187**, 429–434.

Carpiniello, B., Baita, A., Carta, M.G., Sitzia, R., Macciardi, A.M., Murgia, S. & Altamura, A.C. (2002). Clinical and psychosocial outcome of patients affected by panic disorder with or without agoraphobia: Results from a naturalistic follow-up study, *Eur. Psychiatry*, **17**, 394–398.

Cloitre, M., Cohen, L.R., Edelman, R.E. & Han, H. (2001). Posttraumatic stress disorder and extent of trauma exposure: Correlates of medical problems and perceived health among women with childhood abuse, *Women and Health*, **34**, 1–17.

Davidson, J.R., Hughes, D., Blazer, D.G. & George, L.K. (1991). Post-traumatic stress disorder in the community: An epidemiological study, *Psychol. Med.*, **21**, 713–721.

Davidson, J.R.T., Hughes, D.C., George, L.K. & Blazer, D.G. (1994). The boundary of social phobia: Exploring the threshold, *Arch. Gen. Psychiatry*, **51**, 975–983.

Edlund, M.J. & Swann, A.C. (1987). The economic and social costs of panic disorder, *Hosp. Community Psychiatry*, **38**, 1277–1288.

Ettigi, P., Meyerhoff, A.S., Chirban, J.T., Jacobs, R.J. & Wilson, R.R. (1997). The quality of life and employment in panic disorder, *J. Nerv. Ment. Dis.*, **185**, 368–372.

Fallon, I.R., Magliano, L., Graham-Hole, V. & Woodroffe, R. (1996). The stress of caring for disabling mental disorders in a home-based rehabilitation service, *J. Nerv. Ment. Dis.*, **184**, 381–384.

Fava, G.A., Rafanelli, C., Ottolini, F., Ruini, C., Cazzaro, M. & Grandi, S. (2001). Psychological well-being and residual symptoms in remitted patients with panic disorder and agoraphobia, *J. Affect. Disord.*, **65**, 185–190.

Gallagher, J.G., Riggs, D.S., Byrne, C.A. & Weathers, F.W. (1998). Female partners' estimations of male veterans' combat-related PTSD severity, *J. Trauma Stress*, **11**, 367–374.

Grabe, H.J., Meyer, C., Hapke, U., Rumpf, H.J., Freyberger, H.J., Dilling, H. & John, U. (2000). Prevalence, quality of life and psychosocial function in obsessive–compulsive disorder and subclinical obsessive–compulsive disorder in northern Germany, *Eur. Arch. Psychiatry Clin. Neurosci.*, **250**, 262–268.

Hambrick, J.P., Turk, C.L., Heimberg, R.G., Schneier, F.R. & Liebowitz, M.R. (2003). Psychometric properties of disability measures among patients with social anxiety disorder, *Depress. Anxiety*, **18**, 46–50.

Holbrook, T.L., Hoyt, D.B., Stein, M.B. & Sieber, W.J. (2002). Gender differences in long-term posttraumatic stress disorder outcomes after major trauma: Women are at higher risk of adverse outcomes than men, *J. Trauma*, **53**, 882–888.

Hollander, E., Kwon, J.H., Stein, D.J., Broatch, J., Rowland, C.T. & Himelein, C.A. (1996). Obsessive–compulsive and spectrum disorders: Overview and quality of life issues, *J. Clin. Psychiatry*, **57**(Suppl. 8), 3–6.

Hollifield, M., Katon, W., Skipper, B., Chapman, T., Ballenger, J.C., Manuzza, S. & Fyer, A.J. (1997). Panic disorder and quality of life: Variables predictive of functional impairment, *Am. J. Psychiatry*, **154**, 766–772.

Jacobs, R.J., Davidson, J.R., Gupta, S. & Meyerhoff, A.S. (1997). The effects of clonazepam on quality of life and work productivity in panic disorder, *Am. J. Manag. Care*, **3**, 1187–1196.

Karno, M., Golding, J.M., Sorenson, S.B. & Burnam, M.A. (1988). The epidemiology of obsessive–compulsive disorder in five communities, *Arch. Gen. Psychiatry*, **45**, 1094–1099.

Katerndahl, D.A. & Realini, J.P. (1997). Quality of life and panic-related work disability in subjects with infrequent panic and panic disorder, *J. Clin. Psychiatry*, **58**, 153–158.

Katerndahl, D.A. & Realini, J.P. (1998). Associations with subsyndromal panic and the validity of DSM-IV criteria, *Depress. Anxiety*, **8**, 33–38.

Katzelnick, D.J., Kobak, K.A., DeLeire, T., Henk, H.J., Greist, J.H., Davidson, J.R., Schneier, F.R., Stein, M.B. & Helstad, C.P. (2001). Impact of generalized social anxiety disorder in managed care, *Am. J. Psychiatry*, **158**, 1999–2007.

Kessler, R.C., McGonagle, K.A., Zhao, S., Nelson, C.B., Hughes, M., Eshleman, M.A., Wittchen, H.U. & Kendler, K.S. (1994). Lifetime and 12-month prevalence of DSM-III-R psychiatric disorders in the United States, *Arch. Gen. Psychiatry*, **51**, 8–19.

Kessler, R.C., DuPont, R.L., Berglund, P. & Wittchen, H.U. (1999). Impairment in pure and comorbid generalized anxiety disorder and major depression at 12 months in two national surveys, *Am. J. Psychiatry*, **156**, 1915–1923.

Klerman, G.L., Weissman, M.M., Ouellette, R., Johnson, J. & Greenwald, S. (1991). Panic attacks in the community: Social morbidity and health care utilization, *J. Am. Med. Ass.*, **265**, 742–746.

Kollner, V., Schade, I., Maulhardt, T., Maercker, A., Joraschky, P. & Gulielmos, V. (2002). Posttraumatic stress disorder and quality of life after heart or lung transplantation, *Transplantation Proc.*, **34**, 2192–2193.

Koran, L.M., Thienemann, M.L. & Davenport, R. (1996). Quality of life for patients with obsessive compulsive disorder, *Am. J. Psychiatry*, **153**, 783–788.

Koran, L.M., Hackett, E., Rubin, A., Wolkow, R. & Robinson, D. (2002). Efficacy of sertraline in the long-term treatment of obsessive–compulsive disorder, *Am. J. Psychiatry*, **59**, 88–95.

Kuhn, E., Blanchard, E.B. & Hickling, E.J. (2003). Posttraumatic stress disorder and psychosocial functioning within two samples of MVA survivors, *Behaviour Res. Theory*, **41**, 1105–1112.

Lafaye, C., Kennedy, C. & Stein, M.B. (2003). Post-traumatic stress disorder and health related quality of life on female victims of intimate partner violence, *Violence Victims*, **18**, 227–238.

Leon, A.C., Shear, M.K., Klerman, G.L., Portra, L., Rosenbaum, J.F. & Goldenberg, I. (1993). A comparison of symptom determinants of patient and clinician global ratings in patients with panic disorder and depression, *J. Clin. Psychopharmacol.*, **13**, 327–331.

Magee, W.J., Eaton, W.W., Wittchen, H.U., McGonagle, K.A. & Kessler, R.C. (1996). Agoraphobia, simple phobia and social phobia in the National Comorbidity Survey, *Arch. Gen. Psychiatry*, **53**, 159–168.

Malik, M.L., Connor, K.M., Sutherland, S.M., Smith, R.D., Davison, R.M. & Davidson, J.R. (1999). Quality of life and posttraumatic stress disorder: A pilot study assessing changes in SF-36 scores before and after treatment in a placebo-controlled trial of fluoxetine, *J. Trauma Stress*, **12**, 387–393.

Markowitz, J.S., Weissman, M.M., Puellette, R., Lish, J.D. & Klerman, G.L. (1989). Quality of life in panic disorder, *Arch. Gen. Psychiatry*, **46**, 984–992.

Marshall, R.D., Olfson, M., Hellman, F., Blanco, C., Guardino, M. & Struening, E.L. (2001). Comorbidity, impairment, and suicidality in subthreshold PTSD, *Am. J. Psychiatry*, **158**, 1467–1473.

Masellis, M., Rector, N.A. & Richter, M.A. (2003). Quality of life in OCD: Differential impact of obsessions, compulsions and depression comorbidity, *Can. J. Psychiatry*, **48**, 72.

Massion, A.O., Warshaw, M.G. & Keller, M.B. (1993). Quality of life and psychiatric morbidity in panic disorder and generalized anxiety disorder, *Am. J. Psychiatry*, **150**, 600–607.

Meeske, K.A., Ruccione, K., Globe, D.R. & Stuber, M.L. (2001). Posttraumatic stress, quality of life, and psychological distress in young adult survivors of childhood cancer, *Oncol. Nurs. Forum*, **28**, 481–489.

Olfson, M., Fireman, M., Weissman, M.M., Leon, A.C., Sheehan, D.V., Kathol, R.G., Hoven, C. & Farber, L. (1997). Mental disorders and disability among patients in a primary care group practice, *Am. J. Psychiatry*, **154**, 1734–1740.

Ormel, J., Von Korff, M., Üstün, T.B., Pini, S., Korten, A. & Oldehinkel, T. (1994). Common mental disorders and disability across cultures: Results from the WHO collaborative study on psychological problems in general health care, *J. Am. Med. Ass.*, **272**, 1741–1748.

Perugi, G., Akiskal, H.S., Musetti, L., Simonini, E. & Cassano, G.B. (1994). Social adjustment in panic–agoraphobic patients reconsidered, *Br. J. Psychiatry*, **164**, 88–93.

Pohl, R.B., Wolkow, R.M. & Clary, C.M. (1998). Sertraline in the treatment of panic disorder: A double-blind multicenter trial, *Am. J. Psychiatry*, **155**, 1189–1195.

Rapaport, M.H., Endicott, J. & Clary, C.M. (2002). Posttraumatic stress disorder and quality of life: Results across 64 weeks of sertraline treatment, *J. Clin. Psychiatry*, **63**, 59–65.

Rickels, K., Zaninelli, R., McCafferty, J., Bellew, K., Ivengar, M. & Sheehan, D. (2003). Paroxetine treatment of generalized anxiety disorder: A double-blind, placebo-controlled study, *Am. J. Psychiatry*, **160**, 749–756.

Roy-Byrne, P.P., Milgrom, P., Tay, K.M., Weinstein, P. & Katon, W. (1994). Psychopathology and psychiatric diagnosis in subjects with dental phobia, *J. Anxiety Disord.*, **8**, 19–31.

Rubin, H.C., Rapaport, M.H., Levine, B., Gladsjo, J.K., Rabin, A., Auerbach, M., Judd, L.L. & Kaplan, R. (2000). Quality of well being in panic disorder: The assessment of psychiatric and general disability, *J. Affect. Disord.*, **57**, 217–221.

Safren, S.A., Heimberg, R.G., Brown, E.J. & Holle, C. (1996). Quality of life in social phobia, *Depress. Anxiety*, **4**, 126–33.

Savoca, E. & Rosenheck, R. (2000). The civilian labor market experiences of Vietnam-era veterans: The influence of psychiatric disorders, *J. Ment. Health Policy Econ.*, **3**, 199–207.

Schelling, G., Richter, M., Roozendaal, B., Rothenhausler, H.B., Krauseneck, T., Stoll, C., Nollert, G., Schmidt, M. & Kapfhammer, H.P. (2003). Exposure to high stress in the intensive care unit may have negative effects on health-related quality-of-life outcomes after cardiac surgery, *Crit. Care Med.*, **31**, 1971–1980.

Schneier, F.R., Johnson, J., Hornig, C.D., Liebowitz, M.R. & Weissman, M.M. (1992). Social phobia: Comorbidity and morbidity in an epidemiologic sample, *Arch. Gen. Psychiatry*, **49**, 282–288.

Schneier, F.R., Heckelman, L.R., Garfinkel, R., Campeas, R., Fallon, B.A., Gitow, A., Street, L., DelBene, D. & Liebowitz, M.R. (1994). Functional impairment in social phobia, *J. Clin. Psychiatry*, **55**, 322–331.

Schonfeld, W.H., Verboncoeur, C.J., Fifer, S.K., Lipschutz, R.C., Lubeck, D.P. & Buesching, D.P. (1997). The functioning and well-being of patients with unrecognized anxiety disorders and major depressive disorder, *J. Affect. Disord.*, **43**, 105–119.

Sherbourne, C.D., Wells, K.B. & Judd, L.L. (1996). Comorbid anxiety disorder and the functioning and well-being of chronically ill patients of general medical providers, *Arch. Gen. Psychiatry*, **53**, 889–895.

Siegel, L., Jones, W.C. & Wilson, J.O. (1990). Economic and life consequences experienced by a group of individuals with panic disorder, *J. Anxiety Disord.*, **4**, 201–211.

Simon, N.M., Otto, M.W., Korbly, N.B., Peters, P.M., Nicolaou, D.C. & Pollack, M.H. (2002). Quality of life in social anxiety disorder compared with panic disorder and the general population, *Psychiat. Serv.*, **53**, 714–718.

Stein, M.B. & Kean, Y.M. (2000). Disability and quality of life in social phobia: Epidemiologic findings, *Am. J. Psychiatry*, **157**, 1606–1613.

Stein, M.B., Walker, J.R. & Forde, D.R. (1994). Setting diagnostic thresholds for social phobia: Considerations from a community survey of social anxiety, *Am. J. Psychiatry*, **151**, 308–312.

Stein, D.J., Roberts, M., Hollander, E., Rowland, C. & Serebro, P. (1996). Quality of life and pharmaco-economic aspects of obsessive–compulsive disorder. A South African Survey, *S. Afr. Med. J.*, **86**, 1579, 1582–1585.

Stein, M.B., Walker, J.R., Hazen, A.L. & Forde, D.R. (1997). Full and partial posttraumatic stress disorder: Findings from a community survey, *Am. J. Psychiatry*, **154**, 1114–1119.

Stein, M.B., Liebowitz, M.R., Lydiard, R.B., Pitts, C.D., Bushnell, W. & Gerfel, I. (1998). Paroxetine treatment of generalized social phobia (social anxiety disorder): A randomized controlled trial, *J. Am. Med. Ass.*, **280**, 708–713.

Stein, D.J., Versiani, M., Hair, T. & Kumar, R. (2002). Efficacy of paroxetine for relapse prevention in social anxiety disorder: A 24-week study, *Arch. Gen. Psychiatry*, **59**, 1111–1118.

Telch, M.J., Schmidt, N.B., Jaimez, T.L., Jacquin, K.M. & Harrington, P.J. (1995). Impact of cognitive-behavioral treatment on quality of life in panic disorder patients, *J. Consult. Clin. Psychol.*, **63**, 823–830.

Turner, S.M., Beidel, D.C., Dancu, C.V. & Keys, D.J. (1986). Psychopathology of social phobia and comparison to avoidant personality disorder, *J. Abnormal Psychol.*, **95**, 389–394.

Vasile, R.G., Goldenberg, I., Reich, J., Goisman, R.M., Lavori, P.W. & Keller, M.B. (1997). Panic disorder versus panic disorder with major depression: Defining and understanding differences in psychiatric morbidity, *Depress. Anxiety*, **5**, 12–20.

Wang, X., Guo, L., Shinfuku, N., Zhang, H., Zhao, C. & Shen, Y (2000). Longitudinal study of earthquake-related PTSD in a randomly selected community sample in North China, *Am. J. Psychiatry*, **157**, 1260–1266.

Warshaw, M.G., Fierman, E., Pratt, L., Hunt, M., Yonkers, K.A., Massion, A.O. & Keller, M.B. (1993). Quality of life and dissociation in anxiety disorder patients with histories of trauma or PTSD, *Am. J. Psychiatry*, **150**, 1512–1516.

Wenninger, K. & Heiman, A. (1998). Relating body image to psychological and sexual functioning in child sexual abuse survivors, *J. Trauma Stress*, **11**, 543–562.

Wittchen, H.U. & Beloch, E. (1996). The impact of social phobia on quality of life, *Int. Clin. Psychopharmacol.*, **11**(Suppl. 3), 15–23.

Wittchen, H.U., Carter, R.M., Pfister, H., Montgomery, S.A. & Kessler, R.C. (2000). Disabilities and quality of life in pure and comorbid generalized anxiety disorder and major depression in a national survey, *Int. Clin. Psychopharmacol.*, **15**, 319–328.

Zapotoczky, H.G. (1994). Quality of life and OCD, Abstract of Presentation at the 7th European Symposium of the Association of European Psychiatrists Section Committee on *Psychiatric Epidemiology and Social Psychiatry*, Vienna, Austria, 7–9 April 1994.

Zatzick, D.F., Marmar, C.R., Weiss, D.S., Browner, W.S., Metzler, T.J., Golding, J.M., Stewart, A., Schlenger, W.E. & Wells, K.B. (1997). Posttraumatic stress disorder and functioning and quality of life outcomes in a nationally representative sample of male Vietnam veterans, *Am. J. Psychiatry*, **154**, 1690–1695.

Zatzick, D.F., Jurkovich, G.J., Gentilello, L., Wisner, D. & Rivara, F.P. (2002). Posttraumatic stress, problem drinking, and functional outcomes after injury, *Arch. Surg.*, **137**, 200–205.

Zlotnick, C., Franklin, C.L. & Zimmerman, M. (2002). Does 'subthreshold' posttraumatic stress disorder have any clinical relevance?, *Comp. Psychiatry*, **43**, 413–419.

13

Quality of Life in Schizophrenia

Julio Bobes and María Paz García-Portilla

INTRODUCTION

In recent decades, there has been increased interest in the field of quality of life (QoL) in mental disorders. Some events in this field can be considered as historical milestones in the subject, as can be seen in Table 13.1.

Initial interest in QoL in clinical psychiatry began with the change of care policy toward the severely mentally ill, resulting from the introduction and growing use of antipsychotic drugs, as well as other factors. The development and stimulation of the American Community Support Systems funded by the National Institute of Mental Health to promote life in the community for the chronically mentally ill required the conceptualisation of new outcome measures for the evaluation of the effectiveness of such programmes. In relation to this, May (1979) (cited by Skantze et al., 1990) said, 'It is fairly easy to get patients out of the hospitals. The problem is keeping them out; preventing relapse, relieving their distress and improving their quality of life – which is a more difficult task'.

In 1982, Baker and Intagliata, the authors responsible for the evaluation project in New York State, gave five reasons for focusing on QoL as a desired outcome for programmes for the chronically mentally ill: comfort rather than cure, complex programmes require complex outcome measures, keeping the client happy, re-emergence of the holistic perspective and, finally, QoL is a good policy. Simultaneously, in Oregon, Bigelow et al. (1982) developed and applied a concept and measure of QoL as an outcome of mental health services. Since then, QoL has been considered an important goal of mental health services, to the extent that the National Institute of Mental Health (NIMH) in its plan 'Caring for Persons with Severe Mental Illness' selected QoL as one of the major outcome variables to be assessed (Attkisson et al., 1992). Another important event related to the development of the concept was the passing of the Patient Outcome Research Act by the US Congress in 1989. This obliged those conducting clinical trials to include QoL as a basic outcome measure. In Europe, however, the scenario is quite different and QoL is not included among the parameters that have to be evaluated for the approval of new antipsychotic drugs (Committee for Proprietary Medicinal Products, 1998).

As interest in QoL was growing, different authors began to develop instruments to measure the QoL of severely mentally ill patients. Various instruments have since been created, but only a few of them possess a conceptual model, have published psychometric properties and include cultural and language adaptations. In 1996, Lehman and Burns reviewed the characteristics of the QoL instruments more frequently employed in the evaluation of severely ill psychiatric patients. Lehman discusses the same subject in this volume (see Chapter 6). Then, McKenna (1997) specified the need for the development of a responsive QoL outcome measure for schizophrenia. The appearance of the atypical antipsychotic drugs (aripiprazol, clozapine, olanzapine, quetiapine, risperidone and ziprasidone), with different

Quality of Life in Mental Disorders, Second Edition   Edited by H. Katschnig, H. Freeman and N. Sartorius
© 2006 John Wiley & Sons, Ltd

Table 13.1   Historical milestones in quality of life in mental health

Years	Events
1970s	Deinstitutionalisation and development of community mental health programmes
1978	Psychological General Well-Being Index (DuPuy)
1982	First evaluations of community mental health programmes in terms of quality of life (Baker and Intagliata; Bigelow *et al.*; Lehman, Ward and Linn)
1984	Quality of Life Scale (Heinrichs, Hanlon and Carpenter)
1985	New antidepressants: SSRIs (selective serotonin reuptake inhibitor), NSRI (nonadrenaline and serotonin reuptake inhibitor)
1988	Quality of Life Interview (Lehman)
1988	Disability Assessment Schedule (World Health Organization)
1989	Approval of the Patient Outcome Research Act by the US Congress
1990	Atypical antipsychotics
1992	*Quality of Life Res.*, **1**(1).
1992	Quality of Life in Depression Scale (Hunt and McKenna)
1992	Short-Form 36 items (Ware and Sherbourne)
1993	World Health Organization Quality of Life Instrument (WHO)
1994	7th Congress of the AEP (Vienna) on *Quality of Life and Disabilities in Mental Disorders*
1997	Cuestionario Sevilla de calidad de vida (Giner *et al.*)
1998	European guidance on the clinical investigation of medicinal products in the treatment of schizophrenia
2002	Personal Evaluation of Transitions in Treatment (Voruganti and Awad)
2003	Schizophrenia-Quality of Life (Auquier *et al.*)

therapeutic and side-effect profiles from the conventional compounds, promoted further studies and a greater interest in assessing the QoL of schizophrenic patients.

An expression of the growing interest in this field was shown in the organisation by the Association of European Psychiatrists (AEP) of a meeting in Vienna 1994 dedicated to QoL and disabilities in mental disorders. However, in the last few years, the programmes of the Annual Conference of the International Quality of Life Research Organisation have reduced the time spent on the issue of mental disorders and QoL.

As this field evolves, the methodology of its assessment in severe mental disorders does the same; in recent years, several new instruments for assessing QoL in schizophrenic patients have been developed. These include the Seville Quality of Life Questionnaire (Giner *et al.*, 1997), the Personal Evaluation of Transitions in Treatment (Voruganti and Awad, 2002) and the Schizophrenia-Quality of Life (Auquier *et al.*, 2003).

MODELS OF QUALITY OF LIFE IN SCHIZOPHRENIA

Bigelow: Quality of Life as a Mental Health Service Outcome

The Bigelow *et al.* model of QoL was drawn from the needs theory of Maslow and the role theories of Sarbin and Allen (Bigelow *et al.*, 1982; Bigelow, McFarland and Olson, 1991). In this model, QoL results from the interaction between the fulfilment of needs and coping with the demands that society places upon its members. These two factors include, on the one hand, society, with the opportunities it brings for the fulfilment of the patients' needs, and on the other hand, the patients themselves, with their impaired psychological abilities for meeting society's demands.

In this model, mental health services would try to compensate for the deficits in the abilities of psychiatric patients and their consequently impaired participation in the normal opportunity structure. This is done through moderating social demands, supplementing opportunities and restoring abilities.

On the basis of this model, Bigelow, Gareau and Young (1990) developed their Quality of Life Questionnaire, which focuses on satisfaction and performance in important life domains.

Lehman: A General Model of Quality of Life

Based upon the data from two national surveys carried out in the 1970s on QoL in the American population, Lehman developed a general model for chronic mental patients. In this, he considers QoL as a subjective concept, dependent on the following three factors (Lehman, 1988):

1. Personal characteristics
2. Objective QoL indicators in several domains of life
3. Subjective QoL indicators in these same life domains

Objective and subjective indicators are two complementary measures of the patients' life experiences. While the former reflect norms of function and lifestyle, subjective indicators show how patients feel about their lives and are influenced by expectations, prior experiences and perceptions of current conditions.

Skantze and Malm: The Vulnerability–Stress–Coping Quality of Life Model

In their Vulnerability–stress–Coping QoL Model, Skantze and Malm (1994) described QoL as a dynamic concept, influenced by the difference between personal expectations and hopes, on the one hand, and perceived reality, on the other. The model for the evaluation of QoL in schizophrenic patients by Skantze et al. (1990) implied that it is necessary to consider QoL in its physical, social and cultural context, i.e. the person's 'standard of living'. Quality of life is a person's own subjective evaluation of his/her life situation, and thus can only be defined in terms of a subjective index. Based on the results of their studies, Skantze, Malm and their colleagues (Skantze et al., 1990, 1992) suggested that the patients' subjective evaluation of their lives depends more upon their 'inner world' than on the 'outer world'. By contrast, 'standard of living' in this model implies an observer's evaluation of the patient's life situation, and is therefore assessed from an objective point of view. It is not in itself a goal, but a means for achieving personal QoL goals (Skantze and Malm, 1994).

Awad: An Integrative Model of Quality of Life for Schizophrenic Patients Receiving Antipsychotic Treatment

In this circular, multidimensional model, Awad (Awad, 1995; Awad, Voruganti and Heslegrave, 1997) defines QoL as the patient's subjective perception of the outcome of an interaction between three major determinants:

1. Severity of psychotic symptoms
2. Medication side-effects (including a subjective response to antipsychotic drugs)
3. Level of psychosocial performance

This interaction is modulated by other second-order factors such as resources and their availability, premorbid adjustment, personality characteristics and values, and attitudes towards health and illness.
   This model specifically focuses on the effects of psychopharmacological treatments on patients' QoL.

ARE SCHIZOPHRENIC PATIENTS ABLE TO EVALUATE THEIR OWN QUALITY OF LIFE?

Some authors are still concerned with the question of whether schizophrenic patients, due to their lack of insight into the illness and cognitive deficiencies, are capable of self-assessing their QoL. In this sense, Lehman, Postrado and Rachoba (1993), although having demonstrated convergent validity in the perception of QoL between patients and clinicians, recommended caution. They do not minimise their concern about the validity of QoL assessments made by severely mentally ill patients.
   Browne et al. (1996) emphasised the view of several other authors that a clinical evaluation of psychiatric patients' reports of QoL would be desirable. This was because self-reports could be influenced by persistent psychotic symptoms, by the idiosyncratic views and values of these patients, or by

adaptation to adverse circumstances (Lehman, Postrado and Rachoba, 1993). In contrast, Skantze *et al.* (1992) showed that schizophrenic patients experience, feel and are able to report their social deficits, thus supporting the thesis that QoL can only be assessed subjectively.

From a methodological point of view, Lehman (1983a, 1983b) demonstrated that it is feasible to collect statistically reliable QoL data from chronic mental patients, and concluded that subjective QoL assessments can be applied to such individuals. None the less, from a clinical point of view, it was questionable whether these patients' judgements of their well-being can really be trusted, and what would have to be done in the case of any discrepancy between them and the view of clinicians. Such discrepancies have also been reported by Sainfort, Becker and Diamond (1996), using the Wisconsin Quality of Life (W-QOL) questionnaire (Becker, Diamond and Sainfort, 1993) in a sample of 40 schizophrenic patients from that state. The W-QOL questionnaire represents an effort to solve this concern of validity by means of requiring information not only from the patient but, in some areas, also from the clinician and family. Sainfort, Becker and Diamond (1996) demonstrated little agreement between well-being ratings made by service providers and patients, in all domains except symptoms.

Independent of their position with reference to the validity of the schizophrenic patients' assessments, the majority of authors highlight the need for negotiating treatment and service goals between patients, on the one hand, and professionals and politicians, on the other.

CLINICAL STUDIES OF QUALITY OF LIFE IN SCHIZOPHRENIC PATIENTS

Reviewing the various published studies concerning the QoL of schizophrenic patients, we have found considerable differences in the methodology employed, thus making it difficult to establish comparisons. Nevertheless, it can be concluded that, in general, QoL of schizophrenic patients is characterised by the following aspects:

1. It is worse than that of the general population and that of many physically ill patients.
2. Young people, women, married persons and those with a low level of education report a better QoL.
3. The longer the length of the illness, the worse the QoL.
4. Psychopathology, especially the negative and depressive syndromes, correlates negatively with QoL.
5. Lower side-effects and the combination of psychopharmacological and psychotherapeutic treatment improve QoL.
6. Patients integrated in community support programmes show a better QoL than those who are institutionalised.

The Level of Quality of Life of Schizophrenic Patients

Several studies have confirmed the intuitive idea that patients with severe chronic mental illness have an impoverished QoL, compared with that of the general population and many physically ill patients. In this sense, Lehman, Ward and Linn (1982) evaluated the QoL of a sample of residents in board-and-care homes in Los Angeles County, using the QoL interview (QOLI). They found that 56% of the patients felt mostly satisfied or delighted with their life in general, compared to 91% of the general American population who reported the degree of satisfaction with their lives (Andrews and Withey, 1976). Lower levels of satisfaction were reported by Bobes *et al.* (1996a, 1996b), using the QOLI in a sample of 78 private schizophrenic out-patients from Oviedo (northern Spain), who found that only 35% of their patients were mostly satisfied–delighted. However, it is necessary to bear in mind the methodological difficulties when comparing Spanish and American populations. In contrast, Larsen and Gerlach (1996) in Roskilde (Denmark) found that 53 schizophrenic out-patients being treated with depot neuroleptics reported a relatively high QoL level, using the Psychological General Well-Being (PGWB) index (DuPuy, 1978, 1984). The level was almost as high as that of the normal American population.

The mean general life satisfaction score reported by Lehman, Possidente and Hawker (1986) in their community residents from Los Angeles was 4.4, while the mean score for the national population was 5.5. This discrepancy decreased when compared with the scores from a sample of state hospital patients and community residents from Maryland (5.2) (Lehman, Possidente and Hawker, 1986) and with that from a sample of seriously mentally ill patients living in the community in Mississippi (5.3) (Sullivan, Wells and Leake, 1991).

When Lehman, Ward and Linn (1982) compared the QoL reported by psychiatric patients with that reported by socially disadvantaged groups from the general population (low socioeconomic status, blacks and unmarried parents), the differences decreased, although psychiatric patients still tended to be less satisfied. Unmarried parents showed levels of QoL more similar to those of patients. Sullivan, Wells and Leake (1991), on the other hand, found that their patients differed strongly from the black subsample and were more similar to the low socioeconomic group. Bobes *et al*. (1997) compared their private schizophrenic out-patients with women attending a menopausal unit at a university hospital and with haemodialysis patients. All groups were assessed using the medical outcomes study short form-36 (SF-36) (Ware and Sherbourne, 1992). It was found that schizophrenic out-patients showed greater impairment in their emotional roles and social functioning, when compared to climacteric individuals. The same was true in respect of their mental health emotional roles and vitality, when compared to haemodialysis patients.

Skantze *et al*. (1990), in a sample of schizophrenic out-patients from Gothenburg (Sweden) undergoing treatment with depot neuroleptics, reported that 84% of their out-patients could be considered to have a low QoL, when assessed with the Quality of Life Self-report – QLS-100 – even though they had good physical and social standards of living. Later, Skantze *et al*. (1992) reported that QoL and standard of living are independent of each other for schizophrenic patients. In 1983, Lehman had already concluded that subjective QoL indicators were much better predictors of global well-being than objective ones. Browne *et al*. (1996) also reported poor-to-moderate QoL, using the Quality of Life Scale (QLS) (Heinrichs, Hanlon and Carpenter, 1984) in a representative sample of schizophrenic patients attending a catchment area rehabilitation centre in Dublin (Ireland).

The areas of life with the greatest level of dissatisfaction vary between studies. Thus, Lehman, Ward and Linn (1982), with community residents from Los Angeles, identified finance and personal safety as those areas in which patients were more dissatisfied. Finance was also found to be the area with the greatest level of dissatisfaction in both state hospital patients and community residents from Maryland (Lehman, Possidente and Hawker, 1986), and also in seriously mentally ill patients living in the community in Mississippi (Sullivan, Wells and Leake, 1991). Skantze *et al*. (1990) identified the following areas as being those more frequently reported than others as unsatisfactory: work and activities, inner experiences and mental health, contacts with others and money. Kemmler *et al*. (1995), employing the Lancashire Quality of Life Profile (LQOLP) (Oliver, 1991) in a sample of 48 schizophrenic out-patients from south Tyrol (northern Italy), also found finance to be the area with the greatest level of dissatisfaction. Shepherd *et al*. (1996) obtained similar results using the LQOLP in a subsample of patients from private community residential homes in London. In contrast, Bobes *et al*. (1996a), with private out-patients from Oviedo, identified daily activities and health as the areas with the greatest level of dissatisfaction. This is of interest because health is one of the areas with the greatest level of satisfaction reported by several authors (Simpson, Hyde and Faragher, 1989; Kemmler *et al*., 1995; Shepherd *et al*., 1996), as well as one of the areas with the greatest weight in the perception of the global QoL (Mercier *et al*., 1990).

Demographic Factors and Quality of Life in Schizophrenic Patients

In 1983, Lehman, investigating board-and-care residents from Los Angeles County, found that sociodemographic and clinical characteristics have a major influence on the patients' global well-being. Women, married patients and those with a lower educational level were more satisfied with their lives as a whole, compared with other residents. However, Baker and Intagliata (1982), in a sample of 118 community support system clients, did not find a significant association between QoL, on the one hand, and age or sex, on the other. Similar results were reported by Sullivan, Wells and Leake (1992) in a seriously mentally ill population living in the community in Mississippi and by Bobes *et al*. (1996a) in private out-patients, who found that neither age, gender nor marital status influenced satisfaction with life in general (QOLI). However, women significantly reported more satisfaction with their daily activities and family relationships than men.

Meltzer *et al.* (1990), in a sample of treatment-resistant schizophrenic patients from Cleveland (Ohio), failed to find any relationships between age or gender, on the one hand, and QoL, on the other, when they were evaluated with the QLS. However, Browne *et al.* (1996), in a sample of schizophrenic out-patients attending a rehabilitation centre in Dublin (Ireland), found that age was negatively correlated with the total QLS score, this being contrary to the data from the general American population survey, in which the elderly expressed greater satisfaction with life than did younger patients. On the other hand, Shtasel *et al.* (1992), using the same scale in unmedicated patients, found that women revealed a better QoL than men, and specifically showed better functioning in social and relationship spheres.

Skantze *et al.* (1990), using the QLS-100 in out-patients undergoing maintenance treatment with depot neuroleptics, found no significant differences in the level of QoL in relation to age, gender, standard of living or having a modern house. However, QoL was significantly correlated positively with a long survival time (>2 years) in the community. However, in 1992, they reported that older patients and those with a higher level of education presented a significantly lower QoL, while those in employment showed a significantly better picture. In contrast, Browne *et al.* (1996) stated that in their sample, QoL was not influenced by the length of full-time education or by the time since last employment.

The lack of association between gender and QoL, found in a considerable proportion of studies, is described by Browne *et al.* (1996) as somewhat surprising, since it is generally accepted that, on the whole, women have a rather more benign form of illness and a better long-term outcome.

Clinical and Psychopathological Factors and Quality of Life in Schizophrenic Patients

There is considerable concern in QoL research about determining the influence of clinical variables on the QoL of schizophrenic patients. Thus, different studies have focused on variables such as diagnostic subtype, age of onset, length of illness, previous psychiatric hospitalisation, functional level, etc. Even though the overall results are not conclusive, the majority of authors agree that a worse quality is associated with residual type, longer length of illness and previous hospitalisation.

Barcia, Morcillo and Borgoñós (1995), in a sample of 100 schizophrenic out-patients from Murcia (Spain), found a significant association between diagnostic subtype and QoL as assessed by the QLS. The residual schizophrenia was the subtype associated with the worst level of QoL (compared with other subtypes of schizophrenia) and the cycloid psychosis was the subtype associated with a better level of QoL.

In treatment-resistant patients Meltzer *et al.* (1990) failed to find relationships between age at the onset of schizophrenia and length of illness, on the one hand, and QoL according to the QLS, on the other. In contrast, Morcillo, Barcia and Borgoñós (1995), in schizophrenic out-patients from Murcia (Spain), found a significant impairment in the QoL, as measured by the QLS, according to length of illness, viz. the longer the duration of illness, the worse the QoL. Similar results were obtained by Browne *et al.* (1996), who demonstrated a negative correlation between the length of illness and QoL scores. In contrast, Bobes *et al.* (1996b), in private out-patients, did not find any significant correlation between length of illness and quality of life (QOLI).

On the other hand, while Meltzer *et al.* (1990) found an inverse correlation between the number of previous hospital admissions and QoL scores and Browne *et al.* (1996) found a negative correlation between cumulative length of previous hospitalisation and QoL scores, Sullivan, Wells and Leake (1992) and Morcillo, Barcia and Borgoñós (1995) failed to find a significant association between the number of admissions and QoL. Similarly, Bobes *et al.* (1996b) failed to find one between presence or absence of hospitalisation and QoL.

Some studies have demonstrated the existence of a correlation between the level of functioning and QoL. Thus, Baker and Intagliata (1982), in community support system clients, obtained a positive correlation between the level of functioning as measured by the Global Assessment Scale (GAS) and the patients' self-reported QoL (satisfaction with life domains scale, or SLDS), although the coefficient was low in magnitude (0.29). Similarly, Mercier *et al.* (1990) in Canada also found a moderate positive correlation (0.34) between GAS and SLDS scores, and in 1994 found that high GAS scores formed part of the autonomy construct, which appeared to be the most influential factor in promoting patients' QoL. Sullivan, Wells and Leake (1992) also reported a significant positive correlation between

GAS scores and QoL scores (QOLI), while Bobes *et al.* (1996b) found a moderate relationship (−0.43) between disability, as measured by the Disability Scale (DDS) (World Health Organization), and QoL, viz. the lower the level of disability, the higher the QoL.

With reference to psychopathology, a large number of studies agree about its influence on QoL, and particularly emphasise the relevance of negative and depressive symptoms in determining this dimension in schizophrenic patients. Thus, Meltzer *et al.* (1990), studying treatment-resistant patients undergoing treatment with clozapine, reported that both positive and negative symptoms, as measured by the Brief Psychiatric Rating Scale (BPRS), influenced QoL, and that negative symptoms are more important than positive ones in determining this. In the same way, Lauer (1994) reported results from a pilot study in 30 schizophrenic patients by Lauer and Stegmüller (1989) in Germany. Using the QOLI, a significant negative correlation was found between subjective QoL and acute psychopathology as measured by the BPRS. Similarly, Bobes *et al.* (1996b) found significant negative correlations in schizophrenic outpatients between psychopathology, as measured by the Positive and Negative Syndrome Scale (PANSS), and QoL scores (QOLI). However, the coefficients were low, the negative syndrome being the most important influence on these patients' QoL.

Browne *et al.* (1996) in Dublin also found a negative correlation between negative symptomatology (Schedule for the Assessment of Negative Symptoms, or SANS) and QoL (QLS). Tollefson and Andersen (1999) undertook a post hoc analysis of the Tran *et al.* (1997) study in order to investigate the relationship between mood disturbance and QoL in schizophrenic patients. They found that changes in the quality of life (QLS) were inversely related to changes in the disruption of mood (PANSS), and that the strongest correlation was with the 'interpersonal relation' subscale score. In the same way, Revicki *et al.* (1999) and Hertling *et al.* (2003) both found an association between decreases in negative (PANSS) and depressive (Montgomery–Asberg Depression Rating Scale, or MADRS) symptoms and improvements in QoL (QLS and the European Quality of Life Visual Analogue Scale, or EuroQoL-VAS). In contrast, Larsen and Gerlach (1996), while finding a negative correlation between the PGWB index and the patients' rating of severity of illness, did not find any correlation between the patients' subjective assessment of their QoL and the PANSS scores. In respect of cognitive functioning, Velligan *et al.* (2003) found no significant relationship between improvements in cognition and in QoL.

QUALITY OF LIFE AND ANTIPSYCHOTIC DRUGS

Although QoL has been categorised as a distal outcome of antipsychotic therapy of schizophrenia (Lehman, 1996) and it has been stressed that QoL should be considered as important as psychopathology (Naber *et al.*, 2001), relatively few studies have reported data about the impact of antipsychotic drugs on this outcome. Corrigan *et al.* (2003) have stated that findings on this topic are mixed; about half of the studies demonstrate that, in comparison to typical antipsychotics, atypicals significantly increase the QoL of schizophrenia-spectrum patients. Data comparing the efficacy of each of the atypicals are lacking, however. A summary of the published studies is displayed in Table 13.2.

One issue of great concern in the majority of studies conducted is the instrument used for assessing the QoL of schizophrenic patients. The vast majority of published trials have employed the QLS (Heinrichs, Hanlon and Carpenter, 1984), an instrument specifically designed for evaluating the deficit syndrome of schizophrenia and not QoL. Furthermore, this is a clinician-rated instrument whereas, by definition, QoL is a subjective concept that needs to be assessed by patients themselves.

Meltzer *et al.*, with their studies on clozapine, may be regarded as the pioneers in this field. Although they had previously reported (1989) data on the QoL of 31 patients, it was in 1990 that they described 38 treatment-resistant schizophrenics from Cleveland who had been started on clozapine. Using the QLS, they found a significant improvement in the total score between baseline and after six months of treatment. There was an increase of 59.9% in the mean score, and in all four subscales, the interpersonal role and intrapsychic aspects were those with the largest mean increase (72.2 and 70.8%, respectively). In 1992, having studied 25 of these 38 patients over a 12-month period, Meltzer reported very similar results, i.e. a significant improvement in the total score and all subscales. Furthermore, there was a greater improvement in the 'instrumental role' function, which reached similar levels to those of the interpersonal and intrapsychic aspects. In 1993, the group reported

Table 13.2 Quality of life in clinical trials with antipsychotic drugs

Author (year)	Country	Antipsychotic drug	Design	Patients	Instruments	Results
Carrière, Bonhomme and Lemperiere (2000)	France	Amisulpride (400–1200 mg/day) Haloperidol (10–30 mg/day)	4-month double-blind, randomised in-patients	Baseline: 199 (94 AMI, 105 HAL) 4-month: 129 (70 AMI, 59 HAL)	QLS	AMI > HAL
Coloma et al. (2000)	France	Amisulpride (200–800 mg/day) Haloperidol (5–20 mg/day)	12-month open-label, randomised out-patients	Baseline: 488 (370 AMI, 118 HAL) 12-month: 322 (253 AMI, 69 HAL)	QLS	AMI > HAL in QLS total score and in intrapsychic foundations, interpersonal relations and instrumental role domain scores
Rosenheck et al. (1997)	USA (multicentre)	Clozapine (100–900 mg/day) Haloperidol (5–30 mg/day)	12-month open-label, randomised treatment-resistant in-patients	Baseline: 423 (205 CLZP, 218 HAL) 1-year: 178 (117 CLZP, 61 HAL)	QLS	CLZP > HAL among patients who completed their assigned treatment
Essock et al. (1996)	USA (Connecticut)	Clozapine usual care	2-year open-label, randomised treatment-resistant in-patients	Baseline: 227 (138 CLZP, 89 UC)	QOLI	CLZP = UC
Meltzer et al. (1990)	USA (Cleveland)	Clozapine	6-month open-label treatment-resistent patients	Baseline: 38	QLS	Significant improvement in all QLS scores
Montes et al. (2003)	Spain (multicentre – EFESO study)	Olanzapine (5–30 mg/day) Risperidone (1.5–9.5 mg/day) Haloperidol (3.8–30 mg/day)	6-month open-label without randomisation	182 (114 OLZ, 31 RISP, HAL 37)	EuroQol	OLZ and RISP > HAL on EuroQol-VAS scores
Gureje et al. (2003)	Australia and New Zealand	Olanzapine (10–20 mg/day) Risperidone (4–8 mg/day)	30-week double-blind, randomised in- and out-patients	Baseline: 65 (32 OLZ, 33 RISP) 30-week: 29 (17 OLZ, 12 RISP)	QLS SF-36	QLS: OLZ > RISP in the intrapsychic foundations subscale score. SF-36: OLZ > RISP in the role emotional subscale score
Ritchie et al. (2003)	UK	Olanzapine (9.9 mg/day) Risperidone (1.7 mg/day)	Open-label, randomised	Baseline: 66 (36 OLZ, 30 RISP) End: 32 OLZ, 22 RISP	WHOQOL-BREF	Significant improvements in the OLZ group in physical, psychological and health satisfaction domains. OLZ > RISP in the psychological domain score
Voruganti et al. (2002)	Canada	Olanzapine (15–40 mg/day) Risperidone (2–8 mg/day) Quetiapine (200–800 mg/day)	Naturalistic, single-blind, 2–6 years	Baseline: 150 (50 OLZ, 50 RISP, 50 QUET) End: 118 (44 OLZ, 43 RISP, 31 QUET)	QLS SIP	Significant improvements across all groups OLZ = RISP = QUET

Study	Location	Drug (dosage)	Design	Sample	Measure	Results
Ho et al. (1999)	USA (Iowa)	Olanzapine (14.4 mg/day) Risperidone (5.7 mg/day)	6-month open-label	Baseline: 42 (21 OLZ, 21 RISP) 6-month: 26 (13 OLZ, 13 RISP) in-patients	PSYCH-BASE	OLZ = RISP
Tran et al. (1997)	International (9 countries)	Olanzapine (10–20 mg/day) Risperidone (4–12 mg/day)	28-week double-blind, randomised in- and out-patients	Baseline: 339 (172 OLZ, 167 RISP) 28-week	QLS	OLZ and RISP: significant improvements on QLS total and all subscale scores. OLZ>RISP on QLS interpersonal relations score
Hamilton et al. (1998)	USA (multicentre)	Olanzapine (5 ± 2.5 mg/d; 10 ±2.5 mg/day; 15 ± 2.5 mg/day) Haloperidol (15 ± 5 mg/day) Placebo	24-week double-blind, randomised, placebo controlled in-patients	Data from 76 patients (16 OLZ-L, 16 OLZ-M, 22 OLZ-H, 12 HAL, 10 PBO)	QLS	OLZ-M & OLZ-H: significant improvements on QLS total and all subscale scores OLZ-H>PBO on QLS total score. OLZ-M>PBO on QLS total and all subscale scores
Revicki et al. (1999)	International (11 countries)	Olanzapine (5–20 mg/day) Haloperidol (5–20 mg/day)	52-week double-blind, randomised for 6-week acute phase and 46-week extension phase out-patients	Baseline: 1159 (787 OLZ, 372 HAL) 6-week: 600 OLZ, 228 HAL	QLS SF-36	Acute phase: QLS: OLZ>HAL in total, intrapsychic foundations and interpersonal relation scores SF-36: OLZ>HAL in MCS, V and MH. Extension phase: QLS: OLZ>HAL in total, intrapsychic foundations and instrumental role scores SF-36: OLZ=HAL
Velligan et al. (2003)	USA (Texas)	Quetiapine conventional antipsychotics	6-month open-label, rater-blinded, randomised	Baseline: 40 (20 QUET, 20 CAPS) 6-month: 27 (14 QUET, 13 CAPS)	QLS	QUET>CAPS
Bobes et al. (1998)	Spain (multicentre)	Risperidone (3–12 mg/day)	8-month open-label out-patients	Baseline: 318 Month 8: 264	SF-36	At end-point significant improvement in all SF-36 subscale scores and summary measures
Hertling et al. (2003)	Germany and Austria	Risperidone (2–6 mg/day) Flupenthixol (4–12 mg/day)	24-week double-blind, randomised in- and out-patients	Baseline: 153 (77 RISP, 76 FLU) 24-week: 107 (56 RISP, 51 FLU)	EuroQuol-VAS	Significant improvement in EuroQol-VAS in both groups; RISP = FLU

AMI: amisulpride; CAPS: conventional antipsychotics; CLZP: clozapine; HAL: haloperidol; FLU: flupenthixol; OLZ: olanzapine; OLZ-L: olanzapine (OLZ-L): olanzapine 5 ± 2.5 mg/day, OLZ-M: olanzapine 10 ± 2.5 mg/day, OLZ-H: olanzapine 15 ± 2.5 mg/day); PBO: placebo; QOLI: Quality of Life Interview; QLS: Quality of Life Scale; QUET: quetiapine; RISP: risperidone; SIP: Sickness Impact Profile; UC: usual care.

results from all 96 patients who had been admitted to an open trial of clozapine for treatment-resistant schizophrenia at the University Hospital of Cleveland. It was demonstrated that QoL scores only improved in patients who continued clozapine treatment for at least two years, this being an improvement of 242%.

Rosenheck *et al.* (1997) carried out a comparative study of clozapine and haloperidol in refractory schizophrenic in-patients. This was a randomised, one-year, double-blind study at 15 Veterans' Affairs medical centres. A total of 423 patients (clozapine=205; haloperidol=218) were assessed using the QLS. After one year, 117 clozapine-treated patients and 61 taking haloperidol continued their assigned treatment. Among these patients, clozapine was significantly superior to haloperidol in improving patients' QoL.

However, in 1996, Essock *et al.* failed to find any superiority of clozapine over conventional antipsychotics on patients' QoL. Their study was the first randomised cost-effectiveness trial of clozapine. It was a two-year, open-label, randomised comparison of clozapine with usual care in schizophrenic or schizo-affective treatment-resistant in-patients. A total of 227 patients (138 in the clozapine group and 89 in the usual care group) were assessed using the QOLI. Clozapine did not significantly affect patients' QoL: by month 8, both groups experienced equivalent improvements in the QOLI global satisfaction score.

More recently, the other atypical antipsychotics have been studied from the QoL point of view. With respect to amisulpride, Carrière, Bonhomme and Lemperiere (2000) carried out a multicentre, double-blind, randomised study for four months. A total of 199 in-patients with a diagnosis of paranoid schizophrenia or schizophreniform disorder (DSM-IV) were assessed using the QLS. Patients were randomised to receive oral amisulpride (400–1200 mg/day) (N=94) or haloperidol (10–30 mg/day) (N=105). Significantly more patients in the haloperidol than in the amisulpride group withdrew from the study (44 versus 26%). Quality of life was improved in both groups, but the improvement was significantly greater with amisulpride than with haloperidol.

Colonna *et al.* (2000) studied the long-term efficacy and safety of amisulpride in a group of 488 schizophrenic patients. They undertook a 12-month open-label, randomised comparison of 370 patients receiving amisulpride (200–800 mg/day) and 118 having haloperidol (5–20 mg/day). Patients' QoL was assessed using the QLS. Amisulpride demonstrated significantly greater improvements in the total QLS score and in scores on three QLS domains: 'intrapsychic foundations', 'interpersonal relations' and 'instrumental role'.

Recently, a study has compared the safety, effectiveness and QoL effects of olanzapine, risperidone and conventional antipsychotics in first-episode schizophrenia (Montes *et al.*, 2003). The subjects were taken from the EFESO study (a Spanish multicentre, phase IV, observational, six-month open-label study). Patients' QoL was assessed by means of the EuroQol (EQ-5D). Data were obtained from 114 patients receiving olanzapine, 31 receiving risperidone and 37 on conventional antipsychotics. Mean doses were as follows: olanzapine 13.5 mg/day, risperidone 5.4 mg/day, and haloperidol 12.4 mg/day. After six months of treatment, improvement in EuroQol-VAS scores was significantly greater in olanzapine-and risperidone-treated patients than in those receiving haloperidol.

Gureje *et al.* (2003) carried out a multicentre, 30-week, double-blind study comparing the efficacy, safety, use of health care resources, level of functioning and QoL between patients receiving olanzapine or risperidone. Sixty-five patients, either in-patients or out-patients, with a diagnosis of schizophrenia or schizophreniform disorder (DSM-IV criteria) and scores on the BPRS greater than 36 were randomised to receive 10–20 mg/day of olanzapine (N = 32) or 4–8 mg/day of risperidone (N = 33). QoL was assessed using the QLS (Heinrichs, Hanlon and Carpenter, 1984) and the SF-36 (Ware and Sherbourne, 1992). A total of 29 patients (17 in the olanzapine group and 12 in the risperidone group) completed the study. The mean modal doses were 17.2 mg/day (SD 2.8) for the olanzapine group and 6.6 mg/day (SD 1.6) for the risperidone cases. At the end of 30 weeks, olanzapine-treated patients had a statistically significantly greater improvement compared to the risperidone-treated patients in the QLS 'intrapsychic foundation' subscale and in the SF-36 'role emotional' subscale. The olanzapine-treated group reported a statistically significant improvement from the baseline to end-point in the QLS total score, in all QLS subscales except the 'instrumental role' and in all SF-36 scales except the physical. For the risperidone-treated group, a statistically significant improvement was only achieved for the bodily pain scale on the SF-36.

Ritchie *et al.* (2003) compared the impact on QoL of a switch from conventional antipsychotics to risperidone or olanzapine in 66 elderly patients with schizophrenia (mean age 69.6 years). Mean doses were 9.9 mg/day for olanzapine and 1.7 mg/day for risperidone. Quality of life was measured using the World Health Organization Quality of Life [Brief] scale (WHOQOL-BREF). Olanzapine-treated patients significantly improved from the baseline in the physical, psychological and health satisfaction domains, whereas risperidone-treated patients did not show significant improvements on any QoL domain. Treatment with olanzapine was associated with a better response over risperidone on the psychological domain of the scale.

The impact of switching from conventional to novel antipsychotic drugs on QoL was also studied by Voruganti et al. (2002). It involved 150 schizophrenic or schizo-affective patients (DSM-IV) who were considered suitable for a switch, based on an inadequate control of symptoms, subjective reports of side-effects or clinicians' concerns about the risk for adverse effects. The subjects were consecutively switched to risperidone (50 patients), olanzapine (50) and quetiapine (50). Patients were followed up for a period between two and six years. QoL was assessed by means of the QLS and the Sickness Impact Profile (SIP). At the end of follow-up 118 patients remained on novel antipsychotics (44 olanzapine, 43 risperidone and 31 quetiapine). Scores on the QLS and the SIP improved uniformly in the three groups after the switch. There were no significant differences among the three novel antipsychotics.

In another comparative open-label study, Ho et al. (1999) did not find any differential effects of risperidone and olanzapine on patients' QoL. They included 42 schizophrenic (DSM-IV criteria) in-patients, 21 of whom were started on risperidone (mean baseline dose 5.7 mg/day) and the remaining 21 on olanzapine (mean baseline dose 14.4 mg/day). The choice of drug was based on the treating psychiatrist's decision. Quality of life was assessed using the Psychiatric Status you Currently Have-Baseline version (PSYCH-BASE) (Andreasen, 1989) and its longitudinal follow-up version, the PSYCH-UP. The PSYCH-BASE is a structured interview with eight QoL indices: occupational impairment, financial dependence, impairment in performance of household duties, relationship impairment with family members and with friends, enjoyment of recreational activities, satisfaction and overall psychosocial functioning. A total of 26 patients (13 in each group) completed the six-month follow-up interview. At follow-up, there were no statistically differential effects between the two treatments on the eight QoL indices. Significant improvements at the time of follow-up were reported on overall psychosocial functioning in the risperidone group and on impairment in performance of household duties in the olanzapine group.

Tran et al. (1997) compared olanzapine with risperidone in an international, 28-week, double-blind, randomised study. Three hundred and thirty-nine (olanzapine $N=172$, risperidone $N=167$) schizophrenic, schizophreniform or schizoaffective patients (DSM-IV criteria) were assessed using the QLS. In both treatment groups, statistically significant improvements were observed on the QLS total score and on the four subscales from the baseline to end-point. Olanzapine demonstrated a significant greater improvement in the QLS 'interpersonal relations' subscale scores than did risperidone.

Hamilton et al. (1998) evaluated the impact of treatment with olanzapine, compared with haloperidol and placebo, on QoL in schizophrenic in-patients (DSM-IIIR criteria). They undertook a double-blind randomised study, with a six-week acute phase and an extension phase of 46 weeks for the responders. A total of 335 patients were randomised to one of the following groups: olanzapine 5 ± 2.5 mg/day, olanzapine 10 ± 2.5 mg/day, olanzapine 15 ± 2.5 mg/day, haloperidol 15 ± 5 mg/day, and placebo. Data at extension week 24 were reported and QoL was assessed employing the QLS. At end-point, no significant changes in the QLS total and subscale scores were observed for the placebo, olanzapine low-dose or haloperidol groups. In contrast, significant improvements were observed for the olanzapine medium and high doses. The olanzapine medium-dose group demonstrated significant greater improvements in all QLS scores than did the placebo group. The olanzapine high-dose group showed a greater improvement in the QLS total score, compared with the placebo group.

The impact of olanzapine on QoL has also been compared with the impact of haloperidol in a six-week, double-blind, randomised, multicentre trial with a long-term extension (46 weeks) (Revicki et al., 1999). A total of 1159 out-patients with a diagnosis of schizophrenia, schizophreniform or schizo-affective disorder (DSM-IIIR) and scores on the BPRS ≥ 18 were assessed using the QLS (Heinrichs, Hanlon and Carpenter, 1984). The SF-36 (Ware and Sherbourne, 1992) was also administered to the patients in English-speaking countries. Questionnaires were administered at the baseline and at the end of the acute phase of the study (week 6). In the extension phase, they were administered every eight weeks. At the end of the acute phase, data from 828 patients (600 in the olanzapine group and 228 in the haloperidol group) were obtained. Olanzapine-treated patients showed significantly greater improvements in QLS total, 'intrapsychic foundations' and 'interpersonal relations' scores, compared with the haloperidol group. Using the criterion of a 20% increase as clinically meaningful improvement in QLS total scores, 38% of olanzapine-treated patients showed clinically significant improvement in QoL, compared with 27% in the haloperidol group. Results with the SF-36 were similar; the olanzapine group demonstrated significantly greater improvements in the mental component summary scores and in the general health perception, vitality and mental health subscale scores. At the end of the extension phase (week 52), results with the QLS were almost identical: patients in the olanzapine group showed statistically greater improvements in QLS total, 'intrapsychic foundations' and 'instrumental role' scores than haloperidol-treated patients. Clinically significant improvement was obtained in 53% of the olanzapine group, compared with 42% in the haloperidol group. However, with the SF-36, no statistically significant differences were found between the treatment groups.

Velligan *et al.* (2003) studied the effectiveness of quetiapine versus conventional antipsychotic in improving QoL, as measured by the QLS. They carried out an open-label, rater-blinded study in which 40 stable schizophrenic out-patients were randomly assigned to either continue taking their conventional antipsychotic medication or be switched to quetiapine for six months. In the quetiapine group, six patients dropped out, while in the conventional antipsychotic group, seven did. Quetiapine-treated patients had better QoL scores during the follow-up period than those in the conventional group.

Bobes *et al.* (1998) studied the effect of risperidone monotherapy maintenance treatment on the QoL of 318 schizophrenic out-patients (ICD-10 criteria) who had been previously treated with other neuroleptics. Quality of life was assessed employing the SF-36 (Ware and Sherbourne, 1992). At month 8, significant improvement was observed in all SF-36 scale scores and in the summary measures. The greatest improvement was observed in the emotional role scale, followed by the physical role and social functioning measures.

Hertling *et al.* (2003) compared the impact of risperidone and flupenthixol on the QoL of both schizophrenic in-patients and out-patients with mainly negative symptoms (ICD-10 diagnosis F20.0–F20.3, F20.5–F20.9 excluding acute psychosis). They undertook a binational (Germany and Austria), 24-week randomised, double-blind trial in which 72 patients received risperidone and the same number flupenthixol. Patients' subjective QoL was assessed using the EuroQol-VAS and the Patient Satisfaction Questionnaire (Hellewell, 1999). After 24 weeks of treatment, the EuroQol-VAS score significantly increased in both groups, without significant differences between them. In the Patient Satisfaction Questionnaire, flupenthixol demonstrated significant greater improvements in 'feeling more able to cope with stress', 'feeling more relaxed' and 'feeling more able to achieve something' than risperidone.

Ziprasidone and aripiprazol, the newest clinically available antipsychotics, have demonstrated efficacy in a broad spectrum of symptomatology as well as a good tolerance profile. Preliminary data concerning their impact on patients' QoL have are reported to show significant greater improvements than conventional antipsychotics, but definitive data are still awaited.

CONCLUSIONS

In summary, it can be said that nowadays QoL is a consolidated outcome, broadly demanded by patients, families, clinicians and institutions. It is adversely influenced by symptoms, especially negative, cognitive and depressive ones, as well as by treatment-emergent adverse events. In this sense early therapeutic interventions upon the whole constellation of schizophrenic symptomatology may be of great value in improving patients' QoL. Furthermore, atypical antipsychotics, due to their broader efficacy profile and their better tolerability pattern, have demonstrated greater effectiveness in improving the QoL of schizophrenic patients than the conventional ones. However, data comparing the effectiveness of each of the atypicals are still scarce.

REFERENCES

Andreasen, N.C. (1989). *PSYCH-BASE*, The University of Iowa, Iowa.
Andrews, F.M. & Withey, S.B. (1976). *Social Indicators of Well-Being. America's Perception of Quality of Life*, pp. 1–24, Plenum Press, New York.

Attkisson, C., Cook, J., Karno, M., Lehman, A.F., McGlashan, T.H., Meltzer, H.Y., O'Connor, M., Richardson, D., Rosenblatt, A., Wells, K., Williams, J. & Hohmann, A.A. (1992). Clincal services research, *Schizophrenia Bull.*, **18**, 561–626.

Auquier, P., Simeoni, M.C., Sapin, C., Reine, G., Aghababian, V., Cramer, J. & Lançon, C. (2003). Development and validation of a patient-based health-related quality of life questionnaire in schizophrenia: the S-QoL, *Schizophrenia Res.*, **63**, 137–149.

Awad, A.G. (1995). Quality of life issues in medicated schizophrenics: therapeutics and research implications, in *The Treatment of Schizophrenia* (Eds C.L. Shariqui & H. Nasrallah), American Psychiatric Association Press, Washington, DC.

Awad, A.G., Voruganti, L.N.P. & Heslegrave, R.J. (1997). A conceptual model of quality of life in schizophrenia: Description and preliminary clinical validation, *Quality of Life Res.*, **6**, 21–26.

Baker, F. & Intagliata, J. (1982). Quality of life in the evaluation of community support systems, *Evaluation and Progm. Plann.*, **5**, 69–79.

Barcia, D., Morcillo, L. & Borgoñós, E. (1995). Esquizofrenia, calidad de vida y formas clínicas, *An. Psiquiatría*, **11**, 81–87.

Becker, M., Diamond, R. & Sainfort, F. (1993). A new patient focused index for measuring quality of life in persons with severe and persistent mental illness, *Quality of Life Res.*, **2**, 239–251.

Bigelow, D.A., Gareau, M.J. & Young, D.J. (1990). A quality of life interview, *Psychosocial Rehabil. J.*, **14**, 94–98.

Bigelow, D.A., McFarland, B.H. & Olson, M.M. (1991). Quality of life of community mental health program clients: Validating a measure, *Community Ment. Health J.*, **27**, 43–55.

Bigelow, D.A., Brodsky, G., Stewart, L. & Olson, M.M. (1982). The concept and measurement of quality of life as a dependent variable in evaluation of mental health services, in *Innovative Approaches to Mental Health Evaluation* (Eds G.J. Stahler & W.R. Tash), pp. 345–366, Academic Press Inc., New York.

Bobes, J., González, M.P., Bousoño, M., Muñoz, L., G-Quirós, M. & Wallace, D. (1996a). Quality of life in schizophrenic outpatients, in *Annual Meeting – New Research Program and Abstracts* (Ed. American Psychiatric Association), p. 223, American Psychiatric Association, Washington, DC.

Bobes, J., González, M.P., Wallace, D.H., Bousoño, M & Sáiz, P.A. (1996b). Quality of life instruments in schizophrenia: A comparative study, *Eur. Psychiatry*, **11** (Supple. 4), 228.

Bobes, J., González, M.P., Bousoño, M. & Sáiz, P.A. (1997). *Calidad de Vida y Salud Mental*, Aula Médica, Madrid.

Bobes, J., Gutiérrez, M., Gibert, J., González, M.P., Herraiz, L. & Fernández, A. (1998). Quality of life in schizophrenia: Long-term follow-up in 362 chronic Spanish schizophrenic outpatients undergoing risperidone maintenance treatment, *Eur. Psychiatry*, **13**, 158–163.

Browne, S., Roe, M., Lane, A., Gervin, M., Morris, M., Kinsella, A., Larkin, C. & O'Callaghan, E. (1996). Quality of life in schizophrenia: relationship to sociodemographic factors, symptomatology and tardive dyskinesia, *Acta Psychiatrica Scand.*, **94**, 118–124.

Carrière, P., Bonhomme, D. & Lemperiere, T. (2000). Amisulpride has a superior benefit/risk profile to haloperidol in schizophrenia: Results of a multicentre, double-blind study (the Amisulpride Study Group), *Eur. Psychiatry*, **15**, 321–329.

Colonna, L., Saleem, P., Dondey-Nouvel, L., Rein, W. & the Amisulpride Study Group (2000). Long-term safety and efficacy of amisulpride in subchronic or chronic schizophrenia, *Int. Clin. Psychopharmacol.*, **15**, 13–22.

Committee for Proprietary Medicinal Products (1998). Note for guidance on the clinical investigation of medicinal products in the treatment of schizophrenia, London, CPMP/EWP/559/95.

Corrigan, P.W., Reinke, R.R., Landsberger, S.A., Charate, A. & Toombs, G.A. (2003). The effects of atypical antipsychotic medications on psychosocial outcomes, *Schizophrenia Res.*, **63**, 97–101.

DuPuy, H.J. (1978). Self-representation of general psychological well-being of American adults, Paper presented at the American Public Association Meeting, Los Angeles, California.

DuPuy, H. (1984). The Psychological General Well-Being Index, in *Assessment of Quality of Life in Clinical Trials of Cardiovascular Therapies* (Ed. N. Wenger), pp. 170–183, Le Jacq, New York.

Essock, S.M., Hargreaves, W.A., Covell, N.H. & Goethe, J. (1996). Clozapine's effectiveness for patients in state hospitals: Results from a randomised trial, *Psychopharmacol. Bull.*, **32**, 683–697.

Giner, J., Ibáñez, E., Baca, E., Bobes, J., Leal, C. & Cervera, S. (1997). Desarrollo del Cuestionario Sevilla de Calidad de Vida (CSCV), *Actas Luso Esp. Neurol. Psiquiatr.*, **25**(Suppl. 2), 11–23.

Gureje, O., Miles, W., Keks, N., Grainger, D., Lambert, T., McGrath, J., Tran, P., Catts, S., Fraser, A., Hustig, H., Andersen, S. & Crawford, A.M. (2003). Olanzapine vs risperidone in the management of schizophrenia: A randomized double-blind trial in Australia and New Zealand, *Schizophrenia Res.*, **61**, 303–314.

Hamilton, S.H., Revicki, D.A., Genduso, L.A. & Beasley, C.M. (1998). Olanzapine versus placebo and haloperidol: Quality of life and efficacy results of the North American double-blind trial, *Neuropsychopharmacology*, **18**, 41–49.

Heinrichs, D.W., Hanlon, T.E. & Carpenter W.T. (1984). The quality of life scale: an instrument for rating the schizophrenic deficit syndrome, *Schizophrenia Bull.*, **10**, 388–398.

Hellewell, J.S. (1999). Treatment-resistant schizophrenia: Reviewing the options and identifying the way forward, *J. Clin. Psychiatry*, **60**(Suppl. 23), 14–19.

Hertling, I., Philipp, M., Dvorak, A., Glaser, T., Mast, O., Beneke, M., Ramskogler, K., Saletu-Zyhlarz, G., Walter, H. & Lesch, O.M. (2003). Flupenthixol versus risperidone: Subjective quality of life as an important factor for compliance in chronic schizophrenic patients, *Neuropsychology*, **47**, 37–46.

Ho, B.-C., Miller, D., Nopoulos, P. & Andreasen, N.C. (1999). A comparative effectiveness study of risperidone and olanzapine in the treatment of schizophrenia, *J. Clin. Psychiatry*, **60**, 658–663.

Hunt, S.M. & McKenna, S.P. (1992). The QLDS: A scale for the measurement of quality of life in depression, *Health Policy*, **22**, 307–319.

Kemmler, G., Holzner, B., Neudorfer, Ch., Schwitzer, J. & Meise, U. (1995). What constitutes overall life satisfaction of chronic schizophrenic outpatients? Results of a pilot study using the Lancashire Quality of Life Profile, *Quality of Life Res.*, **4**, 445–446.

Larson, E.B. & Gerlach, J. (1996). Subjective experience of treatment, side-effects, mental state and quality of life in chronic schizophrenic and out-patients treated with depot neuroleptics, *Acta Psychiatrica Scand.*, **93**, 381–388.

Lauer, G. (1994). The quality of life issue in chronic mental illness, in *Psychology and Promotion of Health* (Ed. J.P. Dauwalder), pp. 28–34, Hogrefe & Huber, Seattle, Washington.

Lauer, G. & Stegmüller, U. (1989). Zur Lebensqualität chronisch psychisch Kranker, Paper presented at 15 Longress für Angewandte Psychologie on *Psychologie für Menschenwürde und Lebensqualität*, Munich.

Lehman, A.F. (1983a). The well-being of chronic mental patients: assessing their quality of life, *Arch. Gen. Psychiatry*, **40**, 369–373.

Lehman, A.F. (1983b). The effects of psychiatric symptoms on quality of life assessments among the chronically mentally ill, *Evaluation and Progm. Plann.*, **6**, 143–151.

Lehman, A.F. (1988). A quality of life interview for the chronically mentally ill (QOLI), *Evaluation and Progm. Plann.*, **11**, 51–62.

Lehman, A.F. (1996). Evaluating outcomes of treatments for persons with psychotic disorders, *J. Clin. Psychiatry*, **57** (Suppl. 11), 61–67.

Lehman, A.F. & Burns, B.J. (1996). Severe mental illness in the community, in *Quality of Life and Pharmacoeconomics in Clinical Trials* (Ed. B. Spilker), pp. 919–924, Lippincott-Raven, Philadelphia, Pennsylvania.

Lehman, A.F., Possidente, S. & Hawker, F. (1986). The quality of life of chronic patients in a State hospital and in community residences, *Hosp. Community Psychiatry*, **37**, 901–907.

Lehman, A.F., Postrado, L.T. & Rachoba, L.T. (1993). Convergent validation of quality of life assessment for persons with severe mental illness, *Quality of Life Res.*, **2**, 327–333.

Lehman, A.F., Ward, N.C. & Linn, L.S. (1982). Chronic mental patients: The quality of life issue, *Am. J. Psychiatry*, **139**, 1271–1276.

McKenna, S.P. (1997). Measuring quality of life in schizophrenia, *Eur. Psychiatry*, **12**(Suppl. 3), 267s–274s.

Meltzer, H.Y. (1992). Dimensions of outcome with clozapine, *Br. J. Psychiatry*, **160**(Suppl. 17), 46–53.

Meltzer, H.Y., Bastani, B., Young Kwon, K., Ramirez, L.F., Burnett, S. & Sharpe, J. (1989). A prospective study of clozapine in treatment-resistant schizophrenic patients. I. Preliminary report, *Psychopharmacology*, **99**, S68–S72.

Meltzer, H.Y., Burnett, S., Bastani, B. & Ramirez, L.F. (1990). Effects of six months of clozapine treatment on the quality of life of chronic schizophrenic patients, *Hosp. Community Psychiatry*, **41**, 892–897.

Meltzer, H.Y., Cola, P., Way, L., Thompson, P.A., Bastani, B., Davies, M.A. & Snitz, B. (1993). Cost effectiveness of clozapine in neuroleptic-resistant schizophrenia, *Am. J. Psychiatry*, **150**, 1630–1638.

Mercier, C., Renaud, C., Desbiens, F. & Gervais, S. (1990). *The Contribution of Services to the Quality of Life of Psychiatric Patients in the Community*, Health and Welfare Canada, Ottawa.

Montes, J.M., Ciudad, A., Gascón, J., Gómez, J.C. & EFESO Study Group (2003). Safety, effectiveness, and quality of life of olanzapine in first-episode schizophrenia: A naturalistic study, *Prog. in Neuro-Psychopharmacol. & Biolog. Psychiatry*, **27**, 667–674.

Morcillo, L., Barcia, D. & Borgoñós, E. (1995). Esquizofrenia: calidad de vida y años de evolución, *Actas Luso-Esp. Neurol. Psiquiatr.*, **23**, 293–298.

Naber, D., Moritz, S., Lambert, M., Rajonk, F., Holzbach, R., Mass, R., Andresen, B., Frank, P., Rudiger, H., Reinhard, M. & Burghard, A. (2001). Improvement of schizophrenic patients' subjective well-being under atypical antipsychotic drugs, *Schizophrenia Res.*, **50**, 79–88.

Oliver, J.P.J. (1991). The social care directive: Development of a quality of life profile for use in community services for the mentally ill, *Social Work Social Sci. Rev.*, **3**, 5–45.

Revicki, D.A., Genduso, L.A., Hamilton, S.H., Ganoczy, D. & Beasley, C.M. (1999). Olanzapine versus haloperidol in the treatment of schizophrenia and other psychotic disorders: Quality of life and clinical outcomes of a randomized clinical trial, *Quality of Life Res.*, **8**, 417–426.

Ritchie, C.W., Chiu, E., Harrigan, S., Hall, K., Hassett, A., Macfarlane, S., Mastwyk, M., O'Connor, D.W., Opie, J. & Ames, D. (2003). The impact upon extra-pyramidal side effects, clinical symptoms and quality of life of a switch from conventional to atypical antipsychotics (risperidone or olanzapine) in elderly patients with schizophrenia, *Int. J. Geriatr. Psychiatry*, **18**, 432–440.

Rosenheck, R., Cramer, J., Xu, W., Thomas, J., Henderson, W., Frisman, L., Fye, C. & Charney, D. (1997). A comparison of clozapine and haloperidol in hospitalised patients with refractory schizophrenia, *New Engl. J. Med.*, **337**, 809–815.

Sainfort, F., Becker, M. & Diamond, R. (1996). Judgments of quality of life of individuals with severe mental disorders: patient self-report versus provider perspectives, *Am. J. Psychiatry*, **153**, 497–502.

Shepherd, G., Muijen, M., Dean, R. & Cooney, M. (1996). Residential care in hospital and in the community – quality of care and quality of life, *Br. J. Psychiatry*, **168**, 448–456.

Shtasel, P.L., Gur, R.E., Gallacher, F., Heimberg, C. & Gur, R. (1992). Gender differences in the clinical expression of schizophrenia, *Schizophrenia Res.*, **7**, 225–231.

Simpson, C.J., Hyde, C.E. & Faragher, E.B. (1989). The chronically mentally ill in community facilities – A study of quality of life, *Br. J. Psychiatry*, **154**, 77–82.

Skantze, K. & Malm, U. (1994). A new approach to facilitation of working alliances based on patients' quality of life goals, *Nord. Psykiatr. Tiddskr.*, **48**, 37–55.

Skantze, K., Malm, U., Dencker, S.J. & May, P.R. (1990). Quality of life in schizophrenia, *Nord. Psykiatr. Tidsskr.*, **44**, 71–75.

Skantze, K., Malm, U., Dencker, S.J., May, P.R. & Corrigan, P. (1992). Comparison of quality of life with standard of living in schizophrenic outpatients, *Br. J. Psychiatry*, **161**, 797–801.

Sullivan, G., Wells, K.B. & Leake, B. (1991). Quality of life of seriously mentally ill persons in Mississippi, *Hosp. Community Psychiatry*, **42**, 752–755.

Sullivan, G.S., Wells, K.B. & Leake, B. (1992). Clinical factors associated with better quality of life in a seriously mentally ill population, *Hosp. Community Psychiatry*, **43**, 794–798.

Tollefson, G.D. & Andersen, S.W. (1999). Should we consider mood disturbance in schizophrenia as an important determinant of quality of life?, *J. Clin. Psychiatry*, **60** (Suppl 5), 23–29.

Tran, P.V., Hamilton, S.H., Kuntz, A.J., Potvin, J.H., Andersen, S.W., Beasley, C. & Tollefson, G.D. (1997). Double-blind comparison of olanzapine versus risperidone in the treatment of schizophrenia and other psychotic disorders, *J. Clin. Psychopharmacol.*, **17**, 407–418.

Velligan, D.I., Prihoda, T.J., Sui, D., Ritch, J.L., Maples, N. & Miller, A.L. (2003). The effectiveness of quatiapine versus conventional antipsychotics in improving cognitive and functional outcomes in standard treatment settings, *J. Clin. Psychiatry*, **64**, 524–531.

Voruganti, L.N.P. & Awad, A.G. (2002). Personal evolution of transitions in treatment (PETiT): A scale to measure subjective aspects of antipsychotic drug therapy in schizophrenia, *Schizophrenia Res.*, **56**, 37–46.

Voruganti, L., Cortese, L., Owyeumi, L., Kotteda, V., Cernovsky, Z., Zirul, S. & Awad, A. (2002). Switching from conventional to novel antipsychotic drugs: Results of a prospective naturalistic study, *Schizophrenia Res.*, **57**, 201–208.

Ware, J.E. & Sherbourne, C.D. (1992). The MOS 36-Item Short-Form Health Survey (SF-36), *Med. Care*, **30**, 473–483.

WHOQOL Group (1993). Study protocol for the World Health Organization project to develop a quality of life assessment instrument, *Qual, Life Res.*, **2**, 153–159.

World Health Organization (1988). *WHO Psychiatric Disability Assessment Schedule (WHO/DAS) with a Guide to Its Use*, WHO, Geneva.

14

Quality of Life and Childhood Disorders

Klaus Schmeck and Fritz Poustka

INTRODUCTION

In the last 20 years, health-related quality of life (QoL) has become an increasingly important issue in somatic medicine. Formerly, quality of treatment has been equated with removing diseases or symptoms, while mortality was used as the only important measure of outcome in life-threatening illnesses such as cancer. Starting in the 1970s, the focus of attention changed to a more global view of outcome, which included the QoL of survivors as a matter of concern. Moreover, since many diseases have a chronic course, the aim of treatment cannot be cure, but rather the improvement of everyday life.

The use of QoL as a relevant measure of outcome marks a paradigmatic change in the medical view of diseases and their therapy. In addition to such objective criteria as mortality or morbidity, the patient's subjective ratings of his/her living conditions are now considered. This subject-centred approach uses child patients' assessments instead of those done by clinicians or other experts to describe the potential impact of diseases on QoL. Using this concept, the potential risks and side-effects of different treatment approaches have to be considered and in the stage of planning both the potential benefits of treatment and adverse side-effects need to be weighed up (Mattejat and Remschmidt, 1998).

Up to now, no generally accepted definition of QoL has existed. However, as Bullinger (1994) points out, there is a widely accepted consensus of aspects that are necessary for an operational definition: 'Health-related QoL can be understood as a psychological construct that describes the physical, mental, social and functional aspects of the patients' state of health and functioning in their own view' (Bullinger, 1994, translated by the authors). According to Ivan and Glazer (1994), QoL can be seen as a 'novel construct designed to capture essential aspects of psychosocial outcome in chronic pediatric illness that fail to be measured by traditional instruments, which are strictly disease-focused'. This definition can be used equally in child psychiatric disorders.

Although psychiatric disorders are often of a chronic nature and accompanied by a great variety of problems in everyday life, health-related QoL was not a matter of interest in this area until the last decade (Helmchen, 1990; Katschnig and König, 1994). In child and adolescent psychiatry, there is still not enough interest in this issue. In 1993, a World Health Organization (WHO) Working Party concluded that existing measures were inadequate and that there is a need to develop and establish QoL measures for children (Graham, Stevenson and Flynn, 1995). However, in paediatric psychosomatic medicine, QoL has emerged as an important issue. In allergy research with adolescents, for example (Juniper, Guyatt and Dolovich, 1994), or in clinical studies on childhood and adolescent asthma

Quality of Life in Mental Disorders, Second Edition Edited by H. Katschnig, H. Freeman and N. Sartorius
© 2006 John Wiley & Sons, Ltd

(Volmer, 1994), QoL is assessed via specially developed questionnaires. Outcome measures of cancer research often include an assessment of patients' QoL (Diehl *et al.*, 1990; Vance *et al.*, 2001).

A vast array of instruments to assess QoL have been developed (Weber, 1995), but the question has to be raised whether they really measure the same underlying concept. Up to now, there has not been sufficient agreement concerning different definitions of health-related QoL.

With a shortage of financial resources for the health care system, quality assurance becomes even more important. The shorter the money, the more medical services have to demonstrate the quality of their work. With the knowledge of more than 20 years of QoL research, we have to make the choice of a specific therapy not only with regard to relieving symptoms but also with regard to the question of how patient's QoL is affected during and after treatment.

GENERAL ASPECTS OF QUALITY OF LIFE IN CHILD AND ADOLESCENT PSYCHIATRY

In child and adolescent psychiatry, a multidimensional view of patients is preferred. Child psychiatrists not only classify the psychiatric disturbance but other important aspects of the patient's life, e.g. psychosocial living conditions (ICD 10 Axis V) or global level of functioning (Axis VI). In line with general psychiatrists, child and adolescent psychiatrists have claimed for a long time that they already include both the subjective well-being of the patient and living conditions, so that the introduction of QoL as a new concept did not seem to be necessary (Karow and Naber, 2000). However, this view neglects the point that there is a major difference between this multidimensional approach and the QoL concept. The Multiaxial Classification System (MAS) (Remschmidt, Schmidt and Poustka, 2001) is, by definition, an expert rating, whereas the concept of QoL is based on the patient's subjective assessment. This different approach is of especial importance since the level of agreement between the ratings of QoL by patients and clinicians is weak (Juniper, 1995).

One of the major problems in using the concept of QoL, both in general and child and adolescent psychiatry, is the difficult distinction between subjective impairment of well-being and depression. Self-rating questionnaires usually represent the subject's momentary affective status, which is severely influenced by changes in mood. Major shortcomings in subjective well-being may be attributed both to poor QoL or to depressive mood.

Five aspects seem to be crucial for the description of health-related QoL (see Fig. 4.1): the disorder with its impairing symptoms, the treatment, personal characteristics of the patient and the living/

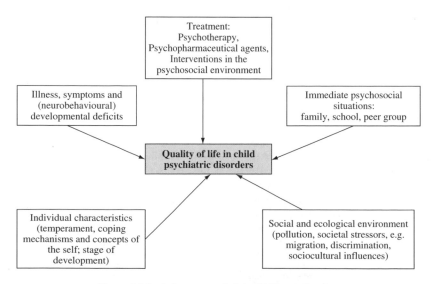

Figure 14.1   Influences on QoL in childhood disorders

upbringing conditions in both the closer psychosocial and broader social and ecological environment (see Bullinger, 1994, who describes disease/treatment, personal characteristics and living conditions as influencing factors for QoL).

MEASUREMENT OF QUALITY OF LIFE IN CHILD PSYCHIATRIC PATIENTS

Measurement of QoL in children has to cope with several problems. The rating of internal states requires a certain capacity of self-reflective functioning. Therefore, psychiatrists mostly have to rely on parents' ratings of their children before the age of 8 or 9 years. However, not enough is known about the relationship between child and parent ratings and there is little information about factors that influence parents' perception of their children's QoL (Vance *et al.*, 2001). Parents have to be aware of their childrens' values, priorities and preferences to rate the latters' QoL successfully. In studies of adult patients, close relatives have seemed to be able to rate patients' QoL, whereas proxy ratings are influenced by distress evoked by the patient (often true for child psychiatric patients with externalising disorders). In the study of Theunissen *et al.* (1998), parents rated their children's QoL to be worse than the children did themselves.

The second problem lies in the dimensions of QoL that have been developed in studies with adults. Not enough is yet known as to whether these dimensions also fit children and adolescents. Further studies are needed to clarify this issue (Ravens-Sieberer, 2000).

In paediatric medicine, several measures of children's QoL already exist (see Table 14.1). Such measures should be developmentally appropriate so that children are able to understand the questions, which should reflect the changing features of QoL with age (Graham, Stevenson and Flynn, 1995). According to these authors, a WHO Child Psychology and Psychiatry Working Party proposed in 1993 that 'new measures should be child-centred, employ subjective self-report where possible, be age-related or at least developmentally appropriate, have a generic core and specific modules, and put an emphasis on health-enhancing aspects of quality of life' (p. 6).

Graham and Stevenson (1994a, 1994b) developed a new instrument for the assessment of health-related QoL in childhood (CQOL). In this questionnaire, 15 main domains of children's lives are covered: (1) getting about and using hands, (2) doing things for self, (3) soiling or wetting, (4) school, (5) out of school activities, (6) friends, (7) family relationships, (8) discomfort due to bodily symptoms, (9) worries, (10) depression, (11) seeing, (12) communication, (13) eating, (14) sleep, (15) appearance.

Mattejat *et al.* (1998) developed the questionnaire ILK (Inventar zur Erfassung der Lebensqualität bei Kindern und Jugendlichen) for use in child and adolescent psychiatric patients as well as in other clinical or non-clinical populations. In 9 items, this short and economical questionnaire covers the areas: (1) school, (2) family, (3) friends, (4) hobbies, (5) physical well-being, (6) mental well-being,

Table 14.1   Tools to assess QoL in children and adolescents

Questionnaire	Age group	Number of items	Rated by
Child Health Questionnaire (CHQ) (Landgraf, Abetz and Ware, 1997)	5–18	28, 50 or 87	Self/parent
Child Health Related Quality of Life (CQOL) (Graham and Stevenson, 1994a, 1994b)	9–15	46	Self/parent
Fragebogen zur Erfassung der gesundheits bezogenen Lebensqualität bei Kindern und Jugendlichen (KINDL) (Bullinger, v. Mackensen and Kirchberger, 1994)	4–16	24	Self/parent
How are you (HAY) (Bruil *et al.*, 1996)	8–13	22	Self/parent
ILK (Mattejat *et al.*, 1998)	6–18	10	self/parent/clinician

(7) total QoL, (8) disease burden, (9) treatment burden. The ILK questionnaire has proven reliability and validity in different German populations (Mattejat *et al.*, 2003).

INFLUENCE OF CHILD PSYCHIATRIC DISEASES ON CHILDREN'S WELL-BEING

For psychiatrically disturbed children and adolescents, as for adult psychiatric patients, QoL does not mean the search for an optimum level of happiness, but rather the reduction of impairment associated with their disease (Katschnig, 1994).

In a recent Australian study by Sawyer *et al.* (2002) on 3.957 children aged from 6 to 17 years, QoL (assessed with CHQ-50) was significantly lower for children with mental disorders, compared with non-disturbed controls. This was not only true for the areas of physical and mental health, but also for the extent to which psychiatric problems interfered with these childrens' daily life. Effect sizes were mostly above 0.80, indicating a substantial effect. Children with mental disorders also showed significantly worse QoL than children with physical disorders. The worst outcome was observed in those patients that suffered from a combination of mental and physical handicaps.

Schizophrenia with an onset in childhood or adolescence has a poorer prognosis than with an adult onset: more than 50% show a chronic course, about 25% attain partial remission and only less than 25% complete remission (Schulz, Martin and Remschmidt, 1994). Schmidt *et al.* (1995) confirmed the poor outcome of patients with a first episode of schizophrenia during adolescence. Four to 18 years after their first episode, 73% had experienced at least one further schizophrenic episode, 72% still required psychiatric treatment, 44% were impaired with regard to education and 58% in respect of social functions.

Schizo-affective psychoses in adolescence also have a poorer prognosis than those with onset in adulthood (Schmidt *et al.*, 1994). Early onset schizophrenic symptoms may reveal an increased vulnerability or higher genetic burden (Schmidt *et al.*, 1994), indicating greater severity and long-lasting impairment. QoL decreases sharply for psychotic adolescents: they show a failure to achieve the expected level of social development with severe deterioration in functioning (e.g. in school) and require psychiatric hospitalisation. All indicators of QoL (Bullinger, 1994) are impaired: (1) physical status by coenesthetic hallucinations and adverse side-effects of neuroleptic medication, (2) mental status by marked lack of concentration, (3) emotional status by paranoid anxieties and depressed mood, (4) behavioural status by expression of bizarre behaviour, (5) social status by withdrawal and lack of satisfying relationships. Longitudinal comparisons between psychotic and non-psychotic adolescent patients showed significantly lower scores on the Global Assessment Scale for the psychotic group at all assessment times (Erlenmeyer-Kimling *et al.*, 1990). In 73%, the disorder started with negative or non-specific symptoms and in 41%, first signs of the disorder appeared before the age of 20. This is very suggestive that the most frequent initial symptoms – poor concentration, subjective thought disorder, lack of energy, suspiciousness and social withdrawal, slowing down and anxiety – influence the neurodevelopmental process of maturation (Häfner, 1995; Häfner and Nowotny, 1995). This could have several implications from reducing information-processing capacity (Arsanow, Brown and Strandburg, 1995) to heightened negative responses from their caregivers (Schmidt *et al.*, 1995).

In externalising child psychiatric conditions, QoL is more impaired by conflicts in social relations (with family members and peers) than by symptomatology itself, so that in disruptive behaviour disorders there is often more desire for change in the surroundings than in the patient him/herself. On the other hand, the low quality of social relations and comorbidity with mild neurological impairment and learning disabilities often leads to low self-esteem, which reinforces the externalising symptomatology. Quite often, conduct disorders are associated with depression. Distractibility, impulsiveness and aggression are common symptoms that disturb others, such as parents, teachers or schoolmates, with consequent failure in school or chronic conflicts at home. Objective impairment is often more serious than the subjective appraisal of the patients themselves.

There is often a very similar situation in chronic and severe eating disorders like anorexia nervosa. Denial of symptoms and good functioning in school and peer groups for a long period can be associated with severe and sometimes even life-threatening somatic changes. Especially at the beginning of the disorder, losing weight leads to appreciation by friends and family members, so that QoL seems to be stable or even increased. It is doubtful, therefore, whether the subjective ratings of QoL of adolescent anorectic patients can lead to reliable and valid statements.

There is a great variety of anxiety disorders in childhood and adolescence, and these have different levels of QoL reduction. For example, in severe conditions of separation anxiety, everyday life is completely disturbed. Three main clinical features can be found: subjective distress, social dysfunction and symptomatic inflexibility (Klein, 1994). Such children are not able to participate in expected, age-appropriate social and academic activities, and complain of somatic problems without medical cause. In extreme cases, school attendance is no longer possible because the patients refuse to leave their mothers. Even in milder cases, QoL of children with anxiety disorders is impaired by constant subjective distress, even in 'normal' social situations.

TREATMENT

The association of QoL and psychiatric treatment has two main issues: (a) in which way does psychiatric treatment influence QoL – positively or negatively?, (b) if complete remission cannot be reached, how can psychiatric treatment help patients to live in an acceptable way?

Psychiatric disorders of childhood and adolescence, such as psychoses, autism, obsessive–compulsive disorders, anxiety or eating disorders, depression, severe hyperkinetic syndromes or conduct disorders, often have to be treated in an in-patient setting for weeks and months. Most patients feel released in the protection of the clinical surroundings. However, especially in the long run, there would be an important improvement in the patients' QoL if they could be treated in day-care settings. The aim of treatment should be maximum help with minimum restriction. After the first days or weeks of crisis intervention, many patients would be able to return to their familiar surroundings for nights and weekends if there is still sufficient psychiatric care during the days. If there is no constant atmosphere of rejection or conflict in the family, this change of treatment setting could increase QoL of child and adolescent psychiatric patients at such a difficult stage of their life. 'Gradual discharge' of young patients from an in-patient to an out-patient status (Poustka, 1982) is rarely a focus of research; up to now, this kind of treatment has not been sufficiently provided and QoL has still not been a main issue in outcome research in this respect.

Psychopharmacological treatment in childhood and adolescence is associated with substantial benefits, but often also with distinct side-effects. These adverse effects can severely influence compliance in adult life:

1. Acute dystonic reactions, for example, are very common if children or adolescents are treated with typical neuroleptics (Taylor, 1994). Especially during the first days of neuroleptic treatment, young patients should be carefully observed and treated with anti-Parkinson medication if necessary.
2. To prevent these dystonic reactions, the use of atypical neuroleptics is more and more recommended in the guidelines. Although the benefits of such treatment are substantial, many adolescents suffer from severe weight gain. Clozapine or olanzapine treatment, for example, leads to a mean weight gain of 4–10 kg, with some adolescents gaining even 40 kg or more. The development of a positive body image – essential for subjective well-being in later life – is severely disturbed.
3. Another adverse effect of many psychopharmacological agents (e.g. neuroleptics, or selective serotonin reuptake inhibitors) is a negative impact on sexual functions. In most cases, however, adolescents do not talk about these problems if they are not asked directly. However, this experience of a body not functioning in the way it should is puzzling and embarrassing.

Problems of compliance also arise in the case of relapse prevention in adolescent bipolar disorder. For these adolescents, who do not have a long history of psychiatric disorder, it is hard to understand that they should bear the acute impairment of QoL caused by side-effects of lithium (e.g. weight gain) to prevent greater impairment (e.g. rehospitalisation) in the future (for the relationship of pharmacotherapy, compliance and QoL see Weber, 1990). Angermeyer (1994) postulates that non-compliance with neuroleptic maintenance therapy is due to its consequences for the patient's QoL. The possibly negative impact of neuroleptics or SSRIs on sexual functions, especially for adolescents, is of high importance and often leads to non-compliance. More than in adult psychiatry, compliance of child and adolescent psychiatric patients depends to a large extent on the compliance of their parents.

Quite often, clinical psychiatric treatment cannot lead to full remission of symptoms (e.g. in psychoses or severe obsessive–compulsive and eating disorders) or the family environment is so noxious that a return to it would destroy the therapeutic effect. In these cases, out-of-home placement is necessary, but especially for older adolescents and young adults, it is very difficult to find adequate placement. It is quite unbearable for an 18 year-old schizophrenic patient to be forced to live in a sheltered residence together with chronic schizophrenic patients of 40, 50 or 60 years of age. Therefore, a very important aspect of the long-term QoL of young psychiatric patients is that they should be placed in surroundings that offer sufficient shelter but at the same time adequate stimulation and social support so that rehabilitation and relapse prevention are possible. At the moment, such places are so rare in Germany that the QoL of young psychiatric patients with chronic courses of disease is often decreased by their actual living conditions. The situation is similar in many other countries.

PERSONAL CHARACTERISTICS OF THE PATIENT

In chronic diseases, especially in conditions of mild to middle severity, there is often a dissociation between symptoms and QoL (Katschnig, 1994). This is due to patients' different premorbid personality traits and actual coping strategies, as well as to different living conditions, discussed below.

Personality traits such as temperamental factors are viewed as having a constitutional biological basis that influences the style of behaviour. Thomas and Chess (1977) state that temperament is 'a general term referring to the *how* of behavior. It differs from ability, which is concerned with the *what* and *how well* of behaving, and from motivation, which accounts for *why* a person does what he is doing. Temperament by contrast concerns the *way* in which an individual behaves' (p. 9). A central concept of temperamental research is 'goodness of fit', which is seen as a protective factor for healthy development. 'Poorness of fit, on the other hand, exists when demands and expectations are excessive and not compatible with the child's temperament, abilities, and other characteristics. With such a fit, the child is likely to experience excessive stress and vulnerability, and healthy development is jeopardized' (Chess and Thomas, 1992, p. 73).

It is very difficult or even impossible for a child to change his/her temperamental style of behaviour (which is postulated as having a biological or genetic basis). Goodness of fit between a child and the environment can mostly be reached by changes in the child's psychosocial environment. For example, parents could try to change their educational style. A long-lasting poorness of fit will produce trouble constantly for both children and their environment.

A different point of view is that of how children are able to cope with the effects of chronic illness. Lazarus and Folkman (1984) define coping with illness as the processes used to register, compensate for or overcome emotionally, cognitively or behaviourally existing or expected stresses that are connected with illness. Thus, the coping mechanisms reveal a concept of how to handle and diminish the negative impacts of chronic illness (Voll and Poustka, 1994). Like children and adolescents with handicaps or chronic somatic diseases, the child psychiatric patients' 'relatively harmonious daily functioning and necessary equilibrium between person and environment is fundamentally shaken over an extended period of time (since, as a rule, the person does not have the psychic means to cope with the serious changes in her/his individual life situation immediately and without complications) and, therefore, the irrevocable losses that have occurred mean that the affected person has to make a complete adaptation' (Voll and Poustka, 1994, p. 310). Coping with illness should lead to the recovery of control as well as maintenance of the optimum level of QoL that is possible after the threatening experience of a psychiatric disorder.

PSYCHOSOCIAL ENVIRONMENT

In comparison with adult psychiatry, it is much more necessary in child and adolescent psychiatry to get information about family functioning in order to understand a child's psychiatric problem. During childhood and adolescence, there is the possibility of watching the development of disturbance and recognising the effects of psychosocial adversities. The younger the child, the more important are parents and other family members for the patient's well-being. Adverse life events in the early psychosocial environment can affect adult psychiatric symptoms (Cadoret et al., 1990). According to the work of Rutter and co-workers (Rutter and Quinton, 1977) six factors have been repeatedly identified (Voll et al., 1982) that are significantly associated with child psychiatric disorder: severe marital discord, low social status, overcrowding or large family size, paternal criminality, maternal psychiatric disorder and the placement of a child in local authority care (Garmezy and Masten, 1994). Because knowledge of a child's psychosocial situation is so essential for understanding the patient's general situation, the MAS (Rutter, Shaffer and Sturge, 1975; World Health Organization, 1991) includes on its fifth axis the assessment of this area (van Goor-Lambo et al., 1990). Ratings are made of abnormal intrafamilial relations, parental psychiatric disturbance, inadequate or distorted intrafamilial communication, abnormal conditions of upbringing, abnormal direct environment, acute adverse life events, social stressors (e.g. migration or discrimination), chronic stressors associated with school or job and adverse life events or situations that are due to the child's behavioural problems or impairments (World Health Organization, 1988; van Goor-Lambo et al., 1990, 1994; see Table 14.1).

According to the concept of vulnerability (Zubin and Spring, 1977; Nüchterlein, 1987), the interaction of biological factors and early psychosocial stressors leads to a disposition towards a certain kind of psychiatric disturbance. Acute psychosocial stressors then trigger the onset of the disorder. Corresponding to this widely accepted theory, there is no disorder without a specific vulnerability, while adverse psychosocial events alone rarely cause illness. Nevertheless, the possibility has to be considered that subjects without a specific vulnerability also suffer from these acute psychosocial adversities. Marital discord, overcrowding, paternal criminality or maternal psychiatric disorder, for example, have a distinct impact on children's and adolescents' well-being, leading to a substantial impairment of their QoL.

Opposite to the concept of vulnerability is that of resilience to stress which helps to understand healthy development under bad conditions (Rutter, 1987). Wyman et al. (1992) demonstrated that caregiver–child relationships play a key role in moderating children's developmental outcomes under conditions of high stress. Stress-resilient children who had been exposed to major life stress reported more positive relationships with primary caregivers, stable family environments, inductive and consistent family discipline practices and positive expectations for their futures.

From another point of view, the child's psychiatric disturbance itself has an influence on family climate and leads to burdens on caregivers (Cook and Pickett, 1987). For example, the behaviour of a boy with hyperactivity and oppositional-defiant disorder can be so annoying that it leads to negative parental reactions and rejection, which again reinforce the child's symptomatology. Usually, if parents' QoL is affected (and this is definitely the case with severe mental disorders in their children), this also affects children's QoL, since they are not able to escape from the negative parental reactions. Therefore, the assessment of family relationships is a crucial aspect of the assessment of QoL in children (see Graham, Stevenson and Flynn, 1995).

ECOLOGICAL AND SOCIAL ENVIRONMENT

The actual somatic and psychological condition of an individual cannot be understood without the effects of constant interactions with both the ecological and social environment. The QoL of children, adolescents and adults are all severely influenced by these factors.

In the discipline of environmental psychology (Ittelson et al., 1974) the dynamic interactions between environmental influences (architecture, urban noise, crowding, etc.) and subjective living conditions are investigated. Environmental medicine (Blumenthal, 1985) adds further important influences on human well-being, such as the effects of pollution, allergens, infectious agents, mutagens or physical agents.

Noise is one of the most comprehensively studied physical agents in environmental sciences. There is no doubt that human functioning is affected by high noise and that noise has to be regarded as an environmental stressor which can produce stress reactions (Spreng, 1984; de Jong, 1993). However, up to now, there have been no data on the question of whether noise exposure leads to long-term damage or even diseases (Griefahn, 1982; Ising and Kruppa, 1993; Stansfeld and Matheson, 2003).

In a field study in northern Germany (Poustka, Eckermann and Schmeck, 1992; Schmeck and Poustka, 1993), the effects of low-altitude flight noise on children and adolescents were examined. The noise of military jetfighters was found to have a significant influence on the level of psychophysiological arousal in children. However, this higher autonomous activity was not associated with a greater amount of medical problems or global psychiatric disturbance, with the exception of higher levels of anxiety in young children who live in an area with frequent low-altitude flight noise.

It would be misleading, though, to come to the conclusion that military aircraft noise does not substantially affect children's life. Beneath the clinical threshold of somatic or psychiatric disorders, we found a distinct impact of military aircraft noise on children's QoL, since most of the children and their families felt constantly annoyed (more than 70%) by the noise and threatened (more than 55%) by the jets themselves (e.g. fear of an aircraft crash in their area). If the living conditions of these children are compared with WHO's definition of health, a substantial difference can be found. The results of this study provide evidence that QoL is an issue that should be included when the effects of pollution or other environmental stressors are investigated. Though definite somatic effects are often hard to prove, the impairment of QoL, which sometimes has an even greater impact on the subjective well-being of the affected population (Aurand, Hazard and Tretter, 1993), also has to be taken into account.

CONCLUSIONS

Many aspects of intervention in child psychiatry are mediated by and reflected in the immediate or wider social environment of the child. Thus, monitoring outcomes of intervention in this special situation of developmental dimensions are influenced by a great deal of reactive responses, which themselves have an impact on maturation, probably biasing educational pathways. Longitudinal observations are lacking of the feedback both of developmental delays and life quality dimensions. New assessment tools have been established, but we are still at the beginning of using these tools in research or clinical routine. The application of the QoL concept to child and adolescent psychiatric patients is still in its infancy.

REFERENCES

Angermeyer, M.C. (1994). Symptomfreiheit oder Lebensqualität: Ziele der Schizophreniebehandlung, in *Schizophrenie und Lebensqualität* (Eds H. Katschnig & P. König), pp. 65–80, Springer-Verlag, Wien.

Arsanow, R.F., Brown, W. & Strandburg, R. (1995). Children with a schizophrenic disorder: Neurobehavioral studies, *Eur. Arch. Psychiatry Clin. Neurosci.*, **245**, 70–79.

Aurand, K., Hazard, B.P. & Tretter, F. (Eds) (1993). *Umweltbelastungen und Ängste*, Westdeutscher Verlag, Opladen.

Blumenthal, D.S. (Ed.) (1985). *Introduction to Environmental Health*, Springer, New York.

Bruil, J., Maes, S., Le Coq, L. & Boeke, J. (1996). The development of the how are you (HAY), a quality of life questionnaire for children with a chronic illness, *Quality of Life Newsl.*, **13**, 9.

Bullinger, M. (1994). Lebensqualität: Grundlagen und Anwendungen, in *Lebensqualität und Asthma* (Eds F. Petermann & K.-C. Bergmann), pp. 17–28, Quintessenz, München.

Bullinger, M., v. Mackensen, S. & Kirchberger, I. (1994) KINDL – ein Fragebogen zur Erfassung der Lebensqualität von Kindern, *Z. für Gesundheitspsychologie*, **2**, 64–77.

Cadoret, R.J., Troughton, E., Merchant, L.M. & Whitters, A. (1990). Early life psychosocial events and adult affective symptoms, in *Straight and Devious Pathways from Childhood to Adulthood* (Eds. L. Robins & M. Rutter), pp. 300–313, Cambridge University Press, Cambridge.

Chess, S. & Thomas, A. (1992). Interactions between offspring and parents in development, in *Vulnerability and Resilience in Human Development* (Eds B. Tizard and V. Varma), Jessica Kingsley Publishers, London, Philadelphia.

Cook, J.A. & Pickett, S.A. (1987). Feelings of burden and criticalness among parents residing with chronically mentally ill offspring, *J. Appl. Social Sci.*, **12**, 79–107.

de Jong, R.G. (1993). Review: Extraaural health effects of aircraft noise, in *Noise and Disease* (Eds H. Ising, & B. Kruppa), pp. 259–270, Fischer Verlag, Stuttgart, New York.

Diehl, V., v. Kalle, A.-K., Kruse, T. & Sommer, H. (1990). 'Lebensqualität' als Bewertungskriterium in der Onkologie, in *'Lebensqualität' als Bewertungskriterium in der Medizin* (Eds P. Schölmerich & G. Thews) pp. 149–167, Fischer Verlag, Stuttgart.

Erlenmeyer-Kimling, L., Cornblatt, B.A., Bassett, A.S., Moldin, S.O., Hilldoff-Adamo, U. & Roberts, S. (1990). High-risk children in adolescence and young adulthood: Course of global adjustment, in *Straight and Devious Pathways from Childhood to Adulthood* (Eds L. Robins & M. Rutter), pp. 351–364, Cambridge University Press, Cambridge.

Garmezy, N. & Masten, A.S. (1994). Chronic adversities, in *Child and Adolescent Psychiatry: Modern Approaches*, (Eds. M. Rutter, E. Taylor & L. Hersov), pp. 191–208, Blackwell Scientific Publications, London.

Graham, P. & Stevenson, J. (1994a). Child Health Related Quality of Life CQOL, Parent Questionnaire, Revised Version, London.

Graham, P. & Stevenson, J. (1994b). Child Health Related Quality of Life CQOL, Child Questionnaire. Revised Version, London.

Graham, P., Stevenson, J. & Flynn, D. (1995) A new measure of health-related quality of life for children: Preliminary findings, Unpublished paper, London.

Griefahn, B. (1982) Grenzwerte vegetativer Belastbarkeit. Zum gegenwärtigen Stand der psychophysiologischen Lärmforschung, *Z. für Lärmbekämpfung*, **29**, 131–136.

Häfner, H. (1995). Epidemiology of schizophrenia. The disease model of schizophrenia in the light of current epidemiological knowledge, *Eur. Psychiatry*, **10**, 217–227.

Häfner, H. & Nowotny, B. (1995). Epidemiology of early-onset schizophrenia, *Eur. Arch. Psychiatry Clin. Neurosci.*, **245**, 80–92.

Helmchen, H. (1990) 'Lebensqualität' als Bewertungskritcrium in der Psychiatrie, in: *'Lebensqualität' als Bewertungskriterium in der Medizin* (Eds P. Schölmerich and G. Thews), pp. 93–115, Fischer Verlag, Stuttgart.

Ising, H. & Kruppa, B. (Eds) (1993). *Noise and Disease*, Fischer Verlag, Stuttgart, New York.

Ittelson, W.H., Proshansky, H.M., Rivlin, L.G. & Winkel, G.H. (1974). *An Introduction to Environmental Psychology*, Holt, Rinehart and Winston, New York.

Ivan, T.M. & Glazer, J.P. (1994). Quality of life in pediatric psychiatry: A new outcome measure, *Child and Adolescent Psychiat. Clinics of N. America*, **3**, 599–611

Juniper, E. (1995). Quality-of-life considerations in the treatment of asthma, *PharmacoEconomics,* **8**, 123–138.

Juniper, E.F., Guyatt, G.H. & Dolovich, J. (1994). Assessment of quality of life in adolescents with allergic rhinoconjunctivitis. Development and testing of a questionnaire for clinical trials, *J. Allergy and Clin. Immunol.*, **93**(2), 413–423.

Karow, A. & Naber, D. (2000). Psychiatrie, in *Lebensqualität und Gesundheitsökonomie in der Medizin. Konzepte, Methoden, Anwendung* (Eds U. Ravens-Sieberer, & A. Cieza), pp. 199–211, Ecomed, Landsberg.

Katschnig, H. (1994). Wie läßt sich die Lebensqualität bei psychischen Krankheiten erfassen? in Katschnig, H. & König, P. (Hrsg.): *Schizophrenie und Lebensqualität* (Eds H. Katschnig & P. König), pp. 1–14, Springer-Verlag, Wien.

Katschnig, H. & König, P. (Eds) (1994). *Schizophrenie und Lebensqualität*, Springer-Verlag, Wien.

Klein, R.G. (1994). Anxiety disorders, in *Child and Adolescent Psychiatry: Modern Approaches* (Eds M. Rutter, E. Taylor & L. Hersov), pp. 351–374, Blackwell Scientific Publications, London.

Landgraf, I., Abetz, L. & Ware, J. (1997). *Child Health Questionnaire (CHQ): A User's Manual*, The Health Institute Press, Boston, Massachusetts.

Lazarus, R.S. & Folkman, S. (1984) *Stress. Appraisal and Coping*, Springer, Berlin.

Mattejat, F. & Remschmidt, H. (1998). Zur Erfassung der Lebensqualität bei psychisch gestörten Kindern und Jugendlichen – Eine Übersicht, *Z. Kinder-Jugendpsychiat*, **26**(3), 183–196.

Mattejat, F., Jungmann, J., Meusers, M., Moik, C., Schaff, C., Schmidt, M.H., Scholz, M. & Remschmidt, H. (1998). Das Inventar zur Erfassung der Lebensqualität bei Kinder und Jugendlichen (ILK), *Z. Kinder-Jugendpsychiat*, **26**(3), 174–182.

Mattejat, F., Simon, B., König, U. *et al.* (2003). Lebensqualität bei psychisch kranken Kinder und Jugendlichen. Ergebnisse der ersten multizentrischen Studie mit dem Inventar zur Erfassung der Lebensqualität bei Kinder und Jugendlichen (ILK), *Z. Kinder-Jugendpsychiat*, **31**(4), 293–303.

Nüchterlein, K.H. (1987). Vulnerability models for schizophrenia. State of the art, in *Search for the Causes of Schizophrenia* (Eds. H. Häfner, W.F. Gattaz, & W. Janzarik), pp. 297–316, Springer, New York.

Poustka, F. (1982). Graduelle Entlassung als teilstationäre Behandlung, *Psychiat. Prax.*, **9**, 155–159.

Poustka, F., Eckermann, P. & Schmeck, K. (1992). Effect of aircraft noise and psychosocial stressors on mental disturbances of children and adolescents – an epidemiological survey in Westphalia, in *Developmental Psychopathology* (Eds H. Remschmidt & M.H. Schmidt), Hogrefe, Göttingen.

Ravens-Sieberer, U. (2000). Lebensqualitätsansätze in der Pädiatrie, in *Lebensqualität und Gesundheitsökonomie in der Medizin. Konzepte, Methoden, Anwendung* (Eds U. Ravens-Sieberer and A. Cieza), pp. 277–292, Ecomed, Landsberg.

Remschmidt, H., Schmidt, M.H. & Poustka, F. (Eds) (2001). *Multiaxiales Klassifikationsschema für psychische Störungen des Kinder- und Jugendalter nach ICD-10 der WHO*, Huber Verlag, Bern, Göttingen, Toronto, Seattle.

Rutter, M. (1987). Psychological resilience and protective mechanisms, *Am. J. of Orthopsychiatry*, **57**, 316–331.

Rutter, M. & Quinton, D. (1977). Psychiatric disorder – ecological factors and concepts of causation, in *Ecological Factors in Human Development* (Ed. M. McGurk), pp. 173–187, North-Holland, Amsterdam.

Rutter, M., Shaffer, D. & Sturge C. (1975). *A Guide to a Multi-axial Classification Scheme for Psychiatric Disorders in Childhood and Adolescence*, Department of Child and Adolescent Psychiatry, Institute of Psychiatry, London.

Sawyer, M.G., Whaites, L., Rey, J.M., Hazell, P.L., Graetz, B.W. & Baghurst, P. (2002). Health-related quality of life of children and adolescents with mental disorders, *J. Am. Acad. Child Adolescent Psychiatry*, **41**(5), 530–537.

Schmeck, K. & Poustka, F. (1993) Psychophysiological and psychiatric tests with children and adolescents in a low-altitude flight region in *Noise and Disease* (Eds H. Ising and B. Kruppa), pp. 301–306, Fischer Verlag, Stuttgart, New York.

Schmidt, M.H., Schultz, E., Blanz, B. & Lay, B. (1994). Verlauf schizoaffektiver Psychosen in der Adoleszenz, *Z. für Kinder- und Jugendpsychiatrie*, **22**(4), 253–261.

Schmidt, M., Blanz, B., Dippe, A., Koppe, T. & Lay, B. (1995). Course of patients diagnosed as having schizophrenia during first episode occurring under age 18 years, *Eur. Arch. Psychiatry Clin. Neurosci.*, **245**, 93–100.

Schulz, E., Martin, M. & Remschmidt, H. (1994). Zur Verlaufsdynamik schizophrener Erkrankungen in der Adoleszenz, *Z. für Kinder- und Jugendpsychiatrie*, **22**(4), 262–274.

Spreng, M. (1984). Risikofaktor Lärm – physiologische Aspekte, *Therapiewoche*, **34**, 3765–3772.

Stansfeld, S.A. & Matheson, M.P. (2003). Noise pollution: non-auditory effects on health, *Br. Med. Bull.*, **68**, 243–257.

Taylor, E. (1994). Physical treatments, in *Child and Adolescent Psychiatry: Modern Approaches*, (Eds M. Rutter, E. Taylor & L. Hersov), pp. 880–899, Blackwell Scientific Publications, London.

Theunissen, N.M., Vogels, T.C., Koopman, H.M., Verrips, G.W., Zwinderman, K.H., Verloove Vanhorick, S.P. & Wit, J.M. (1998). The proxy problem: Child report versus parent report in health-related quality of life research, *Quality of Life Res.*, **7**, 387–397.

Thomas, A. & Chess, S. (1977). *Temperament and Development*, Brunner & Mazel, New York.

Vance, Y.H., Morse, R.C., Jenney, M.E. & Eiser, C. (2001). Issues in measuring quality of life in childhood cancer: Measures, proxies, and parental health, *J. Am. Acad. Child Adolescent Psychiatry*, **42**(5), 661–667.

van Goor-Lambo, G., Orley, J., Poustka, F. & Rutter, M. (1990). Classification of abnormal situations: Preliminary report of a revision of a WHO Scheme, *J. Child Psychol. and Psychiatry*, **31**(2), 229–241.

van Goor-Lambo, G., Orley, J., Poustka, F. & Rutter, M. (1994). Multiaxial classification of psychiatric disorders in children and adolescents: axis five – associated abnormal psychosocial situations. Preliminary results of a WHO and a German multicenter study, *Eur. Child Adolescent Psychiatry*, **3**, 229–241.

Voll, R. & Poustka, F. (1994). Coping with illness and coping with handicap during the vocational rehabilitation of physically handicapped adolescents and young adults. *Int. J. Rehabil. Res.* 1994, **17**, 305–318.

Voll, R., Allehoff, W.H., Esser, G., Poustka, F. & Schmidt, M.H. (1982). Widrige familiäre und soziale Bedingungen und psychiatrische Auffälligkeit bei 8-Jährigen, *Z. für Kinder- und Jugendpsychiatrie*, **10**, 100–109.

Volmer, T. (1994). Klinische Studien zur Lebensqualität bei Asthma, in *Lebensqualität und Asthma* (Eds F. Petermann, & K.-C. Bergmann), pp. 83–98, Quintessenz, München.

Weber, E. (1990). Pharmakotherapie, Compliance und 'Lebensqualität', in *'Lebensqualität' als Bewertungskriterium in der Medizin* (Eds P. Schölmerich, & G. Thews), pp. 133–148, Fischer Verlag, Stuttgart.

Weber, I. (1995). Lebensqualität: Messung und Ergebnisbeurteilung, *Deutsches Ärzteblatt*, **92**(18), 961.

World Health Organization (1991). Multiaxial version of ICD-10 prepared for use by clinicians dealing with child and adolescent psychiatric disorders, Draft, WHO, Geneva.

World Health Organization (1988). Draft multiaxial classification of child psychiatric disorders. Axis five: Associated abnormal psychosocial situations WHO Document MNH/PRO/86. 1, REV. 1, WHO, Geneva.

Wyman, P.A., Cowen, E.L., Work, W.C., Raoof, A., Gribble, P.A., Parker, G.R. & Wannon, M. (1992). Interviews with children who experienced major life stress: family and child attributes that predict resilient outcomes, *J. Am. Acad. Child Adolescent Psychiatry*, **31**(5), 904–910.

Zubin, J. & Spring, B. (1977). Vulnerability: A new view of schizophrenia, *J. Abnormal Psychol.*, **86**, 103–123.

15

Quality of Life in Alzheimer's and Related Dementias

Barry Gurland and Sidney Katz

INTRODUCTION[*]

The consequences of dementia threaten quality of life (QoL) throughout the world. There are currently somewhere between 18 and 38 million persons with dementia living in the world (Alzheimer's Disease International, 1999; World Health Organization, 2001; Wimo *et al.*, 2003). Future trends will only aggravate the already heavy demands on both formal and informal services for the care of persons with dementia. Their number is expected to increase as the older-age groups swell in size, perhaps quadrupling in the next 50 years. The greatest increase will occur in the less-developed countries, where even now more than half of all cases of dementia are found (Prince, 2000).

As the proportion of elderly patients in the population increases, the medical system will face new challenges (Etzioni *et al.*, 2003). Demands for dependent care from both formal (i.e. paid health care professionals or paraprofessionals) and informal (i.e. unpaid family and friends) caregivers are likely to increase (Navaie-Waliser, Spriggs and Feldman, 2002). Bibliometric analysis of keywords in the literature on ethics and dementia during the period 1980–2000 revealed frequent mention of end-of-life decision making and treatment by professionals, as well as QoL issues (Baldwin *et al.*, 2003).

A LANGUAGE FOR QUALITY OF LIFE IN AGEING

Vocabulary

A repository of terms referencing QoL is found in measuring instruments commonly used in both clinical and research work in ageing. These terms usually emerge from social or clinical concerns and form a consensually defined language of QoL, which tends to be increasingly widely shared as it proves useful in resolving treatment, administrative and policy matters, or serves a research agenda.

The language used to describe the needs and challenges faced by elderly people expresses key aspects of QoL and shows what information is needed for another person to respond helpfully. It portrays QoL as the resultant of interconnections between objective and subjective features of body, mind, values, life experiences and anticipations, as well as the environment (Katz and Gurland, 1991).

[*] Because of restraints on space, this chapter deals with the application of quality of life language only to the dementias. We have elsewhere addressed geriatric depression and other mental disorders of elderly people (Gurland and Katz, 1992; Gurland, Katz and Chen, 1997).

Quality of Life in Mental Disorders, Second Edition   Edited by H. Katschnig, H. Freeman and N. Sartorius
© 2006 John Wiley & Sons, Ltd

Classification

We have arranged terms in the language of QoL under 19 domains, as shown in Table 15.1. Each of the domains comprehends a distinctive set of challenges to the adaptations sustaining QoL and lists the related responses that can reflect an individual's efforts to meet that challenge. A method of evaluating the likelihood of the elder's success or failure in responding to these challenges is included. Successful

Table 15.1   Provisional structure and contents of domains of quality of life

Organisation of the structure and content of each domain, and overall evaluation and rationale

Layout of pages in columns

Domain label	Challenge to adaptation	Issues in judging adaptive response

Responses: Examples of the abilities necessary to meet the adaptive challenge in that domain.

Overall evaluation: Criteria for judging adaptive responses to challenges. In each domain, review evidence of failures or inability (e.g. dependence on personal assistance, omissions, infrequency); inefficiency or difficulty (e.g. errors, repetitions, slowness, limited endurance, strain, use of devices); breakdown under stress (e.g. under exceptionally trying conditions, pressure of time, against resistance, in novel situations); deficits in enabling mechanisms (e.g. in motivations, permissions or encouragement, or in access to preferences, assistance, devices or other resources).

Rationale: It is assumed that the degree to which adaptive responses are adequate within and across domains is a measure of that person's potential to achieve their preferred qualities of life. Each domain can be supplementary, complementary and compensatory to the contribution of other domains to this potential. Self-help and helping interventions can be aimed at increasing that potential.

Susceptibility to impairment: Domains affected by dementia. Any and all domains may be eventually impaired in the full course of dementia, and some domains are involved early in certain dementia subtypes but late in others. Domains 4, 8, 13, 19 are often the first to be affected in the early stages of Alzheimer's type dementia; domains 3, 5, 6, 7, 11, 12 in the intermediate stages; 14, 15, 16, 17 in the intermediate to late stages; and domains 1,2,18 in the last stages of Alzheimer's disease. Comorbid conditions usually determine the stage of appearance of domains 9,10.

Definition: A field of operations is a setting in which specified actions can be effected.

Note: Notwithstanding the style of describing abilities, no implications are intended with respect to the exercise of free will, unconscious motivations, or contextual or imposed facilitation or limits.

1 Useful mobility	Move field of operations to optimal site	Can this person physically get to where he/she needs or wants to be, so that he/she can do what he/she needs or wants to do?

Responses: Control head, turn body, sit up in bed, transfer from bed, sit in a chair, crawl, rise from sitting, stand, move around room, move room to room, go up and down stairs, move into street, travel distances outside. Operational fields include: bedside table, tray on bed, seat with a view, seat at writing desk or dining table, bookshelves, chest of drawers, fireplace, wall switch, kitchen, toilet, television set, computer, side walk for recreation, shops, cinema, club, place of worship, friend's house, vehicle, workplace.

2 Basic activities of daily living	Routinely maintain self as operator	Can this person keep his/her body in working order (e.g. taking in food and water, conserving heat, eliminating, cleaning)?

Responses: Feed self (e.g. use fingers, cutlery and utensils to transfer food and fluids to mouth, cut, chew, swallow), dress (e.g. choose, sequence, don), be continent, use toilet (e.g. request, locate, reach, arrange clothes, squat, aim, wipe, flush, rise), groom hygienically (e.g. clean teeth, bathe or shower).

3 Instrumental activities of daily living	Manipulate immediate environment by low technology	Can this person keep his/her living and working areas maintained, properly supplied and producing?

Responses: Cook; prepare snacks, fluids, a meal; work a stove, switches, faucets, locks; clean, tidy, launder, shop, follow lists, pay bills, handle cash, make simple repairs, place and move furniture, perform such basic routines at home, or usual work and place of employment.

| 4 | Technological activities of daily living | Manipulate immediate environment by higher technology | Can this person manage technical apparatus (household appliances) requiring up to date instruction? |

Responses: Use telephone (e.g. touch-tone, directories), operate a coffee machine, regulate the fridge, use a microwave, tune the television, radio; address and mail a letter, adjust spectacles, hearing aid; use a hair drier, camera, home computer, fax; operate devices such as an electric wheelchair, a bicycle, car; open bottles, use household chemicals, self-administer medication.

| 5 | Navigational skills | Find way around operational sphere | Can this person find his/her way around the areas in which he/she customarily live, work and play? |

Responses: Find way around residence, neighbourhood and other frequented places; follow directions, road signs, maps; keep to right side of road; stay within appropriate territory (e.g. not invading other's private areas).

| 6 | Orientation skills | Keep track of movement in time, space and landmarks of operational sphere | Can this person keep track of changes in him/herself and the world around him/her? |

Responses: Keep track of time, continuity and changes in self and others, remain aware of shifts in location and remember placement of objects.

| 7 | Receptive communication | Gather information about the operational sphere | Can this person pick up useful information about the world around him/her and the objects and persons in it? |

Responses: Read instructions, learn, receive communications by some effective mode (e.g. aural: oral instructions or news; visual: written information or observations; special mode: Braille, board or sign language); interpret simple facts, complex facts, signals of impending events, implications of context; gain access to information.

| 8 | Expressive communication | Shape the operational sphere by means of information | Can this person impart information to others so as to obtain needed or desired responses, services or other changes? |

Responses: Send communications (e.g. by oral, visual, body language, special modes) about basic needs, wishes, interests by means of simple or complex instructions or messages, revealing thoughts and feelings; writing letters, telling stories, relaying messages; advising and teaching.

| 9 | Preservation of health | Keep healthy | Can this person's body defend itself and can the person take the necessary steps to preserve his/her health? |

Responses: Avoid dangers and accidents (e.g. burning pots, gas, shock, overflowing water, falling, cutting, attack by others), minimise harmful practices (e.g. alcohol, drugs, smoking, poor nutrition, toxins), promote health (e.g. exercise, preventive measures, early consultation), manage treatment (e.g. make health visits, follow treatment regimes, avoid overdoses or neglect, report side-effects).

| 10 | Comfort and mood | Preserve physical and mental comfort | Can this person's body keep mentally and physically comfortable and can the person take the necessary steps to aid this process? |

Responses: Emotional or mental. Modulate intensity of emotional extremes and suffering (e.g. feelings of being unhappy, sad, tearful, tormented by scruples, lonely, self-depreciated, regretful); limit extent of distracting emotional or attitudinal intrusions into thinking, relationships, interests; contain over-reactions (e.g. prolonged mourning, shame, guilt), anxiety, fear, irritability, regrets; weather stresses (e.g. caused by losses, threats of illness, family tensions). Physical: monitor and adjust comfort; relieve pain and other somatic distress (e.g. interference with sleep, restlessness, poor appetite, unplanned loss of weight, aches and pains, bad taste in the mouth; breathlessness, weakness, fatigue, difficulty swallowing, constipation, nausea, faintness).

Table 15.1   (Continued)

Organisation of the structure and content of each domain, and overall evaluation and rationale

11 Social and interpersonal relations	Preserve social contracts and options	Can this person meet the standards of behaviour of his/her group, manage ordinary civic duties and protect property and rights?

Responses: Keep and nurture relationships (e.g. take an interest in others, engage in social activities, exchange services, stabilise identity); protect, claim and exercise rights, make judgements about the donation of assets, maintain appearances; use community resources, help others, be cooperative, obey the law, desist from objectionable acts (e.g. aggression, noise, soiling, poor hygiene, disorderly appearance, hoarding, making false accusations, other disturbing behaviour), fit into normative patterns (sleep at night, keep appointments), resisting indignities (e.g. loss of privacy).

12 Autonomy	Retain and exercise choice	Can this person make his/her own choices in personal matters?

Responses: Freedom or control with respect to what, when and how one uses existing capacities to conduct one's life, including interests and activities, socialising, clothes, routines, sleeping, food, alternatives in treatment and settings; understanding options, motivation to use options. Exercise of preferences in choosing among the choices for responding to challenges to adaptation in every domain.

13 Financial management	Preserve and wield material resources	Can this person handle his/her ordinary business and bureaucratic affairs?

Responses: Balance chequebook, keep valuables safe, deposit and withdraw cash, keep track of cash and belongings, earn money, maintain a job, save, invest, claim entitlements and benefits, keep financial records, assemble tax records, fill out business and insurance forms, avoid exploitation, remain solvent.

14 Environmental fit	Select and shape the operational sphere	Can this person find or make a suitable place to live, work and receive services?

Responses: Analyse potential of personal environment for satisfactions, make an effort to transform the environment as desired, search for and test better matches between environment and needs, feel able to move, plan budget for desired moves; include features of homeliness, safety, local amenities, opportunities for gratifications; material, economic and intellectual resources; climate, social activities, access to health services, alternative service settings.

15 Motivation and gratification	Extract meaning and pleasure from life	Can this person obtain pleasure, pride motivation and personal fulfillment?

Responses: Act according to own values, follow and enjoy interests, engage in spiritual or aesthetic experience; take pleasure in sexual, tactile and gustatory and other sensory stimulations, get excitement from motor activity (e.g. sports), games, passive entertainment (e.g. reading and TV); obtain relaxation in leisure time; feel productive, useful and appreciated; satisfy personal goals and meaningful aims, sense of mastery, value positive aspects of life despite pain and troubles, feel fulfilled also by altruistic acts and love for others.

16 Self-perceived health	Integrate information on health	Can this person realistically sum up his/her health status and use the information to serve his/her needs?

Responses: View health image realistically (e.g. compared to others of the same age or same condition, previous state); interpret symptoms as indicators of a state of vulnerability or disorder, risk for deterioration or death; understand personal health information, recognise functional capacity and performance standards, know when to seek help for health, understand need for cooperation in treatment and judge response to treatment; appreciate good health.

17 Future image	Integrate information on future	Can this person realistically take into consideration the future and go forward with plans for it?

Responses: Calculate chances of future well-being under various anticipated circumstances; reconcile probabilities of survival or death with probabilities of discomfort or relief; form expectations and strategies for continuing, reshaping or re-establishing past or customary relationships and activities; keep expectations concordant with best information and keep plans keyed to expectations; be capable of reasonable caution but keep up hope for the future despite lack of objective guarantees; accept irreducible uncertainties; prepare for anticipated discontinuities in style of life.

| 18 | General well-being | Integrate information on quality of life | Can this person realistically take into consideration his/her current life and make decisions in that context? |

Responses: Balance and reconcile objective and subjective, positive and negative, and preferred and disfavoured experiences, and the accompanying benefits and costs, over past, concurrent and future time, not dominated by a narrow window in time, modulated by values and taking intensity, duration and extensity into account; be duly aware of the status of each domain; merge hedonistic indulgences and feelings of love for others and empathy for their quality of life; act in accordance with a sense and evaluation of well-being.

| 19 | Effective coordination | Use abilities to best advantages | Can this person carry out initiatives, obligations or commands to best effect and reasonably efficiently? |

Responses: Transfer motivation from various sources in order to inject this into responses to challenges in any and all domains; reconcile conflicts between responses across domains, ensure that responses in different domains are mutually supportive and that skills and capacities in each domain are well used; direct attention to both emotional and pragmatic goals; balance the demands of short- and long-range challenges and express or demonstrate goals beyond immediate needs; effectively plan to achieve domain goals and preserve capabilities of each domain; maintain steady goals; analyse and organise all incoming information for use by each domain (e.g., classifying, abstracting, connecting, weighting by feelings, values and morality), referring learning from experience to improvement of adaptive skills in all domains; synthesising; inducing, deducing, and creating new interpretations relating to planning and acting.

---

adaptive responses put the person in a position to select a preferred QoL while maladaptive responses increase the probability of an impaired quality.

Further discussion will refer mainly to impaired qualities of life. Nevertheless, in principle, it is the profile of impaired and preferred (or positive) qualities that is most useful in understanding the outcomes of mental disorders in the elderly, the needs of both the patient and involved others for relief and help, and the efficacy or effectiveness of treatment.

Severity

The degree to which adaptation (and hence QoL) is impaired, i.e. the severity of maladaptation, is described by intensity and extensiveness terms (Gurland, Katz and Chen, 1997). Intensity conveys the degree of impairment at a stated point in time, usually the present; e.g. by such observable terms as 'complete', 'partial', or 'minimal' and such subjective terms as 'mild', 'distracting' or 'unbearable'. Extensiveness refers to the extent to which impairment pervades the individual's daily life of thoughts, feelings and activities, the frequency and duration of impairment, the number of precipitating circumstances and the breadth of domains affected.

Objectivity and Subjectivity

Objective viewpoints may employ descriptors such as 'unable', 'dependent', 'slow', 'inefficient', 'clumsy', 'dangerous' and 'weak', dealing with observable impairment of adaptive abilities. Subjective viewpoints represent internal states, such as 'distress', 'pain', 'discomfort', 'dissatisfaction' and 'frustration' in carrying out adaptive responses to challenges to maintaining qualities of life. Certain domains seem to warrant terms that lean towards the objective and others to subjective descriptors. Nevertheless, almost all the domains allow either an objective or a subjective viewpoint to be injected into the content of language. For example, basic tasks may be objectively completed, but with a reported sense of discomfort, or may be poorly performed, though to the satisfaction of the patient. Conversely, feelings may be manifested by observable behaviour. QoL language can also be phrased to represent both the objective priorities and subjective perspectives of various parties who have a legitimate involvement in the individual's life: family, formal caregivers, therapists, administrators, planners and policy makers.

IMPAIRED QUALITY OF LIFE DUE TO DEMENTIA[*]

Working Definition of Dementia-Specific Impaired Quality of Life

Quality of life may be deemed to be impaired by a dementia syndrome (caused by Alzheimer's disease, vascular dementia or one of the other subtypes) when, as a result of dementia, a person: (a) objectively fails to adapt to those challenges that particularly rely on cognitive skills or has declined from a best level of these aspects of performance (e.g. in D2, D3, D4, D5, D6, D7, D8, D12, D19) or (b) subjectively has a feeling of discomfort (e.g. D10) during the exercise of cognitively driven processes, is dissatisfied (D15) with the effects of cognitively driven task performance or is otherwise distressed by the effects of the progressive disorder (e.g., D17, D18) or (c) has an unfavourably altered pattern of social relationships (e.g. D11) or (d) has an inadequate margin of cognitive reserve capacity for adaptation in general (any domain).

Observable Markers of Impaired Quality of Life

Characteristic observable failures of adaptation inflicted by dementia include: premature death, disability, dependence, depression, intellectual and physical deterioration, institutional admission and fractures and falls. Certain observable tasks draw heavily on cognitive skills, and therefore can act as specific indicators of deficits in cognitively driven performance (Barberger-Gateau et al., 1992). Functional impairment in everyday activities (D2, D3, D4) is highly related, though not uniquely, to cognitive status (Warren et al., 1989; Nadler et al., 1993; Zanetti et al., 1993). Examples are: selecting appropriate clothes, dressing in the right order and at a reasonable speed (D2), finding the right word (D7, D8), finding objects (D6), managing cash transactions, e.g. paying for purchases and receiving correct change (D13), remembering shopping lists, messages, chores (D3, D7, D9), remembering names (D6, D7, D11), using the telephone or self-administering medication (D4, D9), going out and returning home alone (D5), recognising family and friends (D6, D11) socialising (D11) or managing personal financial and business matters, e.g. paying bills, balancing bank balances and obtaining due credit (D13).

The activities of daily living functions comprise both vegetative-like capacities which are essential for survival, such as feeding, and culturally learned skills, such as dressing. The advent of dependency on someone else to assist in task performance of a highly personal nature, such as the basic or instrumental activities of daily living (D2 to D4), is usually an objective sign of a failure of adaptation. Function cannot be accurately predicted from knowledge of the cognitive status and therefore should be independently assessed (Inouye et al., 1993).

Cognitive dependency increases the risk of neglect or abuse, or of injury from cognitive lapses. Excess mortality may be hastened by malnutrition or dehydration, hidden infections, disruption of medication regimes, side-effects of drugs, and falls and fractures, but also by the underlying neurobiological changes (D9).

Subjective Markers

Subjective indicators of a failure of adaptation as an effect of dementia include feelings of difficulty, anxiety and frustration. The elderly person may be distressed or embarrassed or feel disadvantaged by errors or inability in everyday tasks (D2 to D4). Any observable failure may also challenge adaptation of a subjective nature. In six long-term care sites, 112 residents were assessed using Dementia Care Mapping: QoL was noted to be lower where there was greater impairment in activities of daily living and fewer social contacts and engagements (Ballard et al., 2001). Dislocation from an accustomed and preferred environment (D14), e.g. through admission to a nursing home, or transfer to a caregiver's home, is particularly threatening to QoL.

Memory complaints by elderly people may be focused on failures of specific tasks or may be more diffuse. These complaints are increased in incipient dementia (O'Brien et al., 1992), especially if the

---

[*] Selected examples in the text on challenges to adaptation presented by dementia are cross-referenced to the numbered domains in Table 15.1 by the prefix D and the number of the relevant domain, e.g. D*N*.

complaints are of recent decline (Christensen, 1991), as well as with cognitive deficits not reaching levels warranting a diagnosis of dementia (McGlone *et al.*, 1990; Grut *et al.*, 1993). However, subjective complaints about memory may be misdirected. There are discrepancies between self-perceived and objectively measured memory performance (Hanninen *et al.*, 1994), while memory complaints are common in depression (O'Connor *et al.*, 1990; Feehan, Knight and Partridge, 1991; Grut *et al.*, 1993) and even in older people without any health disorder but with a general tendency towards somatic complaints (Hanninen *et al.*, 1994). Complaints of memory problems are common in elderly people residing in a community, but most of those who complain have neither dementia nor depression.

Depression in Dementia

Rates of depressed mood increase with the onset of dementia (Alexopoulos, Young and Meyers, 1993; Skoog, 1993). Not only are clear-cut depressive disorders increased in this population, but subsyndromal disorders are even more common and cause considerable distress (Thorpe and Groulx, 2001). Symptoms of depression may be among the most frequent initial symptoms of the demented patient, as reported by caregivers (la Rue, Watson and Plotkin, 1993). Depression (D10) as an emotional response to the advent of dementia is to be expected (Kim and Rovner, 1994), but the pathology of Alzheimer's disease has also been directly implicated (O'Brien *et al.*, 1992; Skoog, 1993; Forstl *et al.*, 1994). Severity of depression has been related to communication problems (D7, D8) and the impairment of activities of daily living (D2, D3, D4): instrumental in mild dementia and basic in severe dementia (Fitz and Teri, 1994).

Depression in patients with dementia tends to recover within a few years (Forsell, Jorm and Winblad, 1994). Recovery may be reinforced by changes in neurotransmitter balance or by psychological adaptation (Foster and Cataldo, 1994), and also by treatment. It may also be simulated in some cases by loss of insight and communication ability. Insight into functional deficits is often lost in advanced dementia, especially in those affected people with paranoid delusions (Mangone *et al.*, 1991). Anxiety levels also appear to be lowered in the later and more severe stages of dementia (Koenders *et al.*, 1993).

Behavioural Changes

Behavioural and psychological symptoms of dementia occur in 50–90% of patients with Alzheimer's disease; they can cause premature institutionalisation, increased costs of care and significant loss of QoL for the patient, family and caregivers (Parnetti *et al.*, 2001). Some behavioural problems (e.g. D11) of dementia such as suspiciousness appear to be weakly related to the level of cognitive impairment, being better understood in terms of the patient's individual psychological status (Teri, Larson and Reifler, 1988). An imbalance of different neurotransmitters (acetylcholine, dopamine, noradrenaline, serotonin) has been proposed as the neurochemical correlate of behavioural or psychotic disturbances. Correspondingly, an involvement of some specific brain regions responsible for emotional activities (parahippocampal gyrus, dorsal raphe, locus coeruleus) as well as cortical hypometabolism have been suggested to contribute to these problems (Parnetti *et al.*, 2001).

Longitudinal Course and Outcome

Increasing severity of dementia is regularly accompanied by progressive functional impairment in both basic and instrumental activities of daily living (Kurz *et al.*, 2003). In an 11-year longitudinal study of changes in persons with dementia living at home with a caregiver, the Present Behavioural Examination recorded dementia lasting for a mean of 8.5 years and ending at a stage where around a third of the cohort were unable to walk, more than half were hypophagic, most were incontinent of urine and a substantial minority were incontinent of faeces. The majority died in an institution (Keene *et al.*, 2001). The interval to onset of confinement to home, null activity and null positive affect, as reported by patient proxies, varies with the severity of the dementia (Albert *et al.*, 2001). Among residents of a long-term care facility, a small but significant decline in Alzheimer's Disease Related QoL took place over two years (except for mood), but in half the cohort there was no decline (Lyketsos *et al.*, 2003).

CONTINUUM OF COGNITIVE STATES

Standards

There is no single standard against which to weigh decline, maintenance or improvement of adaptation. Full independence in a task meets a standard that minimises demand for personal care services and maximises the probability of retaining residence in the community. Degrees of failure in independence include assistance in the shape of devices, a restructured or sheltered environment, advice and stand-by supervision, intervention only at difficult steps in the task, joint efforts on the part of the caregiver and care-receiver and, finally, total assumption of the task by a caregiver. Erosion of the margin of reserve for performance of adaptive tasks in a domain may be indicated by changes in efficiency (e.g. speed, errors, repetitions, awkwardness), by a sense of laboured and fatiguing execution of the tasks or by degradation of performance under specially challenging conditions.

Intermediate States

Research within and around the border zone of cognitive health (e.g. the range of cognitive impairment in which both cases and non-cases of dementia occur with comparable frequency) (Gurland *et al.*, 1995) can sharpen many issues. One such issue is whether the dichotomy of normal and disease states embodied in diagnosis is more useful for directing clinical attention to the impact on QoL than is a set of transitional states along a continuum of cognitive impairment. These impacts include interactions between objective and subjective viewpoints during transitions of progressive impairment of QoL as well as labelling effects on both patient and family. Appropriately sensitive indicators of links between changes of cognitive status and changes of QoL within the border zone range of cognitive deficits can open up new avenues for early intervention aimed at preventing unnecessary decline in the maintenance of QoL.

For many purposes, the most salient diagnostic concept of dementia is that which is most clearly related to impairment of QoL. This frame of reference could permit criteria for diagnosis to be adapted to each culture, so as to achieve comparable impacts on QoL. In that case, readily interpretable cross-cultural comparisons can be made of the frequencies of cognitive impairment that reach a level of societal and health concern, as well as the relevant determinants, course, outcomes and resulting family involvement and service utilisation (Gurland *et al.*, 1997).

Context

Adaptation is modified by context, especially motivation and the environment. Therefore, either evaluation of an elderly person's adaptive capacity must be qualified by the context or the context must be optimised to determine potential performance, or kept standard for purposes of comparisons with other subjects or over time. The US/UK cross-national survey found that the prevalence rate of pervasive or clinical depression among older people in New York City and London was similar – about one in eight (Gurland *et al.*, 1983). However, among those who lived at home, ill and disabled New Yorkers were more often depressed than their London counterparts, while the reverse was true for similar patients in nursing homes or other long-term care facilities. Differences in access to personal services was consistent with these subjective variances.

An elderly person is typically highly motivated to perform certain tasks of personal care independently and well; this is a premise for evaluating the tasks of basic activities of daily living (D2), where privacy and initiatives about timing, frequency, pace and style are usually highly valued. It can be assumed that if an individual cannot meet these adaptive challenges independently, it is not for lack of trying. However, caregivers may be motivated to intrude into the patient's prerogatives and usurp initiatives in even the most personal tasks, because it may be easier and quicker for the caregiver to take over the task than to fit into the patient's limits of competence. It has been noted that the giving of supervisory guidance by the caregiver to a patient with dementia is a less common form of help than doing the task for the patient (T. Fulmer *et al.*, personal communication). In other cases, restructuring the home or provision of assistive devices can extend or restore the patient's adaptation and independence.

TYPES OF MEASURES

Some Limitations of Current Measures

In line with the topic of this paper, measurement should serve the purpose of improving the QoL of persons with dementia. In arguing for research to pay detailed attention to the effects of dementia on the person's sense of identity, self-conception, capacities, preferences, values, etc., Schermer (2003) acknowledges the subtleties and complexities facing the techniques of measurement. Schneider (2001) adds that treatment outcomes of dementia should cover QoL, activities of daily living, behaviour, burden on caregivers and economics, as well as cognition. Yet relatively few studies have evaluated subjective health status in patients with dementia (Bureau-Chalot *et al.*, 2002). In addition, there are major difficulties in obtaining consistent, reliable and valid QoL information from persons with dementia, who are likely to have a greater or lesser degree of loss of insight and impairment of communication and understanding.

Demers *et al.* (2000) reviewed the psychometric properties of functional and QoL outcome measures used in drug trials for Alzheimer's disease, covering the Geriatric Evaluation by Relative's Rating Instrument, the Physical Self-Maintenance Scale, the Instrumental Activities of Daily Living, the Blessed Dementia Scale, the Interview for Deterioration in Daily Living with Dementia, the Unified Activities of Daily Living, the Dependence Scale, the Progressive Deterioration Scale and the QoL Assessment. They found that the majority of the scales had serious limitations, particularly in sensitivity to change. Furthermore, statistically significant improvements in tests such as ADAS-cog (Alzheimer's Disease Assessment Scale cognitive subscale) may not be reflected in changes in daily life (Clegg *et al.*, 2001). Nevertheless, according to Spector *et al.* (2003), QoL in Alzheimer's Disease scales have shown sensitivity to treatment effects.

Riemsma *et al.* (2001) surveyed 34 different general health status measures used in studies involving persons with cognitive impairment due to a wide variety of causes. The Sickness Impact Profile and the 36-item Short Form (SF-36) were the most frequently mentioned. The authors concluded that there are no validated instruments available for use in cognitively impaired respondents and little evidence to support the validity of proxy assessments. The French version of the Duke Health Profile was administered to 148 subjects with a mental disorder; help from the interviewer was necessary in 79% of cases and severity of dementia affected the amount of missing data, feasibility, acceptability and reproducibility of the instrument (Novella *et al.*, 2001a).

The ability of the 12-item Health Status Questionnaire and the 12-item Short Form Health Survey to distinguish between people with and without dementia was tested in a door-to-door survey; whereas both measures were found acceptable and valid as health status instruments in large community-based studies of older people, only the Health Status Questionnaire was deemed to be valid for people with dementia (Pettit *et al.*, 2001). The Medical Outcomes Study (MOS) 36-Item Short Form health survey (SF-36) was administered to persons with dementia in a multicentre study and was found to be psychometrically adequate for people with mild-to-moderate dementia, but unsuitable for severe dementia (Novella *et al.*, 2001b). The Canadian Study of Health and Aging employed an 18-item multidimensional measure of well-being, tapping six dimensions of positive psychological functioning, but the internal consistency reliability of subscales was not found to be high (Clarke *et al.*, 2001).

Acton and Kang (2001) call for better and more precise measures to evaluate properly the effects of intervention for caregivers. Modified Grounded Theory allowed themes to be extracted from narratives obtained from persons with mild dementia and from caregivers (Silberfeld *et al.*, 2002). Comparison of these themes with the content of the European QoL (EurQoL) Instrument, Health Utilities Index and Quality of Well-Being (QWB) Scale revealed that essential attributes of the QoL in dementia were missing from those instruments. Post *et al.* (2001), using focus groups of persons with dementia, caregivers and professionals, found that these groups had very different perspectives on the benefits experienced in treatment. Coucill *et al.* (2001) noted that ratings of the EuroQoL EQ-5D instrument for health-related QoL were highly variable across persons with dementia, their caregivers and a doctor. In persons with mild-to-moderate dementia, agreement between self-reports and proxy reports of health-related QoL on the 17-item Duke Health Profile was only poor to moderate (Pettit *et al.*, 2001).

Discrepancies in ratings of QoL between proxies and persons with dementia are greater for subjective rather than objective states (Novella *et al.*, 2001c; Pettit *et al.*, 2001) and widen with increasing severity of the dementia, persons with dementia tending to rate their own QoL higher than is attributed to them by their proxies (Novella *et al.*, 2001c). The French version of the Nottingham Health Profile (NHP) was administered to a large sample of persons with dementia and their family or formal caregivers, most scoring less than 16 on the Mini Mental State Examination (MMSE). With the help of an interviewer, the great majority of items were completed. Test–retest reliability was good, but agreement between patients and their proxies was only just acceptable for physical domains and poor for psychological and social domains (Bureau-Chalot *et al.*, 2002).

Because of communication barriers, indicators of pain are difficult to detect in around one-third of nursing home residents. Focus groups of the nursing staff of three nursing homes generated suggestions for indicators derived from certain repetitive physical or vocal behaviours, other physical signs of pain and changes in the person's usual pattern of behaviour, especially when observed by nurses who knew the person well (Cohen-Mansfield and Creedon, 2002).

Selected Measures

An extensive review of scales useful for the assessment of dementia, including staging, function and behavioural problems, was provided by Kluger and Ferris (1991). The contents of these measures cover the domains previously listed to a varying extent. Schneider (2001) favours the Disability Assessment for Dementia and the Alzheimer's Disease Cooperative Study of Activities of Daily Living scales, and the Behavioral Pathology in Alzheimer's Disease Rating Scale. A straightforward 'Direct Scaling' by caregivers of the overall QoL of persons with mild-to-moderate dementia produced a distribution over five levels (poor, fair, good, very good or excellent), with most in the middle three grades (Karlawish *et al.*, 2001). Application of the Alzheimer's Disease-Related QoL scales has been described by Lyketsos *et al.* (2003). The Daily Activities Questionnaire is aimed at measuring the functional problems of Alzheimer's disease (Oakle *et al.*, 1991).

A new measure of QoL in dementia, the QOL-AD, was tested on a large sample of persons with dementia and their caregivers, with good alpha reliability values; validity claims rest on the positive correlations with independent measures of depression, activities of daily living and pleasant events frequency (Logsdon *et al.*, 2002). Smith *et al.* (2004) have recently developed a questionnaire on QoL in dementia (the DEMQOL) using psychometric techniques on data from a preliminary qualitative phase involving focus groups of persons with dementia and their caregivers.

Yamamoto-Mitani *et al.* (2002) describe the development of a QoL instrument for older Japanese people experiencing dementia (Japanese Quality of Life Instrument for Older Adults Experiencing Dementia, or QLDJ), a three-dimensional construct of interacting with surroundings, expressing self and experiencing minimum negative behaviour. Factor analysis of data from both studies involving experts and a survey of older persons and their formal caregivers in various care settings confirmed the conceptual definitions and showed satisfactory reliability and validity. Terada *et al.* (2002) present the development of the QoL questionnaire for dementia (QOL-D) in Japan. On the basis of a survey, they report that reliability is good to excellent and validity was established to some extent. They suggest that the concept of QoL for elders with dementia in Japan is similar to that in Western countries.

Dementia Care Mapping is undertaken by trained observers who collect detailed information on the types of interactions and activities taking place among both residents and staff on a given day (Kuhn, Kasayka and Lechner, 2002). It is portrayed as offering a comprehensive overview of the quality of care through evaluation of behaviour patterns or processes and well-being or outcomes of persons with dementia (Innes and Surr, 2001). Application to persons with dementia in six care settings disclosed instances both of people with dementia being 'put down' and contrasting instances when well-being was enhanced, suggesting a need for more attention to psychosocial care needs. Fossey, Lee and Ballard (2002), in a study of persons with dementia in long-term care, showed that an assessment period as short as the hour before lunch was significantly correlated with the total assessment period. Nevertheless, Beavis, Simpson and Graham (2002) found that in nine studies between 1992 and 2001 that had examined the efficacy of this technique as an outcome measure the results displayed only moderate validity, while it proved to be very time-consuming.

Structured Tests of Function

Standard tests have been constructed to keep constant the degree of challenge offered by tasks of daily living. These are generally simulations of familiar tasks, often set up in a laboratory and sometimes capable of portability. One example is the Activities of Daily Living Situational Test (Skurla, Rogers and Sunderland, 1988). Materials are arranged in a research site for simulating adaptive capacity in certain domains. The Kitchen Task Assessment (Baum and Edwards, 1993) allows an evaluation of the degree to which a person requires help in preparing a meal. The Structured Assessment of Independent Living Skills assesses functioning in motor skills such as dressing and eating (D2), instrumental tasks (D3, D4), orientation (D5, D6), communication (D7, D8), social activities (D11) and handling money (D13) (Mahurin, DeBettignies and Pirozzolo, 1991).

Sequences of Staging

Measures of stages of deterioration have been developed through statistical techniques, producing from six distinctive stages (Overall et al., 1990) to as many as 16 discernible levels (stages and substages) in the progression of dementia (Reisberg, 1990). Some measures capitalise on there being an orderly progression of staged deterioration. This pattern is captured by the Global Deterioration Scale for Primary Degenerative Dementia (Reisberg et al., 1982), which defines seven stages of severity, based on symptoms and signs and associated neuropsychological test scores. Stage indicators range from (a) complaints of difficulty in finding objects or remembering names, in the very mild stages, through (b) intermediate stages with problems in concentrating, failing at a job or losing the way to (c) forgetting recent general and personal events and showing inability to do complex tasks to (d) dependence on assistance and difficulty in choosing clothes to (e) severe stages of forgetting name of spouse and events of past life, requiring assistance with basic activities and being incontinent, and in (f) the most severe stage, loss of verbal ability and advent of the need for assistance with toilet and eating.

The earliest and latest stages of dementia are the least well documented in terms of their impact on QoL. Changes in frontally mediated behaviours, e.g. apathy and executive dysfunction (rated by knowledgeable informants on the Frontal Systems Behaviour Scale) are common in very early and mild stages of cognitive impairment, even before there has been a functional decline in daily living; these early changes may bring distress to the family as well as impairing the QoL of the person with dementia (Ready et al., 2003). Persons with mild dementia report more depressive symptoms and less life satisfaction than those with more severe dementia (Zankd and Leipold, 2001). Deficits in switching of selective attention, such as occur early in dementia, may impair driving skills and increase the risk of accidents before diagnosis is certain (Parasuraman and Nestor, 1991), especially since Alzheimer cases in the earlier stages of the illness may be active motor car drivers.

CAREGIVERS

Typical Caregivers

In the light of the limited access, availability and affordability of formal care services, the currently estimated 15–25 million informal caregivers in the United States are likely to continue bearing the overwhelming responsibility for the provision of home and long-term care services (Ory et al., 1999). The caregiver is typically a spouse or daughter, but may be a nurse or personal attendant. Women comprise nearly three-quarters of the total number of caregivers and are consequently most under strain (Collins and Jones, 1997; Almberg et al., 1998; Yee and Schulz, 2000).

Stress on Caregivers

Consideration of the caregiver's well-being has been emphasised by several investigators (Rubin et al., 1987; Brodaty and Hadzi, 1990). The caregiver's stress appraisal, rather than years of care-giving, relationship status or education level, is the mediator of the impact on their health (Hooker et al., 2002). Highly burdened caregivers are found where the person with dementia is more behaviourally disturbed and the caregiver has too little time for him/herself or is under financial strain (Coen *et al.*, 2002). A longitudinal study over 18 months of caregiver and recipient pairs reported that the quality of the relationship predicted stress over problem-solving and the caregiver role, as seen in negative attitudes towards the recipient (Burgener and Twigg, 2002b).

An assault on a caregiver's QoL can begin with the first symptoms of dementia in a close family member. Because the disease process impairs language, insight and judgement, family members may be called on to make decisions on behalf of the person with dementia (Karlawish, 2002). Long hours of vigilance and responses to needs and demands can be involved, as well as heavy or sustained personal care chores. The caregiver can feel harassed, burdened, alienated (e.g. the patient forgets his/her name and shared experiences), concerned and distressed (by noisiness of the patient, soiling, interference with social life). The caregiver can also be kept awake at night (Wilcox and King, 1999) because of the sleep disturbances of people with dementia such as insomnia and excessive nocturnal motor activity (Boeve, Silber and Ferman, 2002).

Increases in problem behaviours among persons with dementia are significant predictors of a caregivers' stress and impaired mental health (Kluger and Ferris, 1991; Hooker *et al.*, 2002). Such disturbing behaviour can impair the quality of both the patient's and the caregiver's lives. It affects a substantial proportion of dementia of all types, rates being highest in the more advanced stages of dementia (Teri *et al.*, 1988; Drachman *et al.*, 1992). These behaviours include suspiciousness, hallucinations, delusions, misidentifications, forgetfulness, dependence, wakeful activity at night, wandering, pacing, incontinence, emotional lability, agitation, perseveration, aggressiveness, damaging or injurious acts, and inappropriate public behaviour. Teri *et al.* (1989) add that disorientation, underactivity, no interest in others, poor hygiene, inappropriate dress, muteness, trouble getting out of bed and incontinence of urine are highly stressful to caregivers.

Supports for Caregivers

In many developed countries, there are large-scale social and residential services for the care of people with dementia at home, in assisted living sites and in nursing homes, though family care is still very active (Rice *et al.*, 1993). In less-developed regions of the world the mainstay of these persons is still their informal support network (Wimo *et al.*, 2002).

INTERVENTION

For Impaired Quality of Life in Dementia

Over recent years, an increasing number of publications have described the results of well-designed trials of intervention for dementia that include QoL in their outcome measures. However, there is a patchy record of success in these efforts to improve QoL for persons with dementia or their caregivers.

There is general agreement that attention should first be given to dealing with comorbid disorders and sensory deficits (Herrmann, 2001). Then, non-pharmacological therapeutic strategies should be considered before resorting to potent medication, especially for milder behavioural disorders (Parnetti *et al.*, 2001). According to Baltes and Smith (2003), new endeavours are required to deal with forms of psychological morbidity such as loss of identity and of the sense of control. The initiatives and drive of persons with dementia and their caregivers are also key factors in meeting the challenge to QoL imposed by dementia. Clare (2002) identified themes in these coping strategies as self-protective (e.g. holding on and compensating) and integrative responding (e.g. resisting, but coming to terms with the disorder).

Non-pharmacological

Early diagnosis and ongoing determination of the capacity for making crucial decisions (e.g. in health care, risks of injury, dangers of driving) can help to preserve autonomy and improved QoL for the person with dementia, according to Barbas and Wilde (2001). However, diagnosis itself can induce worries related to fear of others finding out, fears of social embarrassment, long-term dependency needs and being ignored, or can lead to social withdrawal and hypervigilance for evidence of cognitive failure. It can also result in low self-esteem, self-stigmatisation and impaired QoL (Husband, 2000).

In a review covering 157 research studies on intervention for persons with dementia, Burgener and Twigg (2002a) refer to 'well-supported' cognitive–behavioural interventions for cognitive functioning, maintenance of activities, and behavioural symptoms in both the middle and late stages of dementia. In the late stages, the targets of intervention may be nutrition, continence and vocalisation. A fairly large controlled trial of cognitive stimulation therapy showed significant relative improvement for the intervention on the QoL of Alzheimer's Disease Scales, which were regarded as comparable with the results of drug trials (Spector *et al.*, 2003). A placebo-controlled and cross-over design was used to test the efficacy of training in face–name associations and spaced retrieval for persons with probable Alzheimer's disease (Davis, Massman and Doody, 2001); significant improvement resulted in several cognitive parameters, but not to patients' QoL, as assessed by caregivers. Classroom-style rehearsal of information on time, place and persons (i.e. reality orientation) was carried out with 67 elderly people with dementia and compared with 58 controls; significant improvement was noted for behavioural outcomes (Spector *et al.*, 2000).

Evidence of other non-pharmacological intervention (e.g. light therapy, changes in level of stimulation) is still scanty. Koger and Brotons (2000) searched for references to randomised controlled trials of music therapy as an intervention in dementia, but did not find any with adequate quantitative data.

Environmental

Applying the observational method known as Dementia Care Mapping, Kuhn, Kasayka and Lechner (2002) examined the QoL of 131 persons with dementia living in 10 assisted living facilities. Residents in small, dementia-specific sites were worse off with respect to QoL and diversity of interactions and activities than those living in larger, generic sites. Warren *et al.* (2001) similarly compared older people with dementia in residential care centres and special care units, finding that the rates of decline were similar. They add that in residential care centres, there appeared to be more freedom of choice, fewer physical or psychotropic medication restraints and more activities, which may have enhanced QoL. Volicer, Mckee and Hewitt (2001) support the view that the QoL of persons with dementia is enhanced by meaningful activities and avoidance of restraint. Marshall and Hutchinson (2001) relate that nursing literature regards activities for persons with dementia as capable of enhancing QoL through maintaining self-esteem, dignity and roles as well as fostering pleasure and friendships.

In the attempt to minimise the restricting features of a residential setting for persons with dementia, 'subjective exit modifications' (such as camouflage, stripes of tape, concealed latches) have been installed to reduce wandering without obvious barriers. Nevertheless, Price, Hermans and Grimley Evans (2000) could not find any properly controlled trials of the impact of these devices on the frequency of wandering, nor on the QoL of residents.

Pharmacological

The management of behavioural and psychotic manifestations of dementia can significantly improve the QoL for the patient and caregiver (Herrmann, 2001). Medication is often needed for the more entrenched symptoms, but is more effective when combined with non-pharmacological intervention (Parnetti *et al.*, 2001).

Antipsychotics for agitation and aggression have demonstrated modest but consistent efficacy (Herrmann, 2001). Atypical or novel antipsychotic drugs are preferred, especially risperidone, though selective serotonin reuptake inhibitors may also be useful (Parnetti *et al.*, 2001). Low-dose, once-a-day olanzapine and risperidone appear to be equally safe and effective for dementia-related behavioural disturbances and impaired QoL of residents in long-term care facilities (Fontaine *et al.*, 2003).

Robert (2002) points to evidence that loss of cholinergic neurones and a resultant decline in acetyl-choline in brain regions which regulate behavioural and emotional responses may be responsible for behavioural disturbance and psychotic symptoms in dementia, thus providing a rationale for use of anticholinesterases. He states that all such drugs that are in common use improve apathy, depression and anxiety, while rivastigmine additionally improves hallucinations and delusions. In his judgement, there is accumulating evidence that both early and long-term intervention with these drugs improve behavioural and psychotic disturbances, and can thus enhance QoL. The conclusions of a very extensive review of the literature up to July 2000 are that donepezil, rivastigmine and galantamine have a beneficial effect on global outcome measures (Clegg *et al.*, 2001). Galantamine demonstrated clinical benefits on functional ability and behaviour in both Alzheimer's disease and vascular dementia in a controlled study (Kurz, 2002). However, the ability of donepezil to improve QoL remains uncertain (Pryse-Phillips *et al.*, 2001).

A Cochrane Specialized Register search for controlled tests of donepezil effects in all stages of dementia found benefits in activities of daily living and behaviour, but also unpleasant side-effects (e.g. nausea, vomiting, diarrhea and anorexia) (Birks and Harvey, 2003). Another such search (Birks, Melzer and Beppu, 2000) incorporated eight controlled trials of donepezil with 2664 participants, revealing some improvement in global clinical state (assessed by an independent clinician), but no benefits being reported in the patients' own ratings of their QoL. These latter findings led the authors to reserve judgement about the practical importance of these changes to patients and caregivers (see also Courtney *et al.*, 2004). Birks and Flicker (2000) noted that the value of selegiline for symptoms of Alzheimer's disease remains controversial, with only modest benefits observed in some trials and none in others. They carried out a literature search of rigorous research on this medication, but did not find enough evidence to recommend its use in routine practice. They recommend additional studies to evaluate the use of selegiline for the end-points of clinical impression of global change, dependency and caregiver's QoL. Based on another specialised register of the Cochrane, Flicker and Grimley Evans (2001) report that the published literature does not support the use of piracetam (a nootropic) in dementia, because although there are effects on the global impression of change, there are none on more specific measures.

Laboratory and epidemiological evidence of a link between inflammatory mechanisms and Alzheimer disease has led to an interest in the possible benefits of non-steroidal anti-inflammatory drugs. A multicentre, large-scale study of a selective cyclooxygenase (COX)-2 inhibitor (rofecoxib) and a non-selective agent (naproxen) in ambulatory treatment centres (Aisen *et al.*, 2003) included the QoL-AD as an outcome measure, but there was no significant difference compared with the placebo, other than more serious adverse events. Aspirin is widely prescribed in vascular dementia, but Williams *et al.* (2000) could not find any properly designed and unbiased trials of its efficacy reported in the literature.

For Depression and Pain in Dementia

Antidepressant treatment may improve the QoL in depressed people with dementia, but tends to be less effective and is more prone to side-effects than with uncomplicated depression. Hence, non-pharmacological approaches are preferred, unless depression in dementia meets the full criteria for depressive disorder or dysthymia, or persists despite such approaches (Thorpe and Groulx, 2001). Fifty elderly people with probable Alzheimer's disease were randomised to receive inhibitors of cholinesterase (donepezil) alone or with selective serotonin reuptake inhibitors (citalopram), and were followed up for one year; citalopram decreased the depression and improved QoL for both patients and caregivers (Moretti *et al.*, 2002).

Weiner and Hanlon (2001) point to the wide array of non-pharmacological and other effective treatments for different types of pain, including both non-opioid and opioid analgesics, and even tricyclic antidepressants and anticonvulsants. They emphasise that, despite these resources, pain is under-treated in nursing home residents, and opportunities for improving their QoL are thus lost. Also relevant to this consideration is that studies have not shown that the use of feeding tubes prevents malnutrition, pressure sores or aspiration pneumonia, nor that it extends life. This leaves hand feeding as the preferable alternative, because it is more comfortable for the resident (Li, 2002).

For Caregivers

Data from a survey of a representative sample of caregivers to dementia and non-dementia patients produced a path model indicating that well-being was affected by perceived social support, burden, self-esteem and hours of informal care. At the same time, the burden was influenced by behavioural problems, frequency of getting a break, self-esteem and hours of informal care (Chappell and Reid, 2002). The authors hypothesise that the QoL of caregivers could be improved, even with the same burden in their lives. Mutual support groups involving 52 family caregivers in two centres in Hong Kong resulted in significant differences in benefits, compared with controls, for distress levels and QoL (Fung and Chien, 2002).

Schulz *et al.* (2002) reviewed intervention studies for dementia caregivers published from 1996 to 2001; they observed small-to-moderate statistically significant effects on a broad range of outcomes, but only a small proportion of studies achieved clinically meaningful outcomes. They urge that new designs and measures be invoked to realise the promise that intervention studies with caregivers suggest delaying institutionalisation, relieving both major and minor depression and providing valued services. In a meta-analytical review of 30 studies on intervention for informal caregivers of persons with dementia, excluding respite care, Brodaty, Green and Koschera (2003) noted that there were significant benefits for the psychological distress of caregivers and that benefits were more likely to be achieved when the person with dementia was also involved. A comparable meta-analysis by Acton and Kang (2001) focused on support group, education, psychoeducation, counselling, respite care and multicomponent programmes designed to help caregivers cope with the burden of caregiving. Collectively, 27 interventions showed no effect on caregivers' burden, except for the multicomponent interventions, which did significantly reduce the burden.

FUTURE DIRECTIONS

The challenge that dementia represents to the QoL of elders and their caregivers is felt world-wide. This challenge bears not only upon individuals and families but also upon societies, their health and social care systems, and even the stability of their economies. A language capable of describing this challenge in a useful manner is only slowly emerging. To be useful the language should convey to policy makers the impact of dementia on people's lives, lead to an understanding of service needs and contribute to the development and selection of effective interventions.

In this chapter we have proposed and detailed the basic structure and content of such a language. Its potential usefulness was illustrated by demonstrating its relevance to evaluating the impairments by dementia of those adaptive capacities that are necessary to maintain a preferred QoL. Concepts embedded in this prototype language structure can be examined and modified, as data and insights accumulate: with respect to the nature, number and designation of domains; clustering of adaptive and maladaptive responses, subjective and objective viewpoints, perspectives of concerned parties, the relationship between intensity, extensity and severity; the mechanisms of causation and consequence; and the integration of relationships among domains.

There is a widespread effort to develop, test and expand the use of measurement instruments or techniques for QoL in dementia. Interventions directly aimed at improving QoL in dementia are also rapidly expanding. However, still too many interventions remain of unproven efficacy and questions are raised about whether measurement of outcomes in dementia is insensitive to the benefits of interventions. There is bound to be a pattern of reciprocal reinforcements between the search for more sensitive measures and for more efficacious interventions.

Scientific and humanistic approaches to QoL in dementia are needed to constructively face the issues revolving around the refinement of relevant theoretical and empirical understandings, strengthening of therapeutic interventions and empowerment of those directly or indirectly affected.

REFERENCES

Acton, G.J. & Kang, J. (2001). Interventions to reduce the burden of caregiving for an adult with dementia: a meta-analysis, *Res. Nurs. Health*, **24**(5), October, 349–360.

Aisen, P.S., Schafer, K.A., Grundman, M., Pfeiffer, E., Sano, M., Davis, K.L., Farlow, M.R., Jin, S., Thomas, R.G. & Thal, L.J. (2003). Alzheimer's Disease Cooperative Study. Effects of rofecoxib or naproxen vs placebo on Alzheimer disease progression: A randomized controlled trial, *J. Am. Med. Ass.*, **289**(21), 4 June, 2819–2826.

Albert, S.M., Jacobs, D.M., Sano, M., Marder, K., Bell, K., Devanand, D., Brandt, J., Albert, M. & Stern, Y. (2001). Longitudinal study of quality of life in people with advanced Alzheimer's disease, *Am. J. Geriat. Psychiatry*, **9**(2), Spring, 160–168.

Alexopoulos, G.S., Young, R.C. & Meyers, B.S. (1993). Geriatric depression: Age of onset and dementia, *Biolog. Psychiatry*, **34**(3), August, 141–145.

Almberg, B., Jansson, W., Grafstrom, M. *et al.* (1998). Differences between and within genders in caregiving strain: A comparison between caregivers of demented and non-caregivers of non-demented elderly people, *J. Adv. Nurs.*, **28**, 849–858.

Alzheimer's Disease International (1999). Fact sheet 3: The prevalence of dementia, April.

Baldwin, C., Hughes, J., Hope, T., Jacoby, R. & Ziebland, S. (2003). Ethics and dementia: Mapping the literature by bibliometric analysis, *Int. J. Geriat. Psychiatry*, **18**(1), January, 41–54.

Ballard, C., O'Brien, J., James, I., Mynt, P., Lana, M., Potkins, D., Reichelt, K., Lee, L., Swann, A. & Fossey, J. (2001). Quality of life for people with dementia living in residential and nursing home care: The impact of performance on activities of daily living, behavioral and psychological symptoms, language skills, and psychotropic drugs, *Int. Psychogeriat.*, **13**(1), March, 93–106.

Baltes, P.B. & Smith, J. (2003). New frontiers in the future of aging: From successful aging of the young old to the dilemmas of the fourth age, *Gerontology*, **49**(2), March–April, 123–135.

Barbas, N.R. & Wilde, E.A. (2001). Competency issues in dementia: Medical decision making, driving, and independent living, *J. Geriat. Psychiatry and Neurol.*, **14**(4), Winter, 199–212.

Barberger-Gateau, P., Commenges, D., Gagnon, M., Letenneur, L., Sauvel, C. & Dartigues, J.F. (1992) Instrumental activities of daily living as a screening tool for cognitive impairment and dementia in elderly community dwellers, *J. Am. Geriat. Soc.*, **40**(11), November, 1129–1134.

Baum, C. & Edwards, D.F. (1993). Cognitive performance in senile dementia of the Alzheimer's type: The kitchen task assessment, *Am. J. Occup. Therapy*, **47**(5), May, 431–436.

Beavis, D., Simpson, S. & Graham, I. (2002). A literature review of dementia care mapping: Methodological considerations and efficacy, *J. Psychiat. Ment. Health Nurs.*, **9**(6), December, 725–736.

Birks, J. & Flicker, L. (2000) Selegiline for Alzheimer's disease, *Cochrane Database of Systematic Reviews*, (2):CD000442.

Birks, J.S. & Harvey, R. (2003). Donepezil for dementia due to Alzheimer's disease. *Cochrane Database of Systematic Reviews*, (3):CD001190, 2003.

Birks, J.S., Melzer, D. & Beppu, H. (2000). Donepezil for mild and moderate Alzheimer's disease, *Cochrane Database of Systematic Reviews*, (4):CD001190.

Boeve, B.F., Silber, M.H. & Ferman, T.J. (2002). Current management of sleep disturbances in dementia, *Curr. Neurol. and Neurosci. Rep.*, **2**(2), March, 169–177.

Brodaty, H., Green, A. & Koschera A. (2003). Meta-analysis of psychosocial interventions for caregivers of people with dementia, *J. Am. Geriat. Soc.*, **51**(5), May, 657–664.

Brodaty, H. & Hadzi, P. D. (1990). Psychosocial effects on carrers of living with persons with dementia, *Aust. N. Z. J. Psychiatry*, **24**(351).

Bureau-Chalot, F., Novella, J.L., Jolly, D., Ankri, J., Guillemin, F. & Blanchard, F. (2002). Feasibility, acceptability and internal consistency reliability of the Nottingham Health Profile in dementia patients, *Gerontology*, **48**(4), July–August, 220–225.

Burgener, S.C. & Twigg, P. (2002a). Interventions for persons with irreversible dementia, *Annual Rev. Nurs. Res.*, **20**, 89–124.

Burgener, S. & Twigg, P. (2002b). Relationships among caregiver factors and quality of life in care recipients with irreversible dementia, *Alzheimer Dis. Associated Disord.*, **16**(2), 88–102.

Chappell, N.L. & Reid, R.C. (2002). Burden and well-being among caregivers: Examining the distinction, *Gerontologist*, **42**(6), December, 772–780.

Christensen H. (1991). The validity of memory complaints by elderly persons, *Int. J. Geriat. Psychiatry*, **6**(5), May, 307–312.

Clare, L. (2002). We'll fight it as long as we can: Coping with the onset of Alzheimer's disease, *Aging Ment. Health*, **6**(2), May, 139–148.

Clarke, P.J., Marshall, V.W., Ryff, C.D. & Wheaton, B. (2001). Measuring psychological well-being in the Canadian study of health and aging, *Int. Psychogeriat.*, **13**(Suppl. 1), 79–90.

Clegg, A., Bryant J., Nicholson, T., McIntyre, L., De Broe, S., Gerard, K. & Waugh, N. (2001). Clinical and cost-effectiveness of donepezil, rivastigmine and galantamine for Alzheimer's disease: A rapid and systematic review, *Health Technol. Assessment (Winchester, England)*, **5**(1), 1–137.

Coen, R.F., O'Boyle, C.A., Coakley, D. & Lawlor, B.A. (2002). Individual quality of life factors distinguishing low-burden and high-burden caregivers of dementia patients, *Dementia Geriat. Cognitive Disord.*, **13**(3), 164–170.

Cohen-Mansfield, J. & Creedon, M. (2002). Nursing staff members' perceptions of pain indicators in persons with severe dementia, *Clin. J. Pain*, **18**(1), January–February, 64–73.

Collins, C. & Jones, R. (1997). Emotional distress and morbidity in dementia carers: A matched comparison of husbands and wives, *Int. J. Geriat. Psychiatry*, **12**, 1168–1173.

Coucill, W., Bryan, S., Bentham, P., Buckley, A. & Laight, A. (2001). EQ-5D in patients with dementia: An investigation of inter-rater agreement, *Med. Care*, **39**(8), August, 760–771.

Courtney, C., Farrell, D., Gray, R., Hills, R., Lynch, L., Sellwood, E., Edwards, S., Hardyman, W., Raftery, J., Crome, P., Lendon, C., Shaw, H., Bentham, P. & AD2000 Collaborative Group (2004). Long-term donepezil treatment in 565 patients with Alzheimer's disease (AD2000): Randomised double-blind trial, *Lancet*, **363**(9427), 26 June, 2105–2115.

Davis, R.N., Massman, P.J. & Doody, R.S. (2001). Cognitive intervention in Alzheimer disease: A randomized placebo-controlled study, *Alzheimer Dis. Associated Disord.*, **15**(1), January–March, 1–9.

Demers, L., Oremus, M., Perrault, A., Champoux, N. & Wolfson, C. (2000). Review of outcome measurement instruments in Alzheimer's disease drug trials: Psychometric properties of functional and quality of life scales, *J. Geriat. Psychiatry Neurol.*, **13**(4), Winter, 170–180.

Drachman, D.A., Swearer, J.M., O'Donnell, B.F., Mitchell, A.L., *et al* (1992). The Caretaker Obstreperous-Behavior Rating Assessment (COBRA) Scale, *J. Am. Geriat. Soc.*, **40**(5), 463–470.

Etzioni, D.A., Liu, J.H., Maggard, M.A. & Ko, C.Y. (2003). The aging population and its impact on the surgery workforce, *Ann. Surg.*, **238**(2), August 170–177.

Feehan, M., Knight, R.G. & Partridge, F.M. (1991). Cognitive complaint and test performance in elderly patients suffering depression or dementia, *Int. J. Geriat. Psychiatry*, **6**(5), May, 287–293.

Fitz, A.G. & Teri, L. (1994). Depression, cognition, and functional ability in patients with Alzheimer's disease, *J. Am. Geriat. Soc.*, **42**(2), February, 186–191.

Flicker, L. & Grimley Evans, G. (2001). Piracetam for dementia or cognitive impairment, *Cochrane Database of Systematic Reviews*, (2):CD001011.

Fontaine, C.S., Hynan, L.S., Koch, K., Martin-Cook, K., Svetlik, D. & Weiner, M.F. (2003). A double-blind comparison of olanzapine versus risperidone in the acute treatment of dementia-related behavioral disturbances in extended carefacilities, *J. Clin. Psychiatry*, **64**(6), June, 726–730.

Forsell, Y., Jorm, A.F. & Winblad, B. (1994). Outcome of depression in demented and non-demented elderly: Observations from a three-year follow-up in a community-based study, *Int. J. Geriat. Psychiatry*, **9**(1), January, 5–10.

Forstl, H., Burns, A., Levy, R. & Cairns, N. (1994). Neuropathological correlates of psychotic phenomena in confirmed Alzheimer's disease, *Br. J. Psychiatry*, **165**(2), July, 53–59.

Fossey, J., Lee, L. & Ballard, C. (2002). Dementia care mapping as a research tool for measuring quality of life in care settings: Psychometric properties, *Int. J. Geriat. Psychiatry*, **17**(11), November, 1064–1070.

Foster, J. & Cataldo, J.K. (1994). Protection from clinical depression in medical long-term care facilities: Evidence for psychologic adaptation in cognitively intact patients, *Int. J. Geriat. Psychiatry*, **9**(2), February, 115–125.

Fung, W.Y. & Chien, W.T. (2002). The effectiveness of a mutual support group for family caregivers of a relative with dementia, *Arch. Psychiat. Nurs.*, **16**(3), June, 134–144.

Grut, M., Jorm, A.F., Fratiglioni, L., Forsell, Y. *et al* (1993). Memory complaints of elderly people in a population survey: Variation according to dementia stage and depression, *J. Am. Geriat. Soc.*, **41**(12), December, 1295–1300.

Gurland, B. & Katz, S. (1992). The outcomes of psychiatric disorders in the elderly: Relevance of quality of life, in *Handbook of Mental Health and Ageing* (Eds J.E. Birren, R.B. Sloane & E.D. Cohen), pp. 230–248, Academic Press, Los Angeles, California.

Gurland, B.J., Katz, S. & Chen, J. (1997). Index of affective suffering: Linking a classification of depressed mood to impairment in quality of life, *Am. J. Geriat. Psychiatry*, **5**(3), 192–210.

Gurland, B., Copeland, J., Kuriansky, J., Kelleher, H., Sharpe, L. & Dean, L.L. (1983). The mind and mood of aging, pp. 51–52, 105, 121–125, 157–166, Haworth Press, New York.

Gurland, B.J., Wilder, D.E., Chen, J., Lantigua, R., Mayeux, R. & Van Nostrand, J. (1995). A flexible system of detection of Alzheimer's disease and related dementias, *Aging Clin. Expl Res.*, **1**, 165–172.

Gurland, B.J., Wilder, D.E., Lantigua, R., Mayeux, R., Stern, Y., Chen, J., Cross, P. & Killeffer, E. (1997). Differences in rates of dementia between ethnoracial groups, in *Racial and Ethnic Differences in the Health of Older Americans* (Eds L.G. Martin & B.J. Soldo), Chapter 8, National Academy Press, Washington, DC.

Hanninen, T., Reinikainen, K.J., Helkala, E.L., Koivisto, K. *et al* (1994). Subjective memory complaints and personality traits in normal elderly subjects. Second Congress of the PanEuropean Society of Neurology (1991, Vienna, Austria), *J. Am. Geriat. Soc.*, **42**(1), January, 1–4.

Herrmann, N. (2001). Recommendations for the management of behavioral and psychological symptoms of dementia, *Can. J. Neurolog. Sci.*, **28**(Suppl. 1), February, S96–107.

Hooker, K., Bowman, S.R., Coehlo, D.P., Lim, S.R., Kaye, J., Guariglia, R. & Li, F. (2002). Behavioral change in persons with dementia: Relationships with mental and physical health of caregivers, *J. Gerontol. Ser. B – Psycholog. Sci. Social Sci.*, **57**(5), September, P453–460.

Husband, H.J. (2000). Diagnostic disclosure in dementia: An opportunity for intervention?, *Int. J. Geriat. Psychiatry*, **15**(6), June, 544–547.

Innes, A. & Surr, C. (2001). Measuring the well-being of people with dementia living in formal care settings: The use of dementia care mapping, *Aging Ment. Health*, **5**(3), August, 258–268.

Inouye, S.K., Albert, M.S., Mohs, R., Sun, K. & Berkman, L.F. (1993). Cognitive performance in a high-functioning community-dwelling elderly population, *J. Gerontol. Med. Sci.*, **48**(4), M146–M151.

Karlawish, J.H. (2002). Living with dementia: Caregiver perspectives, *LDI Issue Brief.*, **7**(8), June, 1–4.

Karlawish, J.H., Casarett, D., Klocinski, J. & Clark, C.M. (2001). The relationship between caregivers' global ratings of Alzheimer's disease patients' quality of life, disease severity, and the caregiving experience, *J. Am. Geriat. Soc.*, **49**(8), August, 1066–1070.

Katz, S. & Gurland, B. J. (1991). Science of quality of life of elders: Challenge and opportunity, in *The Concept and Measurement of Quality of Life in the Frail Elderly* (Eds J.E. Birren, J. E. Lubben, J.C. Rowe & D.E. Deutchman), pp. 335–343, Academic Press, San Diego, California.

Keene, J., Hope, T., Fairburn, C.G. & Jacoby, R. (2001). Death and dementia, *Int. J. Geriat. Psychiatry*, **16**(10), October, 969–974.

Kim, E. & Rovner, B.W. (1994) Depression in dementia, *Psychiat. Ann.*, **24**(4), April, 173–177.

Kluger, A. & Ferris, S.H. (1991). Scales for assessment of Alzheimer's disease, *Psychiat. Clinic of N. Am.* **14**, 309–326.

Koenders, M.E.F., Passchier, J., Teuns, G., van-Harskamp, F. *et al* (1993). Trait-anxiety and achievement motivation are positively correlated with memory performance in patients who visit a geriatric outpatient clinic with amnestic symptoms, *Psycholog. Rep.*, **73**(3, Pt 2), December, 1227–1231.

Koger, S.M. & Brotons, M. (2000). Music therapy for dementia symptoms, *Cochrane Database of Systematic Reviews*, (3):CD001121.

Kuhn, D., Kasayka, R.E. & Lechner, C. (2002). Behavioral observations and quality life among persons with dementia in 10 assisted living facilities, *Am. J. Alzheimer's Dis. Other Dementias*, **17**(5), September–October, 291–298.

Kurz, A. (2002). Non-cognitive benefits of galantamine (Reminyl) treatment in vascular dementia, *Acta Neurologica Scand.*, **178**(Suppl.), 19–24.

Kurz, X., Scuvee-Moreau, J., Vernooij-Dassen, M. & Dresse, A. (2003). Cognitive impairment, dementia and quality of life in patients and caregivers, *Acta Neurologica Belgica*, **103**(1), March, 24–34.

la Rue, A., Watson, J. & Plotkin, D.A. (1993). First symptoms of dementia: A study of relatives' reports, *Int. J. Geriat. Psychiatry*, **8**(3), March, 239–245.

Li, I. (2002). Feeding tubes in patients with severe dementia, *Am. Family Physician*, **65**(8), 15 April, 1605–1610.

Logsdon, R.G., Gibbons, L.E., McCurry, S.M. & Teri, L. (2002). Assessing quality of life in older adults with cognitive impairment, *Psychosomatic Med.*, **64**(3), May–June, 510–519.

Lyketsos, C.G., Gonzales-Salvador, T., Chin, J.J., Baker, A., Black, B. & Rabins, P. (2003). A follow-up study of change in quality of life among persons with dementia residing in a long-term care facility, *Int. J. Geriat. Psychiatry*, **18**(4), April, 275–281.

McGlone, J., Gupta, S., Humphrey, D., Oppenheimer, S. *et al.* (1990). Screening for early dementia using memory complaints from patients and relatives, *Arc. Neurol.*, **47**(11), November, 1189–1193.

Mahurin, R.K., DeBettignies, B.H. & Pirozzolo, F.J. (1991). Structured assessment of independent living skills: Preliminary report of a performance measure of functional abilities in dementia, *J. Gerontol.*, **46**(2), March, P58–P66.

Mangone, C.A., Hier, D.B., Gorelick, P.B., Ganellen, R.J., *et al* (1991). Impaired insight in Alzheimer's disease, *J. Geriat. Psychiatry Neurol.*, **4**(4), October–December, 189–193.

Marshall, M.J. & Hutchinson, S.A. (2001). A critique of research on the use of activities with persons with Alzheimer's disease: A systematic literature review, *J. Adv. Nurs.*, **35**(4), August, 488–496.

Moretti, R., Torre, P., Antonello, R.M., Cazzato, G. & Bava, A. (2002). Depression and Alzheimer's disease: Symptom or comorbidity?, *Am. J. of Alzheimer's Dis. Other Dementias*, **17**(6), December, 338–344.

Nadler, J.D., Richardson, E.D., Malloy, P.F., Marran, M.E. *et al* (1993). The ability of the dementia rating scale to predict everyday functioning, *Arch. Clin. Neuropsychol.*, **8**(5), September–October, 449–460.

Navaie-Waliser, M., Spriggs, A. & Feldman, P.H. (2002). Informal caregiving: Differential experiences by gender, *Med. Care*, **40**(12), December, 1249–1259.

Novella, J., Ankri, J., Morrone, I., Guillemin, F., Jolly, D., Jochum, C., Ploton, L. & Blanchard, F. (2001a). Evaluation of the quality of life in dementia with a generic quality of life questionnaire: The Duke Health Profile, *Dementia Geriat. Cognitive Disord.*, **12**(2), 158–166.

Novella, J.L., Jochum, C., Ankri, J., Morrone, I., Jolly, D. & Blanchard, F. (2001b). Measuring general health status in dementia: Practical and methodological issues in using the SF-36, *Aging-Clin. Expl Res.*, **13**(5), 362–369.

Novella, J.L., Jochum, C., Jolly, D., Morrone, I., Ankri, J., Bureau, F. & Blanchard, F. (2001c). Agreement between patients' and proxies' reports of quality of life in Alzheimer's disease, *Qual. Life Res.*, **10**(5), 443–452.

Oakle, F., Sunderland, T., Hill, J.L., Phillips, S.L. *et al* (1991). The daily activities questionnaire: A functional assessment for people with Alzheimer's disease, *Physical and Occupational Therapy in Geriatrics*, **10**(2), 67–81.

O'Brien, J.T., Beats, B.H., Katie, H.R. *et al* (1992). Do subjective memory complaints precede dementia? A three-year follow-up of patients with supposed 'benign senescent forgetfulness', *Int. J. Geriat. Psychiatry*, **7**(7), 481–486.

O'Connor, D.W., Pollitt, P.A., Roth, M., Brook, P.B. *et al* (1990). Memory complaints and impairment in normal, depressed, and demented elderly persons identified in a community survey, *Arch. Gen. Psychiatry*, **47**(3), March, 224–227.

Ory, M.G., Hoffman, III, R.R., Yee, J.L. *et al* (1999). Prevalence and impact of caregiving: A detailed comparison between dementia and nondementia caregivers, *Gerontology*, **39**, 177–185.

Overall, J.E., Scott, J., Rhoades, H.M. & Lesser, J. (1990). Empirical scaling of the stages of cognitive decline in senile dementia, *J. Geriat. Psychiatry Neurol.*, **3**(4), October–December, 212–220.

Parasuraman, R. & Nestor, P.G. (1991). Attention and driving skills in aging and Alzheimer's disease. Special Issue: Safety and mobility of elderly drivers: Part I, *Human-Factors*, **33**(5), 539–557.

Parnetti, L., Amici, S., Lanari, A. & Gallai, V. (2001). Pharmacological treatment of non-cognitive disturbances in dementia disorders, *Mechanisms of Ageing Dev.*, **122**(16), November, 2063–2069.

Pettit, T., Livingston, G., Manela, M., Kitchen, G., Katona, C. & Bowling, A. (2001). Validation and normative data of health status measures in older people: The Islington study, *Int. J. Geriat. Psychiatry*, **16**(11), November, 1061–1070.

Post, S.G., Stuckey, J.C., Whitehouse, P.J., Ollerton, S., Durkin, C., Robbins, D. & Fallcreek, S.J. (2001). A focus group on cognition-enhancing medications in Alzheimer disease: Disparities between professionals and consumers, *Alzheimer Dis. Associated Disord.*, **15**(2), April–June, 80–88.

Price, J.D., Hermans, D.G. & Grimley Evans, J. (2000). Subjective barriers to prevent wandering of cognitively impaired people, *Cochrane Database of Systematic Reviews*, (4):CD001932.

Prince, M. (2000). Dementia in developing countries: A consensus statement from the 10/66 Dementia Research Group, *Int. J. Geriat. Psychiatry*, **15**, 14–20.

Pryse-Phillips, W., Sternberg, S., Rochon, P., Naglie, G., Strong, H. & Feightner, J. (2001). The use of medications for cognitive enhancement, *Can. J. Neurolog. Sci.*, **28**(Suppl. 1), February, S108–114.

Ready, R.E., Ott, B.R., Grace, J. & Cahn-Weiner, D.A. (2003). Apathy and executive dysfunction in mild cognitive impairment and Alzheimer disease, *Am. J. Geriat. Psychiatry*, **11**(2), March–April, 222–228.

Reisberg, B. (1990). Alzheimer disease: The clinical syndrome: Diagnostic and etiologic importance, *Acta Neurologica Scand.*, **82**(129, Suppl.), 2–4.

Reisberg, B., Ferris, S.H., De Leon, M.J. & Crook, T. (1982) The global deterioration scale for assessment of primary degenerative dementia, *Am. J. Psychiatry*, **139**(9), 1136–1139.

Rice, D.P., Fox, P.J., Max, W. *et al* (1993). The economic burden of Alzheimer's disease care, *Health Affects (Millwood)*, **12**, 164–176.

Riemsma, R.P., Forbes, C.A., Glanville, J.M., Eastwood, A.J. & Kleijnen, J. (2001). General health status measures for people with cognitive impairment: learning disability and acquired brain injury, *Health Technol. Assessment (Winchester, England)*, **5**(6), 1–100.

Robert, P. (2002). Understanding and managing behavioural symptoms in Alzheimer's disease and related dementias: focus on rivastigmine [review], *Current Med. Res. Opinion*, **18**(3), 156–171.

Rubin, E. H., Morris, J. C., Storandt, M. & Berg, L. (1987). Behavioral changes in patients with mild senile dementia of the Alzheimer's type, *Psychiatry Res.*, **21**, 55.

Schermer, M. (2003). In search of 'the good life' for demented elderly, *Med., Health Care and Philosophy*, **6**(1), 35–44.

Schneider, L.S. Assessing outcomes in Alzheimer disease, *Alzheimer Dis. Associated Disord.*, **15**(Suppl. 1), August, S8–18.

Schulz, R., O'Brien, A., Czaja, S., Ory, M., Norris, R., Martire, L.M., Belle, S.H., Burgio, L., Gitlin, L., Coon, D., Burns, R., Gallagher-Thompson, D. & Stevens, A. (2002). Dementia caregiver intervention research: In search of clinical significance, *Gerontologist*, **42**(5), October, 589–602.

Silberfeld, M., Rueda, S., Krahn, M. & Naglie, G. (2002). Content validity for dementia of three generic preference based health related quality of life instruments, *Quality of Life Res.*, **11**(1), February, 71–79.

Skoog, I. (1993). The prevalence of psychotic, depressive and anxiety syndromes in demented and non-demented 85-year-olds, *Int. J. Geriat. Psychiatry*, **8**(3), March, 247–253.

Skurla, E., Rogers, J.C. & Sunderland, T. (1988). Direct assessment of activities of daily living in Alzheimer's disease: A controlled study, *J. Am. Geriat. Soc.*, **36**, 97–103.

Smith, S.C., Lamping, D.L., Banerjee, S., Harwood, R., Foley, B., Smith, P. *et al* (2004). Measurement of health-related quality of life for people with dementia: Development of a new instrument (DEMQOL) and an evaluation of current methodology, *Health Technol. Assessment* (in press).

Spector, A., Orrell, M., Davies, S. & Woods, B. (2000). Reality orientation for dementia, *Cochrane Database of Systematic Reviews*, (4):CD001119.

Spector, A., Thorgrimsen, L., Woods, B., Royan, L., Davies, S., Butterworth, M. & Orrell, M. (2003). Efficacy of an evidence-based cognitive stimulation therapy programme for people with dementia: Randomised controlled trial, *Br. J. Psychiatry*, **183**, September, 248–254.

Terada, S., Ishizu, H., Fujisawa, Y., Fujita, D., Yokota, O., Nakashima, H., Haraguchi, T., Ishihara, T., Yamamoto, S., Sasaki, K., Nakashima, Y. & Kuroda, S. (2002). Development and evaluation of a health-related quality of life questionnaire for the elderly with dementia in Japan, *Int. J. Geriat. Psychiatry*, **17**(9), Septermber, 851–858.

Teri, L., Larson, E.B. & Reifler, B.V. (1988). Behavioral disturbance in dementia of the Alzheimer's type, *J. Am. Geriat. Soc.*, **36**(1), January, 1–6.

Teri, L., Borson, S., Kiyak, H.A. & Yamagishi, M. (1989). Behavioral disturbance, cognitive dysfunction and functional skill: Prevalence and relationship in Alzheimer's disease, *J. Am. Geriat. Soc.*, **37**(2), 109–116.

Thorpe, L. & Groulx, B. (2001). Canadian Centres for Clinical Cognitive Research. Depressive syndromes in dementia, *Can. J. Neurolog. Sci.*, **28**(Suppl. 1), February, S83–95.

Volicer, L., McKee, A. & Hewitt, S. (2001). Dementia, *Neurologic Clinics*, **19**(4), November, 867–885.

Warren, E.J., Grek, A., Conn, D., Herrmann, N. *et al* (1989). A correlation between cognitive performance and daily functioning in elderly people, *J. Geriat. Psychiatry Neurol.*, **2**(2), April–June, 96–100.

Warren, S., Janzen, W., Andiel-Hett, C., Liu, L., McKim, H.R. & Schalm, C. (2001). Innovative dementia care: Functional status over time of persons with Alzheimer disease in a residential care centre compared to special care units, *Dementia Geriat. Cognitive Disord.*, **12**(5), September–October, 340–347.

Weiner, D.K. & Hanlon, J.T. (2001). Pain in nursing home residents: Management strategies, *Drugs and Aging*, **18**(1), 13–29.

Wilcox, S. & King, A.C. (1999). Sleep complaints in older women who are family caregivers, *J. Gerontol. Psyciat. Sci.*, **54B**, P189–P198.

Williams, P.S., Rands, G., Orrel, M. & Spector, A. (2000). Aspirin for vascular dementia, *Cochrane Database of Systematic Reviews*, (4):CD001296.

Wimo, A., von Strauss, E., Nordberg, G. *et al* (2002). Time spent on informal and formal care giving for persons with dementia in Sweden, *Health Policy*, **61**, 255–268.

Wimo, A., Winblad, B., Aguero-Torres, H. & von Strauss, E. (2003). The magnitude of dementia occurrence in the world, *Alzheimer Dis. Associated Disord.*, **17**(2), April–June, 63–67.

World Health Organization (2001). *Global Burden of Disease Estimates*, WHO, Geneva.

Yamamoto-Mitani, N., Abe, T., Okita, Y., Hayashi, K., Sugishita, C. & Kamata, K. (2002). Development of a Japanese quality of life instrument for older adults experiencing dementia (QLDJ), *Int. J. Aging and Human Dev.*, **55**(1), 71–95.

Yee, J.L. & Schulz, R. (2000). Gender differences in psychiatric morbidity among family caregivers: A review and analysis, *Gerontology*, **40**, 147–164.

Zanetti, O., Bianchetti, A., Frisoni, G.B., Rozzini, R. *et al* (1993). Determinants of disability in Alzheimer's disease, *Int. J. Geriat. Psychiatry*, **8**(7), July, 581–586.

Zankd, S. & Leipold, B. (2001). The relationship between severity of dementia and subjective well-being, *Aging and Mental Health*, **5**(2), 191–196.

16

Quality of Life in Substance Use Disorders

Jason P. Connor, John B. Saunders and
Gerald F.X. Feeney

INTRODUCTION

People use substances in an experimental or recreational fashion to experience sensations of euphoria, sedation or disassociation; the expected effect is one of pleasure. The relationship between humans and the non-therapeutic use of drugs extends back to early human development. Both genetic vulnerability and environmental factors contribute to why some become dependent while others demonstrate little inclination to continue drug use. There is a spectrum of core Substance Use Disorders (SUDs). 'Substance misuse' refers to alcohol or drug use that is counter to prevailing social norms. It is essentially a socially defined concept that has as much to do with the legal, religious, moral and cultural factors within a society as it has to do with the pharmacological properties of a drug. Societal attitudes to alcohol range from total prohibition to deep entrenchment within a culture. Abuse is a diagnostic term in the *Diagnostic and Statistical Manual* of the American Psychiatric Association (DSM-IV revised, 2000) and refers to alcohol or drug use that disrupts social norms, which vary between cultures, genders and generations. Dependence is a more pervasive and long-term disorder, defined as a psychobiological syndrome that arises from repeated and excessive alcohol or other drug use. It consists of a number of behavioural, cognitive and physiological disturbances that tend to cluster in time. The central features are impaired control over the use of a psychoactive substance, a strong desire or craving to take it, a high priority given to substance use, a stereotyped or predictable pattern of use, tolerance, withdrawal symptoms (in some cases) and continued use despite harm. In dependent individuals, substance use becomes central to functioning. SUDs are chronic relapsing states and contribute disproportionately to human morbidity and mortality (Ezzati *et al.*, 2003). They substantially influence health and social functioning which affects Quality of Life (QoL) across a variety of life domains. In this chapter, we examine the relationship between SUDs and QoL. Initially, key issues of comorbidity and the measurement of QoL and these disorders are considered, followed by a review of the current literature.

QUALITY OF LIFE ISSUES IN SUBSTANCE USE DISORDERS

QoL recognises an individual's judgement of personally important aspects of life. Little is known about how people form judgements on their level of satisfaction and well-being. To some, QoL is an

Quality of Life in Mental Disorders, Second Edition   Edited by H. Katschnig, H. Freeman and N. Sartorius
© 2006 John Wiley & Sons, Ltd

existential issue that should be left to 'its idiosyncratic mystery' (Leplege and Hunt, 1997) and question whether there is an optimal level of human functioning to which all human beings should aspire. Well-being has been considered the individual's affective reaction to life circumstances (Okum, Olding and Cohn, 1990), while life satisfaction refers to a cognitive assessment of life's circumstances and may reflect a comparison between aspiration and achievement (George, 1979). For many people, substance use contributes positively to their level of affective and cognitive functioning. For those that abuse substances, the pursuit of well-being though substance intoxication often belies broader dysfunction.

The range of physical, psychological and social processes associated with SUDs make these conditions heterogeneous. A large proportion of people with substance use disorders have a comorbid psychiatric disorder and vice versa. Among American psychiatric populations, between 50 and 70% report comorbid SUDs (Regier et al., 1984; Miller, 1995). Alcohol abuse or dependence increases the likelihood of a depressive disorder between 3 and 4 times (Kessler et al., 1994; Grant and Pickering, 1996), with that risk increasing to sevenfold when associated more broadly with 'drug' abuse or dependence (Grant and Pickering, 1996).

There are higher levels of ill-health and physical impairment among substance misusers than in the general population. The range of target organ damage (in alcohol dependence, e.g. liver disease, cerebellar insufficiency, peripheral neuropathy, pancreatitis, cardiomyopathy) and the infective complications of intravenous drug use (e.g. hepatitis C, HIV) identify substance abusers as a group where QoL issues may include substantial medical illness in addition to psychosocial issues. In SUDs, assessment has conventionally relied on a narrow range of indices of dependence severity, abstinence/relapse, and the extent and pattern of drug consumption. Attempts to appraise both physical and psychosocial functioning as it relates to an individual's QoL is a recent development.

QUALITY OF LIFE CONSTRUCTS AND THEIR MEASURES

With the exception of a new scale designed for drug users who inject (Brogly et al., 2003), no QoL measure has been developed specifically to evaluate individuals with substance abuse or dependence. A range of existing instruments has been applied which captures various dimensions relevant to SUDs. Examples include measures of functionality (e.g. Quality of Well-Being Scale (QWBS), Kaplan, Bush and Berry, 1976), health status (e.g. Rand Corporation Short Form 36 (SF-36), Ware, Kosinski and Keller, 1994), psychological well-being (e.g. General Health Questionnaire (GHQ)-28/12, Goldberg and Williams, 1998), social networks/social support (e.g. Social Support Questionnaire (SSQ), Sarason et al., 1983), life satisfaction and morale (e.g. General Well-Being Schedule, (GWBS), DuPuy, 1984), through to broad generic QoL measures (e.g. World Health Organization Quality of Life Index (WHOQOL-100), World Health Organization, 1998).

Thus, drug and alcohol research has used both the generic construct of QoL, which examines satisfaction with life, and the more specialised construct of Health-Related Quality of Life (HRQL). The implications of studies differ depending on the construct used (generic versus specific) (Rudolf and Watts, 2002). Outcomes are often evaluated through a measurement of health status filtered by the subjective perceptions and expectations of the individual (Testa and Simonson, 1996). However, QoL and health status are distinct constructs, so that favourable intervention effects on health status may not be found in QoL, or vice versa. This raises some questions over the validity of studies that employ health status instruments to assess the QoL construct (Smith, Avis and Assmann, 1999).

QoL measures can also be contextualised by how broad or narrow they assess the construct. In practice, the multidimensional measurement of QoL in addicted patients often means trading-off the relative importance of an assessment that is broader in scope with reduced patient focus, with an assessment that is narrower in scope but reflecting immediate and specific patient QoL needs (see Fig. 16.1).

Global QoL measures (e.g. WHOQoL-100, QoL Interview (QOLI), Lehman, 1988) can be used to assess broadly the major QoL domains among patients with SUDs. Their potential clinical utility lies in the capacity to provide additional data that are not typically captured in an addiction assessment. When collateral substance treatment outcome data are engaged, global instruments can be used as another index of treatment efficacy. Health-related QoL instruments (e.g. SF-36, Nottingham Health Profile (NHP), Hunt, McEwen and McKenna, 1986) have been used in addiction treatment as

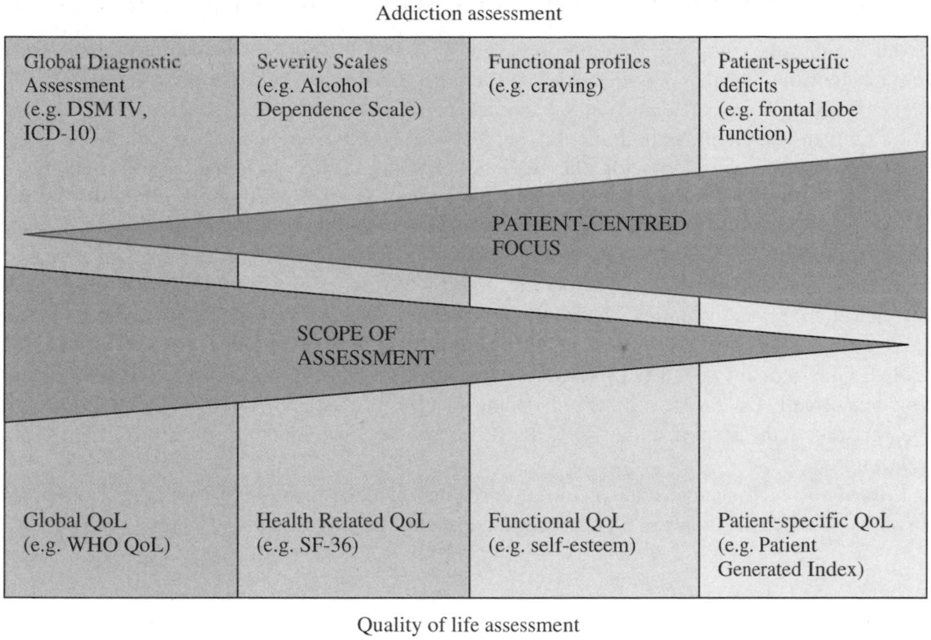

Addiction assessment

Global Diagnostic Assessment (e.g. DSM IV, ICD-10)	Severity Scales (e.g. Alcohol Dependence Scale)	Functional profiles (e.g. craving)	Patient-specific deficits (e.g. frontal lobe function)

PATIENT-CENTRED FOCUS

SCOPE OF ASSESSMENT

Global QoL (e.g. WHO QoL)	Health Related QoL (e.g. SF-36)	Functional QoL (e.g. self-esteem)	Patient-specific QoL (e.g. Patient Generated Index)

Quality of life assessment

Figure 16.1   Relationship between scope and patient focus in addiction QoL assessments

a broad screen of self-reported physical and emotional health. These screening instruments can highlight deficits in central areas of functioning, not usually identified by the narrower but more robust diagnostic measures (e.g. dependence severity scales such as the Alcohol Dependence Scale (ADS), Skinner and Horn, 1984). A more functional assessment applies existing patient information to guide the use of more patient-specific measures. Examples include measures of pain (e.g. McGill Pain Questionnaire (MPQ), Melzack and Katz, 1992), social support (e.g. SSQ, Interview Schedule for Social Interaction (ISSI), Henderson, Duncan Jones and Byrne, 1980) or self-worth (e.g. Self-Esteem Scale (SES), Rosenberg, 1965).

At the most fundamental or patient-specific level, QoL for substance abusing patients should represent the individual's core values. One way this has been approached is by applying standardised interview protocols (e.g. Schedule for the Evaluation of Individual Quality Of Life (SEQOL), Bernheim, 1999). Another approach is for the patient to identify their core values individually, with the assistance of the clinician. In treatment settings, considerations of time and use of resources influence the extent of the QoL evaluation. The disadvantage of an increased patient focus is reduced scope. For the substance abusing or addicted patient, core values may or may not represent clinically useful parameters or goals. Deciding on the optimal balance between the scope and the patient focus of the QoL assessment for these patients will be informed by many factors. Considerations include the immediate and future needs of the patient, the treatment goals, clinical relevance and collateral substance use data (e.g. primary drug type, consumption level, dependence severity, psychopathology, role dysfunction). Katschnig (1997) considers that the QoL concept in psychiatry is meaningful if comprehensive assessment is conducted. The guidelines he advises include a minimum of three assessments (patient, family member/friend, health professional). Evaluation should involve subjective well-being/satisfaction and function (social roles) as well as external living conditions ('standard of living, social supports and networks'). Different life domains should be assessed separately ('multiarea assessment'), which may identify life aspects that are most in need of assistance. The rates of change inherent in the different QoL components should be considered, and Katschnig stresses the need to make explicit whether or not psychopathological symptoms are included in QoL instruments (Katschnig, 1997).

QUALITY OF LIFE RESEARCH IN SUBSTANCE USE DISORDERS

Over the last decade, studies in addiction have emerged that include some form of QoL measure. A review of electronic databases (MEDLINE, Psychinfo, Cochrane Database of Systematic Reviews and The Web of Science) identified 47 studies that used standardised instruments reported to measure QoL in addiction. As both mental and physical health have been shown to be significantly associated with QoL, in reviewing the addiction literature, we attempted to disentangle these constructs by stratifying studies that take into account or control for comorbid health conditions. Here, we have grouped studies that control for psychiatric comorbidity (Category 1), those that control for medical conditions/severity and/or sociodemographic factors (but not psychiatric comorbidity) (Category 2) and studies that do not control for either category (Category 3). The term 'controlled' here refers to studies that either statistically account for possible confounding variables (e.g. covaring models, entering variables as an initial 'step' in hierarchical regression) or using a control or quasi-control group (e.g. substance dependence group ±psychiatric diagnosis). Demonstrating statistically the absence of mean baseline group differences by randomly allocating subjects or comparisons to the normative data of test scores was not considered here as controlling for potential confounds.

In affluent societies, alcohol remains the favourite and most frequently misused drug. Consequently, the majority of the QoL studies in SUDs focus on this substance.

Quality of Life and Alcohol Use

Twenty-five studies were identified that had a primary focus on alcohol use and QoL. Eight of these controlled for psychiatric comorbidity (Category 1). Six studies controlled for medical and/or sociodemographic conditions, but not comorbid psychopathology (Category 2). The remaining 11 studies did not control for either category (Category 3). The most widely used QoL measures across these studies were the SF-36 (seven studies), the Nottingham Health Profile (four studies), the Quality of Life Interview (three studies), the Life Situation Survey (three studies), the Rotterdam Symptom Checklist (three studies) and the 12-Item General Health Questionnaire (three studies).

Alcohol-Related Quality of Life Studies that Controlled for Psychiatric Comorbidity (Category 1)

All these studies reported that coexisting mental disorders or the severity of psychopathology was associated with poorer HRQL among people with alcohol use disorders (Johnson et al., 1995; Drake et al., 1997; Volk et al., 1997; Daeppen et al., 1998; Romeis et al., 1999; Rudolf and Priebe, 1999, 2002; Foster, Peters and Kind, 2002). When coexisting psychopathology was identified and controlled for, the severity of the alcohol use disorder continued to be related to poorer QoL (Volk et al., 1997; Daeppen et al., 1998; Foster, Peters and Kind, 2002). However, Volk et al. (1997) and Romeis et al. (1999) observed that the primary factor in the variation of HRQL was coexisting mental health disorder. Romeis et al. (1999) emphasise that 'the importance of considering the impact of severity, sociodemographics and comorbid physical and mental conditions when researchers and clinicians assess quality of life for recovered and active alcoholics' (p. 660).

Alcohol-Related Quality of Life Studies that Controlled for Medical Conditions/Severity and/or Sociodemographic Factors, but not Psychiatric Comorbidity (Category 2)

Both alcohol dependence (Welsh, Buchsbaum and Kaplan, 1993; Blow et al., 2000) and higher consumption (Foster, Marshall and Peters, 2000; Foster, Peters and Marshall, 2000; Topolski et al., 2001) were associated with lower QoL in alcohol studies that controlled for either medical conditions or sociodemographic data. Data were not presented that afforded an assessment of the relative additional contribution of the medical condition above the disorder of alcohol use. No relationship between alcohol use and subjective well-being was found by Beattie et al. (1993).

Alcohol-Related Quality of Life Studies that Did not Control for Either of the Above (Category 3)

Poorer QoL in these studies related to the presence of alcohol use disorders (McKenna *et al.*, 1996; Bebout *et al.*, 1997; Popovic *et al.*, 1997; McHugo *et al.*, 1999; Foster *et al.*, 2000), severity of dependence (Patience *et al.*, 1997; Foster *et al.*, 1998), relapse status (Foster *et al.*, 1998, 2000) and increased alcohol consumption (Kraemer *et al.*, 2002). Ansoms *et al.* (2000) demonstrated significant improvement in HRQL in those retained in an alcohol treatment programme. In a highly selected group, Gledhill *et al.* (1999) reported no differences in HRQL between previously alcohol-dependent and non-alcohol-dependent liver transplant recipients. One study (Amodeo, Kurtz and Cutter, 1992) reported no association between the length of alcohol abstinence and life satisfaction.

Quality of Life and Other Drugs

Substance abuse other than alcohol misuse involves a wide variety of drugs, administered by a number of routes. A minority use an injectable route. Among intravenous drug users, there are increased rates of alcohol dependence, depression, antisocial personality disorder and suicidality (Dinwiddie, Reich and Cloninger, 1992). Different risk profiles occur across the substances and drug combinations used. Some forms of substance abuse, e.g. solvent abuse, are strongly associated with social disadvantage and low socioeconomic status (Dinwiddie, Reich and Cloninger, 1991). QoL issues in this group are in the early stages of investigation.

Twenty-two studies with a primary focus on substance use other than alcohol and QoL were identified. Seven controlled for comorbid psychopathology (Category 1). Five studies controlled for medical and/or sociodemographic, but not comorbid, psychopathology (Category 2). The remaining ten studies did not control for potential confounding factors (Category 3). The most widely used QoL measures across the 'other substances' studies reviewed were the SF-36 (eight studies), the 90-Item Symptom Checklist (four studies) and the Quality of Life Interview (three studies).

Other Drug Quality of Life Studies that Controlled for Psychiatric Comorbidity (Category 1)

The majority of studies in this category reported that individuals with SUDs reported impaired QoL (Russo *et al.*, 1997; Havassy and Arms, 1998; Garg *et al.*, 1999; te Vaarwerk and Gaal, 2001; Smith and Larson, 2003). Some studies identified that SUDs additionally contributed to poorer QoL for those with psychiatric symptoms (Russo *et al.*, 1997; Havassy and Arms, 1998; Smith and Larson, 2003). Contrasting findings by Garg *et al.* (1999) were that psychiatric comorbidity did not further decrease QoL in people with SUDs. Two studies reported that impairment in QoL was not attributed to an individual's SUD, but rather to psychiatric symptomology (Sherbourne *et al.*, 2000) and homelessness (Bird *et al.*, 2002).

Other Drug Quality of Life Studies that Controlled for Medical Conditions/Severity and/or Sociodemographic Factors but not Psychiatric Comorbidity (Category 2)

All studies in Category 2 reported SUDs contributed to poorer QoL (Dazord *et al.*, 1998; Stein *et al.*, 1998; Zack, Toneatto and Streiner, 1998; Falck *et al.*, 2000; Zullig *et al.*, 2001). One study (Zack, Toneatto and Streiner, 1998) reported that psychiatric patients with a concurrent SUD reported lower QoL when compared with normative data for psychiatric patients with no SUD. QoL impairment was similar across a number of drug classes (i.e. cocaine, alcohol and heroin) (Zullig *et al.*, 2001) and improved with treatment (Dazord *et al.*, 1998).

Other Drug Quality of Life Studies that Did not Control for Either of the Above (Category 3)

The majority of studies that did not control for potential confounds reported that SUDs were associated with reduced QoL (Ryan and White, 1996; Torrens *et al.*, 1997; Perneger *et al.*, 1998; Vignau and Brunelle, 1998; Pani *et al.*, 2000; Mueser *et al.*, 2001; Rehm *et al.*, 2001; Brogly *et al.*, 2003). Half of these studies had a prospective methodology and all reported improvement in QoL following SUD treatment (Torrens *et al.*, 1997; Perneger *et al.*, 1998; Vignau and Brunelle, 1998; Pani *et al.*, 2000; Rehm *et al.*, 2001). Additionally, Ryan and White (1996) showed that people with SUDs had a similar QoL, when compared to normative scores of patients with depression, and also of patients with severe medical illnesses. Harris *et al.* (2000), within a population of individuals using cannabis primarily for medicinal purposes, found that higher QoL was associated with higher rating of cannabis effects and lower side-effect ratings. McCarthy *et al.* (2002) found no relationship between illicit drug use and HRQL.

Current Evidence

There is sound evidence that both higher levels of alcohol consumption and the severity of alcohol dependence correlate with poorer QoL, irrespective of which instruments are used. The degree to which this relates primarily to the alcohol use disorder, rather than to commonly occurring coexisting conditions as well as sociodemographic factors, is not known. Where studies have attempted to control for these factors, they generally report weaker associations between alcohol use and QoL than do uncontrolled studies. Across the QoL studies where alcohol was not the primary drug of abuse, the evidence again identifies poorer QoL among SUDs. Similar to the findings in disorders of alcohol use, there was less support for this association when studies controlled for comorbid psychiatric disorders. In the context of SUD treatment programmes, self-reported QoL improved among those retained in treatment. QoL reported by individuals with SUDs has been shown to approximate to QoL scores for mood disorders and severe medical illnesses.

In addition to issues of what QoL construct has been applied, these studies in SUDs raise other interpretative issues (Stein *et al.*, 1998). The timing of an individual's presentation and subsequent assessment for SUD treatment are often unreported in published studies. People typically seek treatment in times of crisis. This change in functioning may be reflected in lower QoL scores and may over-estimate the relationship between SUDs and QoL (Chitwood, 1985). Population bias occurs from the fact that most studies originate in public substance abuse treatment programmes, whose clients are mostly uninsured, many of whom present only when drug-related complications arise. The factors that influence individuals to seek treatment are often unstated. In many studies, the distinction is unclear between substance dependence and abuse, and it is not stated whether study participants required detoxification. Where studies do distinguish between abuse and dependence, most now apply standard diagnostic criteria. Medical comorbidity is mostly unreported and it is unclear whether overall QoL functioning for the group has been overestimated. Though individuals with SUDs are a heterogeneous population, differences in sample characteristics are often not adjusted for. The pattern of comorbid disorders is clearly different between male and female poly-substance abusers and alcohol dependents (Brady and Randall, 1999; Landheim, Bakken and Vaglum, 2003), yet these gender differences have infrequently been considered in published studies.

CONCLUSIONS

There is increasing support for QoL and health status assessment both in clinical care and in biomedical and health services research. This is partly due to changes in how we think about health and health care and a stronger emphasis on addressing patient satisfaction. Greater importance is attributed to the social consequences of disease. The exponential growth in QoL research over the last two decades has been characterised by a proliferation of instruments that vary widely in their methods of development, content, breadth of use and quality. Compared with some other special-ties in medicine, addiction medicine has been slow to respond to these developments. Although SUDs are common and pervasive problems, they are difficult to study. Standard diagnostic and assessment criteria exist, but these are conditions that reflect both a state of mind and patterns of behaviour that are maintained by a precarious balance of drives. These drives are influenced by a complex of factors including particular genes, biochemistry, patterns of learned behaviour and the social and physical environment. Translating the various domains and components of health into quantitative values that reflect the QoL among these individuals is complex. It comes as no surprise that there has been little uniformity in approaches to the application of QoL measures to individuals with SUDs.

Despite an increase in the number of SUD studies that have included QoL data, there is a paucity of studies that confirm the intrinsic value of these data. In SUD research, few prospective treatment studies with randomised controlled methodology have used QoL as a focal outcome measure. Most studies employed quasi-experimental methodologies and are to be found among the lower bands of the level-of-evidence spectrum, so that their conclusions are necessarily limited. Higher levels of drug consumption and dependence are reflected in a decline in individual functioning, and the emerging QoL literature confirms this observation. Irrespective of the QoL instrument employed, the majority of studies report that the presence of a SUD is associated with poorer QoL. Substance abusers report QoL levels similar to those of chronic medical and psychiatric conditions, reinforcing long-established efforts to engage this patient group in mainstream medical and social services. The presence of under-lying psychopathology is central to QoL issues among these individuals. Where studies take into account coexisting psychiatric conditions, the particular contribution of the SUD component on QoL remains to be identified. The relative contribution of personality disorder and the antisocial lifestyles more so prevalent among substance misusers awaits further investigation.

In treatment of alcohol and other substance use, a limited range of studies have consistently reported improvement in QoL among those retained in formal rehabilitation programmes. In the majority of these studies, QoL has been used as an adjunctive assessment tool. To date, treatments have mainly been directed at conventional outcomes such as reduced drinking or abstinence, rather than at QoL improvement as a primary outcome measure. Interest in QoL as a dependent variable for use in evaluating psychosocial interventions raises important questions about responsiveness and about the ability to measure meaningful and important change in a clinical state. The problem becomes more complex when one considers that individuals may vary in the value they place on a particular treatment benefit, and that the same individual may place a different value on the same benefit depending on his/her circumstances. In addiction, the use of QoL instruments is not established in clinical practice. However, the value of knowledge gained from QoL in SUD research will depend on the practical implications on treatment effects and whether it helps answer questions related to clinical programmes and therapeutic choices. The balance between objective assessment and the indispensable subjective view of the individual is yet to be established.

REFERENCES

American Psychiatric Association (2000). *Diagnostic and Statistical Manual of Mental Disorders*, Fourth Edition, Text Revision (DSM-IV-TR), American Psychiatric Association, Washington, DC.

Amodeo, M., Kurtz, N. & Cutter, H.S. (1992). Abstinence, reasons for not drinking, and life satisfaction, *Int. J. Addict.*, **27**, 707–716.

Ansoms, C., Deckers, F., Lehert, P., Pelc, I. & Potgieter, A. (2000). An open study with acamprosate in Belgium and Luxemburg: Results on sociodemographics, supportive treatment and outcome, *Eur. Addict. Res.*, **6**, 132–140.

Beattie, M.C., Longabaugh, R., Elliott, G., Stout, R.L., Fava, J. & Noel, N.E. (1993). Effect of the social environment on alcohol involvement and subjective well-being prior to alcoholism treatment, *J. Stud. Alcohol*, **54**, 283–296.

Bebout, R.R., Drake, R.E., Xie, H., McHugo, G.J. & Harris, M. (1997). Housing status among formerly homeless dually diagnosed adults, *Psychiat. Serv.*, **48**, 936–941.

Bernheim, J.L. (1999). How to get serious answers to the serious questions: 'How have you been?' Subjective quality of life (QOL) as an individual experiential emergent construct, *Bioethics*, **13**, 272–287.

Bird, C.E., Jinnett, K.J., Burnam, M.A., Koegel, P., Sullivan, G., Wenzel, S.L., Ridgely, M.S., Morton, S.C. & Miu, A. (2002). Predictors of contact with public service sectors among homeless adults with and without alcohol and other drug disorders, *J. Stud. Alcohol*, **63**, 716–725.

Blow, F.C., Walton, M.A., Barry, K.L., Coyne, J.C., Mudd, S.A. & Copeland, L.A. (2000). The relationship between alcohol problems and health functioning of older adults in primary care settings, *J. Am. Geriat. Soc.*, **48**, 769–774.

Brady, K.T. & Randall, C.L. (1999). Gender differences in substance use disorders, *Psychiat. Clin. N. Am.*, **22**, 241–252.

Brogly, S., Mercier, C., Bruneau, J., Palepu, A. & Franco, E. (2003). Towards more effective public health programming for injection drug users: Development and evaluation of the injection drug user quality of life scale, *Substance Use Misuse*, **38**, 965–992.

Chitwood, D.D. (1985). Patterns and consequences of cocaine use, in *Cocaine Use in America: Epidemiologic and Clinical Perspectives* (Eds J.J. Kozel & E.H. Adams), NIDA Research Monograph 91, DHHS 85–1414, pp. 111–119.

Daeppen, J.B., Krieg, M.A., Burnand, B. & Yersin, B. (1998). MOS-SF-36 in evaluating health-related quality of life in alcohol-dependent patients, *Am. J. Drug Alcohol Abuse*, **24**, 685–694.

Dazord, A., Mino, A., Page, D. & Broers, B. (1998). Patients on methadone maintenance treatment in Geneva, *Eur. Psychiatry*, **13**, 235–241.

Dinwiddie, S.H., Reich, T. & Cloninger, C.R. (1991). The relationship of solvent use to other substance use, *Am. J. Drug Alcohol Abuse*, **17**, 173–186.

Dinwiddie, S.H., Reich, T. & Cloninger, C.R. (1992). Psychiatric comorbidity and suicidality among intravenous drug users, *J. Clin. Psychiatry*, **53**, 364–369.

Drake, R.E., Yovetich, N.A., Bebout, R.R., Harris, M. & McHugo, G.J. (1997). Integrated treatment for dually diagnosed homeless adults, *J. Nerv. Ment. Dis.*, **185**, 298–305.

DuPuy, H.J. (1984). The Psychological Well-Being Index, in *Assessment of Quality of Life in Clinical Trials of Cardiovascular Therapies* (Eds N.K. Wenger, M.E. Mattson, C.D. Furberg, *et al.*), Le Jacq, New York.

Ezzati, M., Hoorn, S.V., Rodgers, A., Lopez, A.D., Mathers, C.D., Murray, C.J. and the Comparative Risk Assessment Collaborating Group (2003). Estimates of global and regional potential health gains from reducing multiple major risk factors, *Lancet*, **362**, 271–280.

Falck, R.S., Wang, J., Carlson, R.G. & Siegal, H.A. (2000). Crack-cocaine use and health status as defined by the SF-36, *Addict. Behavior*, **25**, 579–584.

Foster, J.H., Marshall, E.J. & Peters, T.J. (2000). Application of a quality of life measure, the life situation survey (LSS), to alcohol-dependent subjects in relapse and remission, *Alcohol Clin. Expl Res.*, **24**, 1687–1692.

Foster, J.H., Peters, T.J. & Kind, P. (2002). Quality of life, sleep, mood and alcohol consumption: A complex interaction, *Addict. Biol.*, **7**, 55–65.

Foster, J.H., Peters, T.J. & Marshall, E.J. (2000). Quality of life measures and outcome in alcohol-dependent men and women, *Alcohol*, **22**, 45–52.

Foster, J.H., Marshall, E.J., Hooper, R.L. & Peters, T.J. (2000). Measurement of quality of life in alcohol-dependent subjects by a cancer symptoms checklist, *Alcohol*, **20**, 105–110.

Foster, J.H., Marshall, E.J., Hooper, R.L. & Peters, T.J. (1998). Quality of life measures in alcohol dependent subjects and changes with abstinence and continued heavy drinking, *Addict. Biol.*, **3**, 321–332.

Garg, N., Yates, W.R., Jones, R., Zhou, M. & Williams, S. (1999). Effect of gender, treatment site and psychiatric comorbidity on quality of life outcome in substance dependence, *Am. J. Addict.*, **8**, 44–54.

George, L.K. (1979). The happiness syndrome: Methodological and substantive issues in the study of social psychological well-being in adulthood, *Gerontologist*, **19**, 210–216.

Gledhill, J., Burroughs, A., Rolles, K., Davidson, B., Blizard, B. & Lloyd, G. (1999). Psychiatric and social outcome following liver transplantation for alcoholic liver disease: A controlled study, *J. Psychosomatic Res.*, **46**, 359–368.

Goldberg, D.P. & Williams, P. (1998). *A User's Guide to the General Health Questionnaire*, NFER-Nelson, Windsor.

Grant, B. & Pickering, M. (1996). Comorbidity between DSM-IV alcohol and drug use disorders: Results from the National Longitudinal Alcohol Epidemiologic Survey, *Alcohol Health Res. World*, **20**, 67–72.

Harris, D., Jones, R.T., Shank, R., Nath, R., Fernandez, E., Goldstein, K. & Mendelson, J. (2000). Self-reported marijuana effects and characteristics of 100 San Francisco medical marijuana club members, *J. Addict. Dis.*, **19**, 89–103.

Havassy, B.E. & Arns, P.G. (1998). Relationship of cocaine and other substance dependence to well-being of high-risk psychiatric patients, *Psychiat. Serv.*, **49**, 935–940.

Henderson, S., Duncan Jones, P. & Byrne, D.G. (1980). Measuring social relationships: The interview schedule for social interactions, *Psychol. Med.*, **10**, 723–734.

Hunt, S.M., McEwen, J. & McKenna, S. (1986). *Measuring Health Status*, First Edition, Crom Helm, London.

Johnson, J.G., Spitzer, R.L., Williams, J.B., Kroenke, K., Linzer, M., Brody, D., deGruy, F. & Hahn, S. (1995). Psychiatric comorbidity, health status, and functional impairment associated with alcohol abuse and dependence in primary care patients: Findings of the PRIME MD-1000 study, *J. Consult. Clin. Psychol.*, **63**, 133–140.

Kaplan, R.M., Bush, J.W. & Berry, C.C. (1976). Health status: Types of validity and the index of well-being, *Health Serv. Res.*, **11**, 478–507.

Katschnig, H. (1997). How useful is the concept of quality of life in psychiatry?, *Curr. Opinion Psychiatry*, **10**, 337–345.

Kessler, R.C., McGonagle, K.A., Zhao, S., Nelson, C.B., Hughes, M., Eshleman, S., Wittchen, H.U. & Kendler, K.S. (1994). Lifetime and 12-month prevalence of DSM-III-R psychiatric disorders in the United States. Results from the National Comorbidity Survey, *Arch. Gen. Psychiatry*, **51**, 8–19.

Kraemer, K.L., Maisto, S.A., Conigliaro, J., McNeil, M., Gordon, A.J. & Kelley, M.E. (2002). Decreased alcohol consumption in outpatient drinkers is associated with improved quality of life and fewer alcohol-related consequences, *J. Gen. Int. Med.*, **17**, 382–386.

Landheim, A.S., Bakken, K. & Vaglum, P. (2003). Gender differences in the prevalence of symptom disorders and personality disorders among poly-substance abusers and pure alcoholics. Substance abusers treated in two counties in Norway, *Eur. Addict. Res.*, **9**(1), 8–17.

Lehman, A.F. (1988). A quality of life interview for the chronically mentally ill, *Evaluation and Progm. Plann.*, **11**, 51–62.

Leplege, A. & Hunt, S. (1997). The problem of quality of life in medicine, *J. Am. Med. Ass.*, **278**, 47–50.

McCarthy, W.J., Zhou, Y., Hser, Y.I. & Collins, C. (2002). To smoke or not to smoke: Impact on disability, quality of life, and illicit drug use in baseline polydrug users, *J. Addict. Dis.*, **21**(2), 35–54.

McHugo, G.J., Drake, R.E., Teague, G.B. & Xie, H. (1999). Fidelity to assertive community treatment and client outcomes in the New Hampshire dual disorders study, *Psychiat. Serv.*, **50**, 818–824.

McKenna, M., Chick, J., Buxton, M., Howlett, H., Patience, D. & Ritson, B. (1996). The SECCAT survey: I. The costs and consequences of alcoholism, *Alcohol Alcohol*, **31**, 565–576.

Melzack, R. & Katz, J. (1992). The McGill pain questionnaire: Appraisal and current status, in *Handbook of Pain Assessment* (Eds D.C. Turk & R. Melzack), The Guilford Press, New York.

Miller, N.S. (1995). *Addiction Psychiatry: Current Diagnosis and Treatment*, John Wiley & Sons, New York.

Mueser, K.T., Essock, S.M., Drake, R.E., Wolfe, R.S. & Frisman, L. (2001). Rural and urban differences in patients with a dual diagnosis, *Schizophrenic Res.*, **48**, 93–107.

Okum, M.A., Olding, R.W. & Cohn, C.M.G. (1990). A meta-analysis of subjective well being interventions among elders, *Psychol. Bull.*, **108**, 259–266.

Pani, P.P., Maremmani, I., Pirastu, R., Tagliamonte, A. & Gessa, G.L. (2000). Buprenorphine: A controlled clinical trial in the treatment of opioid dependence, *Drug Alcohol Depend.*, **60**, 39–50.

Patience, D., Buxton, M., Chick, J., Howlett, H., McKenna, M. & Ritson, B. (1997). The SECCAT Survey: II. The Alcohol Related Problems Questionnaire as a proxy for resource costs and quality of life in alcoholism treatment. Study of Socio-Economic Consequences and Costs of Alcoholism and Treatment, *Alcohol Alcohol*, **32**, 79–84.

Perneger, T.V., Giner, F., del Rio, M. & Mino, A. (1998). Ràndomised trial of heroin maintenance programme for addicts who fail in conventional drug treatments, *Br. Med. J.*, **317**, 13–18.

Popovic, V., Popovic, I., Lilic, V., Tosic, S., Zlatanovic, L. & Vukic, D. (1997). Some aspects of quality of life of alcoholics, *Quality of Life Res.*, **6**, 700.

Regier, D.A., Myers, J.K., Kramer, M., Robins, L.N., Blazer, D.G., Hough, R.L., Eaton, W.W. & Locke, B.Z. (1984). The NIMH epidemiologic catchment area program. Historical context, major objectives, and study population characteristics, *Arch. Gen. Psychiatry*, **41**, 934–941.

Rehm, J., Gschwend, P., Steffen, T., Gutzwiller, F., Dobler-Mikola, A. & Uchtenhagen, A. (2001). Feasibility, safety, and efficacy of injectable heroin prescription for refractory opioid addicts: A follow-up study, *Lancet*, **358**, 1417–1423.

Romeis, J.C., Waterman, B., Scherrer, J.F., Goldberg, J., Eisen, S.A., Heath, A.C., Bucholz, K.K., Slutske, W.S., Lyons, M.J., Tsuang, M.T. & True, W.R. (1999). The impact of sociodemographics, comorbidity and symptom recency on health-related quality of life in alcoholics, *J. Stud. Alcohol*, **60**, 653–662.

Rosenberg, M. (1965). *Society and the Adolescent Self Image*, Princeton University Press, Princeton, New Jersey.

Rudolf, H. & Priebe, S. (1999). Subjective quality of life in female in-patients with depression: A longitudinal study, *Int. J. Soc. Psychiatry*, **45**, 238–246.

Rudolf, H. & Priebe, S. (2002). Subjective quality of life and depressive symptoms in women with alcoholism during detoxification treatment, *Drug Alcohol Depend.*, **66**, 71–76.

Rudolf, H. & Watts, J. (2002). Quality of life in substance abuse and dependency, *Int. Rev. Psychiatry*, **14**, 190–197.

Russo, J., Roy-Byrne, P., Reeder, D., Alexander, M., Dwyer-O'Connor, E., Dagadakis, C., Ries, R. & Patrick, D. (1997). Longitudinal assessment of quality of life in acute psychiatric inpatients: Reliability and validity, *J. Nerv. Ment. Dis.*, **185**, 166–175.

Ryan, C.F. & White, J.M. (1996). Health status at entry to methadone maintenance treatment using the SF-36 health survey questionnaire, *Addiction*, **91**, 39–45.

Sarason, I.G., Levine, H.M., Basham, R.B. & Sarason, B.R. (1983). Assessing social support: The social support questionnaire, *J. Personality Social Psychol.*, **44**, 127–139.

Sherbourne, C.D., Hays, R.D., Fleishman, J.A., Vitiello, B., Magruder, K.M., Bing, E.G., McCaffrey, D., Burnam, A., Longshore, D., Eggan, F., Bozzette, S.A. & Shapiro, M. F. (2000). Impact of psychiatric conditions on health-related quality of life in persons with HIV infection, *Am. J. Psychiatry*, **157**, 248–254.

Skinner, H.A. & Horn, J.L. (1984). *Alcohol Dependence Scale (ADS): Users Guide*, Addiction Research Institute, Toronto.

Smith, K.W., Avis, N.E. & Assmann, S.F. (1999). Distinguishing between quality of life and health status in quality of life research: A meta-analysis, *Quality of Life Res.*, **8**, 447–459.

Smith, K.W. & Larson, M.J. (2003). Quality of life assessments by adult substance abusers receiving publicly funded treatment in Massachusetts, *Am. J. Drug Alcohol Abuse*, **29**, 323–335.

Stein, M.D., Mulvey, K.P., Plough, A. & Samet, J.H. (1998). The functioning and well being of persons who seek treatment for drug and alcohol use, *J. Substance Abuse*, **10**, 75–84.

Testa, M.A. & Simonson, D.C. (1996). Assessment of quality-of-life outcomes, *New Engl J. Med.*, **334**, 835–840.

te Vaarwerk, M.J. & Gaal, E.A. (2001). Psychological distress and quality of life in drug-using and non-drug-using HIV-infected women, *Eur. J. Public Health*, **11**, 109–115.

Topolski, T.D., Patrick, D.L., Edwards, T.C., Huebner, C.E., Connell, F.A. & Mount, K.K. (2001). Quality of life and health-risk behaviors among adolescents, *J. Adolescent Health*, **29**, 426–435.

Torrens, M., San, L., Martinez, A., Castillo, C., Domingo-Salvany, A. & Alonso, J. (1997). Use of the Nottingham Health Profile for measuring health status of patients in methadone maintenance treatment, *Addiction*, **92**, 707–716.

Vignau, J. & Brunelle, E. (1998). Differences between general practitioner- and addiction centre-prescribed buprenorphine substitution therapy in France. Preliminary results, *Eur. Addict. Res.*, **4**(Suppl. 1), 24–28.

Volk, R.J., Cantor, S.B., Steinbauer, J.R. & Cass, A.R. (1997). Alcohol use disorders, consumption patterns, and health-related quality of life of primary care patients, *Alcohol Clin. Expl Res.*, **2**, 899–905.

Ware, J.E., Kosinski, M. & Keller, S.D. (1994). *SF-36 Physical and Mental Health Summery Scales: A Users' Manual*, New England Medical Center, The Health Institute, Boston, Massachusetts.

Welsh, J.A., Buchsbaum, D.G. & Kaplan, C.B. (1993). Quality of life of alcoholics and non-alcoholics: Does excessive drinking make a difference in the urban setting?, *Quality of Life Res.*, **2**, 335–340.

World Health Organization Quality of Life Group (1998). The World Health Organization Quality of Life Assessment (WHOQOL): Development and general psychometric properties, *Social Sci. Med.*, **46**, 1569–1585.

Zack, M., Toneatto, T. & Streiner, D.L. (1998). The SCL-90 factor structure in comorbid substance abusers, *J. Substance Abuse*, **10**, 85–101.

Zullig, K.J., Valois, R.F., Huebner, E.S., Oeltmann, J.E. & Drane, J.W. (2001). Relationship between perceived life satisfaction and adolescents' substance abuse, *J. Adolescent Health*, **29**, 279–288.

Section V
TREATMENT AND MANAGEMENT ISSUES

17

Psychotropic Medication and Quality of Life

Matthias C. Angermeyer, Reinhold Kilian and Heinz Katschnig

INTRODUCTION

Looking back at the development of the pharmacological treatment of psychiatric disorders, it is clear that in the beginning its primary aim was the reduction of psychopathological symptoms or, ideally, their complete elimination. However, an additional therapeutic objective soon came into being: preventing the recurrence of the acute symptomatology. In the case of schizophrenia, this meant prevention of relapse, whereas for affective disorders, the aim was long-term prophylaxis. Improvement of patients' quality of life (QoL) as a therapeutic aim only appeared on the scene in the early 1990s (Angermeyer, 1994). It was exactly in 1990 that, for the first time, the results of a study on the effect of psychotropic drugs on QoL were published (Meltzer *et al.*, 1990).

Since then, interest in QoL has increased markedly. In the main, this was stimulated by the development of psychotropic drugs of the 'second generation' (i.e. atypical neuroleptics, serotonin reuptake inhibitors) which display fewer side-effects and hence raised hopes that their negative effect on the subjective well-being of the patients might be less severe than that of the earlier drugs. Since then, QoL has increasingly been applied as an outcome measure in clinical trials of psychotropic drugs. Before discussing the results of those studies, we will present a conceptual framework for the assessment of the impact of pharmacotherapy on QoL, which could be of benefit for further studies. (Another concept has been presented by Awad, 1992).

It is useful to distinguish three components of QoL: firstly, subjective well-being, secondly, functioning in social roles and, thirdly, social and material living conditions (Katschnig, Chapter 1 in this volume). All three components can be affected by psychopharmacotherapy. First of all, psychotropic drugs exert a direct influence on subjective well-being, but, beyond that, can have an effect on the level of social functioning – either directly or indirectly – through influencing subjective well-being. Social functioning, then, can have consequences for the social and material circumstances of living. Finally, changes in both level of social functioning and living conditions can have repercussions for subjective well-being (Fig. 17.1). Before discussing the relationship between psychotropic medication and the various components of QoL in more detail, we will briefly describe both the wanted and unwanted effects of these drugs.

Quality of Life in Mental Disorders, Second Edition   Edited by H. Katschnig, H. Freeman and N. Sartorius
© 2006 John Wiley & Sons, Ltd

Figure 17.1   Effect of psychotropic drugs on the three components of quality of life

DESIRED AND UNDESIRED EFFECTS OF PSYCHOTROPIC DRUGS

The main aim of treatment with psychotropic drugs is the reduction or elimination of symptoms. Conventional neuroleptics lead mainly to a reduction of productive psychotic symptoms, in particular of delusions and hallucinations. Antidepressants – as suggested by their name – lead to the lifting of depressive mood, help to restore interest in one's environment and the ability to enjoy life, and reduce lack of motivation as well as the somatic symptoms associated with depression. In addition, they reduce specific symptoms of anxiety disorders, obsessive–compulsive disorders and eating disorders. Lithium and the anticonvulsants carbamazepine and valproic acid are used in the treatment of mania. Benzodiazepines lead to the reduction of anxiety, generally in short-term use.

Long-term treatment with neuroleptics aims at the maintenance of an achieved remission or the prevention of a relapse of the schizophrenic psychosis. Antidepressants serve the same aims with unipolar depression. Lithium and the anticonvulsants are used for prophylaxis against the recurrence of affective disorders.

Unfortunately, however, the effects of psychopharmacotherapy are not only of a positive nature; these drugs also have numerous side-effects that are unpleasant for the patient. They range from psychological and neurological symptoms, over disturbances of the autonomic nervous system (particularly anticholinergic effects and orthostatic dysregulation), gastrointestinal complaints, metabolic disorders (weight gain) and disturbances of sexual function to dermatological side-effects (e.g. allergic rashes). Among the psychotropic drugs of the first generation, benzodiazepines seem to have the least side-effects, at least at first glance. The side-effects of traditional neuroleptics, tricyclic antidepressants, lithium and anticonvulsants appear to be more significant. Further, it becomes apparent that psychotropic drugs of the second generation display a more favourable profile of side-effects, and thus should have a less severe impact on subjective well-being. This is true for atypical neuroleptics, with which fewer extrapyramidal side-effects are observed, and for selective serotonin reuptake inhibitors (SSRIs) and other modern antidepressants due to the absence of anticholinergic effects.

Benzodiazepines have a further advantage in comparison with other psychotropic drugs: the short duration of the latency period before the onset of the desired effect. While the anxiolytic action of benzodiazepines starts after approximately 30 minutes, neuroleptics may take several days until the beginning of their antipsychotic effect. With lithium treatment, it takes at least 10–14 days until the onset of the antimanic effect, and valproic acid requires a similarly long period to cause a reduction of manic symptoms. The antidepressant effect of both tricyclic antidepressants as well as SSRIs and other modern antidepressants may take as long as 2–3 weeks to occur. As far as panic attacks are concerned, their frequency and intensity only eases off after SSRIs have been taken for at least a two-week period, while full protection is only achieved after 6–8 weeks.

However, with the onset of unwanted effects, the situation is quite different. Often, they begin prior to the onset of the desired effects. The anticholinergic effect of tricyclic antidepressants, for example, occurs immediately after the start of treatment, while the agitation and gastrointestinal complaints quite often caused by SSRIs arrive at their maximum between the fourth and the seventh day. The sedating effect of many neuroleptics (which in certain cases might be desired from the therapeutic point of view) occurs before the onset of their antipsychotic effect. Low-dose dependency, which poses a major pharmacological problem with benzodiazepines, only occurs after a prolonged use of several weeks or months.

PSYCHOTROPIC DRUGS AND SUBJECTIVE WELL-BEING

Both psychiatrists and patients would agree that the ultimate aim of psychiatric treatment is to improve subjective well-being. In some cases, though, there might be disagreement about the best way to achieve this objective. Psychiatrists, for example, generally consider the reduction of psychopathological symptoms by means of psychopharmacotherapy as desirable, since in their view symptom reduction automatically means an increase in the patients' well-being. The patients, however, might take a different view. Van Putten, Crumpton and Yale (1975) reported that some schizophrenic patients stopped taking their medication so as to be able to experience again their well-loved delusions of grandeur, as well as pleasant auditory hallucinations. Patients with bipolar affective disorders who undergo long-term prophylaxis not uncommonly miss their 'highs' and find it hard to get used to the new 'middle-of-the-road' state.

Prevention of the relapse of schizophrenic psychosis plays a central part in the clinical reasoning of psychiatrists. Not least, this is motivated by the long-term negative consequences for the patients' social situation (and hence for their QoL) that are almost inevitable with a relapse. Thus, psychiatrists will 'tolerate' the undesired effects of drug treatment more readily than patients, who experience the medication's negative effect on their subjective well-being. That the risk of recurrence of a psychotic episode in the future could be reduced might appear a rather intangible variable, in comparison with the treatment's short-term negative consequences. The issue becomes further complicated by the fact that neuroleptics do not provide 100% protection and that without psychopharmacological treatment relapse may not necessarily occur, although the risk of this is largely increased.

The way in which the effect of drug treatment on subjective well-being is evaluated depends heavily on the subjective importance attached to the various aspects of QoL, which are positively or negatively influenced by the treatment. Young men, for example, might consider sexual dysfunction in the wake of neuroleptic treatment as a particularly grave reduction of their QoL. On the other hand, the weight gain occurring with many psychotropic drugs might represent a serious problem for many women. The meaning of these side-effects and their consequences for patients' compliance with treatment has long been underestimated by psychiatrists (Amering and Katschnig, 1993a).

In addition to these direct pharmacological effects, indirect psychosocial effects of psychopharmacological treatment are important. Firstly, there are the practical implications of this type of treatment, which can have a negative impact on subjective well-being. The simple fact of having to take drugs several times a day, or the regular blood tests necessary during treatment with clozapine, can themselves be perceived as a nuisance. In addition, the limitations on everyday life required with most psychotropic drugs may impose a strain on subjective well-being, e.g. abstinence from alcohol. Regardless of the fact that it can represent a limitation of QoL in itself, this can also lead to embarrassing social situations in which patients have to justify themselves for not drinking alcohol. This involves the risk that they have to disclose their psychiatric disorder. Another practical implication is keeping to a particular diet (with irreversible monamine oxidase inhibitors) or unfitness to drive or operate machinery when taking drugs that may cause a prolonged reaction time (particularly benzodiazepines, sedating tricyclic antidepressants and low-potency neuroleptics).

Beyond these practical concomitants, the symbolic implications of psychopharmacological treatment play an important part in subjective well-being. On the one hand, the awareness that one is taking a drug that has been proved to reduce the risk of relapse in a perceivable manner can give patients a sense of security. No longer do they need to feel at the mercy of the illness. Rather, they have gained – to a certain extent – control over the disorder. On the other hand, dependence on the drug can represent a problem insofar as it is not the patient him/herself who crucially influences the mental state, but an external agent. In addition, taking the drug painfully reminds patients that they suffer from a disease that frequently takes a chronic course. Again and again, patients draw the wrong conclusion – that in order to recover, they simply have to discontinue their drug treatment (Diamond, 1985). The fact that patients have to take medication puts them firmly in the role of the 'mentally ill', with all its negative social implications.

PSYCHOTROPIC DRUGS AND SOCIAL FUNCTIONING

In addition to its effect on subjective well-being, psychopharmacological treatment can affect a patient's level of social functioning. Again, this has both positive and negative dimensions. It may be expected that the reduction of symptoms will create the prerequisite for patients to regain their ability to fulfil the role expectations directed at them by others. However, one problem with treating schizophrenic disorders by means of traditional neuroleptics is that, while being generally successful in suppressing the 'positive' symptoms, these drugs do not (or only marginally) lead to an improvement of negative symptoms such as affect flattening, lack of motivation, anhedonia or concentration deficits. On the contrary, not uncommonly, they may even intensify them. Yet it is precisely these negative symptoms that have a considerable effect on the level of social functioning, after an acute psychotic episode has subsided. Here, some of the newly developed atypical neuroleptics point to progress, as they seem to permit more effective treatment of certain negative symptoms. Antidepressants, besides reducing depressive symptoms, may also have a positive effect on social functioning in general (Stewart *et al.*, 1988) or on specific domains like work performance (Agosti, Stewart and Quitkin, 1991; Mintz *et al.*, 1992), functioning in the home or social relationships (Agosti, Stewart and Quitkin, 1991).

In most cases, however, psychosocial programmes seem to be necessary in addition to pharmaco-therapy in order to achieve an improvement of social functioning, as has become most evident in the treatment of schizophrenia. In panic disorders, the use of antidepressants may often be sufficient to reduce the frequency of panic attacks and then to prevent their occurrence altogether. Nevertheless, behavioural therapy might be required for patients to give up their agoraphobic behaviour, induced by the fear of attacks, and learn to actively engage in their social roles again.

Psychotropic drugs not only positively influence the level of social adaptation but can also affect the latter in a negative manner. This is rooted in their numerous side-effects, discussed above. The negative impact on social adaptation may be illustrated by a few examples from the area of work. Parkinsonism caused by neuroleptics or a lithium-induced tremor can be a severe impairment in performing tasks that require manual skills. Disturbances of visual accommodation due to the anticholinergic effect of tricyclic drugs will represent a grave hindrance for all who have to do much reading. Dryness of mouth caused by the same pharmacological mechanism can be a severe nuisance for those whose occupation requires much speaking (e.g. teachers). The cognitive impairments observed in connection with neuroleptic treatment (concentration deficits in particular) can be an impediment for intellectual activities in general. Artists may experience the reduction of creativity reported for lithium treatment as a serious problem.

Furthermore, patients' social relationships can be affected negatively through the side-effects of psychotropic drugs. This is particularly true for the extrapyramidal symptoms occurring during treat-ment with traditional neuroleptics, as the latter visibly stigmatise those affected. While schizophrenic patients normally are, to a certain degree, in a position to decide whether they want to reveal themselves to suffer from schizophrenia or would rather have their disorder undetected, people suffering from extrapyramidal symptoms are clearly recognisable as being mentally ill, whether they want this or not, producing the 'discreditable' turn into the 'discredited' (Goffman, 1963).

Further, extrapyramidal symptoms, especially hypomimia, as well as motivational, cognitive and affective impairments caused by traditional neuroleptic drugs, aggravate the difficulties in interpersonal interaction and social contact that people with schizophrenia encounter anyway. Also, the weight gain produced by a number of psychotropic drugs can, due to reducing the attractiveness of a person's physical appearance, adversely influence his/her chances of making friends and finding a partner.

PSYCHOTROPIC DRUGS AND SOCIAL/MATERIAL CIRCUMSTANCES

Thanks to their effect on social functioning described above, psychotropic drugs can influence patients' social and material living conditions, both directly and indirectly. Here, too, both positive and negative effects may occur. An example is the capacity to work: an improvement with the aid of psychotropic medication can have a positive influence on patients' financial situation. As a result, they can afford a higher standard of living, which might involve renting a more expensive flat, spending more money on leisure pursuits, travelling, etc. In addition, having an income of their own enables the patients to live more independently and to become more autonomous, as they are no longer dependent on the support of others. Beyond its economic effect, the ability to successfully fulfil the requirements of a job also opens up new fields of social interaction. The workplace being a central source of social contact in our society, having a job is a crucial means for those affected by mental illness to step out of their isolation or to prevent it from happening in the first place. Furthermore, occupational roles can be an important part of social identity. The experience of being 'useful' is therefore likely to stimulate patients' self-confidence, which in turn might encourage them to establish social contacts outside the occupational setting. All this should be beneficial in enhancing their subjective well-being. However, the opposite would be true if patients, due to the severe side-effects of their medication, were eventually no longer able to perform their accustomed tasks – in the workplace and beyond. Hence the 'second-generation' drugs, with their less pronounced side-effects, promise to be a step forward in relation to patients' QoL.

ATTITUDE TOWARDS PSYCHOTROPIC DRUGS AND QUALITY OF LIFE

As the Austrian writer Robert Musil remarked in his famous novel *Man Without Qualities*, people with mental disorders do not only suffer from an 'inferior health (*minderwertige Gesundheit*)' but also from an 'inferior disease (*minderwertige Krankheit*)'. By being given psychotropic drugs, they also receive a type of treatment that is inferior in the eyes of the public. A representative survey conducted in the Federal Republic of Germany in 1990 showed that while psychotherapy was generally held in high esteem by the lay public, psychopharmacotherapy was rejected by the vast majority. People were even more ready to endorse alternative methods such as natural remedies or meditation and yoga than to recommend psychotropic drugs for the treatment of severe disorders like schizophrenia or major depression (Angermeyer, Däumer and Matschinger, 1993; Angermeyer and Matschinger, 1996). In a national survey of the risk perception of prescription drugs undertaken in Sweden in 1988, cigarette smoking, pesticides and alcohol stood out highest in perceived risk, immediately followed by anti-depressants, which were judged the most risky prescription drugs of all, and even more risky than nuclear power (Slovic *et al.*, 1989). Thus the public image of psychoptropic drugs seems to be characterised by a 'pharmacophobia' (Amering and Katschnig, 1993b), though of late there appears to be a change in attitude. In a survey conducted in Germany in 2001, those questioned were more ready to acknowledge the beneficial effects of psychotropic drugs than a decade ago. However, despite changes for the better, the actual situation was far from satisfactory: psychotropic drugs were still met with more disapproval than approval (Angermeyer and Matschinger, 2004).

'OLD' AND 'NEW' DRUGS: THE CASE OF THE ANTIPSYCHOTICS

As stated above, psychiatrists generally consider the reduction of psychopathological symptoms as the most effective strategy to improve patients' subjective QoL (Hansson *et al.*, 1999). However, particularly in the case of schizophrenia, the antipsychotic medication necessary for an effective reduction of symptoms is often associated with severe side-effects (Simpson and Angus, 1970; Mattke, Mobour and Glotzner, 1975; Kemmler *et al.*, 1994; Miller *et al.*, 1995; Larsen and Gerlach, 1996; Gerlach and Larsen, 1999; Awad and Voruganti, 2000; Ritsner *et al.*, 2002). However, only some studies found a significant negative impact of extrapyramidal side-effects on the subjective QoL (Kemmler *et al.*, 1994; Browne *et al.*, 1996; Packer *et al.*, 1997; Ritsner *et al.*, 2002); other studies found no relationship (Larsen and Gerlach, 1996; Gerlach and Larsen, 1999; Kilian *et al.*, 2004). Most experts consider the prevention or at least reduction of negative side-effects of drugs as a crucial task in the process of improving QoL (Naber and Karow, 2001; Naber *et al.*, 2001; Naber, Karow and Lamber, 2002).

With the introduction of the new generation of 'atypical' antipsychotic agents since the 1990s, many psychiatrists expected that the treatment of schizophrenia would become more effective in terms of the improvement of subjective QoL, because – in comparison to conventional antipsychotic agents – these new drugs have a lower risk of inducing severe extrapyramidal side-effects and a greater potential to reduce negative as well as positive symptoms (Angermeyer and Katschnig, 1997; Glazer, 2000; Naber and Karow, 2001; Naber *et al.*, 2001). Meanwhile, several clinical studies on the impact of antipsychotic medication on the subjective QoL of patients with schizophrenia have been carried out. In most of these studies, atypical antipsychotic drugs were found to be superior to conventional antipsychotics in reducing negative symptoms and in producing fewer negative side-effects (Glazer, 2000; Burns and Bale, 2001). However, only some of these studies found that atypical antipsychotic drugs had more positive effects on the subjective QoL than conventional medication (Franz *et al.*, 1997; Bobes *et al.*, 1998; Naber and Lambert, 1998; Awad and Voruganti, 1999; Revicki *et al.*, 1999; Carrière, Bohnomme and Lemérière, 2000; Colonna *et al.*, 2000; Voruganti *et al.*, 2000, 2002; Cook, Goldberg and van Lieshout, 2002). A similar number of studies failed to replicate these results (Awad *et al.*, 1997; Hamilton, Revicki and Genduso, 1998; Hamilton *et al.*, 1999; Stallard and Joyce, 2001; Ritsner *et al.*, 2002; Corrigan *et al.*, 2003). In a recent prospective naturalistic study, Kilian *et al.* (2004) found that subjective QoL was positively related to antipsychotic treatment in general, but no differences were observed between the effects of atypical and conventional drugs. Regarding negative side-effects, the study indicates that patients' subjective QoL was not affected by extrapyramidal side-effects objectively assessed by clinicians, though subjectively experienced side-effects had a negative impact on QoL.

Some authors have suggested that patients' subjective experience of neuroleptic treatment is not only dependent on objective drug effects but also on other factors such as insight into the nature of the illness and the necessity of continuous drug treatment (Awad, 1993; Awad *et al.*, 1995). However, studies on the impact of insight on QoL of patients with schizophrenia found no such relationships (Browne *et al.*, 1998; Doyle *et al.*, 1999; Holloway and Carson, 1999).

Therefore, it is not clear at present whether atypical antipsychotic drugs are more effective in improving the subjective QoL than conventional antipsychotics, nor what factors may prevent patients from experiencing objective positive drug effects. In a recent review Awad and Voruganti (2004) have concluded that there is a positive trend towards a more positive impact on Qol with atypical agents, but that – because of methodological and design limitations of available studies – more independent, well designed and controlled studies are required, including comparisons between different atypical antipsychotics, before the question can be definitely answered.

Moreover, in real-life treatment settings, the combination of both types of antipsychotics is common practice in the treatment of schizophrenia (Clark *et al.*, 2002; Pappadopulos *et al.*, 2002; Weissman, 2002). Presently, the potential advantages or risks of combination therapies are not well understood (Freudenreich and Goff, 2002; Miller and Craig, 2002) and their effects on the subjective QoL have not yet been examined.

CONCLUSION

Although a number of studies on the relationship between psychotropic drugs and the QoL of people with mental disorders have been carried out, many questions still remain unanswered. A largely unresolved problem is the development of suitable instruments for the assessment of the effect of drug treatment on QoL. The impact of psychotropic drugs on QoL seems to be of considerable importance for compliance by patients. Detailed studies investigating the relative importance of the various positive and negative effects of psychotropic drugs on the various domains of QoL, however, still remain to be done. Considering the alarming dimensions of non-compliance – e.g. that only 30–40% of chronic schizophrenic patients regularly take neuroleptic drugs (Naber, 1995) – the need for further research is evident.

REFERENCES

Agosti, V., Stewart, J.W. & Quitkin, F.M. (1991). Life satisfaction and psychosocial functioning in chronic depression: Effect of acute treatment with antidepressants, *J. Affect. Disord.*, **23**, 35–41.

Amering, M. & Katschnig, H. (1993a). Die Wirkungen der Psychopharmaka auf das Sexualverhalten und ihre Bedeutung für die Betreuung schizophrener Patienten, in *Brennpunkte der Schizophrenie. Gesellschaft – Angehörige – Therapie* (Ed. T. Platz), pp. 215–222, Springer, Vienna, New York.

Amering, M. & Katschnig, H. (1993b). Psychopharmaka im Spannungsfeld zwischen Patienten, Angehörigen und Betreuern, in *Brennpunkte der Schizophrenie. Gesellschaft – Angehörige – Therapie* (Ed. T. Platz), pp. 223–231, Springer, Vienna, New York.

Angermeyer, M.C. (1994). Symptomfreiheit oder Lebensqualität: Ziele der Schizophreniebehandlung, in *Schizophrenie und Lebensqualität* (Eds H. Katschnig & P. König), pp. 65–80, Springer-Verlag, Vienna, New York.

Angermeyer, M.C., Däumer, R. & Matschinger, H. (1993). Benefits and risks of psychotropic medication in the eyes of the general public: Results of a survey in the Federal Republic of Germany, *Pharmacopsychiatry*, **26**, 114–120.

Angermeyer, M. C. & Katschnig, H. (1997). Psychotropic medication and quality of life: A conceptual framework for assessing their relationships, in *Quality of Life in Mental Disorder* (Eds H. Katschnig, H. Freeman & N. Sartorius), pp. 215–225, John Wiley & Sons, Chichester.

Angermeyer, M.C. & Matschinger, H. (1996). Public attitude towards psychiatric treatment, *Acta Psychiatrica. Scand.*, **94**, 326–336.

Angermeyer, M.C. & Matschinger, H. (2004). Public attitudes towards psychotropic drugs: Have there been any changes in recent years?, *Pharmacopsychiatry*, **37**, 147–151.

Awad, A.G. (1992). Quality of life of schizophrenic patients on medications and implications for new drug trials, *Hosp. Community Psychiatry*, **43**, 262–265.

Awad, A.G. (1993). Subjective response to neuroleptics in schizophrenia, *Schizophrenia Bull.*, **19**, 609–618.

Awad, A.G. & Voruganti, L. (1999). Quality of life and new antipsychotics in schizophrenia. Are patients better off?, *Int. J. Soc. Psychiatry*, **45**, 268–275.

Awad, A.G. & Voruganti, L. (2000). Intervention research in psychosis: Issues related to the assessment of quality of life, *Schizophrenia. Bull.*, **26**, 557–564.

Awad, A.G. & Voruganti, L. (2004). Impact of atypical antipsychotics on quality of life in patients with schizophrenia, *CNS Drugs*, **18**, 877–893.

Awad, A.G., Hogan, T.P., Voruganti, L.P.N. & Heslegrave, R.J. (1995). Patients' subjective experiences on antipsychotic medications: Implications for outcome and quality of life, *Int. Clin. Psychopharmacol.*, **10**, 123–132.

Awad, A.G., Lapierre, Y.D., Angus, C. & Rylander, A. (1997). Quality of life and response of negative symptoms in schizophrenia to haloperidol and the atypical antipsychotic remoxipride, *J. Psychiat. Neurosci.*, **4**, 244–248.

Bobes, J., Gutiérrez, M., Gibert, J., González, H.L. & Fernández, A. (1998). Quality of life in schizophrenia: Long-term follow-up in 362 chronic Spanish schizophrenic outpatients undergoing risperidone maintenance treatment, *Eur. Psychiatry*, **13**, 158–163.

Browne, S., Roe, L., Gervin, M., Morris, M., Kinsella, A., Larkin, C. & O'Callahan, E. (1996). Quality of life in schizophrenia: Relationship to sociodemographic factors, symptomatology and tardive dyskinesia, *Acta Psychiatrica Scand.*, **94**, 118–124.

Browne, S., Garavan, J., Gervin, M., Roe, M., Larkin, C. & O'Callahan, E. (1998). Quality of life in schizophrenia: Insight and subjective response to neuroleptics, *J. Nerv. Ment. Dis.*, **186**, 74–78.

Burns, T. & Bale, R. (2001). Clinical advantages of amisulpride in the treatment of acute schizophrenia, *J. Int. Med. Res.*, **29**, 451–466.

Carrière, P., Bohnomme, D. & Lemérière, T. (2000). Amisulpride has a superior benefit/risk profile to haloperidol in schizophrenia: Results of a multicentre double-blind study, *Eur. Psychiatry*, **15**, 321–329.

Clark, R.E., Bartels, S.J., Mellmann, T.A. & Peacock, W.J. (2002). Recent trends in antipsychotic combination therapy of schizophrenia and schizoaffective disorder: Implications for state mental health policy, *Schizophrenia Bull.*, **28**, 75–84.

Colonna, L., Saleem, P., Dondey-Nouvel, L. & Rein, W. (2000). Long-term safety and efficacy of amisulpride in subchronic or chronic schizophrenia, *Int. Clin. Psychopharmacol.*, **15**, 13–22.

Cook, P.E., Goldberg, J.O. & van Lieshout, R.J. (2002). Benefits of switching from typical to atypical antipsychotic medications: A longitudinal study in a community based setting, *Can. J. Psychiatry*, **47**, 870–874.

Corrigan, P.W., Reinke, R.R., Landsberger, S.A., Charate, A. & Toombs, G.A. (2003). The effects of atypical antipsychotic medications on psychosocial outcomes, *Schizophrenia Res.*, **63**, 97–101.

Diamond, R. (1985). Drugs and the quality of life: The patient's point of view, *J. Clin. Psychiatry*, **46**, 29–35.

Doyle, M., Flannagan, S., Browne, S., Clarke, M., Lydon, D., Larkin, C. & O'Callahan, E. (1999). Subjective and external assessments of quality of life in schizophrenia: Relationship to insight, *Acta Psychiatrica. Scand.*, **99**, 466–472.

Franz, M., Lis, S., Plüddemann, K. & Gallhofer, B. (1997). Conventional versus atypical neuroleptics: Subjective quality of life in schizophrenic patients, *Br. J. Psychiatry*, **170**, 423–425.

Freudenreich, O. & Goff, C. (2002). Antipsychotic combination therapy in schizophrenia. A review of efficacy and risk of current combinations, *Acta Psychiatrica. Scand.*, **106**, 323–330.

Gerlach, J. & Larsen, E.B. (1999). Subjective experience and mental side-effects of antipsychotic treatment, *Acta Psychiatrica Scand.*, **99**, 113–117.

Glazer, W.M. (2000). Expected incidence of tardive dyskinesia associated with atypical antipsychotics, *J. Clin. Psychiatry.*, **61**, 21–26.

Goffman, E. (1963). *Stigma. Notes on the Management of Spoiled Identity*, Prentice-Hall, Englewood Cliffs, New Jersey.

Hamilton, S.H., Revicki, D.A. & Genduso, L.A. (1998). Olanzapine versus placebo and haloperidol: Quality of life and efficacy results of the North American double-blind trial, *Neuropsychopharmacology*, **18**, 41–49.

Hamilton, S.H., Revicki, D.A., Edgell, E.T. & Genduso, L.A. (1999). Clinical and economic outcomes of olanzapine compared with haloperidol for schizophrenia. Results from a randomised clinical trial, *PharmacoEconomics*, **15**, 469–480.

Hansson, L., Middelboe, T., Merinder, L., Bjarnason, O., Bengtsson-Tops, A., Nilsson, L., Sandlund, M., Sourander, A., Sorgaard, K.W. & Vinding, H.R. (1999). Predictors of subjective quality of life in schizophrenic patients living in the community. A Nordic multicentre study, *Int. J. Social Psychiatry*, **45**, 247–258.

Holloway, F. & Carson, F. (1999). Subjective quality of life, psychopathology, satisfaction with care and insight: An exploratory study, *Int. J. Social Psychiatry*, **45**, 259–267.

Kemmler, G., Meise, U., Tasser, A., Liensberger, D., Schifferle, I., Braitenberg, M., Schwitzer, J., Browne, S., Roe, M. & Lane, A. (1994). Quality of life in schizophrenia: Relationships to sociodemographic factors, symptomatology and tardive dyskinesia, *Acta Psychiatrica Scand.*, **89**, 118–124.

Kilian, R., Dietrich, S., Toumi, M. & Angermeyer, M.C. (2004). Quality of life in persons with schizophrenia in out-patient treatment with first- or second-generation antipsychotics, *Acta Psychiatrica Scand.*, **110**, 108–118.

Larsen, E.B. & Gerlach, J. (1996). Subjective experience of treatment, side-effects, mental state and quality of life in chronic schizophrenic out-patients treated with depot-neuroleptics, *Acta Psychiatrica Scand.*, **93**, 381–388.

Mattke, D.J., Mobour, W. & Glotzner, F.L. (1975). The assessment of neuroleptogenic extrapyramidal syndromes in psychopharmacological research, *Pharmakopsychiat. Neuropsychopharmakol.*, **1**, 36–44.

Meltzer, H.Y., Burnett, S., Bastani, B. & Ramirez, L.F. (1990). Effects of six months of clozapine treatment on the quality of life of chronic schizophrenic patients, *Hosp. Community Psychiatry*, **41**, 892–897.

Miller, A.L. & Craig, C.S. (2002). Combination antipsychotics: Pros, cons and questions, *Schizophrenia Bull.*, **28**, 105–109.

Miller, C.H., Simioni, I., Oberbauer, H., Schwitzer, J., Barnas, C., Kuhlhanek, F., Boissel, K.E., Meise, U., Hinterhuber, H. & Fleischhacker, W. W. (1995). Tardive dyskinesia prevalence rates during a ten-year follow-up, *J. Nerv. Ment. Dis.*, **183**, 404–407.

Mintz, J., Mintz, L.I., Arruda, M.J. & Hwang, S.S. (1992). Treatments of depression and the functional capacity to work, *Arch. Gen. Psychiatry*, **49**, 761–768.

Naber, D. (1995). A self-rating to measure subjective effects of neuroleptic drugs, relationships to objective psychopathology, quality of life, compliance and other clinical variables, *Int. Clin. Psychopharmacol.*, **10**, (Suppl. 3), 133–138.

Naber, D. & Karow, A. (2001). Good tolerability equals good results: The patients perspective, *Eur. Neuropharmacol.*, **11**, S391-S396.

Naber, D., Karow, A. & Lamber, M. (2002). Psychosocial outcomes in patients with schizophrenia: Quality of life and reintegration, *Curr. Opinion Psychiatry*, **15**, 31–36.

Naber, D. & Lambert, M. (1998). Sertindole decreases hospitalisation and improves the quality of life of schizophrenic patients. *Int. J. Psychiat. Clin.*, **2**, S73-S77.

Naber, D., Moritz, S., Lambert, M., Rajonk, F., Holzbach, R., Mass, R., Andresen, B., Frank, P., Rüdiger, H., Reinhard, M. & Burghard, A. (2001). Improvement of schizophrenic patients' subjective well-being under atypical antipsychotic drugs, *Schizophrenia Res.* **50**, 79–88.

Packer, S., Husted, J., Cohen, S. & Tomlinson, G. (1997). Psychopathology and quality of life in schizophrenia, *J. Psychiat. Neurosci.*, **22**, 231–233.

Pappadopulos, E., Jensen, P.S., Schur, S.B., MacIntyre, J.C., Ketner, S., van Orden, K., Sverd, J., Sardana, S., Woodlock, D., Schweitzer, R. & Rube, D. (2002). 'Real world' atypical antipsychotic prescribing practices in public child and adolescent inpatient settings, *Schizophrenia Bull.*, **28**, 111–121.

Revicki, D.A., Genduso, L.A., Hamilton, S.H., Ganoczy, D. & Beasly Jr, C.M. (1999). Olanzapine versus haloperidol in the treatment of schizophrenia and other psychotic disorders: Quality of life and clinical outcomes of a randomised trial, *Quality of Life Res.*, **8**, 417–426.

Ritsner, M., Ponizovsky, A., Endicott, J., Nechamkin, Y., Rauchverger, B., Silver, H. & Modai, I. (2002). The impact of side-effects of antipsychotic agents on life satisfaction of schizophrenia patients: A naturalistic study, *Eur. Psychopharmacol.*, **12**, 31–38.

Simpson, G. & Angus, J. (1970). A rating scale for extrapyramidal side effects, *Acta Psychiatrica Scand.*, **212**, 11–19.

Slovic, P., Kraus, N., Lappe, H., Letzel, H. & Malmfors, T. (1989). Risk perception of prescription drugs: Report on a survey in Sweden, in *The Perception and Management of Drug Safety Risks* (Eds B. Horisberger and R. Dinkel), pp. 90–111, Springer, Berlin, Heidelberg, New York, London, Paris, Tokyo.

Stallard, J. & Joyce, E. (2001). The impact of olanzapine on attitude to medication and quality of life in schizophrenia, *Psychiat. Bull.*, **25**, 378–381.

Stewart, J.W., Quitkin, F.M., McGrath, P.J., Rabkin, J.G., Markowitz, J.S., Tricamo, E. & Klein, D.F. (1988). Social functioning in chronic depression: Effect of 6 weeks of antidepressant treatment, *Psychiat. Res.*, **25**, 213–222.

Van Putten, T., Crumpton, E. & Yale, C. (1975). Drug refusal in schizophrenia and the wish to be crazy, *Arch. Gen. Psychiatry*, **33**, 1443–1446.

Voruganti, L., Cortese, L., Oyewumi, L., Cernovsky, Z., Zirul, S. & Awad, A. (2000). Comparative evaluation of conventional and novel antipsychotic drugs with reference to their subjective tolerability, side-effect profile and impact on quality of life, *Schizophrenia Res.* **43**, 135–145.

Voruganti, L., Cortese, L., Owyeumi, L., Kotteda, V., Cernovsky, Z., Zirul, S. & Awad, A. (2002). Switching from conventional to novel antipsychotic drugs: Results of a prospective naturalistic study, *Schizophrenia Res.*, **57**, 201–208.

Weissman, E.M. (2002). Antipsychotic prescribing practices in the veterans healthcare administration – New York Metropolitan region, *Schizophrenia Bull.*, **28**, 31–42.

18

'Real World' Trials of Psychotropic Medication

T. Scott Stroup and Jeffrey A. Lieberman

INTRODUCTION

Over the last fifty years, the introduction of psychotropic medication has made a major contribution to the fact that most persons suffering from severe mental disorders can live today in the community. One of the goals of new drugs is to improve efficacy and tolerability in order to have a more positive effect on quality of life (QoL) than the earlier ones. Knowledge about the usefulness of medication, in terms of efficacy and side-effects, is usually derived from randomised controlled clinical trials, also called 'efficacy trials', which are regarded as the 'gold standard' for evidence-based medicine. While being scientifically rigorous in establishing whether a drug reduces prominent symptoms and is safe in the short term, such 'efficacy trials' have a number of disadvantages in terms of the generalisability of their results. One of the many reasons for this is the high selectivity of the samples participating in such trials. 'Real world' circumstances, like comorbidity, comedication, compliance and other issues are not addressed in these short-term efficacy trials.

Research studies based on a new paradigm that are designed to answer important questions of major public health significance – in terms of whether psychotropic drugs work in the 'real world' – are now under way. These studies, known as 'practical' or 'pragmatic' clinical trials (PCTs), or 'large simple trials (LSTs)', are expected to yield important evidence about the appropriate use of psychotropic medication for persons suffering from severe mental illness who are living in the community. The goal of these is to examine the effect of pharmacological intervention on a wide range of meaningful outcomes, including QoL, in order to inform clinical and policy decision -makers.

EFFICACY TRIALS

The efficacy of psychotropic medication is established in clinical trials that are designed to meet the requirements of regulatory agencies efficiently. Efficacy trials focus on short-term safety and the reduction of prominent symptoms. In an attempt to isolate the effects of the drug, adjunctive medications are not allowed, or are allowed only under strict or time-limited circumstances. Individuals with medical illnesses or substance use disorders are excluded from participation. Often, the trials are conducted on research units where adherence to the study protocol, including medication dosing schedules, is ensured. Thus, efficacy trials establish the short-term safety of a drug and its ability to ameliorate target symptoms of specific disorders under ideal circumstances.

Quality of Life in Mental Disorders, Second Edition   Edited by H. Katschnig, H. Freeman and N. Sartorius
© 2006 John Wiley & Sons, Ltd

Unfortunately, efficacy trials provide little information about how interventions will work in the real world, where patients make individual choices about the treatments they are offered and where the logistics of costs, convenience and comfort have significant influence. The result is that treatments that have been proven efficacious are less beneficial in typical circumstances than in the ideal circumstances of a short-term efficacy trial. This phenomenon is now commonly known as the efficacy–effectiveness gap (Institute of Medicine, 1985).

When a new pharmaceutical agent becomes widely available, all the evidence about how it works typically comes from efficacy trials sponsored by the pharmaceutical company that has brought the new drug to market. Although these studies are strictly regulated by drug licensing agencies, there can be no doubt that the studies are designed to achieve favourable results for the sponsoring company's new drug. For this reason, efficacy trials are thought by many to have innate biases that limit their internal as well as their external validity.

In addition, efficacy trials do not answer many common, important questions faced by both clinicians and patients. Because a new treatment is compared to placebo or a single standard medication, these studies do not provide direct information on its efficacy compared to all or most commonly used treatments. Efficacy trials are not concerned with many outcomes that are important to interested parties. For example, reductions in symptom scores are likely to be less important to patients than functional outcomes such as social functioning, work, QoL and relapse prevention. Also, efficacy trials are rarely designed to provide the information about the costs or cost-effectiveness of drugs that policy makers may need.

EFFECTIVENESS TRIALS

Effectiveness trials, in contrast to efficacy trials that focus narrowly on disease-related outcomes, such as symptoms and side-effects, examine a variety of outcomes in studies that 'duplicate as closely as possible the conditions in the target practice venues to which study results will be applied' (Bauer *et al.*, 2001). In this explicit attempt to maximise the external validity of the studies, effectiveness trial researchers must still rigorously abide by principles that promote the internal validity of the research (Bauer *et al.*, 2001). For randomised trials, key features promoting internal validity identified by the revised consolidated standards of reporting trials (CONSORT) statement include adherence to eligibility requirements, proper randomisation with successful concealment of treatment conditions until the treatments are assigned, successful blinding if appropriate, adequate sample size and appropriate analysis (Moher, Schulz and Altman, 2001).

Below, we discuss the types of outcomes considered in effectiveness trials and define two types of these – large simple trials (LSTs) and practical clinical trials (PCTs). Then, we describe examples of LSTs and PCTs from within and outside of psychiatry.

EFFECTIVENESS TRIAL OUTCOMES

The relevant outcomes in a clinical research study are, of course, dependent upon the illness and the purpose of the intervention. In some medical fields, efficacy trials focus on changes in a pathophysiological process, e.g. blood pressure or tumour size. These typical efficacy trial outcomes are 'disease orientated' rather than 'patient orientated' because they are not closely related to the types of outcomes that matter most to patients – mortality, functioning and symptoms (Slawson, Shaughnessy and Bennett, 1994). Changes detected in disease-orientated outcomes require assumptions about the benefit that patients may have received. In studies of mental disorders, which currently lack widely accepted physiological markers, efficacy trials tend to focus on reduction in symptoms as measured by a psychometrically sound (valid and reliable) rating instrument. Thus, the outcomes used in efficacy trials of psychopharmacological interventions are reasonably relevant to most patients. However, the reductions of 20–50% in symptoms measured by rating scales that are often classified as a treatment 'response' may have limited meaning to patients with persistent auditory hallucinations, disorganised thoughts or suicidal thoughts. The reliability of symptom ratings, even using the most psychometrically sound instruments, can only be ensured through rigorous training and standardised procedures. Effectiveness trials in psychiatry attempt to measure clear-cut outcomes that are both meaningful to patients and less subject to systematic biases than rating scales.

Remission is a relevant outcome for persons who enter a study with acute or persistent symptoms, functional impairment or disability. Robinson and Schooler (2001) used a multifaceted definition of remission in a re-analysis of data from a study of first-episode schizophrenia. Their definition required no positive symptoms greater than 'mild', no negative symptoms greater than 'moderate', independence (the ability to perform daily activities without assistance), appropriate role function (paid or non-competitive employment or school at least half-time or adequate functioning as a homemaker) and social interactions with a peer at least once a week. This definition of remission, requiring threshold levels of symptom resolution and functioning, is highly appropriate for first-episode patients seeking to resume premorbid levels of functioning.

Relapse, or recurrence of symptoms or disability that reaches a predefined threshold or requires a new intervention, is an outcome that is likely to be important to patients who have achieved remission. One study of schizophrenia that will be described further below used the following criteria for relapse: psychiatric hospitalisation, an increase in the level of psychiatric care, a 25 % increase from the baseline on a measure of symptoms (the Positive and Negative Syndrome Scale, or PANSS), an absolute increase of 10 points on the PANSS for those with low scores at the baseline, deliberate self-injury, significant suicidal or homicidal ideation, violent behaviour resulting in injury to another person or property damage or clinical deterioration ('much worse' or 'very much worse') on the Clinical Global Impressions (CGI) Scale (Csernasky, Mahmoud and Brenner, 2002). This multifaceted outcome is meant to capture significant worsening in patients who have previously achieved some degree of remission and stability.

All-cause treatment discontinuation is the primary outcome in the National Institute of Mental Health (NIMH) Clinical Antipsychotic Trials of Intervention Effectiveness (CATIE) for schizophrenia that is described below (Stroup *et al.*, 2003). This outcome, which is expected to reflect patients' and clinicians' perceptions of efficacy, effectiveness and tolerability, is discrete and clinically meaningful. Treatment discontinuation is important clinically because of many of its causes and consequences. If a patient with schizophrenia stops medication altogether, the risk of relapse and rehospitalisation is greatly increased. If the cause of the discontinuation is inadequate efficacy, poor symptom relief is a significant burden for the patient. Similarly, if the problem is poor tolerability, the patient will have suffered significant discomfort, a potential medical complication or significant morbidity. In the instances when medication changes are required or adverse events must be managed, discontinuation of treatment is associated with significant increases in service use, as well as inconvenience for patients. Thus, although all-cause treatment discontinuation is non-specific because it can be caused by many reasons, alone or together, it is a useful measure of a drug's overall acceptability that is meaningful to patients and their caregivers (BALANCE, 2002).

LARGE SIMPLE TRIALS

Large simple trials have been used in other medical fields, in particular cardiology, with significant impact. Large simple trials have a narrow focus, but on outcomes that are patient-orientated and clearly defined. Treatments are randomised to attempt to control for biases inherent in observational studies. Randomisation is justified by equipoise, the situation in which experts in the field are genuinely uncertain which of the studied treatments is best (Freedman, 1987). Equipoise requires that all of the interventions compared are clinically meaningful, e.g. efficacious drugs used at typical doses that are well tolerated.

LSTs enroll a large number of subjects so that they can detect moderate benefits that smaller trials would miss because of inadequate statistical power (Peto and Baigent, 1998). Research subjects in LSTs are heterogeneous and are recruited from a wide variety of clinical sites, so that they may be representative of typical patients receiving routine care. Eligibility criteria are broad and guided by Peto's 'uncertainty principle' – an individual is eligible if there is substantial uncertainty about which of the studied interventions is appropriate for him/her (Peto, Collins and Gray, 1995).

A key feature of large simple trials is minimal data collection – too much data raise costs and may reduce the reliability of answers to therapeutic questions by making trials less likely to take place or smaller than otherwise possible (Peto and Baigent, 1998). LSTs focus on simple, important outcomes that are relevant to practice and readily measurable. The protocols are simple and flexible so that they can be undertaken in normal practices that make it possible for the results to be applied to these settings. The simplicity of the protocols and the minimal effort devoted to data collection means that routine practice is not significantly disrupted. Large simple trials explicitly avoid the extensive data collection of efficacy trials so that they can enroll large numbers of subjects and have the statistical power to detect relatively small but meaningful treatment effects. By not disrupting routine practice, these studies encourage both patients and clinicians in routine settings to participate and thus enhance the studies' external validity. Thus, LSTs need collaboration from the types of clinicians who see the bulk of relevant patients, rather than the researchers who participate in typical clinical trials.

Antihypertensive and Lipid-Lowering Treatment to Prevent Heart Attack Trial

The US National Heart, Lung and Blood Institute sponsored an important large simple trial known by the acronym ALLHAT (Antihypertensive and Lipid-Lowering Treatment to Prevent Heart Attack Trial). This enrolled more than 42 000 subjects with hypertension and one other risk factor for coronary artery disease. ALLHAT compared the effect of different classes of antihypertensive drugs on both fatal coronary heart disease and non-fatal myocardial infarction. It also examined important secondary outcomes including all-cause mortality, stroke and heart failure. The main finding was that there was no difference in primary outcome between a diuretic, an angiotensin-converting enzyme (ACE) inhibitor, a calcium channel blocker and an alpha blocker. However, on secondary outcomes, the diuretic had advantages. The results supported a conclusion that inexpensive thiazide-type diuretics should be the preferred choice in first-step antihypertensive therapy (ALLHAT, 2002).

The International Suicide Prevention Trial

The International Suicide Prevention Trial (InterSePT) was an ambitious randomised controlled trial (RCT) that enrolled nearly 1000 patients with schizophrenia or schizo-affective disorder who were at high risk of suicide (Meltzer et al., 2003). Multiple international sites enrolled subjects for two years of treatment and follow-up. The study compared the effects of clozapine and olanzapine on suicide attempts, hospitalisation to prevent suicide and ratings of 'much worsening of suicidality'. Study drugs were provided openly, but blinded raters determined when outcomes were achieved. The study was funded by Novartis, the maker of clozapine, and concluded that clozapine was superior to olanzapine in preventing suicide attempts in the target population.

PRACTICAL (OR PRAGMATIC) CLINICAL TRIALS

Practical clinical trials (PCTs) can be thought of as hybrids of efficacy and large simple trials. The key feature of PCTs is that they have hypotheses and study designs that are formulated to provide information to help clinicians and health care policy makers make key decisions (Tunis, Stryer and Clancy, 2003). PCTs try to answer practical questions about the risks, benefits and costs of interventions in the 'real world' or routine clinical situations in which they arise. Like large simple trials, practical clinical trials recruit patients from the types of settings where patients with the condition under study typically receive care, enroll a broad spectrum of study participants and compare clinically relevant interventions over meaningful periods of time. The clinically relevant interventions of PCTs are derived from the real-world choices faced by clinicians and patients. By enrolling research participants who reflect the range and distribution of patients seen in clinical practice, PCTs attempt to enhance the external validity of the study so that it is more likely to be judged useful by clinical or policy decision makers. The use of diverse, typical treatment settings may help to enroll a sample representing the range of people with a specified illness and may mean that the ancillary care they receive is more typical of average care than in research settings. These PCT features may enhance generalisability in a way that specifically addresses a barrier to implementation of research findings by clinicians (Tunis, Stryer and Clancy, 2003).

Follow-up in PCTs is longer than efficacy trials in order to better reflect the course of an illness (Tunis, Stryer and Clancy, 2003). Practical clinical trials differ from large simple trials in that they examine a broad range of relevant outcomes, rather than a single definitive end-point. PCTs examine a range of outcomes that may focus on disease processes as well as those that are of most interest to patients. In addition, practical clinical trials may include a wide variety of outcomes that are of interest to various policy makers. Some outcomes are primarily of interest to clinicians, like changes in metabolic parameters, symptoms and side-effect rating scales. Administrators may be particularly interested in cost-effectiveness. Practical trials also try to include outcomes that are patient-orientated, like QoL, social and vocational functioning, and residential status. Because psychiatric disorders, in the relatively short follow-up periods of clinical trials, are not associated with many discrete outcomes that are not subject to significant measurement bias (like death, stroke or myocardial infarction), a variety of other outcomes have been investigated. These include hospitalisation, relapse, remission, study drop-out and treatment discontinuation.

A Non-psychiatric Practical Clinical Trial

An influential practical clinical trial of importance to policy makers was the US Veterans Health Administration study of arthroscopy for osteoarthritis of the knee (Moseley *et al.*, 2002). Because of a lack of evidence that this procedure was effective, and because arthroscopic procedures were widespread and costly, unlike typical practical trials, this one included a placebo. The study enrolled 180 subjects and randomly assigned them to arthroscopy with lavage, arthroscopy with debridement or sham surgery. The outcomes of interest were pain and functioning, as rated by the patients and trained assessors, who were all blind to the treatment assignments. The important results of this study were that neither type of arthroscopic surgery had advantages over the placebo at any time over two years of follow-up. The authors concluded that the billions of dollars spent on arthroscopy for osteoarthritis of the knee might be better spent elsewhere (Moseley *et al.*, 2002).

A Schizophrenia Relapse-Prevention Study

Csernansky and colleagues (2002) conducted a randomised study that examined relapse prevention in persons with schizophrenia or schizo-affective disorder that had some of the components of a practical clinical trial. The study included a substantial number of subjects (397), compared two effective and commonly used treatments (haloperidol and risperidone) flexibly dosed, followed-up subjects for at least a year and examined a meaningful primary outcome (relapse) in addition to others of importance to both clinicians and patients. On the other hand, this trial had significant limitations that made it less generalisable than most practical trials. All subjects were out-patients who had at least 30 days of medication and housing stability before study entry. Patients with any other DSM-IV Axis I diagnosis, borderline personality disorder, antisocial personality disorder, current substance abuse or dependence, or clinically significant medical illness were excluded. Perhaps the biggest threat to the external validity of this trial was one of the biggest assets to its internal validity – more than 95% of subjects were compliant with their assigned antipsychotic drug regimen. Nevertheless, this important study provided vital information to patients, clinicians and policy makers about the relative effects of two key drugs on relapse prevention in chronic psychoses. The authors concluded that risperidone prevented relapse better than haloperidol.

Practical Trials of Clozapine

Essock and colleagues (1996, 2000) examined the effectiveness of clozapine for persons with long stays in Connecticut state hospitals. The study was intended to be informative to policy makers by comparing the effectiveness of clozapine and conventional antipsychotics and determining if providing clozapine rather than conventional drugs to long-term hospital patients was cost-effective. The study design was designed to examine effectiveness in routine practice – except for randomised treatment assignment, the study protocol mimicked usual state hospital care, with medicines provided open-label. Regarding clinical outcomes, clozapine had no benefit in increasing the rate of hospital discharge, but among those who were discharged, those on clozapine were less likely to be readmitted (Essock et al., 1996). The cost-effectiveness analyses found clozapine to have advantages on some but not all measures (Essock et al., 2000).

Working within the US Veterans Health Administration, Rosenheck et al. (1997) used a practical clinical trial design to examine the effectiveness and cost-effectiveness of clozapine and haloperidol in hospitalised patients with refractory schizophrenia. This randomised, one-year, double-blind study found no significant differences in costs between the two groups but found that clozapine was modestly more effective in reducing symptoms and caused fewer extrapyramidal side-effects than haloperidol.

Together, the Veterans Health Administration and Connecticut studies contributed to perceptions that clozapine is the best available treatment for persons with severe schizophrenia and that it should be widely available, but that its advantages are relatively modest and that continued search for superior treatment strategies is necessary.

Maintenance Treatment of Bipolar Disorder

The Bipolar Affective Disorder: Lithium/ANti-Convulsant Evaluation (BALANCE) trial is based on variation in maintenance treatment for bipolar disorder in the United States and the United Kingdom and uncertainty about the most effective treatment strategy (BALANCE, 2002). The study is a practical clinical trial comparing lithium monotherapy, valproate monotherapy and lithium and valproate combination therapy in maintenance treatment of bipolar disorder. Inclusion in the study is based on the 'uncertainty principle', meaning that the key entry criterion is that neither the clinician nor the patient are sure which of the study treatments is most appropriate (Geddes and Goodwin, 2001). Eligible persons will have an episode of mania, will be considered appropriate for maintenance therapy and will have uncertainty about the appropriate maintenance regimen for their individual situation (BALANCE, 2002). As a maintenance study, only subjects who successfully complete an eight-week non-randomised run-in phase will be randomised (Geddes and Goodwin, 2001). The study will thus attempt to determine the best long-term treatment among persons who are willing to remain on maintenance therapy. The primary outcome is relapse as indicated by hospitalisation or a comparable increase in the level of care. Other outcomes include the use of adjunctive medication, measures of global functioning, deliberate self-harm, QoL, adverse events, medication adherence and rates of study medication discontinuation.

By addressing this practical clinical choice regarding maintenance treatments for bipolar disorder, the BALANCE study hopes to provide information that will prevent clinical decisions being unduly influenced by marketing, i.e. the use of valproate over lithium because valproate is actively marketed (Geddes and Goodwin, 2001).

Comparative Effectiveness of Second-Generation Antipsychotics in Schizophrenia

The Clinical Antipsychotic Trials of Intervention Effectiveness (CATIE) project, sponsored by the US National Institute of Mental Health (NIMH), aims to evaluate the effectiveness of second-generation antipsychotics and a representative first-generation antipsychotic in the treatment of chronic schizophrenia (Stroup et al., 2003). Approximately 1500 subjects with schizophrenia were recruited at more than 50 sites, including community mental health centres, state hospitals, private practices, Veteran's Affairs Medical Centers and university hospitals. In Phase 1, participants were randomly assigned to double-blind treatment with one of five study drugs (olanzapine, perphenazine, quetiapine, risperidone or ziprasidone). Concurrent substance use disorders, comorbid psychiatric illnesses and stable medical conditions were allowed. People with first-episode psychosis and treatment-refractory schizophrenia were excluded because they are known to respond differently to medication than most people with chronic schizophrenia. Those with tardive dyskinesia were not randomised to the first-generation drug perphenazine.

The primary outcome in CATIE is all-cause treatment discontinuation, as defined above. As a practical trial, a broad range of other outcomes will also be considered, including the effects of the study treatments on symptoms, extrapyramidal and metabolic side effects, adverse events, substance use, violent behaviour, costs and service use, neurocognitive functioning, vocational functioning and QoL.

The CATIE Schizophrenia Trial (Fig.18.1) was designed to imitate routine clinical practice with randomisations at clinical decision points where recommendations are uncertain. Participants who discontinue the first randomly assigned medication are offered the opportunity to enter Phase 2 of the study, in which they choose one of two treatment pathways with random assignment. Participants who discontinue the first treatment because of inadequate efficacy are encouraged to enter a trial that compares clozapine to other second-generation drugs. Participants who discontinue the first treatment because of poor tolerability are encouraged to enter a trial that compares ziprasidone to other second-generation drugs. If a participant discontinues the second drug, then he/she can enter a third phase in which an appropriate open-label treatment is chosen based on the individual's clinical situation.

In all phases of the CATIE study flexible dosages of medicines are allowed within ranges that reflect usual care. All other medications, except for other antipsychotic drugs, are allowed unless there is a specific contraindication. The scheduled treatment period is 18 months so that some of the longer-term effects of the study treatments can be observed.

Comparison of Antipsychotic Drugs in First-Episode Schizophrenia

The European First-Episode Schizophrenia Trial (EUFEST) will enroll 600 persons with recent-onset schizophrenia at more than 50 sites in 15 European countries to compare the real-world effectiveness of antipsychotic drugs (Fleischhacker, 2004). The trial will randomly assign one of five antipsychotic drug treatments. The drug treatments are open-label and dosages are flexible. Exclusion criteria are minimal. The primary outcome, like that in CATIE, is retention on the assigned study medicine. Many relevant secondary outcomes will be measured. In an important extension of the practical clinical trial paradigm, a goal of EUFEST is to establish a cohort for naturalistic follow-up of five years. This means that even participants who are not retained on the randomly assigned antipsychotic drug will continue to

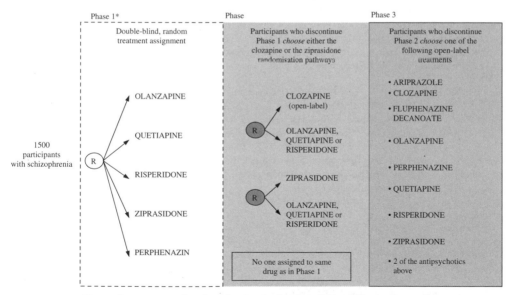

Responders stay on assigned medication for duration of 18-month treatment period

* Phase 1A: participants with tardive dyskinesia do not get randomised to perphenazine
  Phase 1B: participants who fail perphenazine will be randomised to an atypical (olanzapine, quetiapine, or risperidone) before they are eligible for Phase 2

Figure 18.1 CATIE Schizophrenia Trial design

contribute outcome data and that a great deal of information on the history of first-episode psychosis will be forthcoming.

CONCLUSIONS

Practical clinical trials are one important way to evaluate the effectiveness of treatments in real-world settings. The results of such randomised effectiveness trials can be invaluable to decision makers, but they do not provide definitive information about whether the intervention in question will improve practice or clinical outcomes (Essock *et al.*, 2003). Random assignment usefully removes selection biases from trials but does not mimic the way that interventions are assigned to patients in actual treatment settings. If clinicians are able to select good candidates for a new treatment, the beneficial effects may exceed what would be found in a randomised trial, where a new treatment that, for example, required extra effort from a patient would be at a disadvantage (Essock *et al.*, 2003).

In spite of the above-mentioned limitations, practical clinical trials are now an important source of evidence regarding the real-world effectiveness of psychotropic medications. Like other types of clinical trials, practical trials offer considerable design flexibility and can encompass a variety of methods to answer questions about a range of relevant outcomes. The results of recent and ongoing practical trials should yield crucial information to guide clinical and policy decision makers regarding treatment decisions and resource allocation.

REFERENCES

ALLHAT Officers and Coordinators for the ALLHAT Collaborative Research Group (2002). Major outcomes in high-risk hypertensive patients randomized to angiotensin-converting enzyme inhibitor or calcium channel blocker vs diuretic: the Antihypertensive and Lipid-Lowering Treatment to Prevent Heart Attack Trial (ALLHAT), *J. Am. Med. Ass.*, **288**(23), 2981–2997.

BALANCE (Bipolar, Affective Disorder: Lithium/ANti-Convulsant Evaluation) (2002). Study protocol dated 07/2002 available at www.psychiatry.ox.ac.uk/balance/.

Bauer, M.S., Williford, W.O., Dawson, E.E., Akiskal, H.S., Altshuler, L., Fye, C., Gelenberg, A., Glick, H., Kinosian, B. & Sajatovic, M. (2001). Principles of effectiveness trials and their implementation in VA Cooperative Study #430: 'Reducing the efficacy–effectiveness gap in bipolar disorder', *J. Affect. Disord.*, **67**(1–3), 61–78.

Csernansky, J.G., Mahmoud, R. & Brenner, R. for the Risperidone-USA-79 Study Group (2002). A comparison of risperidone and haloperidol for the prevention of relapse in patients with schizophrenia, *New Engl. J. Med.*, **346**, 16–22.

Essock, S.M., Hargreaves, W.A., Covell, N.H. & Goethe, J. (1996). Clozapine's effectiveness for patients in state hospitals: Results from a randomized trial, *Psychopharmacol. Bull.*, **32**(4), 683–697.

Essock, S.M., Frisman, L.K., Covell, N.H. & Hargreaves, W.A. (2000) Cost-effectiveness of clozapine compared with conventional antipsychotic medication for patients in state hospitals, *Arch. Gen. Psychiatry*, **57**, 987–994.

Essock, S.M., Drake, R.E., Frank, R.G. & McGuire, T.G. (2003). Randomized controlled trials in evidence-based mental health care: Getting the right answer to the right question, *Schizophrenia Bull.*, **29**(1), 115–123.

Fleischhacker, W.W. for the EUFEST Study Group (2004). The European first episode schizoprhenia trial (EUFEST), *World Psychiatry*, **3**(Suppl.1), 119.

Freedman, B. (1987). Equipoise and the ethics of clinical research, *New Engl. J. Med.*, **317**(3), 16 July, 141–145.

Geddes, J. & Goodwin, G. (2001). Bipolar disorder: Clinical uncertainty, evidence-based medicine and large-scale randomised trials, *Br. J. Psychiatry*, **178**(Suppl. 41), s191–s194.

Institute of Medicine (1985). *Assessing Medical Technologies*, National Academy Press, Washington, DC.

Meltzer, H.Y., Alphs, L., Green, A.I., Altamura, A.C., Anand, R., Bertoldi, A., Bourgeois, M., Chouinard, G., Islam, M.Z., Kane, J., Krishnan, R., Lindenmayer, J.P. & Potkin, S. for the International Suicide Prevention Trial Study Group (2003). Clozapine treatment for suicidality in schizophrenia: International Suicide Prevention Trial (InterSePT), *Arch. Gen. Psychiatry*, **60**(1), January, 82–91.

Moher, D., Schulz, K.F. & Altman, D. for the CONSORT Group (2001). The CONSORT statement: revised recommendations for improving the quality of reports of parallel-group randomized trials, *J. Am. Med. Ass.*, **285**, 1987–1991.

Moseley, J.B., O'Malley, K., Petersen, N.J., Menke, T.J., Brody, B.A., Kuykendall, D.H., Hollingsworth, J.C., Ashton, C.M. & Wray, N.P. (2002). A controlled trial of arthroscopic surgery for osteoarthritis of the knee, *New Engl. J. Med.*, **347**(2), 11 July, 81–88.

Peto, R. & Baigent, C. (1998). Trials: the next 50 years. Large scale randomised evidence of moderate benefits, *Br. Med. J.*, **317**, 1170–1171.

Peto, R., Collins, R. & Gray, R. (1995). Large-scale randomised evidence: Large, simple trials and overviews of trials, *J. Clin. Epidemiol.*, **48**, 23–40.

Robinson, D. & Schooler, N. (2001). Remission and demonstrating efficacy in clinical trials, Presented at the Annual Meeting of the American College of Neuropsychopharmacology, Waikoloa Village, Hawaii, December 2001.

Rosenheck, R., Cramer, J., Xu, W., Thomas, J., Henderson, W., Frisman, L., Fye, C. & Charney, D. (1997). A comparison of clozapine and haloperidol in hospitalized patients with refractory schizophrenia. Department of Veterans Affairs Cooperative Study Group on clozapine in refractory schizophrenia, *New Engl. J. Med.*, **337**(12), 18 September, 809–815.

Slawson, D.C., Shaughnessy, A.F. & Bennett, J.H. (1994). Becoming a medical information master: feeling good about not knowing everything, *J. Family Practice*, **38**(5), May, 505–513.

Stroup, T.S., McEvoy, J.P., Swartz, M.S., Byerly, M.J., Glick, I.D., Canive, J.M., McGee, M.F., Simpson, G.M., Stevens, M.C. & Lieberman, J.A. (2003). The NIMH-CATIE Project: Schizophrenia Trial Design and Protocol Development, *Schizophrenia Bull.*, **29**(1), 15–31.

Tunis, S.R., Stryer, D.B. & Clancy, C.M. (2003). Practical clinical trials: Increasing the value of clinical research for decision making in clinical and health policy, *J. Am. Med. Ass.*, **290**(12), 24 September, 1624–1632.

19

Psychotherapy and Quality of Life

Gerhard Lenz and Ulrike Demal

INTRODUCTION

In the last 20 years, the concept of quality of life (QoL) has gained importance in the assessment of therapeutic intervention in chronic diseases, e.g. cancer. Measurement of it is becoming increasingly relevant to controlled clinical trials (Guyatt *et al*., 1989). Though QoL is influenced by many factors other than health, health scientists are mainly interested in what is described as 'health-related' QoL.

Quality of life has both a subjective component (well-being, life satisfaction) and an objective one (functioning, social roles), as well as including external circumstances (e.g. standard of living). It is still a matter of discussion how much of each of these components should be included in QoL measurements. The usual criteria for QoL are strongly orientated to standard concepts of normal life without illness. However, illness may change people in different ways and there is great variation between patients in what they consider as priorities in their life, in what they want to achieve and in what can increase their life satisfaction. In his discussion of compliance problems, Linden (1981) focused on the necessity of evaluating both illness concepts and the patients' subjective values and goals, if therapeutic intervention of any type is to be applied appropriately.

Bullinger *et al*. (1993) have stressed the necessity of anthropological and sociological studies to identify cultural variations in the indicators used to define health and well-being, as well as peoples' expectations concerning physical and emotional functioning. International collaboration in medical research needs instruments that are applicable cross-culturally for the assessment of health-related quality of life (HRQL) in clinical trials.

PSYCHOTHERAPY RESEARCH LARGELY NEGLECTS QUALITY OF LIFE

The overarching goal of psychotherapy research is to understand the mechanisms through which such treatment operates and to assess the impact of moderating influences on both maladaptive and adaptive functioning (Akhtar and Samuel, 1995). Outcome-orientated research (Smith, Glass and Miller, 1980; Grawe, Donati and Bernauer, 1994) concerns itself with the scientific evaluation of the effectiveness of psychotherapy. Process-orientated psychotherapy research (Orlinsky, Grawe and Parks, 1994) investigates the extent to which outcome is determined by the interaction of patients' psychopathological characteristics and personality, on the one hand, and therapists' skills, personality and particularly their technique, on the other.

Quality of Life in Mental Disorders, Second Edition   Edited by H. Katschnig, H. Freeman and N. Sartorius
© 2006 John Wiley & Sons, Ltd

In psychotherapy research, much emphasis has been put on issues such as ethics, the nature of control groups, statistics, effectiveness and, in the case of outcome research, on method of treatment and diagnosis (APA Commission on Psychotherapies, 1982). In the measurement of therapeutic outcome, importance has predominantly been put on symptoms and personality factors, but less often on impairment in functioning or subjective distress. The concept of QoL seems to have been of no importance in major reviews of psychotherapy research (Luborsky, Singer and Luborsky, 1975; Smith, Glass and Miller, 1980; APA Commission on Psychotherapies, 1982; Baumann and Reinecker-Hecht, 1986; Bachrach et al., 1991; Bergin and Garfield, 1994; Grawe, Donati and Bernauer, 1994). Interestingly, the QoL of psychotherapists themselves was a matter of concern in one paper (Reimer, 1994), which focused on the lack of life satisfaction and health risks (alcoholism, suicide, marital problems) that seemed to be increased among doctors in general and psychotherapists in particular.

One of the most important reviews on outcome of psychotherapy is that by Grawe, Donati and Bernauer (1994), who reviewed 897 controlled studies of various psychotherapeutic treatments. Each study was evaluated with an extensive assessment instrument containing more than 1000 items in seven major areas: (1) general descriptive information about the study; (2) design and methodology; (3) the patients, therapists and therapy method; (4) validity; (5) measures of main symptoms, personality factors, interpersonal relations, leisure-time behaviour, job performance, sexual behaviour and psychophysiology; (6) evaluation; (7) results (effect size).

For client-centred psychotherapy (mainly for patients with neurotic disorders) significant effects of therapy could be observed on main symptoms and mood. Improvements were also reported in the area of personality and in interpersonal relations (especially in those who had out-patient treatment in groups). The effects of psychotherapy on leisure-time activity were only investigated in one study, in which there was a positive result; effects on job performance were not investigated. Effects on sexual behaviour were investigated in one study, but proved to be without influence. In none of the cited studies were specific instruments used for assessment of QoL. Grawe, Donati and Bernauer (1994) also reported that for psychoanalytic-orientated psychotherapy and short-term psychoanalytic therapies, improvement was found in symptoms, but there was less so in the areas of personality or interpersonal relationships. Job performance was evaluated in one study and improvement was reported.

The methods of weighting in the meta-analytic approach of Grawe, Donati and Bernauer (1994) have been criticised mainly by psychoanalysts (Tschuschke, Kächele and Hölzer, 1994). Bachrach et al. (1991) reviewed findings by psychoanalysts on the efficacy of psychoanalysis: these studies varied in meeting outcome research criteria, but QoL was not used in any of them. The concept of 'quality of life' has mainly been seen as a slogan by psychoanalysts (Hau, 1977). Although some aspects of life satisfaction (wishes for instinctual satisfaction and for protection, acceptance and love) have been seen as very important, they were not primary targets of the outcome measures.

In contrast to psychoanalytic treatment studies, those on cognitive and behavioural treatment are more orientated to the assessment of objective psychosocial functioning and subjective well-being. Again, though, assessments are not carried out with specific instruments for QoL.

In their review of 74 studies on assertiveness-training, Grawe, Donati and Bernauer (1994) report effects of therapy not only on assertiveness but also on interpersonal relations, personality and general well-being. In 62 studies on confrontation therapy (mostly for phobic and obsessive–compulsive patients), the same authors found a significant reduction in symptoms in 90% of patients who had gradual in vivo confrontation. There was also improvement in subjective well-being in 50%, in interpersonal relationships in 30%, as well as improvement in job performance (37.5%) and leisure-time activity (50% reduction of avoidance behaviour). No improvement was found in sexual behaviour or personality factors.

Cognitive therapy (Beck et al., 1979) was initially developed for the treatment of depressive patients and later for anxiety disorders and a wide variety of other conditions, including personality disorder. Grawe, Donati and Bernauer (1994) list 16 studies which reported impressive efficacy, not only on main symptoms but also in the areas of interpersonal relations, personality and leisure-time activity. The National Institute of Mental Health (NIMH) Treatment of Depression Collaborative Research Program (Elkin et al., 1989; Shea et al., 1992) was the first coordinated multisite study initiated by the US NIMH in the field of psychotherapy research. The treatment phase consisted of 16 weeks of randomly assigned treatment with either: (a) cognitive behavioural therapy (CBT), (b) interpersonal therapy (IPT), (c) imipramine plus clinical management or (d) placebo plus clinical management. Follow-up assessments were carried out 6, 12 and 18 months after treatment. Of all patients entering treatment for which there were follow-up data, the proportion who recovered and remained well during follow-up (no relapse of major depressive disorder) did not differ significantly among the four treatments. In cross-sectional analyses of social functioning for the total sample, no significant differences were found among any of the treatment conditions at 6 or 12 months. At 18 months, IPT was significantly superior to imipramine plus clinical management; it differed at a trend level from CBT in global social functioning, but not significantly from placebo plus clinical management. Although some instruments in this study measured aspects of QoL, no specific ones for its assessment were used. Interpersonal therapy, amitryptiline and the combination of both were investigated in an acute treatment study by Weissman *et al.* (1979). IPT proved to be highly effective, especially in combination with the drug. In their one-year follow-up, Weissman *et al.* (1981) found no difference for IPT on clinical symptoms of depression, but it did have a main effect on measures of social functioning.

For marital therapy, Grawe, Donati and Bernauer (1994) list 35 controlled studies. In 29 of these, behavioural marital therapy (BMT) was applied, mainly for marital problems, sexual problems or depression of one partner. In many studies, measurements were only on the main problems or symptoms, but in some they were also on relationships, general well-being, personality or job performance. These studies show an impressive effect of BMT, with significant improvement in the main problems; however, in two-thirds of the measurements, positive effects of the therapy could also be found in other areas (interpersonal relationships, sexual relationship, job performance). Improvement in general well-being only occurred when treatment was given for other than marital problems.

THE EFFECTS OF PSYCHOTHERAPY ON QUALITY OF LIFE IN PATIENTS WITH PSYCHIATRIC DISORDER

Several studies have examined the relationship between QoL and psychotherapy more specifically.

Uncontrolled Studies

In a mainly retrospective investigation of 74 patients with neurotic disorder diagnosed by ICD-9 (WHO, 1978) (anxiety disorder $N = 34$, conversion disorder $N = 9$, obsessive–compulsive disorder $N = 6$, neurotic depression $N = 14$, other $N = 11$), the effects of in-patient behaviour therapy were studied one year after discharge from hospital (Holub, 1990). One area studied was QoL, measured by the scale devised by Plog (1976), with subscales on housing, leisure time, social contacts, job and general satisfaction with treatment. About half of the patients were satisfied in most areas of QoL; the dissatisfaction reported by about 40% was mainly with close relationships and use of leisure time. However, these two areas improved markedly after treatment and scores remained stable at follow-up after one year. Significant correlations were found between successful treatment on a symptomatic level and the following subscales of QoL: general satisfaction with living situation ($p < 0.01$), use of leisure time ($p < 0.01$) and social contacts ($p < 0.01$).

Another investigation (Rubin *et al.*, 1995) measured the QoL in panic disorder patients. Using HRQL ratings (quality of well-being, or QWB), it was found that subjects with panic disorder had suffered a significant decrease in HRQL compared to 'healthy' controls. The disability in panic disorder approached that of illnesses like non-insulin-dependent diabetes. With cognitive behavioural treatment (CBT), the QoL in patients with panic disorder demonstrated delayed but sustained improvement, reaching levels that did not differ from controls.

Demal *et al.* (1996) assessed QoL using the Longitudinal Interval Follow-Up Evaluation (LIFE) (Keller *et al.*, 1987), in a sample of 74 patients with obsessive–compulsive disorder (OCD) treated with CBT and a serotonin reuptake inhibitor. Patients were investigated three times: on the day of admission (baseline), 6 months later (follow-up I) and 12 months after follow-up I (follow-up II). The semi-structured interview format covered the following areas of psychosocial functioning: work, interpersonal relationships with family and friends, sex and recreation. A global social adjustment score (GSA-LIFE) was given, which represented an overall rating. At admission, 18% of the patients showed slight and 82% marked impairment in psychosocial functioning (GSA-LIFE). At follow-up I, after discontinuation of controlled treatment, improvement was evident in symptoms, as well as in psychosocial functioning (14%, no psychosocial impairment; 44%, slight impairment; 42%, marked impairment). A further improvement was observed at follow-up II, where 40% of patients showed no impairment, 30% were slightly impaired and 30% markedly impaired. Of the 40% 'best functioning' patients none had clinical OCD according to the Yale–Brown Obsessive–Compulsive Scale (Goodman *et al.*, 1989). In summary, 44% of the patients showed a significant improvement in QoL (GSA-LIFE), as well as in symptoms, from the baseline to follow-up II.

In another study on patients with panic disorder and agoraphobia, Scheibe *et al.* (1993) found that one-year supportive group psychotherapy improved not only symptoms but also psychosocial functioning (partner relationship, sex, social adjustment) assessed with LIFE and overall satisfaction with life assessed with GSA-LIFE.

In the study of Lenz and Demal (2000), 37 patients with depression or anxiety disorder, who participated in an intensive in-patient cognitive behaviour therapy (CBT) programme for 6 weeks, were interviewed before treatment and 6 weeks after the end of treatment. In addition to other measures, QoL was assessed with the Berlin Quality of Life Profile (Priebe *et al.*, 1995). A substantial reduction in subjective QoL, objective functioning and environmental assets was found at the baseline. At follow-up, according to a clinical global impression, 13.5% of the patients were very much improved and 45.9% much improved; in 26.3%, only slight improvement and in 16.2% no improvement was reported. Quality of life changed for the better in areas like work and education, leisure, housing, social relations, psychological well-being and a global rating of satisfaction with life, but not in marital relations, health in general and finances.

The study of Karterud *et al.* (2003) sought to investigate whether time-limited day treatment programmes for patients with personality disorder (PD) are effective outside well-resourced university settings. All patients ($N = 1244$) who were consecutively admitted to eight different treatment programmes in the Norwegian Network of Psychotherapeutic Day Hospitals from 1993 to 2000 were included in the study. The most common conditions were avoidant, borderline, not otherwise specified (NOS), and paranoid PD. The treatment programmes were based on group therapies and typically consisted of a mixture of psychodynamic and cognitive–behavioural techniques. The treatment followed principles that are considered in contemporary psychiatry as appropriate therapy for patients with PD: (a) an empathic stance; (b) focus on self-experience, affects, self-object failures, interpersonal transactions, cognitive awareness and cognitive assumptions; (c) encouraging problem solving; (d) cognitive behavioural therapy for anxiety symptoms; and (e) pharmacotherapy. The duration of treatment ranged from 8 to 16.5 hours per week and the length of treatment was about 18 weeks, except for one unit, which allowed a longer period (mean of 41 weeks). The goals of the treatment were better psychosocial functioning, reduction of self-destructive behaviour, reduction of symptom distress and interpersonal problems, and enhancement of QoL. Quality of life was measured as a self-report on a scale from 1 to 10 (low to high).

SCID II (Structured Clinical Interview for DSM-II) and MINI (Mini International Neuropsychiatric Interview) were used as diagnostic instruments. Outcome measures included GAF (Global Assessment of Functioning), SCL-90R, CIP (circumplex of interpersonal problems), QoL, work functioning and parasuicidal behaviour, measured at admittance, discharge and 1-year follow-up. As a group, completers with PD improved significantly on all outcome variables from admission to discharge and improvement was maintained or increased at follow-up. Treatment results were best for borderline PD and cluster C patients. Among borderline PD patients, results were good for the completers with respect to global functioning, symptoms distress, interpersonal problems, QoL and self-destructive behaviour, but not for work functioning.

Controlled Studies

De Jonghe *et al.* (2001) compared the efficacy of antidepressants with that of antidepressants plus psychotherapy (combined therapy) in the treatment of depression in 167 patients in a 6-month randomised trial. QoL was measured with the Quality of Life Depression Scale (QLDS). In general, patients found combined treatment significantly more acceptable, were significantly less likely to drop out from it and, ultimately, were significantly more likely to recover. The results also indicated a better QoL in the combined therapy group (see Table 19.1).

Ravindran *et al.* (1999) assessed the efficacy of antidepressant treatment (sertraline) and group CBT, alone or in combination, in patients with primary dysthymia ($N=97$). Patients received either sertraline or placebo in a double-blind design over 12 weeks; in addition, a subgroup ($N=49$) received a structured, weekly group CBT intervention. Both the clinical features of dysthymia and functional impairments associated with the illness (e.g. QoL, stress perception, coping styles) were evaluated. QoL was assessed with the Battelle Quality of Life Scale. This scale is divided into several dimensions including health perception, bed disability days, energy/vitality, cognitive functioning, alertness, work behaviour, home management, social interaction and life satisfaction. Among the patients who responded to drug treatment, the QoL scores were superior to those of non-responders and approached those of non-depressed control subjects. Life satisfaction, social interaction and energy scores among responders to CBT were also considerably greater than those of placebo responders, as well as those of non-responders to CBT. In contrast, among placebo responders, these QoL scores were not improved relative to those of non-responders.

The study of Volpato Cordioli *et al.* (2003) was designed to verify the efficacy of cognitive–behavioural group therapy (CBGT) in reducing obsessive–compulsive symptoms and the intensity of overvalued ideas, as well as improving the patient's QoL. Forty-seven patients meeting DSM-IV criteria for OCD were randomly assigned to either 12 weekly CBGT sessions or a waiting list (control group). Treated patients were followed up for three months. There was a significant reduction in scores on the Yale–Brown Obsessive–Compulsive Scale ($p<0.001$), in the National Institute of Mental Health Obsessive–Compulsive Scale ($p<0.001$), in the Overvalued Ideas Scale ($p<0.001$) and a significant improvement in the QoL in the four domains of the World Health Organization Quality of Life Assessment Scale: physical ($p<0.001$), psychological ($p<0.017$), social ($p<0.018$) and environmental ($p<0.04$). The concomitant use of anti-obsessional medications did not influence the results. The therapeutic gains were maintained and an additional reduction in symptoms was observed during a 3-month follow-up period.

In the study of Guthrie *et al.* (1999), 110 subjects with non-psychotic disorders unresponsive to 6 months of routine specialist mental health treatment were enrolled in a randomised controlled trial. Intervention patients received 8 weekly sessions of psychodynamic–interpersonal psychotherapy, while control patients received usual care from their psychiatrist. QoL was assessed with the EuroQoL 5D (The EuroQoL Group, 1990). This questionnaire is a standard generic instrument for measuring HRQL. It consists of five health domains: mobility, self-care, ability to undertake usual activities, pain and discomfort and anxiety and depression. Subjects randomised to psychotherapy showed a significantly greater improvement than controls in terms of psychological distress and social functioning, 6 months after the trial. Changes in other domains of health status and QoL, however, were much less marked and the study was too small to explore the effects of psychotherapy on QALMs (Quality-Adjusted Life Months).

In a study by Kingsep, Nathan and Castle (2003), 33 individuals with schizophrenia and comorbid social anxiety were allocated to a group-based cognitive–behavioural (CBGT) intervention or waiting list control (WLC). All outcome measures, including the QoL Enjoyment and Satisfaction Questionnaire (Q-LES-Q), displayed statistical improvement in the intervention group compared with no change in the control group. Treatment effects were maintained at a 2-month follow-up.

In the study of Glynn *et al.* (2002), 63 individuals with schizophrenia were randomly assigned to 60 weeks of clinic-based skills training alone or of clinic-based skills training supplemented with generalisation sessions in the community, using an instruction manual. The primary outcome measures were the Social Adjustment Scale (SAS) II and the Quality of Life Scale (QLS) (Heinrichs, Hanlon and Carpenter, 1984). The QLS is a 21-item instrument designed to assess the deficit syndrome concept in individuals with schizophrenia. It examines four domains: interpersonal functioning, instrumental role functioning, intrapsychic factors and possession of common objects/participation in common activities. The QLS was administered at the baseline and then every 12 weeks up to week 60. The pattern of QoL scores suggested that subjects who participated in clinic-based plus *in vivo* amplified skills training improved more quickly and often to higher levels than those receiving clinic-based skills training alone, across the 60 weeks.

Table 19.1 Controlled studies of QoL in psychiatric disorder

Study (year)	Patients	Treatment	Control group	Follow-up	Outcome QoL	Instruments assessing QoL
Ravindran et al. (1999)	Dysthymia $N = 97$	Sertraline and CBT group therapy alone or in combination	Placebo	12 weeks	QoL ↑ in drug responders and in CBT responders	Battelle QoL Scale
De Jonghe et al. (2001)	Depression $N = 167$	Antidepressants plus psychotherapy	Antidepressants alone	6 months	Better QoL in the combined therapy group	Quality of Life Depression Scale (QLDS)
Guthrie et al. (1999)	Unresponsive non-psychotic disorder $N = 110$	Psychodynamic–interpersonal psychotherapy	Usual psychiatric care	6 months	No significant change	EuroQoL
Volpato Cordioli et al. (2003)	OCD $N = 47$	CBT group therapy	Waiting list	12 weeks	QoL ↑	WHO-QoL-BREV
Kingsep, Nathan and Castle (2003)	33 patients with schizophrenia and comorbid social anxiety	Group-based CBT	Waiting list control	2 months	For CBT QoL significantly better than for control group	Quality of Life, Enjoyment and Satisfaction Questionnaire (QLESQ)
Glynn et al. (2002)	63 patients with schizophrenia	Clinic-based skills training supplemented with manual-based generalisation sessions in the community	Clinic-based skills training alone	60 weeks	Improvement of QoL in intervention group more quickly and to higher levels	Quality of Life Scale (QLS)
Spector et al. (2003)	201 people with dementia	CST	'Usual activities'	7 weeks	QoL ↑ in the intervention group	Quality of Life – Alzheimer's Disease Scales

In a randomised controlled trial Spector *et al.* (2003) recruited 201 older people with dementia to test the hypothesis that cognitive stimulation therapy (CST) would benefit cognition and QoL. QoL was measured with the Quality of Life–Alzheimer's Disease Scale (QoL-AD) (Longsdon *et al.*, 1999). This brief, self-report questionnaire has 13 items covering the domains of physical health, energy, mood, living situation, memory, family, marriage, friends, chores, fun, money, self and life as a whole. At follow-up, the intervention group had significantly improved, relative to the control group, on the Mini Mental State Examination, the Alzheimer's Disease Assessment Scale – Cognition (ADAS-Cog) and the Quality of Life–Alzheimer's Disease Scales (QoL-AD).

PSYCHOSOCIAL INTERVENTIONS FOR CANCER PATIENTS

The effect of psychological therapy on the psychosocial adjustment of cancer patients has been evaluated in several systematic studies, but reported results are difficult to interpret, in view of methodological deficiencies. One problem in comparing different studies is the lack of a comprehensive definition of 'quality of life'. In cancer care this concept encompasses a broad spectrum of issues, including physical, social, cognitive, spiritual, emotional and role functioning, as well as psychological symptomatology, pain and other common physical symptoms. Another problem is that different scales and ratings have been used for assessing QoL. Some authors have reported on the effects of 'psychotherapy' or 'counselling' without describing the treatment more specifically, yet full descriptions are required to allow psychotherapy trials to be replicated and valid conclusions to be drawn.

A review of the literature shows that psychosocial interventions are generally applied: (a) to decrease feelings of alienation by talking to others; (b) to reduce anxiety about the treatments; (c) to assist in clarifying misperceptions; and (d) to lessen feelings of isolation, helplessness and being neglected by others. These interventions have the added benefit of encouraging more responsibility to get well and enhancing compliance with medical regimes. Another goal of intervention is improving psychosocial adjustment and the ability to carry out daily activities.

This discussion will focus particularly on those studies where QoL was actually measured. Cunningham (1995) suggested a classification of interventions ordered from low to high in terms of active patient involvement: (a) education programmes providing medical or procedural information; (b) social support, referring to professionally guided support groups; (c) coping skills training, consisting of cognitive, cognitive–behavioural or behavioural methods supposed to modify cognitions or behaviour, as well as techniques such as progressive muscle relaxation, systematic desensitisation, biofeedback or reinforcement schedules; and (d) psychotherapeutic interventions including different kinds of psychotherapy and counselling, such as psychodynamic, existential or supportive therapeutic approaches and crisis intervention.

Regarding the assessment of QoL, different instruments are used. These can focus either on emotional (e.g. Profile of Mood States; McNair, Lorr and Drappelmann, 1971) or on functional adjustment (e.g. Functional Living Index for Cancer, or FLIC; Schipper *et al.*, 1984). QoL instruments can either be classified as global (e.g. Psychological General Well-Being Index; DuPuy, 1984) or disease-specific (e.g. EORTC Quality of Life Questionnaire; Aaronson, Bullinger and Ahmedzai, 1988). They can be either self-reports (e.g. Psychological Adjustment to Illness Scale, or PAIS; Morrow, Chiarello and Derogatis, 1978) or rated by a clinician or observer (e.g. Karnofsky Performance Status Scale; Karnovsky and Burchenal, 1949). Finally, QoL can either be conceptualised as a more stable trait condition (e.g. Cancer Inventory of Problem Situations, or CIPS; Schag, Heinrich and Ganz, 1983) or as a short-term state (e.g. Affect Balance Scale; Bradburn, 1969).

The Karnovsky Performance Status Scale (KPS) (Karnovsky and Burchenal, 1949), as Clark and Fallowfield (1986) point out, is almost invariably used when assessment of QoL is actually made, but its frequency of usage is no indication of appropriateness. This scale, while useful as a measure of health performance status, is not a satisfactory estimation of QoL. Ratings from 0 to 100 are made by the clinician, 100 being normal with no evidence of disease and 0 being the terminal point of the scale, i.e. dead. There are several problems with this method, in particular the assumption that a patient with a low score due to immobility necessarily has a poorer QoL than a patient with a higher score and vice versa. To give an example, an incontinent, wheelchair-bound cancer patient might achieve only 40 on the scale, despite the fact that this patient might have a good social support and experience rich and happy relationships. A breast cancer patient with a score of possibly 80 might, on the other hand, be emotionally crippled by depression, which the scale does not attempt to address. Yet the concomitant loss of libido and self-esteem would give her an extremely poor QoL. Another major criticism is that the scale takes no account of pre-treatment levels of activity. This is potentially serious when comparing the effects of similar biological disease burdens in active, working extroverts with those in more passive, previously housebound patients.

The FLIC (Schipper et al., 1984) measures the quality of cancer patients' day-to-day functioning, including physical and psychological aspects as well as familial and social relations. It contains 22 items, each scored on a 7-point Likert scale. Considerable construct validity data have been published (Schipper et al., 1984), but there is no information on the reliability of the measure. A major criticism is that the FLIC only allows a total score, which incorporates both psychological and physical factors.

The QL Index (Spitzer, Dobson and Hall 1981) was specifically developed for use by doctors to measure QoL in cancer patients. It is quick to complete (one minute on average) and simple to score, administer and analyse. The QL index covers a comprehensive range of QoL dimensions. Five items – activity, living, health, support and outlook on life – are rated on a 3-point scale from 0 to 2, giving a maximum score of 10. The test has a high inter-rater correlation and good correlations between self-rating of patients and those of their doctors. Like all QoL scales, it has some limitations, e.g. giving equal weighting to all items contained in the index.

The PAIS (Morrow, Chiarello and Derogatis, 1978) examines a patient's global adjustment to illness with 45 questions in seven principal psychosocial domains (health care, vocational environment, domestic environment, sexual relationships, extended family relationships, social environment and psychological distress). Ratings for each question within each domain are made on a 4-point (0–3) scale; these generate a PAIS total score, which is a composite score of subjective well-being and objective disability and thus mixes subjective and objective aspects of QoL.

Another scale used is the CIPS (Heinrich, Schag and Ganz, 1984). It is self-administered, requires approximately 20 minutes to complete and consists of 141 problem statements grouped into 21 categories, which are then subdivided under four main headings (personal care, medical situation, interpersonal interactions, miscellaneous). The patient indicates on a 5-point scale, ranging from 'not at all' to 'very much', how much of a problem each statement has been in the preceding month. The instrument appears to be more sensitive than a semi-structured interview, but there are two main criticisms of the test: that no normative data exist yet and that it has only been validated on a small sample. However, the CIPS might be a useful instrument for assessing the psychosocial and physical impact of treatment programmes, with a view to tailoring therapy to cause minimal distress (see Table 19.2).

The results of the study of Lyles et al. (1982) suggest that progressive muscular relaxation and guided imagery can be an effective adjunctive procedure for reducing the side-effects experienced by many cancer chemotherapy patients. Moreover, the relaxation procedure not only helped patients to function better in the clinic during chemotherapy treatment but also at home during the days following these. It was clear from the home record forms and from communication with the patients that those practising progressive muscular relaxation daily 'improved substantially in QoL'; i.e. they had less functional impairment at home.

Gruber et al. (1988) studied the effect of behavioural training on the immune system. Over a period of one year, subjects who had no prior experience with either technique used imagery and relaxation. In addition to several elevated measures of immune system functioning, patients showed improvement in psychosocial functioning.

In the study of Linn, Linn and Harris (1982) counselling was found to be effective in reducing denial but maintaining hope, encouraging patients to participate in meaningful activities, helping them to complete any unfinished business and providing increased self-esteem and life satisfaction. While it was not possible to improve physical functioning or survival in these patients, counselling interventions 'helped to enhance QoL'.

Cella et al. (1993) found significant improvement in QoL, assessed with the FLIC, after an eight-week support group. This group was modelled on principles of wellness in the context of life-threatening illness (Cella, 1990) and the group dynamics related to mutual and peer support.

Table 19.2 Psychosocial interventions and QoL in cancer patients

Study (year)	Patients	Treatment	Control group	Follow-up	Outcome QoL	Instruments assessing QoL
Lyles et al. (1982)	50, mixed cancer	(1) Relaxation guided imagery (2) Talking	No treatment	75 days	QoL ↑	Simple questions about functional impairment at home
Gruber et al. (1988)	10, metastatic cancer	Behavioural training on immune system (relaxation and guided imagery)	–	1 year	QoL ↑	Information from nurses about functional impairment, Karnovsky Performance Status Scale (KPS)
Linn, Linn and Harris (1982)	120, late-stage cancer	Individual counselling	No treatment	1 year	Life satisfaction ↑ QoL ↑	Questions regarding 'life satisfaction', 'social isolation', nurse-rated functional status for daily activities
Cella et al. (1993)	77, mixed cancer	8-week support group	–	8 weeks	QoL ↑	Self report, Functional Living Index in Cancer (FLIC)
Heinrich and Schag (1985)	51, mixed cancer	Stress and activity management group treatment programme (relaxation, cognitive therapy, problem solving, activity management)	Current available care	8 weeks	QoL ↑	6-point scale from 'terrible' to 'excellent', Karnovsky Performance Status Scale (KPS), Psychological Adjustment to Illness Scale (PAIS)
Berglund et al. (1994)	199, mixed cancer	11 structured 2-hour group sessions (physical training, coping skills, information)	No treatment	12 weeks	QoL ↑	Quality of Life Index, Cancer Inventory of Problem Situations (CIPS)
Cunningham, Lockwood and Edmonds (1993)	402, mixed cancer	7 weekly 2-hour sessions (relaxation, mental imagery, discussion, role modelling, emotional ventilation)	–	5 months	QoL ↑	Functional Living Index in Cancer (FLIC)
Edmonds, Lockwood and Cunningham (1999)	66, breast cancer	(1) 35 weekly group sessions (2) 20-week course, cognitive behavioural assignments (3) intensive weekend coping skills training (14 h)	Standard care workbook	4, 8, 14 months	No significant difference between control and intervention group, no improvement in QoL	POMS POMS-SF FLIC
Walker et al. (1999)	96, breast cancer	Relaxation and guided imagery	Standard care	15 weeks	QoL ↑	GQoL (global self rating: Lickert scale from very good to very poor)
Trask et al. (2003)	48, melanoma	Cognitive behaviour intervention (CBI), 4 sessions	Standard care	2 months 6 months	HRQL ↑ HRQL ↑	Questions regarding HRQL

The authors point out that the improvement in overall FLIC scores resulted from changes in its psychological rather than its physical items; i.e. improvement in QoL was primarily in social and emotional dimensions.

Heinrich and Schag (1985) studied the effects of a six-week, structured small group programme. The major components of the group treatment were: education and information (concerning cancer, cancer therapy, the psychosocial impact of cancer, stress and adaptive coping), relaxation exercises, cognitive therapy, problem-solving training and activity management. The latter included a walking exercise component, as well as a contract in order to increase positively valued individual and couple activities. Improvement was found in the treatment group in respect of psychosocial adjustment (PAIS).

Berglund *et al.* (1994) undertook a study with 98 cancer patients who took part in a rehabilitation programme, while 101 patients served as controls. The intervention consisted of 11 structured two-hour group sessions. Physical training, coping skills and information were the primary goals of the programme. Subjects in the experimental group improved significantly in physical training, 'fighting spirit', information, psychosocial functioning and satisfaction with life.

Cunningham, Lockwood and Edmunds (1993) investigated the effect of a brief group programme in coping skills. Subgroups based on religious status, gender, educational level, marital status and previous experience with psychological self-help techniques did not vary significantly, but the overall programme increased coping skills and enhanced psychosocial functioning. It appeared to benefit younger patients somewhat more than older ones. Improvements in quality of physical, psychological, familial and social life were evidenced by the FLIC scores and patients' sense of self-efficacy was also increased.

Edmonds, Lockwood and Cunningham (1999) investigated the effects of long-term group therapy in 66 metastatic breast cancer patients. The intervention consisted of three components: 35 weekly sessions of group meetings which lasted two hours (mutual support, problem-solving, facing the likelihood of one's own death, etc.), a 20-week course of standard cognitive behavioural assignments (monitoring thoughts and behaviour, introducing substitute thoughts and behaviours, exploring resistance to change, developing a more balanced lifestyle) and an intensive weekend coping skills training course (14 hours) during the first 2–4 months of group membership (relaxation, mental imagery, positive affirmations, goal setting). Assessments were at 4, 8 and 14 months. Both control and intervention subjects were also given verbal information and pamphlets on coping with cancer. The control subjects received standard care at the hospital, a workbook and two audiotapes for home practice. Control subjects received telephone calls from the study coordinator at 2, 4, 6, 10 and 12 months in order to maintain compliance in completing the questionnaires. The psychometric results of this clinical trial showed little difference between the control ($N = 36$) and intervention group ($N = 30$). There were no improvements in mood or QoL. It was pointed out that long-term interventions are different in their effects from short-term interventions since, for example, the level of commitment required for a long-term intervention is much greater, both in terms of time and emotional investment.

Another problem is that psychometric tests may fail to pick up important clinical information and clinical impressions. It would be useful to know how sensitive the instruments are to reactions that are observed clinically.

Walker *et al.* (1999) studied the psychological, clinical and pathological effects of relaxation training and guided imagery during primary chemotherapy in breast cancer patients. The 96 patients were randomised to standard care (control group) or to standard care plus relaxation training and guided imagery. In the intervention group, patients were taught both progressive muscular and cue-controlled relaxation. During chemotherapy, patients receiving the psychological intervention were found to have higher GQOL (global quality of life) scores than those in the control group; moreover, the GQOL scores deteriorated significantly during chemotherapy. Therefore the intervention was shown to have beneficial psychological effects: women were more relaxed and easy going, had fewer psychological symptoms and had a higher self-rated QoL during chemotherapy.

Trask *et al.* (2003) compared the impact of cognitive–behavioural intervention (CBI) and standard medical care on distress and HRQL in patients with melanoma. The four sessions of CBI significantly reduced distress and improved HRQL for a period of two months in patients with

Table 19.3   Studies with significant effect (studies with no significant effect)

Intervention type	Compliance	Coping	Affect	QoL	Knowledge
Education/information (5 studies)	1 (4)	1 (4)	4 (1)	– (5)	2 (3)
Behaviour therapy (10 studies)	– (10)	10 (–)	6 (4)	4 (6)	– (10)
Single therapy (13 studies)	– (13)	10 (3)	9 (4)	1 (12)	1 (12)
Group therapy (28 studies)	1 (27)	19 (9)	19 (9)	6 (22)	5 (23)

Translated from Tschuschke, 2003.

melanoma who had medium to high distress, with improved general health evident six months after the intervention.

Cancer patients may benefit from a variety of psychological interventions. Tschuschke (2003) summarises the benefits of psychosocial interventions comparing four intervention types (Table 19.3).

A meta-analysis of 37 controlled outcome studies published between 1970 and July 1999 in English or German focused on the effects of psychosocial interventions on QoL in adult cancer patients (Rehse and Pukrop, 2003). QoL instruments were classified as emotional versus functional, global versus specific, self-report versus observer rating and trait versus state. Psychosocial interventions were classified according to Cunningham, 1995 (see page 237). The duration of intervention was documented both as a continuous and a dichotomised variable. The latter separated short-term (<12 weeks) from long term (>12 weeks) treatment. The overall hypothesis that psychosocial interventions reveal a positive impact on QoL in adult cancer patients was clearly confirmed. The intervention type of educational programmes was more effective (effect size: 0.43) than the other three types. There were no significant differences between the effects of social support (effect size: 0.28), coping skills training (effect size: 0.24) and psychotherapy (effect size: 0.28). This result is inconsistent with single intervention studies, but supports the result from Frischen-schlager, Brömmel and Russinger (1992), who found the highest treatment success rates with structured short-term educational programmes. The observed overall effect size was 0.31 ($d = 0.65$), which could be considered moderate, but this size was moderated by several confounding factors. The duration of intervention emerged as the most important moderating variable, suggesting that psychosocial interventions should be planned for at least 12 weeks. Psychosocial interventions seemed to be more profitable for men than for women or mixed samples. Self-report measures and scales that refer to stable and functional features appeared to be more adaquate than expert ratings and scales that refer to states of shorter duration such as emotional adjustment. It was shown that the patient him/herself is the most relevant person to evaluate his/her QoL. Overall, the results clearly confirmed that psychosocial interventions have a positive impact on QoL in cancer patients.

Most reviews have concluded that psychosocial interventions are efficacious in improving QoL in cancer patients (Fawzy, 1999; Schneiderman *et al.*, 2001; Newell, Sanson-Fisher and Savolainen, 2002). Interventions themselves usually assume one of four common forms: psycho-education, cognitive–behavioural training (group or individual), group supportive therapy or individual supportive therapy. Certain modalities of treatment have been shown to be more effica-cious at one or more points of the illness trajectory. For instance, psychoeducation may be most effective during the diagnosis/pre-treatment time period, when patient information needs are high, but for a later stage adjustment with a more advanced disease, group support may be more effective (Blake-Mortimer *et al.*, 1999). Cognitive–behavioural techniques such as relaxation, stress management and cognitive coping may be most useful during extended treatments (Bottomley, 1997). Thus, interventions to treat distress and improve QoL in cancer patients are widely available, highly effective and standardised.

CONCLUSIONS

The concept of QoL has been well known for a long time in the social sciences when they focus on people's life satisfaction (Bullinger, 1994). In medicine, however, the concept of 'health-related quality of life' is more orientated towards subjective functioning in a somatic, psychological and social perspective (according to the World Health Organization definition of health). In psychotherapy research and treatment, this subjective view of the patient will be of increasing importance in the assessment of the outcome of treatment. Several limitations of this approach, however, have to be taken into account. Thus, on the one hand, subjective well-being will increase during successful psychotherapy (relief from symptoms, reduction of avoidance behaviour, increase in social functioning, leisure-time activities and general well-being, etc.). On the other hand, the increased reality orientation might also reduce subjective well-being, at least in the short term. Patients entering psychotherapy are often unaware of problems, e.g. regarding their marital relationship and during treatment they may discover a variety of difficulties that may decrease their subjective well-being for some time. In addition, many 'objective criteria' in QoL instruments are questionable. The significance of rates of return to work is uncertain, e.g. for those of late middle age at a time when unemployment is high and when early retirement is possible and increasingly attractive. In the case of a patient who moves out of his parents' luxurious apartment to become independent and self-reliant, psychotherapy might be considered successful, although the QoL in terms of housing will decline. Living alone can be considered a success after termination of an unhappy relationship, but also a failure because of difficulties in maintaining contacts with other people. Poor QoL, independent of a psychiatric disorder, e.g. unemployment due to the economic situation, may increase psychological problems and in this case psychotherapy cannot increase QoL.

In some disorders, e.g. depression, QoL and depressive symptoms can hardly be separated, making it difficult to assess QoL. Some newly developed QoL instruments for depression, e.g. the quality of life in Depression Scale (QLDS) (Hunt and McKenna, 1992a, 1992b), mix up QoL and the subjective assessment of symptomatology. Advances have been made in developing assessment devices for QoL that might be integrated in the evaluation of clinical improvement (Frisch *et al.*, 1992).

Despite these difficulties and although theories of QoL have not so far been very conclusive, psychotherapy research can no longer neglect the concept. Both health economic factors and the cost-effectiveness of treatment are important in discussions about the financial coverage of psychotherapy in many countries. The usual assessments of symptoms and personality factors no longer seem to be enough for the evaluation of health, while subjective well-being and objective components of QoL have also to be taken into account.

REFERENCES

Aaronson, N.K., Bullinger, M. & Ahmedzai, S. (1988). A modular approach to quality of life assessment in cancer trials, in *Cancer Clinical Trials: A Critical Appraisal* (Eds H. Scheurlen, R. Kay & M. Baum), pp. 231–249, Springer, Berlin.

Akhtar, S. & Samuel, S. (1995). Between the past and the future of psychotherapy research, *Arch. Gen. Psychiatry*, **52**, 642–644.

APA Commission on Psychotherapies (1982). *Psychotherapy Research. Methodological and Efficacy Issues*, American Psychiatric Association Press, Washington, DC.

Bachrach, H.M., Galatzer-Levy, R., Skolnikoff, A. & Waldron Jr, S. (1991). On the efficacy of psychoanalysis, *J. Am. Psychoanalyt. Ass.*, **39**, 871–916.

Baumann, U. & Reinecker-Hecht, C. (1986). Psychotherapie-evaluation, in Psychiatrie der Gegenwart (Eds Kisker *et al.*) Volume 1, pp. 353–372, Springer, Berlin.

Beck, A.T., Rush, A.J., Shaw, B.F. & Emery, G. (1979). *Cognitive Therapy of Depression*, Guildford Press, New York.

Bergin, A.E. & Garfield, S.L. (1994). *Handbook of Psychotherapy and Behaviour Change*, Fourth Edition, John Wiley & Sons, New York.

Berglund, G., Bolund, C., Gustafsson, U. & Sjoden, P. (1994). A randomized study of a rehabilitation program for cancer patients: The 'starting again' group, *Psycho-oncology*, **3**, 109–120.

Blake-Mortimer, J., Gore-Felton, C., Kimerling, R., Turner-Cobb, J.M. & Spiegel, D. (1999). Improving the quality and quantity of life among patients with cancer: A review of the effectiveness of group psychotherapy, *Eur. J. Cancer*, **35**, 1581–1586.

Bottomley, A. (1997). Where are we now? Evaluating two decades of group interventions with adult cancer patients, *J. Psychiat. Ment. Health Nurs.*, **4**, 251–265.

Bradburn, N. (1969). *The Structure of Psychological Well-Being*, Aldine, Chicago, Illinois.

Bullinger, M. (1994). Lebensqualität: Grundlagen und Anwendungen, in Lebensqualität und Asthma (Eds F. Petermann & K.H. Bergmann), pp. 17–28, Quintessenz, Munich.

Bullinger, M., Anderson, R., Cella, D. & Aaronson, N. (1993). Developing and evaluating cross-cultural instruments from minimum requirements to optimal models, *Quality of Life Res.*, **2**, 451–459.

Cella, D.F. (1990). Health promotion in oncology: a cancer wellness doctrine, *J. Psychosocial Oncol.*, **8**(1), 17–31.

Cella, D.F., Sarafian, B., Snider, P.R., Yellen, S.B. & Winicour, P. (1993). Evaluation of a community-based cancer support group, *Psycho-oncology*, **2**, 123–132.

Clark, A. & Fallowfield, L.F. (1986). Quality of life measurements in patients with malignant disease, *J. R. Soc. Med.*, **79**, 165–169.

Cunningham, A.J. (1995). Group psychological therapy for cancer patients, *Support Care Cancer*, **3**, 244–247.

Cunningham, A.J., Lockwood, G.A. & Edmonds, C.V.I. (1993). Which cancer patients benefit most from a brief, group, coping skills program?, *Int. J. Psychiat. Med.*, **23**, 383–398.

De Jonghe, F., Kool, S., Van Aalst, G., Dekker, J. & Peen, J. (2001). Combining psychotherapy and antidepressants in the treatment of depression, *J. Affect. Disord.*, **64**, 217–229.

Demal, U., Zitterl, W., Lenz, G., Zapotoczky, H.G. & Zitterl-Eglseer, K. (1996). Obsessive compulsive disorder and depression – first results of a prospective study on 74 patients, *Prog. Neuropsychopharmacol. Biol. Psychiatry*, **20**(5), 801–813.

DuPuy, H.J. (1984). The Psychological General Well-Being (PGWB) Index, in *Assessment of Quality of Life in Clinical Trials of Cardiovascular Therapies* (Eds N.K. Wenger, M.E. Mattson, C.D. Furberg & J. Ellison), pp. 170–183, LeJacq Publishers, New York.

Edmonds, C.V.I., Lockwood, G.A. & Cunningham, A.J. (1999). Psychological response to long group therapy: A randomized trial with metastatic breast cancer patients, *Psycho-oncology*, **8**, 74–91.

Elkin, I., Shea, T., Watkins, J.T., Imber, S.D., Sotsky, S.M., Collins, J.F., Glass, D.R., Pilkonis, P.A., Leber, W.R., Docherty, J.P., Fiester, S.J. & Parloff, M.B. (1989). National Institute of Mental Health treatment of depression collaborative research program, *Arch. Gen. Psychiatry*, **46**, 971–982.

Fawzy, F.I. (1999). Psychosocial interventions for patients with cancer: What works and what doesn't, *Eur. J. Cancer*, **35**, 1559–1564.

Frisch, M.B., Cornell, J., Villanueva, M. & Retzlaff, P.J. (1992). Clinical validation of the quality of life inventory: A measure of life satisfaction for use in treatment planning and outcome assessment, *Psycholog. Assessment*, **4**, 92–101.

Frischenschlager, O., Brömmel, B. & Russinger, U. (1992). Zur Effektivität psychosozialer Betreuung Krebskranker – eine methodenkritische Literaturübersicht, *Psychotherapy Psychosomatics Med. Psychol.*, **42**, 206–213.

Glynn, S.M., Marder, S.R., Liberman, R.P., Blair, K., Wirshing, W.C., Wirshing, D.A., Ross, D. & Mintz, J. (2002). Supplementing clinic-based skills training with manual-based community support sessions: Effects on social adjustment of patient with schizophrenia, *Am. J. Psychiatry*, **159**, 829–837.

Goodman, W.K., Price, L.H., Rasmussen, S.A., Mazure, C., Fleischmann, R.L., Hill, C.L., Heninger, G.R. & Charney, D. (1989). Yale–Brown Obsessive Compulsive Scale (Y-BOCS) part I: Development, use and reliability, *Arch. Gen. Psychiatry*, **46**, 1006–1011.

Grawe, K., Donati, R. & Bernauer, F. (1994). *Psychotherapie im Wandel*, Hogrefe, Göttingen.

Gruber, B.L., Hall, N.R., Hersh, S.P. & Dubois, P. (1988). Immune system and psychological changes in metastatic cancer patients using relaxation and guided imagery: A pilot study, *Scand. J. Behavior Therapy*, **17**, 25–46.

Guthrie, E., Moorey, J., Margison, F., Barker, H., Palmer, S., McGrath, G., Tomenson, B. & Creed, F. (1999). Cost-effectiveness of brief psychodynamic-interpersonal therapy in high utilizers of psychiatric services, *Arch. Gen. Psychiatry*, **56**, 519–526.

Guyatt, G.H., Veldhuyzen van Zanten, S.J.O., Feeny, D.H. & Patrick, D.L. (1989). Measuring quality of life in clinical trials: A taxonomy and review, *Can. Med. Ass. J.*, **140**, 1441–1448.

Hau, E. (1977). Lebensqualität – unter psychoanalytischem Aspekt, *Psychotherapie, Medizin Psychologie*, **27**, 6–12.

Heinrich, R.L., Schag, C.C. & Ganz, P.A. (1984). Living with cancer: The cancer inventory of problem situations, *J. Clin. Psychol.*, **40**, 972–980.

Heinrich, R.L. & Schag, C.C. (1985). Stress and activity management: Group treatment for cancer patients and spouses, *J. Consult. Clin. Psychol.*, **33**, 439–446.

Heinrichs, D.W., Hanlon, T.E. & Carpenter Jr, W.T. (1984). The Quality of Life Scale: An instrument for rating the schizophrenic deficit syndrome, *Schizophrenia Bull.*, **10**, 388–398.

Holub, U.M. (1990). Veränderungsmessung im Rahmen eines stationären verhaltenstherapeutischen Behandlungsprogrammes, Thesis, University of Vienna.

Hunt, S.M. & McKenna, S.P. (1992a). The QLDS: A scale for measurement of quality of life in depression, *Health Policy*, **22**, 307–319.

Hunt, S.M. & McKenna, S.P., (1992b). A new measure of quality of life in depression: Testing the reliability and construct validity of the QLDS, *Health Policy*, **22**, 321–330.

Karnovsky, D.A. & Burchenal, J.H. (1949). The clinical evaluation of chemotherapeutic agents in cancer, in *Evaluation of Chemotherapeutic Agents in Cancer* (Ed. C.M. McLeod), pp. 191–205, Columbia University Press, New York.

Karterud, S., Pedersen, G., Bjordal, E., Brabrand, J. *et al* (2003). Day treatment of patients with personality disorders: experiences from a Norwegian treatment research network, *J. Personality Disord.*, **17**(3), 243–262.

Keller, M.B., Lavori, P.W., Friedman, B., Nielson, E., Endicott, J., McDonald-Scott, P. & Andreasen, N.C. (1987). The longitudinal interval follow-up evaluation, *Arch. Gen. Psychiatry*, **44**, 540–548.

Kingsep, P., Nathan, P. & Castle, D. (2003). Cognitive behavioural group treatment for social anxiety in schizophrenic, *Schizophrenia Res.*, **63**, 121–129.

Lenz, G. & Demal, U. (2000). Quality of life in depression and anxiety disorders: An exploratory follow-up study after intensive inpatient cognitive behaviour therapy, *Psychopathology*, **33**, 297–302.

Linden, M. (1981). Definition of compliance, *Int. J. Clin. Pharmacol. Ther. Toxicol.*, **19**, 86–90.

Linn, M.W., Linn, B.S. & Harris, R. (1982). Effects of counselling for late-stage cancer patients, *Cancer*, **49**, 1048–1055.

Longsdon, R., Gibbons, L.E., McCurry, S.M. *et al* (1999). Quality of life in Alzheimer's disease: Patient and caregiver reports, *J. Ment. Health and Aging*, **5**, 21–32.

Luborsky, L., Singer, B. & Luborsky, L. (1975). Comparative studies of psychotherapies: Is it true 'everyone has won and all must have prizes?', *Arch. Gen. Psychiatry*, **32**, 995–1008.

Lyles, J.N., Burish, T.G., Krozely, M.G. & Oldham, R.K. (1982). Efficacy of relaxation training and guided imagery in reducing the aversiveness of cancer chemotherapy, *J. Consult. Clin. Psychol.*, **50**, 509–524.

McNair, D., Lorr, M. & Drappelmann, L.F. (1971). *Manual for the Profile of Mood States*, Educational and Industrial Testing Service, San Diego, California.

Morrow, G.R., Chiarello, R.J. & Derogatis, L.R. (1978). A new scale for assessing patients' psychological adjustment to medical illness, *Psychol. Med.*, **8**, 605–610.

Newell, S.A., Sanson-Fisher, R.W. & Savolainen, N.J. (2002). Systematic review of psychological therapies for cancer patients: Overview and recommendations for future research, *J. Natl Cancer Inst.*, **94**, 558–584.

Orlinsky, D.E., Grawe, K. & Parks, R. (1994). Process and outcome in psychotherapy, in *Handbook of Psychotherapy and Behaviour Change* (Eds A.E. Bergin & S.L. Garfield), Fourth Edition, John Wiley & Sons, New York.

Plog, U. (1976). *Differentielle Psychotherapie*, Volume II, Huber, Bern.

Priebe, S., Gruyters, T., Heinze, M., Hoffmann, C. & Jäkel, A. (1995). Subjektive Evaluationskriterien in der psychiatrischen Versorgung – Erhebungsmethoden für Forschung und Praxis, *Psychiat. Praxis*, **22**, 140–144.

Ravindran, A.V., Anisman, H., Merali, Z., Charbonneau, Y. *et al* (1999). Treatment of primary dysthymia with group cognitive therapy and pharmacotherapy: Clinical symptoms and functional impairments, *Am. J. Psychiatry*, **156**, 1608–1617.

Rehse, B. & Pukrop, R. (2003). Effects of psychosocial interventions on quality of life in adult cancer patients: Meta analysis of 37 published controlled outcome studies, *Patient Education and Counselling*, **50**(2), 179–186.

Reimer, C. (1994). Lebensqualität von Psychotherapeuten, *Psychotherapeut.*, **39**, 73–78.

Rubin, H.C., Rabin, A.S., Levine, B., Auerbach, M., Kaplan, R. & Rapaport, M. (1995). Measuring quality of life in panic disorder, Oral presentation at the Annual Meeting of the American Psychiatric Association, Miami, Florida.

Schag, C.A.C., Heinrich, R.L. & Ganz, P.A. (1984). Living with cancer: The cancer inventory of problem situations, *J. Clin. Psychol.*, **40**(4), July, 972–980.

Scheibe, G., Albus, M., Walter, A.U. & Schmauß, M. (1993). Gruppenpsychotherapie bei Patienten mit Panikstörung und Agoraphobie, *Psychotherapie, Psychosomatik, Medizin Psychologie*, **43**, 238–244.

Schipper, H., Clinch, J., McMurray, A. & Levitt, M. (1984). Measuring quality of life of cancer patients: The functional living index-cancer, development and validation, *J. Clin. Oncol.*, **2**, 472–483.

Schneiderman, N., Antoni, M.H., Saab, P.G. & Ironson, G. (2001). Health psychology: Psychosocial and biobehavioural aspects of chronic disease management, *Annual Rev. Psychol.*, **52**, 555–580.

Shea, M.T., Elkin, I., Imber, S.D., Sotsky, S.M., Watkins, J.T., Collins, J.F., Pilkonis, P.A., Beckham, E., Glass, D., Dolant, R.T. & Parloff, M.B. (1992). Course of depressive symptoms over follow-up: Findings from the National Institute of Mental Health treatment of depression collaborative research program, *Arch. Gen. Psychiatry*, **49**, 782–787.

Smith, M.L., Glass, G.V. & Miller, T.I. (1980). *The Benefits of Psychotherapy*, Johns Hopkins University Press, Baltimore, Maryland.

Spector, A., Thorgrinsen, L., Woods, B., Royan, L. *et al* (2003). Efficacy of an evidence-based cognitive stimulation therapy programme for people with dementia, *Br. J. Psychiatry*, **183**, 248–254.

Spitzer, W.O., Dobson, A.J. & Hall, J. (1981). The QL-Index, *J. Chronic Dis.*, **34**, 585–597.

The EuroQol Group (1990). A new facility for the measurement of health-related quality of life, *Health Policy*, **16**, 199–208.

Trask, P.C., Paterson, A.G., Griffith, K.A, Riba, M.B. & Schwarzt, J.L. (2003). Cognitive–behavioral intervention for distress in patients with melanoma: Comparison with standard medical care and impact on quality of life, *Cancer*, **98**, 854–864.

Tschuschke, V. (2003). Psychologisch-psychotherapeutische Interventionen bei onkologischen Erkrankungen, *Psychotherapeut.*, **48**, 100–108.

Tschuschke, V., Kächele, H. & Hölzer, M. (1994). Gibt es unterschiedlich effektive Formen von Psychotherapie?, *Psychotherapeut.*, **39**, 281–297.

Volpato Cordioli, A.V., Heldt, E., Braga Bochi, D., Margis, R. *et al* (2003). Cognitive–behavioural group therapy in obsessive–compulsive disorder: A randomized clinical trial, *Psychotherapy Psychosomatics*, **72**(4), 211–216.

Walker, L.G., Walker, M.B., Ogston, K., Heys, S.D., Ah-See, A.K., Miller, I.D., Hutcheon, A.W., Sarkar, T.K. & Eremin, O. (1999). Psychological, clinical and pathological effects of relaxation training and guided imagery during primary chemotherapy, *Br. J. Cancer*, **80**, 262–268.

Weissman, M.M., Prusoff, B.A., Di Mascio, A., Neu, C., Gohlaney, M. & Klerman, G.L. (1979). The efficacy of drugs and psychotherapy in the treatment of acute depressive episodes, *Am. J. Psychiatry*, **136**, 555–558.

Weissman, M.M., Klerman, G.L., Prusoff, B.A., Sholomskas, D. & Padian, N. (1981). Depressed outpatients: Results 1 year after treatment with drugs and/or interpersonal psychotherapy, *Arch. Gen. Psychiatry*, **38**, 51–55.

World Health Organization (1978). Mental Disorders: Glossary and Guide to their Classification in Accordance with the Ninth Revision of the International Classification of Diseases, WHO, Geneva.

20

Whose Life Is It Anyway? Quality of Life for Long-Stay Patients Discharged from Psychiatric Hospitals

Julian Leff

INTRODUCTION

Each of us strives to achieve the highest quality of life (QoL) possible within the constraints created by personal, economic and societal factors. There have been many periods in history during which the QoL for some or most of the people has been so abysmal that it has led to death, e.g. the Third Reich, the famine in Ethiopia, the Cultural Revolution in China. Under less extreme conditions, there are still large variations in the QoL within populations, some of which stem from the unavoidable depredations of ill-health. A concern with the measurement of QoL has developed in the past two decades, stimulated by the growth of the consumer movement (Nader, 1973), which led to advocacy organisations for patients and their relatives, and by the escalating costs of health care. The latter faces professionals with uncomfortable choices as to which patients to prioritise, given limited resources. This problem has been sharpened by the development of expensive techniques and apparatus which can keep alive people who would otherwise have faced almost certain death within a short period of time. The painful situation professionals can find themselves in was anticipated by Bernard Shaw in *The Doctors' Dilemma*, in which the doctors have to choose between saving the life of a dull but worthy colleague or an unscrupulous but brilliant artist. In this instance, the professional arbiters of life and death were required to judge the relative value of the contribution each of the two sick men was likely to make to society. Pragmatic considerations of this kind do not currently enter into our decisions about who should receive treatment, although recent suggestions that there should be an upper age limit for certain kinds of medical and surgical interventions presage such a development.

A major controversy in the assessment of QoL centres on whether to include a professional view of the patients' situation as well as seeking the subjective experience of the patients themselves. The salient issues are whether patients are always capable of making a rational appraisal of their situation and whether professionals are able to make a valid judgement of patients' QoL. These issues merit some discussion.

In the past, patients' views about the quality of care they received were almost totally ignored: this was one facet of the paternalism that characterised custodial care. It was easy to dismiss the views of long-stay patients, by asserting that they were psychotic and were likely to make irrational judgements.

Quality of Life in Mental Disorders, Second Edition   Edited by H. Katschnig, H. Freeman and N. Sartorius
© 2006 John Wiley & Sons, Ltd

However, in the case of patients suffering from a functional psychosis, this argument is not supported by the evidence. Weinstein (1979) reviewed 25 studies undertaken between 1956 and 1977 which used questionnaires to measure patients' attitudes towards psychiatric hospitalisation. He concluded that in 13 out of 16 studies in which the appropriate measures were included, length of time in the institution was not related to patients' attitudes.

The study by the Team for the Assessment of Psychiatric Services (TAPS) examined the issue of the reliability of assessing the attitudes of the long-stay patients. Thornicroft *et al.* (1993) used the Patient Attitude Questionnaire (PAQ) to assess the attitude of psychiatric patients towards their treatment settings and staff. To measure test–retest reliability, the questionnaire was administered to 43 long-stay patients in two psychiatric hospitals, on two occasions six months apart. Of the 13 items included in the reliability analysis, only one failed to show satisfactory reliability over time – patients' views on the helpfulness of occupation. It was notable that of all the attitude items retested on the second occasion, 66% of the responses were identical to those given initially. Hence, unreliability of responses cannot be used as a reason to avoid seeking long-stay patients' opinions about their QoL.

The patient's view is obviously necessary, but is it sufficient? In order to answer this question, we need to consider some specific examples in which the patient's judgement is impaired by a psychiatric condition. The most obvious is Alzheimer's disease. Patients with advanced dementia cannot be expected to comment on their QoL, yet this judgement is extremely important, particularly as such patients have been subject to abuse on occasions. We can, of course, use the relative, when one is available, as a proxy for the patient. Otherwise, an independent judge can be asked to assess the quality of the caring environment. This can be in terms of physical and architectural features of the care setting, e.g. using measures derived from the Multiphasic Environmental Assessment Procedure Manual (MEAP) (Moos and Lemke, 1984). It is also possible to make naturalistic observations of day-to-day behaviour and social activity as well as staff activities. This approach was taken in the TAPS study of psychogeriatric services, and showed that there was more staff interaction with patients in the community homes than in the psychiatric hospital. Additionally, patients were noted to spend more time drinking tea in the community homes, which was in accord with the relatives' perception that there was greater opportunity to make drinks for the patients in the community settings. Thus, these two approaches, each of which is a substitute for the patient's expression of satisfaction, concur in indicating a better QoL in the community homes (Wills and Leff, 1996).

Though the necessity for an independent judgement is obvious in the case of demented patients, the argument can be extended to patients with psychotic illnesses. Consider the paranoid patient who decides to withdraw from contact with other people and to live a solitary life. This patient may well express a high degree of satisfaction with his/her chosen lifestyle. However, the psychiatric professional, with the benefit of experience of similar patients, is able to predict that isolation leads to the accumulation of negative symptoms and an eventual deterioration in the QoL, which may be imperceptible to the patient.

A failure to appreciate the ominous nature of some aspects of their lives can also be a feature of non-psychotic patients. In a study of family therapy for marital disharmony and neurotic disorders, Asen *et al.* (1991) found that the therapists were very effective in reducing both critical and over-involved attitudes expressed by parents. Subjects' satisfaction, measured at the end of treatment, correlated positively with reduction in criticism, indicating that they were pleased with the fact that they experienced less anger. However, their satisfaction correlated negatively with reduction in over-involvement. This suggests that they were displeased with the loss of closeness, even though the therapists and researchers knew that if it were not modified, it would lead to continuing problems in family functioning.

Most researchers in this area agree that both the patient's perspective and that of an independent judge are needed to provide a balanced view of QoL. Lehman's scale (Lehman, Ward and Zinn, 1982), which is one of the most widely used, measures objective attributes of QoL and life satisfaction in eight life domains: living situation, family, social relations, leisure activities, work, finances, personal safety and health. Mukherjee (1989) emphasised the importance of including both subjective and objective measures within an assessment battery.

TAPS ASSESSMENT INSTRUMENTS

The choice of measuring instruments is obviously crucial in assessing patients' QoL. For the TAPS study of long-stay patients, a batch of nine schedules was compiled. It was considered desirable, where possible, to use existing instruments with established reliability, for which data would be available for purposes of comparison. However, it proved necessary to adapt some schedules, while in certain areas there was no suitable instrument, so that new ones had to be developed. Each area will be considered in turn.

Personal Data and Psychiatric History

We needed to collect information on the patients' gender, ethnicity and marital status, as well as their living conditions, before they were admitted to the psychiatric hospital. These data were abstracted from the case notes, as well as details of contacts with the psychiatric and forensic services and the diagnosis, currently and at the time of first admission.

Physical Health Index

Many of the patients were elderly and suffered from degenerative diseases of the pulmonary, cardiovascular and musculoskeletal systems. Since poor health, whether mental or physical, reduces the QoL, it was deemed important to assess the patients' physical health as well as their psychiatric states. There were not enough trained staff to examine all the patients physically, so the relevant information was obtained from medical and nursing staff and from the case notes.

Mental State Examination

As with physical health, a high level of mental health contributes to QoL. However, there is often disagreement between patients and professionals over the issue of psychiatric symptoms and treatment with medication. Patients with partial or no insight often maintain that there is nothing the matter with them, when professionals are sure they are suffering from delusions and/or hallucinations. Under these circumstances, the prescription of neuroleptic drugs, which often have unpleasant side-effects, will usually be viewed by patients as reducing their QoL. Professionals, by contrast, will judge that the overall benefit of reducing the likelihood of relapse outweighs the unpleasant effects of drugs. Hence, they will see the drugs as enhancing the patients' QoL. To assess the patients' mental states, we used the Present State Examination (PSE) (Wing, Cooper and Sartorius, 1974), but it was not possible to conduct a full assessment of every patient. Up to one-third of the patients could not be interviewed because they were mute, incoherent or uncooperative. In these cases, it was usually possible to make an assessment of the patients' non-verbal behaviour and mood.

Problems of Social Behaviour

As with psychiatric symptoms, disturbed behaviour may affect the people who come into contact with the patients much more than the patients themselves. In the long run, this will reduce their QoL by alienating friends and relatives who could provide emotional and other forms of support. We chose to use the Social Behaviour Schedule (SBS), which has been validated and found to be reliable by Sturt and Wykes (1986). The SBS covers behaviour stemming from positive symptoms, such as verbal and physical hostility, and from negative symptoms, such as poor hygiene.

Once we began interviewing patients in the community, we realised that there were areas of activity in which the patients operated that were not covered by the SBS. Because it was developed using hospital populations, it was not designed to assess skills such as shopping, using public transport and choosing clothing suitable for the weather. Consequently, we developed a supplementary instrument, the Basic Everyday Living Skills Schedule (BELS), which does cover these important community activities.

Patient Satisfaction

One of the most salient areas of assessment for QoL is the patients' views of the care they receive. These have often been unjustly neglected in the past, on the grounds that long-term psychotic patients were unreliable informants. In fact, as discussed above, we found the PAQ that was developed to have an acceptable test–retest reliability (Thornicroft *et al.*, 1993). From the results of this study, it was concluded that long-term psychiatric patients are able to give clear and consistent views about the care they receive and about the carers.

The Quality of the Environment

A criticism often levelled at institutional care is that it deprives the patient of autonomy, imposing a host of rules and regulations that benefit the staff rather than their clients (Goffman, 1961). We extended the Hospital Hostel Practices Profile (Wing and Brown, 1970) to include questions about the wearing of uniforms by the staff and the availability of privacy, as well as adding a new section on the proximity of amenities such as shops, day centres, parks and cinemas. The latter obviously gains in importance when patients move out of a large institution, where most amenities are provided on site, into residences in the community. The extended schedule is named the Environmental Index (EI).

Social Integration

It is conceivable that long-stay patients discharged from psychiatric hospitals might remain socially isolated from the communities in which they have been relocated. This isolation could be maintained by their neighbours' avoidance of contact with them and by the care staff in their homes overprotecting them from ordinary social interchange with the public. In order to investigate this possibility, it is necessary to define the extent of the patients' social networks, the people included in them and the quality of relationships. Existing schedules were developed for use with healthy individuals and people suffering from neuroses, and were inappropriate for the socially impaired population to be studied. Therefore, an interview was developed that was specifically tailored to the long-stay patients. It is called the Social Network Schedule (SNS) and its validity and reliability have been established (Dunn *et al.*, 1990; Leff *et al.*, 1990).

Economic Evaluation

Collaboration with health economists in the University of Kent Personal Social Services Research Unit was established at the beginning of the TAPS project, and comprehensive costing of patients' care, both inside and outside psychiatric hospitals, is being pursued. In order to record all services received by patients living in the community, a Community Services Receipt Schedule has been developed. Economic data will not be presented in this paper but are available in other publications (Knapp *et al.*, 1990, 1993; Beecham, Knapp and Fenyo, 1991).

The series of schedules used provides a relatively comprehensive picture of patients' QoL, which includes the perspective of the patients themselves as well as the more detached view of the research workers, none of whom were involved in providing services for the patients. The relatives have not been consulted in this study, because all the patients were long-stay initially and only a handful returned to their families on discharge.

DESIGN OF THE STUDY

TAPS was set up in response to a decision by the North East Thames Regional Health Authority (NETRHA) to close two large psychiatric hospitals over a ten-year period. Both hospitals were opened in the Victorian era, Friern in 1851 and Claybury in 1895. Both contained over 2400 patients at their peak in the early 1950s, and both had declined to between 800 and 900 patients each in 1983, the year the closure decision was announced. TAPS undertook to study the effects of closure on the three main patient populations: the long-stay non-demented, the psychogeriatric and patients spending brief periods on the admission wards. Here, the findings for the first of those three groups will be presented.

The long-stay patients were defined as those spending more than one year in hospital, who, if aged over 65, did not suffer from dementia. A small group of patients under 65 with various organic brain conditions was included. A census of the two hospitals was carried out, and identified 770 patients who met these criteria. However, this was not the entire sample, because patients were being admitted to the acute wards until shortly before closure of the hospital, and some of them stayed for more than a year, hence satisfying our inclusion criteria. These new long-stay patients accumulated at a surprisingly high rate, so that the sample size grew to 1166, of whom the new long-stay constituted one-third.

The ideal scientific design would have been to randomise patients to be discharged or to remain in hospital for a further period of time, and to compare the outcomes of the two groups. This was not possible for a variety of reasons, both ethical and practical. Instead, a matched case-control design was adopted. Each patient due to be discharged was matched with a patient likely to stay some time longer on six criteria: age, gender, hospital, total time in hospital, diagnosis and number of social behaviour problems. It was possible to match each discharged patient ('leaver') quite closely with a patient who stayed ('match') for the first four years of the study. In the fifth year, the pool of remaining patients had shrunk to the point where it was possible only to match every two leavers to one patient who stayed. Thereafter the matching procedure broke down, and each patient had to be used as his/her own control, in a 'before and after' design.

The group of patients discharged in the course of a year is designated a cohort. Cohort 1 left the two hospitals between September 1985 and August 1986. Friern Hospital was eventually closed, as planned, in March 1993, by which time eight cohorts had left. The closure programme for Claybury was delayed for various administrative reasons, and the hospital remained open until 1997. For this reason, TAPS ceased to follow up Claybury patients after Cohort 5. A one-year follow-up study has been completed of the first five cohorts of leavers and their matches (Leff et al., 1996). A one-year follow-up has also been conducted of the total long-stay population of Friern Hospital (eight cohorts). A five-year follow-up has also been instituted, because of the importance of monitoring the outcome of these patients, 80% of whom suffer from schizophrenia, over a longer period; this study has been completed on the first two cohorts (Leff et al., 1994). An overview of the variety of follow-up data collected so far will be presented here. Before doing so, however, it is necessary to explain the policy for funding the reprovision of psychiatric care and the nature of the community placements.

'DOWRIES' AND STAFFED HOMES

The problem facing any programme of reprovision for a psychiatric hospital is how to mobilise the resources, both revenue and capital, that are tied up in the hospital. NETRHA's approach to this problem was to attach a 'dowry' to each long-stay patient who was discharged to a newly provided placement in the community. The dowry was calculated by dividing the annual revenue cost of the hospital by the number of patients housed in it. This amounted to £14 000 per year in 1985, and was increased each year to keep pace with inflation. This amount of revenue was added to the budget of the District Health Authority taking responsibility for the patient, and remained in it for an unlimited period. This amount could not be saved from the hospital budget each time a patient was discharged, but only when it was possible to close a whole ward and redeploy the staff. NETRHA recognised this problem and guaranteed to fund double running costs, maintaining the hospital budget as well as transferring revenue to the community, until the requisite savings could be made. They also advanced £20 million in capital for investment in community facilities for Friern patients, with the expectation that this sum could be recovered on the sale of the Friern site, which was prime development land. In the event, this has now happened. Thus NETRHA's financial support of the reprovision programme has been generous, but the health economics team have calculated that the revenue and capital required to develop the community services do not exceed the resources available in the psychiatric hospital.

The capital has been mainly used to buy ordinary houses in the community and to convert them for the patients' use; in most houses, each patient has his/her own bedroom. A high proportion (78%) of the homes have staff resident on the premises. Some of the houses are staffed day and night, and for the most disabled patients the staff-to-patient ratio is as high as 1:1. Some are staffed by nurses who used to work in the two psychiatric hospitals, and are owned by the District Health Authorities. Others are owned and run by voluntary agencies, while a relatively small proportion are privately run. The average number of residents per house is five. The staffed home, an ordinary house in an ordinary street, has turned out to be the standard form of accommodation for the ex-long-stay patient.

OUTCOME FOR THE PATIENTS

Death, Crime and Vagrancy

The worst possible effect on the QoL of discharging patients would, of course, be death. The stress of the move to a strikingly different environment could conceivably result in suicide or exacerbation of an existing physical illness. Alternatively, patients in the community, removed from close scrutiny by hospital staff, might suffer from neglect of physical illnesses which could progress to death. In fact, there was no evidence for any of these possibilities. In the first five cohorts, the death rate during the one-year follow-up was 2.6 for the leavers, compared with 5.2 for the matches – a non-significant difference. The rate in the last three unmatched cohorts was 4.1, which is not different from either the earlier leavers or their matches. There were two suicides among the eight cohorts of leavers and one among the earlier matches.

The public and the media are particularly concerned about the level of violence shown by psychiatrically ill people in the community, especially unprovoked homicidal attacks on strangers. From the point of view of the patients' QoL, however, they themselves are more exposed in the community to the risk of harassment and robbery by criminals, who see them as easy targets. Thus it is important to consider crimes both committed *by* patients and *against* them.

During the first year in the community, of the 695 patients for whom we had information on criminal acts, 20 were either accused or convicted of offences. Some of these were relatively trivial, such as being drunk and disorderly and sending a threatening letter, but there were seven physical assaults on another person. Two patients were admitted involuntarily to psychiatric hospitals following assaults; in addition, one patient was involved in a pub brawl, while another attacked his father with a knife, neither of these being admitted. One patient abducted and assaulted a female patient. Only two patients were sent to prison. One stopped taking his medication, became increasingly paranoid, and threw a cup of tea over a stranger in a cafe. The police were called and he was found to be carrying a knife; he was put in prison briefly, before being transferred to a psychiatric hospital. The second patient was a young man with a dependent personality. On the day of discharge from hospital, he touched the breasts of a woman in the street and was convicted of attempted rape; he was still in prison when interviewed at the one-year follow-up. Nine patients were the victims of crime or accidents, three of them being involved in road traffic accidents. Two patients were victimised at work, two were assaulted and robbed, and one was stolen from. One patient alleged that he had been robbed, but did not proceed with an investigation. While all these incidents are regrettable, neither the rate of perpetration of crime nor of being victimised appears to be particularly high.

The public is naturally concerned about and alarmed by the growing presence on the streets of homeless mentally ill people; this escalating problem is regularly ascribed by the media to the closure of psychiatric hospitals. Certainly, homelessness and the necessity to sleep rough represent the bottom of the scale for QoL. In the TAPS study, only seven out of the total group of 737 discharged patients could not be traced in the first year and are presumed to have become homeless. Of these, four had previously been vagrant before becoming long-stay patients and probably returned to this way of life. It is reassuring to note that during the first year in the community, no patient was lost from a staffed home.

A five-year follow-up has been completed on the first four cohorts, totalling 359 patients. Between the one-year and five-year follow-ups, no additional patients were lost from the study. Thus, the proportion of patients who probably became homeless in the five years after discharge amounts to 1%. This is not a figure to be complacent about, but it is not of a magnitude to account for the alarming rise in mentally ill homeless people, for which there are other probable causes (Leff, 1993).

Psychiatric Symptoms

Patients' mental states were remarkably stable over the one-year follow-up period. The total score on the PSE was 14.76 in hospital and 14.80 in the community. Most of the subscores showed no change over time; in particular, delusions and hallucinations were unchanged. It is possible that there was a transient increase in symptoms in response to the move into the community, but if so, this had settled by the time of the follow-up. In one important area, however, there was a significant change, namely negative symptoms. Because the distribution of scores was markedly skewed, it was necessary to conduct a non-parametric analysis on the scores, dichotomised into 0 and 1+. The proportion of patients with no negative symptoms increased from 39.6 to 44.8%. A further significant reduction in negative symptoms was observed in cohorts 1 and 2 between the first and fifth year follow-up. This improvement is important since negative symptoms are a major obstacle to rehabilitation. These findings also have implications for the theory of institutionalisation. Wing and Brown (1970) demonstrated that the level of negative symptoms exhibited by long-stay patients in psychiatric hospitals varied with the amount of stimulation provided by the staff. These results from the TAPS study indicate that negative symptoms also respond to the increased stimulation consequent on discharge to community settings.

Problems of Social Behaviour

For the total sample of patients, there was a small but significant reduction in the number of social behaviour problems, as recorded with the SBS at the one-year follow-up. However, the earlier matched comparison involving the first five cohorts of leavers revealed a reduction of the same magnitude for patients who remained in hospital. This suggests that rehabilitation has an equally effective impact on social behaviour, whether it is undertaken in the psychiatric hospital or in the community.

The BELS, used to supplement the SBS, revealed a significant reduction of 15% in the proportion of patients with severe problems of compliance with medication when they moved from hospital to the community. This seemed to be related to an alteration in patients' attitude to medication, which will be presented below.

Patients' Satisfaction

Major changes in patients' attitudes were found at the one-year follow-up; these were particularly dramatic with respect to satisfaction with the current care environment. Whereas 33.4% of patients questioned while in hospital wished to remain there, 82.5% wanted to stay in their community homes when seen one year after discharge. This proportion rose to 86% of the first two cohorts interviewed after five years in the community. The main benefit of life in the community, mentioned spontaneously by the patients, was their increased freedom. This aspect of the caring environment was specified by only 3.8% of patients when interviewed in hospital, but by 19.6% when seen in the community at one year, and double this proportion, 38%, after five years.

A more surprising area of attitudinal change that was detected was in relation to the helpfulness of medication. The proportion expressing a favourable view rose from 55.9% in hospital to 72.3% after one year in the community. Presumably, this contributed to the reduction in problems with compliance, observed by the community staff.

The Quality of the Environment

This was the area of measurement that showed the most dramatic change. The total score on the EI fell from an average of 26.2 to 9.9, indicating that there were far fewer rules and restrictions in the community homes than in the two hospitals. It is of interest that the fall in EI score was rather less for the later cohorts than the earlier ones, suggesting that the community care staff were applying more restrictions to the patients with the greatest degree of disability. Even so, the final cohort to be discharged experienced a drop in EI score of 9 points. As indicated above, patients responded very positively to their increased freedom. In fact, their satisfaction grew steadily over the five-year follow-up, even though there was little change in restrictiveness over this period, suggesting that they came to appreciate their freedom more and more with the passage of time.

Physical Health

Over the one-year follow-up, there was an increase of 6% in patients with physical immobility, but this was of the same magnitude for both leavers and their matches, indicating that it was a consequence of ageing rather than of the move to the community. An increase of 8% in patients with incontinence also affected leavers and matches equally. Over the five-year follow-up, the total care received by the patients for physical ill-health increased significantly. Thus, there was no suggestion that patients' physical condition was being neglected.

Social Integration

The size of patients' social networks was no greater after five years in the community than it had been in hospital, but there were major changes in the quality of relationships. After one year in the community, patients had made more friends – an average of two additional friends each. This has to be seen in the context of the total network size, which was only eight on average. Between the one- and five-year follow-ups, there was no change in the number of friends, but a significant increase in the number of confidants. Confidants represent the most intense form of relationship, which clearly took longer to establish than friendships.

It would have been possible for all the patients' meaningful social contacts to have been with other patients and with staff members. However, once they were living in the community, patients established social relationships outside the mental health network, with ordinary people including neighbours, members of church clubs and local shopkeepers. Hence, true social integration was occurring, although not experienced by all the discharged patients.

CONCLUSIONS

The intensive study by TAPS of long-stay patients has shown considerable improvement in their QoL consequent on discharge to homes in the community. In particular, they were living under much freer conditions and greatly appreciated the increased freedom. The great majority of patients wanted to stay in their community homes. Their social networks were enriched by friends and confidants, some of whom were ordinary folk living and working in the neighbourhood. Over the longer term, there was a decrease in negative symptoms, at least for the earlier cohorts to be discharged. The move into the community did not lead to an increase in deaths or suicides, and only a handful of patients were lost from the system. Even this could have been avoided if those particular patients had been placed in staffed homes: four of them had been vagrants before becoming long-stay patients and this should be considered a strong indication that staffed accommodation is required. These improvements in patients' QoL, evident both from subjective and objective appraisals, were not achieved by an unrealistic outlay of revenue and capital. Both types of cost did not exceed the resources available within the psychiatric hospitals (Knapp et al., 1993).

One warning note must be sounded. When Friern Hospital closed in March 1993, there were 72 patients who were judged to be too disturbed for the standard community homes, mostly on account of aggressive or violent behaviour. These 'difficult to place' patients will be found in every psychiatric hospital and require specialised facilities (Trieman and Leff, 1996). The three health districts responsible for the Friern patients chose three different solutions: a locked ward in a general hospital, a locked house in the community and three purpose-built open houses in the grounds of another psychiatric hospital. TAPS is conducting a follow-up study of these units to determine which solution is preferable. Whatever the outcome, this problem will have to be tackled by every organisation intending to close a psychiatric hospital. Creative solutions will need to be found, if the QoL of the most disabled long-stay patients is to be improved.

REFERENCES

Asen, K., Berkowitz, R., Cooklin, A., Leff, J., Loader, P., Piper, R. & Rein, L. (1991). Family therapy outcome research: A trial for families, therapists, and researchers, *Family Process*, **30**, 3–20.

Beecham, J., Knapp, M. & Fenyo, A. (1991). Costs, needs and outcomes, *Schizophrenia Bull.*, **17**, 427–439.

Dunn, M., O'Driscoll, C., Dayson, D., Wills, W., Leff, J. (1990). The TAPS Project. 4: An observational study of the social life of long-stay patients, *Br. J. Psychiatry*, **157**, 842–848.

Goffman, E. (1961). *Asylums: Essays on the Social Situation of Mental Patients and Other Inmates*, Anchor Books, New York.

Knapp, M., Beecham, J., Anderson, J., Dayson, D., O'Driscoll, C., Leff, J., Margolius, O. & Wills, W. (1990). The TAPS Project. 3: Predicting the community costs of closing psychiatric hospitals, *Br. J. Psychiatry*, **157**, 661–670.

Knapp, M., Beecham, J., Hallam, A. & Fenyo, A. (1993). The TAPS Project.18: The costs of community care for former long-stay psychiatric hospital residents, *Health and Social Care in the Community*, **1**, 4.

Leff, J. (1993). All the homeless people – where do they all come from?, *Br. Med. J.*, **306**, 669–670.

Leff, J., O'Driscoll, C., Dayson, D., Wills, W. & Anderson, J. (1990). The TAPS Project. 5: The structure of social-network data obtained from long-stay patients, *Br. J. Psychiatry*, **157**, 848–852.

Leff, J., Thornicroft, G., Coxhead, N. & Crawford, C. (1994). The TAPS Project. 22: A five-year follow-up of long-stay psychiatric patients discharged to the community, *Br. J. Psychiatry*, **165**(Suppl. 25), 13–17.

Leff, J., Dayson, D., Gooch, C., Thornicroft, G. & Wills, W. (1996). The TAPS Project. 19: A comprehensive matched case-control follow-up study of long-stay patients discharged from two psychiatric institutions, *Psychiat. Serv.*, **47**, 62–67.

Lehman, A.F., Ward, N.C. & Linn, L.S. (1982). Chronic mental patients: The quality of life issue, *Am. J. Psychiatry*, **139**, 1271–1276.

Moos, R.H. & Lemke, S. (1984). *Multiphasic Environmental Assessment Procedure Manual*, Social Ecology Laboratory, Veterans Administration and Stanford University Medical Center, Palo Alto, California.

Mukherjee, R. (1989). *The Quality of Life: Valuation in Social Research*, Sage, London.

Nader, R. (Ed.) (1973). *The Consumer and Corporate Accountability*, Harcourt, Brace, Jovanovich, New York.

Sturt, E. & Wykes, T. (1986). The Social Behaviour Schedule: A validity and reliability study, *Br. J. Psychiatry*, **148**, 1–11.

Thornicroft, G., Gooch, C., O'Driscoll, C. & Reda, S. (1993). The TAPS Project. 9: The reliability of the patient attitude questionnaire, in (Ed. J. Leff) Evaluating community placement of long-stay psychiatric patients, *Br. J. Psychiatry*, **162**(Suppl. 19), 25–29.

Trieman, N. & Leff, J. (1996). Difficult to place patients in a psychiatric closure programme: The TAPS project, *Psychol. Med.*, **26**, 765–774.

Weinstein, R.M. (1979). Patient attitudes towards mental hospitalization: A review of quantitative research, *J. Health Social Behavior*, **20**, 237–258.

Wills, W. & Leff, J. (1996). The TAPS Project 30: Quality of life for elderly mentally ill patients: A comparison of hospital and community settings, *Int. J. Geriat. Psychiatry*, **13**(4), 225–234.

Wing, J.K. & Brown, G.W. (1970). *Institutionalism and Schizophrenia: A Comparative Study of Three Mental Hospitals 1960–68*, Cambridge University Press, London.

Wing, J.K., Cooper, J.E. & Sartorius, N. (1974). *Description and Classification of Psychiatric Symptoms*, Cambridge University Press, London.

21

Quality of Life in Mental Health Service Research

Antonio Lasalvia and Mirella Ruggeri

INTRODUCTION

The primary aim of mental health service research is to provide scientific knowledge that helps to improve the health and functioning of people with mental disorders (Ellwood, 1988). Emphasis is increasingly being placed now on the direct measurement of such health outcomes, using standardised measures with proven reliability, validity and acceptability, as well as on the need to favour assessment of outcome in routine clinical practice (Carulla, 1999; Thornicroft and Tansella, 1999; Kissling, 2001).

Modelling of the concept of outcome in psychiatry has come a long way, from the use of morbidity and mortality rates as indicators to the use of data on service utilisation and to the inclusion of social variables in the assessment. Nowadays, it is widely recognised that all these contributions should be combined and that research should move towards routine multidimensional and multiaxial outcome assessment, carried out in the 'real world' of mental health services. This has to consider both subjective and objective variables, and include clinical and social variables, as well as the characteristics of the user's interaction with any service.

In this perspective, quality of life (QoL) has gained increasing importance as a key component in the outcome assessment of the care provided by mental health services. Part of the reason for the steadily increasing popularity of QoL is that it appears to be useful in so many ways (Baker and Intagliata, 1982; Oliver *et al.*, 1996). QoL, for example:

- takes account of improvements in function or distress that fall short of complete cure;
- is holistic and includes a broad range of outcomes that are consistent with the complexities of human life;
- focuses attention on the needs of the individual and so is acceptable to patients and relatives;
- can be applied across disciplines to compare different interventions for different disorders, using the same measure of outcome.

Within psychiatry, it has been suggested that the services for people with severe mental illness address the enhancement of QoL rather than cure. Central to all of these ideas is the use of QoL as an outcome measure.

In the present chapter, we will: (a) provide a brief description of the methodological aspects of the South Verona Outcome Project (SVOP), one of the few examples of outcome evaluation in routine clinical practice within mental health service research; (b) summarise some data on QoL in patients attending the South Verona Community Mental Health Service (CMHS), which is collected in the frame of the SVOP; (c) discuss practical implications of QoL measurement in routine clinical practice, together with the possible future perspectives. Specifically, this contribution will be focused on a series of aspects relevant to QoL measurement in patients attending community-based mental health services.

Quality of Life in Mental Disorders, Second Edition   Edited by H. Katschnig, H. Freeman and N. Sartorius
© 2006 John Wiley & Sons, Ltd

Before analysing in detail the QoL findings of psychiatric patients in South-Verona, it may be useful to provide a brief description of the methodological framework in which data collection was performed.

ASSESSING MENTAL HEALTH OUTCOME IN THE ROUTINE CLINICAL PRACTICE: THE SOUTH VERONA OUTCOME PROJECT EXPERIENCE

The South Verona Outcome Project (SVOP) (Ruggeri and Dall'Agnola, 2000; Ruggeri, 2002) is an attempt to standardise information that clinicians collect and record in periodic reviews of cases in their everyday clinical practice. For service evaluation, it uses the same professionals who are involved in the clinical work.

The project has the following key characteristics: (a) it is in the frame of the routine clinical practice of a well-established and community-based 'real world psychiatric service'; (b) it assesses a comprehensive set of outcome-related variables; (c) there is systematic involvement of both the key clinicians and the patients in the assessments; (d) there are regular checks of the quality of the data collected. Variables belonging to the six main dimensions considered were: global functioning, psychopathology, social disability, needs for care, QoL and satisfaction with service. These were integrated with data on service utilisation and the costs of care.

To ensure compliance by the staff, instructions for a study within the frame of routine clinical practice have to be as simple as possible, and assessments should easily be done in their everyday routine. After having consulted the staff and piloted different alternatives, it was decided that standardised assessment of patients in the CMHS should take place twice a year: from April to June (wave A) and from October to December (wave B). During these periods, all key workers (psychiatrist and psychologists) were asked to assess both first-ever patients and those already in contact with the service at their first or, at latest, second visit in the period. Patients were excluded from the study if they had: (a) been seen only by nurses or social workers; (b) been seen only in the Emergency Department or on a medical ward of the General Hospital, with no other psychiatric follow-up in the period; (c) had only one psychiatric contact, and such a contact had been considered by the key professional to be not suitable for administration of standardised instruments, or only home visits, also considered not suitable for making standardised assessments; (d) had severe cognitive deficits.

In wave A, the assessment was made only by the key professional on the basis of the patient's condition in the previous month, including assessment of global functioning, psychopathology and disability in performing social roles. In wave B, the assessment was made both by the key professionals (as in wave A, plus assessment of needs for care) and by the patients, who are requested to assess their QoL and satisfaction with mental health services in relation to their experience over the previous year. In wave B, a research team was available to help patients completing the instruments, if needed, and to check their understanding of the items and reliability. Confidentiality was fully preserved.

Basing the study design on two waves allowed a more frequent assessment of functioning, symptoms and disability (which are more susceptible to rapid changes) than of needs for care, QoL and service satisfaction (which are considered to change less rapidly).

The SVOP was carried out continually from 1994 to 1997, but also included a series of follow-up studies in 2000 of patients assessed in the early waves of the project (1994 and 1995). The data collection included both subjects still in contact with the service and those whose contacts had been interrupted. Findings on QoL presented in this chapter refer to both cross-sectional studies performed in 1994–1997 and to follow-up studies.

MEASURING LEVELS OF QUALITY OF LIFE IN PSYCHIATRIC PATIENTS

The QoL of patients attending the South Verona CMHS was assessed by the Italian version of the Lancashire Quality of Life Profile (LQOLP) (Oliver, 1991; Lasalvia, Ruggeri and Dall'Agnola, 2000). This is a researcher-led questionnaire about both objective life circumstances and subjective life satisfaction in nine domains: work/education, leisure, religion, finances, living situation, legal/safety, family relations, social relations and health. It includes subjective ratings of overall well-being. The subjective satisfaction ratings are recorded on

7-point 'delighted–terrible' Likert scales. The life satisfaction scores for each domain and for global well-being can be reported individually or combined into a total mean QoL score.

The following data refer to a sample of 285 patients with the full spectrum of psychiatric conditions assessed in the 1994 wave B of the SVOP (Ruggeri *et al.*, 1999b). Sociodemographic and diagnostic characteristics of the sample are reported in Table 21.1, while details on objective and subjective QoL are shown in Table 21.2.

Table 21.1   Sociodemographic and diagnostic characteristics of the sample ($N = 285$)

Gender, female (%)	62.3
Age, years, mean (s.d.)	47.1 (15.5)
Higher education (%)	22.9
Employed (%)	39.0
Unemployed (%)	14.8
Other (retired, homemaker) (%)	46.2
ICD-10 diagnostic groups (%)	
Schizophrenia[a]	18.8
Affective disorder[b]	8.4
Depression without psychotic symptoms[c]	30.7
Other neurosis[d]	18.8
Personality disorder[e]	10.7
Other	12.6
Time since first contact with service (years)	5.99 (5.94)

[a]Includes the following ICD-10 diagnoses: F20, F21, F22, F23, F24, F25, F28, F29, F84.
[b]Includes the following ICD-10 diagnoses: F30, F31, F32.2, F33.3.
[c]Includes the following ICD-10 diagnoses: F32.0, F32.1, F32.3, F32.8, F32.9, F33.0, F33.1, F33.8, F33.9, F34.1, F41.2, F43.20, F43.21, F43.22.
[d]Includes the following ICD-10 diagnoses: F40, F41.0, F41.1, F41.3, F41.8, F41.9, F42, F44, F45, F48, F54.
[e]Includes the following ICD-10 diagnoses: F34, F52, F60, F61, F62, F63, F64, F65, F66, F68, F69.

Table 21.2   Characteristics of the cohort ($N = 285$): subjective and objective components from each domain of the Lancashire Quality of Life Profile in 1994

Objective QoL	
Working time/week (hours) mean (s.d.)	25.03 (16.13)
Earnings/months, (€), mean (s.d.)	554 (455)
Family income /month (€), mean (s.d.)	622 (431)
Leisure activities (number of leisure items checked for past 2 weeks, maximum = 4), mean (s.d.)	2.94 (0.73)
% living unsheltered living	90.4
Personal relations (number of personal relations items checked, maximum = 3), mean (s.d.)	1.60 (1.18)
% who met friend in the past week	63.6
% with physical disability	17.5
Problems with physical illness (number of items checked, maximum = 3), mean (s.d.)	1.34 (0.95)
Problems with mental illness (number of items checked, maximum = 3), mean (s.d.)	1.93 (0.76)
% accused of a crime in the past year	3.7
% being victim of violence in the past year	6.7
Subjective QoL	
Overall well-being, mean (s.d.)	4.17 (1.63)
Work/study satisfaction, mean (s.d.)	4.06 (1.68)
Leisure satisfaction, mean (s.d.)	4.42 (1.16)
Religion satisfaction, mean (s.d.)	4.80 (1.34)
Financial situation satisfaction, mean (s.d.)	3.90 (1.59)
Living situation satisfaction, mean (s.d.)	4.63 (1.16)
Safety/legal situation satisfaction, mean (s.d.)	4.71 (1.32)
Family relations satisfaction, mean (s.d.)	4.69 (1.39)
Social relations satisfaction, mean (s.d.)	4.49 (1.55)
Health satisfaction, mean (s.d.)	4.64 (1.23)

This sample was subsequently followed up at two (Ruggeri *et al.*, 2001) and six years (Ruggeri *et al.*, 2005). Our findings indicate no overall deterioration of either objective life conditions or life satisfaction in this treated-prevalence cohort. Specifically, with regard to objective QoL, in the areas of 'legal and safety' as well as physical disability, where only few patients experienced adverse events, the good QoL condition remains stable over time. On the other hand, in the other objective domains, such as leisure activities and personal relations, the overall cohort condition tends to fluctuate. With regards to subjective QoL, changes occurring over time suggest improvement in key areas of life, such as health, social and family relations, leisure activities and finance, as well as stability in the other areas.

Interpretation of these data would, however, benefit from a comparison with general population estimates, and also with those subjects who have a mental disorder but do not receive such a comprehensive, community-based treatment. Unfortunately, these comparative data are not available at present.

THE LATENT CONSTRUCTS OF QUALITY OF LIFE

Conflicting conceptualisations of QoL have been proposed over time: some definitions (WHOQOL Group, 1993) focus on the subjective appraisal of life, while others base the QoL construct on objective life circumstances (which include health, housing and other material indicators). However, most researchers (Lauer, 1999; Warner, 1999; Katschnig, 2000) believe that both subjective and objective information is necessary to the construct.

With such concerns in mind, we investigated, both cross-sectionally and longitudinally, the differential role of subjective and objective QoL dimensions (Ruggeri *et al.*, 2001). By using a factor-analytic approach, three latent constructs of QoL were identified: (a) subjective satisfaction, (b) objective work/income/leisure and (c) objective living situation/safety. The fact that the subjective and objective components of QoL cluster separately on factor analysis suggests that they measure different underlying constructs. The distinct nature of subjective and objective QoL is highlighted by the fact that each factor was predicted, both cross-sectionally and longitudinally, by different and specific predictors. For example, most of the predictors of the subjective factor were variables reflecting the patient's perspective, such as service satisfaction, self-perceived affect state and self-esteem, whereas both objective QoL factors were influenced by sociodemographic and clinical variables. Thus, younger age, higher education, being married, being employed and non-psychotic, having lower disability and lower negative symptoms predicted a higher QoL in the work/income factor, while being married, having lower positive symptoms and not being admitted to hospital predicted a more stable, safe and non-sheltered living situation.

Since the objective QoL factors were influenced by functioning level and severity of illness and since these latter variables are common targets of mental health services, objective QoL measures may prove to be more responsive than current subjective measures in the assessment of the effect of these interventions. It could be predicted that variables in the work/income factor (e.g. hours of work, earnings and number of leisure activities) and in the living situation factor (e.g. freedom from victimisation and tenure of accommodation) would be valuable in the assessment of rehabilitation outcome. Given the distinct nature of subjective QoL and its lack of association with standard mental health predictors and outcomes, what is to be its role in outcome assessment? Some QoL researchers consider the individual's perception of his/her circumstances to be the central component. Their approach has the merit of empowering the consumer and giving him/her a central role in the development of treatment services. From this point of view, the subjective dimension seems to be essential in painting a complete picture of the person's life, in explaining patterns of behaviour and in providing the subject's interpretation of the personal impact of objective circumstances. Various factors make it difficult, however, to build predictive models around subjective outcomes. These include the tendency towards psychological adaptation or 'response shift', which can occur over time in the subjective appraisal of a person's current state, the multifactorial determination of subjective outcomes and the diverse reaction of different individuals to the same circumstances. For the time being, therefore, objective information may be more suitable in the longitudinal assessment of chronic illness and for building predictive models.

WHAT IS THE EFFECT OF PSYCHIATRIC DIAGNOSIS ON QUALITY OF LIFE?

From an historical point of view, interest in the measurement of the QoL of psychiatric patients was stimulated by the plight of the deinstitutionalised mentally ill and by a parallel interest in assessing such dimensions of daily life as personal safety, isolation, poverty and transience of accommodation (Lehman, 1983). QoL measures have shown success in comparing different populations of people with mental illness in different circumstances and treatment conditions (Lehman, Possidente and Hawker, 1986; Warner *et al.*, 1998). People with serious mental illness display poorer QoL compared with that of the general population or other disadvantaged groups (Andrews and Withey, 1976).

In a series of explanatory cross-sectional investigations by our group (Ruggeri *et al.*, 1999b, 2001, 2002), clinical diagnosis was not shown to be a determinant of both objective and subjective QoL. In fact, people with psychosis did not show lower overall levels of QoL if compared to people with non-psychotic disorders. Diagnosis is not even a predictor of levels of QoL over time. In a two-year follow-up (Ruggeri *et al.*, 2001) and a recent six-year multiwave study (Ruggeri *et al.*, 2005) of a cohort of patients assessed at the baseline in wave B of 1994, after adjustment for other sociodemographic, service use and clinical variables, diagnosis had no effect on either objective or subjective dimensions of QoL.

Differences in specific life domains were found for subjective QoL only; patients with schizophrenia or severe affective disorders had higher satisfaction with quality of health and general well-being, whereas depressed patients without psychotic symptoms showed lower ratings of QoL in the work/education domain (Ruggeri *et al.*, 2002). These latter findings may seem to run contrary to the traditional psychiatric view that patients with psychotic disorders display poorer life conditions than non-psychotic patients, but they are consistent with research showing that patients with schizophrenia tend to overestimate their level of functioning and environmental circumstances – the 'reality distortion fallacy' (Katschnig, 1997). It has also been found that their QoL assessments might be influenced by their degree of insight (Doyle *et al.*, 1999). For patients with mental illness, it has been argued that their own subjective assessment should be supplemented with that of a family member or professional carer (Becker, Diamond and Sainfort, 1993; Sainfort, Becker and Diamond, 1996). This emphasises the caution that researchers and clinicians should use in dealing with the concept of QoL and its measurement, as well as the principle that subjective and objective QoL should be treated as different constructs (Ruggeri *et al.*, 2001).

However, the most important aspect suggested by our findings is that no overall deterioration of objective life conditions and life satisfaction occurred in this sample of patients receiving community-based mental health care. Interpretation of these results, however, would benefit from a comparison with subjects who have a mental disorder but do not receive such a comprehensive, community-based treatment.

IS QUALITY OF LIFE IN PSYCHIATRIC PATIENTS INFLUENCED BY THEIR CURRENT MENTAL STATE?

If the diagnosis does not exert any significant influence on the QoL of psychiatric patients, it would be interesting to ascertain whether mental state, in terms of severity of symptoms in the various psychopathological domains, has any effect on QoL. Using multivariate procedures, we found that overall levels of severity (assessed with the BPRS) had no substantial effect on subjective QoL (Ruggeri *et al.*, 2001, 2002), but a small significant effect on objective QoL factors (Ruggeri *et al.*, 2001). With regard to specific psychopathological dimensions, we found that higher subjective QoL was associated with lower clinician-rated anxiety/depression and higher levels of symptoms of mania. Higher objective QoL in the work/income factor was associated with lower BPRS negative symptoms, while higher QoL in the living situation was associated with lower BPRS positive symptoms. Clinician-rated symptoms made a contribution in explaining the total variance of subjective and objective QoL, but never exceeding 2–3%.

These findings are consistent with most results published in the literature, which report weak correlation (Corrigan and Buican, 1995; Evenson and Vieweg, 1998), if any (Carpiniello *et al.*, 1997; Skantze, 1998; Hansson *et al.*, 1999) between subjective QoL and clinician-rated psychopathology. On the other hand, when the assessment of psychopathology is performed by using patients' self-rated instruments, subjective QoL has been found to be associated with psychopathology (Larsen and Gerlach, 1996; Ritsner *et al.*, 2000), most notably with self-rated depressive symptoms (Sulliven, Wells and Leake, 1992; Carpiniello *et al.*, 1997; Koivumaa-Honkanen *et al.*, 1999). However, these studies did not examine the relationship between psychopathology and subjective QoL by using standardised instruments assessing the full range of psychopathological dimensions from both the clinician's and the patient's point of view. In fact, most research assessing the impact of therapist-rated and self-rated psychopathology on QoL has used either a measure of overall psychopathology or instruments exploring a single dimension of psychopathology, such as depression. To shed new light on the complex relationship between subjective QoL and psychopathology, we undertook a study using both clinician-rated (BPRS) and patient-rated (SCL-90-R) comprehensive psychopathology rating scales (Lasalvia, Ruggeri and Santolini, 2002). We found that in psychiatric patients, subjective QoL is more closely linked to the subjective appraisal of levels of distress, rather than to levels of psychopathology as assessed by clinicians. In fact, using multivariate analyses, subjective QoL appeared to be relatively uninfluenced by clinician-rated psychopathology (only anxiety-depressive symptoms were associated with global subjective QoL, but their contribution to total variance explained was very small), while self-rated levels of distress (particularly depressive symptoms and paranoid ideation) were the strongest predictors. These findings provide further evidence that for patients with chronic mental illness, a low level of symptom severity is not equivalent to good QoL. They suggest that mental health services should focus not only on the simple reduction of psychopathology and/or enhancing levels of functioning, but also on the patient's perceived subjective well-being.

With regard to the impact of the affective state on subjective QoL, we found that depressive symptoms, both clinician-rated and patient-rated, though significant, explained only a small amount of the total variance. This indicated that subjective QoL represents a multifaceted construct, which does not significantly overlap with the affective state (Corrigan and Buican, 1995). Therefore, if caution should be used with affectively disturbed patients, when interpreting the subjective appraisals of their lives ('affective fallacy') (Katschnig, 1997; Atkinson, Zibin and Chuang, 1997), our findings suggest that, to assess outcome in a multidimensional perspective, both subjective QoL and depressive symptoms should be assessed and measured separately. QoL is a more complex concept and not simply a proxy of depressed mood.

HAS THE CLINICAL COURSE ANY IMPACT ON QUALITY OF LIFE?

We have demonstrated that psychiatric diagnosis has no impact on either subjective or objective QoL and that levels of psychopathology, at least as rated by clinicians, exert only a limited effect on the QoL of people suffering from mental disorders. We then explored the effect of another relevant clinical variable – the clinical course – on levels of QoL of psychiatric patients living in South Verona (Lasalvia *et al.*, 2004). The sample of subjects assessed in wave B of 1994 was followed up for six years and their clinical course was retrospectively assessed at follow-up with an ad hoc schedule developed on the basis of the WHO Life Chart Schedule (World Health Organization, 1992) together with Ciompi's (1980) conceptualisations, while taking into account the DSM-IV criteria. By applying multivariate models, adjusted for the effect of psychopathology, we found that the clinical course had an impact on levels of subjective QoL, but with a different effect depending upon the diagnostic category. Specifically, in patients with psychosis (either affective or not), a continuous course predicted poorer overall subjective QoL at follow-up, whereas in non-psychotic patients, a poorer subjective QoL was predicted by an episodic course, with a more pronounced effect in some specific life domains such as global well-being, health and safety. However, the percentage of variance explained by the final models was not higher than 16%. The fact that patterns of clinical course exert different effects, depending on patients' diagnoses, suggests that specific, individualised intervention should be provided to prevent the negative impact of clinical course on the life conditions of persons with mental disorders. To ensure a better subjective QoL for their patients, mental health services should provide specific intervention aiming at: (a) reducing chronicity in people with psychosis and (b) preventing relapse and recurrence in patients with anxiety/depressive disorders.

HAVE PERSONALITY TRAITS ANY INFLUENCE ON SUBJECTIVE QUALITY OF LIFE?

A striking aspect of the studies exploring the predictors of QoL (Ruggeri *et al.*, 2001, 2002) is that the full range of sociodemographic and clinical variables considered in the multivariate analyses explains only a modest percentage of the total variance (less than 14%). The low explanatory capacity found for demographics, diagnosis, psychopathology, disability, function and service use suggests that factors other than these probably play a major role in determining subjective QoL. We have demonstrated (Ruggeri *et al.*, 2001) that overall subjective QoL is associated with higher self-esteem and a positive affect balance. Other potential determinants include individual expectations and personality (trait to be satisfied, capacity to express feelings). Also, the hypothesis that the factors that are associated with QoL vary largely between individuals and so are unable to explain a higher percentages of variance needs to be explored further.

With regard to the effect of personality traits on subjective QoL, we studied (Ruggeri, Pacati and Goldberg, 2003) a sample of patients with a full range of psychiatric disorders, using the Eysenck Personality Inventory. Fairly strong relationships were found between neuroticism and psychoticism, on the one hand, and total subjective QoL, on the other. Among the personality traits, however, only psychoticism had a negative relationship with satisfaction with services. Although neurotics were more dissatisfied with their lives, they were not dissatisfied with the service they received. Graphical models confirmed these findings, showing that psychoticism is the only scale that is negatively related to both subjective QoL and service satisfaction. These effects of personality traits were not influenced by demographic and diagnostic characteristics. As a practical implication of our findings, we suggest that the patient's personality traits, with special regard to psychoticism and neuroticism, should be readily identified in clinical practice, to increase clinicians' awareness of the problems they have to face with these difficult patients.

DOES MEETING SELF-RATED NEEDS IMPROVE SUBJECTIVE QUALITY OF LIFE?

The relationship between QoL and the needs for care in people with mental disorders has been investigated in a number of studies, which consistently reported that patients with a higher number of unmet needs show lower levels of subjective QoL (Bengtsson-Tops and Hansson, 1999; Slade *et al.*, 1999; UK700 group, 1999; Wiersma and van Busschbach, 2001; Hansson *et al.*, 2003). These studies, however, had a cross-sectional design, which did not allow for the provision of any information on the predictive value of needs on QoL over time; they also assessed needs according to one single perspective (either staff or users). This latter aspect is a major limitation, since research has consistently shown that professionals and service users respectively have different perceptions on needs for care (Slade, Phelan and Thornicroft, 1998; Lasalvia *et al.*, 2000; Hansson *et al.*, 2001) and that both views are necessary to provide needs-led individualised intervention.

The first study, which combined a longitudinal design and assessment of both staff and patients' perceptions of needs, was in South Verona within the framework of SVOP (Slade *et al.*, 2004). Needs were assessed by the Italian version of the Camberwell Assessment of Need (CAN) (Phelan *et al.*, 1995; Ruggeri *et al.*, 1999a) and multivariate methods were used for data analyses. Adjusting for the effect of symptomatology, disability or functioning, it was found that a higher number of patient-rated (but not staff-rated) unmet needs predicts lower levels of subjective QoL at one year. This study, however, did not explore how changes in needs would impact on changes in subjective QoL over time; nor did it assess at follow-up patients who were no longer in contact with the service. To overcome these limitations, we carried out a four-year follow-up study to explore the relative impact of meeting needs, rated according to both staff's and patients' perspectives, on subjective QoL of patients assessed at the baseline in wave B of 1995 (Lasalvia *et al.*, in press). This considered both patients still in contact with the service and those who had interrupted their contacts during the follow-up period. It confirmed the central role played by patient-rated (but not staff-rated) needs on subjective QoL. Specifically, both improvement in patients' conditions and the reduction in patient-rated *unmet needs* in the social domain were found to predict an increase in subjective QoL over time. On the other hand, changes in staff-rated needs did not show any significant effect on changes in subjective QoL.

This means that if the goal of mental health services is to improve QoL, then greater emphasis should be placed on needs assessed from the patient's viewpoint. In other words, patients' assessment of their unmet needs should more strongly inform the planning and provision of mental health care. Intervention would then be focused on meeting unmet needs, as well as on symptoms and diagnosis.

ARE THOSE PATIENTS SATISFIED WITH CARE ALSO SATISFIED WITH THEIR LIVES?

The association between subjective QoL and satisfaction with services has been consistently reported in studies both by our group and other research teams (Holcomb *et al.*, 1998; Berghofer *et al.*, 2001; Druss, Schlesinger and Hallen, 2001). A six-month follow-up study on the outcome of care in South Verona used graphical chain models, a new technique that is used to examine the relationship among two variables by taking into account the effect of antecedent and intervening variables. By this technique the relationship between satisfaction with services and psychopathology, disability, functioning and subjective QoL in a group of patients with a full spectrum of psychiatric disorders was assessed (Ruggeri *et al.*, 1998). Higher satisfaction was found to be predicted by low disability at the baseline, but also by improvement in global functioning that occurred in the following six months. Service satisfaction was shown to be closely related to QoL and was its only predictor. These findings were stable over time, since they have been replicated at two years in a recent study which used the same statistical methodology (Ruggeri *et al.*, 2004a). Two other studies in South Verona, specifically exploring the determinants of QoL, with both cross-sectional (Ruggeri *et al.*, 2002) and longitudinal designs (Ruggeri *et al.*, 2001), showed that service satisfaction is the best predictor of subjective QoL, accounting for about 20% of the total explained variance.

More recently, a multisite study of a sample of patients with schizophrenia in five different European countries found that, among all the explanatory variables considered, high satisfaction with life had, after study site, the strongest and most positive association with service satisfaction (Ruggeri *et al.*, 2003). Domains that are very likely to be affected by severe mental illness, such as quality of social relations and health, are those with a higher impact on satisfaction with services.

All these findings seem to confirm that, particularly in long-term care, 'quality of care can become synonymous with quality of life and satisfaction with care an important component of life satisfaction' (Loker and Dunt, 1978). The cross-cultural stability of this association and its predominance over the other associations tested offer the appealing perspective that improvements to patients' subjective QoL can be achieved by providing adequate and individualised care. However, for the time being, caution should be used in interpreting these findings since conflicting results have been obtained about possible confounders. On the one hand, we have demonstrated that subjective and objective QoL have different latent constructs (Ruggeri *et al.*, 2001). Another study has found that self-rated symptoms, subjective QoL, self-rated needs and patient's assessment of treatments are all substantially correlated (Priebe *et al.*, 1998). On the other hand, it has been found that mood interferes with ratings of QoL, but has a small influence on satisfaction with care (Atkinson and Caldwell, 1997). Finally, there is little consensus on the factors that influence subjective QoL in the general population, while results from national surveys do not provide reliable information on cross-cultural differences (Veenhoven, 1993). Achieving further knowledge of these background aspects and implementing follow-up studies on changes occurring over time in both QoL and satisfaction with care might greatly contribute to a better understanding of this issue.

CONCLUSION: AN INTEGRATED MODEL FOR UNDERSTANDING QUALITY OF LIFE IN MENTAL HEALTH SERVICE RESEARCH

A consensus exists among clinicians and researchers that for people with chronic and severe psychiatric conditions mental health services should focus not only on the simple reduction of symptom severity and/or enhancing levels of functioning but also on the patient's subjective well-being and perceived needs. In this perspective, improving QoL seems to be a priority. However, for a long time, several core issues have remain unresolved, thus limiting the practical application of the QoL measurement in mental health care. We have tried to shed some new light here on the complexity of the QoL construct, providing some further insight on its practical usefulness in mental health care and, especially, in community care.

Our data confirmed that two specific components can be detected in the QoL concept – the subjective and the objective factors – which measure two different underlying constructs, convey specific information and recognise different patterns of predictors. Therefore, it is necessary to take into account both aspects when assessing QoL in patients with mental disorders. We also found that psychiatric diagnosis has no effect on either objective or subjective QoL and that patients with psychosis do not display a poorer QoL, compared to people with other disorders. This provides further evidence that, unlike the classic pessimistic prognostic view, in a multidimensional perspective, the outcome of people with severe mental disorders, such as schizophrenia, can be heterogeneous (Ruggeri et al., 2004b). Moreover, we found that patients' sociodemographic characteristics have no influence on subjective QoL, whereas some of them, such as age, education, and marital and occupational status, show some associations with objective components of QoL. Clinical characteristics, such as psychopathology and levels of functioning, have a very limited impact on subjective QoL (on which only patient-rated symptoms exert a significant role), whereas they seem to have some effect on objective QoL. As far as subjective QoL is concerned, self-rated needs for care, some personality traits and, above all, satisfaction with services received are the most important predictors. How can all findings of our studies be combined in an overall integrated model? A detailed description of the proposed model has been fully given in Ruggeri et al. (2005). Here we provide only a brief overview.

We may speculate that sociodemographic characteristics found to be associated with the objective QoL factor, such as being unmarried, being unemployed, lower education and older age, could act as vulnerability factors, which may exert a role in worsening the objective QoL. This depends on the presence or absence of some contextual resources, such as socioeconomic status, cultural level, characteristics of patients' social network and tolerance of the environment. If good resources are available, these vulnerability factors are likely to have a lesser impact on objective QoL, while if they are lacking their potential impact is higher. Therefore, mental health services should be aware of the patient's higher risk for a worsening of his/her objective QoL when vulnerability factors are present and should plan interventions to preserve/ameliorate the wider context within which the patient lives.

Satisfaction with the intervention received has been found to have a central role in predicting subjective QoL. An important role was also played by self-perceived needs for care, affect balance and self-esteem, which are variables strictly related to patients' perception of their overall mental health condition. This suggests that indicators of self-perceived outcome are more important predictors of subjective QoL than indicators strictly related to patients' clinical condition, as observed by the clinician. Therefore, clinicians should systematically take into account the subjective perspective of their patients in everyday practice. They should provide individualised intervention, targeted to improve patients' emotional well-being and self-esteem; this could have a positive effect on patients' satisfaction with life, which in turn might have a beneficial effect on the therapeutic alliance, adherence to treatment and the overall effectiveness of care provided.

REFERENCES

Andrews, F.M & Withey, S.B. (1976). Social indicators of well-being, in *America's Perception of Life Quality*, Plenum Press, New York.

Atkinson, M.J. & Caldewell, L. (1997). The differential effects of mood on patients' ratings of life quality and satisfaction with their care, *J. Affect. Disord.*, **44**, 169–175.

Atkinson, M., Zibin, S. & Chuang, H. (1997). Characterizing quality of life among patients with chronic mental illness: A critical examination of self-report methodology, *Am. J. Psychiatry*, **154**, 99–105.

Baker, F. & Intagliata, J. (1982). Quality of life in the evaluation of community support systems, *Evaluation and Progm. Plann.*, **5**, 69–79.

Becker, M., Diamond, R. & Sainfort, F. (1993). A new patient focused index for measuring quality of life in persons with severe and persistent mental illness, *Quality of Life Res.*, **2**, 239–251.

Bengtsson-Tops, A. & Hansson, L. (1999). Clinical and social needs of schizophrenic outpatients living in the community: The relationship between needs and subjective quality of life, *Social Psychiatry Psychiat. Epidemiol.*, **34**, 513–518.

Berghofer, G., Lang, A., Henkel, H., Schmidl, F., Rudas, S. & Schmidtz, M. (2001). Satisfaction of inpatients and outpatients with staff, environment, and other patients, *Psychiatr. Serv.*, **52**, 104–106.

Carpiniello, B., Lai, G.L., Pariante, C.M., Carta, M.G. & Rudas, N. (1997). Symptoms, standards of living and subjective quality of life: A comparative study of schizophrenic and depressed out-patients, *Acta Psychiatrica Scand.*, **96**, 235–241.

Carulla, L.S. (1999). Routine outcome assessment in mental health research, *Curr. Opinion Psychiatry*, **12**, 207–210.

Ciompi, L. (1980). Catamnestic long-term study on the course of life and aging of schizophrenics, *Schizophrenia Bull.*, **6**, 606–618.

Corrigan, P.W. & Buican, B. (1995). The construct validity of subjective quality of life for the severely mentally ill, *J. Nerv. Ment. Dis.*, **183**, 281–285.

Doyle, M., Flanagan, S., Browne, S., Clarke, M., Lydon, D., Larkin, C. & O'Callaghan, E. (1999). Subjective and external assessments of quality of life in schizophrenia: Relationship to insight, *Acta Psychiatrica Scand.*, **99**, 466–472.

Druss, B.G., Schlesinger, M. & Hallen, H.M. (2001). Depressive symptoms, satisfaction with health care, and 2-year work outcomes in an employed population, *Am. J. Psychiatry*, **5**, 731–734.

Ellwood, P. (1998). A technology of patient experience, *New Engl. J. Med.*, **318**, 1549–1556.

Evenson, R.C. & Vieweg, B.W. (1998). Using a quality of life measure to investigate outcome in outpatient treatment of severely impaired psychiatric clients, *Comp. Psychiatry*, **39**, 57–62.

Hansson, L., Middelboe, T., Merinder, L., Bjarnason, O., Bengtsson-Tops, A., Nilsson, L., Sandlund, M., Sourander, A., Sorgaard, K.W. & Vinding, H. (1999). Predictors of subjective quality of life in schizophrenic patients living in the community. A Nordic multicentre study, *Int. J. Social Psychiatry*, **45**, 247–258.

Hansson, L., Sandlund, M., Bengtsson-Tops, A., Bjarnason, O., Karlsson, H., Mackeprang, T., Merinder, L., Nilsson, L., Sorgaard, K., Vinding, H. & Middelboe, T. (2003). The relationship of needs and quality of life in persons with schizophrenia living in the community. A Nordic multicenter study, *Nord. J. Psychiatry*, **57**, 5–11.

Holcomb, W.R., Parker, J.C., Leong, G.B., Thiele, J. & Higdon, J. (1998). Customer satisfaction and self-reported treatment outcomes among psychiatric inpatients, *Psychiat. Serv.*, **49**, 929–934.

Katschnig, H. (1997). How useful is the concept of quality of life in psychiatry?, *Curr. Opinion Psychiatry*, **10**, 337–345.

Katschnig, H. (2000). Why it is so difficult for persons with schizophrenia living in the community to achieve an adequate quality of life?, *Epidemiol. Psichiat. Soc.*, **9**, 7–10.

Kissling, W. (2001). Who is interested in the quality of everyday psychiatry care?, *Int. Clin. Psychopharmacol.*, **16**, (Suppl. 3), 1–4.

Koivumaa-Honkanen, H.T., Honkanen, R., Antikainen, R., Hintikka, J. & Viinamaki, H. (1999). Self-reported life satisfaction and treatment factors in patients with schizophrenia, major depression and anxiety disorder, *Acta Psychiatrica Scand.*, **99**, 377–384.

Larsen, E.B. & Gerlach, J. (1996). Subjective experience of treatment, side-effects, mental state and quality of life in chronic schizophrenic out-patients treated with depot neuroleptics, *Acta Psychiatrica Scand.*, **93**, 381–388.

Lasalvia, A., Ruggeri, M. & Dall'Agnola, R.B. (2000). Lancashire Quality of Life Profile, in *Come Valutare l'Esito nei Dipartimenti di Salute Mentale*, pp. 173–192, Il Pensiero Scientifico Editore, Roma.

Lasalvia, A., Ruggeri, M. & Santolini, N. (2002). Subjective quality of life: Its relationship with clinician-rated and patient-rated psychopathology. The South-Verona Outcome Project 6, *Psychotherapy Psychosomatics*, **71**, 275–284.

Lasalvia, A., Dall'Agnola, R., Mazzi, M.A. & Ruggeri, M. (2000). The perception of needs for care in staff and patients in an Italian community-based psychiatric service, *Acta Psychiatr. Scand.*, **102**, 366–375.

Lasalvia, A., Bonetto, C., De Santi, K. & Ruggeri, M. (2004). Patterns of clinical course in persons with mental disorders: Which impact on social disability and quality of life? A longitudinal study, *Epidemiol. Psichiat. Soc.*, **13**, 169–190.

Lasalvia, A., Bonetto, C., Malchiodi, F., Salvi, G., Parabiaghi, A., Tansella, M. & Ruggeri, M. Listening to patients' needs to improve their quality of life. A follow-up study in community psychiatry care, *Psychol. Med.*, in press.

Lauer, G. (1999). Concepts of quality of life in mental health care, in *Quality of Life and Mental Health Care* (Eds S. Priebe, J.P.J. Oliver & W. Kaiser), pp.19–34, Wrightson Biomedical, Philadelphia, Pennsylvania.

Lehman, A.F. (1983) The well-being of chronic mental patients: Assessing their quality of life, *Arch. Gen. Psychiatry*, **40**, 369–373.

Lehman, A.F., Possidente, S. & Hawker, F. (1986). The quality of life of chronic patients in a state hospital and in community life, *Hosp. Community Psychiatry*, **37**, 901–907.

Locker, D., & Dunt, D. (1978). Theoretical and methodological issues in sociological studies of consumer satisfaction with medical care, *Social Sci. Med.*, **12**, 283–292.

Oliver, J.P. (1991). The social care directive: Development of a quality of life profile for use in community services for mentally ill, *Social Work Social Sci. Rev.*, **3**, 4–45.

Oliver, J., Huxley, P., Bridges, K. & Mohamad, H. (1996). *Quality of Life and Mental Health Services*, Routledge, London.

Phelan, M., Slade, M., Thornicroft, G., Dunn, G., Holloway, F., Wykes, T., Strathdee, G., Loftus, L., McCrone, P. & Hayward, P. (1995). The Camberwell Assessment of Need: The validity and reliability of an instrument to assess the needs of people with severe mental illness, *Br. J. Psychiatry*, **167**, 589–595.

Priebe, S., Kaiser, W., Huxley, P.J., Roder-Wanner, U.U. & Rudolf, H. (1998). Do different subjective evaluation criteria reflect distinct constructs?, *J. Nerv. Ment. Dis.*, **186**, 385–392.

Ritsner, M., Modai, I., Endicott, J., Rivkin, O., Nechamkin, Y., Barakm, P., Goldin, V. & Ponizovsky, A. (2000). Differences in quality of life domains and psychopathologic and psychosocial factors in psychiatric patients, *J. Clin. Psychiatry*, **61**, 880–889.

Ruggeri, M. (2002). Feasibility, usefulness, limitations and perspectives of routine outcome assessment: The South Verona Outcome Project, *Epidemiol. Psichiat. Soc.*, **11**, 177–185.

Ruggeri, M. & Dall'Agnola, R.B. (2000). *Come Valutare l'esito nei Dipartimenti di Salute Mentale*, Il Pensiero Scientifico Editore, Roma.

Ruggeri, M., Pacati, P. & Goldberg, D. (2003). Neurotics are dissatisfied with life, but not with services. The South Verona Outcome Project 7, *Gen. Hosp. Psychiatry*, **25**, 338–344.

Ruggeri, M., Biggeri, A., Rucci, P. & Tansella, M. (1998). Multivariate analysis of outcome of mental health care using graphical chain models. The South-Verona Outcome Project 1, *Psychol. Med.*, **28**, 1421–1431.

Ruggeri, M., Lasalvia, A., Nicolaou, S. & Tansella, M. (1999a). The Italian version of the Camberwell Assessment of Need (CAN), an interview for the identification of needs of care, *Epidemiol. Psichiat. Soc.*, **8**, 135–167.

Ruggeri, M., Santolini, N., Stegagno, M., Imperadore, G. & Dall'Agnola, R.B. (1999b). Quality of life of psychiatric patients, *Epidemiol. Psichiat. Soc.*, **8**(Suppl. 1), 1–48.

Ruggeri, M., Bisoffi, G., Fontecedro, L. & Warner, R. (2001). Subjective and objective dimensions of quality of life in psychiatric patients: A factor analytical approach. The South Verona Outcome Project 4, *Br. J. Psychiatry*, **178**, 268–275.

Ruggeri, M., Gater, R., Bisoffi, G., Barbui, C. & Tansella, M. (2002). Determinants of subjective quality of life in patients attending community-based mental health services. The South-Verona Outcome Project 5, *Acta Psychiatrica Scand.*, **105**, 131–140.

Ruggeri, M., Lasalvia, A., Bisoffi, G., Schene, A., Knudsen, H.C., Thornicroft, G., Becker, T., Knapp, M., Gaite, L., Tansella, M. & the EPSILON Study Group (2003). Satisfaction with mental health services among people with schizophrenia in five European sites: results from the EPSILON Study, *Schizophrenia Bull.*, **29**, 229–245.

Ruggeri, M., Bisoffi, G., Lasalvia, A., Amaddeo, F., Bonetto, C. & Buggeri, A. (2004a). A longitudinal evaluation of two-year outcome in a community-based mental health service using graphical chain models. The South-Verona Outcome Project 9, *Int. J. Meth. Psychiat. Res.*, **13**, 10–23.

Ruggeri, M., Lasalvia, A., Tansella, M., Bonetto, C., Abate, M., Thornicroft, G., Allevi, L. & Ognibene, P. (2004b). Heterogeneity in outcomes of schizophrenia. 3 year follow-up for treated prevalence cases, *Br. J. Psychiatry*, **184**, 48–57.

Ruggeri, M., Nosè, M., Bonetto, C., Cristofalo, D., Lasalvia, A., Salvi, G., Stefani, B., Malchiodi, F. & Tansella, M. (2005). The impact of mental disorders on objective and subjective quality of life. A multiwave follow-up study, *Br. J. Psychiatry*, **186**.

Sainfort, F., Becker, M. & Diamond, R. (1996). Judgments of quality of life of individuals with severe mental disorders: Patient self-report versus provider perspectives, *Am. J. Psychiatry*, **153**, 497–502.

Skantze, K. (1998). Subjective quality of life and standard of living: A 10-year follow-up of out-patients with schizophrenia, *Acta Psychiatrica Scand.*, **98**, 390–399.

Slade, M., Phelan, M. & Thornicroft, G. (1998). A comparison of needs assessed by staff and an epidemiologically representative sample of patients with psychosis, *Psychol. Med.*, **28**, 543–550.

Slade, M., Leese, M., Taylor, R. & Thornicroft, G. (1999). The association between needs and quality of life in an epidemiologically representative sample of people with psychosis, *Acta Psychiatrica Scand.*, **100**, 149–157.

Slade, M., Leese, M., Ruggeri, M., Kuipers, E., Tansella, M. & Thornicroft, G. (2004). Does meeting needs improve quality of life?, *Psychotherapy Psychosomatics*, **73**, 183–189.

Sullivan, G.S., Wells, K.B. & Leake, B. (1992). Clinical factors associated with better quality of life in a seriously mentally ill population, *Hosp. Community Psychiatry*, **43**, 794–798.

Thornicroft, G. & Tansella, M. (1999). *The Mental Health Matrix. A Manual to Improve Services*, Cambridge University Press, Cambridge.

UK700 Group (1999). Predictors of quality of life in people with severe mental illness. Study methodology with baseline analysis in the UK700 trial, *Br. J. Psychiatry*, **175**, 426–432.

Veenhoven, R. (1993). Happiness in nations. Subjective appreciation of life in 56 nations 1946–1992, in *RISBO, Studies in Social and Cultural Transformation n. 2*, Erasmus University, Rotterdam, The Netherlands.

Warner, R. (1999). The emics and etics of quality of life assessment, *Social Psychiatry Psychiat. Epidemiol.*, **34**, 117–121.

Warner, R., de Girolamo, G., Belelli, G., Bologna, C., Fioritti, A. & Rosini, G. (1998). The quality of life of people with schizophrenia in Boulder, Colorado, and Bologna, Italy, *Schizophrenia Bull.*, **24**, 559–568.

WHOQOL Group (1993). Study protocol to the World Health Organization project to develop a quality of life assessment instrument (WHOQOL), *Quality of Life Res.*, **2**, 153–159.

Wiersma, D. & van Busschbach, J. (2001). Are needs and satisfaction of care associated with quality of life? An epidemiological survey among the severely mentally ill in the Netherlands, *Eur. Arch. Psychiatry Clin. Neurosci.*, **251**, 239–246.

World Health Organization (1992). *Life Chart Schedule* (LCS), WHO, Geneva.

World Health Organization (1993). *The Development of the WHO Quality of Life Assessment Instrument*, WHO, Geneva.

22

The Quality of Life of the Relatives of the Mentally Ill

Maria D. Simon

INTRODUCTION

While patients' quality of life (QoL) has received a good deal of attention in recent years, studies of their informal carers, i.e. family members and relatives, are rare. The few systematic studies of caregivers that have been done have tended to concentrate on carers of the aged and of the chronically physically disabled, but only to a lesser degree of the mentally incapacitated (Herman *et al.*, 1994). Similarly, criteria have been established and instruments devised to measure the QoL of persons suffering from mental illness (Orley, 1994), but no standardised device exists in respect of their carers.

In fact, a good deal is known about this subject, even though the data have generally been collected with other perspectives in mind. The sources of information are for the most part not academic researchers but the carers themselves. Family carers in many countries of the world have been quite articulate in assessing their situation, expressing their needs and campaigning for improvements.

Questionnaire surveys on carers' burdens have been carried out by family associations in the United States (Spaniol, Jung and Zipple, 1985; Johnson, 1990), in Great Britain (Atkinson, 1988) and several other European countries (e.g. France, Spain, Holland, Italy). Among the most recent are an Austrian questionnaire survey in 1993 (Kramer, Katschnig and Simon, 1993) and a comparative survey of ten European countries under the auspices of EUFAMI, the Federation of European Associations of Families of the Mentally Ill, in 1994 (Hogman and De Vleesschauwer, 1996). In considering the determinants of carers' QoL, we shall freely draw on such cumulative evidence, in particular the Austrian and European surveys of relatives' burdens.

GENERAL CONSIDERATIONS

Quality of life is both a composite concept and a subjective category. An individual's QoL is the result of an interplay between personality and situational variables, which no doubt carry different weights in different individuals.

No one factor by itself determines carers' life quality, yet, beyond the multiplicity of personalities and influences in different settings, commonalities can be seen. Caregivers all share a similar fate: their life is dominated by the fact that they take responsibility for their mentally ill family members. They all carry very similar psychological burdens and are exposed to similar situational stressors (Atkinson and Coia, 1995). Their radius of freedom to react to these pressures is limited by external (societal) forces.

Quality of Life in Mental Disorders, Second Edition   Edited by H. Katschnig, H. Freeman and N. Sartorius
© 2006 John Wiley & Sons, Ltd

The principal factors that interact to shape a carer's perception of his/her QoL are: personal characteristics, situational stressors, societal stressors and iatrogenic stressors.

CHARACTERISTICS OF CARERS

The view that the majority of carers everywhere share a number of characteristics is confirmed by the EUFAMI Survey (Hogman and De Vleesschauwer, 1996):

1. The carers' average age is 60 years (some are in their eighties and nineties).
2. The percentage of females ranges from 72% (England and Germany) to 88% (Austria).
3. Approximately 70% of carers are mothers, more often alone than living in a functioning partnership.
4. One of the most striking consequences of carers' age and burden is impairment of their health, beyond what is usual for their years. The following figures from the European survey relate to the Austrian sample ($n = 200$): 91% report health problems, many of them psychological and psychosomatic. The leading complaints were brooding (70%), fatigue (62%), irritability (65%), insomnia (56%) and back pain (51%).
5. A significant minority of carers are partners, grandparents, friends, siblings and adult children, the last of these being sometimes still adolescents. They too are prone to impairment in their normal functioning, development and relationships through the vicissitudes of their carer role. Not enough attention is being paid to their problems.

SITUATIONAL STRESSORS

Sources of situational stress stem from the constant strain that goes with having to care for or live with the presence of one or more mentally ill persons, together with the concomitant friction this causes within the nuclear family environment. Some of these immediate sources of strain are:

1. Existential aspects of living with mental illness in the family, such as constant nervous arousal. According to the EUFAMI Survey, nearly 8% of respondents are caring for two or more mentally ill relatives.
2. Coping with patients' rejection of treatment. According to the European Survey, over 50% of carers take it upon themselves to ensure that the patient takes the prescribed medication.
3. Dealing with patients' aberrations, such as delusions, hallucinations, bizarre behaviour and persecutory ideas (Katschnig, Simon and Kramer, 1994; Simon, 1994). Also, in a high proportion of cases, mental illness exists in conjunction with other types of problem behaviour, such as excessive drug use, substance abuse, alcoholism or sexual deviation (e.g. exhibitionism).
4. Coping with aggressive behaviour from patients. At least eight out of ten carers in Europe have experienced some form of violence from their relative: verbal abuse is very common, damage to property is reported in about 40% and physical violence in 30–40% of cases (Hogman and De Vleesschauwer, 1996).
5. Living in the constant presence of fear and worry, with no relief in sight. There are two dominant fears uppermost in the carers' mind: (a) fear of the future: in the Austrian study (Kramer, Katsching and Simon, 1993) in answer to the question, 'What is your greatest concern?', over 90% replied 'The future – what will happen to my mentally ill family member when I am incapacitated or gone'; (b) fear of a relapse by the patient into acute psychosis. This fear is realistic, and carers' helplessness is compounded in view of the frequent refusal of treatment on the part of patients.
6. Excessive workload. Approximately one-third of the carers from ten countries report that they spend more than 30 hours per week caring for the patient. The highest proportion is reported from Spain (39%) and the lowest from Germany (13%) (Hogman and De Vleesschauwer, 1996). 'Burn-out' is a common complaint and can be accounted for by the sheer duration of caring; more than 50% of the respondents have been caring for the patient longer than 15 years (Kramer, Katsching and Simon, 1993). There is rarely a chance for respite: according to the European survey, 60–90% of the carers felt in need of respite care (Hogman and De Vleesschauwer, 1996).

7. Coping with negative symptoms, such as patients' inactivity, withdrawal, anxiety and frustration. Carers often have to walk the tightrope between activating yet not overstimulating the patient.

8. Living in the presence of suicidal threats and attempts by the sufferer. In the Austrian survey, 61% of relatives reported threats of suicide and 39% suicidal attempts. These are not idle gestures, since it is known that 10% of persons with schizophrenic illness will end their own lives.

9. Family upheaval and break-up: coping with lack of understanding and support from family members, relatives and acquaintances. Rejection of the patient by fathers and siblings is common (Kramer, Katsching and Simon, 1993).

10. Doing justice to the needs and expectations of other family members.

11. Staying 'cool' in the face of overpowering unremitting strain; controlling one's own reactions, so as not to exhibit high expressed emotion.

12. Changing one's life-plan. The care of a mentally ill family member often entails drastic changes in lifestyle. Many carers have to give up or curtail gainful employment, see their career shattered, or have to revise drastically their plans and hopes for the retirement years (Kramer, Katsching and Simon, 1993; Hogman and De Vleesschauwer, 1996). Ageing parents, as well as sibling and children, are denied their age-appropriate roles (Erikson, 1959; Bühler, 1969; Lefley, 1987).

SOCIETAL STRESSORS

The prime cause of societal stresses is indifference and neglect, which accounts for most of the other deficiencies and stigma that beset the carers and their families. This also applies to the lack of research interest in carers' burdens and societal role. The first of these stressors is the inadequacy of services. The families of the mentally ill bear the brunt of the deinstitutionalisation movement, since it is estimated that between 50 and 65% of persons with severe chronic mental illness are cared for by their relatives. Practically everywhere, savings from the reduction of hospital beds have not been redirected to set up an adequate network of community services for treatment, rehabilitation and independent or sheltered living. One of the most glaring deficiencies is the inadequacy of crisis services.

Secondly, there is stigma and social exclusion. Mental illness still stigmatises both the sufferers and their relatives. Since sensationalism in the popular media about 'mad criminals' is rarely counteracted by low-key factual information, the public at large is uninformed about and afraid of persons labelled as mentally ill, and this is generalised to their relatives. In consequence, the social network shrinks, not only for the sufferer but for his carers as well. In the European survey between 25% (England) and 61% (Belgium) of respondents reported having experienced stigma, and between 16% (Ireland) and 65% (Belgium) of the carers are reportedly shunned by their former friends (Hogman and De Vleesschauwer, 1996).

Thirdly, there is extra financial cost. Between 42% (Belgium) and 78% (Spain) of carers cite extra costs as one of their burdens; the European average is 50% (Hogman and De Vleesschauwer, 1996). The fact, mentioned above, that many carers had to give up or reduce outside employment adds to the financial strain.

IATROGENIC STRESSORS

Lefley (1990) has pointed out that some of the most noxious stresses are caused by mental health professionals themselves, and by inappropriate psychiatric services. Among these are:

1. Attribution of familial causation. Although this is less common now than in the past, parent-blaming still persists. According to the Austrian survey, approximately 45% of the carers have experienced blame. In those instances, blame came most often from the sufferer her/himself (34%), quite often reinforced by psychotherapists, 32% from relatives and friends, while 15% were blamed by psychiatrists, 7% by psychologists, and 3% by social workers (Kramer, Katsching and Simon, 1995).

2. Failure of mental health professionals to provide information and support, or refusal to communicate. Many professionals do not realise the crucial role that relatives play as the primary carers in community psychiatry. They do not understand relatives' need for information and support for the

task that has befallen them as a consequence of deinstitutionalisation. In the Austrian survey, 93% of respondents wanted relatives to be given more information about the illness and treatment, and 84% wanted more frequent contact with the patient's doctors (Katschnig, Simon and Kramer, 1994). While most professionals plead pressure of other work for their neglect of carers' wish for information, some refuse contact on principle, pleading confidentiality.

3. Ignorance of the family burden. At the root of professionals' refusal to communicate with the carers is often the fact that they are not aware what caring for a chronic mentally ill person entails. They are not acquainted with the problems of everyday living in these circumstances. Their advice, even if prompted by the best of intentions, often fails to meet the needs of the relatives. Professionals' refusal to communicate with carers and other evasive behaviour is quite likely to be due to their own feeling of helplessness and inadequacy, but this is not admitted; rather, it is glossed over or rationalised.

4. Difficulties of access to in-patient treatment. With the reduction of beds in psychiatric hospitals and of involuntary psychiatric hospitalisation, it has become increasingly difficult in most countries to obtain psychiatric help. Yet emergency situations requiring involuntary hospitalisation occur frequently. The European survey showed that consistently in all ten countries under consideration, approximately 60% of patients have at one time or another been admitted to hospital against their will. The range is from 40% in Holland to 73% in Sweden (Hogman and De Vleesschauwer, 1996). Appropriate crisis services that could prevent an involuntary commitment in many cases are mostly lacking and, as a rule, it is the carer, who is least qualified for this, who has to set the procedure for commitment in motion.

5. Difficulties of access to appropriate out-patient treatment. A significant source of support for carers is appropriate out-patient treatment facilities. In many countries or regions, out-patient community support of chronic patients is lacking or inadequate. Two omissions in particular are glaring:

   (a) Patients are discharged from hospital to their families without a plan for continued treatment or other follow-up. Often, patients will not receive follow-up treatment from the community mental health facility unless they present themselves there, on their own initiative. Many who are the most in need of treatment are not able to do this.
   (b) With a few notable exceptions in Britain and the Netherlands, chronic patients are not provided with a key worker (e.g. case manager, community nurse) who will actively coordinate support and safeguard further treatment (Hogman and De Vleesschauwer, 1996).

What, then, is the result of all the stresses that are brought to bear on the carer? It is grief, confusion, anger, self-blaming, frustration, isolation, guilt-feeling, burn-out, desperation and a breakdown of psychological defences. Normal reactions to the stress situations are unavailable: carers cannot run away and they must not act out their anger. Usually, they cannot even get a rest, while a holiday is an unheard of luxury. With normal outlets blocked, what follows are pathological stress reactions, such as unfocused anger, vague fears, resorting to quack remedies, chronic fatigue and psychosomatic illness. If QoL has something to do with the fulfilment of basic human needs and if these burdens of caregiving are all that life has to offer carers, then his/her QoL is very low indeed.

Is there not another side to caring for a loved and valued family member? Is stress always distress? Since it is sometimes said that stress can be a welcome challenge, are there any compensatory benefits from caring?

BENEFITS FROM CARING

In the Austrian study (Kramer, Katschnig and Simon, 1993), carers were asked whether they had derived any benefits from caring. In the face of the evident burdens, the investigators had low expectations on this point, and were surprised to note that 45% of the respondents reported having benefited. These benefits were quite diverse, e.g. a more profound understanding of the human condition, greater tolerance for deviant behaviour, having found new friends among fellow carers, satisfaction from being needed by someone, satisfaction from having a task in one's old age, meeting a challenge, greater family solidarity in face of adversity, getting closer to one's partner and finding solace in religion.

Even so, it is only a minority that can derive gain from adversity, and these persons have certain exceptional characteristics. They are basically resourceful personalities, are relatively privileged, have joined self-help organisations, enjoy a modicum of economic security and have been able to call on some support not generally available. In other words, they manage to cope. In contrast to them, the majority of carers are overwhelmed by their burdens and can see no mitigating circumstances.

CONCLUSION

In summing up, some common indicators of QoL will be reviewed as they apply to the carers. Katschnig (1994) states that QoL has three dimensions, which will be considered in relation to their significance for caregivers' QoL. They are: (a) objective functioning in a societal defined role; (b) material circumstances (standard of living); (c) subjective well-being.

Carers' societal assigned role is that of primary agents in community care of the chronic severely mentally ill. This assigned role is implicit; it is not socially acknowledged and confirmed with the usual trappings of an office. In order to find satisfaction in a role, it is necessary to be able to muster the means to cope with it, and to be recognised, appreciated and suitably rewarded. Yet as has been amply illustrated above, carers are denied both means and rewards. The means denied to them are the requisite material and immaterial support, while the denied rewards include the withholding of recognition of their role as frontline mental health workers. Thus, their role as primary caregivers can hardly be a source of a fulfilled life.

From the available data, it appears that families of the mentally ill are a cross-section of the general population, so that economic security is no doubt a problem, as it is for many other people. Yet carers, in answering the question about 'the greatest worry' in the Austrian survey (Kramer, Katsching and Simon, 1993), mentioned financial hardships only infrequently as their most pressing problem. This may appear to confirm the findings of a Swedish study of QoL of sufferers (Skantze *et al.* 1992) that the standard of living is a weak indicator of QoL. Nonetheless, we should not underestimate the significance of economic security for the carers' peace of mind.

The factors that interact to determine carers' sense of well-being are subjective as well as objective. The overriding subjective factor is the importance that the carer attaches to the patient's condition. A carer, when asked how she/he feels, will in most instances reply, 'It depends on my ill family member's condition: if he/she is well, I am well; if he/she suffers, I suffer'. The objective factors are the situational and societal burdens and rewards of caring, many of which have been discussed above. The burdens are manifold, but the rewards are rare. On balance, they are hardly conducive to well-being.

DISCUSSION

The conclusion that carers' QoL is low comes as no surprise. However, this could be better if some obvious remedies were applied. Carers should be supported in their own right and not be regarded just as appendages of the patient (Atkinson, 1991). They should be put in a position that enables them to cope and should be given a voice in all measures that affect their life and well-being. The caregiver's role in community care should be made explicit. It should be understood that carers cannot fulfil their assigned task in society without appropriate support and recognition. Just as the QoL of sufferers determines to a large extent the QoL of carers, so an improved QoL for family carers would in turn lead to a better life for the patients.

Any consideration of empowerment for the carers must take note of the crucial role of *family self-help*. No other single factor has been as powerful a resource for improving the lot of relatives. In step with the movement towards deinstitutionalisation since the 1960s, the self-help movement of affected families has evolved from small beginnings into a worldwide network of support groups and lobbies. The activities of family organisations have in no small measure helped to change the climate in psychiatric settings: no longer is 'parent blaming' state of the art. *Families as Allies in the Treatment of the Mentally Ill* (Lefley and Johnson, 1990) may still be more a programme than reality, but the quest is at least no longer regarded as presumptuous. At the local level, carers have found information, help, understanding and sympathy from fellow-sufferers that are often lacking in institutional settings.

In the light of the new importance attached to the QoL issue, some of the family associations have recently begun to re-examine their mission. For example, the long-standing and highly visible family association of Great Britain, formerly called the *National Schizophrenia Fellowship (NSF)* has adopted a new name, *RETHINK Severe Mental Illness*. Acknowledging the independence of patients' and carers' well-being, the organisation names as its prime focus the improvement of the quality of life for all (*The Guardian*, 2002).

REFERENCES

Atkinson, J. (1988). Survey report, *NSF News*, August.

Atkinson, J. (1991). Carers, the community and the White Paper, *Psychiatric Bull.*, **15**(12), 763.

Atkinson, J.M. & Coia, D.A. (1995). *Families Coping with Schizophrenia*, pp. 23–44, John Wiley & Sons, Chichester.

Bühler, Ch. (1969). *Lebenslauf und Lebensziele*, G. Fischer Verlag.

Erikson, E. (1959). *Identity and the Life Cycle*, International University Press, New York.

Herman, H., Schofield, H., Murphy, B. & Singh, B. (1994). The experiences and quality of life of informal caregivers, in *Quality of Life Assessment: International Perspectives* (Ed. J. Orley), pp. 131–150, Springer, Berlin.

Hogman, G. & De Vleesschauwer, R. (1996). *European Questionnaire Survey of Carers*, European Federation of Families of the Mentally Ill (EUFAMI), http://www.eufami.org/index.pl/download/Silent_Partners.pdf.

Johnson, D.L.(1990). The family's experience of living with mental illness, in *Families as Allies in the Treatment of the Mentally Ill* (Eds H.P. Lefley & D.L. Johnson), pp. 31–64, American Psychiatric Association Press, Washington, DC.

Katschnig, H. (1994). Wie läßt sich die Lebensqualität bei psychischen Krankheiten erfassen?, in *Schizophrenie und Lebensqualität* (Eds H. Katschnig & P. König), pp. 241–250, Springer, Wien, New York.

Katschnig, H., Simon, M.D. & Kramer, B.(1994). Die Bedürfnisse von Angehörigen schizophreniekranker Patienten – Erste Ergebnisse, in *Schizophrenie und Lebensqualität* (Eds H. Katschnig & P. König), pp. 241–250, Springer, Wien, New York.

Kramer, B., Katschnig, H. & Simon, M.D. (1993). *Austrian Questionnaire Survey of Relatives of the Mentally Ill*, Ludwig-Boltzmann Institute of Social Psychiatry, Vienna, Austria.

Kramer, B., Simon, M. & Katschnig, H. (1996). Die Beurteilung psychiatrischer Berufsgruppen durch die Angehörigen, *Psychiatrische Praxis*, **23**, 29–32.

Lefley, H.P. (1987). Aging parents as caregivers of mentally ill adult children: An emerging social problem, *Hosp. Community Psychiatry*, **38**, 1063–1070.

Lefley, H.P (1990). Research directions for a new conceptualization of families, in *Families as Allies in the Treatment of the Mentally Ill* (Eds H.P. Lefley & D.L. Johnson), pp. 127–162, American Psychiatric Association Press, Washington, DC.

Lefley, H.P. & Johnson, D.L. (Eds) (1990). *Families as Allies in the Treatment of the Mentally Ill*, American Psychiatric Association Press, Washington, DC.

Orley, J. (1994). The quality of life concept: Theoretical and practical approaches, Paper read at the 7th European Symposium of AEP (Association of European Psychiatrists), Vienna, Austria.

Simon, M.D.(1994) Psychiatriereform und die Lebensqualität von Angehörigen von Schizophreniekranken, in *Schizophrenie und Lebensqualität* (Eds H. Katschnig & P. König), pp. 231–240, Springer, Wien, New York.

Skantze, K., Malm, U., Denker, P.R.A. & Corrigan, P. (1992). Comparison of quality of life with standard of living in schizophrenic outpatients, *Br. J. Psychiatry*, **161**, 797–801.

Spaniol, L., Jung, H. & Zipple, A.M. (1985). Families as a central resource in the rehabilitation of the severely psychiatrically disabled: Report of a national survey, Unpublished manuscript, Boston University, Massachusetts.

The Guardian, UK (3 July, 2002).

23

Consumer Interests and the Quality of Life Concept – Common Ground or Parallel Universes?

Peter Stastny and Michaela Amering

The first edition of this book was published at a time when consumer involvement in service provision and research was in its infancy. In the intervening years, both current and former psychiatric patients have become increasingly active in the areas of advocacy, self-help and empowerment services, and employment-orientated programmes that have special emphasis on peer specialist and other peer support roles. Furthermore, there has also been more than a decade of work by researchers who are self-identified users/consumers/survivors/ex-patients (u/c/s/x)*, addressing such important issues as the impact of self-help programmes and the defining of process/outcome dimensions like recovery, satisfaction with services, quality of life (QoL) and empowerment (Campbell, 1997; Faulkner, 2000; Rose, 2001). These independent and collaborative efforts have already led to the development of joint research agendas (i.e. Trivedi and Wykes, 2002). In reconceptualising outcome and service-participation variables, u/c/s/x researchers have also found it necessary to develop new instruments and research methods that incorporate the priorities identified in earlier work (Dumont and Campbell, 1994; Segal, Silverman and Temkin, 1995: Corrigan et al., 1999; Ralph and Kidder, 1999). The emphasis here has been on self-report measures such as empowerment scales and qualitative assessments, based on semi-structured or observational techniques that give wide room to subjective experience.

Curiously, the QoL concept has received relatively little attention within the panoply of u/c/s/x-driven initiatives, including research programmes, and it appears that neither the efforts of researchers specialising in QoL nor those of u/c/s/x-led scientific endeavours have benefited from significant cross-fertilisation. This is rather surprising in light of the fact that consumer led activism and research

---

* This somewhat awkward and not uncontested terminology arises from the great variety of self-articulated positions and role definitions among current and former psychiatric patients. Clearly, the various terms refer to different ideological positions vis-à-vis the mental health system and their own participation. However, to advance inclusiveness, it has become a widespread convention in the literature (see Estroff, 2004) to combine these titles into the acronym c/s/x, which we have further expanded here to include the European/Anglophone term of service user, thus arriving at u/c/s/x. Whenever readability is of concern, we have chosen to substitute 'user' or 'consumer' for this unwieldy abbreviation.

Quality of Life in Mental Disorders, Second Edition   Edited by H. Katschnig, H. Freeman and N. Sartorius
© 2006 John Wiley & Sons, Ltd

agendas are primarily and explicitly concerned with improving the lives of mental health service users. Therefore, one would have thought that the QoL concept might appeal to consumer researchers seeking to measure the impact of self-help and other user-run interventions. Conversely, QoL researchers are obviously interested in incorporating subjective perspectives of outcome and living circumstances, which might well have involved a dialogue with consumer researchers. Unfortunately, neither of these potential areas of common interest have led to significant exchanges of opinion or collaborative projects in the last ten years. Therefore, a broad understanding is needed of the desired goals and outcomes, as defined by mental health consumers and consumer researchers, before we can understand why an integration of consumer values and QoL has not occurred. Furthermore, such an understanding would help in developing pointers towards a broadening of common ground between these hitherto parallel universes.

One of the earliest studies designed and undertaken by former mental health consumers to shed light on the views, needs and life circumstances of their peers was the Well-Being Project of the California Network of Mental Health Clients (Campbell and Schraiber, 1989; Campbell, 1992, 1997). In cognisance of the fact that 'consumers of mental health services articulate a different set of service priorities and desired outcomes than providers', the organisers began by involving their peers at all levels of design and execution of the study. Specifically, they conducted a 'brainstorming session with 20 people that produced several hundred possible questions for open-ended and scaled formats'. These questions were then prioritised by the group and organised into eight topical areas, one of which was 'well-being definition and quality of life assessment'. The resulting 151-item questionnaire was administered to 331 clients, 87% of whom had been hospitalised in the past, as well as to family members and service providers (shorter instruments). Most clients emphasised socioeconomic factors in response to the question: 'What would make your life better right now?, i.e. 'a decent home, a job, independence, a reasonable income and good friends'. Therefore, it looks as if in this early study, the QoL concept did emerge, but only as one element among the eight subject areas that were articulated by the consumers who designed the questionnaire. More recent work in the United Kingdom summarising areas of interest to consumers who are evaluating their lives came to similar conclusions, and added an emphasis on the nature, extent and quality of relationships to others, including their peers (Faulkner and Thomas, 2002).

In the mid-1990s, a group was formed that included several u/c/s/x researchers to identify desired outcomes for public mental health service recipients, which led to two pilot studies based on concept mapping – a structured group process using multivariate statistical analyses (Dumont and Campbell, 1994). The resulting content domains included 'legal issues, consumer impact on service delivery and system development, oppression and racism, coercion and control, personhood, damaging effects of treatment, alternatives to traditional services, citizenship, quality of life, employment, and validity of research'. According to this process, QoL did have a place among the panoply of outcomes identified by the consumer work groups.

However, by the late 1990s, the notion of 'recovery' had taken centre stage, possibly overriding any earlier interest that u/c/s/x researchers may have had in the QoL concept. For example, a report by Ruth Ralph and Kathryn Kidder in collaboration with the Recovery Advisory Group, consisting of 12 well-known u/c/s/x experts, was entitled 'Can we measure recovery?' and included no specific QoL measures among its listings of recovery instruments (Ralph and Kidder, 1999). Instead, this report lists eight (direct) measurements of 'recovery and healing' along with five instruments that are said to measure certain 'aspects of recovery', including empowerment. The newly emerging framework of recovery and resilience has developed in parallel to the QoL literature, and is primarily driven by u/c/s/x researchers and others who are interested in longitudinal processes or trajectories, rather than cross-sectional representations of symptomatology or life circumstances. The sparse dialogue between these two areas bespeaks the ideological bent of the recovery proponents (i.e. u/c/s/x who are very interested in promoting the view that persons with long-term and serious psychiatric problems can recover, are recovering and can learn strategies to assist in their recovery from their more resilient peers). It also demonstrates the difference among approaches between person- and process-orientated research strategies, often utilising qualitative methods, and cohort-based assessments that incorporate a QoL instrument.

While the work of u/c/s/x researchers began somewhat earlier in the United States than elsewhere, by now several important projects in Great Britain have been completed by consortia of user researchers, leading to comprehensive reports and publications (Faulkner and Nicholls, 2001; Faulkner and Thomas,

2002; Joseph Rountree Foundation, 2003). What stands out here is the limited attention on outcome measures such as QoL in these reports, which are largely based on interviews and surveys of primary stakeholders, i.e persons receiving mental health services and/or involved with user-run organisations. In general, there seems to be a recoiling from any type of cross-sectional assessments in favour of process- and action-orientated methods, especially those not separating interventions from their outcomes and subjective experiences of lives from their measurement. Another tendency among u/c/s/x advocates is to support research that is considered emancipatory by directly improving peoples' lives, for instance if it succeeds in removing them, even temporarily, from the position of research subject, and elevating them to participant observers (Beresford and Wallcraft, 1997). However, user-led research also highlights issues central to users that may have eluded QoL researchers. As examples, the spiritual domains of life and the role of self-help and peer support in recovery are frequently given.

Taking account of these concerns about assessment methods and the definition of outcomes raised by the cited surveys, consumer researchers have begun to develop both qualitative and quantitative methodologies from the bottom up, i.e. using focus groups, concept mapping sessions and individual survivor narratives to generate new instruments that might be more reflective of people in the process of recovering. The methodology of generating this set of new instruments deserves equal attention, under the rubric of 'multistakeholder assessment teams' (Campbell, 1996, 1997). Not unlike the methods of action researchers from the 1980s and earlier, these user-led efforts have emphasised the need for research to be directly useful to the subjects of the study, and are thereby creating feedback loops that are as exciting to the participants as they are methodologically challenging. It is no longer simply a question of triangulating between different types of variables (i.e. qualitative and quantitative data) but also a question of who is looking at whom and what is the role of the research subject in conducting the research of which he/she is a subject.

Given the potential value of this complex work by consumer researchers, one might begin to wonder whether this means that the entire research enterprise in mental health will have to be revamped in response to these important concerns, and whether, in the process, the QOL concept can and will survive. No one seems to be rejecting the fundamental notion of a life with a certain quality, wherein 'quality' emphasises the positive, rather than embodying a neutral concept that may contain both negative and positive attributes. Undoubtedly, such a perspective would raise the question of what to do with all the 'negative' and untoward aspects of life, i.e. to what extent they should be folded into a relatively neutral concept of QoL, or whether they might better be considered as a separate dimension of detractor variables.

Here, a linguistic/transcultural note may be appropriate, considering that the Anglophone notion of QoL, as defined by Lehman and others (Lehman, 1996), may indeed differ from the German proposition of *Lebensqualität*, which has found its way into much of the European research on the subject. When considering the quality of someone's life, American and other English-speaking researchers may be more inclined than their German colleagues to include both positive and negative 'qualities' when making up a comprehensive construct. This type of neutrality might be at the core of some of the main distinctions between consumer-articulated values and professional attempts to approach the subjective assessment of lives. Most of what is being articulated on the user side regarding desired outcomes has decidedly positive connotations, such as recovery, wellness, etc., while notions of QoL continue to embody both the absence or presence of psychopathology as well as factors pertaining to 'regular' life, i.e. a life unencumbered by sickness.

It may be that the German concept of *Lebensqualität* comes closer to the aspects that consumers are looking for among outcome variables that are meaningful to them, rather than 'quality of life'. Strictly speaking, *Lebensqualität* refers primarily to the aspects that make life worth living, i.e. the good stuff that makes a difference between a life of drudgery and a predominantly happy one. The term is not characterised by the absence of distressing elements, but rather by the presence of life-enhancing qualities, thereby steering clear of the many psychopathological and illness/disability-related concepts still contained within QoL instruments. The fact that most users who have publicly articulated their views about desired outcomes have done so in the English language needs to be taken into consideration when trying to understand the distance between professional and consumer views regarding QoL.

In a recent study that sheds light on the extent to which consumer and professional perspectives concerning QoL are divergent (Angermeyer *et al.*, 2001), subjects diagnosed with schizophrenia mentioned 'work, health, leisure activities, social contacts, joy of life and family' most frequently when considering the quality of their lives, while psychiatrists listed 'no or less side-effects of medication, work, social integration, social contacts, independence, social acceptance, psychiatric care and social competence' as their priorities for the lives of patients. 'Work' and 'social contacts' are the only areas of overlap between the opinions of patients and psychiatrists. A surprising finding of another study looking for factors that contribute to positive QoL (Rössler *et al.*, 1999) was that both idiosyncratic views about one's illness and negative assessments of prescribed medication were found to correlate significantly with higher QoL. This may provide a hint that professional definitions of QoL for clients can never fully encompass the broad range of individual views that might be more, or at least equally, important – a fact that has been pointed out by most consumer researchers. In fact, autonomy, individual differences and self-definition may be at the very core of subjective well-being, providing a challenge to researchers using primarily quantitative cohort-based methods.

It is obvious from these divergent priorities that simple, commonsensical, but also idiosyncratic, descriptors are favoured by consumer researchers, while clinicians and more traditional researchers remain inclined towards the use of technical concepts and terms that are not part of the everyday language that people (including, perhaps, clinicians) use when asked to describe their own lives. For instance, 'community integration, resilience, capacity and competence' are fairly abstract sociological terms that most people would not use when thinking about their own lives. Undoubtedly, such a lack of connection might also exist between the accepted terms of user-informed research, i.e. recovery and empowerment, and the everyday language of current and former psychiatric patients.

However, the issue goes well beyond linguistics. Fundamentally different or only minimally overlapping value systems may be at work when contrasting the views of mental health workers (and researchers) with their clientele. Idiosyncrasies, control issues, empowerment, but also dependency, need, consistency and a desire or reluctance to change may all be important factors that have remained outside the QoL framework, but have become key elements of the recovery/empowerment paradigm that permeates consumer-driven research and literature.

Do these efforts invalidate the QoL concept, or should they be informing it in ways that are still unclear? Certainly, neither an understanding and objective assessment of a person's life circumstances nor their subjective views of them should be dispensed with. However, irrespective of the degree to which subjective assessments are built into a QoL instrument, it does not help us to understand a number of processes. Those are the areas in which a person might have arrived at a particular set of life circumstances by finding out to what extent these circumstances may be hindering or promoting further recovery and whether they might be transformed through actions taken by the person or through events occurring in their lives, including psychosocial intervention. It is quite possible, then, that instead of integrating consumer perspectives into QoL concepts, we should be looking at the question the other way round, i.e. the potential for QoL concepts to be integrated into a newly emerging research paradigm that emphasises recovery, resilience and empowerment. In other words, rather than attempting to improve the available QoL instruments by refining and adding elements based on consumer feedback, a reformulated research paradigm that is moving away from pathology and dysfunction might benefit from the sophistication and the findings that QoL researchers have produced over 20 years.

There are several ways to achieve this reversal of directions. Constituting 'multistakeholder work-groups' as proposed by Campbell, Faulkner, Nicholls, Ralph, Loder and other u/c/s/x researchers may provide the appropriate context for the work needed to achieve this cross-fertilisation. Unfortunately, so far, none of the prominent QoL researchers have become part of such a workgroup. Another way might be to seek concepts that could serve as a bridge between the older, more clinically informed paradigm that includes QoL and the new recovery/resilience paradigm. Having identified such concepts, these may in turn serve to stimulate more effective collaboration among researchers interested in QoL and in recovery. The empowerment concept in particular may suit this purpose, since it is a representation of individual capacities that can be brought to bear on a broad range of life circumstances.

This raises the question of whether psychopathological, functional or resilience-related variables can be seen as individual attributes, albeit subject to change. Secondly, can QoL be seen as a snapshot of life circumstances and their meaning for the individual? If so, then empowerment or, stated more simply, the ability to take action may be an important link between them. Furthermore, the old adage that symptoms and functioning must be improved by treatment and rehabilitation before QoL can be affected has repeatedly been challenged (McDonald-Wilson, Rogers and Anthony, 2001). While interventions can take place in both areas, e.g. medication for symptoms and decent housing for homelessness, those that can specifically enhance empowerment may generalise to both areas. In other words, they may ameliorate the subjective experience of symptoms (how the person is dealing with voices) and the experience of social/environmental conditions (available financial resources, housing, etc.).

Interestingly, interventions that aim directly at enhancing empowerment are rarely found within the realm of clinical mental health services. When they can be identified, they are most likely elements of state-of-the-art rehabilitative and self-help programmes.* While it is true that an increasing amount of attention has been placed on enhancing individual coping skills regarding certain symptoms, such as hearing voices, depression, anxiety and stress-related experiences, this has not translated to broader empowering intervention in the clinical realm. It may be of use to conceptualise this type of intervention, especially when considering its impact on outcome and QoL. For example, instituting greater levels of control over life circumstances (e.g. Rodin and Langer, 1977), offering people actual choices in housing and treatment settings (Ware *et al.*, 1992), executing advance directives for mental health with respect to future episodes of incapacity (Amering *et al.*, 1999; Amering, Stastny and Hopper, 2005) and participating in certain types of self-help groups may all be interventions that are likely to enhance empowerment and thereby also have a positive impact on QoL.

In fact, there is some evidence that empowerment may indeed be an important condition or enhancer of QoL, even in the absence of significant changes in living circumstances (Rosenfeld, 1992; Stastny *et al.*, 2001). Interest in empowerment dates back to the early 1980s, primarily through the work of Rappaport and his group. While it has been an important slogan for advocates aiming to improve the situation of u/c/s/x, it has also become increasingly more grounded as a researchable subject, which has led to the development of several empowerment measures (Segal, Silverman and Temkin, 1995; Corrigan *et al.*, 1999).

Apart from awaiting the results of true multistakeholder research groups that combine the expertise of QoL researchers and u/c/s/x, or accepting prematurely the notion that adding the empowerment concept as an essential link between QoL and recovery will resolve these issues, we may need to look further in the published record of consumer/survivors' opinions on these matters. The relationship of QoL to the perceived quality of services (consumer satisfaction) has been a subject of research in only a small number of studies (Holcomb *et al.*, 1998; Ruggeri *et al.*, 2001; Wiersma and van Busschbach, 2001; Ruggeri, Pacati and Goldberg, 2003). However, this issue appears so frequently at the core of consumer concerns that it may indeed be difficult to separate it from an understanding of individual QoL (Estroff, 2004). As can be expected, a similar disparity exists between the areas that concern consumers who evaluate their care and the areas that professional evaluators deem important (Campbell, 1997). Beyond that, if we assume, based on several surveys, that a substantial portion of consumers (>50%) deem the services they receive as less than optimal, and a significant minority rates them as extremely negative (ranging from 10 to 30%), then we should not be surprised to find connections between those assessments of services and individual QoL (Stastny, 2000). Once u/c/s/x and researchers can agree on a set of dimensions essential to evaluating care, e.g. through the work of groups trying to develop report cards for mental health programmes (i.e. Mental Health Statistics Improvement Program, 1996), progress might be made in understanding the relationship between QoL, quality of care and satisfaction with services, especially for those reporting negative experiences in the services they have received.

An interesting relationship was noted by Ruggeri, Pacati and Goldberg (2003), who found a correlation firstly between neuroticism and dissatisfaction with life and, secondly, between psychoticism and dissatisfaction with services. According to this study, when people who scored higher in the dimension of psychosis are dissatisfied with their services, they are also more likely to be dissatisfied with their lives. This connection does not hold true for people with greater problems in the neurotic realm, who may be dissatisfied with their lives but not necessarily with their services. Since most consumers in the

*This information derives from an informal survey conducted between 1998 and 2000 among more than 80 state-run mental health programmes in New York (Penney and Stastny, New York State Office of Mental Health, Albany, 2000).

public mental health sector, especially in the United States, tend to have experience with psychosis, a connection between dissatisfaction with life and with services may be particularly relevant in those settings.

Satisfaction with services and QoL may not be linked directly; their relationship might instead be mediated by the level of unmet needs (Wiersma and van Busschbach, 2001). However, unmet needs as determined by researchers or as expressed spontaneously by consumers and their advocates may not be identical. Therefore, we cannot jump to the conclusion that conventional needs assessment could be a way to resolve this dilemma.

The link between satisfaction with services and QoL may be more significant in those instances when negative (or even traumatic) responses to past services are predominant. This may be especially true concerning involuntary hospitalisation and other coercive intervention, and less so when considering satisfaction with current or past voluntary services. While there are no studies examining this link, there is strong evidence that some in-patient stays continue to be experienced in predominantly negative ways, thereby increasing their potential for long-lasting traumatic effects (Quirk and Lelliott, 2001). Considering long-term in-patients, dissatisfaction with services seems to correlate more strongly with QoL than among a comparable out-patient (i.e. deinstitutionalised) sample, again indicating that hospital experiences may have a greater impact on QoL, contemporarily and thereafter, than services in the community (Shepherd et al., 1994). This would give credence to the many testimonials by consumers who place a great deal of emphasis on their hospital experiences in shaping their subsequent orientation to services and their recovery. Therefore, past negative experiences, especially within hospital settings, may need to be factored into the understanding of current QoL more strongly than satisfaction with contemporaneous services.

Another aspect of the distance between consumer and QoL researchers may be that most QOL research is being conducted with populations defined by a diagnosis of mental illness, primarily schizophrenia, while user researchers are consistently staying away from such classifications. It would be interesting to find out what avoiding those classifications does to the way consumers look at their lives or, conversely, in what way the use of diagnostic classification impacts on consumer views of their QoL. Feeling unencumbered by diagnostic categorisation may open up other issues, such as experiences in the mental health system, perspectives on coercion, disability, stigma and marginalisation, that are equally, if not more, relevant to QoL. Although certain personal idiosyncrasies that might be considered as clinical symptoms by researchers can have an impact on how a person assesses their life, the question would be whether such an impact would outweigh the effects of the other factors that seem to be emerging from research that is led and/or informed by users.

One reason why QoL researchers might be disappointed in the fact that consumer researchers and advocates have not embraced the QoL methodology more broadly is the fact that the former see their work as an opportunity to integrate subjective and objective dimensions. However, it appears that the relationship between subjective and objective dimensions remains problematic within QoL research, as well as in the area of process/outcome assessment in general. Part of the reason for this might be a remaining bias against using subjective measurements, such as described by Warner (1999). He writes that 'those who work with the seriously mentally ill recognize that subjective well-being cannot always be the primary goal of treatment, especially in the case of patients in involuntary treatment'. Warner goes on to say that 'on the other hand, agencies operating in the competitive managed-care market place in the USA, where consumers have considerable power, are likely to give a good deal of weight to subjective satisfaction and well-being measures, showing that consumer involvement is not only an important question in QoL research but also a burning issue for the financing and operation of service delivery in North America'.

In our study of peer specialist services, we found among other things that those clients who benefited from the intervention experienced greater satisfaction in the areas of finance, even though their objective financial situation had not changed. In other words, they were happier with the same amount of money (Felton et al., 1995). This could mean, for example, that they developed additional strategies to stretch their money or that they were more optimistic in general. A similar result in the subjective dimensions of QoL was seen in a study that added consumer advocates to case management services (O'Donnell et al., 1999), raising the issue of whether these extra service funds are wisely invested, given that they primarily affect the subjective dimension.

Table 23.1   Preferred methods and areas of interest in user-led and traditional research

User-led research	Traditional research
Mostly qualititative	Mostly quantitative
Process orientated	Outcome orientated
Process/action	Cross-sectional
Lived experience	Professional concepts
Open re-explanatory framework	Medical model
Person-centred	Diagnosis-centred
Including non-specific factors	Concentration on specific factors
Considering secondary effects	Concentrating on direct effects
Empowerment, recovery	Quality of life

In conclusion, we have to wonder if, and under what circumstances, a narrowing of the gap between user researchers and QoL investigators can be envisioned. In a schematic way (Table 23.1), we are contrasting the current differences in methodological approaches and areas of interest between user-directed and traditional research in mental health. Given the importance of the work that occurs on both sides of the divide, it would be unfortunate if we could not imagine more creative ways of reaching across. At the same time, we need to ask pragmatically whether the integration of user perspectives into the mental health research agenda, driven by a variety of interests, is really feasible and wanted by the majority of stakeholders. Narrowly formulated outcome studies, especially those trying to address the effectiveness of biological (i.e. pharmacological) treatments, may never accept the incorporation of the feedback that is being developed by user researchers. Furthermore, it is equally difficult to imagine where the thrust of user-led research could be heading, given the lack of incentives for conventional researchers (and policy makers) to reach out to users for their expertise and their findings. Whether we have any reason to believe with Faulkner and Thomas (2002) that 'placing user-led research on an equal footing with professional research enables professionals to think more carefully about the values behind scientific evidence' is hard to know. Correctly, these authors go on to say that 'clinical governance' would have to change if user-led research were to be taken just as seriously as the algorithms derived from evidence-based research. Since QoL assessment has not turned out to be the lynchpin in evaluating a more client-centred mental health practice, as some advocates might have hoped for, it remains to be seen whether user-driven research can help advance the hope for better lives, greater recovery and fuller community integration.

REFERENCES

Amering, M., Stastny, P. & Hopper, K. (2005). Psychiatric advance directives: A qualitative study of informed deliberations by mental health service users, *Br. J. Psychiatry*, **186**, 247–252.

Amering, M., Denk, E., Griengl, H., Sibitz, I. & Stastny, P. (1999). Psychiatric wills of mental health professionals: A survey of opinions regarding advance directives in psychiatry, *Social Psychiatry Psychiat. Epidemiol.*, **34**, 30–34.

Angermayer, M.C., Holzinger, A., Kilian, R. & Matschinger, H. (2001). Quality of life – as defined by schizophrenic patients and psychiatrists, *Int. J. Social Psychiatry*, **47**, 34–42.

Beresford, P. & Wallcraft, J. (1997). Psychiatric system survivors and emancipatory research: Issues, overlaps and differences, in *Doing Disability Research* (Eds C. Barnes & G. Mercer), The Disability Press, Leeds.

Campbell, J. (1992). The Well-Being Project: Mental health clients speak for themselves, in the Third Annual Conference Proceedings on *State Mental Health Agency Research*, National Association of State Mental Health Program Directors, Alexandria, Virginia.

Campbell, J. (1996). Toward collaborative mental health outcome systems, *New Directions for Ment. Health Serv.*, **71**, 69–78.

Campbell, J. (1997). How consumers/survivors are evaluating the quality of psychiatric care, *Evaluation Rev.*, **21**(3), 357–363.

Campbell, J. & Schraiber, R. (1989). *The Well-Being Project: Mental Health Clients Speak for Themselves*, California Department of Mental Health, Sacramento, California.

Corrigan, P.W., Faber, D., Rashid, F. & Leary, M. (1999). The construct validity of empowerment among consumers of mental health services, *Schizophrenia Res.*, **38**, 77–84.

Dumont, J. & Campbell, J. (1994). A preliminary report for the Mental Health Reform Report Card Task Force of the MHSIP ad hoc Advisory Group, Center for Mental Health Services, Rockville, Maryland.

Estroff, S.E. (2004). Subject/subjectivities in dispute: The poetics, politics, and performance of first-person narratives of people with schizophrenia, in *Schizophrenia, Culture, and Subjectivity* (Eds J.H Jenkins & R.J. Barrett), pp. 282–302, Cambridge University Press, Cambridge, Massachusetts.

Faulkner, A. (2000). Strategies for living: A report of user-led research into people's strategies for living with mental distress, Mental Health Foundation, London.

Faulkner, A. & Nicholls, V. (2001). *User-Led Research – Towards a Radically Different Mental Health System*, Mental Health Foundation, London; www.mentalhealth.org.uk.

Faulkner, A. & Thomas, P. (2002). User-led research and evidence based medicine, *Br. J. Psychiatry*, **180**, 1–3.

Felton, C.J., Stastny, P. *et al* (1995). Consumers as peer specialists on intensive case management teams: Impact on client outcomes, *Psychiat. Serv.*, **46**, 1037–1044.

Holcomb, W.R., Parker, J.C., Leong, G.B. *et al* (1998). Customer satisfaction and self-reported treatment outcomes among psychiatric inpatients, *Psychiat. Serv.*, **49**, 929–934.

Joseph Rountree Foundation. (2003). Shaping our lives from outset to outcome, Report; http://www.jrf.org.uk/bookshop/eBooks/185935114X.pdf.

Lehman, A.F. (1996). Measures of quality of life among persons with severe and persistent mental disorders, *Social Psychiatry Psychiat. Epidemiol.*, **31**(2), 78–88.

MacDonald-Wilson, K., Rogers, E.S. & Anthony, W.A. (2001). Unique issues in assessing work function among individuals with psychiatric disabilities, *J. Occup. Rehabil.*, **11**(3), 217–232.

Mental Health Statistics Improvement Program (MHSIP) (1996). *The MHSIP Consumer-Oriented Mental Health Report Card. The Final Report on the Task Force on the Consumer-Oriented Mental Health Report Card*, Center for Mental Health Services, US Substance Abuse and Mental Health Services Administration, Bethesda, Maryland.

O'Donnell, M., Parker, G., Proberts, M. *et al* (1999). A study of client-focused case management and consumer advocacy: The Community and Consumer Service Project, *Aust. N. Z. J. Psychiatry*, **33**, 684–693.

Penney, D. & Stastny, P. (2000). Integrating self-help and empowerment services into state-run mental health programs, Unpublished report, New York State Office of Mental Health, Albany, New York.

Quirk, A. & Lelliott, P. (2001). What do we know about life on acute psychiatric wards in the UK? A review of the research evidence, *Social Sci. Med.*, **53**, 1565–1574.

Ralph, R.O. & Kidder, K. (1999). *Can We Measure Recovery? A Summary of Recovery Instruments*, National Conference on Mental Health Statistics, Center for Mental Health Services, Rockville, Maryland.

Rodin, J. & Langer, E.J. (1977). Long-term effects of a control-relevant intervention with the institutionalized aged, *J. Personal Social Psychol.*, **35**, 897–902.

Rose, D. (2001). *User's Voices: The Perspective of Mental Health Service Users on Community and Hospital Care*, Sainsbury Centre for Mental Health, London.

Rosenfeld, S. (1992). Factors contributing to the subjective quality of life of the chronic mentally ill, *J. Health Social Behavior*, **33**, 299–315.

Rössler, W., Salize, H.J., Cucchiaro, G. *et al* (1999). Does the place of treatment influence the quality of life of schizophrenics?, *Acta Psychiatrica Scand.*, **100**, 142–148.

Ruggeri, M., Pacati, P. & Goldberg, D. (2003). Neurotics are dissatisfied with life, but not with services. The South Verona Outcome Project 7, *Gen. Hosp. Psychiatry*, **25**, 338–344.

Ruggeri, M., Bisoffi, G., Fontecedro, L. & Warner, R. (2001). Subjective and objective dimensions of quality of life in psychiatric patients: A factor analytical approach: The South Verona Outcome Project 4, *Br. J. Psychiatry*, **178**, 268–275.

Segal, S., Silverman, C. & Temkin, T. (1995). Measuring empowerment in client-run self-help agencies, *Community Ment. Health J.*, **31**, 215–227.

Shepherd, G., Muijen, M., Dean, R. & Cooney, M. (1994). Residential care in hospital and in the community – quality of care and quality of life, *Milbank Q.*, **72**, 37–47.

Stastny, P. (2000) Involuntary psychiatric interventions: A breach of the Hippocratic oath?, *Ethical Human Sci. Serv.*, **2**(1), Spring, 21–41.

Stastny, P., Nowotny, M., Brainin, M. *et al* (2001). Experienced members of self-help groups report. A comparative analysis of self-help groups in neurology and psychiatry, Final Report, Austrian National Bank, Vienna, Austria.

Trivedi, P. & Wykes, T. (2002). From passive subjects to equal partners. Qualitative review of user involvement in research, *Br. J. Psychiatry*, **181**, 468–472.

Ware, N., Desjarlais, R., AvRuskin, T. *et al* (1992). Empowerment and the transition to housing for persons who are homeless and mentally ill: An anthropological perspective, *New Engl. J. Public Policy*, **8**, 297–314.

Warner, R. (1999). The emics and etics of quality of life assessments, *Social Psychiatry Psychiat. Epidemiol.*, **34**, 117–121.

Wiersma, D. & van Busschbach, J. (2001). Are needs and satisfaction of care associated with quality of life? An epidemiological survey among the severely mentally ill in the Netherlands, *Eur. Arch. Psychiatry Clin. Neurosci.*, **251**, 239–246.

24

Quality of Life of Staff Working in Psychiatric Services

Reinhold Kilian

INTRODUCTION

In 1978, Cherniss and Egnatios (1978a, 1978b, 1978c) presented three main reasons for dealing with the quality of the working life of psychiatric staff which still seem significant today. Firstly, given that satisfying, meaningful and interesting working conditions are increasingly seen as a basic right for both blue-collar and white-collar workers, they should also be considered a right for those working in the helping professions. Secondly, since there are strong indications of positive relationships between job satisfaction and work motivation or performance, quality of working life in psychiatric services seems very likely to be a crucial factor in relation to the quality of service delivery. Thirdly, because people who are better qualified usually have greater possibilities of choosing between different job offers, they are likely to gravitate to those segments of the labour market where working conditions are most favourable. As a consequence, jobs that have poor working conditions are in danger of becoming 'employment slums' through processes of negative selection (Cherniss and Egnatios, 1978b). Whereas the first reason concerns the ethical dimension of work in general, the two others are directly connected with the quality of life (QoL) of mentally ill patients. This is because psychiatric services will only be able to improve the QoL of their clients if they are able to offer working conditions that will be attractive to the more talented, creative and compassionate professionals.

BURNOUT AS A CENTRAL DIMENSION OF QUALITY OF WORK LIFE

Since it was first developed by Freudenberger (1974), the concept of 'staff-burnout' has been increasingly used to describe and analyse a common phenomenon resulting from the particular working conditions in human services. Though the core of the burnout concept consists of a state of emotional exhaustion related to work overload, many authors who have studied such working conditions have extended the definition by including attitudinal, motivational, behavioural and psychosocial aspects. The definition of burnout used by Maslach (1976, 1978a, 1978b, 1979), Maslach and Jackson (1978, 1979, 1981) and Pines and Maslach (1978, 1980) includes the development of cynical and dehumanising attitudes towards clients by service professionals. In contrast, both Perlman and Hartman (1982) and Cherniss (1980) focused more on a decrease in job motivation, performance and productivity, whereas the definition used by the Berkeley Planning Associates (1977) stresses estrangement from both job and clients. Perlman and Hartman (1982) reviewed

Quality of Life in Mental Disorders, Second Edition   Edited by H. Katschnig, H. Freeman and N. Sartorius
© 2006 John Wiley & Sons, Ltd

nearly 50 empirical studies on staff burnout, carried out between 1974 and 1981, and surveyed the definitions of burnout used within these. They concluded that three dimensions constitute the common core: (a) emotional/physical exhaustion, (b) lowered job productivity and (c) over-depersonalisation. All other symptoms and components that had been discussed within the framework of burnout (e.g. low morale, negative self-concept, anger, cynicism, negative attitudes towards clientele, increased emotionality, suspiciousness, overconfidence, depression, rigidity, absenteeism, more time spent on a job, leaving job or drug use) might be correlates, but did not seem to be part of its prime definition.

Irrespective of whether those symptoms will be regarded as primary constituents or as secondary correlates of burnout, they all refer to serious impairments of the QoL of individuals working in these services, as well as to the quality of the services provided. During the last two decades, different theoretical models of the aetiology of burnout and of the factors influencing this have been developed, and there have been many empirical studies within different mental health care settings (Fagin *et al.*, 1996; Benbow, 1998; Leiter, Harvie and Frizzel, 1998; Coffey, 1999; Prosser *et al.*, 1999; Edwards *et al.*, 2000a; Hannigan *et al.*, 2000; Jeanneau and Armelius, 2000; Amstutz, Neuenschwader and Modestin, 2001; Benbow and Jolley, 2002; Cocco *et al.*, 2003; Fawzy *et al.*, 2003). The different theories on the process of burnout will be discussed below, together with an assessment of the significance of these theories for the mental health sector, based on existing empirical studies.

THE AETIOLOGY OF BURNOUT IN HUMAN SERVICES

In contrast to working in an industry or trade, working in the mental health field or in other human services involves direct responsibility for the well-being of other people:

> If a salesperson or factory worker makes a mistake, the consequences usually are not as grave. As Kramer (1974) noted, Ford Motor Company has recalled 500 000 automobiles because of errors in design or manufacture, and this action does not greatly disturb the public. But the recall of clients by a community mental health center because of errors in treatment is unthinkable. The public's reaction would not be so mild (Cherniss, 1980).

Under favourable conditions, this particular characteristic of human service work can be a rich source of accomplishment and satisfaction; many people working in mental health feel, as stated by Florence Nightingale, that 'the nursing of the sick is a vocation as well as a profession.' However, given less favourable conditions, permanent direct involvement with the problems and misery of other people can also become a source of stress and frustration:

> In many health and social service organizations, professionals are required to work intensely and intimately with people on a large-scale, continuous basis. They learn about these people's psychological, social, and/or physical problems, and they are expected to provide aid or treatment of some kind. Some aspects of this job involve 'dirty work', which refers to tasks that are particularly upsetting or embarrassing to perform, even though necessary. This type of professional interaction arouses strong feelings of emotion and personal stress, which can often be disruptive and incapacitating (Maslach & Pines, 1977).

However, the development of staff burnout is not regarded as a direct consequence of these particular characteristics of human service work, but rather of inadequacy either of individual reactions or organisational frameworks, or both (Harrison, 1983; Jeanneau and Armelius, 2000; Humpel, Caputi and Martin, 2001). Within the theory of human stress (Lazarus, 1966; Lazarus and Launier, 1978; Lazarus and Folkman, 1984), human beings interact with their environment through both cognitive appraisal and behavioural activities. Through processes of primary cognitive appraisal an individual defines the meaning and the demands of the situation, e.g. whether a situation is a possible source of stress or not. How the individual actually deals with the perceived demands or threats of the situation, however, depends on secondary appraisal of his/her coping resources. Lazarus and Launier (1978) have shown that this two-part sequence of primary and secondary appraisal, which forms the core of the coping process, will be influenced by both personal and environmental factors (see Fig. 24.1).

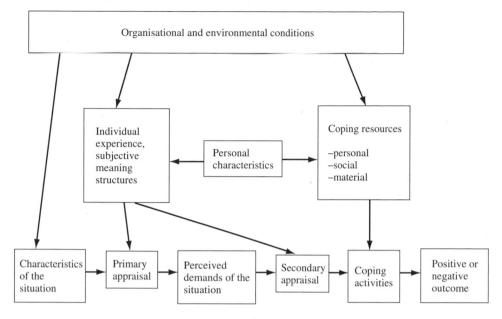

Figure 24.1   The coping process

Within this general model of coping, staff burnout is regarded as a negative outcome of the coping process due to inadequacy of either definitions of the situational demands or of reactions to those demands by the staff members. These again might be caused by either individual, organisational or environmental factors. From the structure of relationships symbolised by the paths of the model, it becomes evident that organisational and individual factors of the coping process are widely inter-connected, so that burnout should not be traced back to one of these factors alone. For conceptual clarity, however, it seems useful to discuss the individual and organisational factors separately, before discussing the interdependencies between the two levels.

THE INDIVIDUAL FACTORS OF COPING AND BURNOUT

Discussing the individual factors of inadequate coping and burnout, Farber (1983) started with the empirically confirmed assumption that those human service workers who tend to show burnout have particular personal characteristics and meaning structures. They are 'emphatic, sensitive, humane, dedicated, idealistic, and people-orientated, but at the same time anxious, introverted, obsessional, over-enthusiastic, and susceptible to over-identification with others' (Farber, 1983). What burnout-prone people lack, in other words, and what Maslach and Pines (1977) saw as a primary precondition for efficient human service work, is the ability to defend against the strong emotional involvement with the client's problems through techniques of detachment. This is because 'by treating clients or patients in a more remote, objective way, it becomes easier to perform the necessary interviews, tests, or operations without suffering strong psychological discomfort' (Maslach and Pines, 1977). As a paradoxical consequence of this lack of detachment, those affected not uncommonly react to the consequent emotional exhaustion with a change to the opposite extreme of over-depersonalisation. This includes the loss of 'any positive feelings, sympathy, or respect for clients or patients' and the development of 'a very cynical and dehumanized perception of these people' (Maslach and Pines, 1977).

In the case of people who work with the long-term mentally ill, Lamb (1979) has stated that idealism and overenthusiasm often lead to unrealistic expectations regarding rehabilitation which, for the most part, cannot be fulfilled by their clients: 'Most of (these staff members) enter the field with enthusiasm and good intentions. But after perhaps a year or two, they get burned out: they lose their enthusiasm; they no longer like their contact with long-term patients; they get bored, frustrated, and resentful. Worst of all, they become ineffective' (Lamb, 1979). Though many experts agree that emotional and person-ality factors play a crucial role in the aetiology of burnout, only a few recent studies provide empirical evidence for this hypothesis (Jeanneau and Armelius, 2000; Humpel, Caputi and Martin, 2001).

Instead of emotional factors, Cherniss (1980) emphasised the importance of learned helplessness within the aetiological process of burnout. Developed by Seligman (1975), this concept proposes that animate beings who are forced into situations in which they have no control over rewards and punish-ments for a prolonged time will develop a generalised feeling of helplessness. This then undermines their motivation to solve problems through active behaviour. Though Seligman developed his theory on the basis of experiments with dogs, the phenomenon has also been found in humans, and its influence on human coping behaviour has been empirically confirmed (Cherniss, 1980). Similar to learned helplessness, the concept of locus of control developed by Rotter (1966) suggests that if, during their learning history, individuals repeatedly find that punishment and reward are not contingent upon their own behaviour, they will develop a generalised external locus of control: 'In general, internal–external control refers to the degree to which the individual believes that what happens to him or her results from his or her own behaviour, versus the degree to which the individual believes that what happens to her or him results from luck, chance, fate, or forces beyond his or her control' (Rotter, 1982). Within the framework of stress theory, learned helplessness and locus of control have become two of the most important individual predictors of coping behaviour (Pearlin *et al.*, 1981; Lazarus and Folkman, 1984). People who feel helpless or who hold an external locus of control have been found to cope with problems in a passive and emotion-focused manner, such as behavioural or mental disengagement, denial, avoidance or drug use. On the other hand people who feel empowered and hold an internal locus of control tend to use more active and problem-focused coping strategies, such as active planning, problem-focused action and seeking social support (Carver, Scheier and Weintraub, 1989). Since passive and emotion-focused coping strategies are closely related to symptoms of burnout, the concepts of learned helplessness and locus of control should also become part of every theoretical concept of the aetiology of burnout (Cherniss, 1980).

Yet another important individual factor in this aetiology has been emphasised by Harrison (1983) within the framework of his social competence model. 'Social competence refers to how one feels about one's capacity to interact with, and therefore to influence the social environment' (Harrison, 1983). Like the concepts of learned helplessness and locus of control, that of social competence stems from social learning theory. In contrast to these former concepts, however, social competence focuses not on the controllability of the environment but rather on the expectations concerning the efficacy of one's own actions. As formulated by the originator of the concept of self-efficacy expectations, Albert Bandura: 'An outcome expectancy is defined as a person's estimate that a certain behaviour will lead to certain outcomes. An efficacy expectation is the conviction that one can successfully execute the behaviour required to produce the outcomes' (Bandura, 1977). Though they are similar to the concepts of learned helplessness and locus of control, those of social competence and self-efficacy expectations enhance the clarity of the burnout model. This is because they offer the possibility of differentiating between individuals who feel that they do not know how to cope with problems and those who know what has to be done, but feel that they lack the necessary skills and abilities to carry out the required activities. Both of these cognitive orientations can become sources of ineffective coping and burnout. However, to prevent staff burnout, it must make a great difference whether learned helplessness or lack of self-efficacy expectations have been suspected as the main causes in a particular work setting.

ORGANISATIONAL AND ENVIRONMENTAL FACTORS OF COPING AND BURNOUT

On the organisational level, Cherniss (1980) saw three components as being particularly relevant for the aetiology of burnout: 'the role structure, the power structure, and the normative structure' (Cherniss, 1980). Based on the role structure, the various tasks and duties resulting from the aims of a particular organisation are allocated to different role patterns, which are commonly associated with the different occupational groups working in that organisation. For the individual worker, the patterns of his occupational role define in more or less detail what he/she has to do, in which way and by which means. Role structures differ widely, not only between particular types of organisations, such as industrial plants or psychiatric hospitals, but also between organisations of the same type and even between individual parts of the same organisation, such as the different wards of a psychiatric hospital. Through research on dysfunctional aspects of organisational role structures, Kahn *et al.* (1964) found that role conflict and role ambiguity are the most important sources of job stress and burnout.

Role overload, as the most overt form of role conflict, indicates that the demands associated with a particular occupational position exceed the worker's abilities and resources. In human services, role overload primarily results from exceedingly high client-to-staff ratios: 'An example is the social worker in one program who was responsible for co-ordinating after-care services for over 200 ex-hospital patients. Responsibility for 20 such clients would begin to strain her capacity to perform adequately; a case load of 200 made it impossible to function effectively' (Cherniss, 1980). Extreme role overload, such as in that example, not only leads to physical and mental exhaustion of the worker but also leaves no opportunity for feelings of success and accomplishment. If the worker is forced to realise that despite all of his/her efforts there is no chance of accomplishing any intended result, the development of burnout seems to be an unavoidable consequence. As an empirical confirmation of the importance of role overload in the aetiology of burnout, studies in several psychiatric institutions came to the conclusion that the larger the ratio of patients to staff, the less staff members liked their jobs, and the more they tried to separate them from their lives (Fagin *et al.*, 1996; Coffey, 1999; Edwards *et al.*, 2000a; Hannigan *et al.*, 2000; Coffey and Coleman, 2001; Humpel, Caputi and Martin, 2001). In the settings with larger patient-to-staff ratios, staff said they would change their jobs if given a chance. They did not seek job-fulfilment or social interaction in their jobs; to them, the best thing about their work was the job conditions, e.g. salary. They limited their after-hours involvement with the institutions or the patients to handling emergency cases (Cherniss and Egnatios, 1978a; Pines and Maslach, 1978; Cherniss, 1980; McCarthy, 1985).

Another form of role conflict that has been found to contribute to stress and burnout in human services results from incompatible role demands. Psychiatric service workers sometimes feel obliged to act as rehabilitation counsellors and agents of social control at the same time, though the adequate fulfilment of the one role often contradicts the fulfilment of the other (Cherniss, 1980; Burnard *et al.*, 2000; Edwards *et al.*, 2000a, 2000b; Hannigan *et al.*, 2000). Role conflicts of this type often result from the human service worker's perception that the bureaucratic demands of the organisation contradict the needs of their clients:

> Professionally oriented helpers tend to believe in and follow a particular set of norms regarding the helping relationship. These norms constitute the professional service ideal, and they are an important part of the culture of professionalism. Unfortunately, human service programs are public institutions that tend to be organized along bureaucratic lines, and there are situations in which the professional service ideal comes into conflict with organizational self interest and the bureaucratic mode of functioning (Cherniss, 1980).

In contrast to role overload and conflicting role demands, role ambiguity occurs when the worker lacks the information necessary for adequate performance of the task (Cherniss, 1980; Wise and Berlin, 1981). As summarised by Kahn *et al.* (1964), role ambiguity includes lack of information along the following dimensions:

(a) concerning the scopes and the responsibilities of the job;
(b) about the co-workers' expectations;
(c) required to perform the job adequately;
(d) about opportunities for advancement;
(e) about supervisors' evaluations;
(f) about what is happening in the organisation.

Several authors have stressed the high prevalence of these dimensions in human service work. For the field of psychiatric services, Cherniss (1980, p. 91) emphasised that a lack of clear feedback concerning the results of one's work, ambiguous goals and criteria for work (such as the goal of psychological growth), the long and uncertain time perspective necessary for results to become visible, and the problem of authorship – that is, not knowing whether a helper's efforts were responsible for positive change in a client' seem to be the most important forms of role ambiguity experienced by the workers. This author sees the reasons for the concentration of these particular modes of role ambiguity in the fact that there is no general consensus of opinion about the right method of psychiatric work: 'For instance, despite hundreds of studies, controversy concerning the efficacy of psychotherapy still exists. There is no clear-cut evidence that psychotherapy is better than benign neglect. Similarly, the superiority of one therapeutic school over another cannot be established conclusively. Thus, the mental health practitioner inevitably must work in a dense of cognitive fog' (Cherniss, 1980). This general problem of mental health services was aggravated by the community mental health movement during the 1970s, because the rapid development of new services that resulted from it entailed new forms of role demands, for which many of the mental health professionals had not received adequate training (Cherniss and Egnatios, 1978a, 1978b). In addition to this lack of training, many of the staff members of the new community mental health services were found to have expressed the feeling that the expectations and the objectives of these new services were not well enough defined (Handy, 1991a, 1991b; Fagin et al., 1995; Coffey, 1999; Prosser et al., 1999; Edwards et al., 2000a; Hannigan et al., 2000; Coffey and Coleman, 2001).

Whereas role conflict and role ambiguity affect the aetiology of staff burnout primarily by overtaxing staff members' abilities to fulfil the demands associated with their occupational roles, there are other aspects of the role structure that produce stress and burnout by understimulation and lack of challenge. Task variety, task identity, and learning opportunities have been identified as very important factors that affect the work satisfaction of human service staff members (Sarata, 1974; Sarata and Jeppesen, 1977; Cherniss, 1980). Task variety and task identity are aspects of the working conditions that are closely connected to the division of labour within a particular work setting. It is known from industrial work settings that high fragmentation of tasks, as in assembly-line work, leads to boredom and loss of meaning, while research suggests that despite its greater variety in relation to assembly-line work, human service work can also be overly fragmented (Sarata and Jeppesen, 1977): 'Thus, a staff member who only teaches basket-weaving to after-care patients during a typical day would lack variety compared with another staff member who does various types of counseling with various types of clients, interspersed with supervision and program development activities' (Cherniss, 1980). Task identity, in contrast to task variety, means that a worker gains an understanding of the whole process of work within the organisation, as well as of his/her own contribution to the final product.

In mental health services, there are great differences in the degree to which the different tasks resulting from a particular rehabilitation programme are assigned to different professionals, such as psychiatrists, social workers, occupational therapists, nursing staff, etc. The more fragmented the rehabilitation process, the less the individual psychiatrist or social worker will be able to obtain a comprehensive understanding of the client's development (Cherniss, 1980). As a possible consequence, the individual staff members may be confronted with the experience that the success of their own efforts depends in great part on forces that they cannot comprehend and that are apparently out of their control. As with task variety and task identity, the learning opportunities offered by a particular occupational role have been identified as an important factor of job stimulation: 'In human service work, helpers often feel that they are giving constantly and getting very little in return. This imbalance is a source of dissatisfaction which exacerbates job stress and burnout. However when helpers believe that they are learning and growing professionally in their work, they begin to perceive that they are getting as well as giving' (Cherniss, 1980).

Considering the different aspects of the role structure and their impact on the process of coping and burnout, the relationships between role conflict and role ambiguity, on the one hand, and task variety, task identity and learning opportunities, on the other, are clearly complex. Because the enlarging of task variety can easily lead to greater role conflicts, and since the reduction of role ambiguity through task fragmentation can lead to decreased task identity, Cherniss (1980) suggested that the ideal strategy to prevent staff burnout in human services would be the development of a role structure that minimises role conflict and ambiguity, while maximising task variety, task identity and learning opportunities.

The possibility of developing such an ideal role structure depends in great part on the power structure and normative structure of the relevant organisation. The degree to which the process of decision making within a human service organisation is hierarchically formalised and centralised seems to be a crucial factor in the aetiology of staff dissatisfaction and burnout (Cherniss, 1980). The results of several empirical studies suggest that restricted autonomy and lack of influence on decision making in these staff members cause feelings of alienation and helplessness (Aiken and Hage, 1966; Pearlin, 1967). Also, staff members often suffer from arbitrary decisions by outside agencies which, in their opinion, are based more on bureaucratic and political needs than on the needs of their clients (Dehlinger and Perlman, 1978). Cherniss and Egnatios (1978c) found that the staff members of 22 community mental health programmes wanted more autonomy than they actually had on 11 aspects of decision making that affected their work.

Whereas role conflict, task variety and task identity are primarily associated with the power structure of a human service organisation, the normative structure, including the goals, norms and ideologies of an organisation or a particular programme, greatly affects the degree of role ambiguity experienced by the staff members. Clarity of the programme contents and methods seems to be a basic precondition for effective and satisfying human service work, but unfortunately the definitions of goals are often too vague or too general for their transformation into practical daily activities. Supporting staff members in their efforts to fill the gap between general goals and their daily practice therefore seems to be a crucial factor in reducing role ambiguity. Cherniss (1980) and Cherniss and Krantz (1983) suggest that the development of a guiding philosophy of treatment would be very helpful for that purpose. This term requires that there are some common principles of daily work that are accepted by all members of the organisation. Such principles may be based on theoretical approaches, such as different therapeutic or educational schools, or on ideological principles, such as religion, but more importantly they should be developed with extensive participation by staff members (Cherniss, 1980; McCarthy, 1985).

THE ROLE OF EMPOWERMENT IN THE PREVENTION OF BURNOUT AND JOB DISSATISFACTION IN MENTAL HEALTH SERVICE STAFF

During the last decade the concept of empowerment (Rappaport, 1981, 1987) has become an important theoretical concept for the prevention of burnout and job dissatisfaction in health care staff (Laschinger and Havens, 1997; Laschinger, Sabiston and Kutszcher, 1997; Laschinger et al., 1999; Laschinger, Finegan and Shamian, 2001; Laschinger, Shamian and Thomson, 2001a; Manojlovich and Spence Laschinger, 2002). The theory of empowerment suggests that offering possibilities of active participation in different settings, such as the general community or the workplace, would help staff to overcome feelings of powerlessness and learned helplessness and therefore to reactivate their hidden competencies for active coping with stress and health hazards (Rappaport, 1981; Wallerstein, 1992). With regard to the individual and the organisational aspects of burnout and job dissatisfaction, discussed above, the empowerment concept provides a theoretical framework for analysing the relationships between both factors. For the particular case of workplace settings, this theory suggests that persons who perceive their job environment as providing them with opportunities to participate in decision making and work organisation, as well as with access to necessary information and resources, will be more able to develop strategies for adequately coping with stressful demands and to contribute productively to accomplishing organisational goals (Kilian and Paul, 1996; Laschinger, Sabiston and Kutszcher, 1997). Relationships between perceived empowerment, coping with job demands and job satisfaction for 154 staff members of a psychiatric hospital have been analysed by Kilian et al. (1997, 2003).

As shown in Fig. 24.2, perceived empowerment is negatively related to perceived job stress (standardised path coefficient=-0.199) and positively related to problem-focused instead of emotion-focused coping (standardised path coefficient=0.210). This indicated that the more people feel empowered in their workplace, the less they perceive their working conditions as stressful and the more they react adequately to stressful job demands. The other path coefficients in the model show a positive effect of perceived job stress (standardised path coefficient=0.359) and a negative effect of problem-focused coping (standardised path coefficient=-0.197) on subjective symptoms and negative effects of perceived job stress (standardised path coefficient=-0.310) and subjective symptoms (standardised

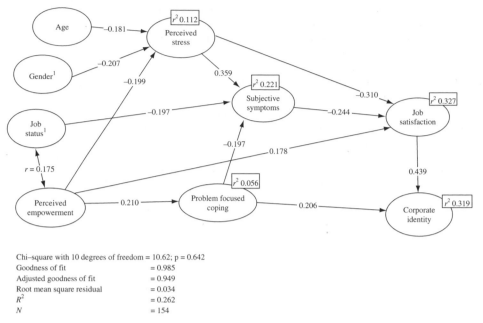

Chi–square with 10 degrees of freedom = 10.62; p = 0.642
Goodness of fit   = 0.985
Adjusted goodness of fit   = 0.949
Root mean square residual   = 0.034
R^2 = 0.262
N   = 154

[1] Dummy coded; 1 = female,
[2] Dummy coded; 1 = physicians, 0 = nursing staff

Figure 24.2 Path model (standardised path coefficients) of the impact of perceived empowerment on job satisfaction and corporate identity

path coefficient = −0.244) on job satisfaction. Furthermore, the path from perceived empowerment to job satisfaction shows a significant positive effect (standardised path coefficient = 0.178), while job satisfaction (standardised path coefficient = 0.439) and subjective coping (standardised path coefficient = 0.206) are positively related to corporate identity. The influence structure indicated in Fig. 24.2 illustrates the key role of empowerment in the process of coping with job stress and work satisfaction. This key role is underlined by a further study examining the effects of perceived empowerment on how mental health staff members cope with the experience of aggressive attacks by patients (Kilian, Paul and Berger, 1998).

As shown in Fig. 24.3, perceived empowerment is negatively related to the experience of violent patient attacks during a 15-month period (standardised path coefficient = −0.260) and positively related to problem-focused coping behaviour after 15 months (standardised path coefficient = 0.329). While the experience of patient aggression during the 15-month period is positively related to burnout (standardised path coefficient = 0.143), problem-focused coping shows a negative effect (standardised path coefficient = −0.349). The additional direct negative effect of perceived empowerment on burnout at time 2 (standardised path coefficient = −0.444) indicates again a key role of empowerment in the process of preventing burnout. Staff members with high feelings of empowerment are less likely to experience a violent attack from a patient, while after 15 months they still coped with job stress in a more adequate and problem-focused way. As the main reason for the negative impact of perceived empowerment on the experience of aggression by patients, Kilian, Paul and Berger (1998) assumed that staff who feel less empowered may be more vulnerable to reacting inadequately in critical situations. This could then result in the escalation of conflicts, while persons who feel empowered may be more capable of coping with the critical situation in a de-escalating manner. Currently, there is still a lack of research on the mechanisms of empowerment and disempowerment in mental health services. However, increasing the experience of empowerment seems clearly to have a crucial role in strategies for the prevention of burnout and its negative impact on the QoL of staff members and patients.

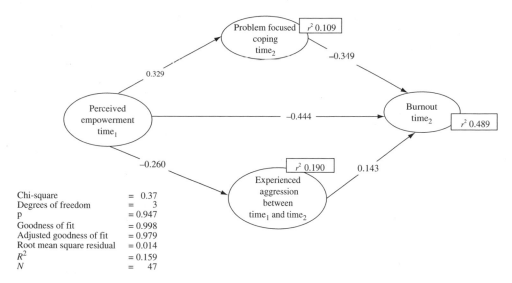

Figure 24.3 Path model (standardised path coefficients) for the role of perceived empowerment in the prevention of patient aggression and burnout

CONCLUSIONS AND OUTLOOK

Research on job stress and burnout indicates clearly that working in mental health services may be harmful to staff members' QoL. However, there is still a great number of people who are willing to face the difficulties of nursing those who are mentally ill and disadvantaged. These people constitute a tremendous human resource, which is essential for each society; losing this resource would have serious consequences for the QoL of us all. Therefore, using the existing knowledge described above for the purpose of preventing people who work in mental health care from burning out and becoming ill should have a high priority in health care policy. Further research is needed to gain a better understanding of the relationships between individual and environmental forces in the process of coping successfully or not successfully with high demands of working with mental disorder. Currently, staff empowerment seems to be an effective strategy, but there is no clarity about the best way to put empowerment into mental health practice. The current trend towards reducing the cost of health care services by saving personnel salaries seems to involve the danger of blocking initiatives to improve working conditions. Any savings from this policy may involve the high price of diminishing the QoL of those people who work for mental health services, as well as those who need them.

REFERENCES

Aiken, M. & Hage, J. (1966). Organizational alientation: A comparative analysis, *Am. Sociolog. Rev.*, **31**, 497–507.

Amstutz, M.C., Neuenschwader, M. & Modestin, J. (2001). Burnout bei psychiatrisch tätigen Ärztinnen und Ärzten. Resultate einer empirischen Untersuchung, *Psychiatrische Praxis*, **28**, 163–167.

Bandura, A. (1977). Self efficacy: Toward a unifying theory of behavioural change, *Psycholog. Rev.*, **84**, 191–215.

Benbow, S.M. (1998). Burnout: Current knowledge and relevance to old age psychiatry, *Int. J. Geriat. Psychiatry*, **13**, 520–526.

Benbow, S.M. & Jolley, D.J. (2002). Burnout and stress amongst old age psychiatrists, *Int. J. Geriat. Psychiatry*, **17**, 710–714.

Berkeley Planning Associates (1977). Evaluation of child abuse and neglect demonstration project. 1974–1977, Volume IX, *Project Management and Worker Burnout*, Final Report, Berkeley, California.

Burnard, P., Edwards, D.F.A., Hannigan, B., & Coyle, D. (2000). Community mental health nurses in Wales: self-reported stressors and coping strategies, *J. Psychiat. Ment. Health Nurs.*, **7**, 523–528.

Carver, C.S., Scheier, M.F. & Weintraub, J.K. (1989). Assessing coping strategies: A theoretically based approach, *J. Personality Social Psychol.*, **56**, 267–283.

Cherniss, C. (1980). *Staff Burnout: Job Stress in Human Services*, Sage, Beverly Hills, London.

Cherniss, C. & Egnatios, E. (1978a). Clinical supervision in community mental health, *Social Work*, **23**, 219–223.

Cherniss, C. & Egnatios, E. (1978b). Is there job satisfaction in community mental health?, *Community Ment. Health J.*, **14**, 309–319.

Cherniss, C. & Egnatios, E. (1978c). Participation in decision-making by staff in community mental health programs, *Am. J. Community Psychol.*, **6**, 171–190.

Cherniss, C. & Krantz, D.L. (1983). The ideological community as an antidote to burnout, in *Stress and Burnout in the Human Service Profession* (Ed. B.A. Farber), pp. 198–212, Pergamon Press, New York.

Cocco, E., Gatti, M., de Mendonca Lima, C.A. & Camus, V. (2003). A comparative study of stress and burnout among staff caregivers in nursing homes and acute geriatric wards, *Int. J. Geriat. Psychiatry*, **18**, 78–85.

Coffey, M. (1999). Stress and burnout in forensic community mental health nurses: An investigation of its causes and effects, *J. Psychiat. Ment. Health Nurs.*, **6**, 433–443.

Coffey, M. & Coleman, M. (2001). The relationship between support and stress in forensic community mental health nursing, *J. Adv. Nurs.*, **34**, 397–407.

Dehlinger, J. & Perlman, B. (1978). Job satisfaction in mental health agencies, *Adm. Ment. Health*, **5**, 120–139.

Edwards, D., Burnard, P., Coyle, D., Fothergill, A. & Hannigan, B. (2000a). Stress and burnout in community mental health nursing: A review of the literature, *J. Psychiat. Ment. Health Nurs.*, **7**, 7–14.

Edwards, D., Burnard, P., Coyle, D., Fothergill, A. & Hannigan, B. (2000b). Stressors, moderators and stress outcomes: Findings from the All-Wales Community Mental Health Nurse Study, *J. Psychiat. Ment. Health Nurs.*, **7**, 529–537.

Fagin, L., Brown, D., Bartlett, H., Leary, J. & Carson, J. (1995). The Claybury community psychiatric nurse stress study: Is it more stressful to work in hospital or the community?, *J. Adv. Nurs.*, **22**, 347–358.

Fagin, L., Carson, J., Leary, J., DeVilliers, N., Bartlett, H., O'Malley, P. *et al* (1996). Stress, coping and burnout in mental health nurses: Findings from three research studies, *Int. J. Social Psychiatry*, **42**, 102–111.

Farber, B.A. (1983). A critical perspective on burnout, in *Stress and Burnout in the Human Service Profession* (Ed. B.A.Farber), pp. 1–20, Pergamon Press, New York.

Fawzy, F.I., Wellisch, D.K., Pasnau, R.O. & Leibowitz, B. (2003). Preventing nursing burnout: A challenge for liaison psychiatry, *Gen. Hosp. Psychiatry*, **5**, 141–149.

Freudenberger, H.J. (1974). Staff burn-out, *J. Social Issues*, **30**, 159–165.

Handy, J. (1991a). Stress and contradiction in psychiatric nursing, *Human Relations*, **44**, 39–53.

Handy, J.A. (1991b). The social context of occupational stress in a caring profession, *Social Sci. Med.*, **32**, 819–830.

Hannigan, B., Edwards, D., Coyle, D., Fothergill, A. & Burnard, P. (2000). Burnout in community mental health nurses: Findings from the all-Wales stress study, *J. Psychiat. Ment. Health Nurs.*, **7**, 127–134.

Harrison, W.D. (1983). A social competence model of burnout, in *Stress and Burnout in the Human Service Profession* (Ed. B.A. Farber), pp. 29–39, Pergamon Press, New York.

Humpel, N., Caputi, P. & Martin, C. (2001). The relationship between emotions and stress among mental health nurses, *Aust. N. Z. J. Ment. Health Nurs.*, **10**, 55–60.

Jeanneau, M. & Armelius, K. (2000). Self-image and burnout in psychiatric staff, *J. Psychiat. Ment. Health Nurs.*, **7**, 399–406.

Kahn, R.L., Wolfe, D.M., Quinn, R. P., Snoek, J.D. & Rosenthal, R.A. (1964). *Organizational Stress: Studies in Role Conflict and Ambiguity*, John Wiley & Sons, New York.

Kilian, R. & Paul, R. (1996). Staff empowerment as a measure of progress in occupational health promotion: Theoretical foundations and baseline data from a health promoting hospital, in *Health Gain Measurements as a Tool for Hospital Management and Health Policy* (Eds J. Vang & M. Kristensen), pp. 172–177, Centre for Public Health Sciences, Linköping.

Kilian, R., Paul, R. & Berger, H. (1998). The role of staff empowerment in the prevention of patient aggression and staff burnout at psychiatric hospitals, in *Feasibility, Effectiveness, Quality and Sustainability of Health Promoting Hospitals* (Eds J.M. Pelikan, K. Krajic & H. Lobnig), pp. 110–113, G. Conrad, Gamburg.

Kilian, R., Paul, R., Berger, H. & Angermeyer, M.C. (1997). Empowerment und Gesundheitsförderndes Krankenhaus, in *Gesundheitsförderung – eine Strategie für Krankenhäuser im Umbruch. Projekte aus Österreich und Deutschland* (Eds A.Grundböck, P. Nowak & J.M. Pelikan), pp. 137–142, Facultas Universitätsverlag, Wien.

Kilian, R., Lindenbach, I., Löbig, U., Uhle, M., Petscheleit, A. & Angermeyer, M.C. (2003). Indicators of empowerment and disempowerment in the subjective evaluation of the psychiatric treatment process by persons with severe and persistent mental illness: A qualitative and quantitative analysis, *Social Sci. Med.*, **57**, 1127–1142.

Kramer, B. (1974). Cited in Cherniss, C. (1980). *Staff Burnout: Job Stress in Human Services*, Sage, Beverly Hills, London.

Lamb, H.R. (1979). Staff burnout in work with long-term patients, *Hosp. Community Psychiatry*, **30**, 396–398, 854.

Laschinger, H.K., Finegan, J. & Shamian, J. (2001). The impact of workplace empowerment, organizational trust on staff nurses' work satisfaction and organizational commitment, *Health Care Management Rev.*, **26**, 7–23.

Laschinger, H.K.S. & Havens, D.S. (1997). The effect of workplace empowerment on staff nurses' occupational mental health and work effectiveness, *J. Nurs. Adm.*, **27**, 42–50.

Laschinger, H.K., Sabiston, J.A. & Kutszcher, L. (1997). Empowerment and staff nurse decision involvement in nursing work environments: Testing Kanter's theory of structural power in organizations, *Res. Nurs. Health*, **20**, 341–352.

Laschinger, H.K., Shamian, J. & Thomson, D. (2001). Impact of magnet hospital characteristics on nurses' perceptions of trust, burnout, quality of care, and work satisfaction, *Nurs. Econ.*, **19**, 209–219.

Laschinger, H.K., Wong, C., McMahon, L. & Kaufmann, C. (1999). Leader behavior impact on staff nurse empowerment, job tension, and work effectivness, *J. Nurs. Adm.*, **29**, 28–39.

Lazarus, R.S. (1966). *Psychological Stress and the Coping Process*, McGraw-Hill, New York.

Lazarus, R.S. & Folkman, S. (1984). *Stress, Appraisal and Coping*, Springer, New York.

Lazarus, R.S. & Launier, R. (1978). Stress-related transactions between person and environment, in *Perspectives in Interactional Psychology* (Eds L.A. Perwin & M. Lewis), pp. 287–327, Plenum Press, New York.

Leiter, M.P., Harvie, P. & Frizzel, C. (1998). The correspondence of patient satisfaction and nurse burnout, *Social Sci. Med.*, **47**, 1611–1617.

McCarthy, P. (1985). Burnout in psychiatric nursing, *J. Adv. Nurs.*, **10**, 305–310.

Manojlovich, M. & Spence Laschinger, H. (2002). The relationship of empowerment and selected personality characteristics to nursing job satisfaction, *J. Nurs. Adm.*, **32**, 586–595.

Maslach, C. (1976). Burned-out, *Human Behaviour*, **5**, 16–22.

Maslach, C. (1978a). The client role in staff burn-out, *J. Social Issues*, **34**, 111–124.

Maslach, C. (1978b). Job burn-out: How people cope, *Public Welfare*, **36**, 56–58.

Maslach, C. (1979). The burn-out syndrome and patient care, in *Stress and Survival: The Emotional Realities of Life-Threatening Illness* (Ed. C.A. Garfield), C.V. Mosby, St Louis, Missouri.

Maslach, C. & Jackson, S.E. (1978). Lawyer burn-out, *Barrister*, **5**, 52–54.

Maslach, C. & Jackson, S.E. (1979). Burned-out cops and their families, *Psychol. Today*, **12**, 59–62.

Maslach, C. & Jackson, S.E. (1981). The measurement of experienced burnout, *J. Occup. Behaviour*, **2**, 99–113.

Maslach, C. & Pines, A. (1977). The burn-out syndrome in the day care setting, *Child Care Q.*, **7**, 100–113.

Pearlin, L.I. (1967). Alienation from work: A study of nursing personnel, in *The Professional in the Organization* (Ed. M. Abrahamson), Rand McNally, Chicago, Illinois.

Pearlin, L.I., Lieberman, M.A., Menaghan, E.G. & Mullan, J.T. (1981). The stress process, *J. Health Social Behaviour*, **22**, 337–563.

Perlman, B. & Hartman, E.A. (1982). Burnout: Summary and future research, *Human Relations*, **35**, 283–305.

Pines, A. & Maslach, C. (1978). Characteristics of staff burnout in mental health settings, *Hosp. Community Psychiatry*, **29**, 233–237.

Pines, A. & Maslach, C. (1980). Combating staff burn-out in a day care centre: A case study, *Hosp. Community Psychiatry*, **9**, 5–16.

Prosser, D., Johnson, S., Kuipers, E., Dunn, G., Szmukler, G., Reid, Y. *et al* (1999). Mental health, 'burnout' and job satisfaction in a longitudinal study of mental health staff, *Social Psychiatry Psychiat. Epidemiol.*, **34**, 295–300.

Rappaport, J. (1981). In praise of paradox: A social policy of empowerment over prevention, *Am. J. Community Psychol.*, **9**, 1–15.

Rappaport, J. (1987). Terms of empowerment. Exemplars of prevention: Toward a theory for community psychology, *Am. J. Community Psychol.*, **15**, 121–148.

Rotter, J.B. (1966). Generalized expectancies for internal versus external control of enforcement, *Psycholog. Monographs: General and Applied*, **80**, 1–28.

Rotter, J.B. (1982). *The Development and Applications of Social Learning Theory*, Springer, New York.

Sarata, B.P.V. (1974). Employee satisfactions in agencies serving retarded persons, *Am. J. Ment. Deficiency*, **79**, 434–442.

Sarata, B.P.V. & Jeppesen, J.C. (1977). Job design and staff satisfaction in human service settings, *Am. J. Community Psychol.*, **5**, 229–235.

Seligman, M.E.P. (1975). *Helplessness*, W.H. Freeman, San Francisco, California.

Wallerstein, N. (1992). Powerlessness, empowerment, and health. Implications for health promotion programs, *Am. J. Health Promotion*, **6**, 197–205.

Wise, T.N. & Berlin, R.M. (1981). Burnout: Stresses in consultation-liaison psychiatry, *Psychosomatics*, **22**, 745–751.

Section VI
POLICY AND PLANNING

25

Quality of Life Measurement in the Economic Analysis of Mental Health Care

Dan Chisholm, Luis Salvador-Carulla and Jose Luis Ayuso-Mateos

INTRODUCTION

The last two decades have seen an ever-increasing interest in and demand for economic analysis of mental health care and policy, fuelled by governments' concerns about rises in health care expenditures (Chisholm, Healey and Knapp, 1997; Singh, Hawthorne and Vos, 2001). Considerations of cost and cost-effectiveness enter into health care reform processes, priority-setting exercises within and across health programmes and regulatory decisions concerning drug approval or pricing. There is no question about the need to include quality of life (QoL) information into such analytical processes. However, the methods for undertaking QoL assessment in economic analyses are relatively new, differ from classical methods of QoL measurement in a number of important respects and, partly because of this, still remain somewhat controversial.

Before addressing the methods, uses and controversies associated with QoL measurement in mental health economic studies, it is appropriate to discuss the broader health policy context within which such developments have occurred. In the light of a growing appreciation at the policy level of the scarcity of resources relative to identified mental health needs, the generation of new tools and methods by health economists in the area of QoL measurement has stemmed from an interest in capturing multiple health outcomes of health interventions (e.g. extension of both the quality *and* the quantity of life) into a composite measure capable of being used for comparative analysis or priority setting across different disease areas. It is easy to forget that for generations, health care decisions and priorities were almost solely determined with reference to that most fundamental (and measurable) of health outcomes, death. Assessment and collection of non-fatal outcomes resulting from different conditions or health intervention at the system level is a much more recent phenomenon, in large part due to the greater measurement difficulties of such an objective. The systematic, empirically based measurement of psychiatric symptoms, for example, can be traced back only as far as two generations ago. For QoL measurement in mental health, it is even less.

Even with the development of improved measures for capturing improvements in morbidity or QoL, non-fatal outcomes continued to be marginalised at the resource allocation or priority-setting level, partly owing to 'rule-of-rescue' arguments (which state the pre-eminent need to intervene against

Quality of Life in Mental Disorders, Second Edition   Edited by H. Katschnig, H. Freeman and N. Sartorius
© 2006 John Wiley & Sons, Ltd

life-threatening health situations or conditions), but also due to the heterogeneous or – compared to death, unstandardised – nature of morbidity indicators (e.g. a resolution of symptoms for depression versus a fall in systolic blood pressure for hypertension). If health economics as a discipline has contributed one key development in the area of outcome measurement, it is the provision of a framework for combining mortality and morbidity into a single, standardised metric that can be used at the population level for determining choices or priorities for action and investment.

MODES OF ECONOMIC EVALUATION

Economics is concerned with maximising the benefits obtained from using scarce resources. Costing of the scarce societal resources needed to implement a health intervention is carried out with reference to the foregone opportunities of that investment, i.e. what would be the next best use of the human or capital resource if not directed towards a particular health intervention such as antipsychotic drug therapy for schizophrenia out-patients. The benefits of intervention, as implied above, can be construed in a number of ways, but will be summarised here in terms of three categories: natural or physical units, utilities and money.

Most economic analyses make use of outcomes measured in natural units, such as lives saved and cases remitted, or in the mental health context, reduced symptoms and improved functioning. The label given to this type of economic evaluation is cost-effectiveness analysis. Condition-specific instruments are the norm for symptomatology measures (e.g. the Hamilton Depression Rating Scale), whereas more generic instruments have been most used for indicating improvements in functioning (e.g. the Nottingham Health Profile, the Medical Outcomes Study Short Form 36 or the World Health Organization's Disability Assessment Schedule II). Such measures are able to generate quite standardised and therefore comparable profiles of a person's health-related QoL or disability across different diseases, but in common with any condition-specific measure fall short of being able to be incorporated into composite outcome measures.

Composite measures of health outcome attempt to capture change in mortality *and* morbidity, examples being the quality-adjusted life-year (QALY) and the disability-adjusted life-year (DALY). The QALY, for example, can be thought of as the product of life expectancy and an adjustment for the quality of the remaining life-years gained. The QALY concept is shown graphically in Fig. 25.1. The key feature of the QALY or DALY relates to the quality or disability adjustment factor for time spent in a particular health state before death. Assessment of this quality adjustment factor is made with reference to expected utility theory, which seeks to reveal the preference associated with different

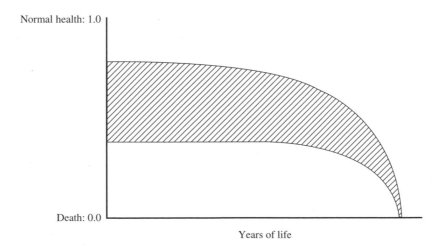

Figure 25.1   Quality-adjusted life-years (QALYs)
Note: The lines show the utility values for untreated severe chronic depression (lower line) and treated depression (upper line). The area between the two lines represents the QALYs gained from treatment.

health states (on a standard interval scale, relative to death and/or full health). According to the utility model, the usefulness of health status measures for priority setting is increased if they incorporate preference measurements and when relevant components (mortality and morbidity) can be aggregated into a single measure. Such an approach, discussed at greater length below, has given rise to the term 'cost–utility analysis' as a particular mode of economic evaluation.

For the final category of outcome measurement, not only the inputs but also the outputs of intervention are converted into monetary units, leaving simple decision rules concerning the worth of a single intervention (monetised benefits should exceed costs) or multiple interventions (choose those with the greatest ratio of monetised benefits to cost). In economic evaluation, this mode of analysis is called 'cost–benefit analysis'. However, there are grave problems in implementing such an approach in psychiatry and related fields, since it requires monetary valuation of all health improvements, including symptom control, improved functioning / QoL or even the loss of welfare associated with medication side-effects (Healey and Chisholm, 1999).

UTILITY MEASUREMENT IN THEORY

Historical Developments

From a historical perspective, the cost–utility approach is based on 'expected utility theory', conceived by Daniel Bernouilli in 1738 and formalised by von Neumann and Morgenstern in the late 1940s. According to this theory, every result of a choice between two alternatives (preference) produces a certain degree of well-being or utility. Subjective utility (the satisfaction derived from the alternative chosen) differs from the objective expected monetary gains on several points, such as risk assumption, choice certainty, degree of probability, or previous experience and cognition. For example, choices concerning gains are associated with risk aversion, while those concerning losses are associated with risk assumption, even when the expected monetary changes are equal for both choices. When certainty is included as an alternative, the low-probability choices are overestimated and the high or intermediate probabilities are underestimated, producing a shift in the risk assumption. The value function provides a description of the relationship between the subjective value and the objective amount that can be gained or lost. Weinstein and colleagues set out the facets of cost–utility analysis in 1977, describing the QALY as the net effectiveness of the alternative in question, expressed by the trade-offs between additional survival and QoL (Weinstein and Stason, 1977). In 1985, the Late Alan Williams pioneered the QALY in the United Kingdom, with a different model based on Rosser and Kind's (1978) Classification of Illness States and its associated matrix for weighting individual 'value of life'. Over the last two decades, further descriptive systems and a variety of valuation techniques have been used in cost–utility analysis (see below).

Key Issues in the Construction of Utility Measures

Utility measures incorporate preference/value measurements and define QoL as a single number or index along a continuum, generally from death (0.0) to full health (1.0). These measures reflect both the health status and the value of the health status to the individual (scores less than zero may reflect health states worse than death) (Becker, 1995; Guyatt, Feeney and Patrick, 1993). Values below '0' are not considered in some standards, even though some respondents, e.g. suicidal patients, may value their health status as 'worse than death'. The main factors in constructing such measures focus on the empirical determination of preferences, the sources of data (people whose valuations are used) and the valuation method (ranking order and systems for aggregating preferences).

The first step towards elicitation of utility scores is a description system for states of health. A number of generic descriptive systems have been developed over the last two decades, such as the EQ-5D (formerly known as the EuroQol), which assesses five dimensions of health-related QoL: mobility, self-care, usual activities, pain/discomfort and anxiety/depression (theoretically allowing for as many as 243 composite health status descriptions). Alternatively, the Health Utilities Index covers eight dimensions: vision, hearing, speech, ambulation, dexterity, emotion, cognition and pain. An obvious concern about such generic descriptive systems is that they may not be particularly sensitive for a given condition such as schizophrenia, particularly when such descriptive systems have been principally developed with reference to physical conditions. One proposed solution to this problem is to develop new descriptive systems for mental health conditions (Chisholm, Healey and Knapp, 1997), as has recently been undertaken for depression in the form of the McSad utility measure (Bennett *et al.*, 2000), which covers six dimensions more relevant to depression (emotion [mood], self-appraisal [self-worth], cognition [concentration], physiology [sleep, energy], behaviour [effort] and role function [ability to work or carry on as usual]).

Concerning the elicitation of preferences, one key debate is related to whether the preference of individual patients can adequately be assessed by others. The point of reference for the election may vary as the individual adapts to a new situation. Thus, ill people adjust to their lives in order to reduce real loss, and rate their health status better than healthy subjects. For example, chronically ill elderly people rate themselves better than their doctors believe them to be (Loomes and McKenzie, 1990). On the other hand, coping strategies such as denial may induce significant choice changes in some groups of patients (e.g. cancer). The internal representation of some health states are more complex than that of others. A lay individual may work out the suffering and consequences of a kidney transplant or a heart attack, but respondents find it difficult to make choices concerning death. Things are even more problematic when choices and risks are set out for conditions far from lay persons' experiences, such as personality disorder or psychosis. The importance of knowledge, information, attitudes and expectations in mental health preferences have been pointed out by Becker (1995). Preference ratings for depression, for example, may be lower than those reported by the general public for the same condition, contrary to what happens with physical conditions, where patients' choices are higher than those expressed by the general public. On the other hand, people may not be the best judges of their own welfare, particularly in those patients with lack of insight or impaired cognitive function, such as mental retardation, dementia and some severely ill psychiatric patients (Shiell *et al.*, 1990). Thus, the preferences of healthy people may be a questionable choice for constructing utility measures of mental health alternatives, and QALYs developed in the context of allocation of acute medical conditions may not be helpful in considering improvements in the outcomes of those with mental illness.

Preferences and values can be obtained from different populations such as healthy individuals, doctors, nurses or other health professionals, expert groups, relatives, patients or even policy makers. For example, the Rosser matrix of health states was obtained from a heterogeneous sample of 70 subjects. The 10 doctors assigned a higher value to the subjective feelings of suffering and resembled the healthy volunteer group in their choices, whereas nurses showed closer agreement to patients' choices. Such heterogeneity questions the overall validity of the results, particularly when major differences can be found in the appraisal of different subject groups. On the other hand, reliability may also be questioned. A reassessment of the Rosser–Kind matrix revealed differences from the original matrix (e.g. the value assigned to 'moderate distress and unable to work' changed from 0.9 to 0.35) (Spiegelhalter *et al.*, 1992). Disability weights underlying the DALY metric were obtained exclusively from experts, with choices being made over six classes of disabilities (Murray and Lopez, 1996).

Several methods exist for placing a value on health state preferences (for a review see Kind, Gudex and Godfrey, 1990; Murray and Lopez, 1996). The most commonly employed techniques are category rating, time trade-off, person trade-off and standard gamble:

1. *Category rating/scaling*. The simplest approach to valuing preferences is to ask subjects to think about health outcomes (for which there is no uncertainty) and to provide a rating or score. The most commonly used technique is the visual analogue scale, a kind of thermometer on which respondents are asked to place a valuation for a particular state of health between 0 and 1 (where 1 equals full health). It is evidently simple to use, but does not take into account uncertainty and/or a person's attitude to risk (unlike the standard gamble).
2. *Time trade-off* elicits how much time an individual would exchange living in one state versus another particular health state (e.g. being healthy). For example, option 1 is being healthy (state A) for 2 years (t_a) and then dying and option 2 is being 5 years (t_b) under treatment with a certain drug for breast cancer (state B) followed by death. Then t_a and t_b are changed until the respondent assigns an equal value to both choices. The 'indifference' ratio t_a/t_b shows the respondent's utility (relative preference) for being treated with the known drug for breast cancer. This method may seem useful

for acute conditions or those with clear-cut time limits, but the way it could be applied to psychiatry is a matter of debate (Shiell *et al.*, 1990).

3. *Person trade-off* asks individuals to choose between curing a certain number of patients in one illness state (or disability class) versus another number in a different class. For example, respondents are asked to make a choice between curing X patients in an A state and Y in a B state. X and Y are changed until the respondent is indifferent to both choices. The X/Y ratio expresses the relative utility of health states A and B.

4. *Standard gambles* ask individuals to choose between the certainty of living in a health state versus a chance of getting well at a probability p and dying at a probability $1-p$. The probability (p) is changed until the respondent is indifferent about the two choices. Here, the utility is represented by the p value. Standard gamble allows decision making under conditions of uncertainty, but its use can be constrained by problems of cognitive overload on the part of respondents.

A key point to note is that, perhaps unsurprisingly, different techniques produce different valuations, with standard gamble valuations tending to produce higher scores than time trade-off, which in turn gives greater values than visual analogue scores (Bennett and Torrance, 1996; Lenert and Kaplan, 2000). An alternative to the composite health state scenario approach described above is the multi-attribute utility (MAU) approach, where each aspect of health is valued separately. Each question asked has several responses, corresponding to different levels of health, each of which is weighted using one of the scaling methods above. The weighted responses are then combined to form the utility value.

UTILITY MEASUREMENT IN PRACTICE: APPLICATIONS IN MENTAL HEALTH

How have utility measures been used to inform mental health policy or resource allocation? We address this question with three illustrations: as a summary measure of population health for disease burden estimates (DALYs attributed to mental disorders), as an outcome measure for population-level cost–utility analysis (DALYs averted by mental health intervention) and as an outcome measure for cost–utility analyses of the treatment of depression in primary care (QALYs gained by intervention).

Global Burden of Mental Disorders

Policy makers and public health experts seek rational guides to set their priorities for health, to evaluate the outcomes of interventions and health care reforms, and to monitor changes over time at local, national, regional or global level. Estimation of needs for health services, their costs and effectiveness require indicators that go beyond measures of death rates or diagnosis alone, and include the 'functioning' of people. To respond to this need, the first Global Burden of Disease (GBD, 1990) study was carried out in the 1990s by the Harvard School of Public Health, in collaboration with the World Bank and the World Health Organization (WHO). The study aimed to provide a set of summary measures that would be comprehensive and provide information on disease and injury, including non-fatal health outcomes, to inform global priority setting for health research and to inform international health policy and planning (Murray, 1996). Aside from generating comprehensive and consistent estimates of mortality and morbidity by age, gender and region, GBD also introduced a new (utility) measure – the disability-adjusted life-year (DALY) – to quantify the burden of disease. The DALY is a summary measure of population health that combines in a single indicator years of life lost from premature death and years of life lived with disabilities. One DALY can be thought of as one lost year of 'healthy' life, and the burden of disease as a measurement of the gap between current health status and an ideal situation where everyone lives into old age free of disease and disability. DALYs are time-based health-outcome measures similar to the quality-adjusted life-years (QALYs), which include weights for time spent in less-than-perfect health, ranging from 0 for perfect health to 1 for death with a higher value, therefore indicating higher disability and a worse outcome. For an illustration of how to calculate DALYs (for bipolar disorder), see Fox-Rushby and Hanson (2001).

The results of the GBD 1990 highlighted the substantial and previously under-recognised burden of neuropsychiatric disorders. The disorders for which the GBD study presented estimates were: unipolar major depression, bipolar disorder, schizophrenia, epilepsy, alcohol use, dementia, Parkinson's disease, multiple sclerosis, drug use, post-traumatic stress disorder, obsessive–compulsive disorder and panic disorder. One of the major findings of GBD 1990, once health estimates were calculated that went beyond mortality to include morbidity (disability), was that conditions such as mental disorders, which disable but do not kill, were found to be a major cause of burden worldwide, ranking as high as cardiovascular and respiratory diseases and surpassing all malignancies combined or HIV. The study showed that unipolar depressive disorders place an enormous burden on society, which was ranked as the fourth leading cause of burden among all diseases, accounting for over 50 million lost years of health life worldwide (Ustun *et al.*, 2004). This high burden is due to a combination of a high prevalence of depression, high impact on functioning and early age of onset. The results of the GBD study have shown variations by country and region, but patterns and trends are remarkably similar worldwide. Mental disorders constitute a large proportion of the global burden of disease, both in developed and developing countries.

Sectoral Cost–Utility Analysis of Mental Health Interventions

To date, there has been only a limited connection made between DALYs and the generation of cost-effectiveness evidence, despite the fact that such a link was a central aim of the GBD study. This link is needed because DALYs are not in themselves sufficient as a mechanism for resource allocation and priority setting in health care. In other words, the size of the attributable burden alone is not sufficient to guide action. For priority setting and resource allocation, a more pertinent question is to ask what is the avertable burden of a particular disease arising from the use of an evidence-based set of interventions and what is the relative cost of their implementation in the target population. Such an analysis can reveal the technically most efficient response to the attributable burden of a particular disease.

Through its CHOICE (CHOosing Interventions that are Cost-Effective) project, WHO recently embarked on a new initiative to assemble databases on the cost-effectiveness of key health interventions in 14 epidemiological subregions of the world (Tan Torres *et al.*, 2003). A comparative cost-effectiveness analysis of interventions for reducing the burden of major neuropsychiatric disorders formed part of this work programme. This project advocates a 'generalised' form of cost–utility analysis, in which costs and effects of both current and new interventions are compared to the starting point of 'doing nothing'. Accordingly, the costs and effectiveness of pharmacological and psychosocial interventions in primary care or out-patient settings provided for psychiatric disorders were compared in a population model to an epidemiological situation representing the untreated natural history of these disorders. Effects have been measured in terms of DALYs averted (i.e. reduced burden), while costs are expressed in international dollars (I$).

Compared to the epidemiological situation of no treatment (natural history), the most cost-effective strategy for averting the burden of psychosis and severe affective disorders in developing regions of the world is expected to be a combined intervention of first-generation antipsychotic or mood-stabilising drugs with adjuvant psychosocial treatment, delivered via a community-based out-patient service model, with a cost-effectiveness ratio in the region of I$ 4200–5500 in Sub-Saharan Africa and South Asia, rising to more than I$ 10 000 in middle-income regions (see Fig. 25.2; Chisholm, 2005). Currently, the high acquisition price of second-generation antipsychotic drugs makes their use in developing regions questionable on efficiency grounds alone, although this situation stands to change as these drugs come off patent. By contrast, evidence indicates that the relatively modest additional cost of adjuvant psychosocial treatment reaps significant health gains, thereby making such a combined strategy for the treatment of schizophrenia and bipolar disorder more cost-effective than pharmaco-therapy alone. For more common mental disorders treated in primary care settings (depressive and anxiety disorders), the single most cost-effective strategy is the scaled-up use of older antidepressants (due to their lower cost, but similar efficacy to newer antidepressants). However, as the price margin between older and generic newer antidepressants continues to diminish, generic selective serotonin reuptake inhibitors (SSRIs) can be expected to be at least as cost-effective and may therefore

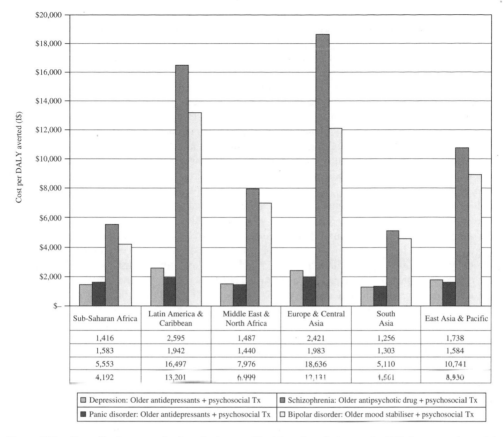

Figure 25.2   Cost-effectiveness ratios for a basic mental health package in low- and middle-income regions of the world

represent the treatment of choice in the future. Since depression is so commonly a recurring condition, there are also good grounds for thinking that proactive care management, including long-term maintenance treatment with antidepressant drugs, represents a cost-effective (if more resource-intensive) way of significantly reducing the enormous burden of depression that exists in developing regions (Chisholm *et al.*, 2004).

The purpose of such an exercise is to locate the relative position of effective and applicable inter-ventions within a wider cost-effectiveness and priority-setting framework in the health care sector. Using the criteria of the Commission for Macroeconomics and Health (2001), the results of this analysis indicate that (a) the most efficient interventions for common mental disorders can be considered very cost-effective (each DALY averted costs less than one year of average per capita income) and (b) community-based interventions for severe mental disorders using older antipsychotic and mood-stabilising drugs meet the criterion for being cost-effective (each DALY averted costs less than three times gross domestic product (GDP) per capita). These findings therefore provide relevant new information to health policy makers regarding the relative value of investing in neuropsychiatric treatment and prevention, and in so doing, may help to remove one of many remaining barriers to a more appropriate public health response to the burden of these conditions.

Cost–Utility Analysis of Depression Treatment in Primary Care

Ten years ago, examples of the application of the cost–utility approach to mental health were hard to find (Chisholm, Healey and Knapp, 1997). Since then, there has been an increasing use of the 'cost per QALY' approach in the economic evaluation of mental health care, following recommendations for such analyses by regulatory bodies in Australia, Canada, the UK, and the US. In the field of depression, for example, cost–utility analyses have now been carried out (all in the US) for screening in primary care (Valenstein *et al.*, 2001; annual and periodic screening cost more than $50 000 per QALY, one-off screening below this threshold), newer versus older antidepressant drugs (Revicki *et al.*, 1997), maintenance treatment for recurrent depression (Kamlet *et al.*, 1992; Hatziandreu *et al.*, 1994), guideline-concordant primary care treatment for women (Pyne *et al.*, 2003) and primary care practice-initiated quality improvement programmes (Schoenbaum *et al.*, 2001). Many of the cost–utility analyses carried out to date employ secondary data and modelling techniques to estimate costs and effects, while others have constructed cost per QALY estimates alongside the conduct of clinical trials.

An example of a cost–utility analysis using a modelling approach is that by Revicki *et al.* (1997), who compared treatment for major depression with: (a) newer antidepressants (nefazodone and fluoxetine), (b) tricyclics (imipramine) and for treatment failures, and (c) a step approach involving initial treatment with imipramine followed by nefazodone. A clinical decision analysis model was developed to simulate the clinical management pathways and pattern of recurrences of major depression for these alternative treatment strategies in order to estimate lifetime medical costs and health outcomes (expressed as QALYs). There were only minor differences in costs and QALYs between nefazadone and fluoxetine, and both of these newer antidepressants were estimated to be cost-effective, compared to imipramine treatment and the imipramine step approach. The ratios of cost to QALYs gained for these newer antidepressants were deemed to be sufficiently low (below $20 000 per QALY gained) to merit adoption of these treatments into the health care system. For example, the extra lifetime cost of nefazadone over imipramine ($1321) resulted in 0.32 added QALYs, giving a ratio of $4065 per QALY gained. Since decision models and their findings are only as good as their underlying assumptions and the quality of the data used to estimate key model parameters, extensive sensitivity analyses were conducted, but these did not alter the basic findings and conclusions. However, the results did not include indirect costs such as changes in work productivity – which are important for a societal perspective – and are not readily generalisable to groups other than the targeted population (in this study, 30-year old women with one previous depressive episode).

An example of the empirically based generation of cost per QALY information is the randomised controlled trial of practice-initiated quality improvement (QI) for depression (Schoenbaum *et al.*, 2001), which involved group-level randomisation of 46 clinics in six community-based managed care organisations in the US, either to a medication or a psychotherapy quality improvement programme (in addition to training and enhanced educational resources). Two QALY measures were derived, one with reference to scores from the short form 12-Item Health Survey (SF-12) plus a standard gamble utility weighting exercise among a local convenience sample, the other with reference to the estimated time spent depressed plus values from the literature for lost utility due to depression. Relative to usual care, average health care costs increased by $400–500 per treated patient, while QALY gains were less than 0.025, resulting in an estimated cost per QALY of $15 000–36 000 (QI medication) and $9500–21 500 (QI therapy). In addition to these health gains, patients exposed to the quality improvement programmes were employed for more days than those receiving usual care.

The envisaged benefit of expressing the results of economic evaluation in these terms lies in the ability to line up the cost per QALY estimated for a wide range of different interventions and diseases, with a view to determining acceptable efficiency against a predefined threshold (of, say, $50 000) or even constructing 'league tables' summarising best and worse buys in the health sector. In practice, there remain significant problems in relying on league tables for the allocation of resources (due to the heterogeneous and context-specific nature of cost–utility studies), while there may be criteria unrelated to efficiency that determine whether a particular intervention is deemed acceptable for reimbursement or inclusion in a defined package of basic health care.

CONCLUSION

Health economists' perspectives on QoL differ significantly from those developed in the medical sector. In medicine, QoL is a status function, while in health economics 'quality of life' is an utility function. In the first case, a subjective rating scale can provide information about the patient's present status in several dimensions related to the QOL construct, while in health economics, the assessment will be based on the individual's preference between two health states. Cost–utility analysis was designed as an economic tool for improving health decision making by producing a common index that would integrate costs and outcomes in order to allow comparisons between different conditions. As demonstrated in the preceding section, utility measures have been put to a number of uses in the mental health field, each of which has contributed to a policy dialogue concerning disease priorities and the relative efficiency of competing interventions. However, cost–utility analysis is founded on a number of assumptions that remain controversial and employs a range of different valuation techniques that often provide different results. Such differences reduce the opportunity to make genuine, consistent comparisons between studies, thereby raising the question of whether the main objective of the cost per QALY methodology has failed.

Whether QoL can be measured in a way that facilitates its comparison with quantitative data (e.g. costs) is a key question in this debate. Most health economists, even those critical to the current available instruments (Loomes and McKenzie, 1990), think that this is possible; they consider present problems as those of a technique in the developmental stage. Some economists, biostatisticians and clinicians are more critical, questioning the overall appropriateness of such techniques for exploring values to be placed on QoL measures that include death, the feasibility of explicit trade-offs between categories and the possibility of misleading results that may lead to unwise or unfair decisions (Brazier, 1993). In addition, a number of instruments for measuring utility do not fulfil quality criteria regarding their reliability, validity and transferability (Lenert and Kaplan, 2000; Cook *et al.*, 2001). The quality criteria of most of the available utility measures (e.g. Quality of Well-Being Scale, Torrance Health Utility Index, the Rosser–Kind Matrix, EuroQol, GBD disability weights) have not been sufficiently tested, particularly their consistency, sensitivity to change, validity and reliability (test–retest, interinformant and interrater reliability if the choices are made by external raters after an interview). Factors such as individual changes in health preferences over time raise serious doubts about the reliability of these measures, particularly in mental disorders. For example, a recent study has shown that the use of a preference-based approach to the construction of EuroQol scores for schizophrenia (and, by implication, other utility measures) produces results that are not appreciably different from a much more simple (non-weighted) descriptive system (Prieto and Sacristan, 2004). More fundamentally, the expected utility approach is based on a series of normative assumptions around risk attitudes and time preferences, whose descriptive validity has been strongly criticised, questioning the overall validity of this model (Loomes and McKenzie, 1990; Cohen, 1996).

Accordingly, there is an important requirement on the part of mental health researchers and policy makers alike to pay close attention to the underlying methods and construction of utility-based estimates of health outcome, but also to acknowledge the potential insights that such approaches can bring to priority-setting agendas in mental health. Finally, it should be emphasised that cost per QALY information should not be advocated as the only criterion for decision making, but as an extra source of data to add to the information currently used.

DISCLAIMER

The views expressed are those of the authors and not necessarily those of the organisations they represent.

REFERENCES

Becker, M. (1995). Quality-of-life instruments for severe chronic mental illness. Implications for pharmacology, *PharmacoEconomics*, **7**, 229–237.

Bennett, K.J. & Torrance, G.W. (1996). Measuring health state preferences and utilities: Rating scale, time trade-off and standard gamble techniques, in *Quality of Life and Pharmacoeconomics in Clinical Trials*, Second Edition, (Ed. B. Spilker), pp. 253–265, Lippincott-Raven, Philadelphia, Pennsylvania.

Bennett, K.J., Torrance, G.W., Boyle, M.H. & Guscott, R. (2000). Cost–utility analysis in depression: The McSad utility measure for depression health states, *Psychiat. Serv.*, **51**, 1171–1176.

Brazier, J. (1993). The SF-36 health survey questionnaire – a tool for economists, *Health Economics*, **2**, 213–215.

Chisholm, D. (2005). Choosing cost-effective interventions in psychiatry, *World Psychiatry*, **4**, 37–44.

Chisholm, D., Healey, A. & Knapp, M.R.J. (1997). QALYs and mental health care, *Social Psychiatry Psychiat. Epidemiol.*, **32**, 68–75.

Chisholm, D., Sanderson, K., Ayuso-Mateos, J.L. & Saxena, S. (2004). Averting the global burden of depression: A population-level analysis of intervention cost-effectiveness in 14 epidemiologically-defined sub-regions (WHO CHOICE), *Br. J. Psychiatry*, **184**, 432–438.

Cohen, J.B. (1996). Is expected utility theory normative for medical decision making?, *Med. Decision Making*, **16**, 1–6.

Commission for Macroeconomics and Health (2001). *Macroeconomics and Health: Investing in Health for Economic Development*, World Health Organization, Geneva.

Cook, K., Ashton, C., Byrne, M. *et al* (2001). Psychometric analysis of the measurement level of the rating scale, time trade-off, and standard gamble, *Social Sci. Med.*, **53**, 1275–1285.

Fox-Rushby, J.A. & Hanson, K. (2001). Calculating and presenting disability adjusted life years (DALYs) in cost-effectiveness analysis, *Health Policy Plann.*, **16**, 326–331.

Guyatt, G., Feeny, D.H. & Patrick, D.L. (1993). Measuring health-related quality of life, *Ann. Internal Med.*, **118**, 622–629.

Hatziandreu, E.J., Brown, R.E., Revicki, D.A. *et al* (1994). Cost–utility of maintenance treatment of recurrent depression with sertraline versus episodic treatment with dothiepin, *PharmacoEconomics*, **5**, 246–264.

Healey, A. & Chisholm, D. (1999). Willingness to pay as a measure of the benefits of mental health care, *J. Ment. Health Policy and Economics*, **2**, 55–58.

Kamlet, M.S., Wade, M., Kupfer, D.J. & Frank, E. (1992). Cost–utility analysis of maintenance treatment for recurrent depression: A theoretical framework and numerical illustration, in *Economics and Mental Health* (Eds R.G. Frank & W.G. Manning), pp. 267–291, Johns Hopkins University Press, Baltimore, Maryland.

Kind, P., Gudex, C. & Godfrey, C. (1990). Introduction: What are QALYs?, in *Quality of Life. Perspectives and Polices* (Eds S. Baldwin, C. Godfrey & C. Propper), pp.57–62, Routledge, London.

Lenert, L. & Kaplan, R.M. (2000).Validity and interpretation of preference-based measures of health-related quality of life, *Med. Care*, **38** (Suppl. 9), II138–150.

Loomes, G. & McKenzie, L. (1990).The scope and limitations of QALY measures, in *Quality of Life Perspectives and Policies* (Eds S. Baldwin, C. Godfrey & C. Propper), pp. 84–102, Routledge, London.

Murray, C.J.L. (1996). Rethinking DALYs, in *The Global Burden of Disease: A Comprehensive Assessment of Mortality and Disability from Diseases, Injuries and Risk Factors in 1990 and Projected to 2020* (Eds C.J.L. Murray & A.D. Lopez), pp.1–98, Harvard University Press, Cambridge, Massachusetts.

Murray, C.J.L. & Lopez, A.D. (Eds) (1996). *The Global Burden of Disease: A Comprehensive Assessment of Mortality and Disability from Diseases, Injuries and Risk Factors in 1990 and Projected to 2020*, Harrard University Press, Cambridge, Massachusetts.

Prieto, L. & Sacristan, J.A. (2004). What is the value of social values? The uselessness of assessing health-related quality of life through preference measures, *BMC Med. Res. Methodol.*, **4**, 10.

Pyne, J.M., Smith, J., Fortney, J. *et al* (2003). Cost-effectiveness of a primary care intervention for depressed females, *J. Affective Disord.*, **74**, 23–32.

Revicki, D., Brown, R., Keller, M. & Gonzales, J. (1997). Cost-effectiveness of newer antidepressants compared with tricyclic antidepressants in managed care settings, *J. Clin. Psychiatry*, **58**, 47–58.

Rosser, R. & Kind, P. (1978). A scale of valuations of states of illness: Is there a social consensus?, *Int. J. Epidemiol.*, **7**, 347–358.

Schoenbaum, M., Unutzer, J., Sherbourne, C. *et al* (2001). Cost-effectiveness of practice-initiated quality improvement for depression; Results of a randomized clinical trial, *J. Am. Med. Ass.*, **286**, 1325–1330.

Shiell, A., Pettipher, C., Raynes, N. & Wright, K. (1990). Economic approaches to measuring quality of life, in *Quality of Life. Perspectives and Policies* (Eds S. Baldwin, C. Godfrey & C. Propper), Routledge, London.

Singh, B., Hawthorne, G. & Vos, T. (2001). The role of economic evaluation in mental health care, *Aust. N. Z. J. Psychiatry*, **35**, 104–117.

Spiegelhalter, D.J., Gore, S.M., Fitzpatrick, R. *et al* (1992). Quality of life measures in health care. III: Resources allocation, *Br. Med. J.*, **305**, 1205–1209.

Tan Torres, T., Baltussen, R.M., Adam, T. *et al* (2003). *Making Choices in Health: WHO Guide to Cost-Effectiveness Analysis*, World Health Organization, Geneva.

Ustun, B., Ayuso-Mateos, J.L., Chatterji, S., Mathers, C. & Murray, C. (2004). Global burden of depressive disorders in the year 2000, *Br. J. Psychiatry*, **184**, 427–432.

Valenstein, M., Vijan, S., Zeber, J.E. *et al* (2001). The cost–utility of screening for depression in primary care, *Ann. Internal Med.*, **134**, 345–360.

Weinstein, M. & Stason, W. (1977). Foundations of cost-effectiveness analysis for health and medical practices, *New Engl. J. Med.*, **296**, 716–721.

Williams, A. (1985). Economics of coronary artery bypass grafting, *Br. Med. J.*, **291**, 326–329.

26

Organisation of Care and Quality of Life of Persons with Serious and Persistent Mental Illness

David Mechanic

INTRODUCTION

Quality of life (QoL) is a broad arena encompassing both objective and subjective components of performance and well-being as well as environmental aspects. Although effective medical and psychiatric care that improves affect and function typically improves QoL in many ways, other aspects are remote from what psychiatrists and other doctors do. Thus, it is essential to distinguish carefully between what can reasonably be expected from high-quality medical interventions and what facets must depend on other social or community initiatives. In adopting QoL as a relevant outcome in evaluating mental health services more broadly, we must be realistic as to what can be expected from one or another intervention. Applying this concept inappropriately or too globally can lead us to underestimate the usefulness of specialised interventions.

This point can be illustrated by the perceived needs of persons with serious and persistent mental illness. We asked clients about the services they were receiving and their needs for more help in some 15 aspects and found that the highest priorities were in those remote from usual conceptions of psychiatric care (Uttaro and Mechanic, 1994). Putting it simply, what clients most wanted was to have the roles and opportunities that most people have: activities to keep oneself occupied and involved, intimate relationships with boyfriends or girlfriends, a job, a decent place to live and money. Psychiatric care tends to focus on medication management, and most respondents were receiving all such help they wanted: only 5% wanted more. In contrast, there was a high level of expressed need for social role restoration and assistance for controlling symptoms and feelings of anger.

These data suggest that improving patients' QoL in many high-priority areas is likely to depend on aspects substantially outside the control of mental health personnel. Such personnel could do a great deal to help the client locate suitable housing, attain disability and social security benefits, get a job and perform appropriately, and the like. However, even in the best of circumstances, they have little control over the housing stock, the adequacy of disability entitlements or the availability of jobs and what these pay. Moreover, their capacity to deal with disorganised families, community stigma and threatening neighbourhoods that lead to victimisation is also quite limited. Yet many of these factors are central to patients' lives and how they perceive them.

As we proceed to examine organisational and financial arrangements that facilitate improved QoL, two other elements must be kept in mind. Firstly, there is now abundant evidence that the association

Quality of Life in Mental Disorders, Second Edition   Edited by H. Katschnig, H. Freeman and N. Sartorius
© 2006 John Wiley & Sons, Ltd

between objective and subjective indicators of QoL is modest. Thus, while it is appropriate to set standards for decent minimal living conditions, these may not be correlated with subjective responses. For example, most people in the community perceive shelter in supervised housing and in public shelters, however limited, as preferable to living on the streets, but some patients see the issue differently. This response can often be attributed to mental illness, but not always: there are many trade-offs in living conditions. Residence in a dilapidated and impoverished area may offer a patient more opportunities for activities and resources to reduce daily boredom than a more middle-class residence, but such residences also increase the probability of victimisation. Clients may prefer the risk because of the need to reduce the awful boredom they feel. Thus, comprehensive judgements of overall QoL are difficult to make without knowing their preferences.

Secondly, it is evident that while one can easily measure global QoL, different factors affect varying dimensions of it. Some general factors such as positive affect and sense of personal control and empowerment relate to many different dimensions of QoL, but even these are related more strongly to some dimensions than to others (Rosenfield and Neese-Todd, 1993). Thus, in studying the impact of any specific intervention, whether in housing, employment or anything else, it is essential to use the correct QoL outcome measure. Simply measuring global QoL may underestimate the value of the intervention.

THE ROLE OF CLIENT AFFECT IN EVALUATING QUALITY OF LIFE

Some studies measure objective aspects of the quality of the patient's environment by having independent raters make the assessment; early important work on the assessment of hospital environments on patients' function, for example, was of this kind. Raters assessed how much time patients spent doing nothing, whether they had a place to keep personal possessions, whether they had basic personal items, etc. (Wing, 1993). Most studies of QoL, however, focus on reports or ratings of clients about their lives and how they perceive them. It is well established that persons with negative affect not only provide more negative subjective responses but also may report objective aspects differently, such as how many friends they have, the safety of their neighbourhoods, the quality of their housing and recreational opportunities available to them.

In the case of 'objective' QoL indicators, it is often possible to check the respondent's report against independent observations or reports by other informants about the same issues. Subjective QoL, however, cannot be validated in the same way. Depressive symptoms at the time of the interview represent perhaps the single best predictor of what people say about their lives, and particularly the subjective aspects (Mechanic et al., 1994). However, there are alternative ways in which this can be interpreted. To the extent that clients regard their lives as dismal, for whatever reason, these are still dismal and that is significant. From a practical standpoint, however, we often want to separate those factors affecting QoL which are associated directly with illness and comorbidities from those due to other factors. In this context, we might regard the effects of depression and other negative affects as artefacts. One corrective approach is to use multivariate statistical techniques that allow the predictors of QoL to be examined, independently of measures of negative affect. In my judgement, it is important to do so routinely in evaluating the wide assortment of factors that affect QoL.

ISSUES IN FINANCING AND ORGANISATION OF SERVICES

The foregoing should already make clear that protecting or enhancing the QoL of persons with serious mental illness extends well beyond even the most excellent medical and psychiatric care. The problem is very much compounded outside hospital, and especially in large urban areas, where mental health personnel have little control over the environment or the client. Hospital care has many disadvantages, but those responsible for the service have control over many aspects of the patient's life including housing, nutrition, supervision and a programme of daily activity. In communities, and particularly in large densely populated urban areas, these responsibilities are dispersed among different levels of government and different sectoral bureaucracies, each with its own goals, culture, priorities and reward structures. Bringing the necessary services together is a formidable endeavour. The primary challenge of community mental health is to direct the efforts of these various bureaucracies to the cases of individual patients and to reduce fragmentation. The problematic areas often include social services, employment and vocational services, housing, social security and disability insurance, criminal justice and even medical care.

Systems of services can only be as good as the quality of the specific interventions they incorporate. In many areas of QoL, we lack sufficient information as to what modalities work best with patients who vary in diagnosis, psychiatric history, dangerousness, age, education, ethnicity and culture, and other characteristics. Attention to family structures and processes is important for all patients, but in some cultural groups it is difficult even to begin without involving the family in organising treatment and care. Many mental health programmes include sheltered work and employment, but relatively few deal well with patients who have high levels of education and skill. Client groups are highly heterogeneous and do not respond uniformly to different forms of intervention.

Whatever the current state of psychiatric and social intervention, effectiveness will also depend on the organisational and financial arrangements for providing services. To address QoL issues, the service package must be comprehensive, flexible and accessible; continuity of responsibility and care must be assured to avoid fragmentation. Moreover, a clinical and financial structure must be in place to ensure that the necessary mix of services, needed at any point in time, can be accessed. The typical service approach directed to this task is case management.

CASE MANAGEMENT

Case management is a term that misleads more than it reveals: the term has now become politically correct and it is applied to models that have little in common (Spitz, 1978; Dill, 2001). Case managers vary in their professional education and skills, ranging in background from graduates in nursing, social work or psychology to those having little training or experience. Case managers may perform a variety of functions; some provide therapy as well as brokering other needed services, while others work entirely on the brokering principle. Some case managers may have considerable control over many of the resources needed, while others can do little more than exhort professionals and bureaucratic officials, who may have little regard for them and are not much influenced. Caseloads may vary from as few as 10 patients per case manager in intensive programmes to as many as 50 or even 100. Case managers often work within bureaucracies, where they are faced with intense conflict between service needs and economics, and where the rewards are greater for with-holding services than for meeting people's needs. Finally, case management may be organised around individuals or teams, be more or less assertive and may be free-standing or organised within a well-planned system of services that assumes continuing clinical responsibility for patients, wherever they might be.

Given this diversity, it should be no surprise that the case management literature gives little guidance. Rarely does it report on the characteristics of patients, medication history and compliance, and many other crucial issues. Some studies find that case management is cost-beneficial, while others find that it increases costs without improving patients' function or QoL (Franklin *et al.*, 1987). In many instances, case management is seen to reduce the use of in-patient care, but only occasionally is it convincingly demonstrated that patients' outcomes are also improved (Olfson, 1990). Most studies have serious selection biases and other methodological problems, and rarely is sufficient information provided on what works well with different subgroups of patients. It seems clear enough that a certain intensity of services is needed to achieve positive effects, but there is no linear relationship between cost and staff intensity, on the one hand, and the quality of the outcomes achieved, on the other (Dietzen and Bond, 1993).

The model of assertive case management, the Program of Assertive Community Treatment (PACT), developed in Wisconsin by Stein and Test (1980) stands out as one of the more successful approaches, supported by the results of reasonably good randomised trials in several countries (New South Wales Department of Health, 1983; Marks *et al.*, 1994). Evaluation of this model showed that highly impaired patients could be cared for almost exclusively in the community. When compared to randomised controls, patients had higher earnings from work, involvement in more social activities, more contact with friends, greater life satisfaction and also fewer symptoms. Economic evaluations of this and other PACT-like programmes suggest that they have higher cost–benefit outcomes than conventional care (Weisbrod, Test and Stein, 1980; Knapp *et al.*, 1994). Most efforts to replicate the programme show that in-patient care can be reduced, but many do not replicate the favourable findings on symptoms and function. Most studies of community care, in contrast to conventional in-patient/out-patient care, find higher patient satisfaction.

Some of these conflicting findings may be due to variations in the assertive case management, contrasting patient populations, varying medication compliance and different evaluation approaches. It is likely that case management works better when organised carefully within an integrated programme of services that assumes long-term clinical responsibility for the patient. Given our limited understanding of how to treat severe and persistent illness, it may be unreasonable to expect long-term improvement in clinical status. However, case management embedded in a comprehensive system should be able to assist patients and improve social functioning, stability of living situation, satisfaction and other aspects of QoL.

ORGANISATIONAL AND FINANCIAL APPROACHES

Stein attributes some of the success of assertive community treatment to Wisconsin's system of financing mental health services and the incentives it established to consider carefully the trade-offs between the use of in-patient care and alternative community services (Stein, 1989). In Wisconsin, the county mental health board received a global budget for services, whether provided on an in-patient or community basis. To the extent that patients in the PACT programme use in-patient services, the charges must be paid from its budget, so that PACT staff have an incentive to consider carefully the necessity for in-patient care. Should they use too much such care, they substantially reduce their community care budget and threaten their own service system and jobs. However, while the financing system in Wisconsin is an enabling structure, it is insufficient. Many other counties with the same funding system have been slow to modify traditional practice; important explanatory factors for this difference include professional inertia, poor leadership and traditional college and university training structures that emphasise psychotherapeutic training. A further barrier is the difficulty of obtaining the necessary conversion funding required during the transition period, when it is essential to retain existing funds while new services are being established.

In the past decade or two, four strategies have been advocated as ways to organise community services to provide more comprehensive care and improve clients' QoL. These include: capitation models of various kinds that seek to modify the typical financial incentives that encourage excessive in-patient treatment; development of comprehensive mental health authorities with an improved capacity to take clinical responsibility and control a broader range of resources; design of hospital and out-patient reimbursement systems that seek to change the goals and priorities of treatment; and application of a variety of managed care approaches, designed to broaden the array of available services while keeping costs under control. All of these approaches require continuing evaluation.

Each approach seeks in one way or another to expand the comprehensiveness of services and allow treatment personnel broader choices in order to facilitate trade-offs between different types of services. They all seek, in one way or another, to address the fundamental problem of fragmentation and to facilitate coordination in providing the services that a seriously mentally ill person might require. They seek in various ways to break down the rigid separation of funding streams and the segmentation among areas of service. They do this in a context in which there are many governmental and bureaucratic barriers that make coordination difficult.

CAPITATION APPROACHES

Capitation involves prepayment of a fixed sum for each patient for a defined range of services, regardless of how many services the patient actually uses. For providers, capitation offers the advantage of knowing their budget in advance and providing sufficient capital to develop new services or acquire new equipment. The payers, in turn, know their costs in advance, transfer financial risk to providers and give providers incentives to use services efficiently. The theory is that being required to function within fixed budgets, providers will make more thoughtful and efficient decisions. Capitation is seen as preferable to global budgets, in that the provider is held responsible for caring for specific patients and not simply for doing the best it can within a catchment area. In the latter case, providers can too easily choose more attractive and less difficult clients and ignore those who may most require services.

The motive behind capitating psychiatric patients is different from the logic of capitation in general medical care, where transfer of financial risk is a central feature (Mechanic and Aiken, 1989). Most seriously mentally ill people who are capitated will need many services, and capitation is valued less for averaging risk than as a device to consolidate resources, to assign clinical responsibility for difficult patients and to encourage comprehensive systems of care. In most instances where such approaches have been used, the focus has been on long-term hospital patients being returned to the community, but capitation has also been applied to out-patients (Babigian and Marshall, 1989). Typically, health maintenance organisations (HMOs) that specialise in mental health are existing community mental health centres that accept clinical responsibility for providing a specified range of services for specific patients, at an agreed price. Thus, the mental health centre can be held accountable for ensuring that these defined patients receive suitable care. Some of the capitation programmes have been broad in scope, encompassing housing, medical care, social services, psychosocial education and other services, in addition to basic medical and psychiatric care. However, implementation of the mental health HMO concept has been difficult, because few people in the mental health field have the financial and managerial capacity to develop and administer these entities. It has taken as much as a decade to put such programmes into place. Diagnosis is a poor predictor of the use of resources in psychiatry (Taube, Lee and Forthofer, 1984) and we lack alternative indicators that are practical for pricing the capitation; therefore providers are reluctant to assume financial risk. Most mental health providers are relatively small organisations, and should they unexpectedly enroll a disproportionate number of very expensive patients, they could be put in great financial difficulty. As a result, complex risk-sharing arrangements have to be negotiated. Moreover, garnering the funds for the needed capitation involves cooperation among varying government agencies, each bound by its own legal and bureaucratic criteria, which is no easy task. American experience indicates that capitated programmes can take long-term hospital patients and care for them at much lower cost than the hospital. However, there is, as yet, no convincing evidence of superior functional or QoL outcomes.

An alternative capitation approach is to 'mainstream' persons with severe mental illness into existing HMOs that have been organised to provide medical care for the broader population (Mechanic and Aiken, 1989). These HMOs contract to provide needed medical and mental health services, although most have had only limited experience with the severely mentally ill. These generic HMOs are expected to provide the needed services, either directly or by contract with specialty mental health providers. Mainstreaming is difficult because persons with serious mental illness have high and unpredictable costs for medical as well as mental health needs, and an adequate methodology is lacking for adjusting capitation payments appropriately. In the most ambitious evaluation of mainstreaming, the largest HMO enrolling the greatest number of mentally ill clients withdrew from the project after only seven months because of the uncertain financial risk (Christianson *et al.*, 1989).

While mainstreaming may work well for persons with less severe disorders, generic HMOs are not organised to provide the range of services needed by persons with severe and persistent disorders. Quantitative evidence is difficult to obtain, but experience suggests that the complicated psychiatric patient does not get adequate care in this context (Schlesinger and Mechanic, 1993). There is also some evidence that patients with major depression fare less well in capitated practice than in fee-for-service practice (Rogers *et al.*, 1993). HMOs differ in their organisational structures, however, so that it is difficult to generalise from one situation to another. Some HMOs control referral very stringently, while others may allow patients to refer themselves to mental health providers. In the mainstreaming demonstration project discussed above, mentally ill enrollees were allowed to self-refer. In a randomised study covering about a year of experience, the researchers found that patterns of use of mental health services were comparable in the HMOs where there were no gatekeepers to referral and in fee-for-service situations. A major difference, however, was that mentally ill patients in the HMO were using public sector services, and most of these services were not being reimbursed by the HMOs (Christianson *et al.*, 1992). In short, the HMOs were cost-shifting to the public sector. It is not clear what services would have been available to mentally ill HMO patients had there not been a broad array of public sector services.

A number of American states are concerned about the high costs of care for disabled persons in Medicaid – a public sector programme that serves poor persons with disabilities. Thus, several are now capitating these patients through community mental health centres and in some instances by mainstreaming them into generic HMOs. In the coming years, we should learn a great deal more about the potentialities and pitfalls of this approach, but experience thus far suggests the need to proceed carefully. The seriously mentally ill, who are not particularly favoured clients under any circumstances, may do poorly in any organisational setting that is not tailored specifically to meet their special needs.

MENTAL HEALTH AUTHORITIES AND EFFORTS AT SERVICES INTEGRATION

Services in large urban areas are especially fragmented, with responsibility often divided among levels of government and medical and welfare bureaucracies that are large, complex and distant from the life of the individual client. It is often difficult to identify who is responsible for the patient's welfare and communication among individuals serving the patient in varying service sectors is commonly poor. Because transportation is easily available, patients travel readily from one jurisdiction to another, often using services in a duplicative and uncoordinated fashion.

One possible solution to this fragmentation is to develop effective mental health authorities that have strong managerial capacity and that take clinical responsibility for organising services, to ensure that patients can gain access to the range of services they need. Such authorities, it has been argued, can organise assertive case management programmes and ensure that every patient is appropriately linked, can develop new housing and other community care services and facilities, and can bring together different funding streams in a way that allows clinicians to make trade-offs across a range of services.

To test this concept, the Robert Wood Johnson Foundation and the US Department of Housing and Urban Development provided $125 million in development funds and housing vouchers over five years to nine large American cities including Philadelphia, Baltimore and Denver. However, experience showed that it was much more difficult to achieve this goal in the complex political environments of these communities than originally anticipated. At the end of five years, most had made progress in developing viable authorities, although the level of accomplishment depended a great deal on where each had started (Morrissey *et al.*, 1994). A careful evaluation of this effort found that these organisations were able to restructure the services environment, and they improved the continuity of care available to patients (Lehman *et al.*, 1994).

From the start, those who designed the intervention believed that the only appropriate criterion for success was the ability to demonstrate that patients' levels of function and QoL would improve as a result of structural reform. The evidence of increased continuity of care would lead to such expectations, but unfortunately the evaluation could show no direct tangible benefit for patients, as measured individually (Lehman *et al.*, 1994). One important goal of the demonstration was to have the mental health authorities gain control over some of the massive funding for mental hospitals, so that a better balance could be achieved between hospital and community care and money could more easily follow the patient. For the most part, however, the authorities were not successful, illustrating again the entrenched power of mental hospital interests.

Five years is a short interval for major structural change, but given the efforts and funds that went into this demonstration, the results are disappointing. The cities were selected because of their leadership, favourable environment and potential for success, yet despite these advantages, their developmental efforts had many false starts and were difficult. More complex cities such as New York, Los Angeles and Chicago were not included in the demonstration, because their potential for developing authorities of this kind seemed less promising. In the light of the careful selection that was made, the accomplishments must be seen as modest, but in retrospect it seems clear that much more attention should have been directed to the quality of the services themselves.

Good structures are enabling frameworks, but ultimately what happens to patients depends on caregivers and the services they provide.

The challenges of integrating services so as to improve psychiatric and QoL outcomes is illustrated by the Access to Community Care and Effective Services and Supports (ACCESS) programme, a five-year demonstration seeking to evaluate strategies for services integration in 18 sites in the United States for improving outcomes among persons with mental illness who were homeless. This programme developed site-specific development strategies by strengthening relationships among local agencies and improving access to and coordination of the services system. The sites used a wide variety of integration strategies including inter-agency coalitions, inter-agency service teams, joint client tracking systems, cross-training of service providers, joint funding and co-location of services (Randolph *et al.*, 1997). Since the programme was focused on the homeless, much effort was given to housing issues. Follow-up of 1340 clients after one year found that the programme was associated with superior housing outcomes, but not with improved psychiatric outcomes (Rosenheck *et al.*, 1998, 2001). This and other large efforts at integration suggest that positive results can be achieved by detailed attention to particular categorical areas, but that it is unrealistic to expect large overall effects across a range of different services challenges. Each specific area affecting different aspects of treatment and QoL such as housing, medication adherence (Zygmunt *et al.*, 2002) and supported employment (Bond *et al.*, 2001) require specific initiatives.

ALTERNATIVE REIMBURSEMENT APPROACHES

Since a dominant assumption of economics is that individuals and institutions will respond to financial incentives, an important approach is to try to build appropriate incentives into reimbursement schemes to achieve particular goals. The single most important example in the American context is Medicare's Prospective Payment System (PPS), which reimburses hospitals by diagnostically related groups (DRGs). Hospitals receive a fixed amount for each case, regardless of the resources they use. The belief is that the incentive of a fixed payment encourages the hospital to be more thoughtful and efficient about how it uses resources than it would be with a cost reimbursement system. The evidence shows that the PPS has saved many billions of dollars (Russell, 1989), without harming the quality of care. However, much of in-patient psychiatric care has been exempt from PPS, because psychiatric diagnosis is a particularly poor predictor of resource utilisation. The United States Medicare programme is now implementing the use of DRGs for in-patient psychiatric services.

Both government and private insurers often use the reimbursement system to attempt to change practice behaviour, and at the most simple level the relative amount paid for varying procedures affects the mix of services provided. In the United States, technical procedures are reimbursed at much higher rates than cognitive services, giving excessive encouragement to the technological imperative. However, efforts have been made in recent years to modify medical reimbursement so as to change this trend. Similarly, mental health authorities are increasingly experimenting with reimbursement incentives to achieve a variety of objectives.

Modifying reimbursement incentives, however, is more complex than may at first appear. Those who design such systems must clearly understand the values of those they are attempting to influence and must have clear conceptions of how changing institutional incentives will affect individual professional behaviour. Hospitals and mental health programmes are complex behavioural systems, with their own ideologies and norms, and the implicit message of reimbursement systems has to be understandable, focused, clear and of sufficient force to effect the desired changes in institutional behaviour. This does not always occur.

New York State, for example, initiated complex changes in its in-patient and out-patient psychiatric reimbursement systems, to achieve a variety of objectives. Among the goals were: (a) to increase in-patient capacity, without adding beds, by reducing the length of stay; (b) to get hospitals to change their case-mix towards more persons with serious and persistent mental illness; (c) to encourage improved discharge planning and linkage between in-patient and out-patient services; and (d) to increase the intensity of out-patient aftercare to avoid in-patient recidivism.

Thus, the state developed a complex payment system that reimbursed hospitals differently for patients with varying diagnostic characteristics and at different rates for varying stages of the in-patient stay. For example, reimbursement was higher for caring for persistently mentally ill patients and for the early part of the in-patient stay. After the average length of stay for a diagnostic category was reached, reimbursement was reduced to 85% of the standard rate, to encourage earlier discharge. Hospitals were also paid an additional sum if a discharged patient in the Medicaid programme received out-patient services within ten days of discharge, as an incentive to improve discharge planning and linkage. Out-patient payments were substantially increased for certain high-priority clients, to encourage greater attention to their needs.

The programme was not succcssful in achieving its ambitious but complicated goals (Boyer and Mechanic, 1994) and, in retrospect, the reasons are clear. The practice environment was much more complex than those who designed the reimbursement system understood, and its implementation was flawed in many ways. Those who were most responsible for implementing the goals at the service level were not directly affected by the incentives and sometimes were not even aware of them. The reimbursement system did not relay clear and forceful incentives, and it also provided various opportunities for 'gaming' the system, which the hospitals understood and used.

Nevertheless, reimbursement approaches remain as viable strategies for achieving some important objectives in mental health services. In most countries in the world, budgeting and reimbursement continues to favour in-patient against out-patient care, and payment approaches are being tried that make it more possible for money to follow the patient. One important approach is to hold the mental health entity responsible for both in-patient and out-patient care within a consolidated budget, thus encouraging thoughtful purchasing of in-patient services. Efforts along these lines continue, and we can anticipate learning a great deal more about how to make financial incentives effective in the years ahead.

MANAGED BEHAVIOURAL HEALTH CARE

In recent years, the managed behavioural health care (MBHC) industry has emerged in the United States as a major participant in organising, monitoring and managing the provision of mental health services (Mechanic, 1999). The industry has grown rapidly with large for-profit firms that offer a wide range of managed care products to state purchasers and private employers, ranging from employee assistance plans to complete networks of services. These services are provided on an administrative basis, on a shared financial risk basis or through full-risk capitation. A survey reported 227 million people enrolled in behavioural health managed care programmes in the years 2002–2003 (*Open Minds Survey*, 2004). Many states now contract with these companies to organise and manage public sector services.

Managed care is a vague term encompassing a range of organisational mechanisms, approaches and strategies, and thus much depends on the details of administration of any programme. Some approaches we have already discussed, such as capitated mental health HMOs and mainstreaming the mentally ill into existing HMOs, and even assertive community care, are examples of managed services. However, the MBHC industry developed largely around the basic idea of utilisation review and the management of high-cost patients. As mental health costs increased, employers contracted with MBHC companies to manage their mental health and substance abuse benefits. As these companies achieved success in reducing costs, the public sector also adopted similar approaches (Mechanic, 1999).

An example of a single company helps us to understand the role of such utilisation management. The Xerox Corporation had good behavioural health care insurance coverage and faced increasing mental health costs. Prior to a utilisation review, the average length of mental health and substance abuse in-patient hospital stays ranged from 29 to 34 days. Following the introduction of utilisation management, the length of stay fell to 13 days in 1993 and 10 days in 1994 (Iglehart, 1996). As utilisation management in mental health became increasingly common, in-patient stays for mental illness and substance abuse in all types of general hospitals fell. By the year 2000, the average length of stay for mental illness in general hospitals was 6.7 days in public hospitals and 7.7 days in proprietary hospitals (Mechanic and Bilder, 2004).

Capitation programmes in managed behavioural health follow three models. The first, already described, capitates general medical HMOs to cover needed mental health and substance abuse services as well as general medical care. Some HMOs organise all these services in-house while others then 'carve-out' behavioural health and contract with other organisations to manage such care. These services can be carved-out in various ways with pharmaceuticals managed separately and with distinctions between mental health and substance abuse services and between services for adults and for children. There are many permutations. In the other two major models, the purchaser (whether an employer or public agency) contracts with a managed behavioural health care organisation. One approach is to contract with a large community mental health centre to provide the designated services on a capitated basis. Such organisations then have the responsibility of organising the network of services and managing them. Alternatively, the purchaser can contract with one of the large for-profit managed behavioural health care companies to organise and manage the network of services covered under the contract. The financial risk may be shared in varying ways, covered benefits may differ and the quality of management and accountability may also vary. Thus, generalisations about these organisations can be difficult. The devil is in the detailed arrangements, the benefit structures, the payment arrangements and adequacy of the capitated rates paid, as well as the quality of the care network and how it is managed.

The evidence is consistent that managed behavioural health reduces costs significantly, largely by reducing in-patient care, by lowering payment to providers, by reducing the intensity of care for many patients and by substituting less expensive mental health personnel for psychiatrists (Mechanic, 1999, 2003). Quality is a more difficult issue to assess and the results are mixed depending on the particular programme studied. Managed care generally increases access to entry into mental health specialty care but reduces the number of visits. On the whole, there is no evidence that quality under managed care is less than in the traditional sector. Evaluations of programmes serving persons with severe and persistent mental illness find mixed results depending on the programme, but differences in outcomes between managed care and traditional programmes tend to be small. Some studies suggest a reduction in services under managed care to the most chronically ill intensive users of care, resulting in some decrements in outcome over time. There are also data showing that poorly executed transitions to managed care can result in discontinuity in medication adherence (Ray, Daugherty and Meador, 2003). One of the most careful long-term studies in the state of Colorado compared three models: traditional fee-for-service, capitated care provided by non-profit community mental health centres and capitated care provided by a for-profit managed behavioural health company. This study examined a wide range of outcome measures and found that managed care significantly reduced costs, with little difference in outcomes among models. When outcomes differed, they favoured the managed care models (Bloom et al., 2002; Cuffel et al., 2002).

The most significant point from a QoL perspective is that all systems of care do an inadequate job of applying established evidence-based understanding to improving outcomes. As the Schizophrenia Patient Outcomes Research Team Client Study found, effective practices are poorly implemented, despite compelling evidence, particularly in the psychosocial areas, including family education and support and vocational rehabilitation (Lehman and Steinwachs, 1998; Lehman, 1999). Moreover, patients with schizophrenia usually did not receive anti-Parkinson medication or antidepressants for comorbid depression. Although depression is now more likely to be recognised and treated, only about one-fifth of patients in the community with major depressive disorders are receiving minimally adequate care (Kessler et al., 2003). Much of the challenge in providing appropriate QoL care for persons with serious and persistent mental illness requires attention to housing and residential care, community support services, supported employment, activities, living skills training and more. Few existing programmes, whether traditional or new, are organised effectively to address these challenges.

From a theoretical viewpoint, managed care offers the potential to develop treatment plans carefully, to select from a broad menu of possible services and to design an integrated and longitudinal strategy for the client's care. The size of these programmes makes it possible to implement management information systems that can track patients and special initiatives to intervene to reduce risk and enhance function. These same structures, however, provide the opportunity to reduce costs by denying services without offering suitable options. Examples of both types of practice are easily identified and thus it is difficult to offer general conclusions without focusing carefully on the particulars of each system of care. Much depends on the skill and training of those who organise services and make case management decisions, the quality of their supervision, and the incentives and reward structures that guide their responses.

THE NEED FOR AN INTEGRATED STRATEGY

As emphasised throughout this chapter, there are formidable challenges in organising effective services for persons with severe and persistent mental illness. Each of the major strategies discussed has some potential, but they are often applied in competing and contradictory ways that give confusing messages. Such strategies obviously work better when they are consistent and reinforce one another (Mechanic, 1991, 2002). For example, assertive community treatment programmes, organised on capitation and supported by a strong health authority that provides technical assistance and community support, are likely to be more stable and politically resilient than free-standing entities. Strong utilisation management procedures, built-in to the programme, are helpful in ensuring that the team remains thoughtful about alternative treatments and its treatment choices. Finally, the incentives affecting budgeting within the capitation framework can help to ensure that money follows best practice and not simply the routines that have become comfortable.

The strategies discussed all remain uncertain, and they may function differently for varying patient populations and in different organisational environments. Moreover, they may affect differently how treatment programmes affect symptoms, function and QoL. Research in this field can only be illustrative and alert us to difficulties (Mechanic, 1996); it cannot provide definitive answers. Situations are too diverse and practices too varied and changing to allow easy generalisation from one instance to another. Perhaps the most useful function of all these initiatives is to induce caregivers to be thoughtful about what they do and about the basis for their treatment and care choices. Certainly that in itself, supported by the active participation of patients and their families in treatment choices, can contribute importantly to making services more responsive to client populations and their QoL.

REFERENCES

Babigian, H.M. & Marshall, P.E. (1989). Rochester: A comprehensive capitation experiment, in *Paying for Services: Promises and Pitfalls of Capitation* (Eds D. Mechanic & L.H. Aiken), pp. 43–54, New Directions for Mental Health Services, No. 43, Jossey-Bass, San Francisco, California.

Bloom, J.R., Hu, T., Wallace, N. *et al* (2002). Mental health costs and access under alternative capitation systems in Colorado, *Health Serv. Res.*, **37**, 315–340.

Bond, G.R., Becker, D.R., Drake, R.E. *et al* (2001). Implementing supported employment as an evidence-based practice, *Psychiat. Serv.*, **52**, 313–322.

Boyer, C.A. & Mechanic, D. (1994). Psychiatric reimbursement reform in New York State: Lessons in implementing change, *Milbank Q.*, **72**, 621–651.

Christianson, J.B., Lurie, N., Finch, M. & Moscovice, I. (1989). Mainstreaming the mentally ill in HMOs, in *Paying for Services: Promises and Pitfalls of Capitation* (Eds D. Mechanic and L.H. Aiken), pp. 19–28, New Directions for Mental Health Services, No. 43, Jossey-Bass, San Francisco, California.

Christianson, J.B., Lurie, N., Finch, M., Moscovice, I.S. & Hartley, D. (1992). Use of community-based mental health programmes by HMOs: Evidence from a Medicaid demonstration, *Am. J. Public Health*, **82**, 790–796.

Cuffel, B.J., Bloom, J.R., Wallace, N. *et al* (2002). Two-year outcomes of fee-for-service and capitated Medicaid programs for people with severe mental illness, *Health Serv. Res.*, **37**, 341–359.

Dietzen, L.L. & Bond, G.R. (1993). Relationship between case manager contact and outcome for frequently hospitalized psychiatric clients, *Hosp. Community Psychiatry*, **4**, 839–843.

Dill, A.E.P. (2001). *Managing to Care: Case Management and Service System Reform*, Aldine de Gruyter, New York.

Franklin, J.L., Solovitz, B., Mason, M. *et al* (1987). An evaluation of case management, *Am. J. Public Health*, **77**, 674–678.

Iglehart, J.K. (1996). Managed care and mental health, *New Engl. J. Med.*, **334**, 131–135.

Kessler, R.C., Berglund, P., Demler, O. *et al* (2003). The epidemiology of major depressive disorder: Results from the national comorbidity survey replication (NCS-R), *J. Am. Med. Ass.*, **289**, 3095–3105.

Knapp, M., Beecham, J., Koutsogeorgopoulou, V. *et al* (1994). Service use and costs of home-based versus hospital-based care for people with serious mental illness, *Br. J. Psychiatry*, **165**, 195–203.

Lehman, A.F. (1999). Quality of care in mental health: The case of schizophrenia, *Health Affairs*, **18**, 52–65.

Lehman, A.F. & Steinwachs, D.M. (1998). Patterns of usual care for schizophrenia: Initial results from the schizophrenia patient outcomes research team (PORT) client survey, *Schizophrenia Bull.*, **24**, 11–20.

Lehman, A.F., Postrado, L.T., Roth, D. *et al* (1994). Continuity of care and client outcomes in the Robert Wood Johnson Foundation program on chronic mental illness, *Milbank Q.*, **72**, 105–122.

Marks, I.M., Connolly, J., Muijen, M. *et al* (1994). Home-based versus hospital-based care for people with serious mental illness, *Br. J. Psychiatry*, **165**, 179–194.

Mechanic, D. (1991). Strategies for integrating public mental health services, *Hosp. Community Psychiatry*, **42**, 797–801.

Mechanic, D. (1996). Can research on managed care inform practice and policy decisions?, in *Controversies in Managed Mental Health Care* (Ed. A. Lazarus), pp. 197–211, American Psychiatric Association Press, Washington, DC.

Mechanic, D. (1999). *Mental Health and Social Policy: The Emergence of Managed Care*, Allyn and Bacon, Boston, Massachusetts.

Mechanic, D. (2002). Improving the quality of health care in the United States of America: The need for a multi-level approach, *J. Health Serv. Res. Policy*, **7**(Suppl. 1), S1: 35–39.

Mechanic, D. (2003). Managing behavioral health in Medicaid, *New Engl. J. Med.*, **348**, 1914–1916.

Mechanic, D. & Aiken, L.H. (1989). Capitation in mental health: Potentials and cautions, in *Paying for Services: Promises and Pitfalls of Capitation* (Eds D. Mechanic and L.H. Aiken), pp. 5–18, New Directions for Mental Health Services, No. 43, Jossey-Bass, San Francisco, California.

Mechanic, D. & Bilder, S. (2004). Treatment of people with mental illness: A decade-long perspective, *Health Affairs*, **23**, 84–95.

Mechanic, D., McAlpine, D., Rosenfield, S. *et al* (1994). Effects of illness attribution and depression on the quality of life among persons with serious mental illness, *Social Sci. Med.*, **39**, 155–164.

Morrissey, J.P., Calloway, M., Bartko, W.T. *et al* (1994). Local mental health authorities and service system change: Evidence from the Robert Wood Johnson program on chronic mental illness, *Milbank Q.*, **72**, 49–80.

New South Wales Department of Health (1983). *Psychiatric Hospital Versus Community Treatment: A Controlled Study*, Sydney, Australia (HSR 83-046).

Olfson, M. (1990). Assertive community treatment: An evaluation of the experimental evidence, *Hosp. Community Psychiatry*, **41**, 634–641.

Open Minds Survey (2002–2003) (2004). Available online at: http://openminds.com/pressroom/mbhoymrbook02.htm, Accessed 14 May 2004.

Randolph, F., Blasinsky, M., Leginski, W. *et al* (1997). Creating integrated service systems for homeless persons with mental illness: The ACCESS program, *Psychiat. Serv.*, **48**, 369–373.

Ray, W.A., Daugherty, J.R. & Meador, K.G. (2003). Effect of a mental health 'carve-out' program on the continuity of antipsychotic therapy, *New Engl. J. Med.*, **348**, 1885–1894.

Rogers, W.H., Wells, K.B., Meredith, L.S. *et al* (1993). Outcomes for adult outpatients with depression under prepaid or fee-for-service financing, *Arch. Gen. Psychiatry*, **50**, 517–525.

Rosenfield, S. & Neese-Todd, S. (1993). Elements of a psychosocial clubhouse program associated with a satisfying quality of life, *Hosp. Community Psychiatry*, **44**, 76–78.

Rosenheck, R., Morrissey, J., Lam, J. *et al* (1998). Service system integration, access to services, and housing outcomes in a program for homeless persons with severe mental illness, *Am. J. Public Health*, **88**, 1610–1615.

Rosenheck, R., Morrissey, J., Lam, J. *et al* (2001). Service delivery and community: Social capital, service systems integration, and outcomes among homeless persons with severe mental illness, *Health Serv. Res.*, **36**, 691–710.

Russell, L.B. (1989). *Medicare's New Hospital Payment System: Is it Working?*, The Brookings Institution, Washington, DC.

Schlesinger, M. & Mechanic, D. (1993). Challenges for managed competition from chronic illness, *Health Affairs*, **12** (Suppl.), 123–137.

Spitz, B. (1978). A national survey of Medicaid case-management programs, *Health Affairs*, **6**, 61–70.

Stein, L.I. (1989). Wisconsin's system of mental health financing, in *Paying for Services: Promises and Pitfalls of Capitation* (Eds D. Mechanic & L.H. Aiken), pp. 29–41, New Directions for Mental Health Services, No. 43, Jossey-Bass, San Francisco, California.

Stein, L.I. & Test, M.A. (1980). Alternative to mental hospital treatment I. Conceptual model, treatment program and clinical evaluation, *Arch. Gen. Psychiatry*, **37**, 392–397.

Taube, C., Lee, E.S. & Forthofer, R. (1984). Drugs in psychiatry: An empirical evaluation, *Med. Care*, **22**, 597–610.

Uttaro, T.C. & Mechanic, D. (1994). The NAMI consumer survey analysis of unmet needs, *Hosp. Community Psychiatry*, **45**, 372–374.

Weisbrod, B.A., Test, M.A. & Stein, L. (1980). Alternative to mental hospital treatment II. Economic benefit-cost analysis, *Arch. Gen. Psychiatry*, **37**, 400–405.

Wing, J. (1993). Institutionalism revisited, *Criminal Behaviour and Ment. Health*, **3**, 441–451.

Zygmunt, A., Olfson, M., Boyer, C.A. *et al* (2002). Interventions to improve medication adherence in schizophrenia, *Am. J. Psychiatry*, **159**, 1653–1664.

27

Quality of Life and Mental Disorders: A Global Perspective

Norman Sartorius

INTRODUCTION

Ideally, a mental health programme should have at its disposal a set of measurement tools that will enable it to reduce errors in the identification and diagnosis of mental illness, allow it to control the treatment process and facilitate the assessment of the impact that the illness has on the patients, their families and communities, and on the health care system. Table 27.1 shows the domains that should be covered by such a set of tools.

The development of this arsenal of tools has been uneven. While major advances have been made in the construction of methods suitable for the assessment and recording of psychiatric symptoms, progress in technology for the assessment of other characteristics of the patient's condition has been much less spectacular. Well-written case histories, for example, are still the best way to depict a patient's life and the circumstances that are relevant for the understanding of the disease process. Instruments for the assessment of the course and outcome of diseases are still not very sophisticated and it is usual to see that investigators restrict themselves to producing global ratings of the course of illness (e.g. 'episodic') and that the ratings of outcome are given in summary terms (e.g. 'favourable'). Operational definitions of the course and outcome that have been proposed by various authors over the years are not generally accepted, and the life of instruments often coincides with the life of the study or, worse still, with the length of funding from a particular source.

Tools suitable for the assessment of the health care system have grown in numbers, often under the influence of changes in funding structure and the insistence of the authorities on quality assurance. They are still more concerned with the process (e.g. how many patients were examined, how long is the waiting period) and input (e.g. how many new services were created) characteristics of a service and remain less trustworthy when it comes to the measurement of: (a) outcome of service interventions or (b) assessment of the impact that a particular set of actions in the health care system had on the society or patient populations as a whole.

Quality of Life in Mental Disorders, Second Edition Edited by H. Katschnig, H. Freeman and N. Sartorius
© 2006 John Wiley & Sons, Ltd

Table 27.1 Domains that should be covered by the set of instruments available to the mental health programme

---

1. Identification and diagnosis

    – Symptoms
    – History of illness
    – Life story
    – Immediate environment
    – Impact of illness
    – Course and outcome
    – Personality
    – Impairments
    – Disabilities
    – Quality of life

2. Control of the treatment process

    – Professional and non-professional care givers
    – Operational features of services (e.g. location of service in relation to catchment area)
    – Process of care
    – Quality assurance
    – Cost
    – Quality of life of staff and caregivers

3. Outcome and impact of services on

    – the patient's illness
    – the performance and structure of the health system itself
    – the satisfaction of the patients and the population with the service

---

APPROACHES TO THE MEASUREMENT OF QUALITY OF LIFE

For a long time, progress in the development of methods for the assessment of quality of life (QoL) has been hampered by profound differences in attitudes to its evaluation. While some considered that the only way to measure QoL was to ask individuals about the goals that they set for themselves and their feelings of how close they had come to them, others felt that the assessment must be based on the measurement of assets and opportunities that people have.

Cell A in Fig. 27.1 corresponds to the first of the above attitudes: QoL will, by 'subjectivists', be measured on the basis of statements that the individuals concerned will make on their feelings about the remaining distance to the goals that they have set themselves. In this framework, it does not matter, for example, what material belongings the individual has: the only thing that matters is whether the

Distance		Goals set by		
		Patient	Family	Society
to goals	Patient	A	B	C
assessed	Family	D	E	F
by	Society	G	H	I

Figure 27.1 Quality of life is equivalent to the distance between persons' positions and their goals. Depending on who defines the goals and who measures how distant they are, the quality of life will be judged to be different (for an explanation of the capital letters see text)

individual whose QoL is being assessed feels that he/she is close to having all the belongings that he/she aims to have. Cell I shows the other extreme: the wider society and its representatives – the government, for example, or doctors representing it – will have to set the goals (e.g. that everyone should have an apartment) and assess whether the person concerned has reached them. If this has happened (e.g. that the person has been placed in an apartment), his/her QoL will be judged to be good. In between are other cells: e.g. in cell E, the position is that the family should set goals for its members and that the members of the family will have to assess the QoL of individuals with reference to whether they are close to the goals that their family considers to be most important.

Over the years, the fervour of the advocates of the two extreme positions abated and it became obvious that both an objective assessment – of the individuals' positions in life, of their symptoms, their capacities – and a subjective assessment by the individuals themselves are important and complementary. The strategy that the World Health Organization (WHO) adopted in its effort to develop cross-culturally-acceptable and applicable methods for the measurement of QoL exemplifies this position (Sartorius, 1993; Sartorius and Kuyken, 1994; Skevington *et al.*, 2004). The definition of QoL proposed by the World Health Organization (WHO) is that QoL is people's perception of their position in life in relation to their goals and the value system they have accepted and incorporated in their decision-making. This definition places primary importance on individuals' willingness and capacity to communicate and participate in the assessment of their QoL. In the WHO Quality of Life Instrument (WHOQOL), a number of domains of individuals' activities have been selected by consulting a large group of scientists and practitioners from different cultures. For each of the domains, a number of 'facets' have been defined and for each of these, an objective assessment (e.g. of the individuals' capacity to walk) and two subjective assessments (i.e. how the individuals feel about their capacity to walk and whether this influences their overall QoL) have been sought.

WHO was not the only one to produce a tool for the measurement of QoL. Numerous individual researchers and research networks have also produced methods for this assessment, and it is fair to say that it is now possible to measure QoL in a variety of health care situations. Not only have methods used for the purpose been improved: it also appears that there is more willingness to apply them. This is certainly so in the services providing care to people suffering from malignant tumours, in long-term care institutions and in services dealing with diseases of long duration, e.g. cardiovascular disorders.

There has also been an increase in the willingness to measure the QoL of relatives of severely ill and impaired people. On the other hand, although it has often been recommended that changes in QoL should be routinely assessed in trials of new medicaments, studies in which this was done are still rare.

MEASURING QUALITY OF LIFE IN PSYCHIATRIC PRACTICE AND RESEARCH

In psychiatric services, the assessment of QoL is still rarely part of routine practice. There are various reasons that could be responsible for this.

1. Symptoms of mental disorder may resemble statements about poor QoL. This is particularly true for symptoms of depressive disorders, of neurotic disorders and of some types of personality disorders.
2. In severe mental disorders, the condition may produce an impairment that makes communication with the assessor difficult. This is clearly the case with certain neurological disorders (e.g. those with aphasia) and mental disorders characterised by cognitive impairment of a severity that makes the comprehension of questions posed by the examiner difficult or impossible.
3. Mental disorders are often accompanied by a stigma that affects all aspects of a patient's life. Stigma will persist even after the symptoms of the disorder have disappeared and may be the main reason for the difficulties that the patient experiences. In such instances, persons without any symptoms of illness may nevertheless report poor QoL because of this difficulty that the stigma of mental illness has created for them.
4. Side-effects of some of the methods of treatment currently used in psychiatry can be serious and impede a precise measurement of the relationship between a specific psychiatric disorder and QoL. A further complication is that certain side-effects can be at the origin of 'secondary' mental disorders

(e.g. depressive disorders emerging as a reaction to tardive dyskinesia or to a severe short-term memory loss after intensive electroconvulsive therapy).

5. Differences between cultures affect the form and severity of mental disorders and the manner in which the information about each of them is obtained. This makes both pooling of data and generalisation difficult, particularly in studies dealing with the QoL of people with mental disorders.

6. In some disorders (e.g. schizophrenia), symptoms such as paranoid delusions or suspiciousness may distort the answers or make it impossible to assess the QoL using methods based on patients' statements.

7. There is the well-known difficulty in reporting one's emotional state – that while the emotion lasts, the individuals experiencing it will not be at their best at observing it, but once the emotion changes, retrospective reporting is bound to be only partially valid. This may be more troublesome in psychiatric patients because it is compounded by the presence of the (temporary or permanent) impairment of cognitive function inherent in many mental disorders.

Despite these difficulties, reliable measurements of QoL of people with psychiatric disorders can be obtained, although in most instances the application of currently available methods requires special training and skills. It also takes time and effort, which health staff in general are unlikely to offer unless a dramatic change happens in their estimation of how important assessment of QoL is for their everyday work.

REASONS FOR MEASURING QUALITY OF LIFE IN MENTAL HEALTH PROGRAMMES

Regardless of difficulties, there are several reasons why the QoL of people with a mental disorder should be measured:

1. Some forms of mental disorders are long-lasting and their symptoms persist when currently available treatments are applied. This does not mean that the mental health services can cease their efforts to help: rather, that further efforts should be directed to improving the patient's QoL, despite the continuing presence of symptoms or impairment.

2. The public health importance of the rehabilitation of the mentally ill and impaired is growing. The number of people disabled because of mental disorders is large – in many industrialised countries, up to 40% of all those disabled owe their disablement to a neurological or mental disorder. Also, there are good reasons to believe that both the absolute and relative numbers of people disabled by these disorders will continue to increase. The extension of the life expectancy of those who suffer from chronic mental disorders will increase the prevalence of these conditions, even if incidence rates remain the same. The growing capacity to save people from dying – e.g. from a parasitic disease involving the brain or from an injury to the central nervous system – may also lead to a greater incidence of organic mental disorders. The ageing of populations increases the numbers of those at risk of becoming mentally ill.

   While treatment of many mental disorders is possible and effective, an important proportion of those affected by a mental disorder will remain impaired and disabled. In current times, it is becoming obvious that their rehabilitation has to be organised, recognising that the central goal of rehabilitation of the mentally ill is the improvement of their overall QoL, as perceived by the patients and their immediate families. Subsidiary goals could be employment or integration into the community, but these should not be seen as imperative; nor should their attainment be considered as the sole or principal indicator of success of a rehabilitation process. A sizeable proportion of the world's population will not have to be employed in the near future and will not be able to find paid work; economic productivity and technological developments have already made many earlier projections of the size of the labour force obsolete. Many of the earlier goals of rehabilitation have now lost their relevance: the QoL of people with disability gains in importance in parallel with the changes in society mentioned above and with the overall increase of priority given to improve the QoL of non-disabled citizens.

3. The tasks of psychiatry do not stop at the prevention and treatment of mental disorders. Psychiatry is a discipline that should assume the leadership in efforts to make health care in general more humane

and inspired by a profound respect for the patient and his/her feelings. Advocacy of the notion that an improved QoL is the central goal of health care is therefore clearly within its responsibility.

4. Psychiatric skills and knowledge could play a crucial role in the development of methods of assessment of QoL. The measurement of QoL has to rely on communication with the individual. Communication skills are clearly in the domain of psychiatry and the disciplines related to it (e.g. psychology), and it is therefore necessary to ensure that these skills and the technical input of mental health programmes are used in the process of developing measurements of QoL in health care.

5. Psychiatric work, particularly in dealing with chronic mental disorder, depends on productive and extensive partnership between mental health workers and the patients' families. The participation of the latter in the process of helping the mentally ill will depend on the changes in the quality of their lives which this partnership brings to them. Mental health programmes must therefore – if they want to continue to rely on the support of the families and communities of the mentally ill – develop ways of measuring the QoL of patients' families and incorporate specific measures to improve it into the plan of operation of mental health and other health services.

ADDITIONAL REASONS FOR MEASURING QUALITY OF LIFE IN HEALTH CARE

Measuring QoL and making its improvement prominent in all health work is an essential corrective to a number of trends in modern health care (see Fig. 27.2). Each of these trends has the potential of dehumanising medical care. When health begins to be conceived as a commodity (1) which should be on the market, purchased and sold to the highest bidder, the ethical underpinnings of medicine are in danger of being neglected. The chief reason for providing medical care is ethical: a civilised society must help those of its members who are sick, distressed or disadvantaged. If medical care is provided for economic reasons, health services will be in competition with all others vying for the resources they need to purchase other commodities. If the ethical imperative to provide care is replaced by financial arguments, both society and patients are likely to lose. Insistence on improved QoL as a main desirable outcome of health care, on the other hand, lifts health care from the market place to the level of equity, which civilised societies are bound to search above all else.

The change of health workers' perception of their own roles has similar consequences (2). As long as health workers see their tasks as part of a humanitarian calling, their satisfaction with the work they do

Trends in health care

(1) Health as a dimension of being - - - - - - - - - - - - ►   health as a commodity

(2) Doctors with a vocation of healer - - - - - - - - - - - ►   professionals of medicine

(3) Eradication of disease - - - - - - - - - - - - - - - - - ►   living with disease and disability

(4) Conceiving pain as inevitable - - - - - - - - - - - - - ►   considering pain as a symptom which doctors should remove

(5) Paternalism and authority of the doctor - - - - - - - ►   agreement and contract with care system

(6) Society and community have - - - - - - - - - - - - - ►   individuals and small groups must
responsibility for the   assume responsibility for their
individual's health   health

(7) Protection of community - - - - - - - - - - - - - - - ►   rights of individuals

(8) Duty to live - ►   right to die

Figure 27.2   Trends in health care

will be high and their motivation to be at the service of their patient will endure. Once they see themselves as health care professionals performing only in relation to the payment they receive, many of the activities they have to perform in order to provide a service will be perceived as a burden. In such a situation, health workers will have their sense of purpose stunted. Being conscious of the inextricable links between the spiritual dimensions of their profession and efforts to increase QoL can help the care provider and the patient to fight the disease in a more effective and satisfactory way.

The gradual growth of awareness that the optimistic predictions of the early twentieth century about the eradication of all diseases by revolutionary new technologies of treatment and prevention (3) are unlikely to be realised imposes the duty to think of strategies that will enable patients to continue living a decent life, despite their chronic diseases. The success of such strategies must be measured in terms of QoL.

The perception of pain as an inevitable part of existence (4) and acceptance of the authority of the doctor (5) both tend to protect the individual from the diminution of QoL that disease and medical intervention can bring. However, there are numerous indications that both of these perceptions are losing strength. Patients less and less frequently conceive pain as an inevitable fact: rather, they see it as a medical problem for which doctors must find a remedy. When this does not happen, patients and their families often interpret continuing pain as the doctor's failure or unwillingness to help rather than as an inevitable part of life and of illness. The change in the acceptance of the authority of the doctor has also affected the perception of illness and QoL. More data about the way in which this change of the doctor/patient relationship affects QoL would be useful in thinking about strategies of health education and in conceiving curricula for students of medicine and other health-related professions.

The change in the assignment of responsibility for health from the society to the individual (6) also has profound effects on the expectations about care and the motivation to undertake an action to improve health. Coercive mass health measures have often protected the health of individuals (7). Now that coercion is by and large becoming an unacceptable way to provide care or prevent disease, the acceptance of preventive measures will depend on the motivation of individuals to do something about their health; this in turn will depend on the trade-off in terms of a perceived gain in health and diminished QoL caused by the measure (e.g. by stopping smoking). The task of public health authorities here will be to assess the impact that the public health measures that they propose will have on the QoL of individuals, in order to be able to estimate acceptance rates for their interventions. They will have to think of ways in which public health and preventive measures can be linked to an increase of the QoL of those for whom they are intended or accept the fact that they will be undertaken only by a small proportion of the target population.

Finally, a trend in health care that has a direct relation on QoL is the current move away from the duty to live (even if this is connected with severe suffering) to a right to die (8). Here the behaviour of individuals will be determined by a number of factors, among which QoL takes a dominant position. It is their continuously diminishing QoL that makes people seek death as an alternative to their miserable existence. The 'duty to live' proclaimed by society and religions will have to be replaced by the wish to live because life, despite difficulties, has elements that are attractive and enhance QoL.

TASKS BEFORE US

If we decide to use the full potential of the concept of QoL, a number of methodological and practical challenges await us. The first of the methodological challenges – and perhaps the most difficult one – is to improve methods for the measurement of QoL in individuals who cannot communicate with the person carrying out the assessment. Children, the demented and other people suffering from disorders impairing their capacity to communicate are not only very numerous, but also the most vulnerable and defenceless. While it is clear that in such instances we can at best hope for an estimate of QoL, we have to make this estimate as valid as possible.

Another major methodological challenge is the identification of those aspects of our instruments that are particularly likely to be difficult to apply in a culture different from the one in which they were produced. Transculturally-valid instruments are necessary, even when the assessments are done in only one institution and when there is no intention to carry out comparative studies involving other investigators in other countries: the millions of migrants and the extraordinary mixture of cultural influences that characterise this century bring different cultures before our door, into all of our work.

A third methodological challenge is to find ways of incorporating QoL assessment into other assessment instruments used in health care. The validity of our measurements, when done in the framework of other examinations, will need to be established; what is more, it will be necessary to identify items in currently widely used instruments that could serve as a proxy for QoL measurement – at least until QoL assessment becomes a routine examination in medicine.

A fourth methodological challenge resides in the necessity to simplify instruments so as to make them usable by health care workers, rather than only by highly trained researchers. Quality of life instruments should be robust and applicable again and again at relatively short intervals; and they must be constructed in a manner that will make it possible to use them, even with people who suffer severe pain or who are otherwise unlikely to participate willingly in evaluation and examination.

The first of the practical tasks that we have to undertake is to ensure that the assessment of QoL and of its changes under treatment become a routine and standard part of the evaluation of any type of new treatment. This requirement is particularly important when new treatments have only marginal advantages over the previously used methods in terms of symptoms, but may be very different in terms of their impact on QoL.

A second practical task is to link the assessment of QoL of all involved in the treatment process – not only of the patient, but also of the family, of caregivers and of health service staff – to quality assurance procedures. These are likely to be used in most of the health care institutions and at regular intervals: if they were linked to an obligatory assessment of QoL, they would gain additional relevance for staff and patients, and this assessment would be given much more prominence and importance.

A third practical task is to introduce the provision of skills and knowledge into the training of health workers. This means that it will be necessary to introduce instruction about QoL concepts and measurement into medical schools and other schools of health personnel, and to make skills of measurement of QoL a part of the examinations and of the supervision process in health services.

Finally, a fourth practical task concerns the development of a common language about QoL. QoL research still suffers from disagreements about methods, lack of definitions and other 'childhood diseases' that relatively new branches of research and practice usually have. An agreement about a common language for work on the assessment of QoL – maybe not in a perfect form, but good enough to be used – might be reached relatively quickly: the chief challenge will not be to produce it but to make everyone in the field use it. Perhaps we should aim, at least in the beginning, at making the commonly agreed system of measurement of QoL a 'second language', i.e. encourage its use in addition to whatever language or terms practitioners or researchers use to talk about QoL. It is to be hoped that in this way (and through the education of all concerned) we shall contribute to the formation of attitudes that will ensure that QoL becomes a central criterion for the success of our work. Eventually the 'second' common language in this field may become accepted as desirable. In the meantime, heightening awareness about the need to improve QoL and its measurement by whatever tools will improve medical care should make a contribution to the search for a better and more humane society in general.

REFERENCES

Sartorius, N. (1993). A WHO method for the assessment of health-related quality of life (WHOQOL), in *Quality of Life Assessment: Key Issues in the 1990s* (Eds S.R. Walker and R.M. Rosser), pp. 201–207, Kluwer Academic Publishers, Dordrecht, Boston, London.

Sartorius, N. & Kuyken, W. (1994). Translation of health status instruments, in *Quality of Life Assessments: International Perspectives* (Eds J. Orley & W. Kuyken), Springer-Verlag, Berlin, Heidelberg.

Skevington, S., Sartorius, N., Amir, M. & the WHOQOL Group (2004). Developing methods for assessing quality of life in different cultural groups. The history of the WHOQOL instruments, *Social Psychiatry Psychiat. Epidemiol.*, **39**, 1–8.

Section VII
OUTLOOK ON THE FUTURE

28

Improving Quality of Life Through Mental Health Promotion

Eva Jané-Llopis and Heinz Katschnig

THE NEED FOR ACTION

At the beginning of the twenty-first century, it seems still necessary to remind the treating professions and those organising and financing mental health services, of the non-disease aspects of mental disorders. It is obviously difficult for those who are engaged in providing treatment to attend to these aspects in their daily practice, not the least because the structure and financing of mental health services often do not allow these aspects to be taken into consideration. As presented and described in this book, most of these non-disease aspects can be subsumed under the concept of 'quality of life'.

The intention of this book has been to describe aspects of quality of life (QoL) in relation to mental disorders as comprehensively as possible and – to a lesser extent – to show how this can be included in managing these disorders. In this chapter, the last in the book, we present emerging concepts related to QoL. These also seem more unfamiliar to those concerned mainly with the management of existing disorders: the public health concepts of 'promotion of mental health' and (to a lesser extent and more implicitly) that of 'prevention of mental disorders'. In contrast to the more descriptive concept of 'quality of life', these two concepts are clearly action-orientated.

In recent decades there have been major advances in the science and implementation of the prevention of mental disorders and the promotion of mental health. In addition to the increasing number of randomised trials, the evidence for their efficacy has been systematically reviewed for specific topics, e.g. depression (Jané-Llopis *et al.*, 2003), and comprehensively overviewed over time (Price *et al.*, 1988; Mrazek and Haggerty, 1994; Herrman, Moodie and Saxena, 2005; Hosman, Jané-Llopis and Saxena, 2006). Recently, an increased interest in 'mental health promotion' has become apparent also at governmental levels. This is documented in two widely distributed publications. The first, *Promoting Mental Health: Concepts, Emerging Evidence and Practice*", has been developed by the World Health Organization (2004a) and is accompanied by a similar publication on the prevention of mental disorders (World Health Organization, 2004b). The second publication, *Mental Health Promotion and Mental Disorder Prevention: A Policy for Europe* (Jané-Llopis and Anderson, 2005a), is supported by the European Commission and is accompanied by a publication presenting the evidence base for the proposed policy (Jané-Llopis and Anderson, 2005b). All these are intended to stimulate policy and argue for actions to be taken by governments. Also, the recent ministerial conference on mental health of the Regional Office for Europe of the World Health Organization

Quality of Life in Mental Disorders, Second Edition   Edited by H. Katschnig, H. Freeman and N. Sartorius
© 2006 John Wiley & Sons, Ltd

(WHO), which took place in January 2005 in Helsinki, placed 'promotion of mental health' prominently on its agenda. But what exactly is to be promoted? What is mental health? And what is promotion of mental health?

Traditionally, clinicians are concerned with treating disorders and aim at restoring health, which they regard as an outcome of their clinical efforts in people who are ill. In their view, therefore, the disappearance of symptoms and the absence of disease are equivalents to health and, if they have achieved this, they regard their task as accomplished. They might be familiar with the concept of prevention of disorders – although not usually regarding it as their business – but they have difficulty understanding the idea that health is something that can be promoted as such.

As a way of trying to bridge the gap between clinicians, who are confronted with the urgent and practical need to manage disease on a day-to-day basis, and those concerned with the public health approach of promoting health (including mental health), the present text explores the relationship between the concepts of 'mental health' and 'mental health promotion', on the one hand, and that of 'quality of life', on the other. From a public health perspective, these concepts are related to each other. During the WHO Conference mentioned, a 'Mental Health Action Plan for Europe' (http://www.euro.who.int/document/mnh/edoc07.pdf) was endorsed. The first of the 12 areas regarded there as requiring action is to 'promote mental well-being for all', with a noteworthy introductory sentence stating that 'mental health and well-being are fundamental to quality of life'.

From a public health perspective, promotion of health can be looked at as the action counterpart of the descriptive clinical concept of QoL. Programmes intended to help the target group to develop personal skills and increase psychological resources of self-esteem, mastery and resilience, obviously intend to improve not only mental health but also QoL. The target groups of mental health promotion include healthy individuals, persons who are at risk of developing mental problems and disorders, and also those who are already ill.

If persons with persistent mental disorders living in the community receive what is called 'psychosocial interventions' by modern community-orientated psychiatry (such as psychoeducation, skills training, providing material and social resources), the intention of mental health workers is certainly to increase their QoL. In our view these 'clinical' activities, in use for a long time, could also be subsumed under the public health concept of promoting mental health. The difference seems to be that the former are usually directed to individual patients in a treatment or management context, whereas the latter, as a public health population approach, are intended primarily to address groups of people.

WHAT IS MENTAL HEALTH PROMOTION?

Mental health promotion aims to achieve mental health and enhance well-being and QoL through the delivery of interventions in an empowering, collaborative and participatory manner. Mental health promotion conceptualises mental health in positive rather than negative terms, endorses a competence enhancement perspective, tries to improve resilience and seeks to create supportive environments. It will also address the broader determinants of mental health (such as macro environmental dimensions of poverty) (Jané-Llopis and Anderson, 2005c). While treatment deals with the mental health of individuals who already have a mental disorder, mental health promotion targets whole populations (including the healthy, those at risk of suffering from mental ill-health and those that are already affected by a mental disorder), as opposed to acting on an individual basis only.

This is in keeping with the fundamental principles of health promotion, as articulated in *The Ottawa Charter for Health Promotion* (World Health Organization, 1986), a landmark document that was published as a result of a WHO Conference in 1986. It defines health promotion as the process of enabling people to increase control over their health and to improve it. To reach physical mental and social well-being, an individual or group must be able to identify and realise aspirations, satisfy needs and change or cope with the environment. Health is understood as a positive concept, emphasising social and personal resources as well as physical capacities (World Health Organization, 1986). The Ottawa Charter calls for five strategies of action for health promotion: building public policy, creating supportive environments, strengthening community action, developing personal skills and reorientating health care.

The following four sections present a set of examples of mental health promotion and, to a lesser extent, interventions for the prevention of mental disorders that have proven to be efficacious across the lifespan. The examples are presented following the lifecycle from infancy to old age, suggesting that interventions early in life are of special importance, since they lay the basis for good mental health and reduce the need for interventions in the later stages.

Promoting a Healthy Start to Life Through Parenting Interventions

Interventions to promote mental and physical health during parenthood aim to develop personal resources and coping strategies as well as creating supportive environments for the individuals and their children to function and develop positively in their surroundings. For example, research in early life has focused on intervening through home-based strategies on the family environment, since mental health is shown to be strongly linked to a healthy and supportive family life. Most home-based interventions are particularly directed to vulnerable children and families, e.g. those with sociocultural, health, psychological and psychosocial vulnerabilities. These types of interventions aim to support parenthood through education on the health and development of the children, enhance responsible and sensitive parenting style, and facilitate the development of healthy parent/child relationships, mostly through focusing on enhancing resilience and competence. These types of interventions have been shown by randomised controlled trials to be efficacious in supporting both parental mental health and the later development of children's competence, functioning and mental well-being. Their impact expands over the years and across social domains.

A classic example of an efficacious home-based intervention that has been implemented and evaluated through randomised controlled trials in different sites is the 'prenatal infancy project', a two-year home visiting programme for low-income, at-risk pregnant women bearing their first child (Olds, 1997, 2002; Olds et al., 1998). This intervention aims to improve maternal and child functioning through improving mother's health behaviour, parental care-giving and the mother's own life course, e.g. by helping them to find work. Several evaluations of the programme have shown wide-ranging health impacts over time both in the mothers and their children. For example, there was an increase in birth weight by up to 400 grams for the newborns, a 75% reduction in pre-term deliveries and a 15% decrease in child abuse during the first years of life for children in the intervention group. At four years of age, in relation to children in the control groups, children held higher IQ scores and made 84% fewer visits to the doctor for injuries and poisoning. In the long term, the intervention has shown important social impacts, e.g. at age 15, these children were 56% less likely to have problems with alcohol or drugs, had 56% fewer arrests and 81% fewer convictions. This programme showed improved health and social outcomes for the mothers also, such as a 38% decrease in emergency-room visits, a 25% reduction in smoking and an 82% increase in employment rates, in comparison to control groups.

Interventions targeting the early years of life to improve parental attitudes and behaviour towards their children not only help mothers at risk but are also successful with mothers already suffering from depression (Gelfand et al., 1996). Mothers experiencing depression tend particularly to be less engaged in their interactions with their babies than non-depressed mothers. A mother–baby intervention, implemented across 20 community mental health centres in the Netherlands, helps new mothers with depression to develop strong attachment with their newborns. A randomised controlled trial has shown increases in the quality of the mother–baby interaction, improved baby attachment over one year and increased mental well-being in mothers who receive the intervention, as opposed to those in the control group (van Doesum et al., 2005).

Finally, a systematic Cochrane review of group-based parent-training interventions, aimed at improving parental psychosocial well-being by providing information and giving instruction in behavioural child rearing strategies, has shown reductions in parental depressive symptoms of around 20% (Barlow and Coren, 2003; World Health Organization, 2004b). These programmes have also shown a positive impact on the children's behaviour and are more cost-effective and successful in the long term than methods that involve working with parents on an individual basis (Barlow and Coren, 2003).

Mental Health Promotion in Children and Adolescents

Psychological interventions to develop coping skills and emotional competence as an individual resource can be found especially in school programmes for children and adolescents (Greenberg, Domitrovich and Bumbarger, 2001). For example, several randomised controlled trials reviewed elsewhere have shown that general cognitive, problem solving and social skill-building programmes in primary and middle school can significantly improve these skills and reduce both internalising and externalising problems, with as much as 50% reductions in depressive symptoms (Greenberg, Domitrovich and Bumbarger, 2001).

In the school setting, another type of efficacious intervention is the ecologically focused programmes that aim to restructure the school and classroom environment, altering contextual variables that can influence students' mental health. These types of interventions aim to provide an environment that is conducive to positive mental health, improves emotional and behavioural functioning, and can reduce symptoms and related negative consequences. For example, the matched controlled study of the 'School Transitional Environment Project' (Felner et al., 1993), which restructured the school environment to facilitate the integration of new pupils in their new school, produced significantly lower levels of stress, reductions in delinquent behaviour and symptoms of anxiety and depression, and improvement in academic progress for the children in the intervention group, as opposed to those in the control group (Felner and Adan, 1988; Domitrovich et al., 2006). Prevention and promotion programmes that focus simultaneously on different levels, such as changing the school ecology as well as improving individual skills, by using a holistic school approach, have proven to be more efficacious than those that intervene on solely one level (Weare, 2000).

Another type of mental health promotion strategy has focused on increasing psychological well-being and coping in groups that are at increased risk for mental health problems, e.g. focusing on improving resilience. For example, children of affectively ill parents are at a substantially increased risk of suffering from a mental disorder later in life (Beardslee, Versage and Gladstone, 1998). A randomised trial on a cognitive-orientated group programme for children with parents suffering from a mental disorder, which aimed to increase coping skills and understanding of the parent's mental illness, showed a decrease in new and recurrent depressive episodes from 25% in the control group to 8% in the prevention condition over the first year after the intervention, and from 31 to 21%, respectively, over the second follow-up year (Clarke et al., 2001). Another randomised trial evaluating the same cognitive group intervention also showed a reduction by 40% of the onset of depression one year after the intervention, when targeted at adolescents who had high levels of depressive symptoms but who did not fulfil the diagnostic criteria for a full-blown disorder (Clarke et al., 1995).

Health care is another setting where mental health promotion can be successfully implemented, e.g. to promote mental health and prevent mental disorders in chronically ill children. Interventions for children in hospitals, for example, have focused on helping children adjust to their disease, both medically and psychosocially, which has helped them to understand their illness and treatment and to overcome psychosocial and developmental issues they might encounter (Aujoulat, Simonelli and Deccache, 2005).

Mental Health Promotion in Adulthood

An important area of intervention for mental health promotion during adulthood is the work environment, where adults spend a large proportion of their time. Legislation and environmental interventions at the workplace have been shown to lead to increases in mental health and well-being as well as reductions in symptoms of anxiety, depression and stress-related problems (World Health Organization, 2004b; Price and Kompier, 2006). Effective strategies include: (a) task and technical interventions (e.g. job enrichment, ergonomic improvements, reduction of noise, lowering the workload), (b) improving role clarity and social relationships (e.g. communication, conflict resolution), and (c) interventions addressing multiple changes directed both at work and employees (Price and Kompier, 2006). These types of interventions have also included specific stress and anxiety management strategies to provide support to employees who are at an increased risk from such mental health problems.

Suffering from unemployment has important consequences for mental health and puts individuals at increased risk for mental disorders. The 'job search programme', targeted at those who are unemployed, aims to improve job searching skills and facilitate the return to the labour market, as well as mitigating the negative mental health effects of unemployment. The evaluation of three randomised trials in the United States and Finland showed that this intervention increased the quality of re-employment, decreased psychological distress and depressive symptoms, and increased self-esteem over two years, especially in those with higher risk for depression at pre-test (Caplan et al., 1989; Vinokur et al., 1991; Price, van Ryn and Vinokur, 1992; Vouri et al., 2002; Vuori and Silvonen, 2005).

In health care, education and support for patients, e.g. to prevent depression in those who have suffered from stroke, results in increased understanding and psychological well-being (Anderson, Hackett and House, 2004). It has also been suggested that interventions which aim to enhance specific psychological resources in different groups of chronic patients may also ameliorate depressive symptoms (Bisschop et al., 2004).

Mental Health Promotion in Older Age

A group of interventions for elderly people that focus on coping with widowhood and bereavement help to reduce depressive symptoms and facilitate better psychosocial adjustment. An effective example is the 'widow-to-widow programme' developed in the United States. This one-to-one outreach and support service is provided by other widows in the community who call on the bereaved on an informal basis. This intervention showed that widows were helped to locate community resources and develop relationships more quickly than the control group and showed fewer depressive symptoms after two years (Vachon et al., 1980; Silverman, 1988). However, only a few of this type of support programme have been evaluated rigorously. Other studies have also found positive changes on outcome indicators (e.g. increased positive affect and support satisfaction, less distress and loneliness) but have used a pre-post design only (e.g. Segal et al., 2001; Stewart, et al., 2001).

Chronic physical conditions such as arthritis or hearing loss are associated with important adverse effects on the QoL of elderly persons. Interventions to learn to cope with some of these conditions have led to increases in mental well-being and QoL. For example, an intervention set in primary care clinics assessed whether hearing aids would improve the QoL of elderly people with hearing loss. A randomised evaluation showed significant improvement in social and emotional function, communication, cognition and depression for those who received a hearing aid compared with those who did not (Mulrow et al., 1990).

Teaching management strategies to deal with chronic diseases and education about the prognosis and the meaning of chronic conditions has shown efficacy in increasing psychological well-being. For example, a Cochrane review of patient education programmes for people with arthritis identified 24 randomised controlled trials evaluating such interventions with an instructions component (Riemsma et al., 2003). The review found significant short-term effects for different outcome measures including psychological status (e.g. depression), although in general these tended to decrease or disappear over time. An effective example of this type of programme is a randomised trial of community intervention to prevent depression in elderly African Americans with chronic pain. The education group received ten-week lectures teaching pain management strategies, including information about arthritic symptoms, skill building, support, group discussions and coping strategies. The programme showed reduced depressive symptoms associated with their condition, which were sustained after two years (Phillips, 2000).

MENTAL HEALTH PROMOTION AND QUALITY OF LIFE: EXPLORING THE UNDERLYING CONCEPTS

Examining the aims of mental health promotion, with the case examples described above, which in several instances encompass improvement of QoL and prevention of psychopathology (defined as a disorder or not), the overlap between the concept of mental health and that of QoL becomes apparent. This section explores the assumptions underlying these concepts and examines how the more clinically orientated concept of QoL and the more public health orientated concept of promotion of mental health might be related to each other.

Promotion, Prevention, Treatment and Rehabilitation

As already stated, promotion of mental health and prevention of mental disorders cannot always be kept separate easily, since, for example, building resilience can serve both purposes, and reducing risk factors, as sought in prevention, is also attempted in health promotion interventions. However, this overlap goes beyond prevention and promotion only. Mental health promotion comprises strategies of enhancement of competence and resilience, creating supportive environments and empowerment. These are the same strategies as are employed in modern community psychiatry, where they are the principles of intervention in both treatment and rehabilitation. Similarly, there is an extensive literature on the potential of other core constructs (such as self-efficacy, sense of control and self-esteem), which have been successfully applied across the spectrum of mental health intervention including promotion, prevention, treatment and rehabilitation. It seems that promotion, prevention, treatment and rehabilitation programmes are more linked to each other than might appear at first, since they all have at their core the overall goal of promoting well-being and QoL (Barry, 2001).

There are many psychosocial interventions used in the treatment and rehabilitation of mental disorders in persons living in the community that are variably called 'psychoeducation', 'skills training', 'guided discovery' or 'learning problem-solving skills' (Bhugra and Leff, 1993; Thornicroft and Szmukler, 2001). They are intended to improve the QoL, self-efficacy and autonomy of patients, and could also be subsumed under the broader concept of 'promotion of mental health'.

In fact, it is often stated that community psychiatry also has to work with the 'healthy parts' of persons suffering from mental disorders. Two programmes developed in Vienna – a psychoeducational programme for persons suffering from schizophrenia, called 'Knowing, enjoying, living better' (Amering *et al.*, 2002), and a family-orientated residential facility, called 'School for living with schizophrenia' (Pension Bettina) (Katschnig and Amering, 1996) – deal with practically the same aims as mental health promotion. Programmes to improve the regime in mental hospitals and carried out many decades ago (Jones, 1952: 'Therapeutic community'; Wing and Brown, 1970: 'Institutionalism and Schizophrenia') might today be subsumed under the broad concept of 'mental health promotion'. However, although these interventions had clear positive connotations when they were implemented, they were formulated in negative terms (e.g. to combat hospitalism or institutionalism). Finally, the emphasis on empowerment, advocacy and self-help groups (both by 'users' and family members) in modern community psychiatry is in line with the principles of promotion of mental health.

All of this underlines that 'there is much opportunity for shared learning and development around the application of these constructs with different populations across the diverse areas of practice' (Barry, 2001), although these often exist in isolation from each other.

Mental Health and Mental Disorders

Mental health is certainly not an easy concept; even the notion of 'mental disorders' is difficult to grasp. Most such disorders can only be diagnosed by a specific pattern of psychopathological symptoms and the longitudinal course of these symptom patterns. This is much less clear than the diagnosis of certain physical disorders which can, in most cases, be validated by specific physical and chemical investigations and procedures. Nevertheless, mental disorders are much more clearly defined (e.g. in ICD-10 and DSM-IV) than mental health is. In a thoughtful discussion on the many uses of the term, Vaillant (2003) has emphasised that one of the most common pitfalls in research on mental health is that different authors attach different meanings to it (see also Katschnig and Schrank, 2004).

The term 'mental health' is used both in a broad and in a very specific sense. In a broad sense, it refers just to the field of *mental* health, as opposed to *physical* health, and covers a large spectrum of conditions ranging from good to bad mental health, i.e. including both its positive and negative poles. Often, however, mental health is just referred to as the positive end of this spectrum, meaning 'good mental' health. In this respect, the term 'mental health' is sometimes used in the sense of mental *health* as opposed to mental *disorders*, which again has led to confusion in defining and understanding the concept. Concerning the negative pole of the field, terms like 'mental ill health', 'mental health problems' or 'poor mental health' have been used. Obviously, these terms include all states of not feeling or not being well psychologically, including formally defined mental disorders. However, at times, 'mental health' is also used to refer to mental disorders. Such uses blur the concept, as in the following example from Lahtinen *et al.* (1999): 'There are many false assumptions concerning mental health. It is, for instance, widely believed that mental ill-health cannot be treated or prevented. The worst social consequence of such false assumptions is the stigma of mental ill-health'. Here obviously 'mental disorders' are meant, since it is these that are associated with the danger of stigmatisation, while states of reduced psychological well-being are usually not.

In mental health promotion, 'mental health' is equivalent to the positive pole discussed above. The WHO emphasises that 'mental health, which contributes to all aspects of human life, can be regarded as an individual resource contributing to the individual's quality of life, and can be increased or diminished by the actions of society' (World Health Organization, 2004a). Mental health has been conceptualised as 'a positive emotion (affect) such as feelings of happiness, a personality trait inclusive of the psychological resources of self-esteem and mastery, and as resilience, which is the capacity to cope with adversity' (World Health Organization, 2004a). This conceptualisation of mental health includes life skills, the ability to manage change and actively influence the social environment, positive self-esteem, enjoyment and experienced well-being. These qualities are considered as values in themselves, not only as signs of absence of illness or disorder (Lehtinen, Riikonen and Lahtinen, 1997). This understanding of mental health follows the same philosophy as the definition of health proposed by the Constitution of the WHO (World Health Organization, 1948).

In addition, certain psychological qualities are considered to be protective against the negative influences of social adversity (e.g. good social competence, well-developed problem-solving skills, internal locus of control, high self-esteem, close relationship with a parent, a supportive social network). These factors can make it easier for people to stay healthy, even during severely stressful times (Hosman, 1997). As has been stated above, modern social psychiatry emphasises such factors as being present to some extent in most persons suffering from mental disorders and regards them as 'healthy components' of their personality, which are valuable for coping with the disorder and for their self-esteem. Equal emphasis should be put on these as on treating symptoms.

Mental Health and Quality of Life

'Quality of life' is a concept for describing the specific life situation of a person. If the concept is used to describe the situation of people who are ill, as is the case in large parts of this book, the term 'health-related quality of life' (HRQL) is used. This concept is mostly restricted to the person's 'subjective' evaluation of his/her QoL.

Katschnig (Chapter 1 in this volume) has argued that if QoL is to be action orientated, it should be conceived in a broader way, as consisting of three components: (a) subjective well-being/satisfaction, (b) functional status and (c) contextual factors. In more detail, this broad approach encompasses: (a) the psychological state of 'being well', often called subjective well-being or satisfaction (the former related more to emotions, the latter more to cognition; both should not refer only to momentary states – as after drinking alcohol – but to an average assessment of a certain living situation) (see also Zissi and Barry, Chapter 3 this volume); (b) the ability to function in daily living situations, both in terms of basic and instrumental skills to care for oneself, as well as of functioning in social roles (see also Wiersma, Chapter 4, and Gurland and Katz, Chapter 15 in this volume); and, finally, (c) environmental assets, both material (sometimes called 'standard of living') and social (in terms of, for example, social support) (see Freeman, Chapter 5 in this volume).

There are apparent similarities between the concepts of mental health and that of QoL, both when the latter is used in the 'restricted' subjective sense and in the broad sense (including the three dimensions just described). The question then arises whether improving mental health can be equated with improving QoL: either in healthy individuals not characterised by any risk factors (just to make them happier), in healthy individuals at risk for developing specific disorders and finally in those who have already developed a disorder. In quite a few of the examples described above, the terms 'mental health' and 'quality of life' are used in a way which indicates that the concepts are, at least partly, overlapping.

The mental health concept, as used in the 'promotion of mental health' movement, covers the first (well-being) and the second (functioning) components of the QoL concept, though the second one in a slightly different meaning. 'Functioning in activities of daily living and social roles' is a descriptive category in the QoL concept (see also Wiersma, Chapter 4 in this volume). In contrast, in the field of mental health promotion, it is a more dynamic concept, meaning coping abilities, resilience and social skills, i.e. psychological properties that enable the individual to function in social roles, in normal life with its ups and downs, stresses and strains, and even to learn from stressful experiences. At least as far as mental well-being is concerned, the QoL and mental health concepts are identical, while as far as functioning is concerned, they overlap to a large degree.

Concerning the third dimension of QoL, i.e. environmental assets, in the 'promotion of mental health' concept this is both a desired outcome of intervention and a target for improving mental health in the two aspects just discussed. However, it does not belong to the concept of mental health as such, which is a psychological concept. The environment is an important target for mental health promotion, in the sense that it must be 'designed' in such a way that it is 'conducive to health' or specifically to mental health. Legislative measures, organisational changes and family interventions, among others, are aimed at changing the environment in the sense that it is helpful for and increases the possibility of improving mental health. The expressions 'healthy society', 'healthy organisations', 'healthy hospitals' and 'healthy companies' imply a metaphoric meaning of the term 'health', if the structure of these entities is regarded as 'healthy'. What such terms refer to in mental health promotion is that these entities should be organised in such a way that they are 'conducive to health' for the people in these organisations.

Thus, if mental health is regarded as an outcome of mental health promotion activities, then it corresponds to the two first components of QoL, i.e. well-being and functioning (viz. 'functioning abilities'). This should anyway be clear, since mental health is a psychological concept, i.e. it concerns individuals. However, as is evident from a number of the examples given above, this outcome is not achieved only by working with the individuals concerned, but also with the environment (e.g. working with the parents of children or policies to improve conditions at the workplace). In that sense, the environmental component is also included in mental health promotion, but, as in the examples quoted, as a means of achieving a specific outcome in the two other components, i.e. well-being and functioning of the target population.

MENTAL HEALTH PROMOTION TO IMPROVE QUALITY OF LIFE

Following the case examples presented earlier in this paper, in the final section, we will attempt to summarise how mental health promotion can be perceived as a way or action to improve 'quality of life'. We shall look at promotion of mental health from the angle of the three components of QoL, well-being, functioning and environmental assets, as most mental health promotion programmes will address several of these aspects. To illustrate this relationship, some of the examples provided earlier, which have been fully referenced elsewhere (World Health Organization, 2004b; Jané-Llopis and Anderson, 2005b), are now summarised under these three components of QoL.

Psychological Well-Being and Satisfaction

Concepts of psychological well-being and satisfaction are central to mental health and QoL, as subjectively perceived. Practically all mental health promotion interventions have as a main aim to improve the well-being of the population, independently of whether this is aimed at directly or indirectly. The centrality of well-being in mental health promotion is also clearly illustrated by the definitions of mental health and mental health promotion provided in this chapter and *The Ottawa Charter for Health Promotion* (World Health Organization, 1986).

As presented above, practically all mental health promotion interventions aim to improve psychological well-being and satisfaction, independently of the setting or age group they target. Interventions to improve psychological well-being in children and adolescents have focused on the development of coping skills, problem solving, emotional competence and resilience as an individual resource. Interventions have targeted all children in a school setting (Greenberg *et al.*, 2001), children at particular risk for a mental disorder, e.g. those with depressive symptoms (Clarke *et al.*, 1995) or those with a parent suffering from mental illness (Clarke *et al.*, 2001), children suffering from a chronic illness (Aujoulat, Simonelli and Deccache, 2005) and children facing a 'fearful' physical intervention such as surgery, in which case a decrease in anxiety symptoms and increase in well-being resulted (Pinto and Hollandsworth, 1989).

In adulthood, mental well-being has been achieved by developing skills and self-esteem in the unemployed, which has also led to decreases in symptoms of depression and increases in life satisfaction (Price, van Ryn and Vinokur, 1992). Other interventions have focused on enhancing well-being of caregivers (Knight, Lutzky and Macofsky-Urban, 1993) such as a psychoeducational intervention for family caregivers of older adults, which led to decreases in depressive symptoms and increases in morale and self-efficacy (Lovett and Gallagher, 1988). Similarly, different types of interventions for elderly people, e.g. to stimulate social support or to provide education for chronic conditions, can lead to increases in mental well-being, life satisfaction and QoL (World Health Organization, 2004b).

Functioning in Social Roles

One aim of mental health promotion is to support individuals' functioning in society so that they can fulfil their roles, which impacts on their own well-being and on the mental health of those in their surroundings. This can be stimulated through creating supportive environments and through changing patterns of life, work and leisure, as advocated by *The Ottawa Charter for Health Promotion* (World Health Organization, 1986). The Ottawa Charter also emphasises the principle of developing personal and life skills that support personal and social development (World Health Organization, 1986). These approaches fit both into the 'functioning' and 'environment' dimensions of QoL. Life skills for social development and supportive environments stimulate individuals' functioning, since mental health is mediated by the interaction between the individual, the environment and its wider social forces. Positive functioning in society will reinforce mental health. Positive mental health will enable individuals to function in society, interact with their surroundings and develop as active and participatory citizens (Jané-Llopis and Anderson, 2005a).

Among the examples presented earlier, mental health promotion in the home setting aims to support parenthood, i.e. the proper 'functioning' as a mother or a father, so that it enhances interaction with their children and supports their own development in their parenting roles (Olds, 1997). Role functioning is also improved through mental health promotion activities in the school setting. In addition to the central role of fostering academic development, schools serve an important role in the health, emotional and social development of students (Weare, 2000). School interventions for children and adolescents focus on enhancing pupils' behaviour and socialisation, as well as aiming to stimulate children's development into adulthood for their positive functioning in society (Domitrovich *et al.*, 2006). Pre-school interventions for children from impoverished backgrounds can, among others, have an impact on role functioning: e.g. one randomised controlled trial showed that, over 20 years, lifetime arrests were reduced by 40% and employment rates increased by 40% for those children who received the intervention (Schweinhart and Weikart, 1998). These supportive activities enhance sociability and stimulate children and adults' daily functioning, with sustained impacts over time.

Environmental Assets

For the psychological and functioning aspects of mental health promotion programmes to materialise, it is necessary that contextual and/or environmental opportunities are available, in which individuals can develop. Therefore, one of the aims of health promotion interventions is to create the environmental and material opportunities that can be conducive to mental health. For example, building healthy public policies puts health on the agenda of policy makers in all sectors, increasing their awareness of the health consequences of their decisions (World Health Organization, 1986). Such policies include legislation, fiscal measures, taxation and organisational change. Improved conditions of work can lead to improved life satisfaction and QoL. As previously presented, environmental policies and approaches to stimulate working conditions that reduce stress and poor mental health in the workplace, including stress management interventions, job redesign, altering time and workload, improving communication and social support, enhance mental health and QoL (Price and Kompier, 2006).

Other existing health and social public policies also have an impact on mental health and QoL, such as policies that increase access to education, housing, urban planning or health care. Mental health and QoL can be compromised by living in neighbourhoods with concentrations of deprivation, high unemployment, poor quality housing, limited access to services and an unfavourable environment (Raudenbush and Earls, 1997). Urban shape, zoning strategies, reduced noise levels and public amenities can promote urban health and help to reduce stress, social dislocation and violence (Jané-Llopis and Anderson, 2005c). Improving housing conditions can lead to positive impacts on individual mental health and social impacts such as perceptions of safety, crime reduction, and social and community participation (Thomson, Petticrew and Morrison, 2001).

FUTURE PROSPECTS

This chapter has explored the relationship between the concepts of mental health and QoL, and presented mental health promotion as an action to improve the QoL of healthy people and of those at risk for developing, and those already suffering from, psychological problems and mental disorders. Although within both medicine and psychiatry QoL is mainly used as an assessment and outcome measure for treatment interventions that are primarily treating symptoms, mental health promotion interventions target QoL directly.

It should have become evident that the QoL field, as it is described in this book, can profit from examining in detail the systematisation of mental health promotion interventions and their effective principles. On the other hand, the advocates of mental health promotion might only be partially aware that, in large parts of modern psychiatry, interventions that could also be understood as mental health promotion have already been applied for a long time. Working with the 'healthy part' of persons suffering from mental disorders is an essential part of modern community psychiatry. This is also a principle of the broader field of mental health promotion.

It is time that these different traditions became closer. Perhaps they need to reframe their concepts in the light of the respective other discipline. The 'big divide' between, on the one hand, those who are under pressing day-to-day demands to help people suffering already from mental disorders and, on the other hand, those who pursue the possibly more logical endeavour of strengthening health and preventing disorders for all, does not seem necessary. Enough common elements can be found in promotion, prevention, treatment and rehabilitation. Bringing the fields closer and learning from each other can only lead to strengthening each discipline and improving mental health and quality of life for all.

REFERENCES

Amering, M., Sibitz, I., Gössler, R. & Katschnig, H. (2002). *Wissen – Geniessen – Besser leben. Ein Seminar für Menschen mit Psychoseerfahrung*, Psychiatrie-Verlag, Bonn.

Anderson, C.S., Hackett, M.L. & House, A.O. (2004). Interventions for preventing depression after stroke, *The Cochrane Database of Systematic Reviews*, Issue 1, Art. No. CD003689.pub2. DOI: 10.1002/14651858.CD003689.pub2.

Aujoulat, I., Simonelli, F. & Deccache, A. (2005). Health promotion needs of children and adolescents in hospitals: A review, *Patient Education and Counselling* (in press).

Barlow, J. & Coren, E. (2003). Parent-training programmes for improving maternal psychosocial health, *The Cochrane Database of Systematic Reviews*, Issue 4, Art. No. CD002020.pub2. DOI: 10.1002/14651858.CD002020.pub2.

Barry, M.M. (2001). Promoting positive mental health: Theoretical frameworks for practice, *Int. J. Ment. Health Promotion*, 3(1), 25–43.

Beardslee, W.R., Versage, E.M. & Gladstone, T.R.G. (1998). Children of affectively ill parents: A review of the past 10 years, *J. Am. Acad. Child Adolescent Psychiatry*, 37(11), 1134–1141.

Bhugra, D. & Leff, J.P. (1993). *Principles of Social Psychiatry*, Blackwell Science, Oxford.

Bisschop, M.I., Kriegsman, D.M., Beekman, A.T. & Deeg, D.J. (2004). Chronic diseases and depression: The modifying role of psychosocial resources, *Social Sci. Med.*, 59(4), August, 721–733.

Caplan, R.D., Vinokur, A.D., Price, R.H. & van Ryn, M. (1989). Job seeking, reemployment, and mental health: A randomized field experiment in coping with job loss, *J. Appl. Psychol.*, **74**(5), 759–769.

Clarke, G.N., Hawkins, W., Murphy, M., Sheeber, L.B., Lewinsohn, P.M. & Seeley, J.R. (1995). Targeted prevention of unipolar depressive disorder in an at-risk sample of high school adolescents: A randomized trial of group cognitive intervention, *J. Am. Acad. Child Adolescent Psychiatry*, **34**, 312–321.

Clarke, G.N., Hornbrook, M., Lynch, F., Polen, M., Gale, J., Beardslee, W., O'Conner, E. & Seeley, J. (2001). A randomized trail of a group cognitive intervention for preventing depression in adolescent offspring of depressed parents, *J. Am. Med. Ass.*, **58**, 1127–1134.

Domitrovich, C., Weare, K., Greenberg, M., Elias, M. & Weissberg, R. (2006). Schools as a context for the prevention of mental health disorders and promotion of mental health, in *Prevention of Mental Disorders: Effective Interventions and Policy Options* (Eds C. Hosman, E. Jané-Llopis & S. Saxena), Oxford University Press, Oxford (in press).

Felner, R.D. & Adan, A.M. (1988). The school transitional enviroment project: An ecological intervention and evaluation, in *Fourteen Ounces of Prevention: A Casebook for Practitioners* (Eds R.H. Price, E.L. Cowen, R.P. Lorian & J. Ramos-McKay), American Psychological Association Press, Washington, DC.

Felner, R.D., Brand, S., Adan, A.M. & Mulhall, P.F. (1993). Restructuring the ecology of the school as an approach to prevention during school transitions: Longitudinal follow-ups and extensions of the school transitional environment project (STEP), *Prevention in Human Serv.*, **10**, 103–136.

Gelfand, D.M., Teti, D.M., Seiner, S.A. & Jameson, P. B. (1996). Helping mothers fight depression: Evaluation of a home-based intervention program for depressed mothers and their infants, *J. Clin. Child Psychol.*, **25**, 406–422.

Greenberg, M.T., Domitrovich, C. & Bumbarger, B. (2001). The prevention of mental disorders in school-aged children: Current state of the field, *Prevention and Treatment*, **4**(1); http://journals.apa.org/prevention/volume4/pre0040001a.html.

Herrman, H., Moodie, R. & Saxena, S. (Eds) (2005). *Promoting Mental Health: Concepts, Emerging Evidence, Practice*, WHO, Geneva (in press).

Hosman, C. (1997). Conceptual clarifications on promotion and prevention, in *Promotion of Mental Health* (Eds D. Trent and C. Reed), Avebury/Ashgate Publishing, Brookfield, Vermont.

Hosman, C., Jané-Llopis, E. & Saxena, S. (Eds) (2006). *Prevention of Mental Disorders: Effective Interventions and Policy Options*, Oxford University Press, Oxford (in press).

Jané-Llopis, E. & Anderson, P. (2005a). *Mental Health Promotion and Mental Disorder Prevention: A Policy for Europe*, Radboud University Nijmegen, Nijmegen; http://www.imhpa.net/actionplan.

Jané-Llopis, E. & Anderson, P. (2005b). *Mental Health Promotion and Mental Disorder Prevention: A Background for a Policy for Europe*, Radboud University Nijmegen, Nijmegen; http://www.imhpa.net/actionplan.

Jané-Llopis, E. & Anderson, P. (2005c). A policy framework for the promotion of mental health and the prevention of mental disorders, in *Mental Health Policy and Practice Across Europe* (Eds M. Knapp, D. McDaid, E. Mossialos & G. Thornicoroft, Open University Press, Oxford (in press).

Jané-Llopis, E., Hosman, C., Jenkins, R. & Anderson, P. (2003). Predictors of efficacy in depression prevention programmes. Meta-analysis, *Br. J. Psychiatry*, **183**, 384–397.

Jones, M. (1952) *Social Psychiatary*, Tavistock, London.

Katschnig, H. & Amering, M. (1996). Neutralität und Autonomie – Leitbilder für die Kooperation mit Angehörigen schizophrener Patienten in einem familienorientierten Wohnheim, in *Integrative Therapie der Schizophrenie* (Eds W. Böker & H.D. Brenner), pp. 377–383, Verlag Hans Huber, Bern, Göttingen, Toronto, Seattle.

Katschnig, H. & Schrank, B. (2004). Prevention of mental disorders and promotion of mental health: Exploring the concepts, in *Mental Health in Europe – New Challenges, New Opportunities* (Eds I. Azueta, U. Katila-Nurkka & V. Lehtinen), Report from a European Conference, Bilbao, Spain, 9–11 October 2003, STAKES, Helsinki.

Knight, B.G., Lutzky, S.M. & Macofsky-Urban, F. (1993). A meta-analytic review of interventions for caregiver distress: Recommendations for future research, *Gerontologist*, **33**, 240–248.

Lahtinen, E., Lehtinen, V., Riikonen, E. & Ahonen, J. (Eds) (1999). Framework for promoting mental health in Europe, STAKES, National Research and Development Centre for Welfare and Health, Ministry of Social Affairs and Health, Hamina, Finland.

Lehtinen, V., Riikonen, E. & Lahtinen, E. (1997). *Promotion of Mental Health on the European Agenda*, STAKES, National Research and Development Centre for Welfare and Health, Helsinki.

Lovett, S. & Gallagher, D. (1988). Psychoeducational interventions for family caregivers: Preliminary efficacy data, *Behaviour Therapy*, **19**, 321–330.

Mrazek, P.J. & Haggerty, R.J. (Eds) (1994). *Reducing Risks for Mental Disorders: Frontiers for Preventive Intervention Research*, National Academy Press, Washington, DC.

Mulrow, C.D., Aguilar, C., Endicott, J.E., Tuley, M.R., Velez, R., Charlip, W.S., Rhodes, M.C., Hill, J.A. & DeNino, L.A. (1990). Quality-of-life changes and hearing impairment. A randomized trial, *Ann. Internal Med.*, **113**, 188–194.

Olds, D. (1997). The prenatal/early infancy project: Fifteen years later, in *Primary Prevention Works*, (Eds G.W. Alblee & T.P. Gullotta), pp. 41–67, Sage Publications, Inc., Thousand Oaks, California.

Olds, D.L., Henderson, C.R., Cole, R., Eckenrode, J., Kitzman, H., Luckey, D., Pettitt, L., Sidora, K., Morris, P. and Powers, J. (1998). Long-term effects of nurse home visitation of children's criminal and antisocial behaviour: A 15-year follow-up of a randomized controlled trial, *J. Am. Med. Ass.*, **280**(8), 1238–1244.

Olds, D.L. (2002). Prenatal and infancy home visiting by nurses: From randomized trials to community replication, *Prevention Sci.*, **3**(3), 153–172.

Phillips, R.S.C. (2000). Preventing depression: A program for African American elders with chronic pain, *Family and Community Health*, **22**, 57–65.

Pinto, R.P. & Hollandsworth, J.G. (1989). Using videotape modeling to prepare children psychologically for surgery: Influence of parents and costs versus benefits of providing preparation services, *Health Psychol.*, **8**, 79–95.

Price, R. & Kompier, M. (2006). Work stress and unemployment: Risks, mechanisms, and prevention, in *Prevention of Mental Disorders: Effective Interventions and Policy Options* (Eds C. Hosman, E. Jané-Llopis & S. Saxena), Oxford University Press, Oxford (in press).

Price, R., van Ryn, M. & Vinokur, A. (1992). Impact of a preventive job search intervention on the likelihood of depression among the unemployed, *J. Health Social Behaviour*, **33**, 158–167.

Price, R.H., Cowen, E.L., Lorion, R.P. & Ramos-McKay, J. (1988). *Fourteen Ounces of Prevention: A Casebook for Practitioners*, American Psychological Association Press, Washington, DC.

Raudenbush, S.W.S. & Earls, F. (1997). Neighborhoods and violent crime: A multilevel study of collective efficacy, *Science*, **277**, 918–924.

Riemsma, R.P., Kirwan, J.R., Taal, E. & Rasker, J.J. (2003). Patient education for adults with rheumatoid arthritis, *The Cochrane Database of Systematic Reviews*, Issue 2, Art. No. CD003688. DOI: 10.1002/14651858.CD003688.

Schweinhart, L.J. & Weikart, D.P. (1998). High/scope perry preschool program effects at age twenty-seven, in *Social Programs that Work* (Ed. J. Crane), pp.148–162, Russell Sage Foundation, New York.

Segal, D.L., Chatman, C., Bogaards, J.A. & Becker, L.A. (2001). One-year follow-up of an emotional expression intervention for bereaved older adults, *J. Ment. Health Aging*, **7**(4), 465–472.

Silverman, P.R. (1988). Widow-to-widow: A mutual help program for the widowed. in *Fourteen Ounces of Prevention: A Casebook for Practitioners* (Eds R.H. Price, E.L. Cowen, R.P. Lorion & J. Ramos-McKay), American Psychological Association Press, Washington, DC.

Stewart, M., Craig, D., MacPherson, K. & Alexander, S. (2001). Promoting positive affect and diminishing loneliness of widowed seniors through a support intervention, *Public Health Nurs.*, **18**(1) 54–63.

Thomson, H., Petticrew, M. & Morrison, D. (2001). Housing interventions and health – A systematic review, *Br. Med. J.*, **323**, 187–190.

Thornicroft, G. & Szmukler, G. (2001). *Textbook of Community Psychiatry*, Oxford University Press, Oxford.

Vachon, M.L.S., Sheldon, A.R., Lancee, W.J., Lyall, W.A.L., Roger, J. & Freeman, S.J.J. (1980). A controlled study of self-help intervention for widows, *Am. J. Psychiatry*, **137**, 1380–1384.

Vaillant, G. (2003). Mental health, *Am. J. Psychiatry*, **160**, 1373–1384.

van Doesum, K.T.M., Hosman, C.M.H. & Riksen Walraven, J.M. (2005). A model based intervention for depressed mothers and their infants. *Infant Ment. Health J.*, **26**(2), 157–176.

Vinokur, A., van Ryn, M., Gramlich, E. & Price, R. (1991). Long-term follow-up and benefit–cost analysis of the jobs program: A preventive intervention for the unemployed, *J. Appl. Psychol.*, **76**(2), 213–219.

Vuori, J. & Silvonen, J. (2005). The benefits of a preventive job search program on re-employment and mental health at two-year follow-up, *J. Occup. Organizational Psychol.*, **78**(1), 43–52.

Vuori, J., Silvonen, J., Vinokur, A. & Price., R. (2002). The Tyohon job search program in Finland: Benefits for the unemployed with risk of depression or discouragement, *J. Occup. Health Psychol.*, **7**(1), 5–19.

Weare, K. (2000). *Promoting Mental, Emotional and Social Health: A Whole School Approach*, Routledge, London.

Wing, J.K. & Brown, G.W. (1970). *Institutionalism and Schizophrenia: A Comparative Study of Three Mental Hospitals 1960–68*, Cambridge University Press, Cambridge.

World Health Organization (1948). *Constitution of the World Health Organization*, Basic Documents, WHO, Geneva.

World Health Organization (1986). *The Ottawa Charter for Health Promotion*, WHO, Geneva.

World Health Organization (2004a). *Promoting Mental Health: Concepts, Emerging Evidence and Practice*, A Report from the World Health Organization, Department of Mental Health and Substance Abuse, in collaboration with the Victorian Health Promotion Foundation and the University of Melbourne, WHO, Geneva; http://www.who.int/mental_health/evidence/en/promoting_mhh.pdf.

World Health Organization (2004b). *Prevention of Mental Disorders: Effective Interventions and Policy Options*, A Report of the World Health Organization, Department of Mental Health and Substance Abuse, in collaboration with the Prevention Research Centre of the Universities of Nijmegen and Maastricht, WHO, Geneva; http://www.who.int/mental_health/evidence/en/prevention_of_mental_disorders_sr.pdf.

Index

Note: page numbers in *italics* refer to tables; the abbreviation QoL = quality of life.

Quality of Life in Mental Disorders, Second Edition   Edited by H. Katschnig, H. Freeman and N. Sartorius
© 2006 John Wiley & Sons, Ltd